*Dublin, 1950–1970*

THE MAKING OF DUBLIN CITY

Series Editors
Joseph Brady, Ruth McManus and Anngret Simms

Joseph Brady and Anngret Simms (eds), *Dublin through space and time, c.900–1900*

Ruth McManus, *Dublin, 1910–1940: shaping the city and suburbs*

Gary A. Boyd, *Dublin, 1745–1922: hospitals, spectacle and vice*

Niamh Moore, *Dublin docklands reinvented: the post-industrial regeneration of a European city quarter*

Joseph Brady, *Dublin, 1930–1950: the emergence of the modern city*

Joseph Brady, *Dublin, 1950–1970: houses, flats and high-rise*

# Dublin, 1950–1970

## HOUSES, FLATS AND HIGH-RISE

*Joseph Brady*

FOUR COURTS PRESS

Typeset in 11pt on 14pt Garamond by
Carrigboy Typesetting Services, for
FOUR COURTS PRESS LTD
7 Malpas Street, Dublin 8, Ireland
www.fourcourtspress.ie
*and in North America for*
FOUR COURTS PRESS
c/o ISBS, 920 NE 58th Avenue, Suite 300, Portland, OR 97213.

© Joseph Brady, the editors and Four Courts Press, 2016

ISBN 978–1–84682–623–8 hbk
ISBN 978–1–84682–599-6 pbk

A catalogue record for this title is available
from the British Library.

All rights reserved.
Without limiting the rights under copyright
reserved alone, no part of this publication may be
reproduced, stored in or introduced into a retrieval system,
or transmitted, in any form or by any means (electronic, mechanical,
photocopying, recording or otherwise), without the prior
written permission of both the copyright owner and
publisher of this book.

SPECIAL ACKNOWLEDGMENT
The author and publishers are grateful to the National University of Ireland
for a grant in aid of publication of this book.

Printed in England
by TJ International, Padstow, Cornwall.

# Contents

**7**
ACKNOWLEDGMENTS

**9**
SERIES EDITORS' INTRODUCTION

**13**
BUILDING THE MODERN CITY

**16**
THE 1950s AND 1960s
The economy – Population dynamics – Change in Dublin's population – Marriage and longevity – Housing – Housing facilities – Overcrowding – Tenure – Occupations – Employment and industry in Dublin – End of the 'servant problem' – The labour force – The agenda for 1950–70 – The maps

**62**
A REVITALIZED HOUSING PROGRAMME
Achievements – The individual schemes – Ballyfermot – Finglas East and West – Walkinstown and Milltown – Coolock and Kilmore – New schemes – Housing costs – Reserved areas – Public utility societies – Support for private housing – Other council areas – Patterns of tenure – Differential rents – Tenant purchase – Selling houses to tenants – Naming and social interaction

**178**
FLATS AND HIGH-RISE
Accommodation in flats – High-rise – Ballymun – System building – The end of high-rise

**240**
HOME OWNERSHIP
The path to ownership – Apartments – Individual housing schemes – Greenhills Estate – Monastery Park – Yellow Walls – Dundrum – Offington Park – The Laurels, Terenure Road – Shrewsbury Lawn, Cabinteely –

Shanganagh Vale – Bayside, Sutton – The ideal home – All electric – Consumption and consumer products – Innovation – Householders' perceptions

### 304
### THE EUROPEAN CONTEXT
High-rise and suburban design – Why not high-rise? – The USSR experience – Other European examples – Building suburbs in the UK

### 330
### THE HOUSING SECTOR AT THE END OF THE 1960s
Housing provision in the city – Owner occupancy – Private rental sector – Multiple occupancy – A new city? – Adequacy?

### 346
### THE SOCIAL AREAS OF DUBLIN, 1971
Social structure – The people in 1971 – Social status in the city – Household characteristics – Labour force – Miscellaneous characteristics – Factorial ecology – Socio-economic status in 1971 – Youthfulness and growth – Other aspects of the socio-economic structure of the city – Dublin's distinctiveness

### 390
### THE WIDER URBAN CONTEXT
The car, the office and the suburbs

### 395
### APPENDICES
1. Detail of selected aspects from the censuses of population
2. The socio-demographic spatial structure of Dublin, 1971

### 417
### SOURCES AND BIBLIOGRAPHY

### 433
### LIST OF ILLUSTRATIONS

### 439
### INDEX

# *Acknowledgments*

When I was completing my MA degree by thesis in UCD in the 1970s, I looked around for a suitable quotation to embellish the work. It was something that was popular at the time! I always liked the work of T.S. Eliot and felt that these lines from *Little Gidding* were very geographical.

> We shall not cease from exploration
> And the end of all our exploring
> Will be to arrive where we started
> And know the place for the first time

I have been studying Dublin for many years now and I think I am getting to the point where I am beginning to understand the processes that have shaped its streetscapes. The previous volume, *Dublin, 1930–1950: the emergence of the modern city*, dealt with a period that I did not experience personally. However, I grew up during much of the time period under consideration here and, more importantly, my lecturers in UCD introduced me to fresh and cutting-edge analysis of the city in the 1960s and 1970s. This was modern and contemporary at the time and we were using all sorts of new approaches and techniques to escape the 'rational description of the earth', which had been the geographical canon. It has been an interesting journey to revisit that material and see what it communicates to me now.

The final chapter in this book was, in another form, the substance of my BA dissertation in geography and became my first formal publication. My analysis is different now, certainly in detail if not in substance, and I hope that I know the place now. My sincere thanks must go to Tony Parker, who introduced me to urban geography and who supervised my three dissertations – surely a penance of some significance. Tony introduced me to the census of population, showed me how to write my first programme in Fortran and has been a great colleague and friend over many, many years. Arnold Horner was another great influence during the time I began my exploration of the city. Arnold's interests are varied and wonderful and from him I learned about maps, chaps, economic processes and so much more. To him my sincere thanks.

It goes without saying but it needs to be written that I owe a continuing debt to my editors. Ruth McManus and Anngret Simms have been great friends and tough critics. Anngret once taught me about European urbanization and, though it is hard to believe at this point, Ruth was once my student. They are both superb scholars and I am lucky that they have devoted so much time to making this text better.

My colleagues and friends in UCD have been invaluable. This and the previous volume are the product of a long period of gestation which benefitted hugely from discourse and argument in all sorts of forums. My thanks are due to Jim Byrne, Alun Carr, John Dunnion, Bryan Fanning, Tom Garvan, Frank Hayes, Andreas Hess, Alun Jones, Michael Laffan, Tim Mooney, Feargal Murphy, Gerald Mills, Niamh Moore, Wolfgang Marx and Ronnie Moore.

Illustrations play a hugely important role in communicating our ideas in this series and this volume is no different. To that end, I wish to acknowledge the value of the Crampton photo archive, now housed in UCD's digital library. I also want to thank most sincerely the late Frank Kelly for his generosity in giving me permission to reproduce material from *Dublin Opinion*. This is a wonderful source of material because it provides a window into what was topical and what was amusing and annoying people. Likewise, my thanks to the staff in Pearse Street Library who provided me not only with crucial material but also provided an oasis of calm in which to work. I am most grateful to Kay MacKeogh who provided me with the fascinating detail on the Walkinstown Utility Society.

Four Courts Press have been great supporters of this series and are a joy to work with. My continuing thanks to Martin Fanning, senior editor, for his patience, skill and huge enthusiasm. I also appreciate greatly the work done by Martin Healy, Anthony Tierney and Meghan Donaldson in getting the work before as wide an audience as possible. Four Courts produce books to the highest standards and they make a vital contribution to the academic world.

Lucy Hogan once again produced an excellent and useful index, greatly enhancing the book. Another vital contribution was made by the National University of Ireland in the form of a publication grant. This was important, not just in monetary terms, but also because of the support it provided.

My mother was a great source of support but also of practical information because the city of which I write was also her city. My deepest thanks, though, must go to Anne for her continuing and unfailing encouragement and support and without whom this book or any other would not have been written.

# Series editors' introduction

It is a great pleasure to introduce the latest addition to our series *The Making of Dublin City*. As with its predecessors, this volume takes a geographical perspective on the city's development, using a wide range of maps and other images to enhance our understanding of the evolution of Dublin during this era. Following on chronologically from Joe Brady's previous book in this series, *Dublin, 1930–1950: the emergence of the modern city*, this volume extends into a time period well within living memory. This time there is a specific focus on the changing nature of the housing stock, the most important land use within the city and, arguably, the one with the greatest day-to-day impact upon its citizens. Its scope extends from the continuing efforts of Dublin Corporation to provide dwellings for the city's poorest citizens, to the creation of exclusive suburbs for the better off. This volume helps to explain why the city's dwellings came to be as they are. Indeed, the decisions made in this period continue to impact to the present day; the most recent census revealed that over a quarter of the current housing stock in Dublin city dates from the twenty-five years between 1946 and 1971.

The changing population dynamics of the city, with on-going rural-to-urban migration and the persistent problems of overcrowding and out-dated housing stock are dealt with in the first chapter. This sets the agenda for the period in question, outlining the needs which had to be addressed in the 1950s and 1960s. Importantly, this volume covers a period of time when the quality of housing in Dublin improved dramatically, and when owner occupancy became increasingly common. The 1946 census returns, while slightly outside of the period, provide a useful snapshot of the work that still needed to be done at the start of the period. Shocking statistics concerning the lack of private water supplies, fixed baths and sanitary facilities remind the reader of how far we have come in the interim.

The volume is book-ended with census data, providing a comprehensive overview of the degree of change in the course of two decades. The 1971 census is analysed in order to conclude the discussion with a detailed examination of the social structure of the city. A series of maps documents the character of the city in terms of socio-economic status, household characteristics and so on, while an appendix is provided for those readers who might wish to delve deeper into the methodological approach for this analysis (factorial ecology).

*Dublin, 1950–1970: houses, flats and high-rise* is concerned with the everyday and the familiar, yet the reader will be intrigued as the story behind the apparently banal dwellings of the city is revealed. The provision of housing is not simply about bricks and mortar, or providing shelter, but involves the lives of individuals and families and, ultimately, decisions about what kind of society is going to be created. Joe Brady examines these more subtle meanings in his exploration of the ideological roots of the high-rise flat on the one hand, and the push to increase owner occupation on the other. As with its predecessor, one of the noteworthy features of this book is the way in which it debunks popular memories, or mis-rememberings, of the past, not least in its handling of the development of the Ballymun housing scheme. Forgotten stories are also rediscovered, including the long-running discussions surrounding the use of the St Anne's estate which lay between Raheny and Clontarf. Although some dwellings were built at its edges, ultimately (and thankfully), proposals for housing on a much greater scale did not come to fruition. Instead, a large proportion of the estate was given over to the beautiful public park which remains a popular and well-used amenity to the present day.

Joe Brady builds on the explanations of the previous volume, which demonstrated how the social areas of housing in the city became ingrained through the locational decisions of Dublin Corporation and private builders, in turn impacted by the availability of suitable building land and serviced sites. We saw, for example, that the north side of the city was much more varied in its social structure than the south side, with smaller pockets of private middle-class suburban housing interspersed with local authority social housing. That pattern was to persist in the period under consideration, which saw the opening up of a new swathe of development land to the north of the city.

Somewhat poignantly, in light of recent developments, this was an era when the end of the housing problem seemed to be within reach. As Dublin Corporation swung into action with a revitalised housing programme following the slow-down caused by wartime shortages, large schemes were constructed at the edges of the built-up area. The genesis of the large-scale individual schemes at Ballyfermot, Finglas East and West, Walkinstown and Milltown, Coolock and Kilmore is outlined. We see the evolution of new areas, the on-going question of cost for housing and the politically-charged issue of differential rents. The significant numbers of suburban 'cottages' produced at this time resulted in renewed anxieties about the future of existing communities linked to loss of population in the city centre. While jobs and services continued to be concentrated in central areas, the high fares and inadequacy of the bus service became a source of discontent for new suburban dwellers in areas such as Ballyfermot and Finglas. Indeed, the high cost of travel was one of the key arguments used to support increased inner city building by Dublin Corporation at this time.

A changing pattern of tenure was a feature of the 1960s as increasing numbers of people moved from renting to home ownership and Dublin Corporation moved from a restricted form of tenant purchase to making all its houses (though not its flats) available for purchase. The idea of the public utility society, discussed in previous volumes in the series, persisted, but the importance of this form of housing provision was on the wane. The preference for one-family self-contained homes remained, in private and public housing, although Joe Brady notes a small number of exceptions as private apartments were gradually introduced to a rather dubious public. A range of private housing developments from around the city is used to illustrate the typical developer-led schemes of the 1950s and 1960s.

While the pattern of constructing large suburban housing schemes and central flat developments by Dublin Corporation persisted, the great departure of the 1960s was the decision to build the Ballymun development at the very edge of the city (and, indeed, partly outside of the area controlled by Dublin Corporation) with both houses and system-built high-rise flats. Joe Brady contextualizes the decision to build high-rise dwellings at Ballymun with a readily-accessible account of its lineage as a significant, ideologically-important aspect of social housing further afield. Typically used to build at high densities in inner city areas, the choice of a high-rise approach for the suburban Ballymun site was, as he explores, largely due to the potential speed of completion using industrial building techniques. In this detailed account, we discover how the project came about and how this radical approach at a first class, high quality solution to the housing crisis ultimately failed to achieve its lofty goals.

As well as looking at the nature of the housing provision, in this volume Joe Brady gives an insight into how these dwellings might have been enjoyed by their occupants. In particular, we learn of the new labour saving devices and other consumer products that were used in the typical Dublin home of the 1950s and 1960s, and the various forms of entertainment which became available. Advertisements give a flavour of the new types of consumer product on offer. The all-electric home, a feature as far back as the 1920s, continued to be heralded, and television sets gradually made their appearance, though it would be a long time before they achieved ubiquity. While the 'universal plan' for suburban houses, which included two reception rooms and a kitchen downstairs, with three or four bedrooms and bathroom upstairs, remained the dominant form, there was now some variation. These include the fashion for American-style 'ranch' houses and the more imaginative internal layouts with open-plan which became a feature in the 1960s. Occasionally, too, we get hints as to the divergent expectations and experiences of the provider and residents of the new housing schemes. For example, in a drive to encourage the use of Irish, from the early 1950s Dublin Corporation named streets in Irish only. Rather than openly complain or agitate for change, the tenants generally simply used the English language versions of the names instead.

As with the other volumes in this series, *Dublin, 1950–1970* looks in detail within the city itself, examining a range of original sources including documents from Dublin Corporation, newspapers and other archival sources, to enhance our understanding. An additional aspect of that understanding is to approach the city from without, in order to set Dublin city within its broader context. This includes not just examining the national policies and political framework of the period, but also turning the lens further afield. By looking at parallels and contrasts with contemporary Britain and continental Europe, extending as far as the Soviet Union, a fuller appreciation of the nature of Dublin's housing is achieved.

*Dublin, 1950–1970* offers something for everyone interested in the city of Dublin. A future companion volume will tackle other aspects of urban change during the same time period, including planning, transport infrastructure and the suburbanization of shopping and office activities. In the meantime, we hope that you will enjoy this book and that it will offer you new insights into our city.

# *Building the modern city*

The subtitle to the previous volume in this series, *Dublin, 1930–1950*, was 'the emergence of the modern city' and this was intended to suggest that characteristic aspects of Dublin that would be readily recognized today had taken form by the end of the 1940s. Foremost among these was the social divide in the city. It is the staple of northside/southside jokes but it has a contemporary reality in that housing south of the Liffey can be upwards of 30 per cent more expensive than its northside equivalent. The housing policies of Dublin Corporation combined with the housing programmes of private developers ensured that any northside/southside divide was further emphasized and fixed. South of the river there was an even more marked contrast between west and east while the maintenance of the coastal (Dún Laoghaire) borough ensured that there would be little encroachment by social housing there. Dublin Corporation built where it had or could get access to land and this directed them to the west of the south county borough because the townships of Rathmines and Pembroke, which maintained their independence until 1930, were largely built up before they were taken under the wing of the city. On the northside, with the exception of parts of Clontarf, the townships were not as successful and were less built up by the time of incorporation, giving Dublin Corporation greater scope. Their building projects produced a much more socially fragmented landscape or a more socially integrated landscape, depending on the reader's point of view. This spatial arrangement was fixed by the end of the 1940s and it would have taken revolutionary zeal to have changed it, if anyone had a mind to do so. The direction of future growth was also determined. Abercrombie's (1941) sketch development plan had noted what was obvious anyway, namely that Dublin had limited possibilities for growth to the south and even less to the east unless the sea was to be driven back. This left the north and the west and the decision to locate the main civil airport north of the city centre was always going to put limits on that expansion. So, westwards it was going to have to be.

The shape of today's road network was also determined during the 1940s. It was a response to a well-developed traffic problem, even with relatively low levels of private vehicle ownership. This had been growing for centuries. Any city that chooses to build on both sides of a river is asking for traffic problems and Dublin built there early in its history. Thus so much of the planning of the city from the seventeenth century was as much about moving goods and people around as it was about providing housing and attractive streetscapes worthy of a capital city. In common with most cities in Europe, Dublin had a radial network that focused on the city centre. The Wide Streets Commissioners had done sterling work in providing wide and straight streets but these were unable to cope with cross-city traffic almost as quickly as they were completed. One answer lay in more and better bridges over the Liffey but a more comprehensive solution was suggested in terms of ring roads and bypasses. Abercrombie's suggestions for these led ultimately, though not without a few detours, to the circular routes such as Collins Avenue and to the inner tangent routes such as along Clanbrassil Street.

If Dublin was going to have a business centre, it was going to be in its south-eastern sector. The rest of the city centre was slipping into genteel decay by the 1940s as the Georgian fabric was showing its age and becoming less and less suited to modern demands. The different fates of the Pembroke and Gardiner families had ensured that the south-eastern sector of the city was spared the downward spiral that occurred elsewhere. By the end of the nineteenth century, the best shopping in the city was located around Grafton Street while the commercial world transformed College Green and Dame Street with the building of fine banking halls and insurance buildings. While Abercrombie had placed his civic centre in the environs of Christ Church cathedral, he had suggested a government quarter for the area around Merrion Square and St Stephen's Green, notwithstanding the plans that the Roman Catholic diocese of Dublin had for Merrion Square. The Fianna Fáil government of the late 1940s had been sufficiently taken by the idea that they contemplated legislation to prevent property speculation in the area.

While it may be readily argued that the nature of the modern housing, traffic and commercial landscape was becoming clear from the end of the 1940s, it would be more challenging to suggest that the city was a centre of modernity in the sense of offering a new and modern view of society. Dublin might have had a bohemian culture for those who liked to take a drink and talk (see Ryan, 1975), but society was still firmly based around the notion of a family where the husband was the bread winner and where only single women were in the labour force. Traditional values were still the norm and except perhaps for a section of the better-off it would be difficult to suggest that Dubliners were much more cosmopolitan or European in their outlook than their rural counterparts. Visitors to the city commented on the conservative appearance of people on the street and a visit to any bookshop would have confirmed the view that Dubliners were equally conservative in their reading tastes, or at least that it had been decided that they would be.

Even though the modern city was being moulded by the end of the 1940s, there was still a lot to do before that shape finally gelled. Housing is such a big topic that it needs a volume of its own and in the pages that follow there will be exploration of houses, flats and high-rise. Other aspects of this changing geography will be analysed in a subsequent volume. Dublin continued to expand its footprint during the 1950s and particularly the 1960s and development quickly spilled over into the county area. Dubliners favoured a low-density city and a three- or four-bedroomed house with a garden and perhaps space for a car was seen as the norm. Dublin Corporation continued as an active house builder, though it slowed its housing provision for some years in the late 1950s, and large developments appeared on the northern edge of the city where most land was available. This was also the period when home ownership became much more common in the private market and the scale of house building, largely in the southern suburbs, reflected a growing city and a more confident economy. Builders sought to build estates but without an 'estate look' and looked for marketing ideas to convince potential purchasers. They found these in the United States rather in the UK, as they might have had in a previous generation, and Dubliners found themselves being offered ranch-style houses, car ports and open-plan designs.

Up to the 1960s, flats were largely a phenomenon of the inner city and were mainly built by Dublin Corporation. The preference in both public and private sectors was for individual houses and flats were built out of necessity rather than conviction. A private sector market in flats began to emerge only in the late 1950s but growth here was slow and imagination often lacking in developments, which were mostly southside. Many seem lacking in character and design when viewed by today's standards. The big housing experiment of the period was with system building and high-rise on the periphery of the city in Ballymun and, for a time, it seemed as if this approach would come to dominate future provision in both public and private sectors. The creation of a high-rise city would have been interesting and private builders toyed with building blocks that would have dwarfed Ballymun. These turned out to be no more than brief pipe dreams for reasons that will be explored within. It is only in the second decade of the twenty-first century that the city is once again ready to embrace the idea of significant volumes of skyscrapers for living.

# The 1950s and 1960s

## *The economy*

It was always going to be difficult in the 1950s to maintain the euphoria of the end of the Second World War. Already at the end of the 1940s there were warning signs in the economy and there must have been a nagging concern that things were going to be more challenging. The immediate post-war years had seen something of a shopping and tourism boom in Dublin with people spending generously and visitors coming from the UK and the United States. The visitors from the UK were lured by the easy availability of goods, especially foodstuffs, which were still scarce at home, while in Dublin there was the residual effect of war and immediate post-war employment in British factories.

But there were dark clouds, captured very well in the pages of *Dublin Opinion*, in the sense that prices were rising and had risen very substantially over the decade. Wages had not kept pace and the affordability of many goods had declined. The previous volume in this series, *Dublin, 1930–1950*, argued that Dublin's economy was already post-industrial so it was hard to see from where would come the growth which would boost incomes. Agriculture

1. 'We're getting the range. We nearly brought him down that time.' The cost of living. (*Dublin Opinion*, 1949, p. 57.)

remained post-colonial in its orientation on primary products, such as live cattle, and industry was largely based on import-substitution. What Ireland needed was export earnings to pay for the imports on which the lifestyle (modest or not) of so much of the population depended.

By the middle of the 1950s, there was a sense of doom in political discourse. Seán Lemass set out the agenda in his comments on the financial statement for the budget in May 1956.

> After two years of this incompetent Administration, we have a deficit in our balance of payments which threatens the future of every man, woman and child living in this country. We have rising prices. We have rising costs of Government. We have a higher and a rapidly increasing burden of taxation. All of that is falling upon an economy in which, as the Minister for Finance admitted here to-day, production is not rising. Any small expansion there was in industrial output last year was offset by the fall in agricultural production because of your incompetent Minister for Agriculture.
>
> (Dáil Debates, 157(1), col. 50)

Allowing for the hyperbole of an opposition reply to a budget statement, it set out the problem for the country very well. Exports were dominated by live cattle and not enough industry while prices for imports were rising. The balance of payments figures could not have been clearer and it was not a sustainable picture in the long run. Taxation was at a very high level and it was argued by de Valera that it had reached its limit, though of course that was capable of reinterpretation. The cost of government was rising and it seemed that there was little possibility of reining it in.

**Table 1.** Value of major domestic exports, 1950–5. (Statistical abstract, 1956, p. 129.)

| Domestic exports | 1950 | 1951 | 1952 | 1953 | 1954 | 1955 |
|---|---|---|---|---|---|---|
| Live animals | £29,274 | £29,807 | £32,345 | £32,647 | £41,585 | £44,617 |
| Food, drink and tobacco | | | | | | |
| Raw or simply prepared | £10,576 | £9,241 | £9,851 | £11,471 | £7,287 | £6,607 |
| Manufactured/prepared | £18,820 | £25,274 | £40,999 | £48,398 | £39,751 | £28,064 |

**Table 2.** External trade, 1940–58. (Statistical abstract, 1959, table 122.)

| Year | Value at current prices (1959) (£) Imports | Value at current prices (1959) (£) Exports | Index of volume 1953=100 Imports | Index of volume 1953=100 Exports |
|---|---|---|---|---|
| 1940 | 46,790 | 32,966 | 56.8 | 70.2 |
| 1941 | 29,530 | 31,733 | 29.0 | 56.7 |
| 1942 | 34,630 | 32,606 | 28.2 | 52.2 |
| 1943 | 26,359 | 27,730 | 21.2 | 41.1 |
| 1944 | 28,531 | 28,799 | 22.4 | 42.9 |
| 1945 | 41,073 | 35,236 | 31.8 | 51.5 |
| 1946 | 72,043 | 38,612 | 57.4 | 53.8 |
| 1947 | 131,335 | 38,568 | 88.2 | 51.3 |
| 1948 | 136,316 | 47,851 | 90.5 | 54.9 |
| 1949 | 130,232 | 58,974 | 90.4 | 66.3 |
| 1950 | 159,394 | 70,452 | 101.2 | 74.6 |
| 1951 | 204,596 | 79,827 | 106.3 | 73.5 |
| 1952 | 172,309 | 99,221 | 88.6 | 89.5 |
| 1953 | 182,480 | 111,517 | 100.0 | 100.0 |
| 1954 | 179,890 | 111,778 | 97.9 | 102.6 |
| 1955 | 207,663 | 107,152 | 107.6 | 95.3 |
| 1956 | 182,849 | 104,276 | 93.0 | 98.1 |
| 1957 | 184,172 | 127,076 | 88.7 | 116.9 |
| 1958 | 198,414 | 125,050 | 100.0 | 113.7 |

The government's own position was hardly more encouraging although they believed that they were doing what was necessary to turn things around. This was the Minister for Finance's (Mr Gerard Sweetman) own assessment of how things stood.

> When introducing the Vote on Account in March I reviewed the economic situation and pointed to certain dangerous tendencies which no Government concerned with the nation's economic health could allow to go unchecked. The balance of trade was deteriorating, savings had declined despite increases in money incomes, consumption was outrunning production and it was becoming difficult to raise adequate capital for local and national development. Remedial action could not await the budget and with Government approval I imposed a special

levy on certain imports of a less essential nature, the proceeds of which would be used to finance capital expenditure.

(Dáil Debates, 157(1), col. 25)

These levies had been introduced in March 1956 with others in the following July as an attempt to discourage imports. These were removed some little time later but they were replaced by customs duties, all designed to try and keep the economy in some kind of balance (Meenan, 1970). Since Dublin was a consumer of resources rather than a producer, it was not a great time to be considering major capital works and even the necessary programmes of housing were under considerable pressure. Fortunately, the end of the 1950s marked a turning point in the economic development of Ireland and set the

*Revenue Commissioners searching for limit of taxation which Mr. de Valera, some years ago, said we had reached.*

**2.** The limits to taxation! (*Dublin Opinion*, 1957, p. 79.)

3. A happy new year! (Cover, *Dublin Opinion*, 1954.)

country on course away from a Third World economy to something approaching the industrial Western economy it is today.

> Our pre-war industrial development was based on home market requirements and protection, and it served the purposes of that time. I think it was the only practical industrial policy then. Because of it, we have secured a basis of industrial organization, a pool of managerial competence and industrial skill on which we can build for the future. Indeed, it would be correct to say that our prospects in the future world situation, as I anticipate it may develop, would be very dim indeed if that pre-war industrial policy of ours had not been so very successful. There is need now to raise our targets and, I believe, also to change our methods. We know that change always produces problems and difficulties, and it is certain that we will experience both, but the problems are not insoluble. The difficulties can in time be solved.
>
> (Dáil Debates, 175(8), col. 938)

Meenan (1970) in his *Irish economy since 1922* quoted the above extract from the speech given by the Minister for Industry and Commerce, Seán Lemass, in 1959 as an indication of the way in which things were to change. These words followed the publication in 1958 of *Economic development* by the then-Secretary of the Department of Finance, T.K. Whitaker, which advocated the planning of the economy in an integrated national way over a period of five to ten years. The report argued that decisions should be taken as to how best to use the resources of the State and that polices should be directed to achieving these aims. It argued that investment was needed by the State in all areas of the economy and that this should be attracted from abroad if it could not be obtained at home. In broad terms the economy was to change from an inward-oriented economy with protectionist policies to an outward-oriented export economy living in the real world with all of the attendant benefits and dangers.

The 1960s were therefore years of optimism, years in which it was hoped that Ireland would break out of the stagnant economic mould into which it had settled and that it would solve its economic ills, raise the living standards of its people, provide employment and rid the nation of the scourge of emigration. The optimism was crystalized in the various programmes for economic expansion, the first of which covered the period from 1959 to 1963. This *First programme* (1958) expected that its implementation would lead to an increase in real national income of some two per cent per annum. If the programme was positive in its economic targets, it was backwards socially in that it sought to pay for the programme of investment in part by reduced expenditure on social capital projects. This echoed what had been stated in *Economic development*, which had argued for a slowing down in housing and other forms of social investment because needs were at last coming into line with provision. This was a debateable position since it depended on where the line with regard to social provision was to be drawn. The State was a long way from meeting the needs of all of those who might be considered vulnerable. It was true that one of the effects of emigration was that demand for housing programmes (at their normal standard of provision) declined during the 1950s. This economic programme was followed by an even more ambitious second programme for the period 1964–70, which set quantitative targets, and which was based on the assumption that Ireland would be a full member of the European Economic Community by 1970. The chief objective of this plan was to raise aggregate real income by 50 per cent over the years 1960–70. This programme was abandoned after two years when it became clear that neither the ambition of joining the EEC by 1970, nor the quantitative targets, especially in employment, would be met. A final attempt was made in the third programme for the period 1969–72 but this fizzled out in a whimper rather than a bang. These failures might suggest that the optimism of the early 1960s was not realized but, as Kennedy (1988) argued, the very act of producing national plans was valuable in that it disseminated knowledge of the requirements for economic growth and made people more aware of the way in which economies worked. As a by-product, this period marked the emergence of the 'economist' in Ireland.

Despite the failure of the programmes to do what was intended, the country experienced considerable growth during the 1960s largely as a result of its new orientation, which allowed it to capitalize on the boom in the world economy of the 1960s. Blackwell (1982), although putting the turning point for the economy at 1961 rather than 1959, noted that the growth rate of output in the Irish economy during the period 1961–73 was more than double what it had been during the 1950s. In fact, the average growth rate of GDP during the 1960s and up to the oil crisis of 1973 was 4.4 per cent per annum.

This growth was very welcome, though it must be remembered that it was not very rapid when viewed in a European context. Other low income economies such as Finland (5.0 per cent), Italy (5.3 per cent) or Portugal (6.9 per cent) put in better performances. Though the gap between the Irish economy and the rest of the world might not have diminished, the growth in the country's wealth was translated into higher living standards at home. There was an increase in personal consumption per head of over 2.6 per cent per annum and disposable income rose considerably. It rose in real terms by a factor of two from 1957 to 1980 despite two oil crises. There were also more subtle changes in society, which were equally important or perhaps more so. Foster (1989) suggested that 'the long-effects of economic expansion may be questionable but the social results were strikingly evident in Ireland during the 1960s' (p. 580). A national television station was opened in 1962 providing a window on a wider world and which gave people an expectation of living standards experienced elsewhere. A free-trade agreement was signed with Britain on 14 December 1965. Free second-level education was introduced in 1967, which opened up the benefits of education to all of the population for the first time. At the same time a programme of new building in universities and colleges was begun and a system of third-level grants was introduced. The result was an increase in participation in education. In 1964, one-quarter of seventeen-year-olds stayed in full time education but by 1979 this had increased to one-half while a two-thirds growth in participation in third-level education occurred during the same period (Rottman, 1982). At the other end of the social spectrum a whole host of reforms and extensions improved the lot of those dependent on the State (McCashin, 1982). A new children's allowance scheme was introduced in 1966, an occupational insurance scheme in 1967 and free travel for those on social welfare old age pensions, later extended to everyone of pensionable age living in the State. In 1970 the Department of Social Welfare introduced invalidity pensions for those who were unfit for work and, in later years, schemes for deserted wives, retirement pensions, unmarried mother's allowances, and prisoners' wives. The changes occurred at the same time as Irish society was becoming more and more urbanized and older verities were coming under pressure (for one example see *Irish Times*, 15 October 1970, p. 6).

## Population dynamics

Censuses of different scale and scope were taken in 1951, 1956, 1961 and 1966 and they showed a national population in decline for most of the period. The data are shown below and these indicate that the population had a significant internal growth dynamic as indicated by the difference between deaths and births. Natural increase would have added about 25,000 people per annum to the population. It was emigration that turned growth potential into relatively modest decline. Estimated by the CSO at 187,111 during the ten years from 1936 to 1946, it accelerated to 119,568 in the five years to 1951 (see *National Commission on Emigration*, 1955). Thereafter, it rose to 196,763 between 1951 and 1956 and reached a peak of 212,003 between 1956 and 1961. It was only in the better economic times of the 1960s that it started to decline. The period between 1961 and 1966 saw modest population growth as emigration slipped to 80,605 during that period.

Population grew by 2.3 per cent between 1961 and 1966 in comparison to a loss of 2.8 per cent in the previous intercensal period, though this growth was unevenly experienced. Leinster exhibited strong growth of 6.2 per cent in comparison to continued losses of 4.2 per cent in each of Connacht and Ulster. The population of Dublin County grew by 10.6 per cent during this period, the highest growth rate in Leinster and in the State. The State's population grew even more rapidly between 1966 and 1971 and increased by 3.3 per cent to 2,978,248. Once again growth was strongest in Leinster, which

"*We've got to admit that the evidence given last evening was pretty convincing.*"

**4.** Commission on emigration. (*Dublin Opinion*, 1948, p. 121.)

grew by 5.9 per cent and though both Ulster and Connacht still registered a decline in population (2.7 per cent and 0.5 per cent respectively), the decline was much reduced when compared to the previous intercensal period.

**Table 3.** Population change in the State, 1946–71. (Census of population, 1971, volume 1.)

| Year | Population | Natural increase | Net emigration |
|------|-----------|------------------|----------------|
| 1946 | 2,955,107 | 173,798 | 187,111 |
| 1951 | 2,960,593 | 125,054 | 119,568 |
| 1956 | 2,898,564 | 134,434 | 196,763 |
| 1961 | 2,818,341 | 132,080 | 212,003 |
| 1966 | 2,884,002 | 146,266 | 80,605 |
| 1971 | 2,978,248 | 148,152 | 53,906 |

The country finally became more urban than rural during the 1960s. There was still a slender majority in rural areas (50.8 per cent) at the time of the 1966 census as a result of an increase of 8.6 per cent in the population of towns of more than 1,500 people (aggregate town areas) while that of the aggregate rural areas decreased by 3.1 per cent. A further increase of 7.7 per cent in urban areas combined with a decline of 1.2 per cent in the rural areas ensured that 52 per cent lived in urban areas by 1971.

**Table 4.** Urban structure, 1971. (Adapted from Census of population, 1971, volume 1, table VII.)

| Population | Percentage change 1961–6 | Percentage change 1966–71 | Total population | Per cent national population |
|---|---|---|---|---|
| Dublin county borough and suburbs | 8.8 | 4.2 | 679,748 | 22.8 |
| Dún Laoghaire borough and suburbs | 24.6 | 17.0 | 98,379 | 3.3 |
| Cork county borough and suburbs | 8.8 | 6.8 | 134,430 | 4.5 |
| Limerick county borough and suburbs | 11.8 | 7.1 | 63,002 | 2.1 |
| Waterford county borough and suburbs | 5.4 | 9.3 | 33,676 | 1.1 |

The data presented in table 4 show the extent to which Ireland was still a nation of small towns in that there were only five towns with a population in excess of 30,000 people. The urban system displayed the characteristic sign of primacy in that the city of Dublin, combining Dublin county borough and Dún Laoghaire, held over 26 per cent of the population or over six times the population of the next largest city, Cork. Between 1961 and 1966, each of the county boroughs grew, though, with the exception of Waterford, the rate of growth was less than previously.

**Table 5.** Urban structure – towns less than 30,000 population. (Adapted from Census of population, 1971, table VII.)

| Population | Number 1966 | Number 1971 | Population 1971 | Percentage change 1961–6 | Percentage change 1966–71 |
|---|---|---|---|---|---|
| > 10,000 | 12 | 12 | 188,586 | 4.7 | 8.7 |
| 5,000–10,000 | 18 | 24 | 120,451 | 5.6 | 8.1 |
| 3,000–5,000 | 28 | 29 | 119,726 | 6.6 | 16.0 |
| 1,500–3,000 | 48 | 44 | 112,608 | 4.0 | 10.7 |

Dublin had grown more strongly than the rest of the country during the 1930s and 1940s and had been the destination of many migrants from the countryside. County Dublin continued to grow steadily during the 1950s and 1960s from a base of 693,022 in 1951 and by 1971 there were 852,219 people there. The 1951 census noted that urban Dublin had outgrown its boundaries with 53,805 people recorded in suburbs outside the city boundary. This with a further 10,565 people in the suburbs of Dún Laoghaire, give a total urban population of 634,473. By the time of the next census in 1956, Dublin had had a boundary extension that took in a considerable portion of land to the north of the city. This meant that the northern suburbs contained only 2,252 persons but the continued expansion into the southern suburbs resulted in a population of 42,755 there with a further 17,302 people in Dún Laoghaire's suburbs. Because most building was accommodated within the new borough boundary, the northern suburban population remained relatively small with 3,287 persons in 1961, an increase of 26.9 per cent on 1956. The march into the southern suburbs was similar in percentage terms, 25.6 per cent, but the numbers were far more significant at 54,553 while Dún Laoghaire's suburbs now contained 20,309. Both northern and southern suburbs grew strongly in the period to 1966 with no change in their relative importance. There were now 5,926 in the northern suburbs but 74,455 persons south of the borough boundary. Dún Laoghaire's suburbs also grew strongly and had 33,042 in 1966, an increase of 62.8 per cent.

In contrast to suburban growth, the county borough saw population decline over most of the period. There were 551,555 people there in 1951 but this fell to 539,476 by 1956 and further to 537,448 in 1961. These were not major decreases but were important pointers to Dublin Corporation as it came

Table 6. Population change in Dublin county borough and Dún Laoghaire, 1951–66. (Census of population, volume 1.)

|      | Dublin county borough | Dún Laoghaire |
|------|-----------------------|---------------|
| 1951 | 551,555               | 47,562        |
| 1956 | 539,476               | 47,553        |
| 1961 | 537,448               | 47,792        |
| 1966 | 568,772               | 51,772        |

Table 7. Urban (aggregate town areas) population change in entire county, 1961–71. (Census of population, 1966 and 1971, volume 1.)

|                         | 1961    | 1966    | 1971    | % increase 1961–6 | % increase 1966–71 |
|-------------------------|---------|---------|---------|-------------------|--------------------|
| Dublin county borough   | 537,448 | 567,802 | 567,866 | 5.6               | 0.0                |
| Dún Laoghaire borough   | 47,792  | 51,811  | 53,171  | 8.4               | 2.6                |
| Suburbs and other towns | 100,540 | 146,574 | 201,493 | 45.8              | 37.4               |
| Total                   | 685,780 | 766,187 | 822,530 | 11.7              | 7.3                |

to an assessment of future housing demand. Growth resumed again in the 1960s as tables 6 and 7 show. Dún Laoghaire's core population remained much the same with 47,562 in 1951 and 53,171 in 1971 but it had significant suburban growth. It did not have the same rehousing pressures but, as Manning Robertson had shown in his prelude to the development plan in 1936, neither did it have much room in which to accommodate growth.

## Change in Dublin's population

Even within Dublin county borough there were variations in population change. There are several explanations possible for changes in population in any given area and more than one may apply. First, large spikes in population might be observed in areas where large housing estates had been built. Despite an earlier decision to the contrary, Dublin Corporation returned to building on a large scale in the 1950s. Some private builders also built on a scale large enough to have this kind of demographic effect in an area. Natural increase would then add further to the population growth because it was usual for young families to be housed in such areas and the death rate was so low as to make little impact. For example, a major building programme by Dublin Corporation in Finglas West between 1951 and 1956 resulted in a thirty-fold increase in the population there and steady growth thereafter. The same effect could be seen in Coolock where it resulted from a combination of public and private building. On the other hand, given what was going on in Dublin, population decline could have been due to slum clearance but it could also indicate areas moving into the older stages of the life cycle. The latter would be particularly the case if the area had been initially built up in one time period and, as a result, life cycle changes would tend to be emphasized.

One of the frustrations that Dublin Corporation had experienced during the 1930s was that, despite their building programme, they did not see the expected reduction in inner city populations or densities. This was attributed in *Dublin, 1930–1950* to migration from the countryside into these areas where there was poor quality but relatively affordable rental property. By 1961, the effect of slum clearance, probably assisted by emigration, was to be seen in the inner city. The population in the north and south inner cities fell in each of the time periods in question and by 1961, the population north and south of the Liffey had reduced by 27.9 per cent and 30.7 per cent respectively. While this was the welcome result of slum clearance, the extent of the decline had implications for the supply of local services, as will be discussed later. The city

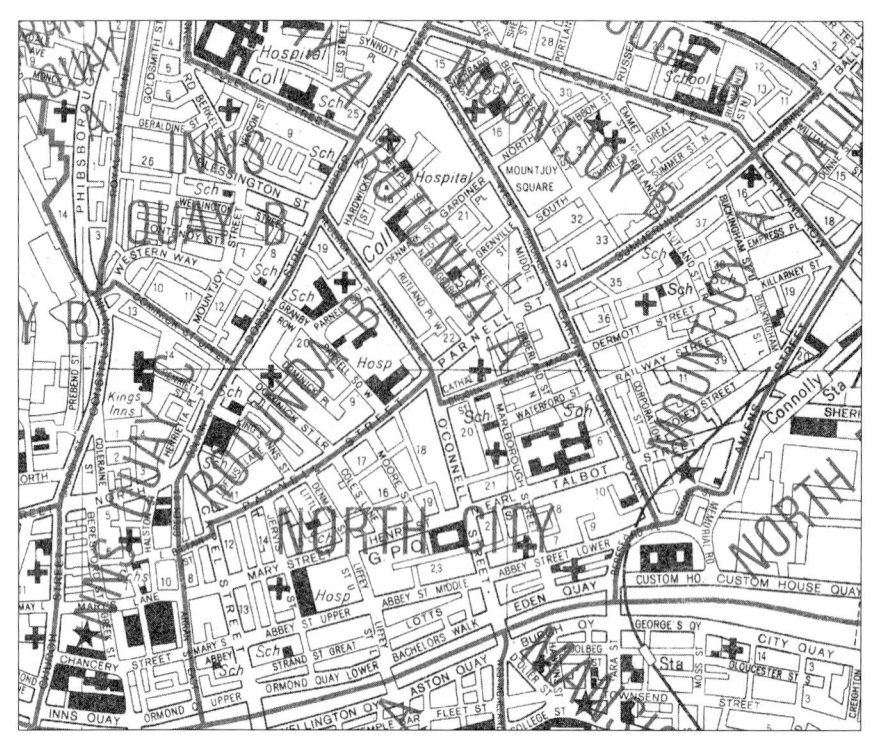

**5.** Northern inner city wards for the 1966 and 1971 censuses. The sub-divisions of each ward were used in 1971.

centre provided both high-order shopping for the city and low-order (day-to-day) shopping for the local population. Both levels of provision now came under threat, the former from the arrival and diffusion of the shopping centre idea and the latter from the removal of the population that sustained it. There was no longer the same need for the number of dairies and groceries, tobacconists and newsagents that were to be found close to the main shopping streets in the city.

As might be expected, there were major declines in wards such as North City where the population dropped by 60 per cent between 1951 and 1966 with big decreases in each of the census periods. Rotunda lost more than 50 per cent of its population over the time period with the greatest decrease experienced between 1951 and 1956. There were similar declines in South Dock and Mansion House while Mountjoy saw a more modest reduction of 35 per cent, spread across the decade and a half.

By 1966, the consequence of redevelopment was that the inner city had only 70.8 per cent of the population it had in 1951. Decline was fairly evenly

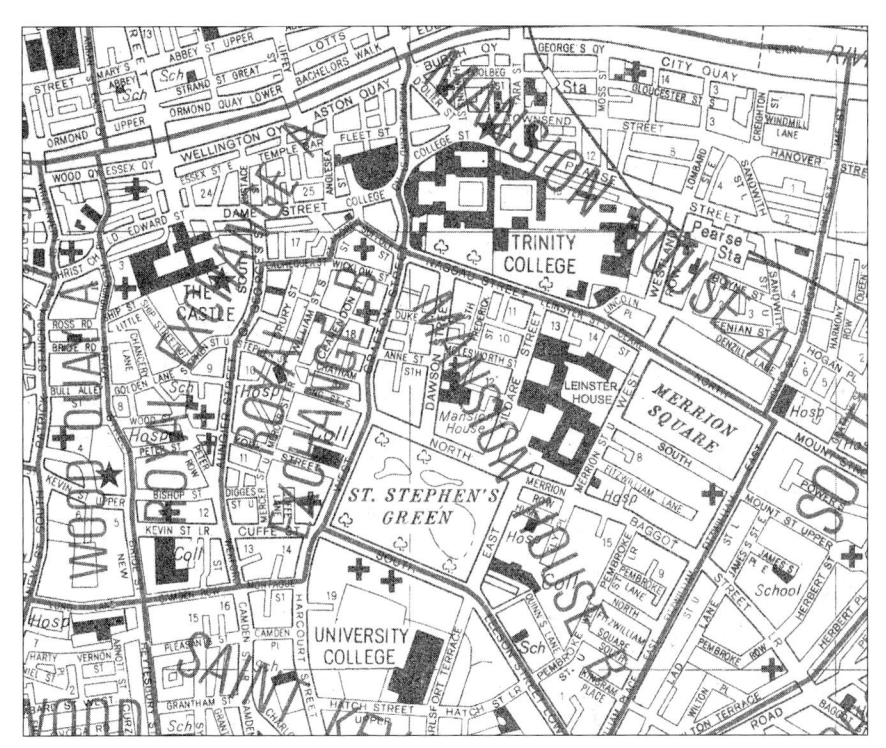

6. Southern inner city wards for the 1966 and 1971 censuses. The sub-divisions of each ward were used in 1971.

balanced though that of the south city was a little greater. It was not just slum clearance that resulted in population decline. Older suburbs had now moved into the later stages of the life cycle (see Appendix 1 for details of population numbers) and places such as Cabra East, Crumlin and Glasnevin saw their populations drop. This was a natural consequence of the building of large estates in Cabra and Crumlin in the 1930s and by 1966 many of the families had been there for over 30 years and the children had left the nest.

In contrast, a few areas grew rapidly and these were responsible for the overall growth in population. Crumlin West, Clontarf East and Rathfarnham all increased by more than 50 per cent but this was nothing compared to the explosion of growth in other parts of Rathfarnham, Finglas, Raheny and Santry where areas were transformed in a very short period of time, rather as Crumlin had been developed in the 1930s.

An insight into the different processes driving population change may be seen by looking at some age-sex pyramids which show the percentage of the population in each of five-year age groups. Unfortunately, the census did not

**Table 8.** Areas of growth and decline, 1951–66. (Census of population, volume 1.)

| Area | 1966 population as a percentage of 1951 population | 1966 population |
| --- | --- | --- |
| Santry | 4,222.4 | 5,792 |
| Coolock | 3,197.3 | 15,596 |
| Finglas West | 3,009.3 | 18,718 |
| Artane | 613.9 | 16,542 |
| Raheny | 488.5 | 6,256 |
| Rathfarnham South | 460.6 | 3,358 |
| Finglas East | 261.5 | 24,557 |
| Ballyfermot | 156.7 | 33,910 |
| Baldoyle | 81.1 | 2,097 |
| Rathfarnham | 76.1 | 14,466 |
| Crumlin West | 75.5 | 1,699 |
| Clontarf East | 49.1 | 21,017 |
| Phoenix Park | −34.1 | 1,907 |
| Mountjoy | −34.9 | 11,402 |
| Inns Quay | −35.9 | 13,078 |
| St Kevin's | −38.6 | 5,900 |
| Mansion House | −38.9 | 8,827 |
| South Dock | −43.7 | 5,818 |
| Royal Exchange | −49.5 | 5,293 |
| Rotunda | −50.4 | 6,757 |
| North City | −60.2 | 2,966 |

provide these data for 1951 or 1956, the period of some of the more dramatic changes, but the data were made available in 1961 and 1966. Finglas West appears as a young and rapidly growing area in the diagram in 1961. The pyramid is broad at the base, indicating the relatively large numbers of children, and it narrows a little through the teenage years. It only broadens out again when dealing with the age groups that contain the parents. As a greenfield development, there were relatively fewer older people. The diagram for 1966 shows that the basic structure had not changed much and that it was still a young area but the period of rapid growth was over and the pyramid had become narrower at the base. Cabra East, in contrast, was a mature area, experiencing some new growth. Its population in 1966 was down nearly a quarter on its 1951 figure but it had been largely stable between 1961 and

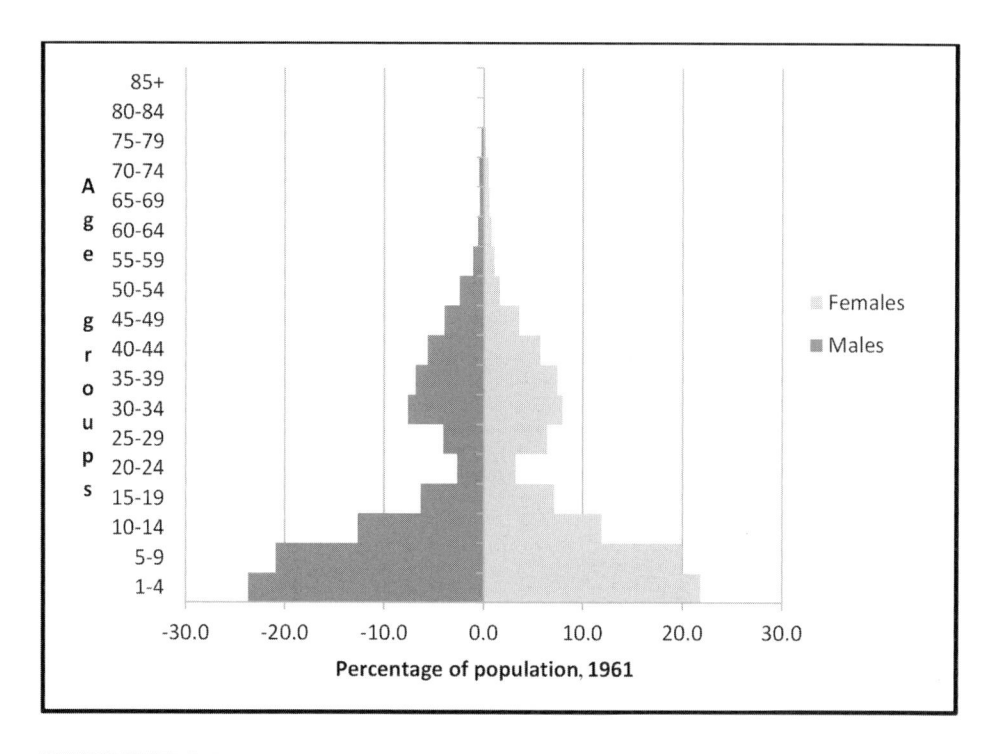

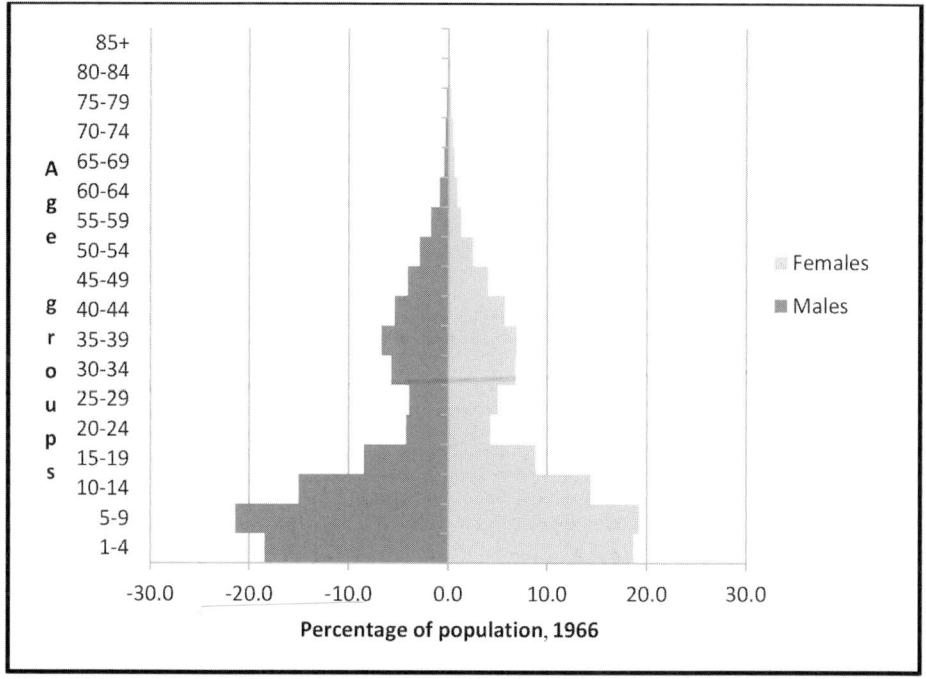

7. Age distributions for males and females in Finglas West, 1961 and 1966. (Census of population, volume 1.)

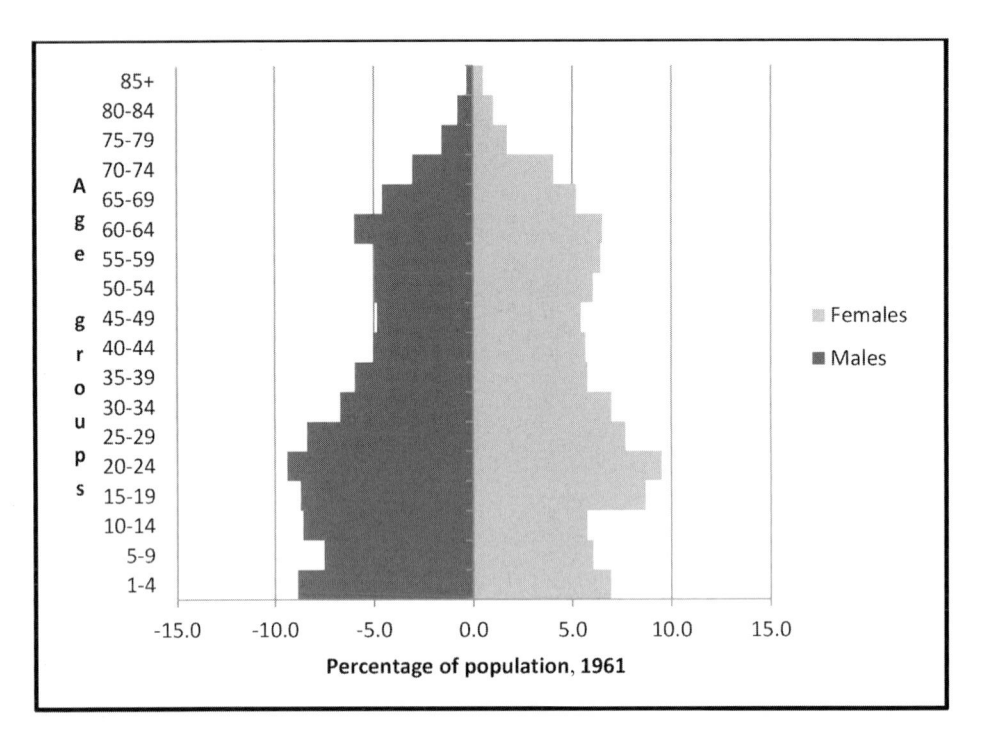

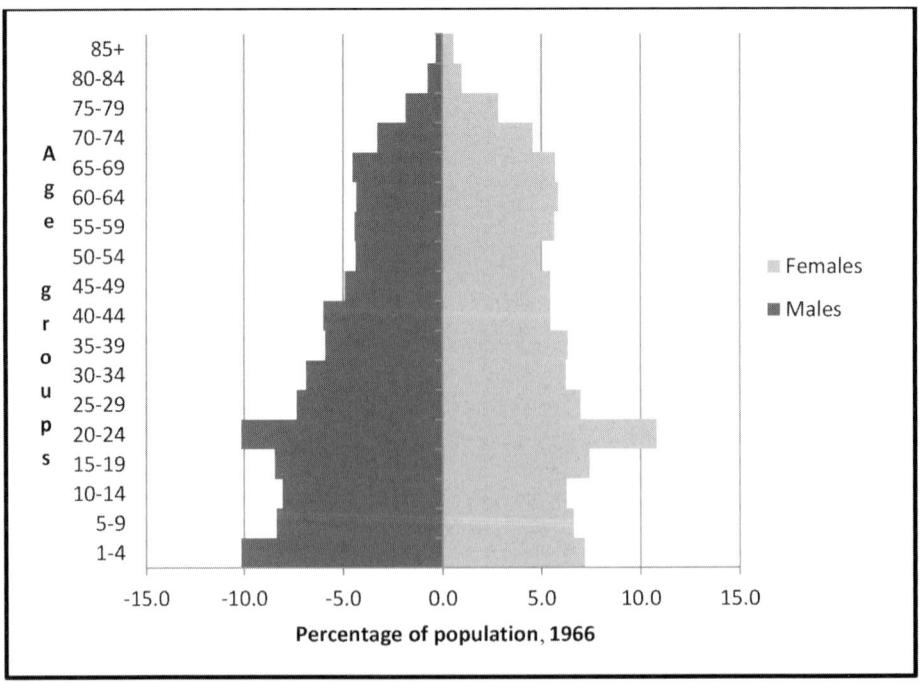

8. Age distributions for males and females in Cabra East, 1961 and 1966.
(Census of population, volume 1.)

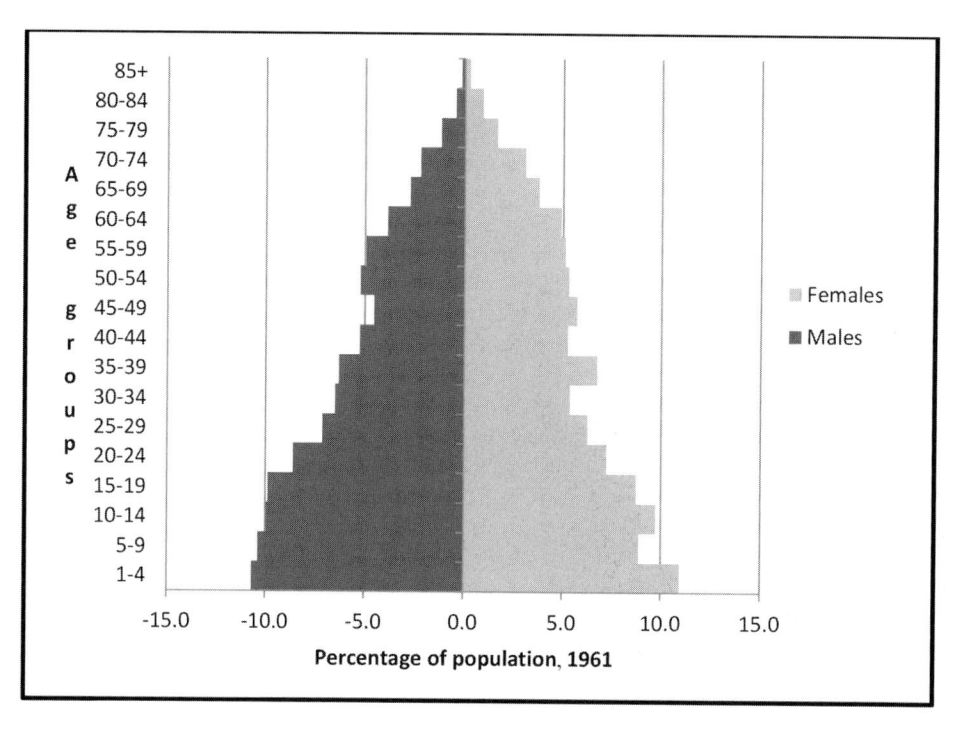

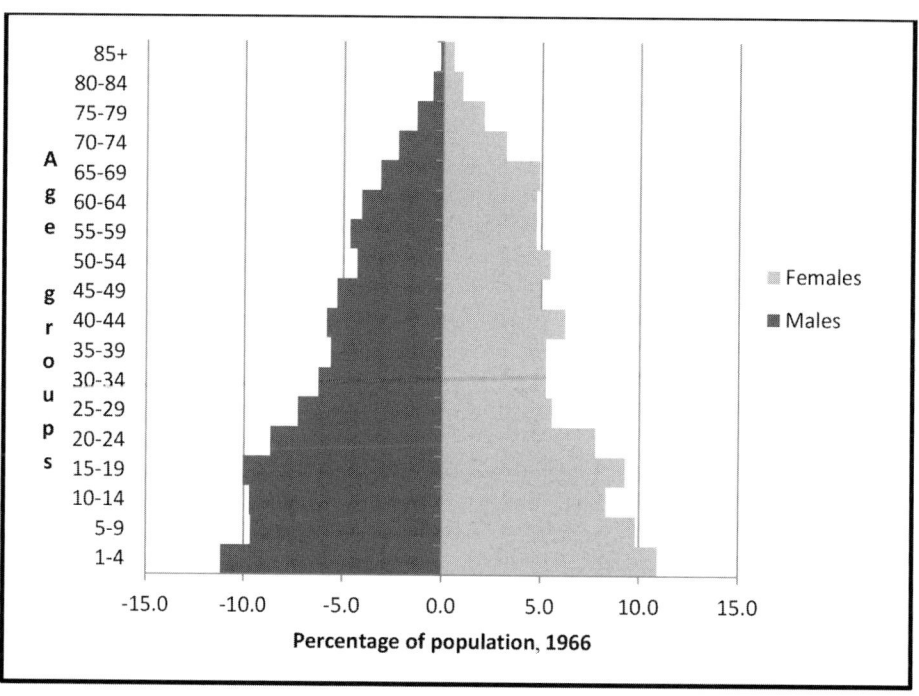

**9.** Age distributions for males and females in North Dock, 1961 and 1966.
(Census of population, volume 1.)

1966. The data show a mature population with significant proportions in middle age and beyond and smaller proportions of children. By 1966, the modest increases in the youngest age groups suggest that some housing had passed to young families and the life cycle was beginning again. This was going to be a more gradual process than its original growth and the dramatic effect of sudden growth was not going to recur. In North Dock the age-sex pyramids show that a mature but growing population, with all age groups being well represented. The fact that there was little change in the structure between the two years suggests that the population decline was the result of slum clearance and not changes in the family structure.

## Marriage and longevity

In 1951, there were far more women than men in the population of Dublin city and Dún Laoghaire. Leaving aside the very youngest age groups, there were no more than 85 or so men per 100 women in the economically active age groups. The most reasonable explanation has to be the impact of emigration, especially as there were over 2,500 more married women than married men. In the older age groups it was not unusual to find more women, given their greater life expectancy. This imbalance was even more marked in Dún Laoghaire where there were only 77 males per 100 women. In 1946 there were 153 married men in city for every 100 single men. Women were a little less likely to be married with a ratio of 140, calculated on the same basis. In 1951, the ratio was little changed at 150 and 141 respectively. Dún Laoghaire offered a greater contrast with 189 married men per 100 single men but only 133 married women per 100 single women. In discussing this in *Dublin, 1930–1950*, it was suggested this reflected a greater population of servants (who tended to be single) and the presence of quite a number of educational and religious establishments in the borough.

Men continued the practice of previous generations by not rushing into marriage. By the age of 30, a small majority of men were married but it was not until 35 years that marriage became the norm for men in the city with over 80 per cent of them in that happy state. Women tended to marry earlier. While few men under 25 were married and only a third of those under 30 years, the figures for women were 15 and 42 per cent respectively. Thereafter, it could be expected that about one in four women would remain single.

**Table 9.** Dublin in 1951, sex ratio and marriage rate. (Census of population, 1951, volume 2.)

| Age group | Dublin county borough |||  Dún Laoghaire |||
|---|---|---|---|---|---|---|
| | Males per 100 females | Per cent males | Per cent females | Males per 100 females | Per cent males | Per cent females |
| 1–4 | 104.9 | | | 102.8 | | |
| 5–9 | 102.2 | | | 98.8 | | |
| 10–14 | 98.9 | | | 94.5 | | |
| 15–19 | 90.4 | 0.2 | 1.0 | 71.0 | 6.7 | 12.2 |
| 20–4 | 85.7 | 7.6 | 14.8 | 71.9 | 34.6 | 40.6 |
| 25–9 | 85.8 | 32.6 | 41.6 | 74.7 | 62.7 | 61.5 |
| 30–4 | 82.4 | 56.0 | 59.5 | 68.5 | 73.8 | 65.7 |
| 35–9 | 83.2 | 71.1 | 67.4 | 82.7 | 83.3 | 69.0 |
| 40–4 | 85.5 | 78.2 | 70.9 | 75.1 | 83.7 | 68.0 |
| 45–9 | 87.5 | 81.2 | 71.5 | 74.4 | 84.8 | 66.2 |
| 50–4 | 83.4 | 81.5 | 72.6 | 72.4 | 85.1 | 69.5 |
| 55–9 | 81.0 | 83.2 | 73.8 | 68.2 | 86.2 | 69.4 |
| 60–4 | 77.1 | 82.1 | 73.9 | 65.5 | 83.9 | 66.6 |
| 65–9 | 71.7 | 80.5 | 73.5 | 63.8 | 81.6 | 66.9 |
| 70–4 | 67.4 | 81.0 | 72.8 | 55.8 | 85.4 | 65.5 |
| 75–9 | 63.4 | 82.7 | 72.8 | 46.2 | 89.5 | 67.4 |
| 80–4 | 53.8 | 84.8 | 71.7 | 61.3 | 94.6 | 64.6 |
| 85–9 | 37.6 | 85.8 | 75.4 | 28.5 | 81.8 | 57.9 |
| 90–4 | 26.1 | 80.4 | 68.2 | 57.9 | 0.0 | 100.0 |
| 95–9 | 11.8 | 50.0 | 61.8 | 0.0 | 0.0 | 0.0 |
| 100+ | 50.0 | 100.0 | 0.0 | 0.0 | 0.0 | 0.0 |

Note: Columns 3, 4, 6 and 7 show the percentage married in the particular age group.

Ten years later and this aspect of the city's population had not changed all that much. The ratio of males to females slipped a little in 1961 but by 1966, it was back at 89 men per 100 women – hardly any change. The city now comprised more married people than before; perhaps it was the better economic climate and it will be seen later that the housing market was more bouyant. In 1951, some 60 per cent of the population over 20 years of age was married, with only small differences between men and women. It was now at 66 per cent with little change between 1961 and 1966. As before, between the ages of 30 and 60 years, the vast majority were married with males a little more likely to be married. In most cases, the percentage exceeded 80 per cent, dropping to the mid-70s in only a few age cohorts.

There was somewhat of a shift towards earlier marriage but not to the degree that men in their early 20s had changed their behaviour. It seems that more 25–9 year olds were getting married and by 1966, some 52 per cent of this age group was married. Women still married younger than men so that 60 per cent of the 25–9 years group was married in 1966 and almost one quarter of those in their early 20s. It was much the same in Dún Laoghaire in 1966. Some 72 per cent of males over 20 were married but only 67 per cent of females. Here too, almost half of the middle 20s, both male and female, were married but it was not until after age 30 that most people were married.

Married or not, Dubliners were living longer and by 1966 a total of 7 per cent of males and 10 per cent of females were over the age of 65 years. Longevity remained unequally available, though. In 1936 the total number of males over 65 years of age in the city was 10,694, compared to 16,766 females. This was 4.9 per cent of the male population and 6.7 per cent of the female population. Only 41 males managed to break the 90 years barrier but 141 females did. By 1946, both groups had seen improvements but the sex gap was still there; 58 males of 90+ compared to 200 women. It was a similar story in 1951, there were 15,471 males over 65 in the city and 23,585 females and though 212 women made it over the age of 90 years only one quarter that number (51) of males survived that long. Dún Laoghaire was not different in this respect either; there were 27 women compared to 11 men over 90.

It got better! In 1961, there were 122 males and 386 females over 90. The Irish life tables published by the CSO for the early 1950s (CSO, 1958) showed that at birth, a man could expect to live for 64.53 years and a woman for 67.08. Having survived the first year of life, the position was a little better and males could expect an additional 66.88 years and females an additional 68.80 years. This was not greatly dissimilar to our nearest neighbour but it would have been better to have been born in the Netherlands because there one could expect 69.4 years for males and 71.5 years for females. France, however, had a lower expectancy of 61.9 years for men and 67.4 years for women and others such as Belgium and Austria were below Ireland in the life tables. These were national figures and, while data were not produced for Dublin specifically, those for urban areas were little less good for men. A male Dubliner could expect only 62.27 years while his female contemporary might reach 66.66. Though a contributory pension scheme had been introduced as part of an improved social welfare system in 1961, the old age pension could not be drawn until aged 70. The expectation was that people would not live to enjoy their pensions. By 1966, there had been improvement and the city was approaching modern life expectancy. The CSO's life tables, published with volume 2 of the 1966 census, showed that by 1967 male life expectancy at birth was now 68.6 years, a change from 57.4 years in 1925–7. For women it was now 72.9 years, a rise from 57.9 years in 1925–7. Even a male Dubliner at birth could now expect to live to 67.2 years but a woman would make it to 72.8.

## *Housing*

While the census of population is a fabulous resource, it is designed as an instrument for determining political representation and policy formation but not for the convenience of the social researcher. There are limits to what may be gathered in each census as there is a limit to the patience and tolerance of the citizens who have a legal duty to comply. The priorities in terms of required information vary from time to time and what appeared in one census might not be gathered in the next or it might be gathered in a manner which is not compatible with what was reported on previously. Thus it was not until 1961 that housing was once more examined in the city, leaving 1946 as the basis for comparison.

Dublin Corporation continued to have to deal with a housing crisis during the 1950s despite the great efforts that had been put into house building since the 1920s. It was a problem that had been exacerbated by the growth dynamic within the population but also because of inward migration to the city by people from the countryside. The CSO estimated that Dublin received net inward migration of 17,959 between 1946 and 1951 (CSO, 1958). The 1950s, though, was to prove to be a very mixed experience for Dublin Corporation as a later chapter will show. While they got off to a very good start, production slowed, due first to delays and then to a policy view that demand was coming into line with supply, at least in terms of how demand was measured. This proved to be a short-lived respite and by the early 1960s, it was necessary to raise the tempo of the programme once again.

Information was given in the 1961 census on a number of aspects of the housing stock. Most of the information of interest here was gathered on the basis of what the CSO called a 'private dwelling', by which they meant the rooms occupied by a 'private household'. While in most of the city this concept was coterminous with a housing unit – most households lived in a single self-contained housing unit – in the older parts of the city it was possible

10. Hillside housing estate, Dalkey. An example of a modern housing development completed in 1959–60 by G. & T. Crampton.

to have many private dwellings in one housing unit. In fact, that was the issue that Dublin Corporation was dealing with.

The data on the age of the housing stock showed that almost 25 per cent of the city's dwellings had been built since 1946 through the efforts of Dublin Corporation and private builders. The data also showed a large volume of very old dwellings in the city. While these were not necessarily in bad condition, it would certainly have been a challenge to deal with housing that was more than a century old and built in very different circumstances. Across the city, some 17.1 per cent of its dwellings pre-dated 1860 while a further 19.8 per cent had been built in the period to the end of the nineteenth century. In fact, over 47 per cent pre-dated 1918. This picture would be greatly changed by 1971 because of extensive programmes of building in public and private sectors and because of the impact of slum clearance.

Looking at the housing stock in the various wards it can be seen just how much Dublin had moved into greenfield sites during the twentieth century. Crumlin, Kimmage, Cabra West and Rathfarnham were areas where there was

Table 10. Wards with highest proportions of old housing in 1961. (Census of population 1961, volume 6.)

|  | Pre-1860 | 1860–99 | 1900–18 | 1919–39 | 1940–5 | Post-1946 | Total dwellings |
|---|---|---|---|---|---|---|---|
| North City | 80.4 | 12.1 | 4.8 | 2.1 | 0.2 | 0.0 | 1,140 |
| Rotunda | 79.0 | 1.7 | 0.2 | 3.6 | 0.0 | 15.5 | 2,303 |
| South Dock | 69.2 | 24.9 | 0.8 | 0.1 | 0.1 | 4.8 | 2,057 |
| St Kevin's | 64.8 | 21.7 | 9.8 | 2.6 | 0.7 | 0.2 | 1,980 |
| Royal Exchange | 61.2 | 16.1 | 3.8 | 7.5 | 2.0 | 9.0 | 1,821 |
| Mountjoy | 59.8 | 13.3 | 10.1 | 8.5 | 2.7 | 5.4 | 3,691 |
| Mansion House | 57.0 | 15.0 | 4.4 | 22.5 | 0.7 | 0.2 | 2,633 |
| Inns Quay | 39.0 | 39.2 | 13.2 | 7.4 | 0.4 | 0.1 | 3,904 |
| Pembroke West | 33.0 | 32.9 | 19.6 | 9.4 | 0.4 | 4.5 | 4,251 |
| Phoenix Park | 32.6 | 56.7 | 4.2 | 4.2 | 0.6 | 1.1 | 353 |

Table 11. Wards with highest proportions of new housing in 1961. (Census of population 1961, volume 6.)

|  | Pre-1860 | 1860–99 | 1900–18 | 1919–39 | 1940–5 | Post-1946 | Total dwellings |
|---|---|---|---|---|---|---|---|
| Santry | 0.2 | 0.1 | 0.4 | 0.5 | 0.7 | 97.7 | 842 |
| Coolock | 0.9 | 1.1 | 0.8 | 1.1 | 0.6 | 95.1 | 1,480 |
| Finglas West | 1.1 | 1.3 | 0.9 | 0.9 | 1.3 | 94.0 | 2,074 |
| Artane | 0.9 | 0.7 | 0.6 | 3.6 | 1.6 | 92.4 | 1,969 |
| Rathfarnham South | 0.2 | 0.2 | 0.0 | 4.1 | 4.4 | 91.2 | 611 |
| Ballyfermot | 0.3 | 0.4 | 1.2 | 5.6 | 1.7 | 90.7 | 5,619 |
| Finglas East | 0.4 | 0.9 | 1.0 | 7.2 | 3.0 | 86.9 | 4,237 |
| Raheny | 1.4 | 2.4 | 1.7 | 15.5 | 3.2 | 75.9 | 808 |
| Crumlin West | 1.2 | 1.5 | 3.7 | 25.2 | 8.9 | 59.5 | 326 |
| Clontarf East | 2.6 | 7.8 | 5.7 | 30.7 | 4.6 | 48.3 | 4,690 |

little settlement before 1918. The concentrations of older houses in inner city areas are also apparent. From the discussion in the previous volume, *Dublin, 1930–1950*, these were the areas of poor families, living in poor housing and the data show that this was still an issue even in 1961. Thus in St Kevin's ward in the south inner city almost all of the dwellings pre-dated 1918. It was not greatly different in Arran Quay, North City, North Dock, Mountjoy or Rotunda wards.

11. Late nineteenth-century DADC housing on John Dillon Street.

12. Vacant lots being used as car parks were a feature of Dublin until the early 1990s. This image shows the Williams and Woods site on Parnell Street in the late 1970s. The flats in the background are on Dominick Street and are now ripe for redevelopment.

In contrast, new housing dominated locations in the north city such as in Kilmore, Edenmore, Coolock, Finglas and south of the city in Ballyfermot. Given the time it takes for the landscape to recover from the trauma of such building it is hardly surprising that these areas were often seen as 'raw'.

In the inner city, even by 1971, there was still quite a stock of older houses despite the clearances and the resulting problem of decay in dereliction. The data now measured units, not dwellings, so they are not directly comparable with 1961 in the inner city. For example, in Mountjoy, despite the considerable renewal of housing as evidenced by the fact that almost one third of its housing units post-dated 1941, it still had 232 units (11.9 per cent) that pre-dated 1860 and another 489 (25.1 per cent) dating between 1860 and 1899. Similarly, in nearby Rotunda, over half of the stock now dated from 1941 but there was still 274 units (23.1 per cent) from before 1861 and a further 171 (14.4 per cent) built before the turn of the century. While much of this housing was in need of renewal, a renewal that would be completed by the early 1980s, the pace of clearance versus rebuilding raised issues of undeveloped and derelict sites. Of course, not all of the stock from the end of the nineteenth century was poor. It is important to remember that there was a stock of solid redbrick artisan houses built by companies such as the DADC (Dublin Artisans' Dwelling Company) in areas around Oxmanstown, Francis and Patrick streets and a variety of other inner city and inner suburban locations.

## *Housing facilities*

One of the measures of housing quality was access to a water supply and a fixed bath. Having to share a water supply or sanitary facilities with other households and the lack of a fixed bath can be reasonable indicators of poorer housing conditions. In the city as a whole, only 10 per cent of dwellings had a shared tap as a water supply but this rose to twenty per cent in the inner city. As might be expected, this was not a characteristic of the newer suburbs and instances of less than one per cent were recorded there. Conversely, this was the reality for a significant proportion of those in the older houses of the inner city. Almost one in two of households in Rotunda and one in three in Inns Quay, Mountjoy and North City had this issue. South of the river the position was somewhat better. The worst area was Royal Exchange where it was one in three and then the nearby Mansion House ward where about 26 per cent lacked a private water supply.

At the time of the 1946 census, just 48 per cent of the city had access to a fixed bath. This lack was a phenomenon of older houses, and not just in the poorer areas, though these were more poorly served. By 1961, the population had potentially greater opportunity to wash at home and 69.1 per cent of dwellings had such an item. Using it on a regular basis was, of course, another matter entirely. That still left almost one in three dwellings without an easy means of washing, though public baths were still provided by Dublin Corporation, such as in Tara Street. Of course, almost all dwellings in the newer suburbs came with a fully fitted bathroom in contrast to older middle-class areas, such as parts of Rathmines and Pembroke, which were just about at the city average. But, areas such as these aside, it was still in the inner city that the problem was most manifest. Without a private water supply, there was no possibility of a fixed bath and thus it was missing in just under two-thirds of housing in inner city areas with the south inner city faring a little better. The figures for Inns Quay, Mountjoy and North City were particularly low at 25.3 per cent, 28.7 per cent and 24.2 per cent respectively. But even here there had been improvement. A visitor to these areas in 1946 would have found that only 14.1 per cent, 15.6 per cent and 7.0 per cent respectively had baths. The functional area of Dublin Corporation had been increased significantly in 1953 and it is fruitful to step back to see what improvement there had been within the area that made up the city (and census area) in 1946. Even within that area, some 33,000 additional dwellings had a bath in 1961 and they accounted for 65.7 per cent of the total, not much worse than the entire city. It can be argued, therefore, that improvement was general if not spectacular. Rotunda, for example, had moved from 9.9 per cent of dwellings with a bath to 38.6 per cent. There had been improvements in all of the poorer inner areas and it was not just the Corporation that was driving improvements. Better washing facilities were also to be found in places such as Rathmines and Rathgar and parts of Ballsbridge where the availability of a fixed bath went up by between 12 and 20 percentage points.

If a dwelling had no private water supply, then a fixed bath was impossible and it also meant that sanitation had to be shared. Here too the improvement discussed above was noticeable. In 1961, just 17.4 per cent had shared sanitary facilities but this was half of the proportion for 1946. As would be expected this was not an issue in the new suburbs, for both public and private housing. It remained an inner city issue, worst in the Rotunda Ward where it reached 60 per cent but even this was an improvement on the 1946 position by almost 28 percentage points. In the remainder of the inner city the chances of having an indoor toilet were around 50/50 but significant improvements were noticeable everywhere, especially in what had been the worst areas.

**Table 12.** Quality of housing facilities in Dublin city, 1961. (Census of population, 1961, volume 6.)

|  | Total dwellings | Shared tap | Fixed bath | Shared sanitary | Per cent flats |
|---|---|---|---|---|---|
| Arran Quay | 4,839 | 15.9 | 23.5 | 24.9 | 40.4 |
| Artane | 1,969 | 0.9 | 95.1 | 1.3 | 2.0 |
| Baldoyle | 330 | 1.2 | 57.3 | 2.1 | 3.3 |
| Ballybough | 2,863 | 20.4 | 38.0 | 31.7 | 39.5 |
| Beann Eadair | 1,506 | 3.1 | 72.6 | 6.1 | 10.0 |
| Cabragh East | 3,954 | 8.4 | 89.1 | 14.0 | 20.3 |
| Cabragh West | 3,733 | 0.8 | 94.5 | 1.2 | 2.4 |
| Clontarf East | 4,690 | 3.2 | 92.5 | 5.9 | 8.5 |
| Clontarf West | 4,627 | 5.5 | 91.5 | 8.9 | 11.3 |
| Coolock | 1,480 | 0.5 | 94.3 | 1.1 | 0.9 |
| Drumcondra North | 3,072 | 2.1 | 93.9 | 2.8 | 3.6 |
| Drumcondra South | 3,571 | 8.8 | 82.8 | 13.2 | 17.6 |
| Finglas East | 4,237 | 0.5 | 90.5 | 1.0 | 0.8 |
| Finglas West | 2,074 | 0.5 | 92.5 | 0.7 | 0.5 |
| Glasnevin | 2,111 | 11.0 | 78.5 | 17.8 | 24.6 |
| Inns Quay | 3,904 | 31.1 | 25.3 | 45.6 | 57.2 |
| Mountjoy | 3,691 | 33.4 | 28.7 | 46.0 | 87.2 |
| North City | 1,140 | 37.8 | 24.2 | 54.7 | 87.4 |
| North Dock | 3,275 | 4.9 | 46.6 | 12.4 | 28.4 |
| Phoenix Park | 353 | 5.7 | 41.1 | 11.6 | 19.5 |
| Raheny | 808 | 1.0 | 93.9 | 1.7 | 2.1 |
| Rotunda | 2,303 | 49.2 | 38.6 | 60.4 | 94.4 |
| Santry | 842 | 0.5 | 96.0 | 1.2 | 0.8 |
| North City Total | 61,372 | 11.5 | 68.6 | 17.1 | 26.2 |
| Ballyfermot | 5,619 | 0.7 | 95.9 | 1.2 | 3.1 |
| Crumlin | 6,649 | 0.7 | 95.7 | 1.2 | 2.8 |
| Crumlin West | 326 | 0.3 | 89.6 | 3.4 | 0.9 |
| Kilmainham | 3,729 | 1.9 | 61.6 | 4.1 | 10.1 |
| Kimmage | 4,455 | 0.9 | 93.0 | 1.9 | 3.5 |
| Mansion House | 2,633 | 19.6 | 54.5 | 36.3 | 90.3 |
| Merchant's Quay | 5,189 | 11.1 | 35.5 | 24.5 | 38.2 |
| Pembroke East | 4,737 | 4.8 | 73.0 | 10.7 | 28.0 |
| Pembroke West | 4,251 | 10.1 | 66.7 | 23.5 | 53.1 |
| Rathfarnham | 3,053 | 1.2 | 87.6 | 2.9 | 10.9 |
| Rathfarnham South | 611 | 0.3 | 94.3 | 0.8 | 1.5 |
| Rathmines East | 4,622 | 11.8 | 84.2 | 23.6 | 43.6 |
| Rathmines West | 6,707 | 13.0 | 70.4 | 28.8 | 56.8 |
| Royal Exchange | 1,821 | 33.1 | 25.2 | 54.3 | 85.4 |
| St Kevin's | 1,980 | 22.7 | 45.3 | 51.4 | 71.3 |
| South Dock | 2,057 | 19.3 | 42.1 | 46.2 | 79.1 |
| Terenure | 3,086 | 5.0 | 88.0 | 9.1 | 13.6 |
| Usher's | 4,269 | 7.4 | 51.1 | 14.8 | 40.6 |
| Wood Quay | 2,619 | 26.3 | 36.5 | 36.9 | 53.4 |
| South City Total | 68,413 | 8.8 | 70.1 | 17.6 | 33.9 |
| Dublin City | 129,785 | 10.1 | 69.4 | 17.4 | 30.2 |

## Overcrowding

Another indicator of housing quality or of potential housing problems is the number of persons per room in a dwelling. The CSO's standard in the 1936 census suggested that a density of more than two persons per room signalled overcrowding (CSO, 1936, p. viii). This concept was maintained in the 1946 census but it was not referred to explicitly in the 1961 census. Nonetheless these data provide one of the few direct points of comparison with 1946 and they show how much had been achieved and how much needed to be done.

In Dublin city some 14 per cent of households lived in dwellings that had two or more persons per room. This was double the position for the county of Dublin and bore unfavourable comparison with Dún Laoghaire's 5.8 per cent. In addition, of that 14 per cent, some 5.5 per cent was at the higher density of three persons or more per room. Nonetheless this was a major improvement on previous times and a clear indicator of the effect of the work undertaken by Dublin Corporation.

The variation in the indicator of high density, 2+ persons per room, is presented below. At the very top of the league was the inner city set of wards of Mountjoy, Rotunda and North City; no surprises there. In these wards, in excess of one third of households had that measure of overcrowding, well over double the average. Yet, this was a big improvement on 1946, when the figure for Mountjoy was 57.3 per cent, Rotunda was 60.8 per cent and North City was up at 55.5 per cent. This demonstrates considerable success for Dublin Corporation and showed the impact of both their renewal and refurbishment policies. The wards that came next in the list were also mainly inner city wards, where upwards of one in five households were in overcrowded conditions. This was also an improvement on 1946 and reductions of over twenty percentage points had been achieved. Thus 52.2 per cent of households in Royal Exchange were in crowded conditions in 1946 but this was down to 24.1 per cent.

It is perhaps surprising to find places such as Kimmage and Ballyfermot among the places with higher rates. Such was the pressure on Dublin Corporation to build houses that they built greater numbers of smaller houses than they would have wished. They regretted having to do this but they felt that a somewhat crowded new house was better than the conditions from which people were being moved. It should also be noted that most of the 'overcrowded' houses in these areas fell into the 'more than two but less than three' persons category. In Ballyfermot just over 3.1 per cent were in the higher density category, with similar figures for Crumlin, though Kimmage was higher at 5.6 per cent.

It is the same small group of inner city wards that emerge once the higher rates of crowding are examined. The city average for rooms with 3 or more persons was 5.5 per cent but in 1961 this type of accommodation was experienced by 28.9 per cent in Mountjoy, 23.5 per cent in Rotunda and 22.8 per cent in North City. There was nowhere outside the inner city where the figure was greater than 10 per cent. Though the problem persisted in 1961, the figures also show considerable improvement. More than half of the households in Rotunda were in this category in 1946 but it was down to one in four in 1961. At the other extreme there were many areas where there was little or no instance of pressure on space. Places such as Clontarf, Rathfarnham, Glasnevin, Artane and Terenure all had percentages that were significantly below average.

This provides an important background to the discussion on housing which comes later. The amount of progress that had been made generated confidence that the housing problem was in sight of being solved. This provided a basis for the slowing down of housing programmes later in the 1950s both because of a lack of money generally and a government anxious to divert what money there was to programmes of economic development. That policy shift was shown to be somewhat premature but the data provided some comfort in justifying a slowdown that might have had to happen anyway.

**Table 13.** Percentage of 1961 households with higher occupation densities along with 1946 figures. (Census of population, 1946, volume 4 and 1961, volume 4.)

|  | Persons per room ||||
|---|---|---|---|---|
|  | 1961 || 1946 ||
|  | 3+ | 2+ | 3+ | 2+ |
| Mountjoy | 28.9 | 40.6 | 49.4 | 57.3 |
| Rotunda | 23.5 | 36.6 | 54.2 | 60.8 |
| North City | 22.8 | 33.1 | 48.3 | 55.0 |
| Mansion House | 18.0 | 28.1 | 30.1 | 42.2 |
| Royal Exchange | 15.6 | 24.1 | 45.0 | 52.2 |
| North Dock | 10.1 | 23.7 | 17.8 | 34.7 |
| Kimmage | 5.6 | 22.7 | 18.8 | 43.3 |
| Merchant's Quay | 11.1 | 21.9 | 28.1 | 37.8 |
| South Dock | 12.2 | 21.2 | 29.8 | 37.1 |
| Ballyfermot | 3.1 | 20.1 |  |  |
| Usher's | 7.6 | 19.2 | 21.1 | 34.3 |
| Cabragh West | 4.4 | 18.8 | 0.8 | 17.1 |
| Inns Quay | 11.1 | 18.5 | 30.8 | 41.1 |
| Kilmainham | 6.2 | 17.5 | 10.8 | 22.9 |
| Arran Quay | 7.0 | 16.0 | 17.6 | 26.4 |
| Crumlin | 3.6 | 15.7 | 5.0 | 22.1 |
| St Kevin's | 9.4 | 15.5 | 22.9 | 29.7 |
| Ballybough | 8.3 | 15.2 | 18.3 | 27.7 |

## Tenure

A changing pattern of tenure was a feature of the 1960s as more and more people moved from renting to home ownership and Dublin Corporation moved from a restricted form of tenant purchase to making all houses available for purchase. In 1946, a total of 75.4 per cent of the households in the city rented their property; home ownership was relatively low. That change was on its way was evident by 1961. The proportion of rental properties had dropped to 60.2 per cent with Dublin Corporation accounting for 28.8 per cent. Ownership had risen by 13.1 percentage points but there was a small drop in the proportion in tenant purchase, probably because some of those included in the 1946 data had since moved into ownership and Dublin Corporation had not facilitated new tenant purchase since the early 1930s.

The trend towards ownership was most marked in the new suburbs in Artane and Santry where almost all dwellings were owned but new developments in older suburbs also showed this change. Ownership jumped by 30 percentage points in Raheny and by 18 percentage points in Rathfarnham and

Table 14. Examples of different patterns of tenure, 1961. (Census of population, 1961, volume 6.)

|  | Local authority tenants | Tenant purchase | Private rented | Owner |
|---|---|---|---|---|
| Santry | 1.0 | 0.0 | 3.3 | 89.7 |
| Raheny | 3.7 | 0.1 | 6.4 | 88.0 |
| Artane | 4.0 | 3.5 | 4.8 | 86.7 |
| Clontarf East | 3.4 | 0.5 | 14.6 | 79.3 |
| Rathfarnham | 6.8 | 1.2 | 17.6 | 71.8 |
| Glasnevin | 0.2 | 0.0 | 34.8 | 63.3 |
| South Dock | 3.3 | 0.0 | 85.6 | 6.8 |
| St Kevin's | 5.1 | 0.0 | 77.9 | 13.6 |
| Royal Exchange | 20.3 | 0.0 | 67.7 | 5.5 |
| Inns Quay | 15.3 | 0.0 | 60.1 | 21.2 |
| Mansion House | 26.3 | 0.0 | 60.0 | 5.7 |
| Mountjoy | 35.8 | 0.0 | 56.4 | 6.5 |
| Merchant's Quay | 22.3 | 3.5 | 55.2 | 17.7 |
| Kimmage | 79.6 | 0.0 | 5.6 | 12.9 |
| Kilmainham | 50.6 | 6.8 | 16.2 | 22.3 |
| Finglas West | 91.4 | 0.6 | 1.7 | 5.3 |
| Crumlin | 64.4 | 0.3 | 17.5 | 17.3 |
| Cabragh West | 60.6 | 0.6 | 4.7 | 30.6 |
| Ballyfermot | 87.3 | 1.0 | 3.8 | 7.2 |
| Finglas East | 26.1 | 7.5 | 14.9 | 50.9 |

16 in Terenure. In contrast, the social housing character of Ballyfermot and Finglas West emerges clearly with over 90 per cent of dwellings in these areas being rented from Dublin Corporation. Finglas East emerged as a much more mixed development because of the activities of public utility and private builders in the east of the area.

Poor housing has already been associated with many inner city areas and while it was a problem that Dublin Corporation had to fix, the data show that the issue was firmly rooted in the private rental market. Private landlords were not as engaged in maintaining or developing their properties as they needed to be, leaving the issue as a re-housing problem for Dublin Corporation. Because new developments in the city, both public and private, were concentrated north of the Liffey, home ownership became more a feature of the northside (39 per cent) than the southside (26.4 per cent). However, this is only a statistical skew since there are no data available for Dún Laoghaire or the suburbs and new properties here were mainly for ownership.

## *Occupations*

T.W. Freeman's classic work on the regional geography of Ireland was first published in 1950. In it, he attempted to produce a regionalization of Ireland that encompassed physical, economic and social characteristics. As he put it, 'as more than one-third of the population of Ireland depend on agriculture for a living, and the landscape is primarily rural rather than urban, it is reasonable to regard farming as the key to the country's social geography' (Freeman, 1950, p. 185). Though industrialization was being promoted in 1950, it still had some way to go. Freeman classified this industry as falling into five classes:

- processed agricultural staples: butter, bacon, tinned meat and sugar.
- drinks, some of which are made from agricultural produce: distilling, brewing, malting, cider and mineral water manufacturing.
- those serving the farmers: milling, farm tools, machinery and fertilizers.
- leather and clothing.
- miscellaneous, chiefly for home supply and mainly comprising bread and tobacco, paper and publishing, timber with furniture, engineering and metal trades. This sector was heavily dependent on substantial imports of raw materials.

In summarizing the position for 1950 and earlier, Freeman came to the view that 'the non-agricultural export of Ireland is remarkably small' (p. 215). By 1960, Freeman had produced a greatly revised edition and he could now offer a perspective of the 1950s. In industrial terms, nothing fundamentally had changed and there was no reason to alter the classification of industry described above. His summation was the 'modern Irish industrial development is of limited scope and depends very largely on tariff protection and on the import of raw materials' (Freeman, 1960, p. 222).

He went on to say that exports must remain largely agricultural in character but they needed to be processed to add value. Industry had not had the desired effect on emigration. 'The provision of 40,000 extra factory jobs since 1945 is a small contribution, but emigrants are moving out at the rate of 40,000 per year; even if one allows for other increases in non-agricultural employment, it is apparent that the modern industrialization, though useful has not solved the country's population problem' (p. 222).

The third edition of his book appeared in 1964 but it did not capture any effects of the programme for economic development. He noted that exports were mainly of agricultural origin but that 'in recent years there has been an increasing overseas sale of manufactures, notably of clothing and footwear' (Freeman, 1964, p. 209). He also commented that 'in such vital industries as chemicals and engineering, Ireland's contribution to export trade is very small, though the current government policy is to attract foreign firms by credits for buying land and buildings and tax concessions on profits arising from new or increased exports. From 1958 to 1963, 160 new firms were induced to settle in Ireland, mainly from Britain, West Germany and the United States' (p. 209). The final edition of his book was printed in 1969 but unfortunately he did not have the data to hand that would have shown the changes in Ireland's economic profile, though he suggested that change was coming: 'although many manufactured goods appear in the list of Irish exports, in most cases – indeed in almost all – they represent only a small return of money to the country. But, as noted above, every effort is now being made to expand overseas trade, partly by increasing the range of goods manufactured in Ireland' (1968, p. 211). Had he been in a position to judge Ireland at the end of the decade, he would have seen that the labour force increased from 1,076,000 to 1,110,000 persons during the years 1961–71. This was an increase of just over 3 per cent, modest in any terms but the significant changes were in its composition. Whereas in 1961 there were 360,000 employed in agriculture, this fell to 272,000 by 1971, a drop of approximately 25 per cent. This decline was marked by a corresponding growth in employment in industry and services which increased from 252,000 and 405,000 respectively to employ 320,000 and 457,000 by 1971. By 1971 an industrial economy had emerged with 24.5 per cent employed in industry and 41.1 per cent employed in services. Given the locational attributes of many of these economic developments, these sectoral changes encouraged urbanization, a phenomenon that continued during the 1970s.

## Employment and industry in Dublin

It has been argued above that the wealth-generating engine of the Irish economy was solidly based in agriculture. There is nothing wrong, *per se*, with such an economic focus if the product was high value. The issue was that it was largely unprocessed and fitted well the colonial model of raw materials out and industrial goods in. Dublin, for all its population and infrastructure, relied on an inefficient export platform to supply it with the imports it needed.

Dublin in the 1940s was characterized by service employment and relatively little industrial employment. The clothing and hosiery industry together with the boot and shoe industries had major concentrations in Dublin. There were elements of protected industries in car assembly, and the food industries, including the drinks industry, were very important. However, even though there were 1,685 industrial establishments in Dublin by the early 1950s, employment totalled only 88,160 and much of this was production for the domestic market. Dublin needed considerable funding in order to develop its potential and to solve its problems. In the 1950s, there was no sense of where this wealth was going to come from and therefore no basis on which to build for the future of Dublin.

The words of James Meenan writing in 1957 are instructive. The occasion was the publication of a volume on Ireland as part of a visit by the British Association for the Advancement of Science. The piece formed the second part of three papers on the city of Dublin and offered a discussion of *Dublin in the Irish economy*. In his view:

> The bulk of Irish industry will depend on the fortunes of the Irish market, on its size and on its prosperity; and thus the cities, most of all Dublin, must depend on its rural areas. A city such as Belfast, which is in its own right a large importing and exporting area, might not be affected by the fortunes of its hinterland. Dublin is not in that position. Its future, and indeed the future of the country as a whole, would seem to depend on the emergence of a social and economic structure in the Irish countryside which will at once be productive and acceptable to those who form it.
>
> (Meenan, 1957, p. 243)

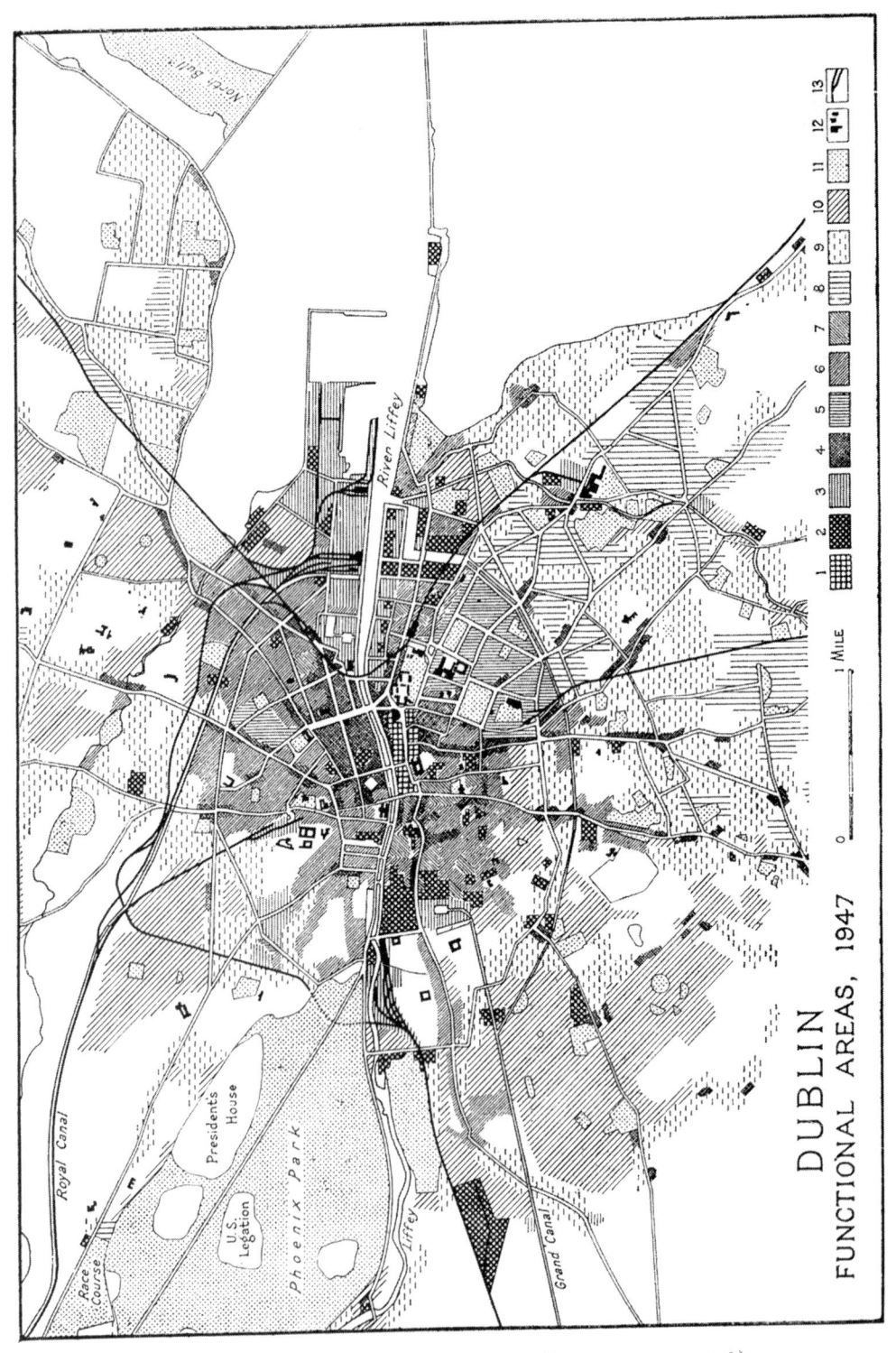

13. Functional areas in Dublin city centre. (Freeman, 1950, p. 236.)
Note: 1: Commercial Core, 2: Factories, 3: Transport and Warehouses.

**14.** New offices for Esso in Stillorgan, completed in 1960.

In others words, there was no clear idea as to how Dublin was to be sustained. Dublin relied on importing many of its needs and industry, in the view above, was doomed to serve only the local market. Therefore, everything depended on some undefined transformation of agriculture to meet all needs. Freeman's (1960) description of the location of industry in Dublin suggested that factories were:

> spread through the city and only near the docks is there any marked factory-warehouse belt ... Guinness, the vast brewery, is to the west of the commercial centre: its barges on the river go to the firm's wharf on the quays for export. Most of the goods produced in factories are intended for the home market, as in various other capital cities, and a trend of recent years has been to establish factories outside the city altogether, in such places as Finglas to the north.
> (Freeman, 1960, p. 267)

Despite the significant industrialization of the country during the 1960s, the categories used in official figures did not highlight those changes. Bannon et al. (1981), writing on the problems of growth and decay in Dublin, offered a comparative table on the occupational structure of Dublin from 1926 to 1977. The data for 1946 to 1971 are reproduced below.

**Table 15.** Occupational structure in Dublin (including Dún Laoghaire). (Adapted from Bannon *et al.*, 1981, p. 55.)

|                          | Percentage of employment |      |      |
|--------------------------|--------------------------|------|------|
| Occupation               | 1946                     | 1961 | 1971 |
| Producers and repairers  | 27.7                     | 29.8 | 26.2 |
| Transport workers        | 9.3                      | 9.3  | 12.6 |
| Workers in commerce      | 11.4                     | 12.0 | 10.8 |
| Public administration    | 7.3                      | 2.2  | 2.3  |
| Professional occupations | 8.8                      | 9.3  | 10.9 |
| Service occupations      | 14.1                     | 11.4 | 10.3 |
| Clerical                 | 9.9                      | 16.7 | 17.6 |
| Other                    | 11.6                     | 9.3  | 9.3  |

The data for 1971 are not strictly comparable with those of earlier years since the earlier ones refer to the combination of the county borough and Dún Laoghaire and the 1971 refer to the Dublin sub-region, a larger entity. However, the level of aggregation is such that this is not a big problem. Taking a broad view of service occupations, and not just the category with that name, it can be seen that Dublin's increasing economy was dominated by these types of jobs.

This is not to suggest that industrialization was absent from Dublin. Just as the decade saw the creation of suburban shopping centres, so the suburban industrial estate emerged. There was no longer room for industry within the city centre and the capacity of the suburbs to offer land for single storey expansive operations was a winner. There was also an inevitable shake out of the industrial sector as older protectionist-era industries fell before the wind of an open market and were replaced by the new industries such as chemical and electronics. This process accelerated after EEC membership in 1973 and Ireland had a turbulent time, not helped by two oil crises. The 'Telesis' report of 1980 (NESC, 1980) showed that indigenous industry continued to decline in importance during the 1970s and although it accounted for two-thirds of Irish industry, it provided only 30 per cent of Irish exports of manufactured goods. Jobs in textiles, clothing and footwear, which had been important in the central city area, all continued to decline in the face of competition from cheaper imports. The growth was to be in electrical, electronic and mechanical engineering companies and in the chemical and pharmaceutical industries, none of which needed central locations.

What the figures presented in table 15 do not show, however, was the significant change within the services industry. There had been a shift away from those involving physical labour. So, for example, there was a huge change in the employment structure of the port. The jobs that replaced them were in the skilled and specialist information handling areas – white collar jobs. It was these jobs that drove the transformation of the city centre and the creation of its office sector.

## End of the 'servant problem'

Domestic servants had been a perennial feature of the employment landscape of Dublin. Their numbers had declined in the 1930s and 1940s as society changed, houses became smaller and people generally could not afford to pay them. Indeed, there was a constant complaint in the 1930s that such was the difference between the pay available in the UK and in Ireland that Ireland was no more than a training ground for servants.

Domestic servants were predominantly, though not exclusively, female. In 1951, there were 7,187 female servants 'living in' in the county borough and a further 3,854 'living out'; there were 309 and 580 males respectively. The position in the Dún Laoghaire borough was that there were 1,706 live-in servants and 549 living out. Only five years previously, there had been over 15,000 females described as domestic servants in the city. The *Irish Times* noted in 1955 that it was still hard to engage domestic servants. This was despite improvements in wages and conditions which had reduced the flow to Britain to some degree. This was a matter that the *Irish Times* returned to from time to time and they noted in the same year that employment agencies were suggesting that it would be impossible to obtain domestic help within a few years. It seemed that very few girls were entering domestic service because they could get higher wages and work shorter hours in factory jobs. As a result 'most of those who answer the "domestics wanted" advertisements now are either untrained or partly-trained girls or else elderly women' (*Irish Times*, 1 June 1955, p. 8). There were also suggestions from time to time that what was needed was a formal programme of education. One advocate of that was John O'Mahony, headmaster of Thurles Vocational School who argued that the status of the female domestic needed to be raised: 'get her a decent wage as a skilled worker and, at the same time, equip her to be a good housewife' (*Irish Times*, 6 March 1954, p. 3). There may well have been sufficient employers in Dublin for greater numbers of servants, had such been available.

These housewives would not have been seduced by the increasing number of supposed 'labour saving devices' on the market nor taken comfort in the fact that there was no room for a servant in the smaller middle-class houses, which were increasingly the norm.

By 1961, there were only 4,098 women described as being in 'private domestic service' and a further 1,086 in Dún Laoghaire. The fact that the numbers held up better there is interesting and is a pointer towards the higher social status of the area and the proportion of larger houses which were more difficult to keep. By 1966, the classification had changed somewhat to 'maids, valets and related workers' but then there were 3,370 in the city and 795 in Dún Laoghaire. This marked the effective disappearance of what was once the most important source of female employment in the city.

## *The labour force*

An overview of the labour force may be obtained by looking at gainful employment and non-gainful employment, as used in the census. This classification is based on a person's self-assessment of whether s/he is active in the labour force. Gainful employment describes a circumstance in which a person is normally employed for financial gain and it also includes those who are temporarily unemployed. Non-gainful employment includes those who work but are not remunerated as well as those described as being retired or students. The largest group included in this are women working in the home – the key characteristic being the lack of remuneration. Purely for convenience and ease of reading, a reference to being in employment here and later in the text will be a reference to being in gainful employment. The total male labour force in Dublin city in 1951 was 175,051 but this had declined to 169,303 by 1961 before rising to 182,148 in 1966. It has already been noted that there were far more females in Dublin than males and this was also reflected in the size of the labour force.

Male employment was highest in 1951 at 86.2 per cent and thereafter it fell slightly to 81.5 in 1966, mainly due to younger people staying longer in school. It was always lower in Dún Laoghaire for that reason and so it remained over the years, coming in at about three to four percentage points lower.

The female labour force was larger and stood at 210,937 in 1951. It did not fall during the 1950s and had reached 219,368 by 1966. Employed women remained a minority of those aged over 14 years and the proportion actually fell from 41.4 per cent to 38 per cent in 1966. A majority (53 per

**Table 16.** Involvement in the labour force, 1951–66. (Census of population, various volumes.)

|  | Males | | | Females | | |
| --- | --- | --- | --- | --- | --- | --- |
|  | 1951 | 1961 | 1966 | 1951 | 1961 | 1966 |
| *Dublin county borough* | | | | | | |
| Gainfully occupied | 86.2 | 82.7 | 81.5 | 41.4 | 39.0 | 38.0 |
| Not gainfully occupied | 13.8 | 17.3 | 18.5 | 58.6 | 61.0 | 62.0 |
| *of which* home duties | | | | | 52.4 | 52.9 |
| *Dún Laoghaire* | | | | | | |
| Gainfully occupied | 82.9 | 77.6 | 76.9 | 37.6 | 34.9 | 33.5 |
| Not gainfully occupied | 17.1 | 22.4 | 23.1 | 62.4 | 65.1 | 66.5 |
| *of which* home duties | | | | | 52.2 | 53.6 |

cent) were devoted to home duties. This was similar in Dún Laoghaire, though there was a higher percentage of women in continuing education there. Therefore, the traditional image of the man at work and the woman in the home still held good during the 1950s and into the mid-1960s.

## The agenda for 1950–70

Dublin looked to the beginning of the 1950s with a mixture of optimism and trepidation. The city looked as if it would continue to grow and there was a renewed sense of possibilities in political and socials circles that real progress could be made in alieviating its most intractable problem – that of housing. Because poor housing was the visible manifestation of many aspects of poverty, there was confidence that in dealing with housing that it would deal with other issues too. The future of the city lay in the implementation of a rational approach to planning. It had long been recognized that the city needed to be conceived of and dealt with as an entity and not as a series of more-or-less connected elements. There was a long-term agenda to deal with transport, infrastructure, civic architecture and all of those aspects of life and economy that go to make up a city. Unfortunately, the Corporation had chosen not to share its plans with the general citizenry and the implications of this will be discussed later. It was also unfortunate that the economic fortunes of the State were about to take a turn for the worse. The economy had never been particularly robust but the 1950s brought home the stark reality that it cost more to run the State than was available. Therefore, what was achieved during the 1950s was all the more remarkable because every shilling of expenditure was under scrutiny; indeed, it was unclear that there would be a future supply of shillings.

Ironically, the problem of high levels of emigration gave Dublin Corporation a breathing space that allowed it to get closer to meeting the needs of its priority groups. Housing conditions had improved significantly by 1961 and the figures show the extent of the clearance of slum areas and older housing. It was not a utopia. There were still people living in poor conditions and there were still areas with poor conditions but there was a feeling that these problems could be dealt with in time. The wisdom of this perspective will be explored.

The city of Dublin can hardly be said to have been an economic power house during the 1950s. Because the country continued to rely on agricultural exports for its wealth, the city remained a consumer of resources. Most employment continued to be in various branches of service provision and even by a most generous interpretation of 'industry', no more than one-third of jobs were industrial and not enough of these were in the traded sector. Rather, the industrial sector tended to deal with the supply of the local market and depended greatly on imported raw materials, thus limiting its value added. This was a serious problem in a badly skewed balance of payments deficit. Fortunately, for both the State and the city, this was set to change and that change would result in a dramatic alteration in the urban landscape. The 1960s were set to see a boom in the commercial sector and the development of a major office sector in the city. This would have big implications for the built environment, both positive and negative. The clearances by Dublin Corporation had left a lot of unused property in various states of decay and this was ripe for redevelopment. Unfortunately, though, the location of this land did not always coincide with the locations that developers preferred.

From a demographic perspective, it cannot be said that there were any dramatic changes revealed by the censuses of the 1950s and early 1960s. People were living longer but the family and married life remained the norm. Though the city's population continued to grow, the effect of emigration could be seen in the population structure of the city. The spatial distribution of that population continued to change. The inner city, long abandoned by the middle classes, was now being emptied of the working classes. Growth was concentrated at the edge of the city at increasing distances from the centre. The city was well on its way to being a doughnut city – a city characterized by low population in the centre and growth on the edge. As will be discussed

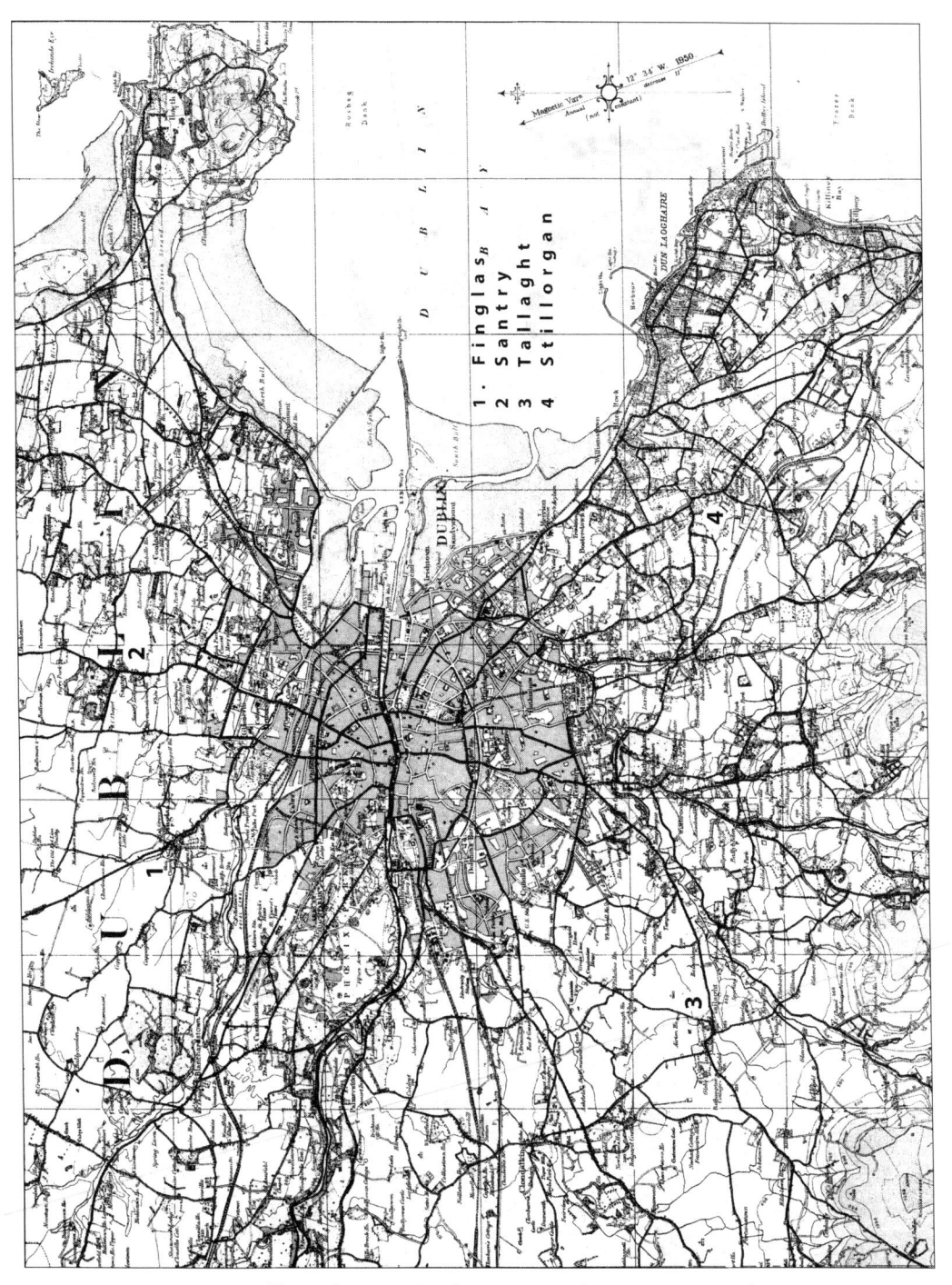

**15.** Dublin in the 1940s. (Ordnance Survey plan, 1:63,360, 1950.)

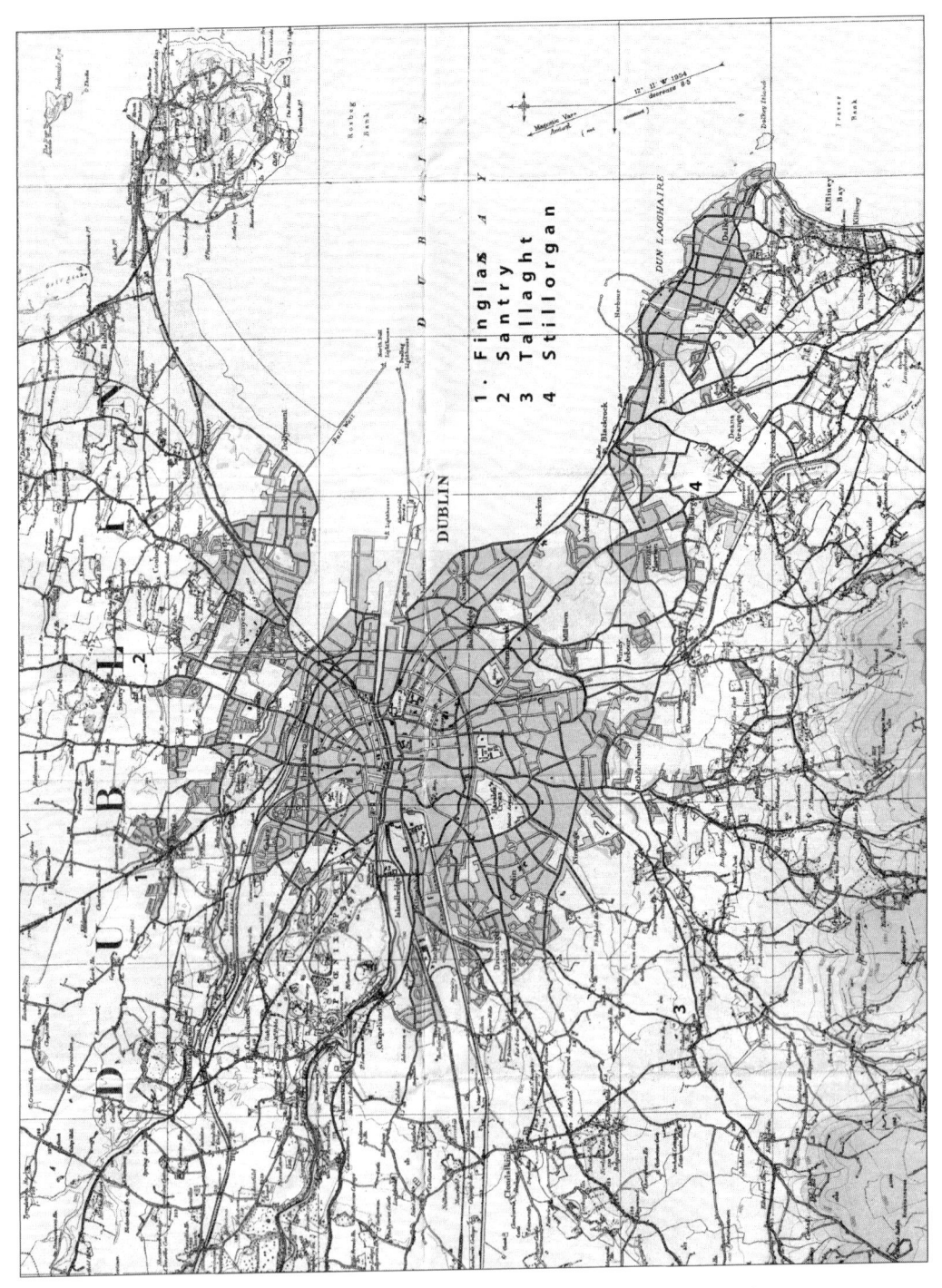

16. Dublin in the early 1950s. (Ordnance Survey plan, 1:63,360, 1954.)

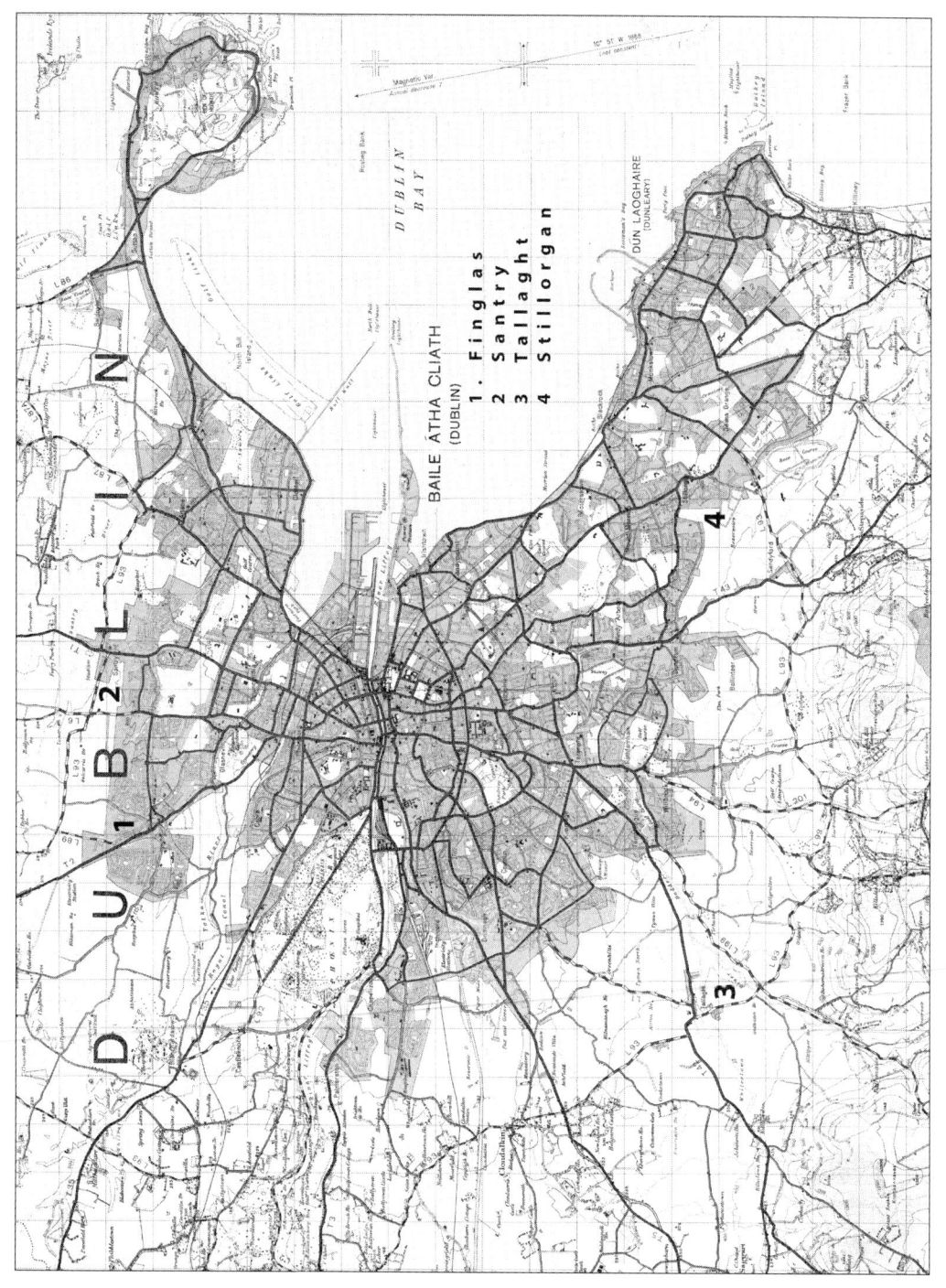

17. Dublin in the mid-1960s. (Ordnance Survey plan, 1:63,360, 1966.)

later, despite awareness that this was not a good idea, the growth tended to be unbalanced demographically. Large suburbs comprising young married couples were developed in both the public and private sectors with a resulting imbalance in the demand and supply of resources.

## *The maps*

The Ordnance Survey produced a map of the Dublin region at a scale of one inch to one mile (1:63,360) in 1950. As with many maps, the information dates to an earlier but unspecified time but it can be taken as providing a view of the city in the 1940s. It shows a quite compact city with the county borough built up and while the suburbs to the south of the city are clearly visible, they have not yet coalesced into a single urban landscape. Within the county borough there were significant blocks of unused land, especially in the north city to the north of Griffith Avenue but this was in institutional hands, for example the Christian Brothers campus on Griffith Avenue. The persistence of these properties as green space as development leapfrogged them is a feature of the later maps.

The edition published in 1954 showed the next ring of expansion quite clearly. This was especially so on the northside where development on either side of Collins Avenue was shown. In this map, the transformation of Finglas into a suburb was well underway, in dramatic contrast to the previous edition. Artane, Coolock and Raheny also showed signs of growth and the importance of major routeways as conduits of development emerged, leaving the land between them to be filled in later. South of the river, the suburbs were obvious in south County Dublin but they were still spatially discrete. Mount Merrion, Stillorgan, Dean's Grange and Rathfarnham were all visible on the map but there was the potential for further significant growth.

By 1966, the effect of infill was clearly visible. There was now a continuous belt of development along the northern edge of the city from Finglas in the west through Santry and Kilbarrack and along the coast to Sutton. The institutional land bank had the effect of providing a green lung for the city in addition to preserved spaces such as the undeveloped Tolka Valley, which provided a buffer between Finglas and the remainder of the city. The city had also expanded to the west and housing was evident in Lucan, Palmerstown and Chapelizod but no sign was yet visible of what was to come further west in Clondalkin or Finglas. South of the river the map showed that the various suburban areas in the county had now joined to form a belt of continuous urbanization.

The maps show the creation of an additional ring of development and the gradual infilling of space within that ring. Dublin now had a problem with further growth and further and more distant suburban development would be necessary. It was not until the 1990s that much of the institutional land would come onto the market and until then it remained as green space, though not necessarily accessible to the public. The foothills of the Dublin mountains had now been reached and the airport would have to leapfrogged to the north. There had been suggestions from time to time, including from Abercrombie, that some of the coastal zone from Sandymount to Blackrock could be reclaimed for housing but that had never been seriously contemplated. This left only the west and this was soon to be the direction that the city would take (see Horner 1985, 1992).

# A revitalized housing programme

## Achievements

By most measures Dublin Corporation had done well since it began its housing programme in earnest in the 1920s. It had over 18,000 housing units on its rental books by the end of the 1940s and, in addition, it had completed the earlier tenant purchase schemes in Marino and Drumcondra. This building programme had transformed the map of Dublin as new suburbs appeared north and south of the Liffey and the city's footprint had expanded dramatically as people were introduced to new locations such as Cabra, Finglas, Crumlin, Drimnagh and Kimmage. For those who had moved to these locations, the quality of housing was far better than they had previously experienced. Though houses were small relative to family size, and smaller in many cases than would have been wished by the Corporation, they had substantial gardens and all houses had indoor plumbing with baths and toilets, facilities not universally enjoyed in the private housing sector. The earlier schemes were also designed on the basis of trying to ensure a social mix by locating the social housing built by the Corporation in close proximity to houses built for purchase. The principle was that this would permit the development of a more socially balanced community and sustain a greater range of services than might otherwise be available. It was a matter of regret that this concept had to be diluted somewhat as the scale of housing schemes grew larger but it was the Corporation's intention to return to it as circumstances allowed. The need for houses meant that building could not always be as the local authority would have wished and stylistic variation was another aspect that had to give way in the desire to build as many as possible. The Marino scheme was notable for the great variety in house types with a number of types on single streets. It gave the impression of a gradual evolution of an area rather than a single estate. By the end of the 1930s, house style had been reduced to two basic house types with some minor variation from scheme to scheme.

Despite these difficulties, all of the statistics bar one were indicative of a very good performance, especially with the resources available to the Corporation. The indicator on which they were not doing so well was that of need. It seemed that no matter how fast the building programme added to the housing stock that the need remained as great as ever. The data discussed in the previous volume (Brady, 2014) suggested that immigration to the city from the countryside was such that the poor areas of the city were replenished almost as fast as their population was being rehoused. The census figures show that population in inner city areas did not fall in line with the population rehoused in the suburbs.

This necessitated, in the early 1940s, that the Corporation begin a programme of acquiring and renovating the tenement blocks of the inner city, something that went against the grain. It was born out of a realization that it would be too long before the Corporation could house these people and the conditions in which they were living were unsustainable. It was known that the private landlords were not investing in keeping these houses habitable and there must have been concern to manage this circumstance before it got out of hand and placed an impossible burden on resources. Money was always in short supply and this resulted in the city authorities being in an almost permanent state of having to focus on what they called the priority housing group. These were people with the lowest incomes and the largest families and it goes to explaining the mismatch between housing size and provision mentioned above. The houses which the Corporation built were in line with what it could afford – the minimum reasonable size – but they were small in terms of the families that they needed to house. The Corporation had also largely abandoned tenant purchase because they believed that the group that they were housing could not afford it. In fact, they could not charge economic rents and thus there was always a drag on their finances as increased housing provision also increased the continuing day-to-day costs. This could be met only from the rates and whatever grants and special loan treatment was available from the government. Their focus on the priority group left a substantial stratum of the city's population outside the scope of housing provision – people who might normally expect to be housed by the city. They were low income people but they had fewer children than the priority group or they might not meet some of the other requirements such as residency. These people were dependent on the rental market and a particular form of rental provision developed to suit them.

The debate about suburban houses or cottages versus inner city flats was never resolved but the balance was always in favour of the suburbs. It was a very simple equation. The only way to provide sufficient housing in the inner city was to build towering blocks of flats at very high density. The technology to do this did not exist until the end of the 1940s but, more importantly,

"*I don't wish to appear unduly pressing, but I think you will agree that there is some case for moving my application one or two up in the list.*"

**18.** The demand for housing. (*Dublin Opinion*, 1948, p. 231.)

Dublin Corporation was never convinced that there was virtue in this approach. In the immediate post-war years, they examined the various experiments that had been tried in Britain during the war years but did not see anything that they felt would improve on what they were doing. They valued the idea of providing people with their own space, their own gardens, but this also seemed to provide the best value in terms of return for capital employed. Their tenants did not always agree and, as will be seen below, there was always a substantial cohort that preferred the tightness of their local inner city community to the 'wilds' of the suburbs.

The city recognized that it was running out of land and, in the absence of the implementation of the recommendations of the 1938 Tribunal, it either would have to seek a boundary extension or develop some means of building its housing on county council land. It chose to seek a boundary extension and, after protracted negotiations, it managed to obtain an additional 6,891 acres (2,790ha) (Report 1951/74). The expansion was mainly on the north side of the city but with some 340 acres (138ha) on the southside in Ballyfermot and Walkinstown. This is discussed in more detail in volume 7 in this series, where there is a discussion on development land.

**Table 17.** Housing provision by Dublin Corporation, 1945–63.

| Financial year | Dwellings provided by Dublin Corporation |||
|---|---|---|---|
| | Houses | Flats | Total |
| 1945–6 | 557 | 77 | 634 |
| 1946–7 | 422 | 34 | 456 |
| 1947–8 | 476 | 77 | 553 |
| 1948–9 | 604 | 171 | 775 |
| 1949–50 | 1,245 | 329 | 1,574 |
| 1950–1 | 2,253 | 335 | 2,588 |
| 1951–2 | 1,410 | 572 | 1,982 |
| 1952–3 | 1,903 | 297 | 2,200 |
| 1953–4 | 1,262 | 91 | 1,353 |
| 1954–5 | 1,282 | 640 | 1,922 |
| 1955–6 | 1,148 | 163 | 1,311 |
| 1956–7 | 984 | 580 | 1,564 |
| 1957–8 | 848 | 173 | 1,021 |
| 1958–9 | 294 | 166 | 460 |
| 1959–60 | 266 | 239 | 505 |
| 1960–1 | 94 | 183 | 277 |
| 1961–2 | 282 | 110 | 392 |
| 1962–3 | 372 | 271 | 643 |

Despite the problems of shortages during the war, the city managed to complete a significant number of houses, though not on the scale that would have been wished. As the 1940s came to an end there was renewed hope that it would be possible, with government aid, to sustain an accelerated housing programme. This was also going to include a renewed element of private housing integrated into the public schemes and there would be a re-evaluation of tenant purchase. The targets which were set for the first years of the 1950s were ambitious but the ground work had already been put in place for what was to become Finglas East and Finglas West. A useful summary, reproduced above, was given in the Dáil in response to a question on 25 June 1963 by William Norton of the Labour Party to the Minister for Local Government, Mr Neil Blaney (Dáil Debates, 203(11), col. 1553).

There was a rapid pickup in building once the supply problems caused by the Second World War eased and in the first five years of the 1950s, just over 10,000 housing units were completed. Most of these were houses and most were suburban but there was a considerable amount of flat building too, concentrated in central areas. Though output was good, the City Council became concerned in the early 1950s that it was not good enough. They passed a somewhat dramatic motion at a special meeting on 31 March 1952.

That as the Members of the City Council are seriously disturbed and shocked by the terms of the Report dated 20th February, 1952, submitted by the Principal Officer, Housing Section, to the Housing Committee, wherein it is indicated that approximately 1,050 houses less than our recognized target for the year will be built in 1953, we require the City Manager to prepare and furnish to each Member of the City Council within fourteen days a comprehensive report …

(Minutes, 31 March 1952)

It was explained to them that it was not a dramatic failure in the system but that a slowdown had resulted from a change in the manner whereby the Department of Local Government gave permission for development. They were no longer prepared to sanction elements of a scheme before they had considered the entire scheme. This had caused delays to Ballyfermot, Chapelizod, St Anne's and Rathfarnham. In fact, the process from design through to compulsory purchase (if necessary) and onto building was a lengthy if not tortuous one. The Corporation made a compulsory purchase order for Power's Court (near Lower Mount Street) in 1956 but it was refused by the Minister only in March 1958 (Minutes, 10 March 1958). Similarly, an order made for the Chamber Street / Cork Street area in December 1956 was approved by the Minister only in May 1958 (Minutes, 5 May 1958). The concern of the Council was an indication of their desire to get houses built because, by any measure, what was achieved in the early 1950s was impressive. Even with the delays, they were building in the order of 2,500 dwellings per year and for a while it looked as if they would get to a point where supply was in balance with demand, at least for the priority group.

Output began to fall rapidly after mid-decade and only 6,000 units were completed in the second half of the decade. Between 1958 and 1963 only 2,277 dwellings were provided and almost half of these were flats (969). There were issues relating to the availability of money which contributed to the slowdown, especially pressure in relation to loans under the Small Dwellings Acquisition Acts, but the main factor was emigration. As a result of emigration, Dublin Corporation saw its vacancy rate rise to a high of 1,605 units in 1960, way in excess of its building programme. The number of vacancies had been in the low hundreds up to the middle of the 1950s but began to rise rapidly thereafter. There were seasonal flows in the vacancy numbers but the figures below show the total number of families from the waiting list that were allocated dwellings each year and the net number of

Table 18. Dwellings occupied and net vacancies, 1950–60.

| Year | Dwellings handed over | Net vacancy | Total |
|---|---|---|---|
| 1950–1 | 2,588 | 194 | 2,782 |
| 1951–2 | 1,982 | 256 | 2,238 |
| 1952–3 | 1,209 | 215 | 2,424 |
| 1953–4 | 1,353 | 358 | 1,711 |
| 1954–5 | 1,922 | 605 | 2,527 |
| 1955–6 | 1,302 | 763 | 2,065 |
| 1956–7 | 1,564 | 986 | 2,550 |
| 1957–8 | 1,021 | 1,294 | 2,315 |
| 1958–9 | 460 | 1,393 | 1,853 |
| 1959–60 | 505 | 1,605 | 2,110 |
| 1960–1 | 279 | 1,260 | 1,539 |
| Total | 15,185 | 8,929 | 24,114 |

vacancies. These show a steady increase between 1950 and 1960 to the point where housing provision was driven by the vacancies in the system and not new building (Report 109/1961).

The slowdown in 1957 was sudden but that year's decline was due to the co-incidence of a number of factors (Report 90/1957) which were unlikely to be repeated. Two building contractors had failed and there was a delay in getting a contract prepared for a direct labour scheme. Two schemes experienced strikes while spiralling costs forced the cancellation of two flat schemes. Thereafter, it was a conscious decision by Dublin Corporation to delay the start of projects that they had planned. As the City Manager noted in 1962, when 'the substantial and continuously increasing vacancy rate was noted and considered in 1956, this resulted in a suspension of new development proposals and some delay in placing new housing contracts' (Report 132/1962).

In response to a question from Councillor Dowling in March 1959, the Manager provided a list of where vacancies existed (Minutes, 2 March 1959, p. 41). It can be seen that they were to be found in both suburbs and inner city flat developments. There was a concentration in Ballyfermot but vacancies were to be found in many suburban locations and almost all flat developments. The data were presented in terms of what was available to particular categories of family and it can be seen that there were possibilities for a variety of family types.

| Type | Vacant Houses | Vacant Flats |
|---|---|---|
| Husband, wife, 1 child in one room | Ballyfermot<br>Finglas | Fatima Mansions<br>St Teresa's Gardens<br>Sean McDermott St<br>Gardiner St<br>St Brigid's Gardens<br>St Laurence's Mansions<br>Corporation Place<br>Foley Street<br>Hollyfield Buildings<br>Mt Pleasant Buildings |
| Husband, wife, 2 children in one room | As above +<br>Coolock Donnycarney | As above +<br>Avondale House<br>Liberty House<br>St Mary's Mansions<br>St Joseph's Mansions<br>O'Devaney Gardens<br>Phil Shanahan House |
| Husband, wife, 3 children in one room | As above +<br>Cabra<br>Whitehall<br>Crumlin (N and S) | As above +<br>Ballybough House<br>Emmet Buildings<br>Oliver Bond House<br>St Audoen's House<br>Marrowbone Lane Flats<br>James' St Flats |
| Husband, wife, 3 children in two rooms | Ballyfermot<br>Finglas | Fatima Mansions<br>St Teresa's Gardens<br>Sean McDermott St<br>Gardiner St<br>Summerhill<br>St Brigid's Gardens<br>St Laurence's Mansions |

In his 1959 report stating his opposition to a nine-storey flat block in Gardiner Street, the City Manager expressed the view that the housing crisis had now been brought under control. The waiting list was then at 6,736 and the details provided to the Council in September showed that more than half of the applications were from single people, childless people or families of three persons – people most unlikely to be housed. Almost 800 families with four or more persons occupied one room and a further thousand families of the same size occupied two rooms. In his report the Manager was able to confirm that 'the Corporation has offered or is in a position to offer, a house to every eligible family of four persons in one room (About 300 families of three in one have been offered accommodation)' (Report 69/1959, p. 318).

**Table 19.** Relationship between family size and rooms occupied, 1959.

| No. of rooms occupied | Family sizes |||||||
|---|---|---|---|---|---|---|---|
| | 1 | 2 | 3 | 4 | 5 | 6+ | Total |
| 1 | 472 | 638 | 698 | 441 | 200 | 150 | 2,599 |
| 2 | 106 | 262 | 419 | 478 | 257 | 227 | 1,749 |
| 3 | 24 | 80 | 130 | 89 | 98 | 125 | 546 |
| 4 | 4 | 50 | 60 | 91 | 48 | 109 | 362 |
| 5+ | 3 | 10 | 22 | 37 | 20 | 52 | 144 |
| Sub-tenants | 33 | 119 | 271 | 154 | 37 | 36 | 650 |
| Condemned | 224 | 164 | 122 | 76 | 46 | 54 | 686 |
| Total | 866 | 1,323 | 1,722 | 1,366 | 706 | 753 | 6,736 |

Source: Minutes, 7 September 1959, p. 203.
Notes: The table does not include 377 applicants under the newly wed scheme. Sub-tenants = Corporation sub-tenants. Condemned = Occupiers of condemned and acquired property.

The Corporation was not moved to extend its housing programme to those further down the priority list. This might have been one response to an easing of the pressure but the reasons for not so doing must lie in the difficult financial times. Money was difficult to obtain and the State was under great pressure in providing loans. It will be noted below that the State tried, unsuccessfully, to reduce its commitments to housing support. The Corporation also had been devoting its resources to the housing issue, some might suggest to the neglect of other aspects of its brief. If there was now a breathing space, it was a space in which the authorities could get a grip on the other needs of the city. As will be discussed later, the Corporation's housing stock was always a burden on its finances. It never could charge economic rents and therefore the more houses it had on its books, the more expensive was the city to run.

In the event, the vacancy safety valve proved to be of short duration. A slowdown in vacancies was noted in 1960 and this was followed by a rapid decline. In 1961, there were only 856 net vacancies and by 1962, the figure was down to 700. It was time to increase housing production again (Report 132/1962) but the problem was that it took both time and money to do this. The Corporation's own estimates suggested that it took not less than five years to get a project from inception to completion and that double that time could pass in individual cases with the need for compulsory purchases of land, the necessity to have ministerial approval, the inevitable sworn public enquiry about the compulsory purchase as well as the practical matters of planning, developmental works and actual building.

It was not panic to begin with. The City Council decided to take a five-year view of building requirements in 1961 so that it could provide an orderly system of employment for tradesmen and workers (Report 109/1961). This report from the Assistant City Manager noted that there were 7,199 registered applicants for housing, of which 4,279 were of families of three or under and 2,920 of four persons or over, leaving some 1,024 single people. Thus, in terms of the priority group, the Corporation did not have a major issue in terms of housing provision. At that time, there was a total of 826 dwellings under construction, though the rate of building of houses had declined and, unusually, more central city flats were being built than suburban houses or cottages. The locations were as follows:

**Table 20.** Location of construction projects, 1961.

| Schemes | Flats | Cottages |
|---|---|---|
| Finglas | | 312 |
| Rathfarnham | | 20 |
| Donnybrook | 52 | |
| Rathmines Avenue | 74 | |
| Chamber Street | 58 | |
| Mercer Street | 104 | |
| Bridgefoot Street | 143 | |
| North Clarence Street | 63 | |

The proposals for the next five years involved the building of 1,300 city centre flats and 4,300 houses in the suburbs, subject to ministerial approval. Flats were planned for Rutland Avenue, where work was about to commence on 53 flats and 4 cottages, while tenders had been received for a scheme of 30 flats and 4 cottages in Union Place / Grove Road. It was anticipated that tenders would be sought within the following eighteen months for the following list of flat developments.

| | |
|---|---|
| Braithwaite Street | 14 |
| North Strand Road | 73 |
| Botanic Avenue | 36 |

(The above proposal for 'old folk accommodation' on Botanic Avenue was the subject of objections from the St Columba and Glasnevin Residents' Association which were rejected (Report 175/1961).

| | |
|---|---|
| Marrowbone Lane | 110 |
| Hill Street | 20 |
| Lower Dominick Street | 58 |
| St Vincent Street West | 108 |

**19.** Tender request for flat blocks on Botanic Avenue, 1961.

In addition there were layout plans for approximately 500 flats in Lynch's Place (30), Basin Street Upper (64), Dominick Street Upr/Dorset Street (130), Kevin Street Lower/Bishop Street (66) and Charlemont Street (210). Sites had been acquired in Marrowbone Lane, Pimlico, Grenville Street, Gardiner Street, Cuffe Street and Guild Street where it was anticipated that 300 flats could be provided and a number of compulsory purchase orders were in train.

The big schemes would once again be suburban and the focus on inner city flat schemes had been no more than temporary. While there was

### TENDER

#### BARDAS ATHA CLIATH

ERECTION OF THREE TWO-STOREY BLOCKS OF FLAT DWELLINGS AT BOTANIC AVENUE HOUSING AREA

Tenders are invited for the erection of the above-mentioned two-storey blocks containing thirty-six Flat Dwellings, in accordance with Contract Documents which can be inspected at the office of the Dublin City Architect, 6 Mountjoy Square, Dublin 1.

Copies of Bills of Quantities and Form of Tender may be obtained at the offices of the Housing Department, Exchange Buildings, Lord Edward Street, on payment of a deposit of fifteen guineas, which will be refunded to each Contractor who submits a bona fide tender not subsequently withdrawn.

Bills of Quantities, properly priced in detail, must accompany tender under separate sealed cover with Contractor's name endorsed thereon. The Corporation will not be bound to accept the lowest or any tender.

Tenders must be delivered to Dublin Corporation, Housing Department, Exchange Buildings, Lord Edward Street, not later than 12 noon on Tuesday, 16th January, 1962.

**20.** The Botanic Avenue scheme as completed.

capacity for over 4,000 new houses in Edenmore, the project was still in the early stages of development but tenders had been received for 600 dwellings in Raheny. The Manager's view was that a calm approach was needed and that they should not be spooked by the rapid increase in the applications list. Many, if not the majority of these applications would not meet the necessary criteria. He estimated that there was an urgent need for about 3,000 dwellings but that these could be supplied within about two-and-a-half years. There was a need for a further 5,000 dwellings but they could be provided in a measured way 'with as much urgency as conditions permit' (Report 132/1962). There were already 1,000 dwellings in the pipeline and more than 4,000 would be provided by the schemes under development. The Minister (22 May 1963) addressed the issue in the Dáil when he was asked to comment on the housing list in Dublin. It was suggested by Brendan Corish that Dublin Corporation was able to deal only with families where there were five people or more in one room. The Minister's information was more positive and he offered the following.

> I am informed that at 1st April, 1963, 4,159 applicants were on the Dublin Corporation's effective waiting list, including 542 single persons and 382 families of 2 persons. 1,903 of these families are living in overcrowded conditions, 1,165 are subtenants in Corporation dwellings and 601 families and 490 single persons are living in dwellings that have been acquired or condemned.
> 
> (Dáil Debates, 203(1), col. 119)

He went on to say that:

> I should like to see more houses built, of course, in Dublin. So would everybody else. The effective additional steps that might be taken certainly evade me at this moment and I would be obliged for useful suggestions that would bring a quicker remedy than the Dublin Corporation can effect.
> 
> (Dáil Debates, 203(1), col. 120)

This was disingenuous because the Minister was already looking at the possibilities offered by system building and his officials had been looking at practice elsewhere. Nonetheless, it seemed to those in the Dáil that the problem was within bounds. Certainly, Dublin Corporation had to ramp up its housing programme but there was no suggestion that this would not or could not be done. What was at issue was the time lag and all were agreed that the reasons for this lay in decisions taken in the 1950s. It was anticipated that output would increase significantly once projects already in train came to fruition. Within a month, however, there was to be a dramatic change.

## *The individual schemes*

As wartime shortages began to ease, so the housing programme of Dublin Corporation began to gather momentum. At the end of 1949, Dublin Corporation's Housing Committee approved a revised layout for 340 houses for the Milltown scheme and it was making plans for an architectural competition for housing on part of the St Anne's Estate (Report 7/1950). The big suburban schemes, such as Crumlin, were well underway and there were further contracts to Jennings for 198 houses in Captain's Lane and to Crampton for a further 126 houses in Ballyfermot, which was an extension to their contract for the Sarsfield Road area. These areas continued to be important building locations during the early 1950s but the northside gradually took on far greater importance with the Finglas East and West developments, while from the middle 1950s on there was building in Coolock, Raheny and Edenmore. There were other small contracts such as that given to Frank Kenny and Co. for 72 houses in Howth for £81,174 and there were some small excursions into the county area.

Two points of principle were agreed. The first was recognition that in future housing schemes, contracts for building of shops should be made at the same time as contracts for dwellings to ensure that people could shop locally. The second was that the Corporation should take possession of all houses in tenement areas where compulsory purchase orders were in place and set about providing alternative accommodation. The latter was likely to have a significant impact on the housing list in the short term, at least.

Plans for further developments were agreed during 1950 and these involved both flat schemes and cottage schemes. The Finance Committee recommended that a sum of £4.887m be raised on the expectation that a grant of £1.603m would be forthcoming from the Transitional Development Fund on the basis of £600 per flat and £400 per cottage. The Transitional Development Fund had been set up in 1946 as a source of funding for a broad range of projects such as developments in mining, rent subsidization, local authority housing schemes (*Irish Times*, 5 June 1946, p. 1). It was designed to smooth the transition from a wartime economy to normal times and was originally intended to have a life of two years but it was still operating in 1950. The schemes were outlined in the report of the Finance Committee (Report 44/1950).

These proposals were further refined and the report given to the Council in March 1952 set out the locations in which development was expected to continue into the middle 1950s. This was a good outcome though the earlier targets had been missed for reasons already outlined.

Table 21. Housing programme for four years as envisaged in January 1951. (Minutes, 31 March 1952, p. 88.)

| Scheme | Houses | Estimated completion ||||
|---|---|---|---|---|---|
| | | 1951 | 1952 | 1953 | 1954 |
| *Cottages* | | | | | |
| In progress at 1/1/51 | 2,244 | 1,850 | 394 | | |
| To be started | | | | | |
| Ballyfermot Lower | 278 | | 278 | | |
| Finglas West | 444 | | 444 | | |
| Milltown | 266 | | 266 | | |
| Philipsburgh Avenue | 204 | | 204 | | |
| Finglas East | 1,100 | | 600 | 500 | |
| Bluebell | 358 | | 300 | 58 | |
| Wilkinstown | 458 | | | 258 | 200 |
| Donnybrook | 230 | | | 230 | |
| Ballyfermot Upper | 644 | | | 644 | |
| Rathfarnham Lower | 600 | | | 300 | |
| Chapelizod | 1,000 | | | | 1,000 |
| St Anne's | 950 | | | 300 | 300 |
| Coolock/Raheny | 1,000 | | | | |
| *Flats* | | | | | |
| In progress 1/1/51 | 574 | 474 | 100 | | |
| To be started | | | | | |
| NCR Road (section 1) | 272 | | | 128 | 144 |
| North Strand | 36 | | | | 36 |
| Whitefriar Street | 32 | | | | 32 |
| Dolphin's Barn | 284 | | | | 284 |
| Vicar Street | 84 | | | | 84 |
| Reconditioning | 413 | 113 | 100 | 100 | 100 |
| **Total** | | 2,437 | 2,686 | 2,518 | 2,480 |

In addition, sums were voted for playgrounds in the schemes in Ellenfield and Benmadigan Road and for the acquisition and conversion of 4–8 Mountjoy Square. The North Circular Road scheme was destined to become O'Devaney Gardens. Crumlin West became Walkinstown though both Walkinstown and Wilkinstown were used interchangeably for some time. Wilkinstown was the name of the area on the 6-inch (1:10,560) ordnance survey maps while Walkinstown Avenue was originally Wilkinstown Avenue. Though Walkinstown was used less often at first to describe the area it ultimately displaced the original name.

## *Ballyfermot*

The first houses in Ballyfermot were completed in 1948 but the suburb is mainly a creation of the early 1950s with most construction completed by 1955. The first phase of the scheme saw houses completed or nearing completion on the following roads by 1950.

| Year | Location | Houses |
| --- | --- | --- |
| 1948 | Lally Road | 164 |
|  | Sarsfield Road | 49 |
| 1949 | Ballyfermot Road | 96 |
|  | Ballyneety Road | 80 |
|  | Decies Road | 173 |
|  | O'Hogan Road | 65 |
|  | Landen Road | 418 |
|  | O'Moore Road | 73 |
|  | Thomond Road | 226 |

By offering a number of contracts simultaneously, the Corporation was able to achieve impressive output in Ballyfermot. It was said that houses could be completed in four months from start to finish and it was even suggested that when the scheduling worked perfectly that an eight week turnaround was possible. This was at the price of variety in design and the houses followed the patterns that had been used in the 1940s. For the most part, houses were three- and four-roomed with a kitchenette. Because these houses were reserved for priority cases, most tenants already had substantial families and so overcrowding was an issue from the beginning. Since people were moving from the tenements and slums of the city centre, the houses was nonetheless a huge improvement on what they had experienced before. Houses were built in short terraces of four and six with no specific provision made for cars

21. The first phase of Ballyfermot. (Geographia plan, 1: 15,840, 1958.)

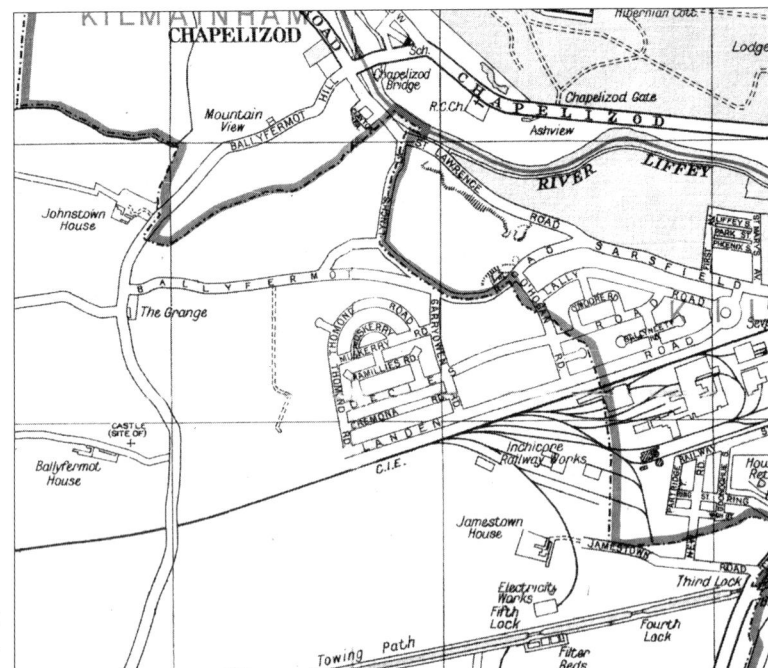

22. *(below)* Ballyfermot completed. (Geographia plan, 1: 15,840, 1967.)

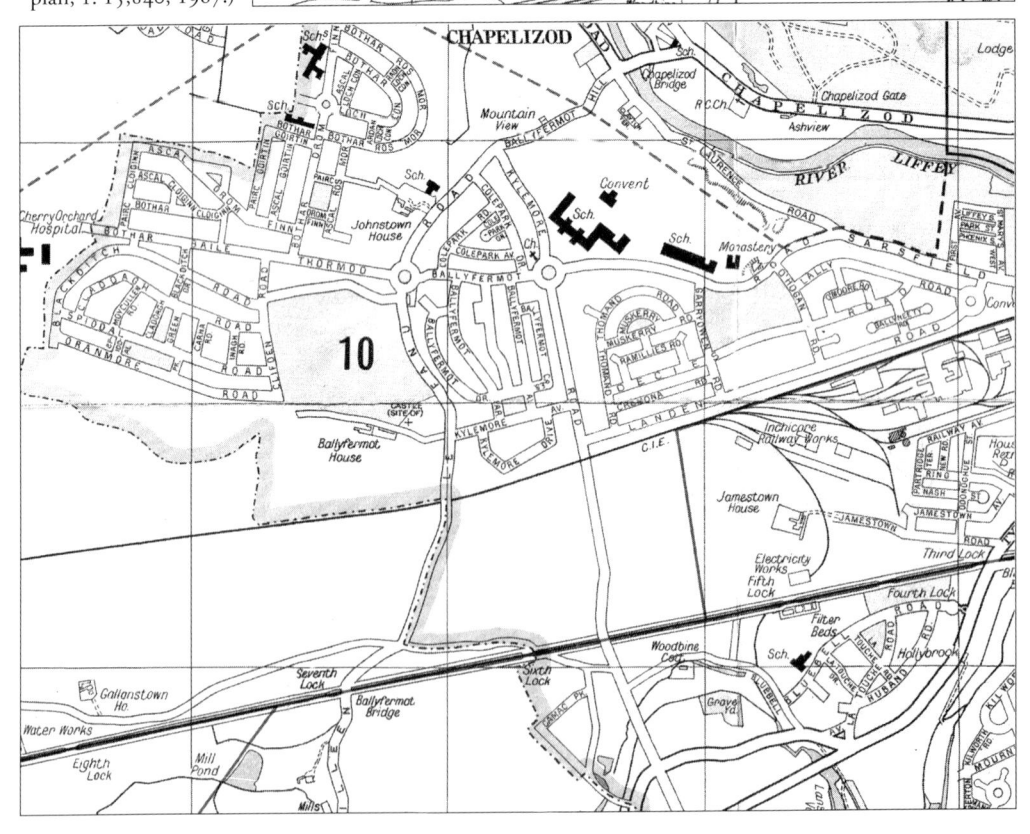

though houses had substantial gardens front and rear. Semi-detached houses tended to be confined to junctions. The use of terraces, therefore, continued to be a factor differentiating social housing from private housing, especially south of the river. Most were faced with concrete and there was relatively little use of red brick. A coloured brick course was used to break the line of the first storey from the ground floor and the roofs were concrete tiles, rather than slates. Occasionally, houses were built with a small projecting roof at right angles to the main roof, as they had been previously in Ellenfield and Cabra, which allowed some additional space for the front rooms. The two-bedroomed houses typically had a floor area of 70 sq. m (about 750 sq. ft) but with considerable potential for extension into the garden space.

The suburb spread in a westward direction as additional contracts were approved. McInerney and Sons had a tender approved in 1950 for 190 houses (Report 78/150), followed later in the year by an additional tender for 212 houses. In 1951, a plot was obtained from the Office of Public Works (OPW) and tentative plans were developed for a further 968 dwellings comprising both flats and houses. The following year, the Housing Committee approved the general layout plan for what was called Ballyfermot Upper and in 1953 Jennings was given a contract for 230 dwellings for the sum of £279,360, a gross cost per dwelling of £1,215.

**23.** An example of housing style in Ballyfermot. It did not differ greatly from earlier schemes.

| Year | Location | Houses | Location | Houses |
|---|---|---|---|---|
| 1950 | Ballyfermot Avenue | 114 | Ballyfermot Crescent | 122 |
|  | Ballyfermot Road | 52 | Kylemore Avenue | 84 |
|  | Kylemore Drive | 136 | Kylemore Road | 160 |
|  | Ramillies Road | 83 | Cremona Road | 181 |
|  | Muskerry Road | 89 | Garryowen Road | 35 |
| 1951 | Ballyfermot Drive | 156 | Ballyfermot Parade | 132 |
|  | Le Fanu Road | 112 |  |  |
| 1952 | Ballyfermot Road | 8 | Colepark Avenue | 56 |
|  | Colepark Drive | 62 | Colepark Road | 72 |
|  | Le Fanu Road | 52 |  |  |
| 1953 | Colepark Green | 30 | Carna Road | 30 |
|  | Claddagh Road | 136 | Clifden Road | 28 |
|  | Inagh Road | 28 | Oranmore Road | 164 |
|  | Spiddal Park | 8 | Spiddal Road | 124 |
| 1954 | Drumfinn Avenue | 114 | Drumfinn Road | 80 |
|  | Gurteen Avenue | 58 | Gurteen Road | 20 |
|  | Lough Conn Avenue | 24 | Lough Conn Road | 118 |
|  | Lough Conn Terrace | 16 | Blackditch Road | 152 |
|  | Claddagh Green | 16 | Moycullen Road | 32 |
| 1955 | Ballyfermot Road | 96 | Cloiginn Avenue | 62 |
|  | Cloiginn Park | 58 | Cloiginn Road | 64 |
|  | Gurteen Park | 54 | Lough Conn Drive | 16 |
|  | Rossmore Avenue | 68 | Rossmore Road | 132 |
| 1956 | Blackditch Road | 74 |  |  |

The approximate sequence of building in the area is set out above. This gives a total of just over 4,850 dwellings (mostly houses) provided between 1948 and 1955. It excludes the nearby Inchicore development as well as some additional housing added later.

This meant that by 1956, there was an approximate population of 30,000 people in Ballyfermot, more than in most Irish towns. A creation on this scale went against the axiom developed in the late 1930s that the Corporation would not build again on the scale of Crumlin because of the difficulties in community formation that resulted. There was never a formal eschewing of that view, more perhaps a realization that houses needed to be built. There was, however, adherence to the notion that shops should be provided at the same time as housing and, for example, the tender given to Jennings in 1953 specified that there was to be six residential shops. The Corporation invited tenders for these shops and chose an interesting mix from applicants. There was to be a butcher, a grocer, a chemist, a tobacconist and newsagent, a

24. Tender for residential shops in 1957 in Ballyfermot. Note that it was not always easy to get tenants. (*Irish Independent*, 8 October 1957, p. 1.)

> **BARDAS ATHA CLIATH**
> RESIDENTIAL SHOPS TO LET
> Offers are invited for the yearly tenancy of the following residential shops:—
> 4 PAIRC DROM FINN, BALLYFERMOT: for business other than Victualler, Grocery, Fish and Chips, Drapery, Chemist, Greengrocery, Ladies' and Gents' Hairdressing.
> 116 O'DEVANY GARDENS, NORTH CIRCULAR ROAD: for businesses other than Chemist, Grocery, Tobacconist, Fish and Chips
> Application forms are obtainable at the Housing Department, Exchange Buildings, Lord Edward street, on payment of a tender fee of £10 10s. which will be refunded to persons who submit a bona fide tender not subsequently withdrawn.
> Offers in a sealed envelope and addressed as directed must be lodged at the Housing Department, Exchange Buildings, Lord Edward street, not later than 12 noon, Friday, 8th February.

hardware shop and, most interestingly, a fish and chip shop. This mix came to be the standard one in 1950s developments, as will emerge in the discussion below. Later provision comprised ten residential shops in Pairc Droim Finn (Drumfinn Park), built in a long terrace, of which five were initially let to two groceries, a drapery, a tobacconist and a greengrocer. It did not always prove easy to find tenants for residential shops or to keep them.

Schools were in place early and by 1956 there was a boys' school run by the De La Salle Brothers that catered for 1,600 while the girls were looked after by the Dominicans who, at the time, were also building a secondary school. Nonetheless, there was pressure on school numbers and there was a need for pupils to travel out of the area. The other element maintained from previous developments was the provision of green space and recreational areas. Houses were provided with large gardens and there was quite an amount of casual green space in the location. Formal parks were also provided such as the California Hills Park, Markievicz Park and Le Fanu Park, incorporating amenities such as playing pitches.

The area itself, encompassing around 500 acres (200ha), was relatively self-contained. It is bounded on the north by the river Liffey and on the south by the main railway line out of Kingsbridge (Heuston) Station. More than that, the main routes out of the city did not go through Ballyfermot and traffic was much more local than would be expected in a large suburb so close to the city. This might have assisted in community development and helped foster a sense of identity. Unfortunately, it seems to have done the opposite and Ballyfermot rapidly developed the label of a 'problem area'. This was enumerated in a piece in the *Irish Times* in March 1955. The big problem was unemployment and this ramified into all other areas of life and generated a high level of discontent. The early onset of the problem meant that people did not have time (or take the time) to settle into a new and raw environment and residents often sought to return to the tenements from which they came. There were three focuses to the annoyance of the tenants. The first was the local shops. There were accusations of price gouging, a process whereby prices are higher in areas where there is little alternative. Thus, for example, one tenant argued that:

> Last week coal was 1s. 2½d. a stone here while it was selling in Dublin City at 1s.: eggs were 3s. a dozen when they were selling in a Thomas street shop at 2s. 4d.: potatoes were 3s. 4d. a stone when they were selling at 3s. in town.
>
> (*Irish Times*, 19 March 1955, p. 4)

High bus fares contributed to this sense of injustice. The area was not particularly badly served by buses but it was felt that it was too expensive to travel in and out of the centre. This was seen by people as the alternative shopping location and it was pointed out that 10d. was too much to pay to go shopping. This relative isolation was also experienced in terms of entertainment opportunities which, it was argued, were concentrated into the city centre.

The final element was the differential rent system. After June 1950 new tenancies, as most of these were, were subject to the differential rent system, which saw people paying rent on the basis of their circumstances. For some, this represented quite an increase on the rents that they had been previously paying if they had been Corporation tenants. However, those who had been in private accommodation would likely have been paying a lot more than any differential rent. Rent payment became a major problem when unemployment struck and the rent did not rapidly respond to the changed circumstances. Such was the problem of increased poverty consequent on unemployment that the Sisters of Charity of St Vincent de Paul were providing 1,000 cheap meals every day (*Irish Times*, 26 March 1955, p. 20).

This level of discontent caused a major problem for community development. There was a significant element in the population who wanted to get out of the area and back to the city centre. The new flats which were being built in Newfoundland Street (St Bridget's Gardens) were seen as an earthly paradise which was denied to those in Ballyfermot. There was a belief that only the wealthy (relatively) would be housed there. The City Manager was asked in 1957 whether there was a policy to refuse all transfer requests from Ballyfermot (Minutes, 2 December 1957). The answer was that there was no such policy but that transfer requests were considered on the basis of reasons and length of tenancy as well as the condition of the house which was to be surrendered. It would have been relatively difficult to leave Ballyfermot. Differential rents would have applied to the new tenancy too – there was no going back to fixed rents – and rents had the potential to be high but the main difficulty in moving people back was that priority in central locations was given to those who had a job or an economic association with the city centre. The unemployed were therefore at a particular disadvantage.

By 1958, a large proportion of the Corporation's vacancies were in Ballyfermot (Minutes, 2 March 1959). The reader is reminded that vacancies varied from day to day, so these figures represent only a snapshot on the given day.

|  | Total vacancies | Ballyfermot vacancies |
| --- | --- | --- |
| 30 November 1958 | 238 | 69 |
| 31 December 1958 | 196 | 53 |
| 31 January 1959 | 197 | 44 |

It is perhaps not surprising that the area developed a reputational issue early on. Whether general or not, certainly some people in Ballyfermot felt that it was not a good address. Thus the *Irish Times* quoted Martha Pender:

> When we were living in the city in Hardwicke place, the seven of us who were old enough to go out to work always found plenty to do. Now we are in Ballyfermot, and the 14 of us are old enough to work but we can't get anything to do. Often we haven't the price of the bus fare to the city to go and look for a job and when I say where I live that is the end of every job.
>
> (*Irish Times*, 19 March 1955, p. 4)

The problems were not the specific making of Dublin Corporation. The quality of housing was good though the geography of self-containment probably contributed to the tenants' sense of isolation. Much of the problem had to do with the generally poor economic circumstances of the country.

More imagination on the part of CIE might have diminished the feeling of isolation by the provision of a structured fare system but it was unemployment that was at the root of things. It was to take many years and the dedicated work of large numbers of community activists, including the local Catholic clergy, to turn the area around. 'New town blues' was a phrase created by the British media to describe the experience of many who migrated to new towns in the UK in the post-war period. They experienced feelings of isolation and loss as they were removed from the support networks that they had previously enjoyed. Ballyfermot was not a new town and not nearly as spatially distinct from the city as the UK new towns were. However, the hankering expressed for life as it was in the slums suggests that the phenomenon may well have been the same.

## *Finglas East and West*

Dublin Corporation was running out of land in the early 1950s. This prompted a boundary extension to the city which was the subject of protracted negotiations between city and county in the late 1940s and early 1950s. While this added dramatically to the area of the city, most of the addition was to the north of the city with the result that the focus for large scale house building shifted there. Acquiring land was one step, the other was a significant infrastructural investment in sewers. The north Dublin drainage scheme opened up the northern part of the city to development and set the stage for most of the new housing schemes of the 1950s.

In 1950 the comprehensive layout for the Finglas scheme was agreed by the Corporation's Town Planning and Streets Committee. At that time, Finglas was still a small village to the north-west of the city. It was a long way from the centre but its landscape had not been entirely untouched by large-scale building. The St George's Public Utility Society built 100 houses on Jamestown Road in the 1930s (*Irish Times*, 6 February, 1933, p. 2). These were four-, five- and six-roomed houses, described as semi-bungalows and rented on the basis of a deposit of between £30 and £40 and then a tenant purchase scheme, as was common at the time.

The businesses in Finglas were intimately involved in the provision of food to the city. Much of the land was used for milk production or for the production of cattle for the Dublin market. The idea of turning this land into a housing development did not go down well with all of the landowners and there was quite a level of objection when the public inquiry into the

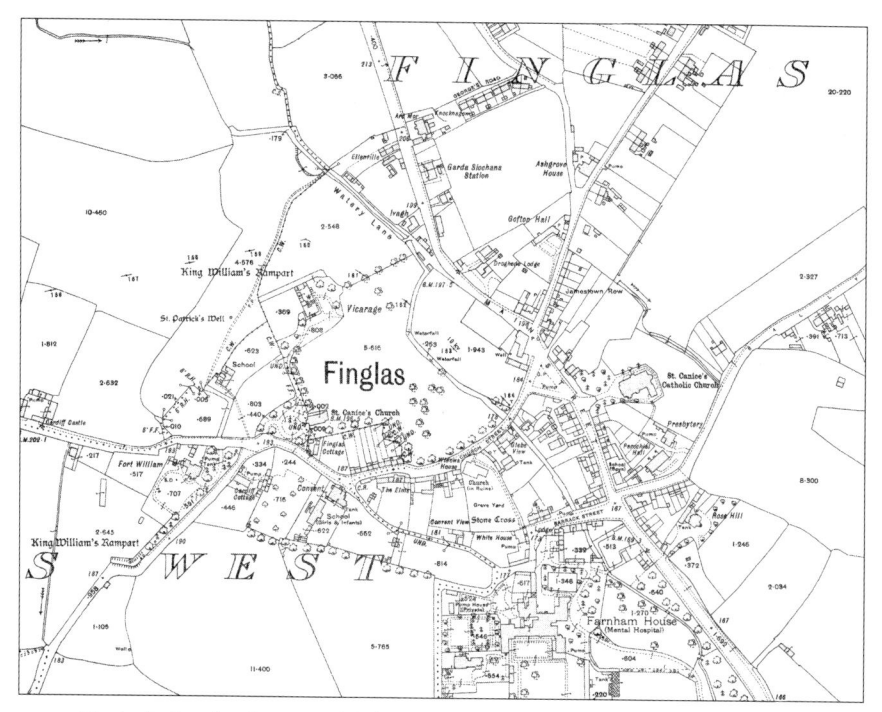

**25.** Finglas before development. (Ordnance Survey plan, 1:2,500, Sheet 14(XIV), 1939.) Its medieval character is still evident in this plan.

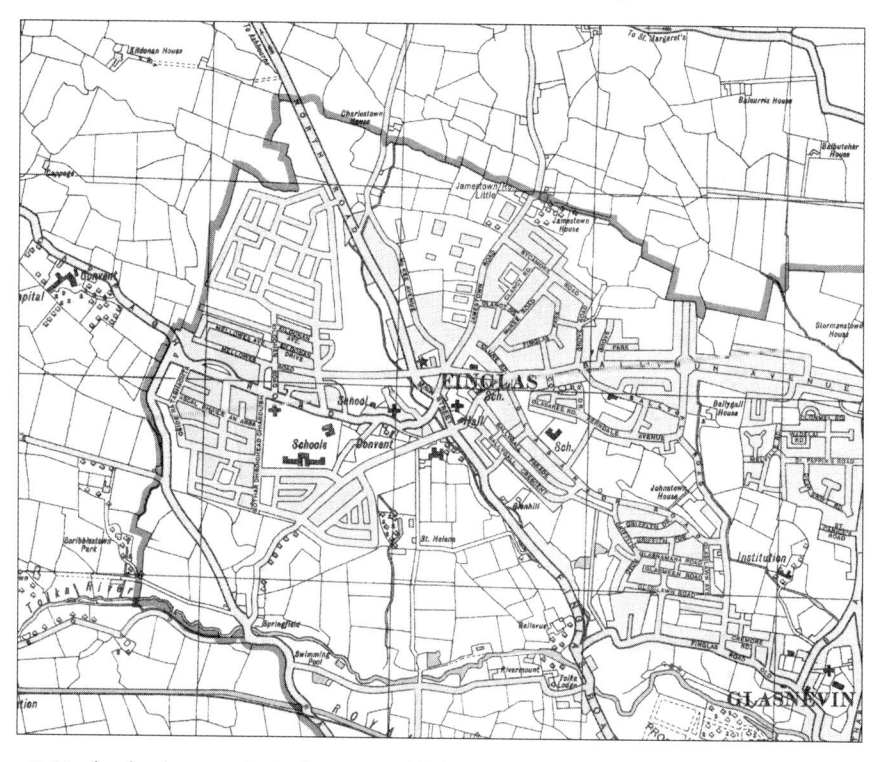

**26.** Finglas development in the late 1950s. (Ordnance Survey plan, 1:25,000, 1959.) Note the spatially discontinuous nature of the development on both sides of the main road.

compulsory purchase order for 200 acres (81ha) in Finglas West was held in 1951. At that hearing it was stated that the intention was to build about 3,500 houses as part of the Finglas scheme but the ultimate intention was to house about 30,000 people in the Finglas area. This planning difficulty was overcome and the process of awarding tenders began, using the same mechanism as used elsewhere. The houses were built in phases with a number of builders engaged at any one time. Building to the west and east of the village was undertaken simultaneously but there was greater emphasis on the east side in the early days. While shops were included, there was an odd decision in relation to Finglas West. A tender for 184 houses in Finglas West was accepted from Messrs. E. O'Sullivan in 1950. As part of this tendering process, it was decided to provide only six residential shops in the initial stages because of the existing level of provision in Finglas village, though this was a good distance away (Report 97/1950). By 1952, the first dwellings were completed – a total of 687 houses and 40 flats.

| Year | Location | Houses | Flats |
| --- | --- | --- | --- |
| 1952 | Ballygall Crescent | 140 | 0 |
| | Ballygall Parade | 138 | 32 |
| | Ballygall Place | 26 | 0 |
| | Ballygall Road West | 32 | 0 |
| | Collins Drive | 42 | 0 |
| | Collins Green | 12 | 0 |
| | Collins Row | 6 | 0 |
| | Glasanaon Road | 61 | 0 |
| | Glasaree Road | 50 | 0 |
| | Cappagh Drive | 52 | 8 |
| | Kildonan Road | 8 | 0 |
| | Liam Mellowes Avenue | 120 | 0 |

Most of the first completions were in the eastern section. The area was bounded by Finglas Road, Ballygall Road East and Jamestown Road. The houses were largely of uniform design, three- or four-roomed with concrete render as the facing and concrete roof tiles. Gardens were provided front and rear and, though the roads were wider than in previous generations, garage space was not provided. They were a little different to previous variants in that a small porch was provided but there was even less internal variation compared to earlier schemes. The most interesting was Ballygall Crescent where short terraces of houses between it and Ballygall Parade (mostly three roomed) were

27. Standard houses at Ballygall Crescent.

set at right angles to the street. This reduced footfall and there was no provision for through traffic. There were gardens front and rear but having no walls between the gardens resulted in an open landscape between the two perpendicular streets. This approach was repeated at Cappagh Drive but it does not seem to have been popular. It will be seen later on that this was one of the suggested standard layouts from the UK Housing Manual but there seemed to have been a preference by Dublin Corporation for the more standard 'on street' design.

Cappagh Drive, Kildonan Road and Mellowes Avenue (later Liam Mellowes Avenue) were in the western section of the scheme. These were quite a distance from the houses in the eastern section and would have been somewhat isolated in the early days. Though the roads were narrower, the basic design was the same and while there were both three- and four-roomed houses, there was a greater concentration on three-roomed houses with reasonably sized gardens front and rear with metal railings. These early developments at Finglas were cotemporaneous with significant public utility society building. The scale of this activity was unusual in a Dublin context and rivalled the work being undertaken by Associated Properties in Wadelai, described in the previous volume in this series.

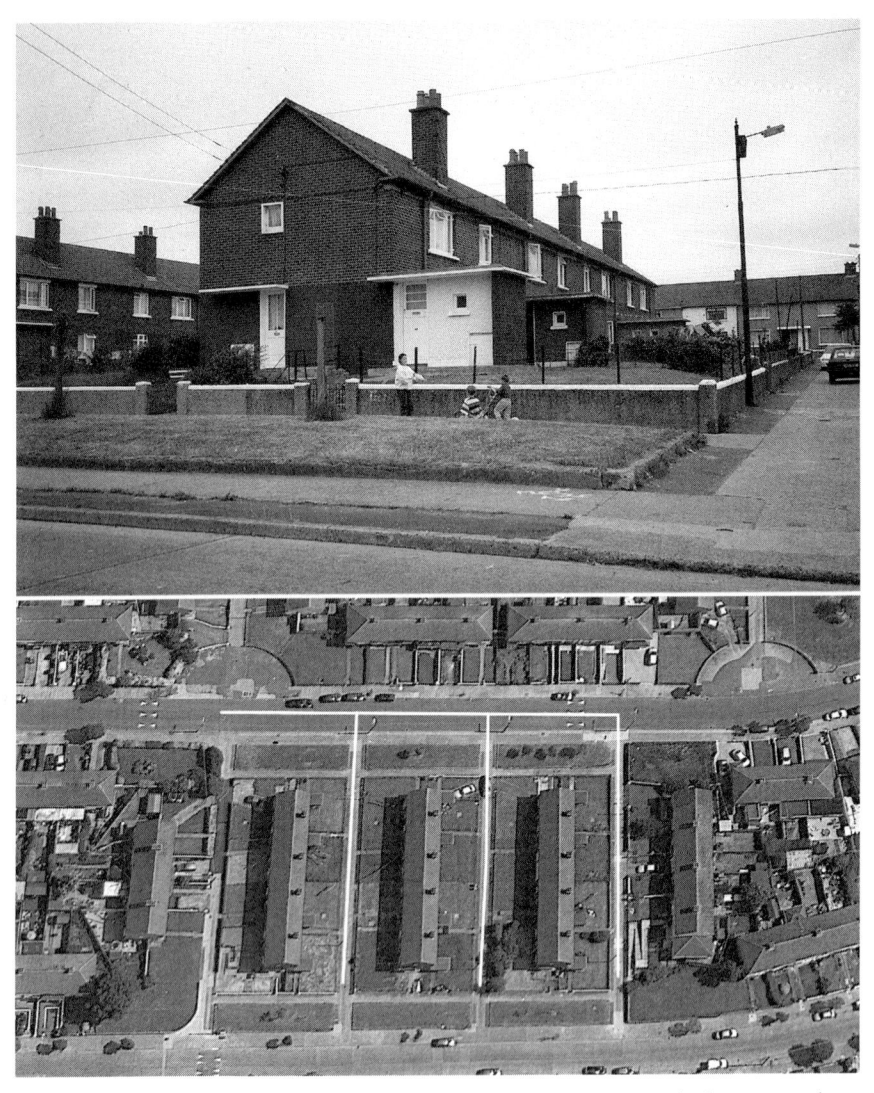

**28.** Houses at right angles to road at Ballygall Crescent. The access to the houses is wide enough for a car to pass, which somewhat diminishes the value of the concept.

Development in Finglas East was largely complete by the early 1950s with only small additions made thereafter. From then on, the focus moved to Finglas West, an area with very little previous development. It can be seen from table 22 that development was steady right into the middle of the 1960s but that the pace of development was greater in the early years, 1956 being the apex. The Corporation approved two tenders by its direct labour unit in 1956 (Report 6/1956), one for 112 houses at a cost of £135,804 and

**Table 22.** House building in Finglas East and West, 1953–65.

| Year | Finglas East | Finglas West |
|---|---|---|
| 1953 | 362 | |
| 1956 | | 734 |
| 1957 | | 302 |
| 1959 | 82 | 184 |
| 1960 | | 40 |
| 1961 | | 252 |
| 1962 | | 330 |
| 1963 | | 190 |
| 1964 | 18 | 122 |
| 1965 | | 102 |

**Table 23.** Later additions to Finglas East.

| | | Houses | Flats |
|---|---|---|---|
| 1953 | Collins Place | 18 | 24 |
| | Finglas Place | 42 | 0 |
| | Glasanaon Place | 4 | 0 |
| | Griffith Drive | 76 | 0 |
| | Griffith Parade | 78 | 0 |
| | Griffith Road | 144 | 0 |
| 1959 | Beneavin Road | 8 | 0 |
| | Ferndale Avenue | 38 | 0 |
| | Glasanaon Road | 36 | 0 |
| 1964 | Finglas Place | 18 | 0 |
| 1966 | Finglas Road | 18 | 0 |

the second for 176 houses at a cost of £207,255 so that, in gross terms, these houses cost the city about £1,200 each. A later tender awarded to Crampton at the end of 1958 for 80 houses worked out at almost £1,400 in gross terms, suggesting a significant increase in costs (Report 26/1959).

Later development in Finglas East was largely confined to filling in gaps between the earlier development and the houses being built by the Ballygall Public Utility Society. The latter had built around Griffith Road since the early 1950s and because of this, Dublin Corporation succeeded in creating a mixed development with significant private housing in close proximity to a large social housing scheme. This was not always entirely welcomed by the private residents and there was the usual concern expressed about the impact of such

**29.** Housing on Ferndale Road, Finglas.

proximity on property prices. This was noted at a meeting of the Finglas East Development Association in 1953 when the chairman complained that the area had once been a residential area but there were now factories close by as well as a Corporation estate which they had not been told was in prospect when they bought. They were seeking a fifty per cent reduction in the valuation of their houses, which in turn would halve the amount of rates payable (*Irish Times*, 20 February 1953, p. 1).

The list which follows gives the approximate sequence of building in Finglas West, which was about as peripheral as it was possible to be. As with Ballyfermot it was circumscribed by its local physical geography. The Tolka Valley, a substantial physical feature in this part of the river's course, formed the southern boundary while the main Finglas road ran to the east. Although that road was not the physical barrier that it is today, the area was cut off from the more developed Finglas East with its better range of facilities. To add to any sense of isolation, the earlier tenders were at the western edge of the city with infill towards the city taking place only in later times. The houses were of the same basic design as used elsewhere, with variation in porch design being the most significant difference between the various contracts.

## A REVITALIZED HOUSING PROGRAMME

| Year | Location | Houses | Location | Houses |
|---|---|---|---|---|
| 1956 | Abbotstown Ave | 108 | Abbotstown Drive | 48 |
| | Abbotstown Road | 72 | Cappagh Road | 36 |
| | Cardiffsbridge Ave | 78 | Cardiffsbridge Road | 60 |
| | Deanstown Green | 34 | Deanstown Park | 38 |
| | Deanstown Road | 44 | Ratoath Avenue | 92 |
| | Ratoath Drive | 16 | Wellmount Green | 26 |
| | Wellmount Park | 18 | Wellmount Ave | 20 |
| | Wellmount Crescent | 44 | | |
| 1957 | Deanstown Avenue | 32 | Deanstown Drive | 10 |
| | Dunsink Avenue | 80 | Dunsink Drive | 42 |
| | Dunsink Green | 34 | Dunsink Park | 38 |
| | Wellmount Drive | 10 | Wellmount Road | 56 |
| 1958 | Dunsink Gardens | 40 | Dunsink Road | 26 |
| 1959 | Barry Road | 14 | Casement Drive | 42 |
| | Casement Grove | 60 | Casement Park | 68 |
| 1960 | Kilshane Road | 40 | | |
| 1961 | Barry Drive | 40 | Barry Green | 18 |
| | Barry Park | 84 | Barry Road | 18 |
| | Kildonan Road | 36 | Liam Mellowes Avenue | 4 |
| | Liam Mellowes Park | 52 | | |
| 1962 | Barry Avenue | 8 | Barry Avenue | 18 |
| | Barry Avenue | 31 | Casement Drive | 41 |
| | Casement Green | 45 | Casement Park | 8 |
| | Plunkett Avenue | 24 | Plunkett Drive | 40 |
| | Plunkett Green | 34 | Plunkett Grove | 6 |
| | Plunkett Road | 18 | Plunkett Road | 57 |
| 1963 | Cappagh Avenue | 48 | Cappagh Road | 6 |
| | McKelvey Avenue | 62 | McKelvey Road | 36 |
| | Ratoath Avenue | 6 | Ratoath Drive | 16 |
| | Ratoath Road | 16 | | |
| 1964 | Casement Park | 6 | Casement Road | 10 |
| | Casement Road | 74 | Dunsink Road | 16 |
| | St Margarets Road | 12 | Wellmount Road | 4 |
| 1965 | Cappagh Avenue | 4 | Casement Road | 4 |
| | Plunkett Avenue | 40 | Plunkett Crescent | 36 |

There were well-justified complaints that shopping facilities were inadequate for the growing population. There were constant gripes about the cost of bus fares to go shopping elsewhere and even a trip to the better shopping facilities in Finglas East was quite an expedition. Though Dublin Corporation had plans to build residential shops as part of the development, it seems that the initial six shops provided had to serve a local population of

30. Aerial view of Finglas West; Kildonan Park is in the upper area of the image.

31. Mellowes Park in Finglas West built by W.&T. Crampton in 1960–1.

about 15,000 (*Irish Times*, 13 January 1964, p. 9). Sites were reserved for shops but the Corporation was slow to allocate them. For example, in 1956 it was noted that they had serviced sites for 25 shops in Finglas West in the area south of Mellowes Road and 24 sites to the north of this road. They had made a similar provision of 28 shops in Finglas East (Report 93/1956).

32. General tender for shops in Finglas West in 1961.

**BARDAS ATHA CLIATH**
**SITES FOR RESIDENTIAL SHOPS**
**at**
**FINGLAS WEST**

The Corporation has sites available for leasing at the Finglas West Housing Area for the erection of residential shops.

Full particulars may be obtained at the Housing Department, Exchange Buildings, Lord Edward Street.

Tender forms are available on payment of a fee of £10 10s. 0d., which will be refunded to applicants who submit a bona fide tender which is not subsequently withdrawn.

The highest or any offer will not necessarily be accepted.

The latest date for the receipt of tenders is 12 noon on **Tuesday, 7th March, 1961.**

## Walkinstown and Milltown

The southside schemes in the early 1950s were different in scale to those on the northside. Even with the extension of the city boundary, the area available for building was much more limited. The developments had more of the character of infills than major extensions of the city as in the case of Finglas West.

The Milltown scheme was announced in the late 1940s and was well underway as the 1950s began. Approval was given to plans prepared by Messrs McDonnell and Dixon (Architects) for 232 dwellings with 6 residential shops (Report 97/1950). The final total turned out to be a little higher with 237 houses and 49 flats being completed by 1952. The houses comprised short terraces, as was usual, but with the additional element of a hip roof at right angles to the terrace on some of the mid-terrace houses. An additional element in this development was the need to act on conditions in Milltown village. The village of Milltown claimed to pre-date the Anglo-Normans but its older housing had fallen into ruin by the 1950s and was regarded as unfit for human habitation. This led to a clearance order being sought by Dublin Corporation in 1951 that encompassed most of the village and involved the displacement of 60 families comprising 247 persons. They were housed in the new development close by and the demolition did not begin until that housing was complete. However, this also resulted in the transformation of the area as the original site, being prone to flooding, was no longer felt to be fit for residences. The eighteen-foot road (5m) which passed through the village was widened to 30 feet (9m) with a widening of Milltown Bridge to 50 feet (15m). A stretch of the Dodder riverbank was reserved for a park with a car park provided.

| Year | Location | Houses | Flats |
|---|---|---|---|
| 1952 | St Columbanus Place | 13 | 37 |
| | St Columbanus Road | 102 | 0 |
| | St Columbanus Avenue | 52 | 0 |
| | St Gall Gardens North | 14 | 12 |
| | St Gall Gardens South | 8 | 0 |
| | Patrick Doyle Road | 48 | 0 |

The sequence shows that a relatively large number of flats were included in the scheme but these were low density and in the form of duplexes rather than blocks.

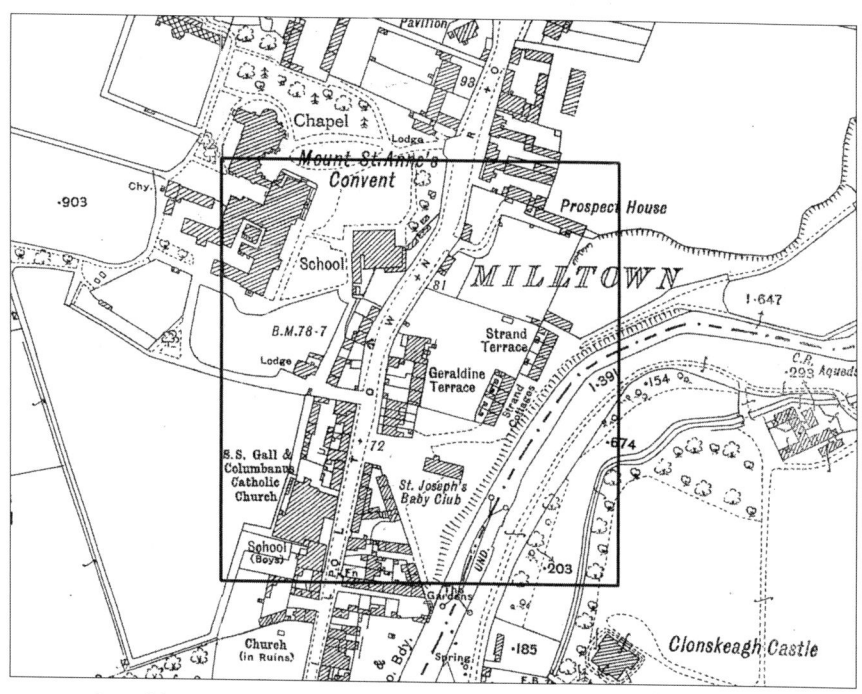

33. Site of the Milltown clearance. The main locations are enclosed in the rectangle.
(Ordnance Survey plan, 1:2,500, Sheet 22(4), 1936–7.)

SCHEDULE ABOVE REFERRED TO.
The area to which the Order relates is bounded as follows:—

" On the North by the lands of Mount St. Anne's Convent and Milltown Hill. On the East by Milltown Hill and Main Street. On the North again by Main Street and No. 7 Geraldine Terrace. On the West by the rere of Nos. 4, 5, 6 and 7 Geraldine Terrace. On the North again by land between Geraldine Terrace and the rere of Strand Cottages. On the West again by land at rere of Nos. 1, 2, 3 and 4 Strand Cottages. Again on the North by land adjoining the northern boundary of No 4 Strand Cottages. Again on the West by land north of and adjoining No 4 Strand Cottages. On the North again by No. 5 Strand Terrace. On the West again by Nos. 5, 6, 7 and 8 Strand Terrace. On the North again by land between the River Dodder and Strand Terrace and the River Dodder. On the East again by the centre line of River Dodder, Milltown Bridge and Old Bridge. On the South by the road leading to Old Bridge. On the West again by Main Street. Again on the South by Main Street and the Lodge and lands of Saint Philips's. Again on the West by the lands of Saint Philip's and the lands of Mount St. Anne's Convent. On the North, West and North again by the grounds and Church of Saints Gall and Columbanus and Main Street. Again on the West by Main Street On the South again by Main Street and the grounds of the Church of Saints Gall and Columbanus. On the West, South, West and South again by the grounds of the Church of Saints Gall and Columbanus, and on the West, North and West again by the lands of Mount St. Anne's Convent. The portion coloured Grey on plan is excluded from above area."
Dated this 28th day of July, 1953.

34. Compulsory purchase order for Milltown clearance, 28 July 1953.

Walkinstown (or Wilkinstown) was completed about the same time. The compulsory purchase order was published in March 1950 (*Irish Times*, 31 March 1950, p. 9) and the housing was complete by 1955. Included in the scheme was provision for private housing which is discussed below. The development quickly took on its own identity and its own church, the church of the Assumption, was opened in August 1956. The approximate sequence of completion in Walkinstown was as follows.

| Year | Location | Houses |
| --- | --- | --- |
| 1953 | Walkinstown Drive | 80 |
|  | Walkinstown Green | 32 |
|  | Walkinstown Parade | 52 |
|  | Walkinstown Avenue | 146 |
| 1954 | Walkinstown Park | 102 |
| 1955 | Walkinstown Crescent | 54 |

Walkinstown seems to have had somewhat more investment in design in that Walkinstown Green offers a vista on the church from the main artery, Walkinstown Avenue, replicating a design feature provided in the earlier Cabra scheme. The church sits on a large site in the distance, with a great deal of green space both around and before it. The shopping area was located at the junction of Walkinstown Green with this green area, providing an intermediate focus for the street. Additional character and distinction was given to this route by building the houses in red brick.

## *Coolock and Kilmore*

As well as the self-contained St Anne's scheme, which is discussed separately below because it was a renewed excursion for Dublin Corporation into tenant purchase, the largest development area which remained to the city was in Coolock. With the completion of the northern sewerage system, this area was ready for building from the middle of the 1950s. Planning for the scheme began in earnest with the usual public inquiry into the compulsory purchase order for the lands. This took place in December 1954 and involved about 602 acres (240ha), a considerable plot of land. It was estimated that the entire project would cost about £6.5m and would result in about 4,700 houses. Following well-established norms, at least 10 per cent of them would be provided for persons or groups building for themselves. This time, the Corporation envisaged the development as comprising three 'precincts':

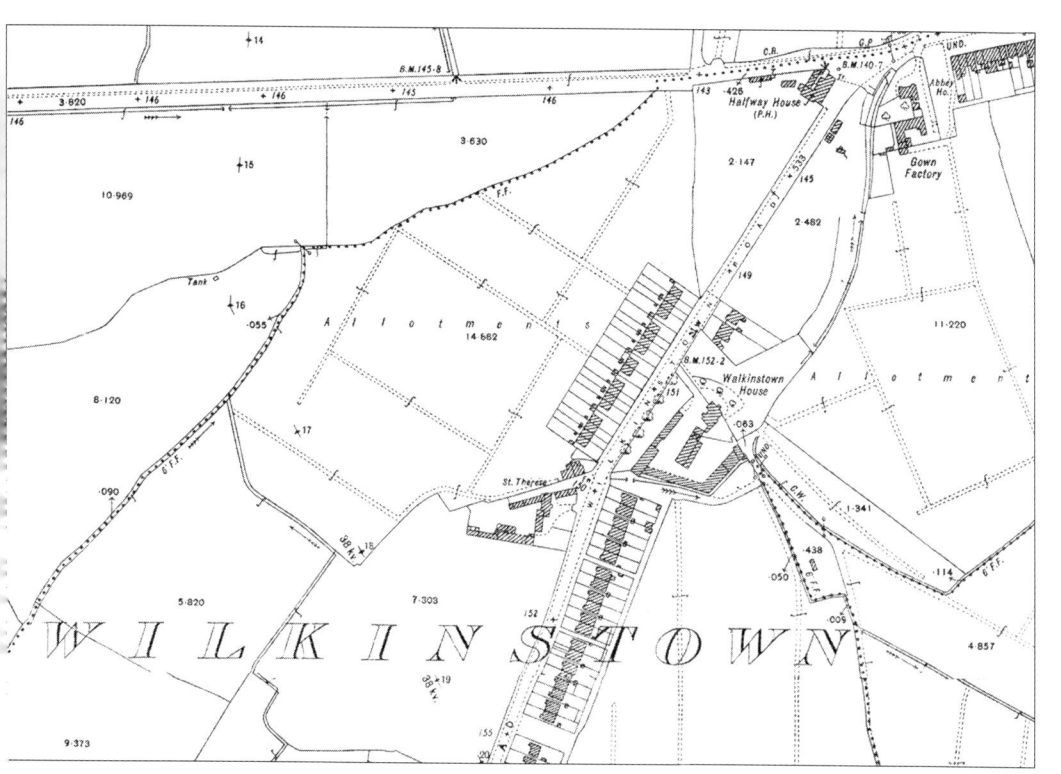

**35.** *(above)* Wilkinstown /Walkinstown before development. (Ordnance Survey plan, 1:2,500, Sheet 18 (XIII) and Sheet 22(I), 1943.)   **36.** *(below)* Walkinstown as completed. Note the symmetrical relationship around Walkinstown Green. (Ordnance Survey plan, 1:18,000, 1969.)

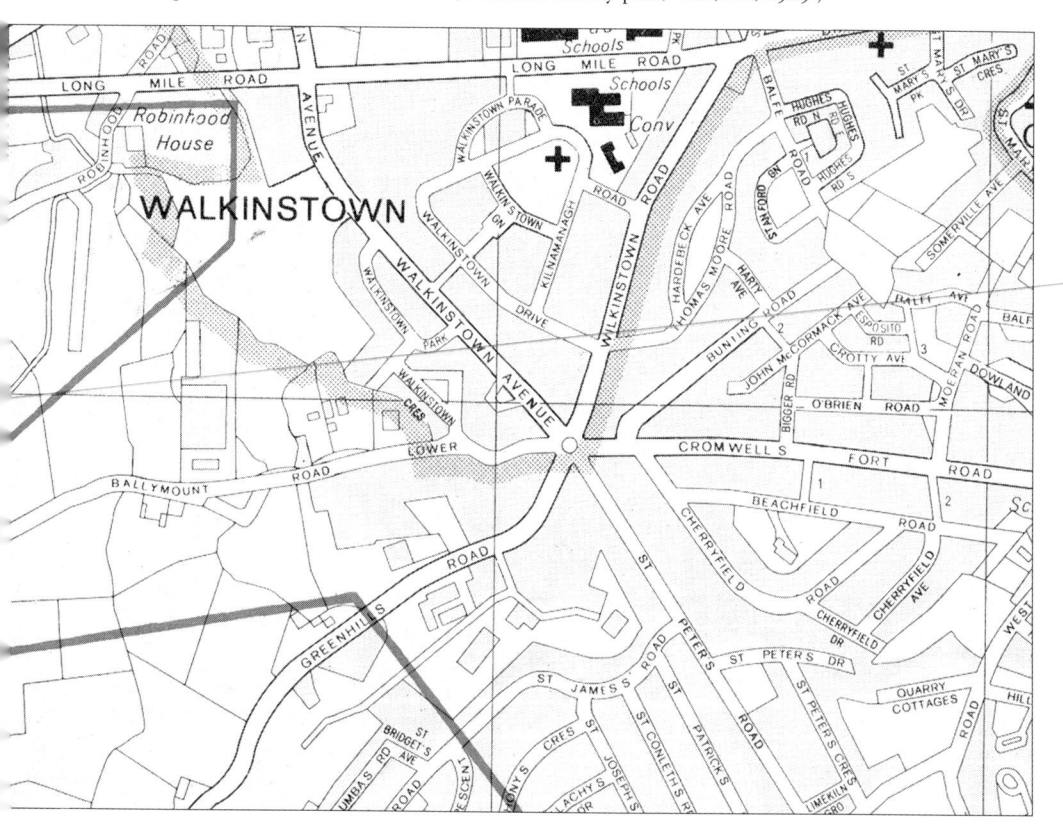

37. The vista at Walkinstown Green as seen from the air. (Google earth.)

Kilmore, Bonnybrook and Edenmore. The planned density was about eight houses to the acre in gross terms or about 12.5 houses to the acre in net terms, in keeping with the usual practice. The concept was that each would be a self-contained community with its own public buildings, open spaces, playing fields, primary schools and shopping centres. In the case of Kilmore and Edenmore, a site was reserved for a church, while it was envisaged that the Bonnybrook scheme would be served by Coolock village where a new church was being built. Some limited form of light industry was also envisaged.

The plan suggested that Edenmore would have 1,250 houses and 30 shops with a school for 1,500 pupils. Its location at the edge of the city meant that it was likely that it would be extended further by taking in the Kilbarrack area. Bonnybrook was envisaged to have in the order of 2,200 houses and about 50 shops with primary school provision for 2,700 children. The third element in the scheme, Kilmore, would have 1,300 houses, 30 shops and about 1,600 school places. As in the Finglas scheme, it was intended that the existing shopping facilities in Coolock and Raheny would be integrated into the development. The additional provision was for mainly low-order shopping and the number of shops intended suggested that the Corporation realized that the hinterland of these shops had to be small or that people would otherwise have little choice in what was an undeveloped and largely rural area.

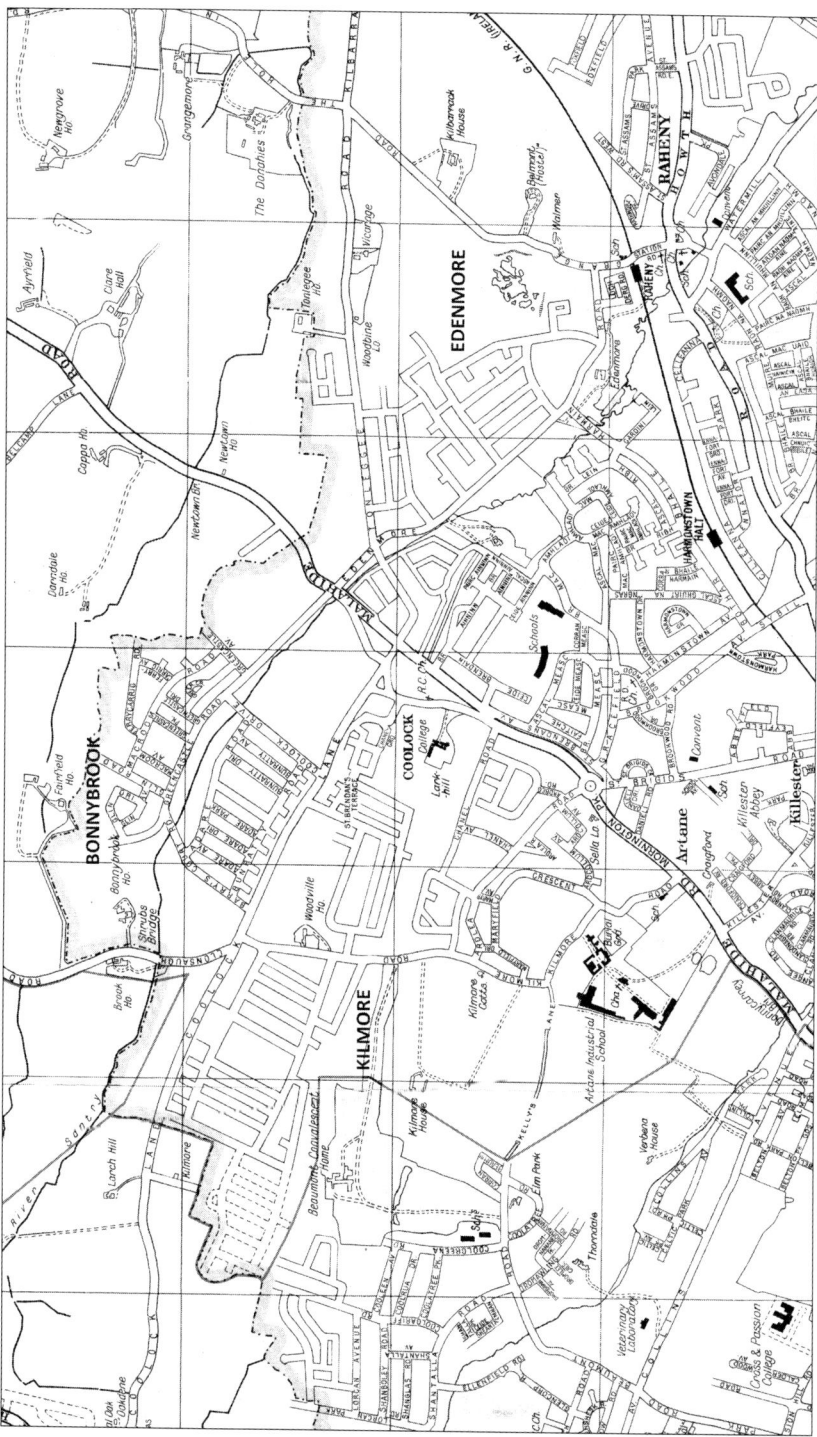

**38.** Outline of the Bonnybrook, Kilmore and Edemore scheme as of the mid-1960s. Note the spatial extent of the development and the manner in which it encompassed other developments.

The area was about the same distance from the city centre as Finglas, a maximum of about 4.5 miles (7km), and there was now the potential to improve the connectivity of both locations by the completion of one of Abercrombie's planned outer ring roads whose route ran through the district. As it transpired, it did not quite work out as smoothly as intended. However, the Oscar Traynor Road linked with Tonlegee Road provided an east west link from the Dublin–Belfast Road (and later with the M1/M50) across Malahide Road to the coast.

Building was slower to get going than was originally anticipated for the reasons outlined above. The initial focus was on the space between Raheny and Coolock in an area that was situated north of the railway line and immediately to the west of the Santry River park. The names Ennel, Lein, Mask (Measc) and McAuley identify most of the roads built during this period. The latter deviates from the focus on lakes to honour Catherine McAuley, founder of the Mercy Sisters, who was born locally in Stormanstown House. The design of the houses followed the standard model with good front and rear gardens. There was a great deal of open space provided, giving an airy sense to the area though, as was common, it proved very difficult to do anything with the space other than look at it. The list below gives the approximate completion dates. The names were originally approved in Irish and the 'lough' has now been largely dropped from the names of the roads in English.

| Year | Location | Houses | Location | Houses |
|---|---|---|---|---|
| 1956 | Lough Mask Crescent | 28 | Lough Mask Road | 20 |
|  | McAuley Avenue | 38 | McAuley Park | 38 |
|  | Lough Ree Road | 92 |  |  |
| 1957 | Harmonstown Road | 76 | Lough Lein Gardens | 38 |
|  | Lough Lein Park | 48 | Lough Derg Road | 42 |
|  | Lough Mask Avenue | 64 | Lough Mask Drive | 36 |
|  | Lough Mask Green | 26 | McAuley Drive | 60 |
|  | McAuley Road | 20 | Lough Ree Avenue | 56 |
| 1958 | Lough Ennel Avenue | 16 | Lough Ennel Drive | 62 |
|  | Lough Ennel Park | 36 | St Brendan's Park | 14 |

There was quite a gap in time before development gathered pace and it was the early 1960s when development began at Edenmore. Tenders were sought in May and August 1962 for the first phases and the gross average cost per house ranged from £1,700 to £1,800. This phase was located on the other side of the Santry River and bounded by Tonlegee Road. The eponymous streets in the district were completed by 1964 and in that same year CIE announced the operation of a new bus route, the 28, running from Eden Quay to the Edenmore estate. An indication of the sequence of building can be obtained from the list below of approximate completion dates.

| Year | Location | Houses |
|---|---|---|
| 1963 | Edenmore Crescent | 126 |
| | Edenmore Gardens | 62 |
| | Edenmore Green | 48 |
| | Edenmore Grove | 78 |
| | Edenmore Park | 64 |
| 1964 | Edenmore Drive | 60 |
| | Springdale Road | 66 |

The building of Kilmore followed with work commencing in July 1963 and this development was located south of the main west-east artery, the Oscar Traynor Road, the name having been agreed in 1966 (Report 101/1966). The first houses were completed by 1965 and 994 had been built by 31 December 1966 but another 150 houses were added later on as Dublin Corporation ramped up its housing programme.

| Year | Location | Houses | Location | Houses |
|---|---|---|---|---|
| 1965 | Greencastle Crescent | 72 | Ferrycarrig Avenue | 40 |
| | Ferrycarrig Road | 92 | Glin Road | 48 |
| | Greencastle Avenue | 38 | Greencastle Drive | 36 |
| | Greencastle Road | 86 | Macroom Avenue | 18 |
| | Macroom Road | 129 | Bunratty Avenue | 64 |
| | Bunratty Drive | 32 | Bunratty Road | 227 |
| | Coolock Drive | 32 | Edenmore Avenue | 150 |
| 1966 | Adare Park | 44 | Glin Avenue | 37 |
| | Glin Drive | 66 | Greencastle Park | 20 |
| | Adare Avenue | 42 | Adare Drive | 40 |
| | Adare Green | 24 | Barryscourt Road | 22 |
| 1967 | Cromcastle Road | 85 | Kilmore Road | 6 |
| | Castlekevin Road | 68 | Cromcastle Avenue | 68 |
| | Cromcastle Drive | 64 | Cromcastle Green | 36 |
| | Cromcastle Park | 32 | Kilbarron Road | 108 |
| | Trim Road | 12 | | |
| 1968 | Ballyshannon Avenue | 34 | Ballyshannon Road | 158 |
| | Castletimon Road | 95 | Dundaniel Road | 72 |
| | Kilbarron Avenue | 74 | Kilbarron Drive | 68 |
| 1969 | Castletimon Drive | 20 | Castletimon Avenue | 40 |
| | Castletimon Green | 22 | Castletimon Park | 28 |
| | Kilbarron Park | 38 | | |

**39.** Housing on St Brendan's Park, Raheny.

**40.** Housing on Adare Park, Bonnybrook, though Coolock is more generally used as the district name.

**41.** Housing on Cromcastle Park, Kilmore.

**42.** Housing on Edenmore Avenue.

As had become the norm by now, local shops were provided in small blocks at central locations but the advent of the shopping centre concept added a new dimension. Edenmore was provided with a neighbourhood centre of nondescript design but the provision of parking there was recognition of the new role of the car. Of greater significance, the decision to build a district-level shopping centre provided the area with much high-order shopping facilities than would have been the case previously. The Northside Shopping Centre, designed to service the entire community, offered 56 shops when it opened in 1970.

It cannot be said that any of the precincts was particularly distinctive in design terms though they did feature the concept of a distributor road system, which was designed to ensure that only local traffic entered the area. One additional feature was the avoidance of development along the main arteries. Thus there is very little housing that fronts onto Oscar Traynor Road with houses either backing on to it or at right angles. It means that no sense of a streetscape was created on the boundary artery.

As building progressed the Corporation found itself in competition with private builders for a diminishing bank of land. There had been considerable private building in Raheny cotemporaneous with Dublin Corporation and it seemed that there was a market for lower cost private houses in the area. In 1962, Messrs Gallagher and Company sought permission to build on 95 acres (38ha) that they had obtained in Kilbarrack. Permission was refused by the Corporation on the grounds that the land was needed for social housing. The company appealed to the Minister for Local Government who decided in their favour. The basis of his decision was that the company was going to build houses for the same market segment as Dublin Corporation but would do so far faster than the Corporation planned to. They were given permission on 7 May 1963. Dublin Corporation had moved away from tenant purchase in the early 1930s because it felt that its tenants could not afford the costs. There was now sufficient evidence that a proportion of Corporation tenants or potential tenants could afford to purchase their own houses, if they could get access to credit and if the purchase terms were reasonable. The developers sought to tap that market by offering to sell houses to those who were nominated by the Corporation, if the Corporation would but let them build the houses. The Corporation was not in the mood for such co-operation and instead ignored the reality of the Minister's decision by making a compulsory purchase order for the Swan's Nest area of Kilbarrack in July 1963. The area involved was 329 acres (133ha) but included the area for which permission had already been given. The required public inquiry was held on 15 October 1963. Among the objectors were Mr Frank McInerney and Mr Matthew Gallagher, both significant builders. They pointed out that they already held a considerable portion of the land, for which they had planning approval, and were ready to proceed to develop it. They suggested that Dublin Corporation did not need the land, given their rate of building in recent years and that they, the developers, would be able to get houses built in half the time that the Corporation could. Indeed they noted that they might be the very companies ultimately asked to build for the Corporation, if the latter got the land. This was not an unlikely possibility since both had been involved in building in the Raheny and Finglas schemes. They further argued that the Corporation's policy of dislocating people from the city centre was poorly conceived and they should concentrate instead on building in the city centre. The Corporation, it was said, was not facing up to reality and that 'having buried its head in the sand ... it is presenting a part of its anatomy which must be a great temptation to the Ministerial foot' (*Irish Times*, 16 October 1963, p. 6). The Minister did apply his foot to some extent, noting that the matter had been decided earlier in 1963 in relation to the 95 acres but he did give his permission for the Corporation to acquire 224 acres (91ha) in October 1964. It was a dogfight that became political very quickly and it seemed that Dublin Corporation came to the view that it would have to fight 'for Raheny acre by acre' as one unnamed official was quoted as saying some time earlier (*Irish Times*, 11 September 1963, p. 11).

The matter was revived and was the subject of vigorous debate in the Dáil in late February 1968 on the occasion of the Fine Gael Planning Appeals Bill, 1967. The previous Minister was accused of having interfered in the planning process to the advantage of the builders. The current Minister, Mr Boland, denied this in his typically robust style; 'I was dealing with the false, slanderous allegations made by Deputy Cluskey here and which were so widely and maliciously publicized' (Dáil Debates, 232 (12), col. 1836). He had pointed out that while Dublin Corporation had yet to develop any portion of the land for which they had been given approval, the private builders had 900 houses nearing completion on the portion of land that they retained. He once again maintained that, as they were building for the same market as Corporation tenants, the provision of such housing could only be welcomed (Dáil Debates, 232 (10), col. 1607).

It was not just about competition for land, though. It was also about balance. A sense of this concern is obtained from a letter to the *Irish Times* which was published on 7 September 1963 (p. 13). The letter was from a local resident and was a long discourse on the issue. The writer made reference to the fact that it did not make sense to transfer the land from builders who were prepared to build at that moment while the Corporation was unlikely to be able to build for up to eight years. The point was also made that the

Corporation should concentrate its efforts on inner city redevelopment. To move people out to the suburbs was to put burdens on them as well as dispersing closely-knit city communities. In addition, it was clear to the writer that the people who would occupy these privately-built houses would vacate council housing and thus make space for new tenants. These were very much the arguments that were to be made a little later on at the hearings on the compulsory purchase. However, one additional point was one of balance. As the writer put it:

> Every argument is in favour of allowing this area to be developed immediately by private builders. With the vast amount of municipal housing which has been provided in Harmonstown and Edenmore, it is necessary if any sort of balance development is to be preserved in the area. Houses can be provided immediately. A very real sense of grievance and injustice will be removed from a great number of people in the adjoining estates who have, at very great sacrifice, provided themselves with their own houses. They are decent, respectable citizens who, whether you agree with them or not, genuinely think the Dublin Corporation treat them with contempt and arrogance.
>
> (*Irish Times*, 7 September 1963, p. 13)

It was always a tricky thing on the north side of the city to get an appropriate balance between public and private housing. As has been shown before, the area was much more mixed than south of the river where a clear west-east social gradient had been developed. The Edenmore development had been quite a large one and there had also been a significant amount of private building. In the event, the Kilbarrack development went ahead and the Briarfield, Thornville and Rosemount elements were completed by 1970 with over 700 houses.

## *New schemes*

In 1967, the Corporation adopted a building programme that would see them through to the first quarter of 1971 (Report 129/1967). As of 1 July 1967, they had a requirement for 8,518 dwellings and a prospective need for 11,040, giving a total requirement of 19,558. Taking into account new dwellings which were ready to be handed over and making a conservative assumption about vacancies, their view was that they would need to supply 17,219 new units. There were five elements to their strategy to achieve this with the following number of dwellings being produced by each:

- building for people on the waiting list   7,836
- a programme of purchase house and private sites   7,078
- new housing sites in urban development areas   500
- new housing areas   500
- acquisition of additional land for purchase houses/sites.   2,000

The latter three were somewhat speculative but it can be seen that the Corporation was now going to be greatly reliant on getting people to build or purchase their own houses under the various assistance programmes and that was going to supply about 40 per cent of the requirement.

The building programme included the major Kilmore and Ballymun schemes and these would produce a total of 2,798. The remainder would come from new developments with Kilbarrack as one of the larger programmes (1,498 units) and also Finglas South/Tolka Valley (1,030 units). However, these were still only at the compulsory purchase order stage and therefore some time away. The remainder was divided between schemes which were in the process of being formulated (2,945 units) and a much more speculative plan for sites which were being acquired (1,400 units).

The purchase houses and sites programme was also someway off into the future. The plans were for Kilbarrack, where development works were in train, and then for schemes in Howth, Baldoyle, Ballymun Avenue, Tallaght and Rathfarnham. This would not be sufficient, though, and it would be necessary to get lands in Kilbarrack and Darndale, Blanchardstown and Clonsilla, Dunsink, Santry and Poppintree. Much of this development was outside the city (the county borough boundary) and the Corporation was now embarking on developments which would involve them directly with the County Council.

The urban renewal areas which could yield a total of 500 units were in:

- Charlemont Street/Albert Place West
- North Brunswick Street/Smithfield/Haymarket
- Westmoreland Park, Ranelagh
- New Street/Clanbrassil Street
- Newmarket/Coombe
- Bride Street/Golden Lane.

There were seen to be possibilities for another 500 units in locations such as:

- Portland Row
- Phibsborough Road
- Dorset Street Lower
- Ballybough
- Macken Street
- Clanbrassil Street Upper
- Brown Street South
- St Mary's Terrace, Sarsfield Road
- Inchicore and Bluebell.

They had provided 1,964 dwellings in the period 1 April 1967 to 31 March 1968 and it was confidently expected that the total in each of the financial years 1968–9 and 1969–70 would reach 3,000 dwellings (Minutes, 3 February 1969). This was in line with the building programme which had been adopted in 1967.

## *Housing costs*

Since the social housing provided during the 1950s was never intended for sale, it is not possible to determine what its price would have been and how it compared to private housing. The best that can be done is to look at the tender prices, which give a good indication of building costs but exclude important elements such as site acquisition and a profit margin. The following shows the estimated average cost in Corporation schemes during the 1950s together with the name of the developer. The data for cottages show a steady increase in cost over the years across all categories. By 1956, the cost had risen by at least 20 per cent on 1950 with the smaller three-roomed houses costing on average 25 per cent more. The increase on the five-roomed house had been less dramatic at 17 per cent but the Council built relatively few of them, except in their tenant purchase schemes.

The data confirm that flat developments were more expensive in every category than suburban houses. The difference in price was not consistent but, for example, McInerney was able to be build a four-roomed house in Coolock-Raheny in 1956 for an average cost of £1,683 but the same company charged £2,124 for a four-roomed flat in Bluebell. The cost of flat building also rose during the 1950s by amounts which were substantially ahead of suburban cottages.

**Table 24.** Tender costs in a range of cottage developments, 1948–56.

| | Cottages | | | |
|---|---|---|---|---|
| | | Rooms | | |
| Year | 3 | 4 | 5 | Location (developer) |
| 1948 | 1,026 | 1,191 | | Sarsfield Road (Fearon) |
| 1949 | | 993 | | Captain's Lane (Jennings) |
| 1950 | 1,214 | 1,388 | 1,554 | Milltown (Mc Inerney) |
| 1951 | 1,016 | 1,137 | | Finglas East (Redmond) |
| 1951 | | | 1,460 | Annadale |
| 1952 | 1,374 | 1,439 | 1,571 | Ballyfermot (Jennings) |
| 1953 | 1,423 | 1,527 | 1,605 | Ballyfermot (Redmond) |
| 1954 | 1,304 | 1,379 | 1,551 | Ballyfermot (Jennings) |
| 1955 | 1,533 | 1,657 | 1,774 | Coolock – Raheny (Fearon) |
| 1956 | 1,518 | 1,683 | 1,814 | Coolock – Raheny (McInerney) |

**Table 25.** Tender costs in a range of flat developments, 1948–56.

| | Flats | | | |
|---|---|---|---|---|
| | | Rooms | | |
| Year | 3 | 4 | 5 | Location (developer) |
| 1948 | | 1,506 | 1,850 | St Teresa's Gardens (Dempsey) |
| 1949 | | 1,274 | 1,512 | Irishtown (Crampton) |
| 1950 | | 1,463 | 1,804 | C. Mooney Gardens (Irish Estates) |
| 1951 | 1,270 | 1,813 | 2,301 | North Strand (Rooney) |
| 1952 | 1,533 | 1,918 | 2,260 | O'Devaney Gardens (McInerney) |
| 1953 | 1,532 | 1,949 | 2,332 | Whitefriar St (Rooney) |
| 1954 | 1,357 | 1,794 | 2,226 | Hardwicke St (McInerney) |
| 1955 | 1,485 | 1,680 | 2,025 | Dolphin's Barn (McInerney) |
| 1956 | 1,601 | 2,124 | 2,442 | Bluebell (McInerney) |
| 1957 | | 2,458 | | Gloucester Place (McGee) |

## *Reserved areas*

The principle of reserving areas for private housing in council housing areas was a long established one and has been discussed in detail in previous volumes in this series (McManus, 2002; Brady, 2014). The policy was given new life during the 1950s and the principle was established that ten per cent of all sites in a development should be for private housing (Report 40/1951). The underlying idea had been that local authority housing areas benefitted from the co-location of people with higher incomes. There was an element of social grooming involved in that it was felt that the tenants would take their cue from the people in the better-off houses but there was a practical reason too. The presence of people who were better off would increase the average income of the area and thus sustain a wider range of goods and services than might otherwise be the case. The most impressive reserved area was that provided as part of the Drumcondra scheme in the late 1920s (see McManus, 2002). The reserved area was to the north of the Corporation housing area on rising ground. Each of the housing providers in the reserved area produced a distinctive type of house, with the commercial builders showing the least imagination. The reserved area was much larger in area than the Corporation's own housing area and was a distinctive urban area in its own right and not just the finishing touch. Nothing quite like that occurred again but reserved areas tended to comprise individual streets within schemes and there was a tendency to use routeways or boundaries for such housing, the idea being to provide a good 'finish' to the estate. Crumlin Road is a good example of this where twenty four sites were given to the Irish Ex-servicemen's Utility Society (Report 96/1950) in 1950. The Clancy Building Group was allocated eight sites there with others going to the Post Office Staff Society (Report 62/1951). Similarly, when the Brickfields site in Crumlin was being developed, it was decided that Brickfield Drive would be the reserved area. Here eight sites were given to the Anglesea Public Utility Society in 1951, though there was concern that since this served a lower income group, they would build at a standard only slightly above Corporation specifications (Report 62/1951). Here too the Irish Ex-servicemen's Utility Society were given eight sites (Report 83/1951), while the Dublin Typographical Housing Group was allocated two sites (Report 99/1951), with seven sites going to individuals. It was a similar story in the Captain's Lane area where an initial sixty sites were made available in 1950 with others coming later.

Originally, the housing sites in reserved areas were made available to organizations such as public utility societies or private builders who then sold the houses to suitable purchasers. However, the categories covered for grant purposes under the Housing Amendment Act of 1948 resulted in the Corporation coming to the view that it could not treat these formal entities differently to groups of individuals or even individuals. This was undoubtedly one of the factors in the ultimate disappearance of public utility societies from the housing landscape; the complexity of setting up and maintaining a society was no longer needed.

The process which was now followed was that invitations to apply for sites were published in the newspapers and a vetting process was undertaken to determine the final allocation. It changed little over the years, as the advertisements shown below demonstrate. Interest was high in the early years of the 1950s and, for example, an allocation of 54 sites on the west side of Swords Road in Larkhill in 1950 attracted some 371 applications, mostly from groups of individuals. The names and addresses of the successful applicants were published by the Corporation and it seems that most groups were small, few comprised more than four persons. They were a diverse collection of people. Judging by surnames, some may have been related but with most there was nothing to indicate any kind of association or relationship. They came from across the city; some lived in private accommodation, some lived in Corporation housing while others were in tenements. Thus the 'Doherty Group' comprised four persons:

| William Henry | 38 Chelmsford Road |
| Joseph Harvery | 207 Blackhorse Avenue |
| Patrick Doherty | 127 Leinster Road |
| Patrick Sherry | Merville Cottages |

In that particular allocation, there was only one public utility society involved – the Dublin Civil Servants' Building Society – and they were given four sites. A similar opportunity in Captain's Lane on a site fronting Armagh Road and St Agnes' Park, this time for 60 private dwellings, produced 139 applications (Report 35/1950). Most applicants intended to use professional builders and sometimes they engaged builders who were already operating in the area, such as the Chalet Building Company whom the McMahon Building Group intended to use. The Albert Building Group's (unsuccessful) application was unusual in that they intended to do the building themselves in their spare time, using an initial capital outlay of £500 as a seed fund and then using each completed house to fund the next one. The same approach was used when the Corporation developed in Rathfarnham, for which a compulsory purchase process was begun in 1950. In 1956, it allocated the first seventeen of the forty-eight sites it had reserved for private building as follows (Report 7/1956):

| Irish Ex-servicemen's Public Utility Society | 4 |
| Flanagan Group | 4 |
| Anglesea Group | 4 |
| Service Housing Society | 2 |
| Woodvale PUS | 2 |
| Individual | 1 |

Two sites were reserved also for a parochial house, though it was later decided not to proceed with this (Report 71/1959). An additional four sites were later allocated to the Woodvale PUS with thirteen sites going to the Marian Home Building Society, five sites to the General Housing Society, two to the Sundrive Building group and three sites to individuals. Though interest in these sites was high, as mentioned above, it seems that there were often difficulties in the follow through. There are many instances in the documentation of the reallocation of sites because the original purchaser was no longer in a position to complete the transaction. This became more marked as the 1950s progressed and, for example, in 1957 it proved necessary to reallocate eighteen sites in the Rathfarnham scheme. Four sites were given to the Woodvale PUS and two each to the Gygax group, Cosgrave group, Power group and to the O'Donnell group. This process was even more marked in 1958 when there were numerous reallocations and when the final six sites were allocated in 1960, there was a stipulation that the dwelling was to be built within six months (Report 69/1960).

The rationale for allocating sites in this manner was outlined during the official opening of a housing scheme in Finglas in 1954. There was not much said about social balance on this occasion, rather it was about the impact on housing demand. The Co-operative Home Building Society Limited had completed a scheme of 24 houses on Cappagh Road and a reception was held in the Royal Hibernian Hotel following the official opening and blessing (*Irish Press*, 4 February 1954, p. 8). These houses were right in the centre of the Corporation's building programme in Finglas West but they were different in that they were semi-detached houses, quite in contrast to the houses around them. Such a contrast was characteristic of the Marino and Drumcondra schemes but it was not universally the case in later developments. The importance of this form of private building was emphasized by the attendance which included John Garvin, the Secretary of the Department of Local Government who was representing the Minister, the Lord Mayor and the chairman of the Housing Committee. John Garvin made the point that anything that reduced the housing burden on the local authority was welcome. The Lord Mayor noted that the men who were buying the houses were people whom it might be expected that the Corporation would house and so it was good to see such building being undertaken privately. Mr T.C. Gerald O'Mahony, the solicitor for the building group, made the point that the people buying the houses in this way were no threat to private builders because they would never be able to put together the deposit needed by private

## SITES FOR PRIVATE DWELLING-HOUSES

The Corporation is prepared to consider applications for leasing sites for the erection of dwelling-houses at Crumlin Road (Brickfields), Captain's Lane and Ballyfermot.

Particulars and Forms of Applications may be obtained at Housing Department, Exchange Buildings, Lord Edward Street.

Applications must reach the Housing Director, Exchange Buildings, Lord Edward Street, not later than 12 noon on Wednesday, 11th April, 1951.

P. J. HERNON,
City Manager and Town Clerk.
City Hall, Dublin.
16th March, 1951.

## CORPORATION OF DUBLIN
### SITES FOR PRIVATE DWELLING-HOUSES AT

Collins Park, Donnycarney—13 Sites
Glasnaon Rd., Finglas East—20 Sites
Nephin Road, Cabra West—10 Sites

The Corporation hereby invites applications for sites, to be let on lease, for the erection of private dwelling-houses at the above areas.

Full particulars and Forms of Application are obtainable at the Housing Department, Exchange Buildings, Lord Edward St., Dublin. Completed Application Forms in sealed envelopes and endorsed as directed must be lodged at the Housing Department, Exchange Buildings, Lord Edward St., not later than 12 noon on Friday, 11th December 1953.

P. J. HERNON,
City Manager and Town Clerk.
City Hall, Dublin.
19th November, 1953.

**43.** Invitations for tenders in the 1950s.

## BARDAS ATHA CLIATH
### BUILDING SITES
### FOR PRIVATE HOUSES AT
(1) Malahide Road, Coolock.
(2) Edenmore Road, Raheny.
(3) Watermill Road, Raheny.

Tenders are invited for the leasing of fully-developed sites for private dwellinghouses at the above locations.

Application forms and full particulars may be obtained at the Housing Department, Exchange Buildings, Lord Edward Street, on payment of a tender fee of £10 10s. 0d. This fee will be refunded only to applicants who submit a bona fide tender which is not subsequently withdrawn.

Tenders, in sealed envelopes, and endorsed as directed, must be lodged at the Housing Department, Exchange Buildings, Lord Edward Street, not later than 12 noon on Friday, 29th July, 1960.

The highest or any offer will not necessarily be accepted.

## Bardas Atha Cliath
### BUILDING SITES
### for
### PRIVATE HOUSES
### at
### TOLKA ESTATE, OLD FINGLAS ROAD

Tenders are invited for the leasing of 45 sites for private dwellinghouses at Tolka Estate, Old Finglas Road.

Full particulars are obtainable at the Housing Department, Exchange Buildings, Lord Edward Street, Dublin, 2.

Tender forms may be obtained on payment of a tender fee of £10 10s. 0d. This fee will be refunded only to tenderers who submit bona fide tenders which are not subsequently withdrawn.

The latest date for the receipt of tenders is 12 noon on Friday, 28th June, 1963.

**44.** Invitations for tenders in the 1960s.

contractors. So, in sum, this was a good way to get people off the housing list and enable them to provide for their own housing in a manner which met their resources. At the same time, these houses were not cheap, weekly payments were £2, considerably ahead of rents in the area. The deposit was £100 for a house that cost about £1,900 and though funding was provided as well as a government grant of £285, it cannot be said that these people came from the lowest income group.

Building groups in reserved areas came in a variety of forms. One group that was a little different to the others and which figured in a number of schemes was the Magnificat Family Guild. They were mentioned in the previous volume in this series in connection with reserved areas on Collins Avenue. They wrote to the Corporation in 1950 noting that they had allocated the twenty-six sites that they were given and asking for further ones. They sought sites particularly suited to a lower income group – people whose income would not be greatly different to those housed in the Council schemes. It was usual to expect houses on reserved sites to be of a higher standard but such was the housing need that the Corporation was willing to facilitate any group that would add to the stock. Accordingly, they were given sixteen sites on Lower Crumlin Road, land which had originally been purchased from the Dublin Brick Company (Reports 1950/51). They returned from time to time seeking additional sites and, for example, were granted six sites in Collins Park in 1956 (Report 52/1956 and 91/1956).

As in previous years, Dublin Corporation seized on other opportunities as they arose. In 1950, the Glass Industry Housing Society sought a plot for their members – all employees of the Irish Glass Bottle Company. An important element in the proposal was the fact that the society was sponsored by the company and the Corporation were satisfied that a better class of house would result. On that basis, they were given a plot of 3 acres and 2 roods (1.5ha) on Dundrum Road, on the site previously owned by the Dublin Laundry. In a similar vein, the Odeon Building Society, for employees of the Odeon Cinemas, sought sites for thirty houses in 1951. They were offered fourteen sites in Crumlin on the Brickfields site (Report 40/1951). The Lord Mayor, Senator Andrew Clarkin, attended the opening of the first four houses in the scheme in September 1952. The houses were described as having three bedrooms and two reception rooms and cost £1,500 each. The mayor was quoted as saying that it showed the 'value of cooperation between employers and employees in a unity of spirit' (*Irish Times*, 21 September 1952, p. 7).

**45.** One style of housing on Bóthar Ainninn.

Another opportunity to assist in the provision of private housing was taken in Walkinstown. The Corporation had acquired 20 acres (8ha) from the Chalet Building Company. That company had developed housing on the adjacent land and the deal struck with the Corporation was that they could lease back a portion of the 20 acres on which to build 45–50 houses for clients nominated to the Corporation by the company. The first twenty sites were allocated in 1951 (Report 68/1951) with the remainder allocated over the next few years.

The process continued into the 1960s and ten sites were made available on the Malahide Road and a further twenty-one sites at the intersection of Edenmore Road and Watermill Road. Construction moved to Bóthar Ainninn (St Brendan's Park) in 1962 and some thirty-two sites were allocated over the course of the year (Report 99/1962, 111, 148, 166). As before changes in leases continued to be a regular feature of Corporation reports, such as 57/1962, which dealt with Watermill Road and Edenmore Road. The turnover in early purchasers was quite marked with relatively few of the original grantees in place on, for example, Watermill Road, in the late 1960s. By this time, public utility societies were disappearing from the process and there was a shift towards allocating the sites to building companies, who then submitted lists of recommended purchasers to the Corporation for approval. Thus Bóthar Ainninn was largely developed by Messrs Curtis and Farrelly, who were local builders, and by J.A. Lawler, who was also responsible for many of the houses on Edenmore Road.

Though the housing layout was planned early on, building on these streets sometimes took place over an extended period with small batches of sites being released as required. Thus Curtis and Farrelly were given three sites in 1962 (Report 111/1962) and a further two sites in 1963 (Report 62/1963) while J. A. Lawler was given two sites in 1963 (Report 65/1963), all of which were on Bóthar Ainninn. On other occasions though, the Corporation sought tenders for a larger number of sites as when they advertised for 45 sites at the Tolka Valley Estate on the Old Finglas Road in February 1963 (Report 169/1963).

The Corporation was nothing if not flexible and was prepared to consider any initiative that would increase the housing stock. The Housing Committee approved in January 1964 the placing of an advertisement stating that the Corporation was prepared to purchase suitable new or older dwellings for families on the waiting list. The same committee recommended early in 1965 that the proposed sites for sixteen semi-detached houses and three bungalows at the junction of Howth Road and Brookwood Avenue be offered to tenants who were prepared to surrender their dwellings with the greater incentive of not having to pay for the site (no site fine) (Report 4/1965). This generated a lot of interest and it was necessary to allocate the sites by lot. The people came from all over the city, with no particular pattern evident (Report 155/1965). This approach was repeated in 1966 when eight sites were offered on Beaumont Road (Report 48/1966). Again, such was the interest in this that the allocation had to be by lot. This bolstered the view that there was an untapped capacity among Corporation tenants to purchase houses and so they scaled up the offer when they offered 288 houses for sale at Coolock/Kilmore (Report 68/1967). This was to be done on the basis of 200 houses for existing tenants, 44 for those on the waiting list and 44 sub-tenants on the waiting list. As noted in the minutes, 'The Corporation, in addition to the provision of sites, has agreed to assist the provision of dwellings by the erection of houses for sale in which it is considered that priority should be given to Corporation tenants and persons on the approved waiting list. Applications for such houses, which will be provided at Coolock/Kilmore were invited on 29 July last and are under consideration' (Minutes, 4 September 1967). It was agreed to provide further houses for sale with 16 provided on St Columbanus Road, 18 on Ballygall Road East and 54 in Coolock/Kilmore. The first draw for the Coolock houses took place in 1968 and was for 144 houses with a further 70 sold in May (Report 65/1968). The interest from the various strata was

**46.** Advertisement inviting applications for Coolock houses. (*Irish Independent*, 29 July 1967, p. 22.)

### BARDAS ATHA CLIATH
### PROVISION OF HOUSES FOR SALE
### Coolock/Kilmore Area

NOTICE TO TENANTS OF DUBLIN CORPORATION DWELLINGS AND APPLICANTS ON THE APPROVED WAITING LIST FOR CORPORATION DWELLINGS

The Corporation proposes to erect a number of semi-detached houses at Coolock/Kilmore for sale to Corporation tenants and persons on the approved waiting list.

**DEPOSIT £150
LOANS AVAILABLE
LOW WEEKLY OUTGOINGS**

Persons in the groups mentioned who are interested may obtain particulars at the **Housing Department, 24/26 Jervis Street, Dublin 1**, where applications should be lodged as soon as possible.

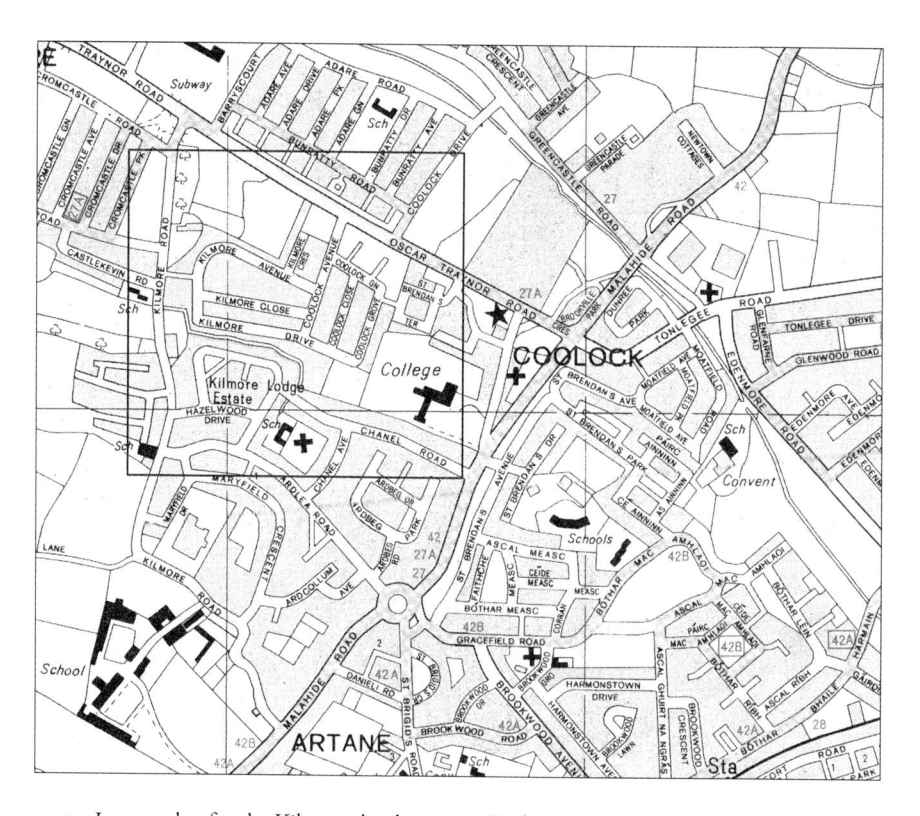

**47.** Layout plan for the Kilmore development. (Ordnance Survey plan, 1:18,000, 1969.)

**48.** Houses on Kilmore Avenue.

significant. There were 453 applications from tenants, 371 on the approved waiting list and 253 from those who were sub-tenants. The houses, on Coolock (now Beechlawn) Avenue, Green, Close and Kilmore Avenue and Crescent, were priced at £3,362 but with State and supplementary grants, this reduced to £2,665. A deposit of £150 was required with a loan provided by Dublin Corporation at 7.5 per cent over 35 years (Report 49/1968). Even without the grants, this was a good price and at the low end of what was available in the private sector at the time. Once the grants were factored in, this price was very attractive indeed as the asking price for houses in the area at the time was between £3,300 and £3,850. The houses reflected the designs in the private sector in that they were semi-detached with garages and the development had a distinctive spatial identity with its own access to the Oscar Traynor Road, the main road. The houses on St Columbanus Road, Milltown (Report 110/1968) and Ballygall Road East (Report 118/1968) attracted similar interest. Ten of the planned eighteen houses in Milltown went on sale and there was 181 applications from tenants, 87 from those on the list and a further 171 applications from sub-tenants. The terms were the same as for Coolock above. This initiative did not mark the end of the other approaches to housing provision. In 1969, a total of 32 sites were made available at Kimmage Road Lower in groups of 8 for four small-scale builders. It was a case of continuing to use every means possible to boost the housing stock.

## Public utility societies

By 1950, public utility societies had been part of the housing landscape for over thirty years. These co-partnership societies had been pioneered by the work of Canon Hall and the St Barnabas Public Utility Society in East Wall (McManus, 2002) and were a useful contribution to the housing programme, though the usefulness of this funding mechanism was now diminishing. The main focus of utility society building in Finglas East was concentrated in the eastern part of the district. The Red Park Utility Society had a block of sites between Glasilawn Road, Glasilawn Avenue and Glasmeen Road while the Tolka Estate was another private development to the north of this between Glasmeen Road and Glasnamana Road. It was different in that it was originally under the control of Dublin County Council but passed to Dublin Corporation with the changes to the city boundary. The agreement was that the houses would be built on a tenant purchase basis by Dublin Corporation but the allocation of houses would be done by Dublin County Council. The Finglas Housing Society was particularly active in the early 1950s and they developed Finglas Park, a long semi-circular avenue that linked McKee Road at two points. It was sold on the basis of being only three miles (5km) from the city with a bus service from Eden Quay. Each house offered three bedrooms, two reception rooms, a bathroom, a kitchenette and had gardens front and rear but in terms of physical appearance they were only a little different to what Dublin Corporation was building nearby. The houses were pebbledashed with concrete tiles on the roof and with similar porch design. Most of the houses were in terraces but there were subtle differences to the Corporation houses in terms of the enclosing walls and the availability of semi-detached and end-terrace houses. These were provided with space for garages and cost £1,750 for the former and £1,645 for the latter. Terraced houses were a little cheaper, reflecting the fact that there was no room for a car, and were available at £1,545. The level of grant was £285 in all cases. The financing was also very good, with the availability of the deposit being the important limitation. A purchaser needed a deposit of £160 for a terraced house, £260 for an end-terrace house and £285 for a semi-detached house. This allowed the society to advance a loan of £1,100 with a repayment schedule of 27s. 6d. over 30 years but purchasers were liable for ground rent and rates. The repayments were less than the maximum differential rents that could be charged in council housing and it was possible for families in social housing to be paying more than those who were purchasing their own property. This

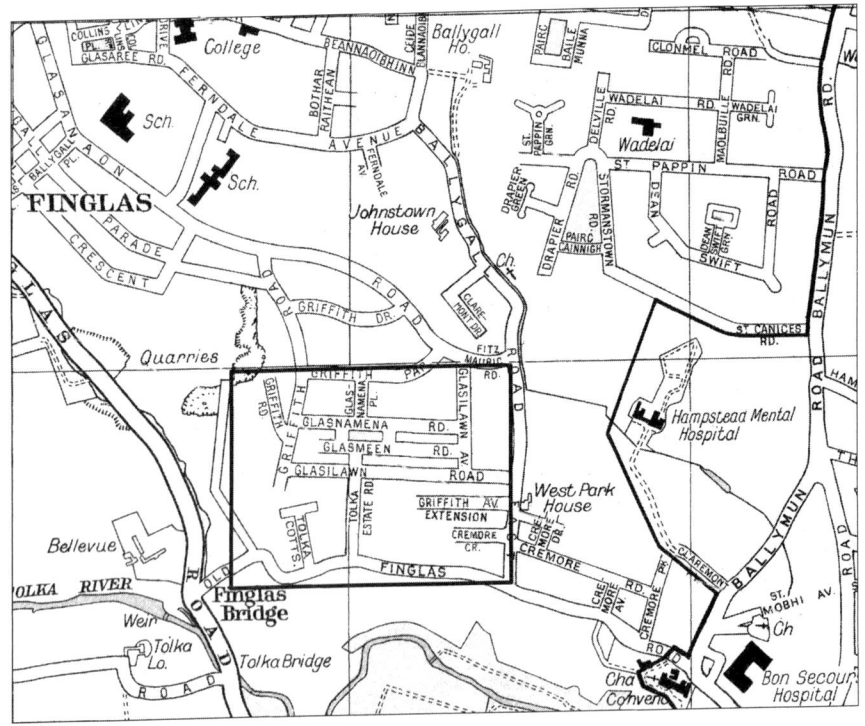

49. The developments of the Red Park Utility Society, Tolka Estate and Ballygall Public Utility Society. (Geographia plan, 1:15,840, 1967.)

scheme was completed by early 1952 and the society was wound up in February, all debts having been cleared. By this time they had completed 520 houses for the 'working class' (their description), a spectacular achievement. This method of funding was not how a traditional public utility society worked. The practice had been that a society was kept in existence until the houses had all been paid for because of the central role which repayments had in the funding of the society. In this case, the funding was at arm's length, with the society operating more like a building company. Once the houses were sold, the society folded its tents and left the purchasers to deal with the loan providers. However, that was not the end of their building activities in Finglas.

As they were completing their Finglas Park development, they were moving their focus of activity to Ballygall Road. Transformed into the Ballygall Public Utility Society, but with the same business address initially, they offered houses on Ballygall Road, which later became Ballygall Road East, with the locus of their building opposite the then extant Ballygall House (Hillcrest). This was on the eastern side of Finglas East and it was marketed as being Glasnevin

50. Advertisement by Ballygall Public Utility Society. (*Irish Independent*, 23 February 1952, p. 5.)

**BALLYGALL PUBLIC UTILITY SOCIETY Ltd.**

HOUSES ARE AVAILABLE FOR SALE AT BALLYGALL RD., GLASNEVIN, three miles from the centre of the city and opposite Ballygall House. Each house contains two reception rooms, three bedrooms, a bathroom and lavatory, a kitchenette and a fuel shed, and hot water, electricity and gas laid on. There are gardens front and back, and the houses are situated in very healthy surroundings looking over Dublin towards the Wicklow Mountains.

END TERRACE HOUSES, with garages, are available for £2,160, less Government Grant, £285. Net £1,875. This figure includes law costs, stamp duties and all other costs in the case of Irish Citizens. A **deposit of £275** will secure an end terrace house, as the Society will itself advance £1,600 of the purchase price, repayable with interest at 5 per cent per annum, over a period of 30 years by weekly instalments of £2. The Annual Ground Rent is £12.

INSIDE TERRACE HOUSES are available for £2,060, less Government Grant, £285. Net £1,775. This figure includes law costs, stamp duties and all other costs in the case of Irish Citizens. A **deposit of £175** will secure an inside terrace house, as the Society will itself advance £1,600 of the purchase price, repayable with interest at the rate of 5 per cent per annum, over a period of 30 years by weekly instalments of £2. The Annual Ground Rent is £12.

THE DEPOSIT in each case includes £1 in respect of a share in the Society which is taken up by the purchaser, who thereby becomes a member of the Society.

If the purchasers do not wish to borrow from the Society, applications can be made by them to the Dublin County Council for advances under the Small Dwellings Acts.

The houses can be inspected on any Monday, Tuesday or Friday between the hours of 10 a.m. and 4.30 p.m., or on any Thursday afternoon between the hours of 1.30 and 4.30 p.m., by application to the Timekeeper on the site. Any further information can be obtained from : —

THE SECRETARY,
**BALLYGALL PUBLIC UTILITY SOCIETY, LTD.**
23 CLUNE ROAD, FINGLAS

rather than Finglas. The houses were built with the same specifications as above though with a more distinctive design on a much wider and much busier road. The price was considerably in advance of what they advertised in Finglas Park. This time they did not differentiate semi-detached houses from end of terrace houses but the price in 1951 had risen to £2,160 while a terraced house now cost £2,060. A garage was included with the end-terrace house but this would not explain the significant increase in price. The grant was unchanged and, taking a deposit into account, it meant that loans were now of the order of £1,600 with a repayment schedule of £2 per week for 30 years. By 1953, they had changed their approach. Now they offered semi-detached houses but with a deposit of only £50 being required. There was also the prospect of a supplementary grant for suitable applicants. This followed from a provision in the Housing (Amendment) Act of 1952 which allowed a local authority to provide a supplementary grant of up to 50 per cent of the State grant. It was aimed primarily at people who were either local authority tenants or who were eligible to be tenants, as long as in the latter case they were resident for five years in Dublin. This will be explored in greater detail below. Their prices continued to rise and by 1953 a superior semi-detached house (*their description*) would have cost £1,987 10s. net of the State grant. Taking a deposit of £50 and assuming a full supplementary grant of £137 10s. meant that a loan of £1,800 was required. A term of 35 years was assumed with monthly repayments of £9 15s. This was towards the high end of prices, even for a superior semi-detached house, on the north side of the city and it seems that they had problems selling. Certainly in 1954, the society was selling sites for £200 on Ballygall Road (*Irish Press*, 24 September 1954, p. 15). The society finally went into voluntary liquidation in November 1963, though with all its debts paid in full.

The business approach by the Ballygall Public Utility Society appears not to have been untypical for the times. The Walkinstown Utility Society obtained a plot of ground just over 2.5 acres (1ha) for £5,000 in the late 1940s and proceeded to build houses there in the early 1950s – a scheme of 50 on Balfe Road East and Moeran Road. The members were allocated a plot and the society undertook to build a house there within a period of one year. The houses were three-bedroomed with a kitchen, dining room and sitting room and were built mainly in terraces of six, though semi-detached houses were built at the road intersections. The price in January 1952 was £1,540 and the purchaser was required to pay £130 at the signing of the agreement and a further £50 when the roof was on. The balance was due on completion. While the society promised to pay to the purchaser any State grants which they managed to raise, there was no guarantee. Additionally, the agreement to purchase the house was entirely separate to any arrangement which might be put in place to raise the funds necessary to complete the purchase. In other words, it was not quite the co-partnership society of an earlier period and much more akin to a modern building society. As with the Ballygall Society above, the society went into liquidation when its building was complete. Formal notice of liquidation was made on 26 October 1953 with all debts having been settled.

Thereafter, public utility societies began to fade from the building scene in Dublin as they were gradually eclipsed by other forms of financing. Some continued to build into the 1970s; the St Canice's Housing Society took on the provision of 64 detached and semi-detached houses in the Coolock development on land acquired from the Christian Brothers (Report 106/1967) while the South Dublin Co-operative Housing Society was active in the Dún Laoghaire borough. As a new co-operative organization, the St Canice's National Housing Society went against the trend and their Coolock development was their first. They were an organization of engaged and newly married couples and they had 300 members by February 1967. They were well organized and quite active in the public domain and they went on the offensive in 1970 when they criticized the decision of Dublin Corporation to make 300 acres (120ha) available to private developers to build houses that would qualify for grants. They challenged the City Manager to a public debate on the matter (*Irish Press*, 17 August 1970, p. 7). They claimed they were being edged out of the market by these large-scale developments and builders were not interested in their small-scale projects. Their situation was made even worse by restrictions on the land being made available to them; they had been promised 5 acres (2ha) by Dublin County Council in Kilbarrack, they were given only two. A similar shortage of land meant that they could only develop seventeen houses on Tonlegee Road in 1970.

It was in the natural order of things for public utility societies to come and go. Nationally, there were 276 public utility societies in 1962 and in that year some twenty-five were in liquidation. The 1960s and 1970s were characterized much more by the winding up of many societies. Sometimes this was done in an orderly fashion as their business was completed and sometimes simply because they had failed to make returns for some years to the Registrar, a good indication that they were not functioning. Some names which would be familiar to those reading these volumes disappeared during this time. The Dublin Building Operatives PUS had its registration cancelled in May 1970 (*Irish Times*, 26 May 1970) while An Saorstát, the St Mobhi and the Saorstát Civil Service public utility societies disappeared in 1971.

## *Support for private housing*

Such was the housing need that support extended into what would normally be seen as the private sector. It might be surprising to have a section on support for private housing in a chapter dealing with Dublin Corporation but McManus (2002) argued that it was a mistake to see the public and private housing sectors as distinct; rather they needed to be seen as either end of a continuum with more complex arrangements characterizing the middle ground. The State was anxious to keep the housing lists as low as possible and therefore extended support to those with modest incomes who were sufficiently well off to be able to afford their own housing in the right circumstances. Dublin Corporation had its reserved areas where it made sites available to selected occupiers. It also helped these people with access to funds.

It assisted public utility societies and other groups. However, assistance was not necessarily confined to developments immediately adjacent to their own schemes. Theoretically, at least, they were prepared to assist anyone obtain housing. One of the points that will be made in relation to private housing is that owner occupancy was quite low in Dublin and low compared to non-urban areas. Houses were more expensive and it was difficult until the early 1960s for purchasers to raise relatively big loans. This is where the Small Dwellings Acquisition Acts were important. The primary legislation dated from 1899 but it was amended so many times over the years that it was far distant from its original purpose of helping tenants purchase from landlords. It was permissive rather than obligatory and Dublin Corporation was not required to provide support under the Acts. However, support under the SDAA became a central plank of Dublin Corporation's housing policy so that, for example, between 1948 and 1957, the Corporation spent £25.2m under its own housing programme but £8.84 million under the provisions of the SDAA. The latter assisted 5,879 families to buy their own homes (Report, 132/1962).

The supports available in the 1950s were a housing grant of £275 to anyone building or providing new dwellings for themselves within the size limits of the scheme. In addition, from 1953 onwards, Dublin Corporation decided to make a supplementary grant available to certain classes of purchasers. Then, the SDAA kicked in and ensured that a loan (also within limits) was made available to complete the purchase. It was a loan, not a grant, so it did not have the same financial implications for Dublin Corporation as other supports but it still required resources to manage.

The grant was provided under the provisions of the 1948 Housing Act. Like many such grants, it was initially intended as short-term stimulus. In this case, houses had to be completed by April 1950 but the time period was extended again and again. The maximum grant was £275 to a private individual who was building or reconstructing but £285 to a public society for new dwellings. This was a maximum for dwellings of at least 5 rooms connected to a main drain and was reduced for four-roomed and three-roomed dwellings. It was a substantial sum of money at the time, though its widespread availability might suggest that builders simply factored it in the house price. It was also available for quite significant houses. Although a minimum of 500 sq. ft (46 sq. m) was needed for grant purposes, the 1950 legislation increased the maximum to 1,400 sq. ft (130 sq. m) while a later amendment in 1952 allowed houses that were under reconstruction to be even larger. Social housing in Dublin was generally closer to 900 sq. ft (84 sq. m) and most three-bedroomed semi-detached houses would not come close to the limit. Over time the effect of the grant was diminished as house prices increased and no corresponding increase in the value of the grant was authorized. It was confirmed at the same levels for both private individuals and public utility societies in the Housing Act, 1966, though the maximum area could now be 1,500 sq. ft (139 sq. m).

A supplementary grant, payable by the Corporation, was also available in some circumstances from 1953 onwards. This had been provided for in the 1952 legislation but it was up to each local authority to decide whether it would pay it.

The income limits and the amount payable were set out in section 10 of the 1952 Housing (Amendment) Act.

i. if his family income does not exceed £208, 100 per cent. of the relevant grant,
ii. if his family income exceeds £208, but does not exceed £312, 66⅔ per cent. of the relevant grant,
iii. if his family income exceeds £312 but does not exceed £365, 50 per cent. of the relevant grant, or
iv. if his family income exceeds £365 but does not exceed £416, 33⅓ per cent. of the relevant grant.

These amounts were varied from time to time as were the other conditions which applied to the award. Thus, the amendment in 1956 made it easier for people to obtain the higher level of grant funding. Under the 1954 Housing (Amendment) Act grants were paid on a sliding scale based on the family income which was the aggregate income of the applicant and every member of his family who lived with him. This was altered in the 1956 Act so that only the income of the applicant and his spouse was taken into account. The income bands were also widened with the outcome that more people should have been eligible for higher supplementary grants (Report 1957/25).

| Annual family income not to exceed | percentage of State grant payable |
| --- | --- |
| £364 | 100 |
| £481 | 66⅔ |
| £546 | 50 |
| £624 | 33⅓ |

Up to this point in March 1957 a total of £274,404 had been advanced under the supplementary scheme. This was further amended under the Housing (Loans and Grants) Act of 1962. This removed the gradual scale and allowed the Corporation to decide the nature and scope of the scheme and the classes of persons or types of houses which could be eligible. The overarching condition was that the grant made by the Corporation could not exceed the amount of any grant made by the Minister. The revised rules for the supplementary grant were approved by the Council on 8 February 1963. These set out that the grant could not exceed 50 per cent of the State grant and that the combined income of husband and wife could not exceed £832. In addition, an applicant had to be a native of Dublin (city or county) or have been resident or employed in Dublin for the preceding four years. Applicants were required to be married and, if council tenants, they had to surrender that tenancy. Finally, it was a requirement that a grant recipient live in the house for at least three years or repay the grant in default, though leeway was given to remit this in exceptional circumstances (Report 13/1963). The crisis that resulted from the need to deal urgently with condemned buildings in 1963 coincided with a further easing of the terms, designed to get people out of the Corporation system. The maximum grant was increased to 100 per cent of the State grant for tenants who surrendered a tenancy or to persons on the official waiting list (Report 144/1963).

Table 26. Supplementary grants paid, 1953–62.

| Year | Category 1 | Category 2 | Category 3 | Total |
|---|---|---|---|---|
| 1953–4 | 0 | 0 | 2 | 2 |
| 1954–5 | 12 | 22 | 437 | 471 |
| 1955–6 | 88 | 44 | 805 | 937 |
| 1956–7 | 93 | 46 | 657 | 796 |
| 1957–8 | 51 | 32 | 440 | 523 |
| 1958–9 | 66 | 22 | 279 | 367 |
| 1959–60 | 67 | 26 | 304 | 397 |
| 1960–1 | 63 | 42 | 311 | 416 |
| 1961–2 | 50 | 38 | 358 | 446 |
| 1 April to 31 July 62 | 30 | 19 | 159 | 208 |
| Total | 520 | 291 | 3,752 | 4,563 |

Notes: Category 1: Based on applicant's income irrespective of other qualifications.
Category 2: Applicant was a tenant who surrendered a Corporation house.
Category 3: Applicant was a person eligible for a Corporation house.

The relative importance of supplementary grants can be seen in the table above which was provided to councillors in September 1962 (Minutes, 10 September 1962, p. 275). It showed that a total of 4,563 payments had been made since 1953, the first year the Corporation had sanctioned such a payment, and this had come to a total of £603,028. Unlike loans under the Small Dwellings Acquisition Act which had been self-financing, these grants had to be paid for out of Corporation funds and were a charge on the rates of about £46,000 in 1962–3.

There were no income limits for those in category 2 and 3 and it can be seen that the grants were much more important in taking people off the housing list or preventing them getting on to it than in terms of freeing up Corporation housing. Nonetheless, a contribution of 500 grants over almost ten years was important in the housing drive. This left the Small Dwellings Acquisition Act as the source of the remainder of the funding. The Acts were something of a mystery in that they were designed to provide access to funding for people of modest means. That term was never defined and it was left, in the case of Dublin Corporation, to the City Manager to define what that was. The benefit to a person qualifying as a person of modest means was that they got a mortgage of up to 95 per cent (90 per cent in earlier times) of the purchase price at an attractive price. The money had been raised using the better credit rating of both State and Corporation and, certainly in the 1950s, was a very important source of such mortgages. Building societies were cautious about to whom they loaned money and they baulked at loans in excess of 75 per cent.

While the City Manager had discretion to determine who got a loan, the amount of that loan was limited by legislation. The 1952 legislation set a limit of £1,600 as the maximum advance generally but up to £1,800 for a house located in the Dublin city or county, Dún Laoghaire or the district electoral divisions of St Mary's, Bishopstown, Blackrock and Douglas in Cork. This set an effective limit on house prices for some considerable time. It was theoretically possible for people to buy more expensive houses by having the SDAA account for a smaller proportion of the price. However, such people were unlikely to be good candidates for an SDAA loan. The concept of a 'subsidy house' – one that could be bought via an SDAA loan – became very important in the difficult times of the early 1950s when more expensive houses were difficult to sell. There was constant pressure therefore to increase the limit.

While the amounts advanced under SDAA loans were ultimately to be repaid, they remained as a debit on both the balance sheet of the Dublin

Corporation and the State and therefore a drag on other borrowing. Thus there was a move in 1956 to encourage the banks, building societies and other lenders to lend to the same degree. They were offered a guarantee that the local authority would bear two-thirds of any loss they suffered because of a loan default on the amount advanced in excess of what would usually have been the case. This could be considerable since such loans tended to be for no more than 75 per cent of the price and for a term of twenty years.

As the Minister for Local Government, Patrick O'Donnell, put it in the debate on the second stage on Thursday, 19 July 1956.

> The facilities available to borrowers under a guarantee scheme will be similar to those provided by local authorities under the Small Dwellings (Acquisition) Acts, in that a guarantee will only be given for advances made for the purchase or erection of new houses for owner-occupation, and that advances will not exceed £1,800 in Dublin City and County and Dún Laoghaire, and Cork City and its immediate vicinity, and £1,600 elsewhere. Subject to these limits, the societies will advance up to 95 per cent. of the market value, exclusive of a grant under any enactment. The minimum deposit required from the borrower will be 5 per cent. Some of the societies are prepared to make advances repayable over 35 years. Interest will be at the rate charged by the society in its normal course of house financing.
>
> (Dáil Debates, 46(8), col. 635)

If a purchaser felt that he qualified as a man of modest means, then there was a complicated process to be completed before the money would be advanced. It involved the following stages as outlined in 1960 (Minutes, 13 June 1960, p. 175):

- examination of plans in relation to the general control of building.
- determination of valuation on which loan will be based.
- examination of title and generally of security on which the mortgage will be based.
- technical examination of the completed house or of the partially completed house on which an interim payment is based.
- each of the foregoing stages requires certificate by the responsible officers before the authorization for payment is submitted to an authorized by the Manager.

Both State and Dublin Corporation were anxious that loans should continue to be available during the 1950s and into the 1960s but, at the same time, there was always a degree of tension between State and Corporation over the level of provision and about who was paying for it. The amount involved was considerable. When the city authorities came to consider a scheme to allow tenants to purchase their houses in 1961, it was noted that by that time the number of houses being purchased and supported under the scheme had risen to 8,101. The outstanding loan which the Corporation had on its books for these houses was then £10.86m (Report 91/1961).

Despite the economic difficulties of the 1950s, loans under the SDAA continued to be advanced but there was a spat between State and Corporation in the 1950s which demonstrates just how parlous were the finances of both parties and also how sensitive was the question of SDAA loans. The process was that each year the Corporation sought approval from the State to advance a certain amount of money under the SDAA. This was in addition to the funding it sought to continue its capital programme, mainly house building for the working classes. On 19 September 1955, approval had been sought for a loan of £2m and the Minister for Local Government sanctioned this on 29 November (Report 19/1956). However, trouble was not far away as the Secretary of the Department of Local Government, John Garvin, informed the Council in December 1955 that the Government proposed sweeping changes to the SDAA process. Specifically, he said that:

- the State was not in a position to provide any further assistance under the SDAA;
- Minister for Finance suggested that the Corporation should sell its older houses to tenants and so increase its capital resources;
- Minister for Finance suggested that the Corporation should approach banks or insurance companies to see if they would finance the purchase of houses by those recommended by the Corporation, with a guarantee if necessary;
- there was no objection to the Corporation raising its own loan to finance operations under the SDAA;
- Corporation was advised to reduce loans to a minimum.

It is fair to suggest that the Corporation was stunned and this was expressed in a motion passed on 30 January 1956. This 'rejected the Government proposition of transferring to the Corporation the responsibility of financing loans under SDAA and request[ed] the City Manager to inform the Department of Local Government that unless funds [were] made available housing under this branch will cease with consequent unemployment and disastrous slowing down of housing' (Minutes, 30 June 1956). To give effect to this, it was proposed to process only those applications which had been received prior to 21 November and for which it was believed that funding was in place.

The City Manager upped the ante further by suggesting that it 'might be wise, in consultation with the Minister, to consider whether in present circumstances, it [was] wise to enter into further extensive commitments for other capital works on the assumption that capital money would be available' (p. 35). The rationale behind this was that the Department's initiative had come as a bolt from the blue and the Corporation felt that they had been utterly undermined. They felt that they had had an understanding of what would or would not be approved and projects had been advanced in many cases before final approval had been obtained. In fact, an earlier decision of the Department not to approve any portion of a scheme in advance of the development of plans for the entire scheme made such an approach a necessity.

This response seems not to have been expected by the Department and the Corporation was asked immediately not to proceed with their decision to terminate consideration of new applications until consultations could be had with the Ministers for Finance and for Local Government. The result of the consultation was recognition that the original proposal had been a step too far. It is not clear whether this was a mistake on the Department's part or a hand of poker. In any event, the Corporation's position became very clear when, following the Department's suggestion that they try the market, they sought an overdraft of £870,000 from Bank of Ireland to meet a temporary shortfall in their capital account. The bank had a long-standing relationship with the Corporation and the request was for a temporary facility only but it was refused on 29 March. Appeals to the highest level within the bank to reverse the decision produced much hand-wringing but no result. The Corporation then applied to the Minister.

Shortly afterwards the Taoiseach, Mr John A. Costello, contacted the Corporation with a deal. He commented that he was doing so because the Minister for Local Government was unavailable and he wanted the matter settled quickly. The Taoiseach explained that the problem had been that the State needed to see the full extent of demands on its resources from its various departments before it could respond to the needs of the Corporation. They now had that information and had discussed the financing of the housing

"I'm afraid, Kathleen, I'll have to be giving you a bit of a squeeze!"

51. The need for austerity. (*Dublin Opinion*, 1956, March cover.)

programme. Lest it be misunderstood, there was recognition of the 'onerous obligations of Dublin Corporation and the desire of the Government, on social grounds, of continuing to devote a high proportion of national resources to meeting essential housing needs' (Minutes, 16 April 1956, p. 120).

They were given approval for borrowing of £4m, of which £1m (that required for SDAA) loan was to come from the Local Loans fund, another vehicle for raising finance but from which Dublin and Cork city councils were excluded. This was the first time that Dublin Corporation had been given access to this fund. In return, the Corporation was to use its best endeavours to raise the £3m on the market but with the assurance that the State would step in if this could not be done. Given the experience with the overdraft, nobody can have believed that the Corporation would be able to raise a loan of £3m. The Corporation was satisfied with this arrangement and expressed its satisfaction to the Taoiseach.

There was obviously still some hope on the government's part that the total of loans advanced could be kept under control while still maintaining the appearance of a fully funded scheme. This was assisted by an instruction from the Ministers for Finance and Local Government that while the Corporation could have the £1m for loans under SDAA, these loans were to be restricted to those who qualified for supplementary grants (Report 29/1956).

The Government must have felt that they had done well by the Corporation, especially as capital within the country was very scarce. They had offered a long term national savings bond in February 1956 in the hope of raising £20m but had managed only to get £8.4m. They surely expected the Corporation to get on with their programme. The good relations which seemed to have been reflected in the motion of thanks back in the spring had turned sour by the autumn with Dublin Corporation being accused of sabotaging the housing programme by playing politics with loans under the SDAA. There was a counter charge that the housing programme was being damaged by the delays that the Department of Local Government had imposed on the approval of projects. It was said that nobody was going to make commitments when it was unclear if the money was going to be forthcoming. The political accusation was that the State had run out of money but that rather than say so, they had resorted to a tactic of delays. Mr Robert Briscoe TD, and also a member of Dublin Corporation and a sometime member of the Housing Committee, put it thus.

> As a result of that, and accepting the Minister for Finance's view as being a correct one, that no authority had a right to sign firm, formal contracts unless they knew that the money would be available, we in the Dublin Corporation announced that unless we had confirmation that the money for the particular transaction would be available we were not signing the contract. [...]
>
> The Minister now knows that it was not the Lord Mayor of Dublin or the Dublin Corporation who put all the small house builders out of existence and who caused all the unemployment in connection with that particular category of work, but that it is the result of his own actions, decisions and instructions.
>
> (Dáil Debates, 160(14), col. 2045)

In so far as the facts about the SDAA can be ascertained from a political argument, Dublin Corporation proceeded to allocate grants under the SDAA until the £1m which had been approved had been allocated. The restrictions on the availability of loans had reduced the number of suitable applicants and it seems that there were people who had entered into contracts on the basis that they would qualify found themselves without any means to complete their contracts.

The Corporation then announced that they would not consider any further applications until the question of future funding had been decided. It was their view that they had no money to fund SDAA loans into the future. The Government's view was somewhat different. They said that they had funded Dublin Corporation in 1956 to the tune of £4m, of which £1m was to go to SDAA loans. When the Corporation had come to the Government later in the year and said that it would be useful if they could know what the funding position for the next year would be, the Minister for Finance, Mr Sweetman, had agreed with them. They were told that they could rely on funding of £4m in the coming year for the same purposes. The Corporation took that to mean that they could control the allocation of the funding under the various heads and they decided that they needed all of the money for the capital programme, leaving nothing for the SDAA. The Minister took the view, strongly, that when he said 'same purposes' that he meant that £1m was to go to housing under the SDAA. He gave a lengthy and annoyed explanation in the Dáil about what he meant and, in essence, he expected words to take the normal meaning ascribed to them. So when he said 'same purposes', he assumed that the Corporation would allocate the money to the same range of activities for which funding had been previously allocated. He was not demanding exactly the same proportions but:

> what I do say, and say quite categorically, is that when a local authority is given funds for a purpose covering several items they are bound to make a reasonable allocation out of those funds for each of the several items for which the funds have been allotted ... The Dublin Corporation, on their own initiative, changed the purposes; and to exclude one purpose, with whatever motive they did that exclusion, was not a procedure that should be carried through.
> (Dáil Debates, 160(14), col. 2077)

The political charge was that the Corporation had made the announcement of a lack of funding for SDAA loans while a by-election was being contested in South-West Dublin as a result of the death of government TD, Peadar S.

Doyle. The result saw a Fine Gael seat move to Fianna Fáil. This political charge was given extra credence by the fact that some £215,000 was 'found' for SDAA loans in the weeks following the election. This, the Corporation claimed, resulted from their inability to make other necessary commitments on foot of the delays noted above.

The Minister was not prepared to tolerate this and he communicated his view to the Corporation. Mr Robert Briscoe TD, during the Dáil debate, put it that the Minister had sent a 'bluff letter to the Corporation last week instructing us to spend £500,000 on S.D.A.A. housing' (col. 2042). While the import of the letter might have been that, in fact it was sent by the Departmental Secretary, John Garvin, and was couched in milder terms.

> It seems to him [Minister] that having regard to his assurances in his letter of 6 July with regard to the financing of the capital programme it should be possible for the Corporation to meet their requirements under other heads and at the same time provide for issues of not less than £500,000 under SDAA (Minutes, 3 December 1956).

In any event, the Corporation took the view that it was time to lower the temperature. The Housing Committee had recommended a provision of £215,000 for loans under SDAA at its meeting on 23 November but the Council voted on 3 December to ask the Housing Committee to see if they could find any additional funds to bring the total up to the £500,000 requested. This they did in early January 1957 when they determined that a projected drop in house building would allow the required money to be spent under SDAA (Report 5/1957). This shows how sensitive was provision under SDAA. It was not the Corporation's top priority but any cutbacks in provision had an immediate political effect as well as an effect on the building trade and the people involved.

This allocation was sufficient as demand for funding under SDAA fell in parallel with other falls in housing demand. Figures presented to the Council in 1960 (Minutes, 13 June 1960) show that applications had halved in the five years since 1955. The dip in 1957 was a consequence of the row described above between the Corporation and the Government.

| Year ended | Applications received | Year ended | Applications received |
| --- | --- | --- | --- |
| 31 March 1955 | 1,450 | 31 March 1958 | 621 |
| 31 March 1956 | 1,196 | 31 March 1959 | 608 |
| 31 March 1957 | 335 | 31 March 1960 | 730 |

This allowed some relaxation in the conditions under which funding was made available to applicants. A requirement had been introduced in 1956 that applicants should also qualify for the supplementary housing grant. This meant that they were either tenants of the Corporation or eligible to be tenants and that they had been resident in Dublin and it also defined what was a 'modest income' in a rather crude way. Under these revisions, SDAA loans became more widely available and could be made to those with incomes under £832 per annum, regardless of whether they qualified for a supplementary grant (Report 73/1957). Since SDAA loans were resumed after 1948, they had been confined by Dublin Corporation to new building as an incentive to increase the housing stock. A further revision (Report 40/1959) provided that loans could now be made for previously occupied houses of amounts up to the lesser of 85 per cent of the house price or £1,700. This meant that houses with a value of more than £2,000 were outside the scheme. As usual, applicants were required to have been resident in Dublin city or county for a continuous period of not less than three years and they were required to live in the house for a period of at least three years post purchase. They were required to have a disposable income of at least £7 per week after all outgoings with a maximum income of £832 per annum though the Housing Committee of Dublin Corporation recommended that this minimum be raised to £8 per week (Report 56/1960 and noted in Minutes, 2 May 1960). The maximum income threshold was waived in the case of a Corporation tenant surrendering a house.

As the housing crisis manifested itself once again, there was further adjustment of the SDAA to make it more attractive. It was recommended to the Council that the ceiling on the value for previously occupied houses be raised to £2,500 with a maximum possible loan of 95 per cent. However, for a while the Minister did not budge on his 1962 instruction to limit loans to £2,000 (Report 25/1964). A further consideration of the scheme (Minutes, 5 October 1964) led to the maximum loan being increased to £2,250 and a council tenant who was surrendering a council house could expect to receive a loan of up to 99 per cent of the purchase price. These loans were now governed by section 11 of the Housing (Loans and Grants) Act of 1962 though they still tended to be called 'SDAA' loans and the figures for 1965 and 1966 (Minutes, 6 March 1967) showed their continued importance but increasingly only for those buying at the lower end of the market. The increases in the size of loan available did not keep pace in any way with the housing market and an SDAA loan did not figure in the considerations of most middle-class people.

Table 27. Loans and supplementary grants (new houses).

|  | SDAA | | Supplementary | |
| --- | --- | --- | --- | --- |
| Period | Number | Average amount | Number | Average amount |
| First half 1965 | 154 | £2,158 | 272 | £168 |
| Second half 1965 | 244 | £2,236 | 208 | £190 |
| First half of 1966 | 247 | £2,320 | 157 | £187 |
| Second half of 1966 | 218 | £2,408 | 184 | £203 |

Although the figures also show that the amount of the supplementary grant was not enormous, the maximum was £275 for a tenant or someone on the housing list, it was an important additional element in the affordability of any house. Since they were introduced in 1953 and up to the end of October 1967, a total of 6,942 grants had been provided at a cost of £993,169. While SDAA loans were self-financing, the burden of supplementary grants fell on the rates and was not insignificant, being estimated as being £75,000 in 1967 (Report 139/1967). The Corporation was always open to ideas to extend the reach of the supplementary grant scheme, despite the cost implications. In 1968 it was decided to amend the SDAA scheme for loans for new and older houses (Report 88/1968). Loans on new houses could now be offered to people who lived outside the Corporation functional area with the maximum loan raised to £3,000. The minimum disposable income to sustain such a loan was raised to £10 10s. While the maximum loan for older houses could also reach £3,000 it was still confined to those in the functional area of the Corporation and to those who were tenants surrendering a house or on the approved waiting list or in cases of extreme hardship.

It has been noted above that not all those who were approved for reserved area sites followed through on their allocation. Equally, not all those who took up SDAA loans were able to service them and this became an increasing problem in the 1950s. For some time, it was unclear to Dublin Corporation as to what they could do or indeed what they wanted to do. Somewhat reluctantly, they got into the business of repossession and they leased the houses to tenants on a temporary basis. This was done by soliciting offers for the leasehold in the newspapers and an example is reproduced below where they offered a variety of properties across the city (*Irish Press*, 25 June 1960, p. 19). The Minister for Local Government gave permission in May 1961 to sell houses which had been funded under SDAA and repossessed and which had been let on temporary leases. This was slow to take off but the process was

**52.** Advertisement for leasehold interest in SDAA houses. (*Irish Press*, 25 June 1960, p. 19.)

> BARDAS ATHA CLIATH — Offers are invited for the leasehold interest in each of the following properties: 42 Harmonstown Ave., Artane: 7 North Rd., Finglas: 20 Harmonstown Ave., Artane: Site 80 Beneavin Estate, Finglas: 3 Ballymun Park, Ballymun: 47 Ballygall Rd. East, Finglas: 26 Coolgreena Rd., Beaumont: 64 Cooleen Ave., Beaumont: Site 47, North Rd., Finglas: 26 Dromawling Rd., Beaumont: 57 Harmonstown Ave., Artane: 47 Avondale Park, Raheny: 37 Avondale Park, Raheny: 12 Coolatree Road, Beaumont: Site 1087, Grove Park Estate, Finglas. Further information about these houses may be obtained at the Housing Department's Offices at 56 Dame Street. Offers in sealed envelopes marked "Offer for S.D.A.A. House No. 2/60" and addressed to the Assistant City Manager, Housing Department, Exchange Buildings, Lord Edward St., will be received up to but not later than 12 noon on 8th July, 1960. The highest or any offer will not necessarily be accepted.

in place by 1963 when houses on Coolatree Road, Dromawling Road and Harmonstown Road were sold for prices that ranged from £1,720 to £1,800 (Report 4/1963 and 62). A much larger disposal took place in February 1964, revealing a degree of pent-up demand. There were seventy houses involved and an analysis of the locations does not reveal any particular concentrations. They were located in all of the major developments that had taken place since 1948 and this meant that most were on the north side of the city. There were houses on Sycamore Road in Finglas, in Beneavin Drive, Park and Road, Shanowen Park, Harmonstown Avenue, Shantalla Drive and Road, Ferndale Road as well as Killester Park, Collins Park and Gracefield Avenue. Prices ranged from £1,720 to £1,850 and the sale in each case was to the tenant/occupier (Report 22/1964). Later on that year there were two further sales of 16 houses and 9 houses respectively and this was followed by 16 successful sales in 1965. Broadly the same locations were involved with some southside houses in Braemor Grove, Milltown Drive and Landscape Crescent fetching much higher prices in the range £2,230 to £2,300.

## Other council areas

As a later discussion will show, Dublin Corporation dominated the social housing sector in terms of the sheer numbers of dwellings it provided and maintained and the activities in the other council areas were of a much lower intensity. It would not be until the 1970s when the city's housing schemes spilled over in large volumes into locations such as Tallaght, Clondalkin and Blanchardstown. Because Dún Laoghaire is a port, it has its own urban structure and the characteristics that would be expected in a medium-sized Irish town. Part of that was a need for social housing for its own working-class population and there had been provision going back to the beginning of the twentieth century. The borough's own analysis was that as building became possible following the end of the Second World War, there was a need for an additional 1,000 houses to add to the 1,977 dwellings that had been provided to that point. By October 1950, some 409 houses had been completed, 314 were in the process of being built and there were plans for a further 162. This led them to state in 1952 that they had seen the end of their housing problem; this was a proud statement given the very different position within the city (*Irish Times*, 20 September 1952, p. 3).

The main scheme of the late 1940s and early 1950s was in Sallynoggin (Belton Estate) and the Dunedin estate where three- and four-roomed houses together with three-roomed flats were provided. These were of standard size for the time, not particularly spacious, with 850 sq. ft (79 sq. m) provided in the bigger houses, 730 sq. ft (68 sq. m) in the smaller with 450 sq. ft (42 sq. m) provided in the flats. The use of culs-de-sac, though, removed through traffic from the area and ensured that it had its own clear identity. The borough agreed to raise a loan of £200,000 for the Belton estate and £25,000 for the Dunedin estate in May 1949. They also decided in 1950 to acquire four acres (1.6ha) at Daleview in Ballybrack with a view to building 36 houses on the site which they believed would meet the needs of the Ballybrack area.

At the opening in 1951 of a tranche of 164 houses in Sallynoggin, one of the bigger tenders, there was certainly a sense that things were going well, though Mr T.C. O'Mahony, housing director, was clear that building still needed to continue. He felt that there was a still a need for 800 houses in the borough. Indeed, in 1952, buoyed up by the success of their programme, the Corporation invited applications from all those who were still in need of accommodation. They received 417 applications, of which 111 had not been in the system before. In addition, they expected to receive 50 to 100 new

## A REVITALIZED HOUSING PROGRAMME

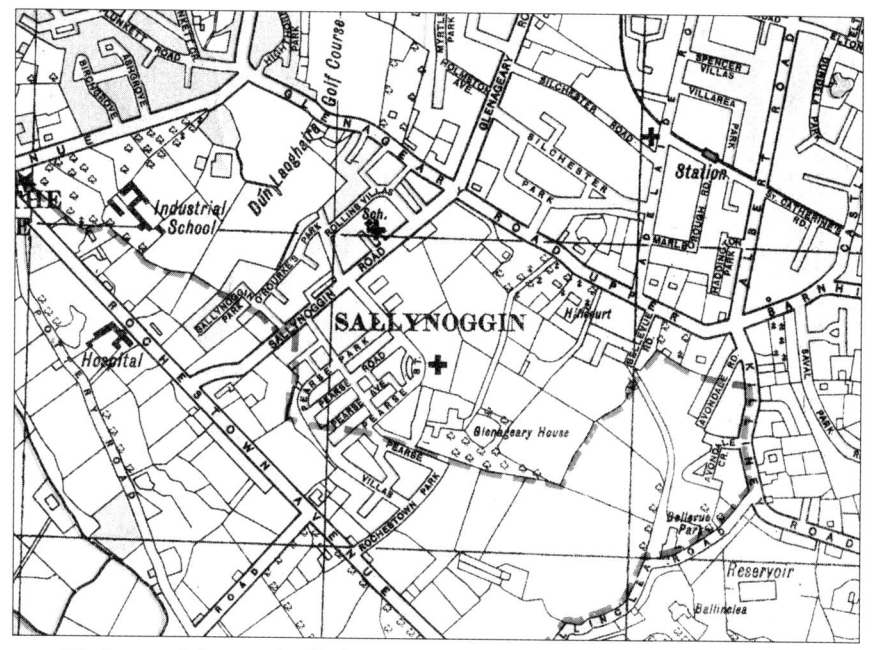

**53.** The layout of the completed scheme in Sallynoggin. (Ordnance Survey plan, 1:25,000, 1959.)

**54.** Housing in Sallynoggin.

applications each year, pointing to the need for a small, managed programme of house building.

As part of that managed programme, the borough completed two schemes off Kill Avenue in Monkstown in 1957. The Ashgrove Park development contained 72 houses while the Casement Park scheme had 40 houses. The latter houses had three bedrooms, a living room and parlour with a kitchenette, bathroom and wc. Gardens were provided front and rear and the rents ranged from 24s. to 28s. per week. The Ashgrove Park scheme was similar in provision. The building of these schemes was not entirely without controversy. An objection was made to the compulsory purchase of the land on which the Casement Park houses would eventually be built. The argument was that the presence of local authority houses would diminish the value of local private property by at least 25 per cent. In 1959, the borough returned to Kill Avenue and sought land at Kelly's Field to build eight houses. Houses dominated the building programmes but in 1957, they agreed to a tender from McInerney for the construction of 112 flats at Mounttown.

They continued to build in the same fashion during the 1960s. Thus, they completed a scheme of 142 houses at Rockford (Stradbrook) in Blackrock. These houses cost around £2,200 each to build and the rents were fixed at 50s. per week. With the completion of this scheme in late 1965, they had 123 registered applicants on the housing list who were deemed to be in immediate need of rehousing and another 148 who were potentially in need and who would have to be dealt with in the near future. Taking stock at this point, it was calculated that the borough then had 3,529 dwellings of which 1,579 had been built since 1947. Dún Laoghaire was also running out of land and it was estimated that all they had would permit the completion of an additional 400 dwellings (*Irish Times*, 1 December 1965, p. 4). They too were going to have to move into the county area.

As with Dublin Corporation, Dún Laoghaire borough provided sites to private individuals or public utility societies and also awarded loans under the SDAA schemes. One example of a public utility society was that of the Dún Laoghaire Home Builders' Public Utility Society which was active in the late 1940s and early 1950s. These were mainly members of the building trades and the 10 houses which they completed in late 1949 on Hyde Road were estimated to have cost only £1,050, which reduced to £765 after the application of the government grant. This was remarkably low at the time for three bedrooms, parlour, living room and a total area of about 900 sq. ft (84 sq. m) and was closer to 1930s prices. Tenant purchase was also provided

55. Alpine Gardens Public Utility Society. (*Irish Times*, 18 February 1950, p. 10.)

> ALPINE Gardens Public Utility Society—Beautiful semi-detached Bungalows at Dundrum, double-fronted, two bay windows, brick frontage; 3 bedrooms, 2 reception rooms, bathroom and w.c. combined, kitchen, fuel store; garage £75 extra; coved ceilings in principal rooms; hard-wall finish, with best quality wallpaper; most attractive fittings and fireplaces, etc.; on bus route; lease 900 years; G.R. £15: price £1,600, plus Grant: £1,475 loan available, repayable £2 3/11 per week; deposit £125. Further particulars from T. C. Gerard O'Mahony, Solicitor, 32 Molesworth street. Phone 62449.

for from time to time as when the borough decided to make 28 houses available for tenant purchase and the advertisement seeking applications appeared in May 1954 (*Irish Times*, 8 May 1954, p. 9). These were provided for families who were living in unsuitable accommodation and who could afford the deposit of £50 plus legal costs. They also had to show that they could meet the repayments, estimated at about £2 per week, without causing hardship to themselves or their family. In the county area, the Alpine Gardens Public Utility Society offered three-bedroomed double fronted bungalows in Dundrum for £1,600 in 1950 after the grant was taken into account. Even allowing for the fact that a full loan was available, less the deposit of £125, these were not serving the working classes. In May of that year, they had one bungalow available in Dundrum for the slightly increased price of £1,633 and they were selling sites on North Avenue, Mount Merrion for four-bedroomed detached houses with two reception rooms, large kitchen, garden and outhouses at a cost of £2,200 after the grant. This was clearly not the typical public utility society.

## Patterns of tenure

### Differential rents

The introduction of differential rents was seen by Dublin Corporation as the solution to a difficult problem. It needed a sufficient income from its tenants to maintain the houses and their associated services but many of its tenants, especially given that they were priority tenants, were not in a position to pay economic rents. For some, even the standard rent was a heavy load but there was a substantial minority who could afford to pay more than the standard rate. As its housing stock increased, so did the maintenance and debt repayment requirement and it came to consume an increasing proportion of the annual budget. To run a budget in which the existing housing stock was heavily subsidized from the Corporation's other sources of income made no sense, since this would merely diminish the capacity to build new houses, houses which were sorely needed.

The introduction of differential rents had been recommended by the 1939–43 housing inquiry but it had not been approached initially with enthusiasm by the Corporation, though they recognized the financial exigencies. The reasons were not difficult to see and were set out by the City Manager, Dr Hernon, in a report to the Housing Committee in April 1946 (Report 31/1946). It was simple arithmetic in that in order that some tenants would pay less rent, others would have to pay more. There would be enthusiasm for the former but there needed little consideration to determine the reaction to the latter. Despite Dr Hernon's concerns, it was inevitable that such a system would be introduced and work was undertaken during 1949 on developing a system (Report 31/1949). The choice was between two basic systems. In one, subsistence allowances are calculated for all members of the family. The rent is determined on all or a large portion of the remainder of the income. In the second system the rent is a fixed portion of the family income with only a small number of adjustments. The second system had the benefit of simplicity and it was favoured for that reason and because a similar system was operating in Cork. The maximum rent was determined as something close to economic cost while the minimum rent was set at a level sufficient to cover the rates. The scheme was approved in May 1949 with the proviso that it should apply only to new lettings. The approval of the Minister was sought and it was given. He required, however, that an economic rent should be fixed for every type of dwelling brought into the scheme. By this he meant the full cost of providing and maintaining the dwelling with no grants or subsidies taken into account and including a suitable amount in lieu of rates. Within this, approval was given to fix maximum and minimum rents and it was received on 5 June 1950.

The reaction of tenants was hostile once people found out that some currently paying between 10s. and 12s. per week were likely to see increases to 27s. 6d. per week. Moreover, it seems that some councillors were taken by surprise and seem not to have understood the full implications of what they had approved. This began a process, which was to continue for many years, of the Council trying to undermine the system they had introduced. By summer 1950, the level of opposition was such that the Corporation decided that the scheme would apply only to lettings made since 26 June 1950. In November 1950, they decided to appoint a special sub-committee to examine various proposals put forward for amendment of the system. This produced some changes and the decision to limit the rents to new lettings had some effect but discontent continued to simmer and occasionally bubbled over. Those who were lucky enough to remain on fixed rents knew well that if they ever wanted to move, they would face the differential system.

The system that was eventually introduced required that tenants pay up to one-sixth of their income, though a house provided to a newly married couple would potentially be more expensive and cost up to a maximum of one-fifth of income. Various discounts were applied. The first 10s. of income was discounted and an allowance of 5s. per child of school going age in excess of two children was also given. Rent for a four-roomed house varied from 6s. 6d. per week to 33s. per week while that for a five-roomed house ranged from 7s. 6d. to 36s. 6d. per week. There were some six-roomed houses and these could cost up to 40s. per week while one-roomed flats had a minimum of 2s. 6d. per week but could range to a maximum of 12s. 6d.

For the next few years there was an almost constant stream of proposals that ranged from amendments to the scheme to attempts to abandon it. It is clear that many councillors were under pressure from their constituents and they were more prepared to tolerate pressure on the rates rather than on rents. Thus in 1951, there was a proposal from the special sub-committee of the Council which would have had the effect of lowering the rents. This proposed an abatement of 1s. per week for every unemployed child in the house under the age of 16 years. The motion approved the levying of £22,000 on the rates for each 3,000 new houses built. This was put to the Council and approved at its meeting on 14 August 1951. The matter was returned to as part of consideration of further proposals from the special sub-committee in 1952 (Report 3/1952). This proposal would have discounted the first 25s. of income from the rent calculation and also would have reduced the maximum rent by an amount equivalent to the grant available to persons providing housing for letting under section 19 of the 1948 Act. The report was approved at the Council meeting on 4 February 1952 (Decision 51) but discussion on the specifics of the proposal was deferred to the March meeting. At the 3 March meeting the Council approved a motion in Councillor Larkin's name which sought more detailed information on the cost involved. The Assistant City Manager returned to the Housing Committee with an estimate of £48,364 as the cost of implementation of the proposed reduction in 1952–3 (Report

26/1952). Taking a sample of rents it was shown that the following changes would occur.

|  | Average rent present scheme | Average rent per motion | Fixed rent pre-differential scheme |
|---|---|---|---|
| 4-roomed cottage | 17s. 1d. | 11s. 9d. | 14s. 7d. |
| 4-roomed flat | 16s. 3d. | 12s. | £1. 1s. 11d. |
| 3-roomed flat | 13s. 10d. | 9s. 9d. | 14s. 6d. |

He showed that the reductions would be substantial but would also have the unexpected effect of lowering differential rents below fixed rents in many cases. The matter was raised at the 7 April meeting without conclusion. Finally, it was referred to a meeting of a committee of the whole house on 15 September (Report 84/1952). This led to the adoption of the proposal first proposed at the beginning of the year in Report 3/1952.

This example demonstrated the constant twisting and turning of the Council and the problems caused when all of the adjustments proposed to charges were downwards. The initial charges had been based on what was necessary to preserve the rental income and the Corporation had not attempted to price gouge its better-off tenants. Therefore, any one-sided rebalancing was going to have a significant income effect.

It was one thing to propose and approve these changes, it was quite another to have them implemented. Proposals were made on a regular basis and a ritual developed whereby the councillors demanded certain changes and the City Manager explained why they could not be afforded. In 1955, the demand was that the total rent would not exceed one ninth of family income compared to the then limit of one sixth. In 1956, the City Council, acting on a recommendation of the Housing Committee (Report 35/1956), recommended that overtime should not be included in the calculation of income and that cost of living increases awarded in salaries should not be the basis for a rent increase. They also asked that the discount allowed in families where there were four or more children of school age be increased to 7s. 6d. per child.

This was considered at the Council meeting on 9 April. The City Manager rejected the proposal on the basis that there was no provision in the budget for them. It was estimated that the measure would cost £76,700 per year and would be a burden on the rates at a time when businesses were struggling. There had been an important shift, however, in the power balance. Section 4 of the City and County Management (Amendment) Act of 1955 provided that by vote of the Council a Manager could be compelled to act in a particular way, provided it was lawful. Thus it now lay in the power of the Council to compel these changes in the differential rents system. Indeed the City Manager reminded the councillors of this possibility in his report. However, though the Council decided to pass the resolution calling for the differential rents to be amended as set out above, they did not attempt to do so under section 4. This now became the pattern with proposals being made, motions being adopted but the Council never taking the nuclear option of forcing the Manager to comply. A further example can be seen in the outcome of a deputation to the Council from the Ballyfermot Newly-Weds Association in 1956. There had been approximately 610 such lettings and the assessment of rent was based on one-fifth of salary and the maximum rent was a little higher than usual. The proposal was that the rents be based on one ninth of the gross family income with no deductions made in respect of children, principal income holder or any other reason. This would cost the Corporation some £14,500 per year. The newly-weds did not get this but the Housing Committee recommended that they be moved into the standard scheme at a cost to the city of £6,350 (Report 142/1956). It was considered at the Council meeting of 7 January 1957 (Decision 24) and it went as expected. The Manager stated that it could not be afforded and would not be done except under a section 4 motion, which was not forthcoming. The matter was referred back to the Housing Committee who decided on 2 December 1957 to undertake a comprehensive review of the differential rents system to ensure equity to tenants and ratepayers (decision 354).

Though the level of differential rents was a constant source of complaint, they were never economic rents. Figures provided for Ballyfermot in 1958 showed that as loan charges to fund housing increased, the gaps between differential rents and economic rents widened.

|  | Average per week | |
|  | Differential rent | Economic rent |
| --- | --- | --- |
| May 1950 to July 1953 | £1 0s. 3d. | £1 12s. 0d. |
| September 1953 to November 1953 | £1 0s. 4d. | £2 7s. 9d. |
| November 1954 to May 1956 | £1 1s. 4d. | £2 6s. 7d. |

The issue of differential rents was going to remain a problem as long as there were people on fixed rents. People on differential rents could see those in similar circumstances to themselves paying perhaps one third of the rent that they were paying. It was recognized (or hoped) that the problem would go away once all tenants were on a differential rent system but that was not going to happen any time soon. Indeed, the Corporation began to experience significant levels of rejection of new houses from those with fixed rents. Part of the reason for rejection was probably the greater distance from the centre but the certainty of moving to a differential rent system was certainly a factor. This must have been a factor in the decision to raise fixed rents in April 1957, though it was not going to be significant. The decision was to raise rents by 3*d.* per room per week from 8 April with the provision that tenants could go onto the differential rent system if hardship resulted. The effect was diminished by the exclusion from the increase of 3,454 houses which had been built prior to 1932, reducing the income to the Corporation by £5,500. A further increase of 2*d.* per room (discounted to 1*d.* per room for pre-1932 houses) was applied in 1960.

Threats of rent strikes were common and Dublin was not the only centre of agitation. The *Irish Times* reported in April 1957 that members of the Corporation Tenants' Association in Finglas were threatening to go on strike. By this time there were 15,000 tenancies in the differential rent system of which 900 were in the Finglas East scheme. The grievances were the same: inclusion of overtime, and 'snooping' by the Corporation in that people had to make annual declarations of income which were certified by their employers. One tenant was quoted as saying 'we are being treated like serfs, and we're just about fed up with it' (*Irish Times*, 26 April 1957, p. 3). It is hard to know what level of sympathy was felt for them by the general body of the population. Even the maximum rent of 36*s.* 6*d.* was below the economic rent for a five-room house of 52*s.* 3*d.* The *Irish Times* suggested that there was 'folklore' that people were doing very well under the system and far better than the 'white collar ratepayers' who helped to keep the schemes going.

There are not much comparative data available but the 1961 census gathered some information, reproduced in table 28. These data include Corporation rents and even only the rough comparison that is possible with the figures given above would suggest that Corporation rents were good value, all other things being equal. The next shock to the system came in 1962 when the Corporation moved to increase rents generally. This had been on its way for a long time. Data for 1959 had shown that prices had fallen in that year and that for the first time in many years increases in wages had been achieved on a basis other than inflation (*Irish Times*, 1 January 1960, p. 6). This did not lead to an immediate increase in rents, these matters always took time, but it did provide an opportunity to consider such an increase. For the meantime,

**Table 28.** Rent per month in 1961. (Census of population, 1961, volume 6, table 19a.)

| Monthly rent | Number of dwellings |||
|---|---|---|---|
| | Dublin City | Dún Laoghaire | County |
| Under £1 | 1,577 | 59 | 496 |
| £1 to £1 10s. | 4,593 | 264 | 941 |
| £1 10s. to £2 | 5,226 | 738 | 644 |
| £2 to £3 | 15,154 | 785 | 730 |
| £3 to £4 | 14,657 | 823 | 612 |
| £4 to £5 | 7,015 | 773 | 542 |
| £5 to £7 10s. | 20,257 | 1,169 | 1,228 |
| £7 to £10 | 5,236 | 691 | 550 |
| £10 to £12 10s. | 4,365 | 654 | 446 |
| £12 10s. plus | 3,029 | 535 | 582 |
| Average in shillings | 101.59 | 123.43 | 110.53 |

there was the usual debate between the elected councillors and the city authorities. Both knew where their powers lay and neither was prepared to push the argument to its limits. In May 1961, the Council was asked not to include overtime in assessing differential rents of young families where there was only one earner. It was also proposed that in future assessments of rent that a reduction of 10d. should be applied for each child, that the discount for the principal earner be increased to £1 and that of other earners to 10s. A final stipulation was that should the head of household become unemployed the practice of considering the next highest earner as the principal earner should be discontinued (Minutes, 15 May 1961). The response of the authorities was that the rate for the year had been passed on the basis of charges being what they were. These proposed changes would cost between £100,000 and £150,000 per year and there was no source for this income (*Irish Times*, 16 May 1961, p. 1). Notwithstanding this, the motions were passed. Thus the councillors could keep faith with their constituents without bursting the budget. Within the context of any budget, there was a simple balance between the rates levied on all households and businesses and the rents achieved from tenants. This balance was a matter of political discourse. The higher the rates, the lower the rents could be and vice versa. Mr Seán Dunne argued in the Dáil in November 1961 that:

but over the years it has developed in such a fashion that it has been manipulated by those represented in Dublin Corporation as they are represented in every local authority throughout Ireland whose sole concern is not the overriding drive or thought to house the working people at the lowest possible rents but whose sole concern is entirely different – to maintain rates at as low a level as possible. This differential rent system has been developed in such a way that the working class people of Dublin, in that huge reservoir of labour which keeps the wheels of industry turning in this city, that huge mass of workers living in Ballyfermot, are literally suffering as a result of this system.

(Dáil Debates 192(2), col. 292)

There were many shades of that view expressed during the debate and even the Government response recognized that there was concern about the method of determination.

The review was begun in 1962. It was pointed out that the level of rent had not increased since the system was introduced whereas the cost of maintaining housing had risen, especially in recent times. By this time, some 40 per cent of housing was under the differential system so the points of comparison between fixed and differential rents remained as live as ever. However, though it took many months to complete, the only result was that the maximum rent payable increased by 10 per cent in April of 1964. Meanwhile, the same process was underway in County Dublin. There the increase in the maximum from £2 2s. to £3 13s. affected only seven people. It applied to those earning more than £23 10s. per week and having four or more children. In the county only 185 in total were affected by increases.

It was inevitable that the issue would be revisited soon. This occurred in October 1965 and quite a detailed presentation was given by the Assistant City Manager, Mr R. O'Brolchain (*Irish Times*, 15 October 1965, p. 6).

|  | Max. rent | Min. rent | Required income to pay max rent |
|---|---|---|---|
| 1-roomed flat | 37s. 6d. | 2s. 6d. | £12 5s. |
| 2-roomed flat | 52s. 6d. | 3s. 6d. | £16 15s. |
| 3-roomed flat/house | 87s. 10d. | 5s. | £28 16s. 6d. |
| 4-roomed flat/house | 96s. 10d. | 6s. 6d. | £31 10s. 6d. |
| 5-roomed flat/house | 109s. 9d. | 7s. 6d. | £35 8s. 6d. |
| 6-roomed flat/house | 120s. | 10s. | £38 10s. |

However, this was still a proposal which would apply only to new lettings and it did not involve an increase in the minimum rent; it was a long way from a reform of the total system.

The rents that would be paid under the new system are outlined above. It was noted that tenants with an income sufficiently large to require them to pay the highest rent would not normally be found in what was called the 'working classes' (Report 83/1965). Indeed, the term 'working class' was seen increasingly to be outmoded and no longer descriptive of the group which needed housing.

The data presented on the distribution of income types showed that while individual incomes might not be particularly high, household incomes could be considerable. The report presented data on the basis of 1,133 recent lettings and these showed that almost one-third of families had annual incomes in excess of £900 with some, at least, having upwards of £3,000.

| Annual family income | No. of families | Per cent of families |
| --- | --- | --- |
| Up to £728 | 398 | 35.0 |
| £728–£936 | 368 | 32.5 |
| £936–£3,120 | 367 | 32.5 |

This was a point reiterated in the Dáil in October 1966 when the Minister, Mr Neil Blaney, stated that 'it is known that there are something like 100 tenants in the Corporation scheme — it is a very small percentage — with family incomes of over £60 per week. There are a few thousand with family incomes of over £30 per week' (Dáil Debates 224(8), col. 1117). These families could easily afford the new rents. While it was argued that the proposals would double some rents, he went on to say that it had not been sufficiently noted in the focus on increases that rents would decrease for 35 per cent of tenants.

The Assistant City Manager had come to the Council asking that the increases be in place by 1 December (Report 80/1965). Naturally, this did not happen, so he returned with an interim proposal which would have seen the new system introduced but only in Ballymun. The reason for this was that building in Ballymun was coming to the point where the first tenants were going to move in and all would be on the differential rent system. He wanted the matter fixed in advance so that there would not be an issue of having to increase the rents there so soon after the first tenants arrived.

Once again the contentious nature of differential rents became obvious when the matter was discussed at the Council meeting on 17 January 1966.

Rather than simply vote on the report, Councillor Larkin, whose record in opposing differential rents had been consistent for over a decade, moved the following motion.

> Council disapproves of the proposed maximum rents contained in the proposals from the assistant City Manager in Report 180/1965 for the following general reasons (a) the absence of any detailed information on the cost of the dwellings referred to in the Report; (b) the failure of the Minister for Local Government to increase the level of subsidy payable from central government funds; (c) the lack of information from the Department of Local Government at this date as to what specific additional assistance will be made available in respect of this Scheme in accordance with the promise made to the deputations from the Corporation which met the Minister for Local Government prior to the Council approving of the Ballymun Project; (d) Council does not accept the proposition that the maximum differential rents shall equate with the full economic rent of the dwelling in question and while recognizing that the increased allowance contained in the proposal would be of benefit to tenants in certain income brackets, consider that the proposed maxima are not justified.

While the objection under (d) was a long-standing one and indeed it had for many years been council policy to fix the maximum rent below the economic rent, the other objections presented an impossible dilemma for the city authorities since most of the objections lay outside the remit or control of the Council. The meeting of a Committee of the Whole House duly took place on 31 January 1966 and the proposal was eventually adopted at a Council meeting on 7 February 1966. However, at the same meeting, the City Manager got an interim agreement on rents. His report restated the position that everybody knew, namely, that there had been few alterations in the scheme since it was introduced and that it had not been fundamentally reviewed. Perhaps with a well-practiced sigh, he noted that it had not proved possible to obtain agreement on this new proposal and so he asked for an interim agreement that would apply to new lettings and re-lettings of vacancies (old houses). This was the perennial solution to any problem since it affected only a minority of those in the scheme. This produced a complicated scheme with two sets of 'new' rents. One scheme applied to all lettings of new dwellings after 28 February 1966 and to vacancies which occurred in houses first let since 1 January 1960. The other applied to lettings in dwellings which were first let between 1932 and 31 December 1959.

He tried to sell the scheme on the basis that though the rents were increasing there were also increases to the allowances. These allowances were particularly directed towards larger families with incomes under £14 per week and he estimated that 35 per cent of all applicants would be paying less. The reduction ranged from 1s. 9d. per week to 7s. 6d. for families with five children. He also pointed out that people would have to be in receipt of a substantial income in order to pay the maximum rents. In order to pay the maximum weekly rent for a 5/6-roomed dwelling, an income of £1,612 per annum would be needed (Report 14/1966).

The rules for determining income were the same as proposed for the scheme in Ballymun but, as Councillor Larkin noted, the Manager had amended his original proposal and this resulted in a reduced maximum rent for a one-roomed dwelling of £1 12s. 6d. rising to £4 15s. for a five-roomed dwelling. Even that was not sufficient and a further concession which protected successors in tenancies from the increase was agreed. Others disagreed with the principle that was being developed in the Manager's proposals of encouraging people who could afford it out of renting and into ownership (*Irish Times*, 8 February 1966, p. 14). The Manager's interim solution was eventually passed on 7 February but there was no indication of how 'interim' the solution was going to be. It was a complicated system as indicated by the mechanism for rent determination.

Interim mechanism for determination of differential rents
from 28 February 1966

- By taking the principal income (whether that of father, mother, son, daughter, etc.) and reducing it by £1.
- This income shall be further reduced by subtracting further sum of 10/- per week in respect of each child under the age of 16 years who has no income and resides with the parents or guardians.
- Payments under the Children's Allowances Acts shall not be included in the calculation of weekly income.
- To the principal income there shall be added the income of every other member of the household excluding the first 10/- per week of income in each case, and subject to maximum of £4 each such member.

- In the calculation of family income, no account shall be taken of certain increases in Social welfare and other allowances in accordance with the scales sanctioned by the Minister for Local Government from time to time for the existing differential renting scheme.
- Within the maximum and minimum limits rent shall be assessed at one-sixth of the combined family income and shall be rounded off to the nearest three pence in each case.

Table 29. Rents payable under the March interim scheme.

| Type | New | Old | Minimum |
|---|---|---|---|
| 1 Room | 32s. 6d. | 25s. | 2s. 6d. |
| 2 Room | 47s. 6d. | 35s. | 3s. 6d. |
| 3 Room | 75s. | 60s. | 5s. |
| 4 Room | 85s. | 67s. 6d. | 6s. 6d. |
| 5/6 Room | 95s. | 75s. | 7s. 6d. |
| Newly-wed | 75s. | 60s. | 5s. |

Note: The 'New' column was the proposed maximum rent for new dwellings from 28 February 1966 and all vacancies occurring in houses first let from 1 January 1960.
The 'Old' Column was the rent for lettings from 28 February 1966 for all vacancies which occurred in dwellings first let from 1932 to 31 December 1959.

The attempt to turn the interim solution into something more durable was made early in 1967. The Manager presented a report to the Housing Committee, which once again sought to increase both fixed rents and differential rents. Although he accepted a number of compromises which were put forward by the Housing Committee (Report 12/1967), he was unable to agree to a reduction in the overall level of increases. He pointed out, once again, that because differential rents had not risen and because rates were integrated into the rents, this meant that tenants under the differential rent system had not seen any increase in their rates. The gap between these people and the ordinary ratepayer had widened to the point that since 1950 'the total rate increase amounted to 23s. 3d. in the pound on the rateable valuation. The result is that all tenants under the Differential Rents Scheme are now paying 23s. 3d. in the pound less than all other ratepayers. This has resulted in putting a very heavy burden amounting to £230,000 per annum on the remainder of the ratepaying community and, as the Council are aware, rates are being levied irrespective of the means of the ordinary ratepayer' (Report 13/1967, p. 48).

The proposal this time was to increase only the maximum rents. This would cover the deficiency in rates and also allow some reductions in rent for those on lower incomes. Those on the minimum differential rent paid no rent at all since their entire payment was only a contribution to the rates. The Manager was prepared to tolerate that 'while the ordinary ratepayers of limited means have not the privilege of getting any reduction in their rates, the present arrangement should continue as regards rates payable by the differential rent tenants who are below the maximum'. However, he could see 'no justification at all for allowing it to continue in respect of the well-off tenants who are in a position to pay the new increased rent and whose incomes are known to compare more than favourably with those of the ordinary ratepayers' (p. 49). Those on fixed rents would see an increase to reflect the increased cost of maintenance and administration. Again, in most cases, the rent obtained would still be below the average cost of administration and maintenance.

What the Manager proposed was a complex system, similar to the interim one, where there would be different differential and fixed rents depending on when the tenancy was first taken out as well as being based on income and family size. It was based on the principle that there had to be a compromise since the Council represented all citizens and not just Council tenants and that there was a widely held view that ordinary people were paying much more than council tenants with similar incomes. However, the Council once again came to the view that no increase was justified. It voted on 6 February that neither the process for determining rents or the increases proposed be accepted.

The saga was about to come to an end at least for a while in that the Minister for Local Government, Mr Kevin Boland, intervened and made a proposal on 28 February. He had been apprised of the Council's decision by letter on 7 February and came to what he hoped would be a Solomonaic judgment. He noted that there had been a legal requirement for differential rents to rise in line with increases in rates. This had not been done and it now needed to be done. He, therefore, approved an increase in differential rents in line with rate increases but did not approve any increase in the rent element. For those on fixed rents, he noted that he had no power in this area but he suggested that the increase should not exceed that now being applied to the main differential rent rate, that applying to dwellings first let during the period 1 January 1954–27 February 1966. The price for this agreement was that a tenant purchase scheme for all houses was to be submitted as quickly as possible.

In fact, the Minister rewrote the rental system and produced the following set of rules. The City Manager was happy to agree to these proposals and they were put to the Council on 14 March 1967. After a lengthy debate and the insertion of six recommendations, the Manager's proposals were adopted by nineteen votes to eleven.

- Proposals for a tenant purchase scheme for all houses should be submitted to the Minister as soon as possible. In this connection, the Minister would be prepared to agree to sales under section 90 of the Housing Act, 1966, when in operation, at a discount from the market value of the house, calculated at a rate not exceeding 2% a year for each year after 5 years during which the tenant has been continuously in occupation of the house or any other house of a local authority, subject to a maximum discount of 30%. This discount is to be calculated in each case from the date on which the tenancy started, i.e., the benefit cannot be transferred on succession;
- In the assessment of the income of a subsidiary earner for the purposes of schemes (A), (B) and (C) for the first £3 of income should be disregarded and the rent should be based on the remainder of his income in lieu of the current methods of assessment of income in such cases;
- The first £1 (instead of the first 10/-) of the income of the principal earner should be disregarded so as to bring Scheme (A) into line in this respect with Schemes (B) and (C);
- All changes in tenancy arising on or after a date in the near future to be decided by the authority, either from vacancies, inter-transfers, succession or otherwise, should be subject to the new tenant going on to the appropriate differential rent scale. In this connection, the Minister has no objection to the application of Scheme (B) to new tenancies in dwellings first let on or after 1st January, 1954;
- The existing inclusive differential rent scales should be amended as soon as practicable so as to indicate separately the basic rent and the rates in each case, and the rates should be regularly adjusted in accordance with statutory requirements;
- The Corporation should ensure that the cost of culpable damage to dwellings by tenants is as far as possible recovered from the responsible tenant.

This ended the matter in the Council for a little while but it would be wrong to suggest that opposition to the system outside the council chamber melted away. The silence that ensued was a consequence of the abolition of the Corporation by ministerial order on 24 April 1969 because of its failure to strike a rate sufficient to meet the financial obligations of the city. Tenant opposition actually grew and became more organized so that the potential for rent strikes was greater at the end of the 1960s than it had been at the beginning of the 1950s. The concept of differential rents had not become ingrained into the system, probably because there was still a substantial minority of tenants who were on fixed rents and whose continued tenure was a focus of discontent for those on similar incomes who were paying much more. Thus Mr Larkin, addressing the two-day convention of the National Association of Tenants' Organizations (NATO), suggested that 'action was the only answer. There was no use in setting up a commission to inquire into the situation and it would take a lot of jail space to cater for 250,000 people' (*Irish Times*, 2 September 1968, p. 13).

By then systems of differential rents were widespread throughout the country and were pretty well universally disliked. From the perspective of the Corporation tenant, it is possible to understand why the system was so disliked. It differentiated the recent tenant from the older tenant and it took more from those who had greater income. Thus people living in exactly the same houses side by side on the same street could be paying very different rents. The fact that there was a progressive nature to the rent in that it was related to income was not seen as a positive feature. There was an expectation that people should enjoy their additional income and not have to put more of it into their houses. Neither was it appreciated that even for the highest earners that the rents were considerably below the economic rent. Corporation tenants could point to the private sector where rents were fixed regardless of income and that people with more money were free to do with it as they pleased. There was also the perennial argument that the basis on which income was determined was draconian and that it failed to recognize the day-to-day needs of families. Indeed, it was this aspect that engaged the Council over the twenty years of the scheme as they tried to tweak this element and that element. It was a source of 'common knowledge' that families with similar incomes could end up paying different rents because of the way in which the income was made up.

On the other hand, there were many ordinary ratepayers whose incomes were not greatly dissimilar to those in Council tenancies. Granted that those in Council housing tended to be those with larger families and whose households could therefore be more expensive to run. Against that, these households were not responsible for repairs and maintenance. It was felt by many that Council tenants were getting away with rents that were too low and that an unfair burden was being placed on the ratepayers. The ratepayer was often characterized as comprising businesses and wealthy householders but most people had to pay rates. To rub salt into the wound, the rates were based on the Primary Valuation (Griffith) of the site and this had not been revised in a century. It did not reflect the size or condition of the dwelling, the desirability of the residential area or the ability of the occupants to pay.

It was also 'common knowledge' that there were methods whereby Council tenants could reduce their assessable income with the complicity of employers or by having family members temporarily move out as assessment day approached. As with all such 'common knowledge', there is no factual basis on which to judge whether these were fair points or not. What is easier to conclude, though, is that there was no common ground on how best to provide the income which the city needed. The rent from Corporation housing was not covering the cost with the result that rates had to be higher or income was unavailable for other worthy city projects. Neither was a solution to be found during the 1970s.

## *Tenant purchase*

Dublin Corporation's initial suburban estates in Clontarf (1905) and Marino and Drumcondra in the 1920s had been for tenant purchase. However, it was quickly realized that this was not a suitable vehicle for the people at the bottom of the housing needs spectrum and a policy shifted towards renting from the early 1930s onwards. Indeed, as has been shown in the previous volume in this series, this was not out of line with the approach in the building sector generally. Most people in private housing were also renters and home owners were a minority throughout the 1930s and 1940s. It seems though that once the Second World War ended and the shortages in building materials began to end, the Corporation began once to look more favourably at tenant purchase. There was certainly interest in the idea from about 1948 but it was not until 1951 that interest was crystallized in a proposal. A meeting was held with the Minister for Local Government on 5 December 1951 concerning the Corporation's proposals in relation to the houses that they were building at Philipsburgh Avenue, later named Annadale. The Minister was favourably disposed to tenant purchase becoming a feature of the Corporation's building programme and he reminded the deputation that though he intended in forthcoming legislation to give an entitlement to rates remission to such purchasers, there should be no further burden on rates as a result of tenant purchase schemes (Minutes, 18 July 1952). It was pointed out to Dublin Corporation that though section 17 of the 1950 Housing Act set out the mechanism for tenant purchase, the intention was that local authorities would not make use of it until after reasonable provision had been made to provide houses for the working classes. However, the Minister intervened to say that he felt that that provision (the work of another Minister in another government) was really intended for ordinary local authorities throughout the country. If it was applied to Dublin, there would never be provision for tenant purchases. He also felt though that there should be a limit on the proportion of houses provided for newly-weds and tenant-purchasers. After some more discussion it was agreed in principle that at least 80 per cent of new building should be directed towards meeting the needs of the working classes and no more than 20 per cent towards newly weds and tenant purchase.

The Corporation's reflection on this led them to the view that it was desirable in all housing areas to get a mixture of either private housing or more expensive social housing through tenant purchase schemes. This was adopted as policy by the City Council on 18 July 1952.

On paper, it was a cautious policy and the principle of a mixture of housing tenures was not seen as an absolute necessity in every scheme. In addition, the idea of a particular percentage being allocated to newly-weds or tenant purchase was to be seen in overall terms rather than within each scheme. They then threw caution to the winds and decided to experiment by allocating the entire Annadale scheme of 204 houses off Philipsburgh Avenue to tenant purchase. The scheme was advertised in the newspapers on 26 January 1952 and potential purchasers were advised that they needed a deposit of £50 and that they had to be assured that they could afford the weekly payment of £2 without hardship. People had a month to apply with completed applications required by 29 February. The level of demand for the Annadale scheme was high with 1,650 applications and the Corporation must have felt that they could choose tenants who had the capacity to pay. The cost was £1,800 per house, about the same as the public utility societies in Finglas were offering, with rents of about £2 per week (which included rates and ground rent) over a 35-year period.

Future intentions were set out in the table presented to the Housing Committee in 1952 (16 July 1952). The figures show some considerable

DUBLIN CORPORATION.
PHILIPSBURGH AVENUE
TENANT PURCHASE SCHEME.

Applications are invited from persons with families for 204 tenant-purchase houses at Philipsburgh Avenue.

Applications will only be considered from persons in a position to pay a deposit of £50 and all legal costs. Applicants must satisfy the Corporation that they are in a position to meet the outgoings (estimated at £2 per week) without causing hardship to their families, and that their present accommodation is unsuitable to their needs.

Only applications on the official forms will be considered. These forms, together with particulars of the scheme, may be obtained on application to the Housing Department (Tenancies Branch), Exchange Buildings, Lord Edward Street, as and from Monday, 28th January, 1952, between the hours of 10 a.m. to 4 p.m. on Mondays to Fridays, and between 10 a.m. and 12 noon on Saturdays.

Applications, enclosed in envelopes marked on the outside "Philipsburgh Avenue," and addressed to the Housing Director, Exchange Buildings, Lord Edward Street, Dublin, must be received not later than Friday, 29th February, 1952.

P. J. HERNON,
City Manager and Town Clerk.
25th Jan., 1952. City Hall, Dublin.

**56.** Advertisement for Annadale scheme. (*Irish Independent*, 26 January 1952, p. 11.)

**57.** The Annadale development to the north-west of the Croydon part of the Marino scheme. (Geographia plan, 1:15,840, 1958.)

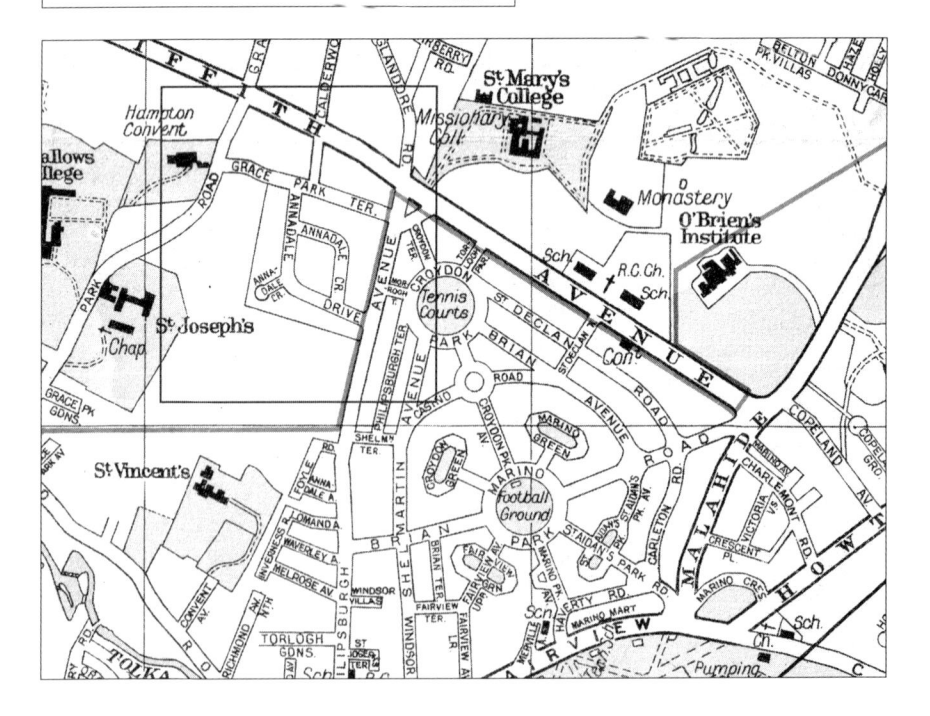

**58.** Housing on Annadale Drive. (*Irish Independent*, 23 September 1952, p. 6.)

**59.** Housing in the Annadale scheme in 2014. Its basic character remains unchanged.

variation with some schemes not being deemed suitable. A varying percentage was provided in other schemes and to the list should be added the 40 tenant purchase dwellings in Milltown and 46 in Finglas West (this group of houses faced the church site) (Report 102/1953). At the other extreme, the proposal for St Anne's represented a dramatic escalation with a decision to provide 600 houses for tenant purchase and none for weekly tenancy.

Table 30. Tenant purchase schemes in progress or predicted, 1952.

|  | Tenancy | Tenant purchase | Total |
|---|---|---|---|
| *Schemes completed in 1951* | 2,271 |  | 2,271 |
| *Schemes completed in 1952* | 716 | 68 | 784 |
| *Schemes in progress on 1 July 1952* |  |  |  |
| Exclusively tenancy schemes | 1,492 |  | 1,492 |
| Balance of Annadale |  | 178 | 178 |
| Finglas East | 920 | 32 | 952 |
| Wilkinstown | 364 | 12 | 376 |
| *Future cottage schemes* |  |  |  |
| Donnybrook | 114 | 26 | 140 |
| Ballyfermot Upper | 644 |  | 644 |
| St Anne's |  | 600 | 600 |
| Rathfarnham | 368 | 112 | 480 |
| Ballyfermot Upper / Chapelizod | 660 | 110 | 770 |
| Flats and reconditioning | 666 |  | 666 |
| Total | 8,215 | 1,138 | 9,353 |

Note: Source: Minutes, 18 July 1952. Note that in addition sites for about 450 private houses were included in these schemes.

The St Anne's scheme had been in gestation since the early 1930s when the estate was put on the market. It was regarded as one of the finest remaining estates in the country with almost 500 acres (200ha) and a fine house. It had once been the residence of Lord Ardilaun and it had passed to his nephew, the Hon. B.J. Plunket, former bishop of Meath. Though the property came on the market in the early 1930s, it was not until the end of the decade that Dublin Corporation acquired it and dealt with some difficult issues in relation to various lease holders. This gave them plenty of time to consider to what use the property was to be put. They came to no clear conclusions. It was suggested that up to 3,000 houses could be accommodated on the site but they were conscious that this was close to a well-developed middle-class area and the residents were none too happy at the prospect of another 'Marino'. The water was tested for a proposal designed to meet this objection. It was suggested that only a better class of house would be built on the site and that it would be for the better-off workers, those who earned between £3 10s. and £5 per week and who had comparatively small families. These would be able to afford four- and five-roomed houses (*Irish Times*, 27 February 1937, p. 15). This was not met with enthusiasm by the locals and the idea was not pursued. There were other proposals for the estate, which included a house for the

President or the Lord Mayor. When Abercrombie suggested keeping it as a park, it added another dimension to the discussion. He argued that Dublin needed a number of regional scale parks and that St Anne's was a perfect opportunity to provide one for the north-east of the city.

> In situation, level and natural beauty, the St Anne's Estate is admirably adapted for use as one of the Metropolitan Parks for recreation and large scale playing fields and we suggest that the fine Mansion and gardens attached might be used as folk museum.
> (Abercrombie, 1941, p. 47)

Abercrombie's intervention ended the discussion about using the entire park for housing and it also got Dublin Corporation out of the difficult relationship that it had with the local residents. A further complication was that the mansion was gutted in a fire on Christmas Eve of 1943. It is a measure of the times in that there was more concern for what was being stored there than for the house itself. It was being used as a store for ARP and Red Cross supplies and there was deep concern that there had been severe losses. In fact, the *Irish Times* reported 'no big loss at St Anne's', noting that the loss to the stores was far less than had been feared because so much was stored in the basement (8 January 1944, p. 10). The house, however, was a total loss but it was insured for £100,000 so Dublin Corporation effectively got the entire estate for £40,000 and no longer had to worry about what to do with the house.

In the post-war period, debate continued about the use of the estate. While the City Manager, Dr Hernon, was making plans for the demolition of the house, the City Council passed a motion unanimously on 11 November 1946 asking that the estate become a memorial to those who died in the course of Irish freedom, especially those who had been involved in the 1916 Rising. Rather than demolish the house, it was suggested that it be used as library or an archive focused on the Rising. There was a later suggestion that a national athletic stadium be built there and it seems from exchanges in the Dáil that nobody really knew who was proposing what. The Minister for Local Government, Mr Murphy, was aware of a proposal to set up an inter departmental committee to look at the siting of a national stadium on a portion of the estate. Others commented on the decision of the Corporation that it should be a national memorial site, though one TD believed that the Corporation had decided on the Phoenix Park (despite the fact that the Office of Public Works controlled the park). Others worried that there could be a deflection from the decision to put housing on it. The Minister summed it up thus

> There are proposals for the utilization of portions of the estate for the construction of a national memorial park; there are proposals for the erection of a national stadium; there are proposals for the construction of houses, for the erection of a maternity convalescent home, and for the erection of a secondary school. All these projects will get due consideration at the earliest possible moment.
> (Dáil Debates, 110(4), col. 365)

Full-scale use of the estate for housing seemed to be back on the agenda for a little while in 1948 when a draft housing plan for Dublin noted that 3,582 houses could be developed on the site. That never seems to have been a serious proposal. The decision of the Corporation to resume making grants under the Small Dwellings Acquisition Act in 1948 (*Irish Times*, 26 July, p. 5) re-opened the prospect of using the land for better quality houses (Report 79/1950) and they even agreed to commission an architectural competition in 1949 (Report 7/1950). By 1952, the project had been scaled back and a proposal was made to the City Council by the Housing Committee to build 930 dwellings in a mix of three-, four- and five-roomed houses. There were sites reserved for 60 private houses. This would have left a considerable parkland free of development but the proposal produced a furious response from the locals (*Irish Times*, 16 May 1952, p. 6), what the Corporation referred to as strong public agitation (Minutes, 18 July 1952). The *Irish Times* was on the residents' side for a 'special correspondent' noted that 'Clontarf has always been a high class housing area, thanks to the care exercised by the Corporation. Superior houses, like any other commodity lose their individual values when they are grouped with inferior dwellings'. This caused the Corporation to drop 62 houses from the scheme which would have backed directly onto this older housing. This produced a reconfiguration of the scheme into 154 three-roomed houses, 564 four-roomed and 90 five-roomed, the latter being for tenant purchase.

Further agitation continued, with the locals suggesting that all of the houses be for tenant purchase. The positive reaction the Corporation had previously received from the Minister about tenant purchase proved very helpful and the Corporation set about a re-examination on that basis. The three-roomed houses were dropped and a revised scheme for 404 four-roomed and 322 five-roomed houses was developed. Further consideration, however, led the Council to the view that four-roomed houses were also unsuitable for the development. The proposal was amended for a scheme of approximately 600 five-roomed tenant purchase houses plus the 60 private houses and the residential shops. This was put to the Council and agreed at its meeting on 18 July 1952.

In their announcement of the scheme in 1954, the most ambitious tenant purchase programme that the Corporation had attempted for decades, the Corporation emphasized the quality of the opportunity. It was aimed at those of their tenants who had bettered themselves and who had raised themselves above the classes for whom the houses that they occupied were originally intended. They described that a –

> unique opportunity is now presented to those families in keeping with their improved conditions and on a site which, for the beauty of its setting, cannot be surpassed in the City of Dublin or its environs.
>
> By availing of this opportunity to transfer to this high class residential area the families will be helping themselves on the road to further progress, and, by vacating their present dwellings, will also be helping their less fortunate fellow-citizens who are still compelled to live in overcrowded and insanitary conditions in the slums of Dublin.
>
> (*Irish Times*, 3 February 1954, p. 7)

The advertisement appeared the following day (*Irish Times*, 4 February 1954, p. 4) inviting applications. As part of the redesign it had also been decided to build the houses at the Raheny end of the estate, away from the 'superior houses' in Clontarf. The remainder of the estate was later developed into the park that exists today. There was no deposit required and it was estimated that legal outlays would come to no more than £20. The rents were set at £2 3s. 9d. for end-terrace houses and £2 1s. 7d. for mid-terraced houses. Though the Corporation maintained its principle of building in short terraces, it also stayed firm to its view that these should be houses of a better kind and they were three-bedroomed with two reception rooms, kitchen and separate bathroom etc. The cost of the houses worked out at £1,625, reduced after State and Corporation grants to £1,075 and payable over a thirty-five-year period.

**CORPORATION OF DUBLIN**

**TENANT-PURCHASE SCHEME FOR HOUSES ON ST. ANNE'S ESTATE.**

Applications are invited from tenants of existing Corporation weekly-tenanted dwellings for transfer to the new houses now being erected on the St. Anne's estate at Raheny. Up to 90% of the 600 houses to be provided will be reserved for approved Corporation tenants and the terms of sale have been made specially attractive for such tenants. There will be no initial deposit and the only outlay will be the actual out-of-pocket legal expenses, estimated at about £20.

The estimated outgoings, including rates and insurance, will be £2-3-9d. per week for an end house and £2-1-7d. per week for an intervening house in a terrace.

The houses contain 2 sittingrooms, 3 bedrooms, kitchen, separate bathroom and w.c., etc.

Full particulars and Forms of Application may be obtained at any of the estate offices or direct from the Housing Department, Lord Edward street.

Completed Application Forms should be lodged in the Housing Department as soon as possible, but not later than Monday, 22nd February, 1954.

P. J. HERNON,
City Manager and Town Clerk,
City Hall, Dublin,
2nd February, 1954.

60. Advertisement for St Anne's housing scheme. (*Irish Independent*, 4 February 1954, p. 4.)

By July 1954, the Council was in a position to approve the names for some of the new roads, though the English versions are now used: Bóthar na Naomh, Pairc na Naomh, Raon na Naomh, Raon an Mhuilinn, Ascal an Mhuillinn, Pairc an Mhuillinn, Ascal Naomh Áine, Ardán Naomh Áine, Raon Naomh Áine (Report 54/1954). By 1955, they were in a position to approve a further tranche of street names: Bóthar Bhaile Mhuire, Ascal Mac Uáid, Ascal Cnoc Síbile, Ascal Bhaile Bheite, Bóthar an Easa, Ascal Nainicín, Ascal Bhaile Thuaidh. The scheme was coming to completion in 1956 when a tender process was approved for the provision of shops on the usual model (Report 116/1956).

Despite the effort put into the development, the response was disappointing. While there had been an enthusiastic response to the Annadale development, it seemed that the market did not need as many as 600 such

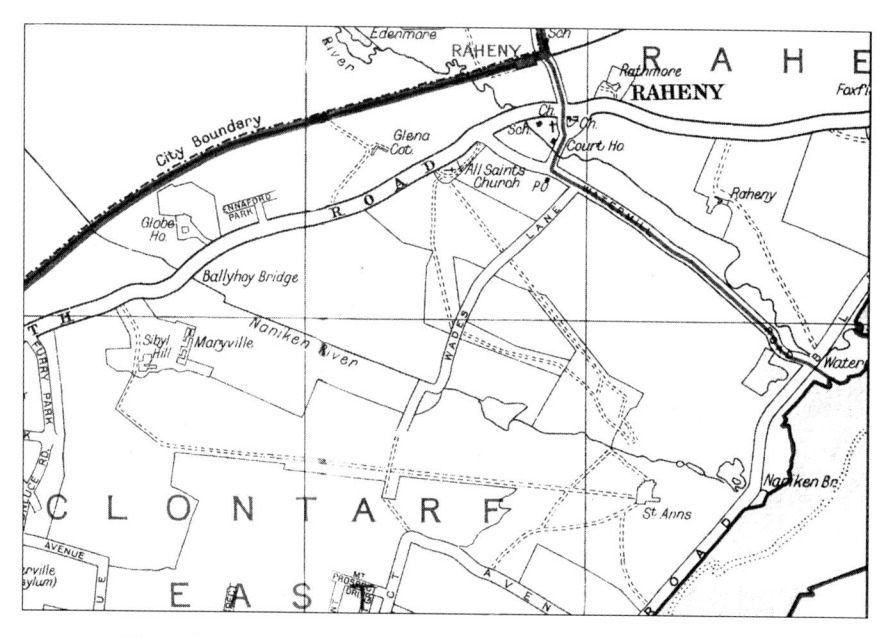

**61.** The St Anne's area before development. (Geographia plan, 1:15,840, 1958.)

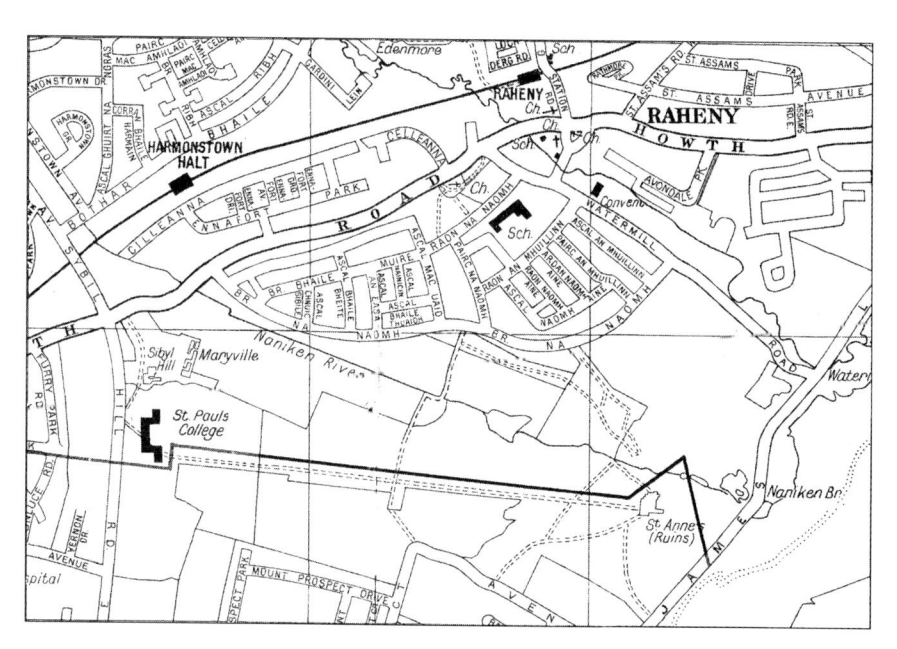

**62.** Layout for St Anne's housing scheme. (Geographia plan, 1:15,840, 1967.) Note the Corporation's Coolock scheme, discussed above, across the railway at Harmonstown Halt.

houses. By the end of June 1955, only 273 of the houses had been taken. Even this was after a relaxation of the supplementary grant requirements that purchasers be already tenants of the Corporation or had lived in Dublin for at least five years. There was a further concession which allowed those about to be married to apply. While the houses were eventually let, the slowness prompted Dublin Corporation to review its policy on tenant purchase and it did not attempt provision on the St Anne's scale again. It had to deal as well with the phenomenon of people seeking to surrender houses which they were purchasing under the tenant purchase system. In the tough economic times of the 1950s, people found themselves unable to keep up payments and for some emigration was the solution. This was not the end of the concept of tenant purchase, though, just a slowing down, and it continued to feature in the schemes of the 1960s. The Minister continued to promote it as in the speech which he gave in Athlone later in 1955 when he said that 'the policy of tenant-purchase, so far as it could be found practicable and economic was a wise one. Home ownership made for independence and self-reliance – traits of character which go to make politically healthy nations' (*Irish Times*, 17 September 1955, p. 9). The idea of houses for purchase was retained as part of the large Coolock, Kilmore, Edenmore development of the 1960s and, for example, some eighteen sites were provided on Edenmore Road in 1963.

*Selling houses to tenants*
A feature of tenant purchase schemes was that they were so designated from the beginning. Marino and Drumcondra quickly moved out of the Council sphere as the tenancies matured and people came to own their properties. The later schemes remained rental schemes even though the economic circumstances of the tenants might have changed as they moved through the life cycle and found themselves with a disposable income which could have supported purchase. There were schemes which facilitated this but all required that the person move from their home. Keeping the housing stock within public control was never an ideological position for the Corporation, as it was in the United Kingdom. Indeed, they worried that as the housing stock grew ever larger, an increasing amount of money was needed each year to keep the housing stock in good condition. This meant that the drain on Corporation resources was set to continue to rise as economic rents were not charged, even in schemes in which the differential rent system applied. The idea of selling houses to current tenants did not figure strongly on the Corporation's agenda, though. The Housing Committee noted a letter from the Minister (11 June

# A REVITALIZED HOUSING PROGRAMME

63. Example of housing in St Anne's.

**BARDAS ATHA CLIATH**

Purchase-Type Houses — Coolock/Kilmore Section 4A

## SHOW HOUSES

Show Houses at Oscar Traynor Road (Coolock end) will be open for inspection on Saturdays and Sundays between 3.00 p m. and 6.00 p.m.

Persons desirous of viewing these houses are invited to attend during these hours.

Additional purchase-type houses will be available later in this and other Housing Areas, and applications will be invited in due course by public advertisement.

64. Kilmore purchase houses advertisement. (*Irish Press*, 3 May 1968, p. 15.)

1953) in which he set out his view as to the minimum return that should be obtained if such sales were to be accommodated. He suggested that the sale price should be greater of (a) the outstanding balance on the loan raised to build the house or a sum reflecting the annual rent (exclusive of rates). This was to be calculated on the basis of the following table (Report 17/1955).

| Houses built prior to 1922 | 10 years rent |
| Houses built 1922–31 | 15 years rent |
| Houses built 1931–46 | 20 years rent |
| Houses built post-1946 | 30 years rent |

The Council took no action at that time, though the Association of Municipal Authorities in Ireland regularly advocated a tenant purchase scheme for existing tenants as in September 1956 (*Irish Times*, 19 September 1956, p. 7) or the following year (*Irish Times*, 21 September 1957, p. 4). The idea was revisited in 1961 in a report produced by the Housing Committee. The data provided by the Assistant City Manager revealed that the housing stock controlled by Dublin Corporation had now risen to 42,637 units and, as noted above, this housed of the order of 40 per cent of the city's population. Most of the units were in weekly tenancies (37,310) with only 5,327 in tenant purchase. This left the Corporation with an accumulated debt of £31.245m for housing, about three times the debt associated with loans under the SDAA. The cost of housing was borne by three actors: tenants, State and ratepayers. The tenants provided about 60 per cent of the costs in terms of rents. A further 20 per cent came in the form of State support and was ultimately provided by taxation. The remaining 20 per cent was funded by the ratepayers (Report 91/1961).

The reply gives some insight into why a scheme had not been previously developed for existing tenants. It was acknowledged that the position of the Corporation was that tenants were entitled to own their own houses, just like anyone else. The problem was that they were worried as to how they would finance it. The issue was the residual debt charge and what would happen when the houses moved into private hands. The Corporation was concerned that the State would take the opportunity to end any subsidy and, in fact, would be anxious to seize any such opportunity. The rates would hardly be able to sustain any increase in demands. The tenants had shown an interest in becoming owners but it was not at all clear that they had either the capacity, or the interest, to take on an increased financial burden.

'Sure they'll only be young once … and, anyway, the Corporation is paying for the repairs.'
**65.** Housing maintenance. (*Dublin Opinion*, 1954, p. 108.)

This was the major issue. There were additional concerns about who would take responsibility for maintenance of both houses and areas. Should the maintenance costs be transferred to the tenants or should the Council continue to pay them? In favour of the latter approach was the argument that the Council's investment needed to be protected but it was argued against the position that private estates were not supported in anyway by the developer or the mortgage providers. However, they needed to look only to the Marino scheme and the more recent Annadale scheme to be reassured on that front. They were also concerned about speculation but it was possible to ensure that a speculative profit could not be made by any tenant who purchased a house. In essence, it came down to devising a scheme which would not see an increase in the debt that the Corporation had to bear in terms of servicing loans nor one which would put an unsustainable burden on the purchasers.

It had to be agreed that only houses would be included in the scheme. It was not seen as feasible to include any of the 8,876 flats for practical and pragmatic reasons. They also had to decide whether the loss of the State subsidy on debt charges would prove an unsustainable problem. The debt on each estate was different, reflecting the funding environment at the time of building and the interest rate which was charged. A decision needed to be taken as to whether there would be different terms for each estate, reflecting the particular funding position, or whether an average for the city would be applied to each house. A further point of principle was whether the length of tenancy should be a factor in determining the price. The argument here was that longer term tenants might be deemed to have paid off varying amounts of the house if they had been in a tenant purchase scheme. Thus their purchase price should be discounted by some percentage.

All of this gave the Housing Committee a great deal of food for thought and they decided that they were not quite ready for such a momentous decision. Thus, in the time-honoured manner, they deferred any decision pending clarification and confirmation that State funding would be preserved in any such scheme (Report 91/1961 and *Irish Times*, 30 June 1961, p. 1). As was often the case with such measures, this was only the opening salvo in a long campaign, which saw increasing support for tenant purchase among tenants and the political establishment.

As noted above, the Minister finally gave the necessary impetus to the scheme when he made approval on much-needed increases in rental income conditional on early approval of a purchase scheme. He also set the terms of the scheme and the City Manager had little to do but to endorse them. In his report to the Council (13/1967) the Manager set out the basic terms of the scheme. It would operate based on a market valuation of the house with a maximum reduction of up to 30 per cent for continuous tenancy. Loans would be advanced at 7.5 per cent compared to the 8.5 per cent generally available at the time. Houses built after 1932 were available for purchase; older houses on a case-by-case basis. Prices were anticipated to range from £1,200 for older three-roomed houses to £2,300 for newer houses of the same size. Four-roomed houses would cost between £1,400 to £2,500 and five-roomed houses at between £2,600 and £3,000. It was estimated that these provisions affected some 33,000 houses and had the potential to transform the landscape of tenure in the city (Minutes, 12 June 1967). It took a while for the offer to be made to tenants as there were some issues that required clarification. The Housing Committee at its meeting on 19 May recommended that the offer not be made until these matters were cleared up. They did not like the capping of the maximum discount at 30 per cent nor the requirement that a minimum tenancy of five years be completed before any discount was offered. They were also unhappy that the concept of continuous tenancy did not provide for succession. However, by October, agreement had been reached and the process was begun (Report 127/1967).

The reaction was mixed. The first National Convention of the National Association of Tenants' Organizations in Liberty Hall passed a resolution calling for the value of property to be based on its original value and not current value (*Irish Independent*, 11 September 1967, p. 10), a somewhat utopian view given the level of Corporation rents. People, they said, were interested in purchasing their houses but not at these prices. An estimated 40,000 people from seventeen tenant associations marched from Parnell Square in November to protest against the rent increases and the scheme for tenant purchase. They met the Minister for Local Government, Mr Blaney, and then moved to City Hall where their protest was handed to the City Manager. There was a quieter reaction that was more eloquent. The Assistant City Manager reported in June 1968 as the first of the houses was about to be transferred that over 5,000 applications had been received and more were coming in by the day (Report 84/1968). Whatever the protests, there was an evident demand for purchase and the shift towards home ownership was now inexorable.

The repayment periods were potentially quite long and the purchaser was not liable for stamp duty or any part of the Corporation's legal costs in dealing with the matters. The Corporation also undertook to ensure that the house was in a good state of repair before the sale was completed. The repayment period was a maximum of 20 years for a house built before 1932 but these were considered on a case-by-case basis anyway. For the other houses it was 35 years for any house built after 1948 and 30 years for a house built between those dates. There were some terms and conditions but these were as might have been expected. The purchaser was expected to keep the house in good repair and to live there and could not mortgage or sublet the property without the consent of the Corporation. It took time to process all the requests and the reports of the Corporation contained monthly records of disposals through 1969. By 10 December 1969 it was reported that 2,376 houses had been transferred (Report 173/1969). A sense of the prices involved can be obtained from some examples. A four-roomed house on Carnlough Road which was valued at £1,620 was sold for £1,100 after a discount of £520 for continuous tenancy. A three-roomed house on St Attracta's Road was valued at £1,250 but attracted a discount of £375. As a final example, a four-roomed house on Dunmanus Road was also valued at £1,620 but here the discount was £486. These were incredibly good prices and less than half of what was being asked in the private sector at the bottom end of the market.

## Naming and social interaction

Dublin Corporation's policy of mixing its residential areas between purchasers of various types and renters was designed to produce a more socially diverse urban environment. This was further encouraged by the assistance given to public utility societies and other groups of private builders. The people involved did not cover the entire spectrum of social classes in the city and it was often argued that they were essentially the same social groups but with different individual family circumstances. However, even slight differences, if they were so, were important. As Festinger, Schachter and Back showed in their 1950 seminal study of Westgate West spatial closeness (propinquity) did not guarantee that friendships would occur.

If there was going to be tension between the various groups, then one way in which it might be manifested was in the naming of streets and districts. Street names were decided by Dublin Corporation. Sometimes it was a very simple process and it does not seem that a lot of time was needed to come to a conclusion. They took the name of some of the plots of ground or townlands and used variants of gardens, avenue, road, drive, park or crescent. Sometimes a theme suggested itself and the lakes of Ireland were used in the Coolock scheme. Flats complexes needed a little more consideration and the names of saints were favoured – St Teresa's Gardens, St Laurence's Mansions, St Bridget's Gardens. Lourdes House was chosen for a flat complex in North Gloucester Place and St Jude's Gardens for one in Railway Street (Report 56/1960). Dublin Corporation was not known for irony so it is difficult to understand why anyone could consider that what was being provided could be a 'garden' or a 'mansion'. The coupling of the saint's name with the use of 'mansion' or 'garden' suggested something even more exotic. Names of famous people, either national or local figures, were sometimes used. Dermot O'Dwyer House and Rory O'Connor House were chosen as names for blocks in the Hardwicke Street complex (Report 54/1957) while Phil Shanahan House was chosen for a block in the Newfoundland Street scheme (Report 42/1957). In 1958, it was decided to name the flats in Gloucester Place after Sean Treacy (though this was later reassigned to a flat complex in Buckingham Street (Report 56/1960)) and those in Orchard Road after Tom Clarke (Report 17/1958). The late Lord Mayor and TD, Alfie Byrne, was commemorated in Grenville Street (Report 51/1958). Sometimes, though, inspiration was lacking and the flats were just named after the streets in which they were located – Hogan Place or Gardiner Street.

As part of the Corporation's drive during the 1950s to encourage the use of Irish, street names were in Irish only (Minutes, 2 March 1953). This was not a conspicuous success and in 1962 it was decided to revert to a bilingual system (Report 170/1962). There was remarkable little agitation among tenants to have street or flat names changed and they simply used the English names in preference to the Irish ones. One formal change was that from Bóthar Ainninn to St Brendan's Park. Of the 58 residents who were eligible to vote, 49 returned a ballot with 46 in favour. The Council had no difficulty in agreeing to the change. While the reason for seeking the change was not recorded, it was probably no more than the impossibility of pronouncing the name of the street and there were other St Brendan's around (Minutes, 2 November 1964).

Although private developers required the approval of the Corporation when it came to naming, they usually did not meet resistance from either Corporation or residents. Changing a name, though, required a formal process. Even Dublin Corporation itself was not exempt from this. After all, even though they (and many others, but not the *Irish Times*) had referred to Sackville Street as O'Connell Street ever since the erection of the eponymous monument, they still had to go through a formal process to give legal effect to the change. They finally proposed the change in May 1924 along with the change of Queen's Square to Pearse Square, Great Clarence Street to Macken Street, Wentworth Place to Hogan Place and Denzille Street to Fenian Street (Minutes, 5 May 1924). At that time, the vote of a majority in number and value of the ratepayers was needed to effect a change. This became more egalitarian and property owners could petition the Corporation for a name change on the basis of one person/one vote. This still involved the holding of a plebiscite and it was a lengthy process and not without cost to the Corporation. If four-sevenths of the owners agreed to the proposed change then the Corporation might, in its absolute discretion, approve the change.

There are examples of a name change being sought from an Irish version, such as when those on part of Cill Eanna agreed to change the name to Ennafort Road. A total of 75 of the eligible 112 voters were in favour (Minutes, 6 September 1965). Sometimes what seemed minor issues motivated residents to the point that they sought a name change. The residents of Foxfield Drive and Foxfield Avenue sought a new combined name of Foxfield Drive. While the larger residents' group in Foxfield Avenue voted in favour, those in Foxfield Drive did not. That was the end of the matter as far as the Corporation was concerned (Minutes, 3 February 1964). Residents agreed to a change from Maywood Crescent to Maywood Lawn (22 of the 35 eligible voters in favour, Minutes, 2 May 1966) while others sought to have a portion of Harmonstown Road changed to Harmonstown Rise (Minutes, 5 September 1966). The discarded names were sometimes recycled by developers in other parts of their schemes.

It did not happen very often but an important catalyst for seeking change was when residents perceived that new development might impact adversely on their property values. In 1950, there was a petition from residents on Kimmage Road East requesting that their road be renamed to Terenure Road West (Report 58/1950). Kimmage did not have the same cachet as Terenure. The usual process was followed and it was reported in February 1953 that 75 residents had voted in favour with 19 against and two abstentions. The request for the name change was granted (Minutes, 2 February 1953). Not successful, however, were the efforts of one group of residents who sought to change Ballyfermot Hill to Chapelizod Hill in 1958. Following a vote only 16 of the 32 residents agreed to the change and the matter was dropped (Minutes, 1 December 1958). A successful attempt at a change was that from Clonmel Avenue to Ballymun Park in August 1958 (Minutes, 18 August 1958). This was to be a relatively short-lived change for reasons outlined below and is indicative of the relatively high standing that 'Ballymun' had as an address at the time.

Occasionally, a developer got it wrong. One such felt that there was no problem in using variants of the nearby main road for his development. However, within six months of permission being granted to the developers of the Cameron Estate in Coolock to name the streets Tonlegee Avenue, Drive, Grove, Gardens and Close, the purchasers of the houses looked for a change to Glendassan Road, Glenroan Road, Glenfarne Road, Glenwood Road and Glenayle Road, respectively (Minutes, 4 July 1966 and Report 93/1966). It seemed that some of the residents did not like the connotations of 'tonlegee'. Getting four-sevenths of all residents to support a proposal, and not just four-sevenths of those who voted, was quite a high barrier. In the above case only the residents on Tonlegee Grove and Tonlegee Gardens met the threshold required and had the name change approved (Minutes, 6 March 1967). While those living on Tonlegee Drive supported the name change by a significant majority, 28 in favour from 38 votes returned, this was not four-sevenths of the electorate of 72 people. The Corporation, though, was generally quite accommodating in giving people a second chance. At the meeting of the Council on 6 November 1967, Councillor Stanley Coggin asked the City Manager what 'precautions are envisaged by the Corporation authorities to protect the market values of the Tonlegee Road houses which have already

# A REVITALIZED HOUSING PROGRAMME

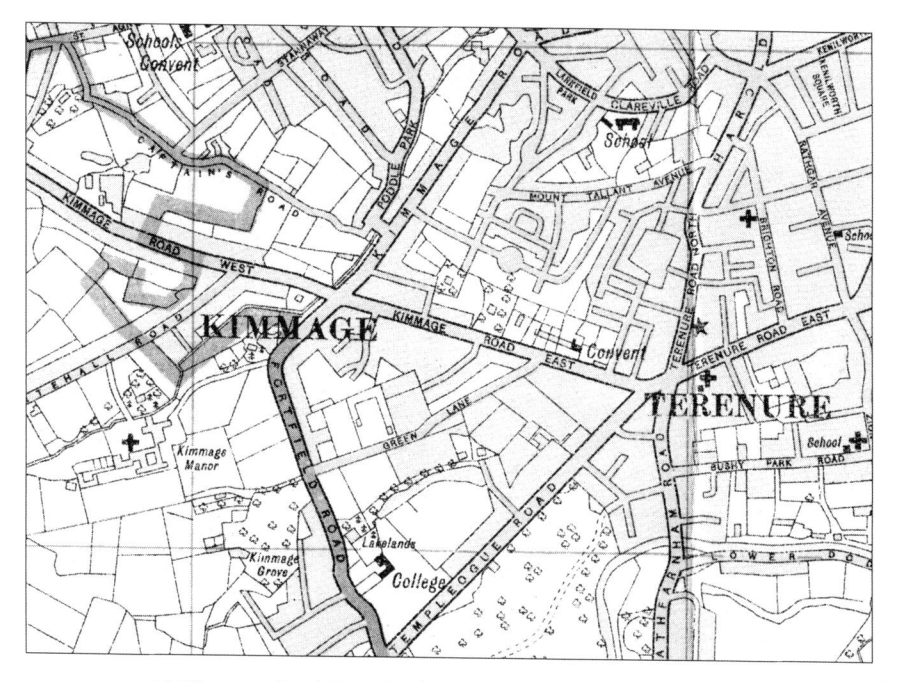

**66.** Kimmage Road East. (Ordnance Survey plan, 1:25,000, 1948.)

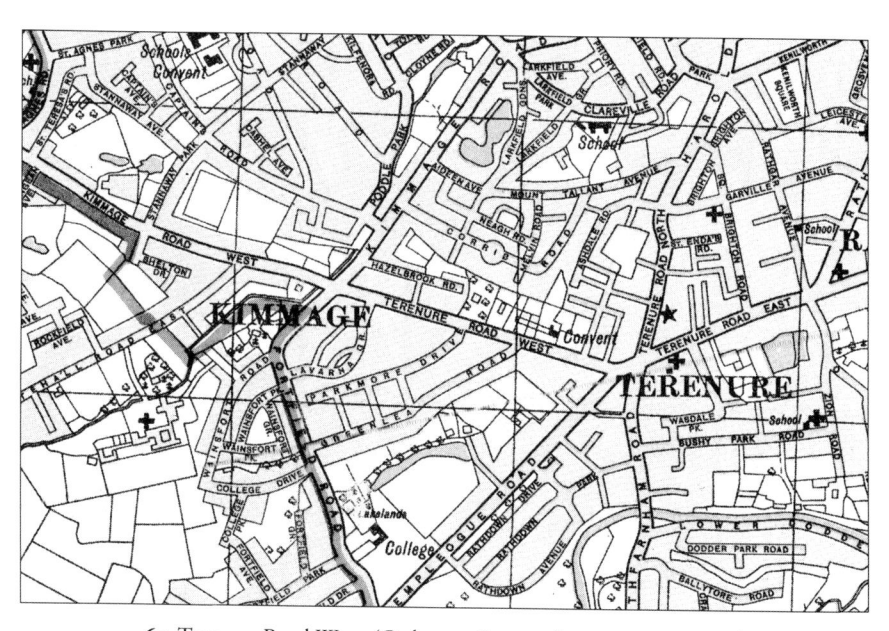

**67.** Terenure Road West. (Ordnance Survey plan, 1:25,000, 1959.)

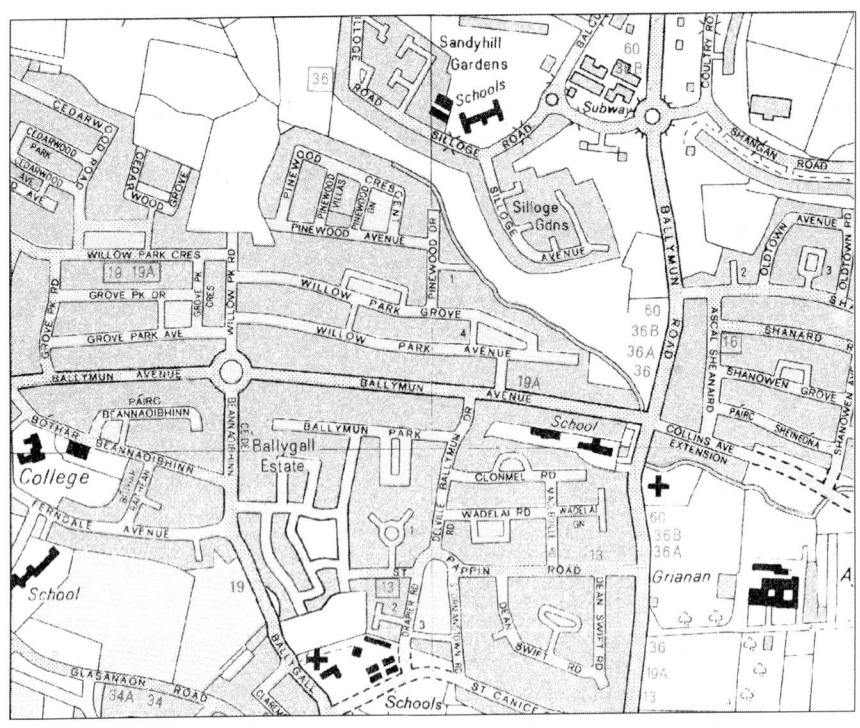

**68.** Ballymun Avenue. (Ordnance Survey plan, 1:18,000, 1969.)

deteriorated according to the owners due to previous Corporation schemes in the area. He got little reassurance and was told that the Corporation planned an additional 458 houses in the area, of which 254 would be for purchase. The Corporation, however, facilitated a rerun for the plebiscite for those on Tonlegee Close and this time there was no difficulty in getting the required majority for a change to Glenayle Road (Report 158/1968).

Harmonstown Road was mentioned above and it featured once again when one group of residents sought to differentiate themselves from another. In 1966, approval was given to residents on a portion of Harmonstown Road to change the name to Brookwood Rise, a total of 40 residents from a possible 51 residents having voted in favour (Report 156/1966). This aimed to differentiate the private part of the road, from Brookwood Avenue to the railway station, from the Council part. However, the other residents did not like this and they complained that there was no mechanism in the process that allowed one portion of a road to be consulted and not the entire road. The law agent agreed and, accordingly, it was decided to authorize a plebiscite to see if the remaining residents wanted the name change also, which had the

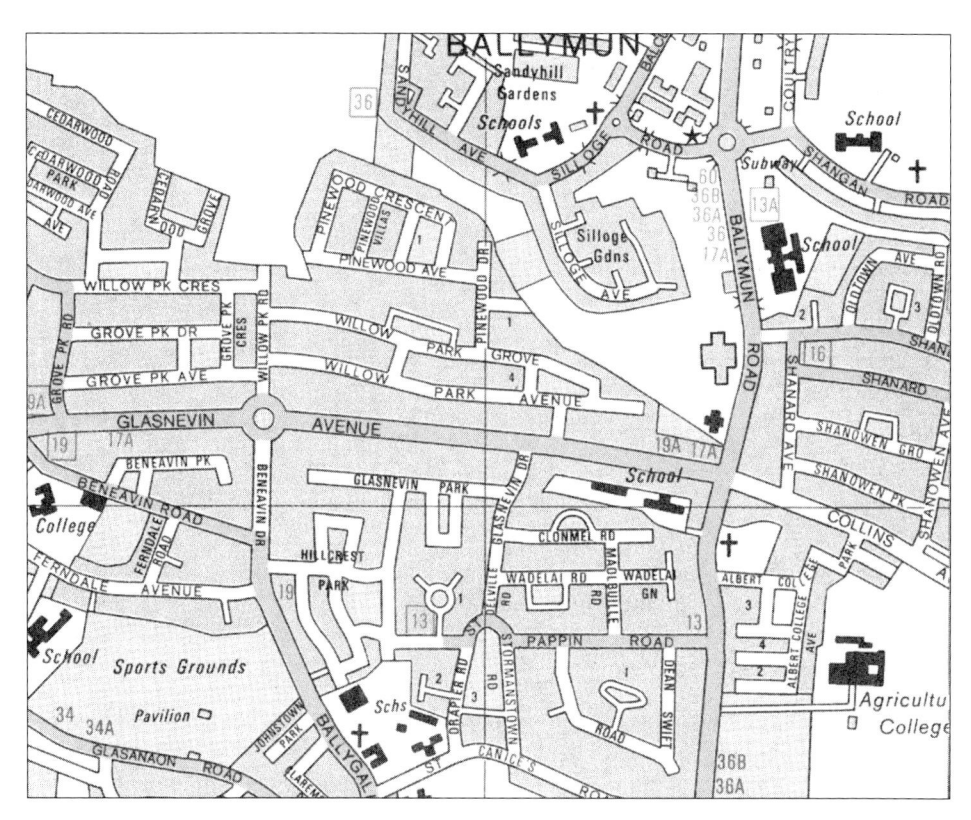

**69.** Glasnevin Avenue. (Ordnance Survey plan, 1:20,000, 1979.)

potential to produce a very different outcome to the one already sought (Report 4/1968). In the event, nothing changed and the name changes just at the railway station. The change process in Harmonstown continued though with a change to Brookwood Lawn from Harmonstown Grove later in 1968 (Report 64/1968).

The resistance by the Corporation to change in the case of the environs of Ballymun was out of character. As the reputation of Ballymun began to slide in the early 1970s, there were requests from the longer established residents of Ballymun Drive and Ballymun Park for a name change, replacing 'Ballymun' with 'Glasnevin'. The plebiscite was held in 1973 with the vote going against change in Ballymun Drive but the larger Ballymun Park voted by 73 to 12 out an electorate of 101 for change. Normally that would have resulted in change but in this case no action was taken and it was allowed to sit. This was the time when the city was under the rule of commissioners rather than the Council but that is probably not the reason. Granted, when the Council was restored the change to Glasnevin Park was agreed (Minutes, 7 October 1974) and a rerun of the process for Ballymun Drive was facilitated (Report 76/1974) which resulted in approval of the name change on 2 September 1974. It was the same Council, though, that refused to allow a plebiscite for Ballymun Avenue in 1975, though the issue was revisited and the name was finally changed to its present Glasnevin Avenue on 7 November 1977. Ballymun Avenue was the main artery running west to east as the extension to Collins Avenue and a change there was hugely symbolic since it confined Ballymun to a much smaller spatial area. This reluctance to permit the change in both cases was probably an indication of final attempts to halt the slide of its perception. It would have been useful if Ballymun referred to a more mixed area and not just the new social housing development.

Names were one issue but access was another. Developers building private housing sometimes ensured clarity of identity in that their road systems did not join up with any council schemes in the vicinity. The case of Belton Park has been referred to in volume 2 of this series. Sometimes, previously agreed road schemes came as a shock to residents as their estate took shape. This was the case with Ferndale Avenue, which today is in either Glasnevin or Finglas depending on one's perspective. Glasaree Road was part of the Council's housing development in Finglas East and the intention was that it would be linked by a road to Ballygall Road East. This road was eventually completed in 1956. By then, the private development of Keogh and the Ballygall PUS, the Ferndale Avenue part of which was given Council approval in June 1954, had been completed. It was now a case of linking two previously separate housing areas. With the completion of the road, there began an agitation by some residents of Ferndale Avenue to have the connection between it and Glasaree Road closed. This was the subject of two proposals to the City Council prior to a lengthy report on the matter in May 1960 (Minutes, 2 May 1960). Part of the argument of the residents was that the road had not appeared on the draft planning scheme and they had been unaware of it until work began on its construction. In fact, it was pointed out by the City Manager that the road had always been part of the plans for the council housing in the area and that negotiations had taken place with Keogh about altering his housing layout to fit better with the alignments of the Corporation road layout. It was also pointed out that fourteen loans had been sanctioned under the SDAA for residents of Ferndale Avenue. The line of the new road was clearly outlined on these plans so it was impossible for residents to argue that they had bought in ignorance of the plan. The final nail was that the law

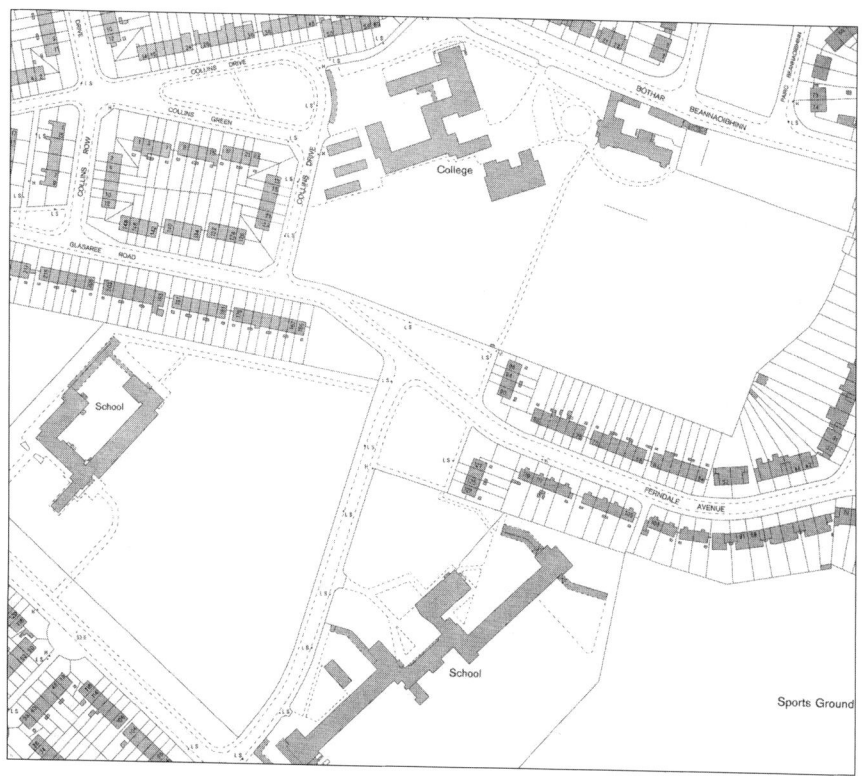

70. The connection between Glasaree and Ferndale roads. Note the awkwardness of the connection between these two roads. (Ordnance Survey plan, 1:1,000, Sheet 3131(18), 1974.)

agent pointed out that once a road was designated, it remained a road forever and there was no mechanism to close a road which was in use and in the public interest. Thus the matter ended.

The fact that such a great deal of attention was given to the concerns of the residents of Ferndale Avenue is indicative of how little agitation there was generally. Despite the examples given above, people seemed either happy or acquiescent in terms of the geographical relations that they had with their neighbours. Petitions to change names were few and far between and generally a serious deterioration in perception seemed necessary before change was sought. The sudden and downward slide of Ballymun produced such a response in parts but not universally across the area. Similarly, the building of private apartments on what had been part of Sean McDermott Street in the 1980s prompted the extension of Cathal Brugha Street to encompass those apartments. However, the process and the arguments were noteworthy only because they were exceptional.

# Flats and high-rise

## Accommodation in flats

By the beginning of the 1950s, there was a considerable number of flat developments either completed or in development in the city centre and, with only a few exceptions, to live in such a purpose built flat block was to live in social housing. These were located throughout the inner city in places such as Newfoundland Street, Rialto and Dolphin's Barn. Others were in development such as those on North Gloucester Place or North Clarence Street and a major scheme was in preparation for a site just off the North Circular Road near to the Phoenix Park. In 1950, it was reported that the Corporation had decided to name part of the Newfoundland Street scheme as St Bridget's Gardens. The saintly theme was continued in the decision to name the scheme on Donore Avenue as St Theresa's Gardens but while the idea of 'gardens' was maintained, O'Devaney Gardens was the chosen name for the scheme off the North Circular Road (Report 79/1950). These developments comprised large blocks of flats, generally four storeys, with considerable open space around them and courtyards often between the blocks. In 1952, the city sought funding for an additional 392 flats in Dolphin's Barn, 32 in Whitefriar Street, 44 on Lower Gardiner Street and 32 in Power's Court. The intention was to build 2,625 flats by 1956, about 500 per year. They did not quite reach that target, as the figures given in an earlier chapter indicate, but upwards of 2,000 flats were completed.

The debate about central city flats versus suburban houses was as old as the housing programmes of the city and they have been discussed in detail in previous volumes in this series. There was a cost argument. It was cheaper to build in the suburbs but tenants had to endure high bus fares to get to their jobs in the city centre. There was a community argument. It was said that the strong support structures of inner city communities were lost in the new suburbs. However, the quality of housing and life was better in the suburbs where there was more light and better air. It was also argued that it was impossible to rehouse all inner city residents in the inner city without recreating slums. While most housing in the 1950s and 1960s was to be built in the suburbs, there was increased support for more inner city building, driven to a large degree by complaints of inadequate bus services and high

**71.** Layout plan of O'Devaney Gardens. (Ordnance Survey plan, 1:1,000, Sheet 3263-2 and 3, 1972.)

fares. It has been noted above that high bus fares were a focus of discontent in Ballyfermot and Finglas and the problem was that, of necessity, each new suburban development was further and further from the city centre where jobs and services continued to be concentrated. Despite many calls to do so, CIE did not or could not introduce lower fares. Things were a far cry from the position less than 20 years before when the new developments in Kimmage and Crumlin were seen as 'Siberia' (Behan, 1965). These were now rapidly becoming inner suburbs. Thus, when it was decided to redevelop Lower Dominick Street by demolishing the Georgian houses and building new flat blocks, there was considerable agitation to keep as many of the residents there as possible. The Lord Mayor, Alfie Byrne, sent a telegram of support to a meeting of the Dominick Street and District Development Association in 1954 in which he said 'High bus fares in housing schemes in outskirts are an increased burden on citizens. Keep up pressure for more city flats and with the aid of my colleagues in the Corporation you will succeed' (*Irish Times*,

**72.** Aerial view of O'Devaney Gardens in 2014 as it awaits demolition. It was to have been redeveloped under a public-private partnership between the city council and developer Bernard McNamara but the deal collapsed in 2008.

24 November 1954, p. 3). A speaker at that meeting noted that she had been impressed by the anxiety of old people to 'live out their lives in Dominick Street, even in the appalling conditions prevailing there'.

It was important to provide decent housing and the Housing Committee recommended in 1956 that the schedule of accommodation in future flat schemes be such that the greater part of flats would have three or more rooms, the equivalent in the eyes of the Corporation of a four-roomed suburban cottage. The proposed distribution was (Report 73/1956):

| Flat size | per cent |
| --- | --- |
| 1 room | 15 |
| 2 room | 25 |
| 3 room | 50 |
| 4 room | 10 |

This left the Corporation with a dilemma. There was now greater enthusiasm for inner city flat schemes but there was little land available. The only solution was to build higher and thus began a flirtation with high-rise. It was to be some time before they were prepared to contemplate what would be

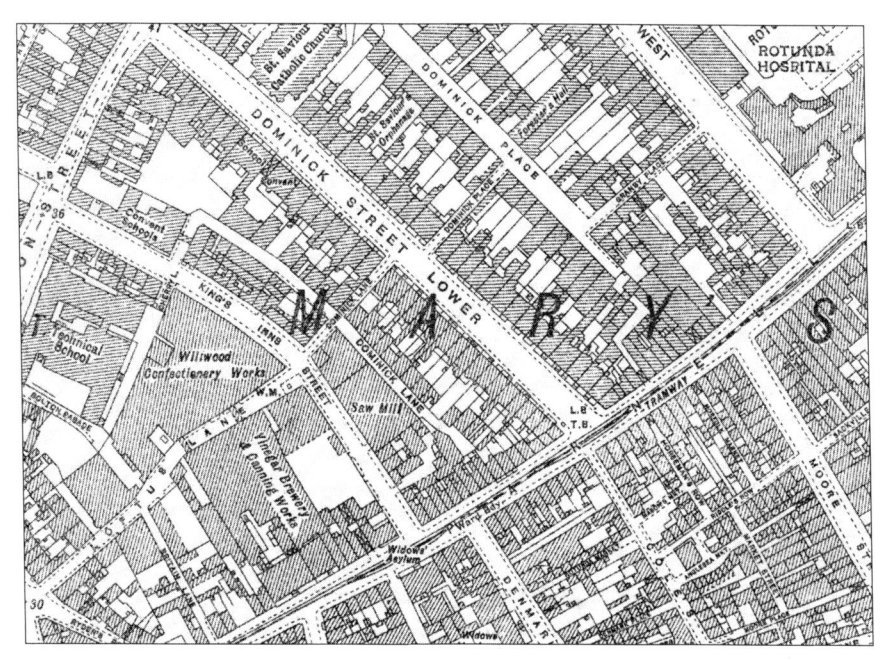

**73.** Dominick Street before redevelopment. (Ordnance Survey plan, 1:2,500, Sheet 18(VII), 1939.) Note the size of the Georgian houses on the north-western side of the road.

**74.** Dominick Street with its flat complexes. Note the amount of unbuilt space which resulted from the development. (Ordnance Survey plan, 1:1,000, Sheet 3263–5, 1972.)

seen as true high-rise and this will be discussed below. What they began to consider was whether it was feasible or desirable to move from the standard of no more than five storeys to perhaps nine-storey blocks. They undertook this review in 1956 and to be fair to them, they did not blindly accept the case for higher buildings. Their review noted that building higher did not necessarily save ground space since taller blocks needed a larger footprint (*Irish Times*, 1 February 1956). Nor did they come to any rapid conclusion. When the time came to rebuild in Dominick Street, and in the general slowdown of the 1950s this did not happen until 1959, the decision was to build three five-storey blocks and to try one nine-storey block. The scheme would provide a total of 124 flats, divided into 31 one-roomed flats, 31 two-roomed flats and 62 three-roomed flats (Minutes, 13 January 1958). The contribution of the nine storey block was 35 flats comprising 2 one-roomed, 32 two-roomed and 1 three-roomed. The approval for the nine-storey block was conditional on more work being done on the plans.

The decision to proceed was taken by the Housing Committee on 31 July 1959 in recognition of the 'high cost of acquisition of central city areas and the necessity for intensive development in these areas' (Report 69/1959). This had not been taken lightly. It had been pointed out to them that costs were likely to be higher pro rata than for the standard blocks of five storeys and the subsequent requests for tenders were done with a view to ascertaining whether this perception was solidly based in fact. When the tenders had been examined, the City Manager's report came (Report 69/1959) down firmly against the building of the block. His view was that there was no good reason to adopt a high cost solution, especially as no additional housing would be achieved by building high. The need to maintain the overall density of the scheme within norms ensured that there would be no gains in that respect. He made the argument that the cost of building and maintaining the housing stock was a growing burden on the rates, given that the Corporation was now housing about 40 per cent of the city's population in their 42,112 dwellings. The housing rate had risen from 3*s*. 2*d*. in 1950/1 to 5*s*. in 1959/60 and the Corporation was under constant pressure from the Minster for Local Government to keep housing costs down, especially given the extent of the State subsidy.

When the tenders were examined, the conclusion was that the cost of building nine storeys would work out at least 20 per cent greater per square foot than a five-storey block and at least 29 per cent greater for a two-roomed flat than the norm. The Manager pointed out that the costs in parts of the Gardiner Street scheme were already significantly in excess of what was regarded as the standard cost and the Department of Local Government had already signalled that it wished costs reined back to the standard level. While he could not predict the Minister's response to a request to fund the nine-storey block, his view was that permission was unlikely. The estimated all-in cost of a three-roomed flat in the tower block was £3,167 compared to £2,280 for a standard three-roomed flat such as had been built in Vicar Street. Both were more expensive than a suburban cottage of four rooms which could be built in Finglas for £1,700. In addition, the annual maintenance costs of a three-roomed flat in a tower block was over 30 per cent greater than that of a standard flat. While differential rents would be charged, the economic rent could not be. This would have resulted in an annual cost to the Corporation of £142 6s. 1d. per three-roomed flat in the tower block. This compared to the annual cost of £69 12s. 10d. for a three-roomed flat and only £36 6s. 11d. for a four-roomed suburban cottage.

When the consultant architect, Desmond Fitzgerald, read in the newspapers of the concern of the Corporation over his proposed nine-storey block, he mounted a strong defence. He argued that the comparative basis was not correct and that it was more economical to build a nine storey-block on expensive central land. What stunned the Corporation, however, was his assertion that he could reconfigure the block by reducing the size of flats bringing those more into line with the reduced useable area recently adopted by the Corporation and so save at least £100 per flat. The response from the City Manager was one of surprise: 'I am personally aware that from the initiation of the scheme the necessity for economy in costs, consistent with acceptable standards, was emphasized to you as well as the necessity for getting the work under way without avoidable delay' (Minutes, 21 September 1959, p. 210). This was accompanied by a request to submit a revised scheme urgently. The architect duly submitted revised plans designed to achieve these savings but the Corporation was not impressed. Not only did the revision not make it clear how the £100 saving was to be achieved, it was also found that the floor area of the revised flats was below standard.

The Housing Committee in the form of Councillors Larkin and Carroll made a final attempt to have the matter referred back to them. However, the Council decided to accept the City Manager's report and thus to replace the nine storey block with one of five storeys. In truth, the Corporation as a whole never really bought into the idea of high-rise, even in the city centre. They were convinced that the costs were too high or, in the words of M.J. Mullen on the night of the debate, the proposal was 'reckless and extravagant'.

75. New design for flats as used in Donnybrook. The Corporation reverted to a more standard design with internal stairs later in the decade.

76. Tower access design on Macken Street – city centre location.

77. Front view of tower access design on Chamber Street.

The city authorities also introduced a new design for flats. The first of its kind was opened in Gardiner Street in 1960 and it was the subject of a detailed piece in the *Irish Times* on 7 January (p. 7). They had a distinctive roof whereby the pitched roof was set back and a wide parapet provided. This, it was explained, was a reference to the surrounding Georgian architecture. Despite this odd feature, the most distinctive element was that access was by means of circular towers which were separate from the buildings and connected to the various levels by bridges. Most of the accommodation was in the form of maisonettes over two storeys with some one person (mainly for old folk) and 8 two-roomed flats on the ground floor. The 28 three-roomed maisonettes contained an entrance hall, living room, balcony and kitchen downstairs with two bedrooms and a bathroom upstairs. Features of this design were the shared services so that rubbish was tipped directly from each maisonette into a central rubbish chute where it was gathered at the base of the tower. From there it was easy to collect it in specially adapted refuse trucks. The blocks featured a central drying room and a small communal grassed area and recreational space. There were no lifts and the *Irish Times* writer saw no issue with this. Indeed it was noted that the 'splayed treads of the precast steps are designed for a normal comfortable rise close to the core. This will have the

78. Rutland Street flats, 1969. An alternative flat design.

79. The same design used in four blocks in Charlemont Street.

80. The tower access design in Gardiner Street before the redevelopment of the west side of the street.

advantage that by walking close to the outer wall, older people will have a much easier climb, and mothers bringing prams up to the maisonettes can rest them on each step'. Of course, none of the shared services ever worked as intended.

These became a common design across the city where the authorities hoped to build 46 flats in Buckingham Street and 50 flats in Railway Street by 1960. The target for 1961 was 82 flats in Love Lane and 84 in Gardiner Street.

There was also an end to the policy of refurbishment of tenements which the Corporation had reluctantly embraced in the 1940s. Many tenements were in private hands and the owners, in many cases, had failed to maintain them. Enforcing its own standards would have required that the tenements be condemned, immediately adding to the housing crisis. So the Corporation began a process of acquisition and renovation of a great deal of Georgian Dublin. Alderman Alfie Bryne was an enthusiastic supporter of this policy and put on the record in June 1950 a statement with which many would doubtless have agreed.

> That in view of the growth of Dublin and the sending out of the City of the citizens to housing accommodation many miles away from their employment, schools, churches, dispensaries and shopping centres, with extra bus fares added to their rents and higher charges for electricity, and losses in certain cases of benefits – the Council directs the Officers

in charge of the reconditioning of houses in the tenement areas of the City to speed up the work of re-conditioning by putting on more men to do the necessary work in North Great George's Street, Gardiner Street, Buckingham Street, Grenville Street, York Street, Summerhill, Temple Street, Temple Place, Hardwicke Street, Hardwicke Place, Mercer Street, and in all other places acquired or to be acquitted for reconditioning by the Corporation.

(Report 58/1950)

As was noted above he continued to be concerned about the costs of suburbanization but this was the other half of the equation. He was content to have reconditioning as a speedier solution to the problem. The process worked after a fashion and people were pleased with the outcome in the short term. The *Irish Times Pictorial* published a piece in 1953 in which the work was lauded. It noted of Summerhill that before 'their "beauty treatment" these houses were slum dwellings. Now each house contains three- and four-roomed flats with all modern conveniences, and none of the Georgian drawbacks' (4 April 1953, p. 7).

This was always going to be a temporary reprieve. Even by then, housing policy had returned to clearance and the buildings and projects mentioned above were among the last of the 1940s undertakings. Upper Diggis Street, Mercer Street and Cuffe Street were approved for clearance in 1952. This involved 349 people in 109 families with 115 children (Report 44/1952). Hardwicke Street was made ready for redevelopment in 1953. The houses were bricked up and were scheduled for demolition in a year or two. The *Irish Times* asked:

> What is going to happen to these fine, symmetrical buildings, those wide thoroughfares, those beautiful fanlights, elegant hall doors, artistic wrought iron window protections? [...]
> Why not restore these fine old houses and turn back the clock by restoring the residential status of the area? [...]
> We asked a Dublin Corporation spokesman what were the plans for the future of Hardwicke place and area. He said: 'It has been decided to demolish the houses, which are in a very poor state of repair, and to put in their place Corporation flats for working-class families'.
>
> (*Irish Times Pictorial*, 24 October 1953, p. 3)

**81.** Upper Rutland Street, Summerhill, waiting for redevelopment in the late 1970s.

The list of streets that Alderman Byrne mentioned as worthy of renovation comprised a great deal of the inner city but by the early 1950s, a clearance order was their most likely fate rather than reconditioning. In 1954, the Corporation accepted a recommendation that an area around Tyrone Square and Place be cleared (Report 61/1954). This affected 34 families who had 33 children. This was followed in 1955 by a decision to seek a clearance order for Lower Dominick Street (Report 5/1955), referred to above. Further orders in the same year were for Basin Street (Report 113/1955) and for Power's Court and Stephen's Lane (Report 114/1955). These affected respectively 38 families with 119 persons, of which 38 were children and 29 families in which there was a total of 91 persons.

The list of projects for which a loan of £3.596m was approved in 1955 shows that there was only one reconditioning project in the inner city. By 1962, there were growing complaints about the quality of the reconditioned tenements and the fact that they compared poorly with what was being built at the time (Minutes, 5 November 1962). It seems that they had once again begun their slide into decay.

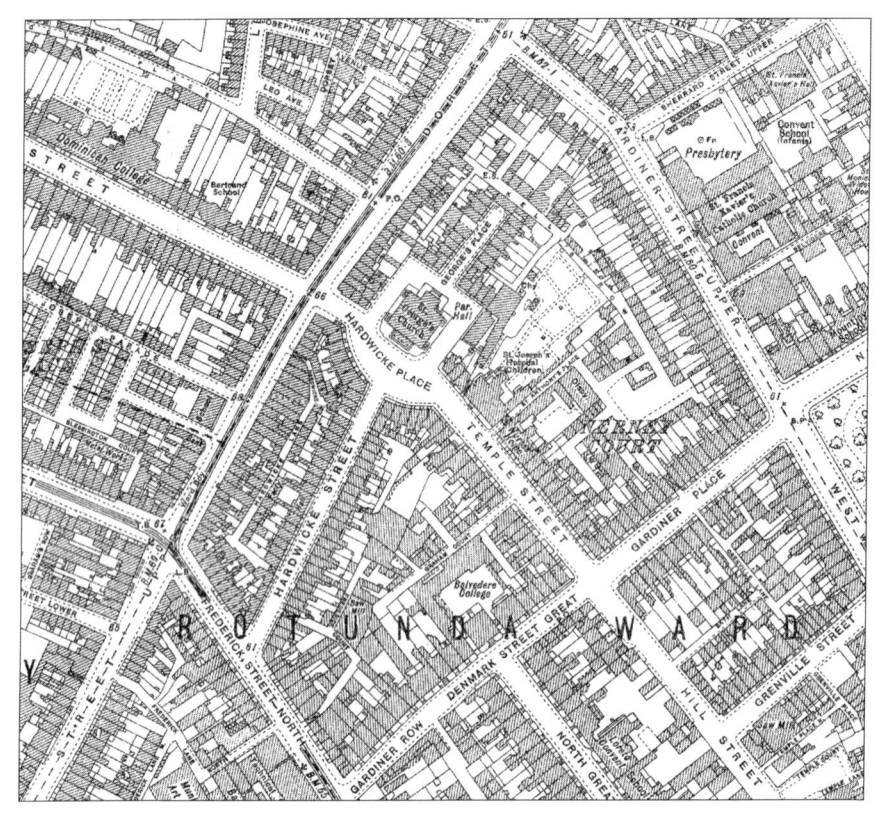

**82.** Hardwicke Street before redevelopment. (Ordnance Survey plan, 1:2,500, Sheet 18(VII), 1939.)

**83.** Hardwicke Street flats. The new flat complexes maintained the geometry of the street with its focus on St George's church. (Google Earth.)

**Table 31.** Projects for which funding was sought in 1955. (Report 7/1955.)

| Location | Cottages | Flats |
|---|---|---|
| Coolock/Raheny | 750 | |
| Finglas | 900 | |
| Finglas West | | 150 |
| *Meath Street/South Earl Street (Reconditioning)* | | 41 |
| Gloucester Place | | 63 |
| Hogan Place | | 63 |
| Love Lane | | 42 |
| Buckingham Street | | 66 |
| Rathmines Avenue | | 52 |
| Bridgefoot Street | | 120 |
| Total | 1650 | 577 |

## *High-rise*

Dublin came late to the world of true high-rise, high-density housing and might never have built any had circumstances been a little different. By the end of the 1960s, the problems associated with high-rise provision were becoming manifest across Europe and it was increasingly realized that it was not a panacea for the need for large volumes of social housing. Dublin Corporation had been building flat complexes for generations but had expressed little interest in going higher than the four or five storeys which they were building in the inner city. They had explored the possibilities of system and pre-fabricated building at the end of the 1940s but the decision to undertake a huge development at Ballymun came out of the blue and they were as much taken by surprise as anyone.

There is an important correlation between high-rise and high density for the main justification for housing people in high-rise buildings is that the density which can be achieved allows a larger number of people to be housed in the same area compared to conventional housing. It was a particularly attractive option in inner city areas where the problem was often the replacement of densely populated slums. As Dublin Corporation had long understood, it was not possible to rehouse all of the local population in decent housing and suburban locations were necessary. High density had the added advantage of permitting a high level of services since the threshold populations for such provision were easily reached and exceeded. However, high-rise buildings were both expensive to build in inner city locations and to maintain

> # DEPARTMENT OF LOCAL GOVERNMENT
> # HOUSING
> ## PROJECT OF 3,000 DWELLINGS AT BALLYMUN, DUBLIN
>
> The Minister for Local Government proposes to arrange on behalf of Dublin Corporation for the provision of approximately 3,000 dwellings with associated amenities on a site at Ballymun, Dublin.
>
> The urgency of the housing situation requires that these dwellings should be provided as speedily as possible consistent with a high standard of layout, design and construction and to acceptable costs. In these circumstances consideration will be given to proposals employing new building methods and techniques.
>
> Subject to an acceptable proposal being forthcoming from a competent building interest, it is desired that responsibility for planning the project and for all development and construction works should be undertaken by the proposers.
>
> A mixed development is visualised comprised mainly of flats, including a proportion of high-rise buildings with some two and three-storey family housing. Planning will be on the basis of a supplied schedule of housing requirements and will provide for associated amenities, including landscaping.
>
> Contoured site-plan, schedule of housing requirements and other details will be available to principals on application to the undersigned. Individual firms who on examination of these documents express their interest on 18th July in undertaking the project, and whose capacity and ability to do so are accepted, will be invited to submit outline proposals to the Minister. Subject to detailed negotiation with selected firms in response to these preliminary proposals, it is desired to enter into a contract with the minimum of delay to ensure that the erection of dwellings will commence as soon as possible without upset to the existing structure and balance of the building industry.
>
> J. GARVIN,
> Department of Local Government, Secretary.
> Custom House, Dublin 1.

84. Expressions of interest for Ballymun development. (*Irish Press*, 24 June 1964, p. 6.)

and, in the absence of high density, there was little argument in their favour. High-rise was a well tried solution to the problems of inner city renewal when Ballymun came to be built. What was different was that Ballymun was deeply suburban, beyond the edge of the city at the time. It seemed that the attractiveness of high-rise had more to do with the speed with which housing could be provided than issues of population retention and service provision.

## *Ballymun*

The Ballymun scheme is of interest for many reasons, particularly because the role of the Minister and Department of Local Government points up the degree of centralized control which has always been a feature of urban governance in Ireland. It was an initiative of the Minister and he drove the project from the very beginning. The advertisement seeking expressions of interest to build the scheme was placed by the Department and not Dublin Corporation. It was John Garvin, the Secretary General of the Department, who was the person to whom enquiries had to be made and not the city manager.

The decision to try a bold experiment in Ballymun was the result of the coincidence of two events. The proximate catalyst for the scheme was two tenement collapses in 1963 that resulted in fatalities. The second was the desire of University College Dublin to divest itself of a substantial parcel of land to the north of the city. The first housing collapse took place on 2 June 1963 when 20 Bolton Street collapsed into the street. Two elderly people, Mr and Mrs Maples, were both killed in the collapse. However, the second collapse had greater impact. This occurred on 12 June 1963 at about 4 p.m. in Fenian Street when two four-storey houses, nos. 3 and 4, collapsed. The impact on the city was far greater because the causalities this time were two children, Linda Byrne (8) and Marie Vardy (9) who had the misfortune to be passing the houses at the time of the collapse. There had been tenement collapses before, often with fatalities, and these had not resulted in such a dramatic response. What was different this time was their closeness in time and the fact that two children had been killed. The Minister demanded a public inquiry and it took place later in the month.

The City Council was well aware that there were condemned buildings in the city which were still occupied. Figures provided to the Council in 1962 revealed that there were 2,217 persons in such buildings (Minutes, 5 November 1962), distributed as follows:

| Family size | Persons |
| --- | --- |
| 2 | 580 |
| 3 | 603 |
| 4 | 408 |
| 5 | 260 |
| 6+ | 366 |

While it was recognized that, once condemned, a building should have been de-tenanted immediately, the realities of life required that this be done on a gradual basis as new housing became available. Equally, housing which had been emptied could stand for some time before redevelopment cleared them away. What the inquiry showed was a grey market in which supposedly empty condemned houses were being quietly re-let and a Corporation that did not have the resources to check all of the old decaying tenements. It did not own these houses and it was the responsibility of the owners to take all

DUBLIN. FLATS COLLAPSE IN FENIAN STREET: THIS SCENE COULD HAVE BEEN TAKEN AFTER AN AIR RAID IN WORLD WAR II. FIREMEN AND RESCUE WORKERS RUSHED TO THE SCENE, WHERE TWO FOUR-STOREY TENEMENTS CAME APART ON JUNE 12. TWO CHILDREN WERE BURIED AND DIED IN THE RUBBLE. (*Radio photograph.*)

85. Fenian Street housing collapse. (*Illustrated London News*, June 1963.)

measures to ensure their safety. It was pointed out that none of the houses that collapsed had obvious structural defects and the clear implication was that other collapses were likely but their location was unpredictable.

The arguments raised here had occurred some generations previously and on that occasion the Superintendent Medical Officer for Health, Sir Charles Cameron, was criticized for not enforcing the sanitary laws to the maximum degree. The 1913 Housing Inquiry stated:

> We regret to state that in many cases the conditions laid down by the Corporation are not complied with. Sir Charles Cameron having taken on his own shoulders the responsibility of dispensing in certain cases with the Bye-laws governing tenement houses and with the conditions laid down by the Corporation in regard to rebates, we feel that we can lay little blame in regard to these matters on the Corporation as a body, though we think that they cannot be entirely absolved from censure, as

it was their duty to keep themselves informed of the manner in which their Superintendent Medical Officer of Health carried out their orders. In extenuation of the want of rigid enforcement of the laws, it was put before us by Sir Charles Cameron and others that the stringent enforcement of the sanitary laws might inflict great hardship, as it might lead to the eviction of a number of people. While we cannot dispute the truth of this plea were the enforcement of hitherto dormant powers suddenly and drastically exercised, we cannot help coming to the conclusion that had a judicious but firm administration of the powers already given been exercised during the last 35 years since the passing of the Public Health Act, 1878, it should have been possible without any undue hardship being inflicted to have produced a better state of affairs than exists at present, and especially as at one time during this period the population of Dublin reached the lowest point it has touched for 60 years.

(Housing Inquiry, 1914, p. 13)

It was the same argument in 1963. A rigid enforcement of the bye-laws would have resulted in homeless people, who would have to be housed by the Corporation and they did not have the resources to do so.

This time they had to act and the Corporation moved quickly and dramatically (*Irish Times*, 15 June 1963, p. 11). Notwithstanding the suggestion that recent bad weather had played a significant part in the collapses, no one was prepared to take the chance that these were simple random events. There followed a rigorous process of inspection and of clearance which resulted in a large number of people requiring housing on an urgent basis. The Housing Committee recommended at its meeting on 14 June that the existing system of priority allocation be suspended forthwith, that priority for housing be reserved to families being displaced from dangerous buildings and that all provisional notifications to people of new tenancies and advance offers be cancelled. In essence it meant stopping the housing drive, just as it was gaining momentum, with the consequence that demand would quickly build up (Report 101/1963).

The situation needed a swift review and this revealed a picture that as of July 1963, there were 444 houses and 338 flats under construction while work was about to commence on 334 houses and 150 flats. A tender had recently been accepted for 66 flats while a decision to add to existing developments would yield an additional 35 one-roomed flats in Dolphin House and 140 three-roomed maisonettes in Marrowbone Lane. This gave a total of 1,508 dwellings under construction or about to commence. Tenders would be sought for 341 flats and 66 cottages within six months and development works were underway for 485 flats and 700 cottages. This gave a grand total of 3,100 dwellings coming on stream within the next years (Report 120/1963).

By November, a total of 459 dangerous buildings had been identified, of which 101 had been reported in the previous six weeks but they had also managed to house some 675 families (including single people). By 8 November, some 202 families of three plus people had been given police removal orders. This latter was proving increasingly necessary as, despite the dangers, many did not want to move from their condemned buildings. Allied to this, the Corporation had 201 families comprising more than six persons each living in one-roomed units, while there were 787 living in unfit buildings. There was also 123 families and single persons awaiting displacement from dwellings which were in compulsory purchase areas and whose rehousing was necessary to permit clearance and redevelopment (Report 176/1963).

While it can be seen that, over time, the housing programme would have met the need, the issue was that this focus on condemned dwellings had caused temporary unsustainable pressure. As a result the Corporation was forced to contemplate the previously unthinkable – the provision of temporary and pre-fabricated accommodation. This went against the grain because it had always been an axiom of the Corporation that good quality housing should be provided, combined with a fear that the temporary often became the permanent.

The Housing Committee recommended that 100 temporary dwellings should be obtained for those who could not be housed, even as priorities – mainly aged single people and two person families (Report 120/1963). As a first step the Department of Local Government gave approval for 30 caravan-type dwellings (Report 151/1963). Later in 1963, they were given permission to erect 100 temporary dwellings with sanction for 100 more, should they be needed. It was agreed that these should be located within existing schemes and the following locations were chosen (Report 183/1963).

| Love Lane | O'Devaney Gardens | Gloucester Place flats |
| Church Street | Ringsend Park | Rathmines Avenue |
| Power's Court | Bridgefoot Street | Vicar Street |
| Cork Street | | |

The Corporation had been busy during the second half of 1963 dealing with the emergency but there was time in January 1964 to step back and review their position and this is set out here.

**Table 32.** Housing provision in January 1964.

|  | Flats | Cottages | Total |
|---|---|---|---|
| *In progress* at 1 June 1963 | 464 | 380 | 844 |
| *Commenced* 1 June to 31 December 1963 | 391 | 544 | 935 |
| **Other accommodation** |  |  |  |
| (temporary, fire stations etc.) |  |  |  |
| Provided | 88 |  | 88 |
| To be provided | 65 |  | 65 |
| Total | 1,008 | 924 | 1,932 |

They expected to begin construction of an additional 2,309 dwellings before 31 March 1965. The sequencing of these projects, together with those already in train, would result in 1,186 dwellings being ready by March 1965 with a total for the year of 1,991 (Report 2/1964). This would be followed by 1,727 dwellings (537 flats and 1,168 cottages) in 1966/67. Vacancies would add to this total but these numbers were falling. The Corporation had stepped up its programme as quickly as it could and put into production more housing during the second half of the year than it had in progress before that.

They were in trouble in the short term. The houses were coming on stream quite quickly but the need was growing even more quickly. By February 1964, they had rehoused a total of 847 families and 115 single persons from dangerous buildings but they had done this by not providing housing for anyone else. They were under pressure to relax this and a small move was made on 2 December 1963 when it was agreed to allocate 5 per cent of new dwellings in Edenmore and Finglas to those families of six plus persons living in one-roomed accommodation as long as the claims of those families from dangerous buildings were not prejudiced. This is a measure of how bad things had become. The group that they were facilitating was at the top of the priority groups and even here the offer was contingent. They began to feel that they were getting on top of the problem in April. At that point they estimated that they would have about 1,150 dwelling units in 1964/5, comprising 750 new dwellings and 400 vacancies. They needed, they reckoned, about 1,000 dwellings to rehouse all families of 3 or more people from dangerous dwellings. This suggested that they could increase the allocation to other needy families to 10 per cent of new housing (Minutes, 6 April 1964).

By June the position was reported to the Council (Minutes, 1 June 1964) that a total of 1,816 families had been displaced and their circumstances are outlined below. In addition there were 327 families of 3+ persons, 178 couples and 247 single persons who were in the process of having their properties condemned and being served with police removal notices.

**Table 33.** Displaced families, June 1964.

| Family size | Displaced | Rehoused | Did not accept offer | Found own housing | Not offered |
|---|---|---|---|---|---|
| 3+ | 1,060 | 990 | 33 | 37 | 0 |
| 2 | 309 | 176 | 32 | 18 | 83 |
| 1 | 447 | 193 | 51 | 44 | 159 |
| Total | 1,816 | 1,359 | 116 | 99 | 242 |

The number of those not accepting an offer of rehousing was relatively large, especially given the circumstances of their previous housing. Couple this with the fact the police orders were necessary in many cases to ensure that houses were vacated and it is perhaps possible to see why the Corporation had not acted with greater vigour before the 1963 collapses. They were aware that large numbers of people were living in condemned houses but they were also aware that many of these people were not in the priority group and therefore would not be housed by the Corporation. They did what they could for the people who were displaced but the offers were often in less than ideal locations; those Corporation developments that had vacancies were often the less desirable ones. Some groups they could not house at all and there was a particular problem with the elderly single group. It is easy to understand why people would have preferred what they had even though it was often dirty, unsanitary and downright dangerous. It was a home and integrated with their local support networks. It might be asked why the housing programme was allowed to slow down during the latter years of the 1950s when there was this unsatisfied demand and the answer is simply that the Corporation felt it beyond their resources to extend their scope outside the priority group; there were simply too many to house if an entitlement had been established. Unhappiness with forced displacement and either poor offers or no offers spilled out into public unrest and this was capitalized upon by the Dublin Housing Action Committee in the late 1960s who sought, *inter alia*, the declaration of a housing emergency. A useful discussion of their activities is provided in Hanna (2013).

The crisis finally seemed to be coming under control by November. By that point over 16,000 buildings had been surveyed and 2,668 dangerous building notices had been served with de-tenanting required in 913 houses. However, the important point was that the rate at which dangerous buildings were being identified was going down. It was not being suggested that the problem was over but rather that the worst areas of the city had been dealt with and it might be expected that a lower proportion of houses would be found dangerous in the future (Minutes, 2 November 1964). In their December 1964 report (Report 186/1964), the Housing Committee recommended a return to the normal system of priorities, a proposal which was approved by the Corporation in January 1965. However, it was not business as usual and the decision was hedged with conditions. These were:

- that priority be given to persons displaced as a result of dangerous buildings operations and that the existing rules applicable to such cases continue to apply.
- that consideration be then given to those families who were offered new flats immediately prior to the emergency and whose offers were subsequently withdrawn. A large number of these became dangerous buildings cases and were dealt with as such. The numbers remaining are:
  – families of three persons or over    22
  – couples (Elderly)    11
  – single persons (Elderly)    13
- that elderly single persons and elderly couples displaced from dangerous buildings who have got no offer be now considered.
- that families displaced from dangerous buildings who refuse offers and have appealed for a further offer be considered on a equal basis with overcrowded families of the same size.
- that resumption of the Newly-Wed scheme be deferred.
- that consideration be given to families of 5 persons or over evicted, through no fault of their own, by private landlords.
- that over-holders of Married Quarters in Military Barracks be considered on an equal basis with overcrowded families of the same size.
- that the remaining categories – (a) C.P.O. cases, (b) Section 23 and 25 cases, (c) T.B. and other medical cases recommended for priority by the C.M.O. and (d) the overcrowding category be dealt with as prior to the emergency.
- a resumption of rehousing as proposed will involve the provision of housing accommodation for the many classes mentioned above. It must be emphasized that they can only be rehoused according as dwellings become available and there should be no expectation that they can all be dealt with at once. It must also be understood that the allocations will have relation to the suitability of the accommodation

on offer for the applicant's family. This may mean that smaller families will be housed in the smaller dwellings in advance of large families for which suitable accommodation is not available at the time.

(Report 186/1964, p. 666)

As the crisis further diminished, there was an opportunity to deal even more leniently with those displaced from condemned dwellings. A motion approved by the Council in 1966 allowed that 'all legitimate tenants dispossessed from dangerous dwellings shall in future receive accommodation and that married couples being displaced shall receive standard accommodation in cases where satisfactory evidence as to pregnancy is produced' (Report 66/1955). The improvement can be seen in the figures for 1967 which suggested that there were now only 149 families living in condemned dwellings (Minutes, 3 April 1967). By 1969, it was reported that 29 families were living in dangerous buildings and a further 99 families were living in conditions regarded as unfit. However, these families had expressed particular preferences for relocation and had to wait until these became available. This improvement in the housing system allowed the annual draw system for newly weds to be resumed in 1966 when 200 houses were made available (Report 71/1966).

Another consequence of the problem was that the Corporation was now amenable to other solutions. The Housing Committee, having considered reports from the city architect and chief quantity surveyor, recommended that further enquiries be made into the possibility of using system building for flats (including high-rise) and cottages. It was not an unqualified burst of enthusiasm, for system building was to be considered only as an addition to the already approved programme (Report 16/1964). There was also an easing of the policy of building flat blocks only in central areas. They gave approval for the construction of nine five-storey blocks in the Coolock/Kilmore scheme. It was made clear, though, that the question of providing flats in 'perimeter areas' was to be based on the merits of each location and subject to an examination of the costs involved in providing 'several central heating' in such flats (Report 81/1964). The report was duly noted by the Council on 1 July 1964. They were built only to four storeys and there were eight blocks, rather than nine, but they were an unusual feature on the edge of the city and they still stand out in an otherwise low-rise landscape.

This gave far greater focus and impetus to the developing ideas of the Minister in relation to system building and industrial methods. Dublin

**86.** The flat complex on Kilmore Road (recently refurbished).

Corporation found themselves having to stop their normal programme just as they had been powering it up. This would have knock-on effects for some years in the absence of a special intervention. The Minister saw in industrial approaches the opportunity to make a significant impact on the housing list and not just in Dublin. For some time Minister Blaney had been building support within the Government for a major housing drive that would eliminate unfit housing all over the country. There was talk of spending upwards of £50m and the Minister was in a hurry. He indicated his frustration when moving the estimate for his Department in July 1961. He said that some local authorities had been slow in getting to grips with the problem and that 'he had repeatedly told local authorities that there was no financial or other restriction on their plans to eliminate unfit and overcrowded housing conditions' (*Irish Times*, 5 July 1961, p. 5). In saying this, it seems that he had become more and more convinced that industrial building would be a fruitful path because of the prospect of significant time savings. They might also be cheaper since they reduced the need for skilled labour on site with a consequent reduction in costs.

The question of the site for such a development was then to be addressed. Normally, it would have been expected that such a development would take place in an inner city location. However, the scale of what was planned made it extremely difficult to find a suitable location, though ones could have been found had it been necessary. There was space in the docklands that would have met the need, for example. This is where another set of interests coincided.

UCD had determined in 1959 that the facilities that it operated at the Albert College in Glasnevin were no longer suited to the study of agriculture. The separation of the students from the remainder of UCD was not desirable and the city was encroaching on the farm lands. The Faculty of Agriculture submitted a request for a sum of £740,000 for a building on the new Belfield campus and at the same time, it sought a new farm for applied teaching (McCartney, p. 392). This ultimately led to the acquisition of the Lyons estate in 1962, a location even further from the campus, for the sum of £100,000. The sale of the Albert College lands was one element in the financing of these projects and the university sought the necessary approvals for both sale and purchase from the appropriate Minister. This was approved in spring of 1962.

Had the lands been immediately suited to housing, the best outcome for UCD would have been to sell on the open market. The difficulty was that the lands were not designated for inclusion in the new north Dublin sewerage system and this meant that housing use was impossible. The Housing Committee agreed to a proposal from UCD that negotiations be initiated with a view to the acquisition of the land by the Corporation (Report 78/1963). It seems that the Minister saw the possibility of the property as a location for social housing and a joint committee was established between UCD, the departments of Agriculture, Finance and Local Government to determine how best to dispose of the lands. The upshot was that UCD offered the lands for sale to Dublin Corporation and the offer was accepted (Report 78/1963). It took until February 1964 for the process to be finalized and a price of £442,000 was agreed for the 359 acres (145ha) – a lot less than the capital costs involved in rebuilding the College at Belfield. It was also agreed at a joint meeting of the Housing and Streets committees that an outline plan be adopted and that technical and legal officials negotiate the details with UCD (Report 24/1964 and Minutes, 17 February 1964).

It is difficult to judge whether UCD got a good deal. As development land the site would have been worth a lot more but it became development land only because Dublin Corporation decided that it should. One councillor, Frederick J. Mullen, was intrigued to know how it came to pass that a site, which was reported to the Corporation as unsuitable for housing a year before, was now suitable. The answer was convoluted. Indeed, the land had been excluded from the calculations for the new Dublin sewerage system because it was felt that it would remain in agricultural use. When it was proposed initially that the land would be used for housing, it was found that there was no spare capacity in the sewerage system because it had all been committed to

**87.** The UCD land available for development, shaded grey.
(Ordnance Survey plan, 1:25,000, 1962.) Adapted from Power (2000).

current or future developments. However, the City Engineer found that by tweaking this and that and adding this and that capacity that the system could accommodate another 62,000 people, all at a cost of £350,000. It seemed to be that where there was a will (or a Minister), there was a way (Minutes, 6 April 1964). UCD may also have garnered some goodwill both for the funding of the replacement facilities and for support for the more ambitious move to Belfield and it seems most unlikely that UCD would have done anything other than respond positively to any suggestion made by the Minister. This land was divided into two separate areas, bisected in an east/west direction by Ballymun Avenue. It was on the more northerly 212 acre (86 ha) site that the Ballymun housing scheme was to be constructed. There was the theoretical complexity that approximately half of this portion of the site was in the county but that seems not to have impinged on anyone's thinking.

The local population did not respond with great enthusiasm to the suggestion of a large social housing programme on its doorstep. Figure 87 shows that the northern part of the site was in a relatively undeveloped area. The southern part, however, was already surrounded by housing. A telegram was sent to the Council meeting of 7 February from the Ballymun Residents' Association.

> The residents of this area protest in the strongest possible terms against the proposed development of the land previously held by the Albert Agricultural College on the grounds that development in the manner proposed must have the effect of lowering the values of their holdings and that in addition the cost will be subsidised by the already overburdened taxpaying public. We request postponement of any decision in the matter pending further representations.
> A.G. O'Hanlon, 29 Ballymun Ave., Dublin.
> Chairman of Ballymun Residents' Association.

A deputation met with the Housing Committee on 3 April 1964 and there was a request from the Gaeltacht Park Residents' Association for a meeting too. The latter were content when it became clear that the southern part of the land holding was not to be used.

Concerns were greatly allayed when the association was afforded the opportunity to see the plans in City Hall on 8 January 1965. One element which they liked very much was a parkland which would lie between the older development and the new scheme. The formal response from the association emphasized this point.

> The committee feel very strongly that the Parkland between the existing development and the new proposals should be well fenced and protected in the interest of the present inhabitants and the new occupants. In particular, the committee feel that the entrances to the Parkland should have gates which would be closed at nighttime, as is the Corporation's practice with other Parklands under their supervision.
> (Minutes, 11 January 1965)

They were also pleased that the community centre would be built early in the project. So with a suitable cordon sanitaire in place, the committee placed on record that: 'subject to the above reservations, the committee are entirely satisfied that the proposals will form an excellent scheme, far superior to anything ever attempted in the country before, and will add immensely to the amenities and well-being of the area'.

This was to be the high point of the relations between those in the older residential areas and the newcomers. Disenchantment began quite soon after the first tenants moved in and led ultimately to a signal change in the perception of Ballymun as a good residential address. Some years later this resulted in the renaming of Ballymun Avenue to Glasnevin Avenue and to the general renaming of what had been 'old' Ballymun to Glasnevin North.

## *System building*

The Minister kept up the momentum by meeting Dublin Corporation in September 1963. It was agreed that a technical group of officials from his Department and the Corporation would be formed to examine how a housing programme might be developed to meet current needs. While he maintained his opposition to temporary dwellings, he was persuaded by Dublin Corporation that they were necessary in the short term, given the renewed focus on the removal of people from dangerous buildings.

While this was going on he was pursuing his agenda in relation to system building. An interesting advertisement was placed in the main newspapers in August by the Secretary of the Department, Mr John Garvin (*Irish Times*, 23 August, p. 12). He asked for representations on the extent to which housing output could be increased by changes to the organization of the building industry and by the use of non-traditional building methods. He asked for proposals which could be drawn to the attention of public authorities or private persons interested in the provision of houses.

The advert went on to state that there was considerable interest in the provision of economically priced houses and flats. It was noted that the then total output was about 2,000 units by local authorities and about 6,000 from private entities with the aid of grants. The annual output of flats was about 300, mainly by Dublin Corporation, and there was demand for units of between one room and five rooms, recognizing that buildings above five floors would need lifts. Private house building in Dublin mainly comprised semi-detached houses with a garage and a floor space of between 850–1200 sq. ft (80–110 sq. m). About 2,000 of these were being produced annually, while Dublin Corporation was producing about 500 mainly terraced houses for renting. He noted also that there were concentrations of demand in Cork,

> **GOVERNMENT NOTICE**
>
> DEPARTMENT OF LOCAL GOVERNMENT
>
> ## HOUSING
>
> ### INVITATION TO BUILDING INTERESTS
>
> The Minister for Local Government wishes to ascertain the extent to which the provision of housing could be expedited if the building industry's present system of organisation and methods were supplemented by non-traditional systems. He accordingly invites proposals from building interests for the provision of houses or flats by non-traditional techniques or systems. Any such proposals will be examined with a view to seeing whether they could be brought to the notice of public authorities or private persons interested in the erection of dwellings. No obligation to adopt any particular system will be involved.
>
> Substantial demand exists for economically-priced houses and flats from persons who wish to be owners of their dwellings as well as from persons eligible for local authority housing.
>
> The present annual building output supervised by the Department of Local Government is about 2,000 dwellings provided by local authorities and 6,000 for private ownership with the aid of grants.
>
> The spread of building is as follows:
>
> FLATS:
> Present annual building rate about 500, mostly for renting by Dublin Corporation. There is scope for development in the output of flats of diverse size from one to five rooms. Flats about 5 storeys would require lifts.
>
> HOUSES:
> Present annual building rate in the Dublin area is about 2,000 for private ownership, mainly semi-detached with garage, and 500 for renting by Dublin Corporation, mainly terraced. Average sizes (internal dimensions) 4/5 rooms, from 850-1,200 square feet.
>
> Concentrations of demand exist in the County Boroughs of Cork, Limerick and Waterford and in a number of urban districts. In the areas outside County Boroughs and Urban Districts, the chief need is for houses on small farms and the Minister wishes to stimulate the demand for such houses. The present annual building rate in rural areas is over 3,000, including 600 by local authorities. Houses are usually 4/5 roomed, from 750-900 square feet and are generally required to be serviced.
>
> Discussions with Departmental representatives to facilitate any concerns which may be interested in submitting proposals can be arranged through the Housing Authorities Section of the Department.
>
> J. GARVIN,
> Secretary.
> Department of Local Government,
> Custom House, Dublin.

88. Expression of interest in alternative housing approaches.
(*Irish Times*, 23 August 1963, p. 12.)

Limerick and Waterford and in a number of other unspecified urban districts. It seems from this that the Minister was anxious to see the extent to which non-traditional methods might be encouraged in all parts of the housing provision spectrum. He did not see it as a solution to social housing only but was interested to see how it might be applied more generally.

However, he had greater direct influence with local authorities and there was a particular pressing need with Dublin Corporation. He set out his position in October 1963 at the annual meeting of the National Building Agency in Dublin (more will be said about this agency below). This was in the context of legislation that he hoped to introduce into the Oireachtas soon, though it was not until 1966 that it would be enacted. He said that he wanted more flexibility and more co-operation among local authorities on a regional basis and a recasting of housing eligibility on the basis of need. He noted that private house building was at the highest level ever but he was disappointed with what the local authorities were doing. He referred to the fact that output should never have been allowed to fall to the levels that it had reached and he was not satisfied that any local authority was going fast enough with its housing programmes. And this is where his interest in system building came into focus. He noted that his Department had undertaken an examination of the relevance of new building techniques so that they would be in a position to determine what was technically feasible and whether they would assist in the expansion of housing which he wanted (*Irish Times*, 5 October 1963, p. 1).

As he had noted, his Department had been building up its knowledge of system building for some time and the Minister had increased his own familiarity with system building by a visit to France in October 1963, during which he examined the Balency method of construction, the one ultimately used in the construction of Ballymun. It now remained to see what Dublin Corporation was going to do to address the housing problem. They were steered more and more towards a system building project particularly as they were allowed to understand that such a project would be in addition to their normal housing programme. In fact, the Minster told them as much at a meeting which he held with Dublin Corporation on 10 February 1964. He told them that the Albert College site was a suitable location for a project of 3,000 dwellings, to be built at the rate of 1,000 per year. He advocated system building techniques and he emphasized to them that this would be a supplementary housing programme. If they agreed, he would get the development to be carried out by an outside housing agency and, as well, he would increase the level of support for slum clearance generally (*Irish Press*, 11 February 1964, p. 1). In all, he set the agenda out for them very clearly. All they had to do was formulate a proposal to him in those terms. However, first, he proposed that a delegation go and see these various approaches and a fieldtrip was organized in April when a number of systems were viewed in France, Sweden and Denmark. This was augmented by a demonstration in Dublin of the Barets system for members of Dublin Corporation and Dún Laoghaire borough in February (*Irish Times*, 29 February 1964, p. 10).

The delegation that went on the fieldtrip was a large one. Ten councillors, including the Lord Mayor, where accompanied by seven officials, including the Assistant City Manager and by four officials from the Department of Local Government. The agenda for the fieldtrip was developed by the Department of Local Government and they chose the sites. The trip took place from

Monday 6 April to Saturday 11 April and they visited Paris, Copenhagen and Stockholm. They saw systems which were based on three processes and the sites they visited were classified on that basis.

| | | |
|---|---|---|
| A. Systems in which wall and floor elements were cast in a factory, transported to the site, and there erected. | | |
| B. Systems in which wall and floor elements were factory cast and the floor elements were cast *in situ*. | | |
| C. Systems in which all castings were done on the site and there erected. | | |
| Paris | Camus | A |
| | Balency and Schuhl | B |
| | Barets | C |
| Copenhagen | Jesperson | A |
| | Larsen and Neilson | A |
| Stockholm | Skarne (incorporating Siporex) | A |
| | Sundt | C |

The report of the group was positive but they recognized the limitations of their knowledge. The phrase 'appears to be' was used quite a lot as they noted that 'the introduction of some form of industrialized building methods as part of the Corporation's housing programme appears to be feasible and that the techniques involved appear to be capable of adaptation to our requirements in Dublin' (Report 62/1964).

The selling points for the adoption of system building were that superstructure works could be completed in about half the time. It was the time element that was particularly attractive. The process was more labour efficient and could be undertaken with few skilled tradesmen and it was suggested that the cost of these buildings would be approximately the same as those built by traditional methods. These benefits would be achieved only if the buildings were multi-storey – literally, economies of scale. That scale made possible the use of district heating systems and it was noted that these were a feature of practically all the schemes. This was desirable because of the difficulties otherwise encountered in trying to provide independent heating to each flat in a large unit. The high-rise nature meant that lifts were provided in all of the schemes. This was not a feature of Corporation schemes to that point, it had been carefully avoided, and they felt it worthy of mention. However, they were more reassured that multi-storey flats had 'provided a seemingly satisfactory form of community development in the cities visited'.

While the report was positive, the group recognized that they were not in a position to verify the claims made to them. They pointed out that they had seen a lot and travelled a lot in a short time and could not offer a complete technical evaluation of the systems seen. They also made the point that there were systems other than the ones that they had seen. The group did not have the luxury of taking time to develop their knowledge and understanding and they pointed out that in one project in the UK that a period of two years passed between the taking of the decision and the delivery of the first prefabricated unit. Notwithstanding these caveats, the group also made the point of noting the circumstances in which the city found itself. At a post trip meeting, they agreed:

- that an additional 1,000 dwellings a year for the next three years would be required to supplement the set programme which is being carried out by traditional building;
- that, without disturbing its set programme, if the Corporation could get an additional 3,000 houses on a separate (new) site, or sites, they would favour it;
- that, provided agreement on the question of cost can be reached, and subject to the co-operation of the Trade Unions concerned, these 3,000 extra dwellings should be provided by new system building which, after inspection, they are satisfied could provide acceptable dwellings without disturbing the set programme;
- that, as the Corporation's technical and other staffs are fully engaged in dealing with the set housing programme, the task of providing the additional 3,000 dwellings should be carried out by an outside agency.

This was adopted as the visiting group's report with one councillor dissenting. It suggests that the Corporation recognized that it badly needed dwellings and if system building could provide them, they would take them, as long as they did not have to undertake the project themselves. Thus, their concerns about whether the claims of the various systems could be met would not turn out to be their problem to resolve.

This report was adopted by the City Council on 4 May 1964 with five members dissenting and the process of further investigation of the systems proceeded. This detailed analysis was reported to the Housing Committee in May (Report 82/1964) and it trod a careful line between recognizing the opportunity that system building would provide and wondering if it was the way to proceed. They were clear that it was important that the system chosen suited the type of housing that they wanted and not the other way around but, having said that, the officials felt unable to choose between the various systems. Though they offered criticisms of some, it seemed to them that all of the systems seemed capable of producing what was needed and that there was no particular reason for rejecting any one of them, on the basis of what they knew. They reiterated an earlier point that they were aware that systems other than the ones inspected might also do the job. Whatever system was chosen, they suggested that only one be used for the project. The assessment that the planning officer had made of the site was that there was about 169 acres (68ha) which could be used for dwellings and the ancillary requirements such as schools, churches, shopping centre. It was felt that it would be possible to produce 3,000 dwellings on the site. However, this would involve a large number of one-roomed flats, used largely to accommodate elderly people, and they were concerned that this might produce a social problem. They suggested the dwellings might comprise 750 one-roomed, 100 two-roomed, 500 three-roomed and 1,650 four-roomed dwellings, each flat to have a kitchenette, bathroom and toilet. What is noteworthy in their report is that it lacks an enthusiastic endorsement of high-rise. The officials suggested that with a density contemplated of upwards of 60 habitable rooms per acre (148/ha), it might be possible to provide the 3,000 dwellings without having to go over four storeys in height and still have a number of compact two- or three-storey family homes. They posed as many questions as they answered and wondered whether the Corporation was prepared to accept the implications of providing flats in a peripheral area such as Ballymun. They also noted the cost and it was going to be much more expensive than cottages, especially if they went high. Though flats of four/five storeys cost fifty per cent more than traditional two-storey cottages, this rose to 90 per cent when tall blocks were built. It was this baseline against which the costs of system building would be judged and not the cost of cottages. Ultimately, they suggested that a good balanced solution might be found in a mix of two- or three-storey houses at high density for larger families with a predominance of full family sized flats (minimum three bedrooms) in the form of four-storey walk-up blocks. Some one-, two- and three-roomed flats could be provided as determined by the nature of the waiting list and these could be either walk-up flats or high-rise.

The questions they posed to the Council in relation to what they were prepared to accept were difficult ones (Report 71/1964).

- Is the Corporation prepared to provide the accommodation required, mainly by way of flats?

- If flats there are acceptable, should they be confined to four storeys in height or should they, or at least some of them, rise higher with lift services? In this connection the officers point out that four to five storeys would cost approximately 50% more than 2-storey cottage construction and high-rise flats approximately 90% more than 2-storey cottage construction.
- Is the Corporation prepared to provide family size flats (say 3 bedrooms) for married couples with small but expanding families?
- To what extent are two and three-storey houses to be provided?
- Is the Corporation prepared to provide central space heating in some or all of the dwellings?
- Is the Corporation prepared to accept forced ventilation for internal sanitary accommodation, lobbies, etc.?

With their eyes open and following discussion, the Housing Committee came to the view that it was prepared to accept these characteristics for this development. It should be noted, however, that this was in the context of Ballymun only and in the context of the Minister agreeing to meet the costs. There was no suggestion that system building was going to be extended to the Corporation's own programme of house building. In addition to a recommendation that approx. 3,000 dwellings should be provided at Ballymun they decided the following.

- To recommend that the dwellings should be mainly provided by flat development, including a proportion of High-rise Flats (in excess of four storeys in height). Committee noted that flats of this type would cost from 50% to 90% more than cottages built in two storeys. In this regard, the committee stressed the indication given by the Minister for Local Government in connection with revised subsidy from central government in the event of the Corporation deciding to build flats similar to those built on the continent and in Britain.
- The committee agreed to recommend the provision of family sized flats, i.e., flats containing mainly three bedrooms.
- It was also agreed to recommend that a percentage of two and three storey houses be provided in the area.
- The committee decided, in the light of the contents of the first report on System Building, to recommend that central heating (space) be provided in all flats built in accordance with industrial building practice. A further report to be submitted on the question of providing central water heating.

- The committee recommend the acceptance of forced ventilation for internal sanitary accommodation, lobbies, etc.
- The committee, having considered the recommendation in the Schedule of Accommodation, directed that while accepting the necessity for the number of dwellings, further examination might be made of the sizes of the various units.

The report was adopted at the Council meeting of 25 May but with the change that the schedule of accommodation be altered to 400 one-roomed and 450 two-roomed flats (Minutes, 25 May 1964). On 1 July 1964, the Corporation formally passed the resolution to set the project in motion (Minutes, 1 July 1964, p. 178). This stated that:

> Approximately 3,000 dwelling units be provided on the Albert College site to supplement the housing programme of the Corporation and … that the Minister for Local Government be requested to undertake through an agency to be selected by him, the planning and subject to prior agreement between the Corporation and the Minister as to the portion of the cost of the scheme to be borne by the Corporation, the development of the site and the provision of the dwellings on behalf of the Corporation.

It would interesting to know what would have happened if, by some mischance, the Corporation had failed to pass this resolution for they already had indicated their acceptance of the proposal to the Minister. In fact, the advertisement asking firms to express an interest in the project was already in the main newspapers in June. It appeared in the *Irish Press* on 24 June and in the *Irish Independent* and *Irish Times* on 27 June. By that time a contoured site plan, schedule of housing requirements and other details were available. The scheme was to comprise mainly flats, including a proportion of high-rise buildings with some two and three-storey family houses. This level of preparation had clearly being going on for months and they took place in parallel with the Corporation's decision-making process. In essence, after their meeting with the Minister in February, the only input needed from the Corporation was their acquiescence. The Minister did not even wait for that to be given formally.

The Minister said as much in the Dáil in June. This was on the occasion of the debate on Vote 28 – Local Government on 2 June. He set out the process whereby the Ballymun scheme was developed and it is clear that he saw himself as the driver at every point of the process. It all developed out of a realization that:

> Housing construction forms a very large part of the operations of the building industry as a whole, in fact so large a part that its problems are largely those of the industry itself and that it is within the industry itself the changes which will give us speedier construction must take place. Notwithstanding this, I felt that my own intervention in this field was essential unless the possibility of greater social progress was to be lost. I accordingly decided that the ground should be prepared to enable me to consider whether specific techniques or systems not hitherto used in this country for housing would be necessary to supplement the output being achieved by present methods.
> (Dáil Debates, 210(3), col. 342)

The Ballymun project was a test of the process as well as meeting a particular need. He noted that:

> the Corporation accepted my advice to investigate the possibilities of new building methods and techniques, with a view to using them to produce dwellings over and above the number which they could produce in the normal programme by traditional methods, and the use of an agency other than the Corporation if this would expedite the project.
> (Dáil Debates, 210(3), col. 345)

This is an important point. While the Minister had to be asked by Dublin Corporation to undertake the project, he asked them to ask him. It was the peculiarities of spatial governance that prevented the Minister from acting as his own agent on the city's territory. The Minister maintained the polite fiction that he was responding to an initiative of the Corporation while the reality was that they were responding to one of his. The city authorities were quite content to allow the Minister to build (within certain limits) as long as they did not get saddled with the costs and as long as this was in addition to the usual allocation for capital buildings. They would get 3,000 dwellings that they badly needed far more quickly than might otherwise be the case. They were beyond the range of their experience in building on this scale and it seems that had they been building on their own initiative, they would have built cottages. After all, they continued to develop their nearby housing projects in that way and there was never a suggestion that they should be redesigned and this was long before any of the issues with Ballymun began to emerge.

This left two major decisions to be taken. The first related to the systems that would be used and the consortium that would build it. The Corporation recognized that they did not have the expertise to decide between the various systems, therefore, it would be the Minister's choice. The second related to the outside agency that would develop the scheme. In the latter case, the National Building Agency was the obvious choice. The agency had been operating on a temporary basis since 1961 but had been given a statutory basis in the eponymous Act of 1963, which was debated in December. In the course of that debate the Minister stated that its job was to build houses and associated services to facilitate the industrial development of the country in circumstances where they could not be provided by the local authority or private enterprise. The impact of the agency to that point had been relatively modest. On the industrial front, it had assisted to varying degrees in the provision of 285 houses for industrial workers throughout the State. It also had a role in the provision for State employees and it was in the process of providing 530 Garda houses. The Ballymun project was far greater than anything the agency had been involved with to that point and that is perhaps why the Minister was coy for so long as to whether the agency would be involved. Thus he issued a statement of 5 August 1964 denying reports that the NBA had been selected (*Irish Times*, 6 August, p. 2). It seems, though, that the decision was taken quickly thereafter and by late August the agency had been given the role of planning, development and construction of the project on behalf of Dublin Corporation.

There was a lot of interest in the project and by the deadline for submissions, some 89 firms or groups had responded. A shortlisting process was quickly undertaken and detailed submissions were requested from six consortia. It was made apparent early on that Irish involvement in the project would be an important criterion, both in terms of the use of materials and in the actual construction. The chosen consortium was that of Hadens and Cubitt (London) and Sisk in association with Balency and Schuhl, with Sisk providing the Irish connection and the others providing the system approaches to be used. This was announced to the public by the Minster on 2 February 1964 who explained that a contract was expected to be completed within four weeks. It was seen by some as rather unusual that the company would have been awarded the deal without the specifics of the contract being agreed. However, it proceeded on that basis, with the main specification in terms of cost being that the project should not exceed what it would have cost in terms of time, labour and money had it been built by traditional methods. This was an acceptance that time (rather than money) was likely to be the main saving, though the trades union had been rather concerned with the implications of the project because of the lack of a need for skilled persons in what was, in essence, an assembly process. It seemed that the Minister wanted the project completed and was prepared to tolerate higher costs than might otherwise be the case.

Dublin Corporation had nothing to do until the Minister felt he could report on progress towards the end of 1964. He wrote to the Lord Mayor on 4 November and a delegation met with the Minister on 13 November at which he briefed them on progress. The Minister attended a meeting of a Committee of the Whole House on 8 January 1965 and made a presentation with scale models and diagrams. A lot of progress had clearly been made. The plan was for 3,000 dwellings, of which 450 would be houses. The houses were to have a floor area of about 950 sq. ft (88 sq. m), bigger than the standard council house, and would have three bedrooms, two reception rooms, two toilets and a bathroom and all would have central heating. The flats would vary in size but be essentially on the same scale as current Corporation provision, meaning that the three-bedroomed flats would have the same space as the houses. The flats, too, would have central heating and the blocks would range in height from four storeys to fifteen storeys but most of them would be eight storeys high. Blocks in excess of four storeys would have lifts. The fifteen-storey blocks were included as 'features of the development' and would provide specially for 'small adult households of one, two and three persons' (Report 2/1965). There was an early intention not to house families with small children in the tall blocks.

The plan included provision for road improvements, landscaping and churches, schools, community buildings and a shopping centre but the immediate aim was to provide the 3,000 dwellings for those in need. This was the point at which alarm bells must have begun to ring in the heads of the councillors for the Minister asked them to consider the desirability of 'facilitating the implementation of the general plan as far as practicable simultaneously with the provision of dwellings, in particular through the co-ordination of services directly provided by the local authority'. The Minister had mentioned only housing but the Corporation had assumed that the other elements would be provided simultaneously and by the Minister. He remained coy about the final costs, though he now argued that substantial savings would be made on construction compared with traditional methods. There must have been some concern that the Corporation might get the dwellings but that the ancillary provision would be left until sometime later.

In later discussion that day, the Corporation accepted the recommendation of the City Manager, who advised them that an opportunity existed to obtain adjacent land by consent at Balbutcher and Balcurris. This was for a substantial site of 152.32 acres (62ha) for £220,000. They also passed a motion accepting the Minister's scheme but it also stated that they wanted the shopping centre provided at the same time as the housing. They also noted that they were not giving the Minister carte blanche in relation to costs and that the matter of the proportion of costs to be borne directly by the Corporation still remained to be sorted out.

The specific terms of the motion of agreement were:

> The Committee on the motion of Councillor P. J. Burke, TD, seconded by Alderman T. Stafford recommended that the Scheme be accepted subject to the following addendum: That the Minister for Local Government be requested to arrange for the construction of a town centre incorporating shops, public halls, swimming pool, library, clinic, etc., at the same time as the dwellings are being built special arrangements to be made for the provision of small shops in the area pending the completion of the town centre and subject to the general conditions specified in Council decision in report 71 of 1964 and to the general condition that Irish labour and Irish materials be used and to the insertion in Contract Documents of a clause governing the employment of Trade Union Labour similar to that in Corporation Contracts.
>
> (Report 2/1965, p. 4)

The Minister responded quickly to the resolution and the details of the project began to crystallize. The Minister wrote to Dublin Corporation on 28 January 1965 and confirmed an earlier intention to appoint the National Building Agency to enter into the contract with the developers. Although there was still a degree of vagueness about the final cost, it now emerged that the project was likely to cost £9,109,808. This level of precision was odd given that the basis of the contract was that of target cost. This was meant to be a maximum cost based on the design as agreed but subject to variation in the light of adjustments that might be found to be necessary. The Minister was very pleased with this figure and it was confirmed by the Corporation's own chief quantity surveyor that to build five-storey flats and two-storey houses would cost of the order of £9,678,673. However, the quantity surveyor made the not unreasonable point that the Corporation had never built on the scale intended and that it was likely that they could have found savings on that basis. The Minister countered that items such as car parking and children's play areas were not usually costed as part of a Corporation tender and he made the point that he had specifically asked that the Corporation ask him to include these. This provision as well as the main road island and the pedestrian bridges were costed at £401,000.

Despite the dance of 'asking the Corporation to ask him', the Minister was driving the project and despite the Corporation's view, it was he who determined the housing schedule. The proposal was now for 3,021 dwellings of which 400 would be 5-roomed houses. The Corporation was in favour of a large number of one-roomed flats, given the nature of the housing list, but the Minister decided instead to provide 725 two-roomed flats instead of the 450 suggested by the Corporation and to reduce the number of one-roomed flats to 52 to be provided in the two-storey accommodation. The argument could 'be justified by the growing demand for accommodation for one and two person households and by reference to the economics of system building'. It seems that the Minister felt he had superior information to that of the Corporation and the amended schedule comprised the following.

| Flats | |
|---|---|
| 4 rooms | 1,574 |
| 3 rooms | 490 |
| 2 rooms | 725 |
| 1 room | 52 |
| Cottages (5 rooms) | 400 |

It was also decided that all houses and flats would have central heating with lifts being provided in blocks of over four storeys. Parking was to be provided for between 500 and 600 cars with provision made for small local shops, if required. The roads at 24ft (7.3m) would be quite wide and 'in the long-term interests of the Corporation' it was intended to provide drainage for an area much greater than the scheme.

In their consideration of the Minister's plan, the Corporation once again noted that they would not have built flat blocks on the perimeter of the city but they recognized that they could not have fitted as many dwellings on the site, nor provided housing as quickly. Even so there remained three issues. The Minister did not commit to the provision of the shopping centre as the Corporation had suggested. He said that he was giving it consideration but he hoped that the Corporation would recognize the need to be getting on with the project in the meantime. Thus, the shopping centre was not going to be part of the main contract and this should have been a worry. The financing did not include provision for the substantial landscaping that would be required and it was unclear who would bear that cost. The final worry, perhaps the most important, was that there was as yet no reassurance for the Corporation as to from where the money was going to come. The City Manager made the point explicitly that the Minister had not indicated any special subsidy for the scheme. All he could do was point to what the Minister had said in his White Paper on Housing. He quoted the Minister as saying that to lighten the burden which would fall on the rates as a result of building high, special subsidies will be payable for flats of six or more storeys. Special subsidies will also be proposed for dwellings which require abnormal expenditure because of location, siting and form of construction. This was as good as it got from the City Manager's point of view and he recommended that the Corporation proceed to ask the Minister to proceed in the terms the Minister had outlined. The City Council duly agreed but put into its resolution a requirement that a suitable subsidy be paid and that the cost and type of central heating be explored further. It had been a long time since central heating had been considered for flats but on that occasion in 1938 the cost had been seen as unsustainable for tenants. Perhaps that was in the mind of the Council.

Another matter that was in the mind of one councillor at least was the need to finish off the development with private housing. The principle of reserved areas for private housing was long established, though the degree to which it had been used in recent years had varied. Councillor John J. Walsh asked the City Manager about plans for such housing and while the answer indicated that the officials had this in mind for Ballymun, there was some vagueness of what form it would take. The Manager replied that:

> In addition, an Coiste Teaghlachais has agreed that 23 acres on Collins Avenue extension will be preserved for Corporation tenancy dwellings and that 45 acres near the southern boundary of the College lands will be reserved for private housing. The Corporation is not yet in

possession of all these lands. Details of the layout will be considered by An Coiste as soon as possible.

(Minutes, 1 March 1965, pp 66–7)

The final step was the necessary approval by Dublin Corporation of a resolution to request the Minister to authorize the National Building Agency to enter into a contract for the approximately £10m involved. The enthusiasm for the project was clear in an editorial in the *Irish Times* the following day and in other coverage in the paper. There was a lot they liked, such as the range of accommodation being offered and the provision of employment. They also liked the idea that:

> Ballymun, as planned, will make history in Ireland at least, in that dwellings, shops, schools, churches, planting and play spaces will all be started – and – finished within the same period of time. From the point of view of the consumer (that is, the man or woman or child who has to live there), the question of whether or not the project is 'system-built' from factory-made units, or constructed along traditional lines is of very little importance. What does matter is that, according to the Minister and his advisers, the use of system-building will enable an equivalent standard of dwelling to be provided much more quickly, and at equal or even reduced cost than would be possible by traditional methods. [...]
>
> It seems likely, from the forward-looking way in which Ballymun has been planned, that it may well become a technical and economic showpiece for the rest of Europe... At its very lowest, it is an important pioneer scheme, the physical and economic development of which must be watched with the keenest interest.
>
> (*Irish Times*, 3 February 1965, p. 4)

Despite this statement of enthusiasm, the concerns still existed. In the debate in Dublin Corporation, Mr Denis Larkin, chairman of the housing committee, urged that no time should be lost in building the town centre despite the pressing need for housing. He also noted that the cost of landscaping had still to be provided for. The latter was not just decoration. It was part of the plan to separate people from traffic and to soften the angular nature of the building. It had also been promised to the other residential areas nearby to allay their concerns about the nature of the scheme.

This was a problem for the future, though, and now it was time to get the project underway. There was a site visit and photo opportunity for the Minister and members of the consortium on 22 March. The formal inauguration took place on 31 March and the development was now referred to as a 'satellite town', which the Minister hoped would be called Ardglas.

The scheme involved houses and flats. The houses were to be built using the Cubitt system, which was relatively new at the time. This involved using a light steel frame to which was first fixed the roof and first floor. Thus the house was completed from the top down, rather than the bottom up. They had a conventional look to them with a conventional roof and were built in short terraces. Progress on their construction was reported to be satisfactory in September 1965. The building of a number of prototype houses had gone well. The only issue relating to the completion of houses was the phasing of other necessary works and it was reported to the Council that the first houses would be available on 1 December with six houses per week being completed after that (Minutes, 6 September).

As it happened, the first 21 houses became available to be handed over to the NBA by the end of January 1966. This was about two months behind schedule but this was attributed to bad weather. It was still anticipated that the entire project would be completed on time. Indeed, the data show completion dates of 1967 for houses on roads such as Coultry, Shangan, Sandyhill and Balcurris.

The flats were the more distinctive and controversial part of the development and there was a longer lead-in time for them because of the necessity to build the factory for the pre-cast units. The first phase of these was due in March 1966 when it was anticipated that 79 units would be available. By year end, it was expected that 697 flats would have been built. However, these too fell behind schedule and by the beginning of 1967, the project was three months in arrears. This was blamed on bad weather and labour problems. In essence, these were block buildings, using the Balency method which had been around since the late 1940s. It involved using pre-cast reinforced slabs which were slotted into place using cranes. There were specialized blocks that carried the services and the floor units contained the heating coils and wiring. It meant that once the slabs were fitted together, so were the services. It also meant that should anything go wrong with the services, it would be a considerable labour to get access to them. This became manifest later as the heating systems failed to deliver what was promised, producing tropical conditions in one flat and arctic conditions in a

89. Ballymun from the air.

90. Aerial photograph of the Ballymun development.

neighbouring one. The first flats were handed over in March 1967 when 128 flats in the four-storey units were taken over by the NBA. The tenants moved in the following month.

The matters of the town centre and landscape still remained to be resolved. Despite the natural wariness of the Council and their desire to see firm commitments, in late 1965 there was no sense of any real difficulties. Indeed the briefing given to the Council from the Department of Local Government (Minutes, 2 September 1965) was very reassuring on both fronts. It was reported that: 'in summary, the present rate of progress achieved by the coordination of planning, design and construction indicates that the erection of the 3,021 dwellings proposed can be achieved within the contract period and that it will be possible for the Minister to arrange for the concurrent provision of the Town Centre and related amenities requested by the Corporation'.

Progress was made on the landscaping question and a programme was agreed with the Minister and approved by the Council in November 1965. It was intended that at least 36 acres (15ha) of open space would be provided in addition to the incidental open space of roads and such like. Two-thirds of the provision was to be in the form of parks with the principle that nobody should be more than one quarter of a mile (.4km) from such a park. There would be playgrounds for older children situated in conjunction with the parks and with some play equipment. Younger children would be accommodated in smaller units of about 1–2,000 sq. ft (90–180 sq. m) which would be located close to family-size houses. Playing fields would be provided but outside the housing area. In addition, the entire area was to be landscaped and this 'would involve planting flowers, shrubs, trees, laying out gardens, parks, playgrounds and all incidental open spaces, providing benches, shelters, paving, pools, fountains or other ornamental features, and attending to any details or incidentals with the purpose of enhancing the appearance of both the public and private spaces between the buildings of the scheme' (Minutes, 11 November 1965). The cost was estimated at £172,564 over and above the expenditure already approved and the Minister was requested to make available to the Corporation 'an amenity grant or subsidy in respect of this portion of the project to an extent of not less than 50 per cent of the expenditure'.

This was all very good and positive. Even more so was the statement attributed to the Minister that he understood the vital importance of this aspect of the project. The report to the Corporation noted that:

> The Minister stresses the great importance of this aspect of the overall development. Apart from the visual and aesthetic considerations arising, an adequate landscaping provision raises environmental standards and provides a favourable atmosphere for the development of a good social and community outlook among the residents. It is to be expected that in the long run the success of the Ballymun Project, socially and aesthetically, will depend to a significant degree on the landscaping treatment. The lack of adequate provision of this kind has been a major deficiency in some large-scale municipal housing developments in the past.
>
> (Minutes, 11 November 1965, p. 283)

This was both a very perceptive and prophetic statement by the Minister.

**91.** A tower block in Ballymun. Note how the communal services had been abandoned.

There were many innovative features to the Ballymun project and the provision of heating was among them. This was addressed in detail during 1965 and considered by both the Housing Committee and a Committee of the Whole House. The final choice proved to be a fateful one. Various choices were explored on behalf of the NBA by J.A. Kenny and Partners, Consulting

**92.** A view of a spine block.

**93.** The view from the main roundabout, shopping centre on the left.

Engineers. This included examination of the use of existing public utilities or on-site combustion, district heating from a central boiler house or the provision of local boiler houses to serve sections of the project, alternative forms such as underfloor coils and warm air, the merits of full heating and of heating for livingrooms, kitchens and halls with partial heating to bedrooms, the implications of individual metering and the comparative capital and running costs of different systems on the basis of alternative fuels comprising oil, gas, anthracite (peas, grains or duff), turf (machine won and briquettes) and electricity (Report 65/1965).

For the flats it was suggested that heating would be provided by embedded floor coils in living room, kitchen and hall, to give 68°F, 60°F and 55°F respectively (20°C, 15°C, 13°C) but without giving the tenant control by metering. Hot water supplies would, however, be metered. While there was a suggestion that there could be either one large district boiler house or three or four local ones, the final decision was for a single district boiler house that would be oil fired.

The houses proved more difficult. The Corporation wanted them included in the district heating system but the Minister felt that this would be too expensive to achieve because of the capital costs involved. He told them bluntly that he would not do this and that they would be told later whether they should 'choose' to use gas for all of the dwellings or to introduce an all-electric system for the houses that were still under construction (Report 86/1965). The Council took it on the chin but requested that the central heating system in the houses should be tenant-controlled and they asked further that the central boiler house be extended to provide heating for the community centre, schools and shops. They were also of the view that the Corporation should own the boiler house.

Although there had been considerable progress by 1966, the speed of building was not in line with everyone's expectations and on 9 January the Housing Committee expressed concern over delays in handing over houses and flats (Minutes, 9 January 1967). They asked that urgent representations be made to the Minister for Local Government on the question of the cost of heating, the early development of the town centre and the provision of a central television service (Report 71/1966). This unhappiness spilled over into a meeting of Dublin Corporation on 12 June 1967 with Mr Michael Mullen TD quoted as saying that the delay in completing the Ballymun housing scheme was bordering on a public scandal. He noted that they had been promised that the approach would result in units being built faster but this had not happened. The last flats had been promised for May and this had not happened. This seems somewhat harsh criticism, given that housing was being provided and it was housing that the Corporation could not have provided itself. However, it might have had something to do with the fact that the

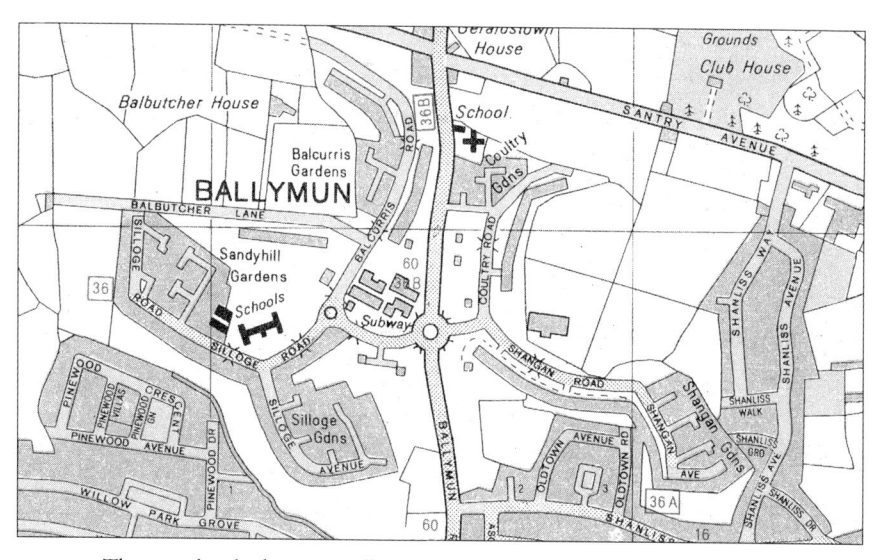

**94.** The completed scheme at Ballymun. (Ordnance Survey plan, 1:18,000, 1971.)

Corporation found that the original promise that the Corporation would be facilitated in raising its output had not been kept. Mr Larkin had made this point at a meeting of Dublin Corporation in January when he complained that the Corporation's housing output had fallen since 1965 and that 1968 would see the lowest ever. This, he argued, was because of a direction of the Minister for Local Government which resulted in a reduction in the capital programme (*Irish Times*, 10 January 1967, p. 8).

The handover of dwellings continued during 1968 and it was reported to the City Council in February that offers had been made to 1,697 families, of which 266 were refused (Minutes, 5 February 1968). A further 28 people accepted the initial offer but later returned the keys. It took until December 1968 before the scheme was officially complete. On 19 December, the Minister attended an event at which the last slab was fitted into place. By that time, 2,616 flats had been completed, of which over 2,000 were occupied. A further 452 houses were occupied and over 200 additional flats were nearing completion. By the end of March 1970, there was a total of 3,265 dwellings in Ballymun. There were now seven towers but as each tower provided only 90 flats the greater part of the flats were in the eight storey 'spine blocks' which were linked together to form long facades, giving them their title. The towers had been named after the leaders of 1916 and the roads named Coultry, Balcurris, Shangan (Report 18/1967) and Sandyhill (Report 137/1966).

There is no doubt that it was an impressive achievement and a valuable contribution to the housing stock. It had cost a great deal of money. In November 1968, it was reported (Report 58/1969) to Dublin Corporation that only £453,000 of the original £9.975 million allocated to the project remained and the Council was asked to ask the Minister to raise an additional £1m. This was agreed to on 13 January 1969. Later in 1969, there was a need for further funding as the final accounts began to take shape. The cost had risen to a total of £11.961m, mainly as the result of two additional blocks of flats. The loan element in that was £11.75m and the Corporation was asked to ask for an additional loan of £700,000 in the hope that this would mark the end of the costs (Report 147/1969). What was less clear was whether it would have been possible to build conventional houses for the same amount and in the same time. It will be remembered from above, that the bar had been set low for this project. Speed of construction was to be the main advantage and other costs were acceptable as long as they did not exceed traditional costs. A paper in 1965 (Fleming, 1965) showed that the adoption of non-traditional methods did not, of itself, yield any savings. It depended very much on the costs of the various inputs, especially the relationship between building wages and those in other industries. The research on cost comparisons was sketchy but the author suggested that the available data in the UK indicated that costs for non-traditional approaches were 8 to 9 per cent higher when all elements were factored in. The conclusion was that in the British Isles, that although the use of non-traditional methods might satisfy the desire for speed in construction, there was unlikely to be a radical shift away from traditional methods because of the relationships between labour and material costs. It was suggested that economy was likely to be found in the evolution of traditional methods.

## *The end of high-rise*

The initial reaction to Ballymun was positive as reported in an *Irish Times* piece entitled 'Ballymun – soaring new town' (21 October 1968, p. 12). The early tenants liked the quality of the accommodation, especially in comparison to what they had left. There seemed little concern that children had relatively little supervision once they left the flats and there was a feeling that the playgrounds were good. There was only one dissenting view in that piece. She was a young mother who found living in the towers an isolating experience and who was concerned about a lack of recreational facilities for both adults and children.

As time went on, however, more and more people identified with her issues. Some of them were inherent to high-rise and some were inherent to Ballymun. Those that related specifically to Ballymun had at their kernel the fact that the town was not completed as it should have been. Services were not provided at the same time as housing and many essential services were lacking several years later. It was not for the lack of warning about this. The City Councillors had asked time and time again that facilities and landscaping be put in at the same time as the houses.

It took until February 1967 before the shopping centre got underway in any serious manner. The Minister sought expressions of interest from developers and it was mid-year before it was agreed that the shopping centre should be built by a consortium of Cubit and Sisk. This was considered to be the most advantageous since they were already the developers of the housing and were on site. It was felt that they could get up and running faster than any of the other interested parties.

The Minister made a proposal to the Housing Committee and it was considered in August 1967. The suggestion was for 111,800 sq. ft (10,440 sq. m) of retail space, including supermarkets, department stores and licensed premises with a total parking provision for 440 cars. There would also be petrol filling stations, cinema, a ballroom and a bowling alley. It was to be done in two phases with the first completed within twenty months and comprising 75,820 sq. ft (7,045 sq. m) of shopping, a petrol filling station, a small amount of office accommodation and car parking for 200 cars. The remainder was to be completed within thirty-two months.

The Minister's proposal also provided that sites be reserved for community buildings, e.g., swimming pool, clinic, Garda station and community hall, and these sites were to be made available free of charge to the Corporation or 'their nominees for the purpose of providing such building any time up to three years after the completion of the scheme'.

In addition, the developers sought exclusivity in that they wanted the Corporation to guarantee that the 'Corporation will not sponsor another shopping development in the catchment area of Ballymun'.

While the Corporation must have been pleased that the shopping centre was going ahead at last, they must have noted that they were being left to provide the community facilities and it seemed that the Minister did not see a role for himself in that. In any event, the Corporation voted to accept the proposal at its meeting on 21 August 1967, though it did not accept the requirement to prevent competition within the catchment area. At best, this

95. The town centre in Ballymun.

was going to leave people without proper shopping facilities for two further years and the Corporation found it necessary to provide temporary shopping facilities and to provide for five out-of-centre shops (Minutes, 3 February 1968).

In October 1968, an overall position regarding the development of Ballymun was given. The schools were coming on stream with one already in operation and work was about to begin on a second. The site for the church had been taken over by the authorities. A number of children's play areas had been provided and more were set to be provided when the sites had been agreed with the Tenants' Association.

However, though matters were progressing with the shopping centre, progress was still slow (Minutes, 7 October 1968). Permission had been granted for 44 shops, one supermarket, two department stores and two licensed premises, together with the necessary car parking and work was underway. The time scale for completion by the chosen developer, the Green Property Company, was envisaged as:

| November 1968 | Supermarket |
| February 1969 | 9 shops |
| April 1969 | 7 shops and one department store |
| July 1969 | 8 shops and second department store |
| August 1969 | Remainder of shops |

At that time, a temporary supermarket was operating and arrangements had been made to let a lock-up shop at Silloge Road, which was expected to open that month.

It was envisaged that work would commence on the swimming pool in 1969 and sites had been earmarked for the other community facilities. The pool did not happen in 1969 and the Minister for Local Government, Mr Molloy, was still dealing with the issue in 1971. This time it was over a row as to whether the pool had been promised by the developers as a gift. The Minister replied.

> In reply to Deputy Dowling, who put what was the most important question, I am fully in favour of the provision of a swimming pool in Ballymun as an amenity for the residents of Ballymun and the surrounding area. I would assure the Deputy that as soon as the local authority can agree on a site—I understand they have suggested a site south of the Ceannt Tower and that discussions are going on with residents about this location—and when they present full proposals to me I will have the matter favourably considered.
> (Dáil Debates, 256(10), col. 1924)

Over three days (22–4) in July 1971, the *Irish Press* ran a series called 'the real Ballymun'. It was a generally positive series about the town. It accepted that the area was still young and that it needed time to develop. It recognized that there was a lot going on in terms of community development. The comments quoted from residents were mostly positive and it was seen generally as a good place to live. However, it was also noted that the area had no church, no bowling alley, no cinema and no swimming pool. For an area which housed a large number of young families there was nothing in the evening for the parents to do, except visit one of the two pubs. There was no nursery or crèche for the legion of young children roaming unsupervised. There was a suggestion that Ballymun could do more for itself but it was the comment of one resident that suggested that there was no effective residents' association that produced a most interesting reply.

The purpose of the response was to show that Ballymun had a very active tenants' association, the Ballymun Estate Tenants' Association, and in so doing it gave a very useful insight into the issues that were being faced. The swimming pool, library and community centre still had not been provided and it was not clear when they were going to be. A post office had been recently opened and there had been some improvement in the provision of buses. The central heating system was not working. People did not have control over the heating in their own flats and for three months of the year they did not have it at all. The lifts did not work on a regular basis and families with small children were housed at the very top of the towers, despite the early official recognition that this was not a good idea. There was an absence of play areas and people missed garden spaces, even if they never had them in their downtown tenements. The relationship with Dublin Corporation had broken down. Rents were relatively high because of the operation of the differential rent scheme but they felt there was no recognition of that. As he put it: 'the area of conflict is too great to go into in any detail here. I will mention only the following: drainage, flooding, lift maintenance, central heating, blocking of underpasses, tiling of old folks' ground floor hall ways in Sandyhill and Coultry, internal decorative work for old people unable to do so themselves, seating around the estate and of course the recent rates increases. The list is by no means complete' (*Irish Press*, 6 August 1971, p. 8).

The heating system was a particular disappointment. Ballymun was an important experiment in district heating in that heating was not produced in individual units but rather in a central facility and then piped to each of the housing units. The coils were built into the floor panels prior to installation to provide underfloor heating. It should have been a great engineering and economic success but it never worked properly and remediation was extremely difficult because of the manner whereby the flats had been constructed. It proved expensive for the tenants to run. As early as 1967, there were complaints that heating bills were working out at three times what had been expected and that its operation was unsatisfactory. At that time, the response was that these were teething problems and that tenants had to manage their own heating, though it was acknowledged that it seemed that some tenants did not have the means to control their heating. The expectation was that the cost would be less than 15s. per week (Minutes, 6 February 1967). However, this continued to be a problem until the decision to redevelop the area in the 1990s.

The problems with the Corporation and State in terms of the provision of facilities could have been fixed but some of the issues were inherent in high-rise generally. By the time that Ballymun was nearing completion, the problems associated with housing young families in high-rise blocks were already becoming well known.

Taylor, writing in 1973, enumerated many of the difficulties that arose when people, especially families with young children, were housed in high-rise apartments. They lost the immediate connection with the street. This might seem obvious but it seems important to people that they experience the day-to-day comings and goings of neighbours on the street. This served to reduce any sense of isolation while the feeling that life was being lived in the company of others added to a sense of security. In these flat complexes, tenants were subjected to a greater degree of control in terms of the management of the buildings. There were more rules about what might be done and what might not be done. There were rules about the use of equipment, there were rules about decoration. The communal areas were often unattractive and many times not enough effort was devoted to their maintenance and cleaning.

Such rules and controls have now become the common currency for those living in apartment blocks or in gated communities but this was not the case in the 1960s. While similar rules would have applied in normal flat complexes run by Dublin Corporation it seems that matters were more difficult in Ballymun. There were early complaints in Ballymun about graffiti in the common areas and general disruption in the use of common spaces such as those provided for drying of clothes. Soon it became commonplace to see washing lines strung across the balconies. It was a mistake to provide open access to all the flat blocks and to fail to clean graffiti immediately. These communal spaces soon became unusable.

The lift became an essential facility in every block, yet the experience across the UK was that these were often cheap, slow and unreliable. Jephcott reported that waiting times of over ten minutes were reported in the lifts at the Red Road scheme, Glasgow. This was contemporary with Ballymun and was built between 1964 and 1969. Even as they were being built, the high proportion of children housed in the towers and the inadequate lift provision created a reputation for juvenile delinquency (Horsey, 1990). This was exactly the experience in Ballymun. It was said that the lifts could not cope with the abuse given to them by gangs of children and youths. Certainly, the lifts became part of the folklore of Ballymun, part of its image – the scenes with the horse Tír na nÓg in the lift from the film *Into the West* is typical. However, given open access to the blocks, the lifts should have been designed to take the heavy use and even abuse.

The lifts in Ballymun were an issue almost immediately but this was put down to problems of misuse and vandalism (Minutes, 4 March 1968) and not to any problems inherent in the equipment. Pickets were placed on City Hall and Leinster House by the Ballymun tenants' association in May 1970 with the association claiming that two thirds of the lifts were out of order at any one time (*Irish Press*, 5 May 1970, p. 3). The Minister for Local Government, Bobby Molloy, declared in the Dáil on 9 June 1970 that they were not of poor design and quality and that his information was that they were working. However, he noted that maintenance was a matter for Dublin Corporation.

> I do not accept that the lifts in Ballymun are of poor quality. On the contrary, I am advised that these lifts are of sophisticated design and robust construction. Their design commenced in September, 1965. Manufacture began soon afterwards and continued, up to last year, during the course of construction of the flats. The National Building Agency Limited accepted the lowest tender for the supply of the lifts which had to comply with an exacting standard specified by them. The lifts were so designed that their operation would be unaffected by adverse weather conditions, and that they would be used internally, in accordance with normal practice.
>
> Dr Byrne: The Minister must be aware that the majority of those lifts are subject to severe weather conditions and are not used internally, that all the lifts of the eight storey blocks are open to the weather, have rusted and are continually breaking down?
>
> (Dáil Debates, 247(5), col. 657)

This was still an issue in 1971 when an *Irish Independent* reporter found that lifts were out of order in almost all of the blocks visited. Stories were reported of six-day waits for lifts to be repaired and of their going out of service almost immediately (*Irish Independent*, 7 July 1971, p. 9).

In flat complexes all over the UK, the provision of recreational space became troublesome and the position in Ballymun was no different. Many flat complexes were, of themselves, high density but they were often in islands of open space. This was provided by the planners as some form of amenity for the residents. The towers or blocks certainly enjoyed good light as a result but they could derive precious little else from the amenity. The problem was that because the land was accessible to everyone, it was accessible to nobody. For one person to make use of it was to deny potentially the enjoyment of it by somebody else. The only way to ensure that such infringements did not take place was to have strict rules. Thus, in the Lee Bank redevelopment area in Birmingham, there were great swards of green space. Lest anyone might use them, there were prominent notices:

**96.** Enjoying the amenity in Lee Bank, Birmingham. (Taylor, 1973.)

> PLEASE DO NOT WALK OR PLAY ON THE GRASS. This area has been laid out as an amenity to be enjoyed by all the tenants on the estate. Will you please help to preserve its appearance by preventing damage in the area. JJ. Atkinson, Housing Manager.
>
> (Taylor, 1973, p. 100)

It is hard to understand how the planners believed that these commonage spaces were ever going to be used. There was space enough for private gardens or for allotments or for playing pitches but without the designation of particular uses, the land was destined to remain unused. The phenomenon can still be observed in estates built in the 1980s and 1990s where houses surround vast urban meadows that offer only grass.

Landscaping had always been a key concern in Ballymun. It was recognized early on that this was going to be a challenge and there was constant pressure on the Minister by the Council to provide the necessary funds. These were provided only on a piecemeal basis and slowly; the argument being that landscaping could not be properly completed until the building works were done. The Housing Committee considered the issue in detail in 1966 and approved the following resolution.

Estimate by Department of Local Government that cost of Landscaping, grassing–£26,513; Trees–£30,300; Fencing–£11,000; Consultant's fees–£13,500, be approved as maximum figure and subject to an amenity grant of not less than 50% of the gross cost being paid by the Minister for Local Government, approved. Report to Council.

This included a 'buffer zone' or 'planting belt on the southern perimeter between the project site and adjoining private development areas. This provide[d] for planting of trees (50/- each) at 30 ft intervals in the shelter belt and infilling with forestry planting' (Report 155/1966). They were still waiting for confirmation from the Minister that they could get the subsidy on 6 November 1967 and 1968 was well advanced before the Department made a decision to provide £50,000 for landscaping (Report 163/1968). In fact, what was ultimately done was disappointing. There were no pools, no ornamental features, no seating. The reality was as described above and visible in the pictures here – flat blocks rising out of a sea of grass with an occasional lonely tree.

Domestic concerns about the safety of high-rise living also prompted rules. In Edinburgh the Fort Leith estate displayed notices: 'Children are not allowed to play on Balconies. By Order City Architect'.

This was despite the fact that the spaces were originally designed as 'play decks'. The issue of safety left parents with a terrible dilemma. Outside was open space, fresh air, but that was a long way away and it might be a long time away too, given the unreliability of the lifts. Children were out of the effective control of their parents once they left the flat. Small wonder, therefore, that many parents chose not to permit their children to leave their flats.

As time went on, it became common for local authorities in the UK to heed a growing body of advice that families with young children should be housed on the ground floor. This did not always happen but by the early 1970s, the Greater London Council had a policy to offer families with children under twelve years accommodation on or below the fifth floor. In their introduction to their report on *Families in flats*, Littlewood and Tinker (1981) noted that 'the acceptance of multi-storey living to a nation of house dwellers has been far from wholehearted, and public concern has continued unabated for over 25 years about the difficulties, particularly for families with young children. Many studies have been unanimous in concluding that these are the ones for whom living off the ground poses severe problems' (p. 5). By the late 1970s, this realization that multi-storey accommodation led to problems had prompted some countries to change their policies. Finland had

**97.** Landscaping in Ballymun in 1980 around the blocks, a decade following completion. Here the towers rise from great swards of grass and car parking.

**98.** Mature landscaping along Ballymun Road in 2005.

moved to building more low-rise, the Netherlands decided to avoid going above six storeys where possible. Dublin Corporation, itself, had decided to avoid going higher than three storeys while Hungary, Belgium and the Netherlands were trying to allocate only lower level flats to families (Littlewood and Tinker, 1981, p. 13). Dublin Corporation had no such luxury in allocation. Because most of their clients were families with at least three, if not four, children it was necessary to house them in the flat blocks (Minutes, 12 June 1967).

The outcome in Ballymun was described as 'the Ballymun neurosis' at the annual meeting of the Irish Medical Association in April 1970. A motion was passed urging planners to provide recreational facilities in new housing estates. Dr Mowbary pointed out that 'above the seventh floor in these 15-storey "Alcatrazes" in Ballymun, the mother and children are usually incapable of getting to the ground because half the time the lifts are out of order'. It was noted that delinquency was often the outcome when there was a lack of recreational facilities and a lack of privacy was a factor in family disruption. It was noted that 'most other countries had come to realize that these multi-storey flats and large housing schemes were not the solution to a housing problem and it had been found that blocks of flats above the height of four storeys brought about a ghetto mentality' (*Irish Press*, 3 April 1970, p. 3).

Ballymun was a bold experiment and a radical approach to trying to solve a housing crisis. Credit must be given to the Minster for driving the project through its various stages and for getting the money necessary to build the complexes. It was all done with high hopes and great expectations and there was never any sense that anything other than first class was being attempted. This was manifest in the selection of the tenants in that getting a dwelling in Ballymun was seen very positively. However, while a great deal of attention was paid to the building methods, it seems not enough time was devoted to looking at the sociological and psychological issues of high-rise flat blocks. The experience, especially in the UK, should have been enough to raise warning flags and to ensure, at least, that the facilities worked and that the ancillary services that were promised arrived at the same time as the tenants. Disillusionment quickly set in and this was manifested by a very rapid turnover of people. Everyone was a renter; they could afford the higher rents, and there was a quick return to the housing list as people sought to get housing in better locations. People were prepared to put up with broken lifts, bad heating and an absence of recreational and other services only for so long. A study entitled *Ballymun: the experiment that failed* was completed in 1974 and was based on a survey of 10 per cent of the population. While it has all of the limitations associated with sample surveys, the responses confirmed the issues as reported in newspapers and other media. Of particular interest was that over half of those surveyed intended to leave and only half of them had been there in 1971. The high turnover was not good for community building and helped reinforce the image of Ballymun as being in a downward spiral. Ballymun quickly became an address not to have and the name changes to streets in the locality was a potent sign of this. While Dublin Corporation built multi-storey blocks in other locations, nothing was ever attempted again on the scale of Ballymun. Dublin Corporation was not alone in coming to the conclusion that high-rise had a limited future. The same decisions were being taken in the UK and, although the Roehampton Alton Estate received the accolade of being declared a grade II protected structure because there was nothing else quite like it, most others have suffered the same fate as the Ballymun blocks, the last of which was demolished in September 2015.

# Home ownership

## The path to ownership

The 1971 census showed that there were 93,459 dwellings which were owner occupied in the built-up metropolitan area, which included the county borough (city) area, the Dún Laoghaire borough and the north and south suburbs. Most of these dwellings were within the city and only 2,000 or so were located in the northern suburbs, mainly in Lucan and Blanchardstown. Dún Laoghaire had 7,332 such units, more than twice the number of local authority rentals, and owner occupancy dominated the south county area where there were 27,811 owner-occupied dwellings, mostly conventional houses, out a total housing stock of just over 34,000.

Prices had risen during the 1940s so that £1 of goods available in 1940 would have cost £1.55 in 1950. There are no specific indices available for housing costs but using the general index and 1950 as a base, a consumer would have needed an additional 30 per cent in 1955 and a further 50 per cent by 1960 to buy the same goods. Prices increased steadily during the 1960s and the index reached 1.8 by 1965 and got to 2.1 by 1969. So over the twenty years, the amount of money available to a consumer would have had to more than doubled in order to buy the same things. The pace of increase was fairly steady over the period but the trend was always upwards. If anything, house prices increased at an even faster rate, at least during the 1960s. As a point of comparison, over the past 20 years, the index increased by 59 per cent using 1993 as a base year.

Builders were not in good spirits in the early 1950s. Their recovery in the post-war period had been hampered by the imposition of restrictions on private building to ensure that building resources were available to strategically important projects and for smaller, cheaper houses. This limited, except by permit, building projects where the cost of materials exceeded £500 and had a dampening effect on speculative building. By 31 May 1950, the Minister for Industry and Commerce, Mr Morrissey, was hoping to be able to end these restrictions as soon as possible (Dáil Debates, 121(7)) but it was to be February 1952 before they were finally removed. By then the building industry was complaining that though there was demand for private houses, there was little capacity in the market to purchase them. It seemed that prospective buyers could not or would not put the money together. As early as 1950, auctioneers were complaining that there were too many houses in the higher end of the market for which buyers could not be found. One auctioneer was quoted as saying that 'all over the city suburbs – at Mount Merrion, Foxrock, Blackrock, Clonskea (sic), Terenure, Dundrum, Roebuck, Clontarf, and in the Dún Laoghaire area – hundreds of houses are lying empty. These are homes that cost about £3,500 to build and were intended for sale at from £4,000 to £6,000'. He added that in the Stillorgan area alone there were about 300 houses vacant' (*Irish Times*, 6 January 1950, p. 7). It was not only at the high end of the market that the problem existed. The view expressed in 1952 by a cross section of builders was equally gloomy; in the previous eighteen months the cost of 'modest' three or four-bedroomed houses had increased from £2,000 to £2,300 or way ahead of the general increase in prices. They estimated that because of increases in wages in the building trade and rising costs generally that a further increase of seven or eight per cent was in the offing. It was said that timber had increased in price by 44 per cent, cement by 37 per cent, lead by 103 per cent and copper by 50 per cent. This meant that the required deposit was now of the order of £250 or £300 and people could neither afford this or the long term commitment of a loan at what were high rates of interest. It meant that builders were left with houses on their hands and it was estimated that, as a consequence, building activity had decreased in the Dublin area by 15 per cent (*Irish Times*, 31 May 1952, p. 16). Prices were also running ahead of what would be supported under the newly revived SDAA loans system. The maximum that could be advanced was not indexed and, even by 1951, it seemed that some builders had been priced out of that vital market. One builder complained to the *Irish Times* that he had eighteen houses for sale on the site of the Norwood Tennis Club in Ranelagh but he was finding it hard to sell them because they were priced at £2,400 (*Irish Times*, 10 November 1951, p. 2). The building trades union agreed as they complained about a steep rise in seasonal unemployment. They claimed that there were 100 craftsmen idle in Dublin for the first time in many years and that there was also a large number of labourers unemployed (*Irish Times*, 5 January 1952, p. 5).

People wanted and needed houses but there was general agreement that houses had moved beyond peoples' ability to purchase. At the dinner of the Dublin and District House Builders' Association in Dublin in December 1954, the Secretary of the Department of Local Government, Mr John Garvin, suggested that demand for all types of new housing in the Dublin area showed no sign of being satisfied. However, he made the point that the output of private builders should be directed towards houses within the means of the lower income groups and that was where government subsidies were directed. The builders for their part complained that this was all well and good but they often had to wait months to get loans which were awarded under the SDAA system and that this pushed costs upwards (*Irish Times*, 6 December 1954, p. 6). The upshot of this was that speculative builders who built houses in the price range above what Dublin Corporation would support for an SDAA loan were very much out on a limb. They were dependent on a relatively small cohort of people who had access to a substantial deposit, upwards perhaps of 25 per cent, and could afford the significant repayments of a commercial mortgage. That builders came to rely on those who could access SDAA loans is evidenced by the outcry that resulted when the Government engaged in a stand-off with Dublin Corporation over who should pay for the loans, a matter discussed in detail in an earlier section (see *Irish Times*, 25 June 1956, p. 7).

There was a price readjustment that began to make itself felt by 1955. By then auctioneers were speaking of artificially high prices in the post-war years and that the market was coming back into equilibrium. In the annual review for 1954, Daniel Morrissey and Sons, auctioneers and valuers, suggested that 'vendors became more realistic in their reserves, the property market became more stable and the number of sales increased (*Irish Times*, 6 January 1955, p. 8). They reckoned that there was good demand for modern houses in the £2,500 to £5,000 price range as well as houses convenient to the city centre costing up to £1,500. Still, it was estimated in April 1956 that there were 3,000 newly completed houses in the Dublin area for which it was difficult to find buyers notwithstanding the government's attempt, by means of a guarantee, to get commercial lenders to provide loans of up to 95 per cent at the lower end of the market.

Matters did not improve greatly for some time and many builders decided that survival lay in contract work rather than in speculative building. This put even greater emphasis on the housing programme of Dublin Corporation in sustaining the building trade at a time when it was winding down that programme in the light of money shortages and increasing vacancy rate. It also re-emphasized a point made above that building outside the range of the subsidy house was a dangerous endeavour. The pressure on subsidy houses continued and there were constant calls to have the limit for loans under the SDAA increased so that bigger (and more expensive!) houses could be built.

The real impact of the squeeze on all areas of the business was seen in unemployment figures. By early 1958, employment in the trade had stabilized but at a level that saw significant numbers of people without work. The data showed that on 28 December 1957, 3,178 builders' labourers were out of work compared to only 1,602 in July 1950. In that same year skilled workers were hard to come by and only 49 masons, 36 plasterers, 120 carpenters and a similar number of painters were out of work but at the end of 1957 the figures were 208 masons, 443 plasterers, 780 carpenters and 403 painters.

By 1959, in the view of a trade union spokesman, reported in the *Irish Times*, 'the building trade is at a very low ebb. We cannot gauge the unemployment position properly because many of the operatives have emigrated. Some of them have taken their families with them to England' (*Irish Times*, 14 April 1959). This was to prove to be the low ebb and by 1962 builders were reporting that there was brisk business with prices significantly higher compared to 1958. The better availability of credit was cited as one of the reasons. Throughout the late 1950s, there had been severe credit restrictions in both Ireland and the UK and money was expensive. The Educational Building Society put it thus at its annual general meeting in 1959.

> The continuance of severe credit restrictions resulted in an increased rate of withdrawals by investors ... With the lowering of the bank rate in the latter period and the consequent stimulation of public confidence, the Society has been in the position to resume its normal working.
> (*Irish Times*, 25 May 1959, p. 10)

Only a year later, there was considerable improvement and the 'early part of the year under review was marked by an increasing inflow of investment owing to the relaxation of credit restriction in 1958'. So both the availability of credit at a reasonable price and the increased confidence in the market had worked a change. As a result the EBS reported that 'the increasing demand for home-ownership has been well maintained throughout the year. The amount advanced in 1959 was £748,132 – the comparative figures for 1958 are £489,052' (*Irish Times*, 31 March 1960, p. 10). One of the effects of this was to push prices upwards as there seems to have been quite a level of pent-up demand and people seemed prepared to spend upwards of £4,000 on a house, well in excess of any possibility of SDAA support. There was particular interest in houses that were closer to the city but given that most new building had to be further out from the city in the suburbs, this pushed prices higher in suitable locations.

This was quite a turnabout from the stagnation of the 1950s and the surge was not a short-lived one as prices continued to rise steadily. It was now a case of demand exceeding supply and it seems that people were prepared to pay huge increases in prices. In a review of the property market for 1962, it was suggested that houses of all types had increased by between 25 per cent and 50 per cent and some houses in desirable locations had increased by more. People were prepared also to buy the larger, more expensive houses as long as they were in desirable areas such as the southern suburbs of Dublin. Even the more humble three-bedroomed houses that were available at the beginning of the decade for £2,500 had reached £3,000 to £3,500 by 1962 and there was a steady demand (*Irish Times*, 22 December 1962, p. 10). This had a significant knock on effect on the price of land and there was an increasing difficulty in getting land in Dublin at a reasonable price. Land was now selling in the southern suburbs for £3,000 an acre (£7,500 per ha).

By 1964, it was described as a seller's market and there was no difficulty selling houses in the £3,000 to £5,000 bracket. The trend towards people being prepared to buy bigger continued and prices of up to £7,000 were now being asked and obtained in the better residential areas. Where the area had a particular cachet, such as Killiney, prices became stratospheric. A new bungalow on one-quarter of an acre sold for £14,000 and a solid Victorian house for £12,000. Even the more standard four-bedroomed detached house was selling at £7,500 and there was no problem getting buyers for new houses with central heating in the £6,000 to £8,000 range.

There was also a surge in the purchase of properties to convert into flats. These new tenements were concentrated in areas close to the city centre, especially in Rathmines where the large Victorian townhouses were particularly suited to this purpose. With the imposition of greater control under the 1963 Local Government (Planning and Development) Act, the rate at which houses were purchased for conversion slowed somewhat but the trend continued and they were seen as good investments.

The following year was found to be no different and it continued to be a seller's market with demand exceeding supply in all categories and the standard house was now seen as lying in the £3,500 to £7,000 range. There seemed to be no difficulty in raising large mortgages but there was some concern that this could not go on. The *Illustrated London News*, in a short report on the General Election in 1965, noted that Dublin was now more expensive to live in than London and that there was a fear that galloping inflation could ruin much of the economic growth (*Illustrated London News*, 3 April 1965, p. 7).

**99.** Dun Emer in Dundrum. (*Irish Times*, 21 June 1967, p. 56.)

# DUNDRUM
## Real Home Value!

### DUN EMER
### SANDYFORD ROAD, DUNDRUM
**4 BEDROOMS — SEMI-DETACHED — CENTRAL HEATING — GARAGE — CHOICE LOCATION**

**LOCATION:** Dun Emer is a pleasant new development situated on Sandyford Road, a few minutes from Dundrum village and only four miles from Dublin City centre. There is a very good shopping centre in Dundrum, ¼ mile from the site.
**CENTRAL HEATING:** Oil-fired central heating system. In addition to circulating warm air through discreetly placed grills, heats the domestic water.
**GARDENS:** Walled front and rear. Each house is provided with concrete drive and concrete paths front and rear.
**BUS SERVICE:** No. 44 from Burgh Quay, Dublin, stops at the entrance to the site.
**ACCOMMODATION:** Ground Floor is on the open plan style with dining and lounge areas combined to give maximum space. Large bright window extending from floor. Beautiful tiled fireplace with mahogany overmantel. Kitchen: Sink unit with single drainer in stainless steel. Wall cabinets and worktops faced with plastic. Vinyl tiles are fitted to kitchen floors.
**First Floor:** 4 Bedrooms. Each room is provided with one power point.
**Bathroom:** With panelled bath, wash-basin and pedestal. Tiled half-way up walls. Vinyl tiles are fitted to bathroom floor.
**OUTSIDE:** Garage having patent up-and-over door. Fully insulated. Fuel Store: Concrete block construction.

**LOANS AVAILABLE TO SUITABLE APPLICANTS** — **£4,400** nett

VIEW HOUSE OPEN DAILY (Saturday and Sunday 3—5.30 p.m.) or by appointment

for central heating SHELL BP

**PARAMOUNT HOMESTEADS LTD.**
40 UPPER MOUNT STREET, DUBLIN
TEL. 62294

By 1967, despite the ever-increasing price of land, there was a variety of housing developments under way in Dublin and these were captured in a supplement to the *Irish Times* in June 1967. They listed thirty-seven developments in the city and county area that varied in scale from ten to over a thousand. One feature of the distribution that will not surprise is that only six of the developments were on the north side of the river and all of these were suburban, in Castleknock, Finglas, Grange in Raheny and two in Howth. The remainder were south-side with the greatest concentration in the south-eastern sector of the city. The supplement also noted more suburban development and the importance of Malahide, Swords, Lucan and Killiney as locations for owner occupancy was clear.

The houses on offer were mainly semi-detached or detached, though there were a small number of terraces and while three-bedroomed was available, more and more houses tended to be four- or five-bedroomed, further differentiating themselves from council housing if location was not sufficient enough. The price range reflected the differences in size and location. Nothing was available below £3,000 and it was possible to pay in excess of £7,000. Dun Emer on Sandyford Road was a middle range development while Offington Park in Howth was at the higher end and these are discussed in more detail below.

As has been noted elsewhere, the trend towards the provision of central heating as standard had continued during the 1960s and the majority, but not all, of the developments now offered it. Whatever interest there had been in hot air or underfloor systems had waned and most systems were now oil fired, usually incorporating a back boiler as well.

Developers sought to emphasize the unique features of each estate and even complained that Dublin Corporation's planning rules were a drag on creativity. Even so, at least one architect saw the dominant design as 'dullsville'. In the *Irish Times*, Eoin McVeigh put it this way:

> New development at Dullsville on unsurfaced through road. Open-plan living with continuous 'through air' windows. Delightful planned kitchen with 'picture-window' view of twenty-five similarly delightful kitchens. Fitted presses behind all four kitchen doors. Master-bedroom fitted with generous (3ft x 1 ft) built-in wardrobes; 3 other beds, two suitable for dwarfs only. Close to shops, schools and glue factory. Show house open sunny weekends.

He argued for purchasers to take greater control of the process on which they were spending huge amounts of money. For example, he suggested that notwithstanding the modernists who advocated open-plan for living space, the demands of different members of the family not to mention radio, television and records made it imperative to have at least two living spaces – one near the kitchen as a 'day space' and the other as an adult 'evening space'. He noted that there were car magazines that provided detailed information on how to take any car apart. What was needed was the same level of advice for house buyers, which he then went on to offer in summary. He finished with the advice that should any potential purchaser come across a house which met or exceeded what was advised and was beautiful, he should not write to the Editor about it but buy it and settle down unobtrusively (*Irish Times*, 21 June 1967). Doubtless he would also have agreed with another complaint, which

100. Range of developments available. (*Irish Times*, 22 November 1969.)

> **THE BUILDERS' AUCTIONEER**
> OFFERS
> **NEW DEVELOPMENTS**
> at
> **DUN LAOIRE • KILLINEY • GLENAGEARY**
> **DALKEY • BRAY • SKERRIES • MALAHIDE**
> FROM £6,500 — £30,000
> BOOKING DEPOSITS FROM £100
>
> **BUILDERS!**
> SITES FROM £1,000 — £6,000
> SUBSTANTIAL FINANCE AVAILABLE IF REQUIRED
> We are anxious to act for additional builders now, or builders who will require land or sites in the future.
> For quick, prompt, personal attention consult
> **J. P. MAGUIRE & CO. LTD.**
> Tel. 680243    THE PROPERTY HOUSE,    Tel. 683990
> BALLSBRIDGE

was that the contractors were using electric wire as elastic and not providing nearly enough sockets. It was noted that the minimum required in local authority houses in the UK was 20 sockets in a typical three-bedroomed house. This was not a standard often found in private houses in Dublin. In fact, the advertising feature for Dun Emer (figure 99) made a virtue of the fact that there was one socket in each of the bedrooms.

As the decade was coming to an end, the same patterns were manifest. Houses were being built in Malahide, Portmarnock, Chapelizod, Lucan, Dundrum, Cabinteely, Killiney, Glenageary and Dalkey. It cannot be said that designs were wildly exciting but the earlier trend towards more bedrooms was maintained and there were more detached houses than heretofore, though in some cases the term 'detached' was more a legal one than a spatial one, given the lack of space between houses. Prices had also continued to rise and purchasers could expect to pay in the range £7,500 to £10,000 and there were opportunities to spend up to £30,000.

For example, B.&R. Builders offered at Taney in Dundrum 'executive type' detached bungalows with varied external finishes and full central heating, four

> **BELGROVE LAWN**
> Chapelizod    Co. Dublin
>
> Belgrove Lawn is not an estate. It is a small development, just beside Chapelizod and on the edge of Phoenix Park, portion of which it overlooks.
>
> These houses, the front of which is coloured bondstone and light dash, are especially atractive.
>
> Oil-fired automatic central heating (central brick unit portway)
>
> ACCOMMODATION (approximate measure):
>
> Ground Floor: Tiled entrance porch.
> Hall: 18' x 8'. Concealed stairs, hanging cloakroom under. Also cloakroom with w.c. and w.h.b., off hall.
> Lounge: 15' x 12'. Diningroom 12' x 10'. Kitchen, 14' x 10' 6". Beautifully fitted with tiled floor and wall presses, all factory made Spot lights over working area.
> First Floor: Hot linen press. Four bedrooms—15' x 11', 12' x 10', 10' 6" x 10', 10' x 8'. Bathroom with coloured combination suite. Walls and floor tiled.
> Outside: Garden front and rere (walled). Drive-in paths, concrete. Garage, 20' x 8' 6". Coal bunker.
>
> **PRICE £6,250**
> Show House completely furnished
>
> Apply:
>
> **P. BYRNE**
> **BUILDER**
> BELGROVE LAWN, CHAPELIZOD
> (Turn opposite West County Hotel)
> Phone 888476

101. Belgrove Lawn. (*Irish Times*, 30 August 1969, p. 14.)

well-proportioned bedrooms, two reception rooms and a fully fitted kitchen from £9,750 (*Irish Times*, 22 November 1968, p. 16). A nearby development by Crosspan offered 'luxurious detached properties' on Ballinteer Road, including two spacious reception rooms, fitted kitchen, ground floor cloakroom, four bedrooms, bathroom, full central heating, garage and car port from £7,975. They claimed that this was still a rural setting but only four miles (6km) from Dublin. If one was prepared to look to the western edge of the city then what was described as a 'cleverly designed' semi-detached four-bedroomed house was available at Belgrove Lawn, Chapelizod, for only £6,550. It was not immediately apparent from the outside view of the houses where the cleverness lay in the design but it seemed to be a selling point. However, large houses were available in all locations and nearby Vesey Park in Lucan had five bedrooms and three reception rooms in a detached dwelling for £10,200. Similarly, Brennan and McGowan offered 'Parkview' in Castleknock from £10,000 for which the purchaser got 'luxury' detached bungalows and houses on a secluded site overlooking the Phoenix Park, but for those with more modest ambitions a 'town house' was available on Terenure Road West for £6,500.

The figures show a dramatic increase in prices over the period. For much of the time buyers were playing catch-up as their income did not regain the

## PORTMARNOCK BY THE SEA

**FRANK DUNNE LTD. • BUILDER • PORTMARNOCK VILLAGE**
### Luxury Ultra-Modern Detached Houses

Four bedrooms, all with fitted wardrobes; oil-fired central heating; large fully-fitted kitchen-cum-breakfastroom; separate diningroom/study; large lounge; bathroom and separate shower room; open tread mahogany staircase; gardens front and rear; carport. PRICE £8,450 Also available in the immediate area—Luxury three-bedroomed houses, £5,500; four-bedroomed houses, £5,750; detached houses, £7,500, and one beautifully appointed existing detached residence, £8,000.   TELEPHONE: SITE OFFICE 350877

102. Portmarnock by the sea. (*Irish Times*, 30 August 1969, p. 14.)

purchasing power which it had before the Second World War. Salary increases were limited in the 1950s to largely 'cost of living' adjustments and this did nothing to encourage people into the market. This was analysed by Nevin (1963) and he determined that largely as a result of wartime statutory controls, 'earnings rose some 14 per cent less than consumer prices between 1938 and 1946, and until the early 1950s the rise in real earnings was doing no more than recover this wartime erosion of real wages. By mid-1962 the real value of industrial earnings was thus some 40 per cent. greater than in 1938, and the annual average increase over the period 1938–62 as a whole was only about 1.4 per cent' (p. 4).

It was only in the 1960s, as increases in salaries exceeded the cost of living increases, that people began to have the confidence to exploit the newly improved credit market and take on significant debts. There is no comprehensive database on salaries, let alone a sense of the purchasing power of salaries, but some indications can be gleaned from what was going on in the civil and public service. In 1961, an increase was granted of between 15 per cent and 18.2 per cent to executive and higher executive officers – middle ranks. The salary for a married executive officer rose to £1,215 per annum while his higher grade counterpart enjoyed an increase to £1,580. It was pointed out that this was not sufficient to restore them to the relative position that they enjoyed in 1939. Clerical officers were paid £815 per annum while a clerk typist, almost invariably female and single, was paid the much lower rate of £494 per annum. By 1966, the married higher executive officer was earning £2,060 while the executive officer was at £1,600 and by September 1969, there had been further increases to £2,385 and £1,870 respectively. These were maximum payments at the top of the scale and for married men only (the age of equal pay is sometime off) but they provide a yardstick against which the house price increases can be measured. They are also useful in that the system of analogues then operating ensured that the level of increase was applied widely in the public service. Private sector salaries are more difficult to pin down but a survey undertaken in 1967 by Associated Industrial Consultants and reported in the *Irish Times* gave some generic figures. They also suggested than increases between 1963 and 1967 needed to be of the order of 35 per cent to maintain purchasing power.

The following year an IMI survey indicated that the majority of executive salaries were under £2,000 per annum and they found that only 100 out of

Table 34. Executive salaries in 1967. Survey relates to salary only and does not include fringe benefits. (*Irish Times*, 23 February 1968, p. 14.)

| Title | Upper Quartile | Median |
|---|---|---|
| Chief Accountant | £2,820 | £2,720 |
| Cost Accountant | £1,966 | £1,700 |
| Works Manager | £2,845 | £2,249 |
| Chief Engineer | £2,800 | £1,923 |
| Production Controller | £2,120 | £1,550 |
| Purchasing Manager | £2,500 | £1,900 |
| Personnel Manager | £2,600 | £1,930 |
| Head of Design / Research | £3,125 | £2,400 |
| Sales Manager | £3,000 | £2,500 |
| General Manager | £2,900 | £2,130 |

the 8,225 who responded earned more than £5,000 per year (*Irish Times*, 31 January 1969, p.1). In September 1969, Guinness sought to hire two experienced management accountants with a salary range of £2,625 to £3,500, the Ulster Museum sought a Director for between £4,045 and £4,620 and a leading Dublin firm wished to hire a public relations executive at £2,500 per annum. Otherwise, female office assistants in the ESB could expect £953 at the top of their scale while the *Irish Times* needed a junior clerk typist (female) at £15 15s. per week.

## *Apartments*

The difference between a 'flat' and an 'apartment' these days can have much more to do with who is inhabiting the dwelling than anything inherent in the building itself. Dublin Corporation had been building flats for rental in the city centre since the early years of the century but there had been no such developments for the middle classes or owner occupiers. Indeed, with the exception of a few small enclaves in the southern part of the inner city (see McManus, 2011), the middle classes had deserted the inner city and were not set to return until the 1990s. Therefore, the building of self-contained flats, they were not yet generally called 'apartments', for the middle classes was a novel phenomenon of the early 1960s, though owner occupancy was to come a little later. This was quite different to the conversion of older houses into multiple occupancy, a process which was well underway in Rathmines, Rathgar and also in Drumcondra.

The first developments were leasehold and perhaps the most impressive was that on the banks of the Grand Canal, near Leeson Street Bridge – the Mespil development. Advertisements appeared in the national newspapers in June 1954 for modern self-contained flats and centrally heated bedsitting rooms available for immediate letting. The development was added to over the years and by 1967, there were eleven flat blocks comprising 256 flats, all managed by Irish Estates Management Ltd. The apartments ranged from single rooms to three bedrooms and they were well appointed with lots of electrical sockets and, by 1967, cable television. Phones were not easy to have installed in 1960s Dublin; it was not unusual for five years to pass between the placing of an order and the installation of the phone. Thus explains why a selling feature was that provision was made in the apartment for the installation of a private telephone. It was up to the renter to work the oracle. The estate was self-contained with its own gardens and was aimed at business and professional people. A three-bedroomed flat would have cost £230 per year plus rates while a two-bedroomed flat was available for £202. There were three one-roomed flat types and these were £172 10s. per annum while the bedsit was at £130. There were additional costs and the tenant had to play electrical charges as well as a 'decoration fee' which varied from £18 to £8. However, there was the offer of two-thirds rates remission for the first five years. Security of tenure was not a feature of these rentals, even for the middle classes and following a one-year tenancy, it was renewable from month to month.

The final phase of this scheme was begun in 1970 with the erection of another six-storey block which contained 36 two-bedroomed flats. This brought the total number of flats in the entire Mespil complex to just under 300.

It was not until the middle 1960s that apartment living was provided with a more dramatic architectural statement. This undoubtedly was influenced by the trend towards high-rise in Ballymun but any comparison would have been short lived. This was Ardoyne House on the edge of Herbert Park, which was completed in 1966 by Albion Securities, at an estimated cost of £350,000, and it managed to combine a secluded location with dramatic and panoramic views over the city; a characteristic it has managed to retain. Over eleven floors were 44 two- and three-bedroomed apartments, two of each per floor, with the twelfth floor occupied by two four-bedroomed penthouse apartments. They were provided with balconies, gas central heating and an extremely high level of finish with brass and mahogany featuring in the fittings. The entrance was designed to be managed by a concierge and very generous parking space was available. But they were not an overwhelming success to begin with. People were not prepared to pay the very high rents that were required, rents which would easily purchase a substantial house elsewhere. Rents which increased with elevation could easily top £1,000 per year and by 1968 only one third of the apartments had been let. This prompted a most unusual phenomenon in property terms, a rent reduction. So, for example, the rent for a two-bedroomed apartment on the ninth floor was reduced from £1,025 to £850 while a three-bedroomed apartment on the third floor, originally on offer for £975, was reduced to £825; but in all cases there was an additional service charge which varied from apartment to apartment but was around 2 per cent of rental (*Irish Times*, 11 June 1968, p. 12). By any measure these were expensive and they sought to place apartment living at the very acme of residential options.

Ardoyne House did not spark a trend towards high-rise living, despite the qualities of the particular build. The middle classes saw no particular need or

**103.** The Mespil complex in the early 1970s. (Ordnance Survey plan, 1:1000, Sheet 3264–16, 3264–21, 1973.)

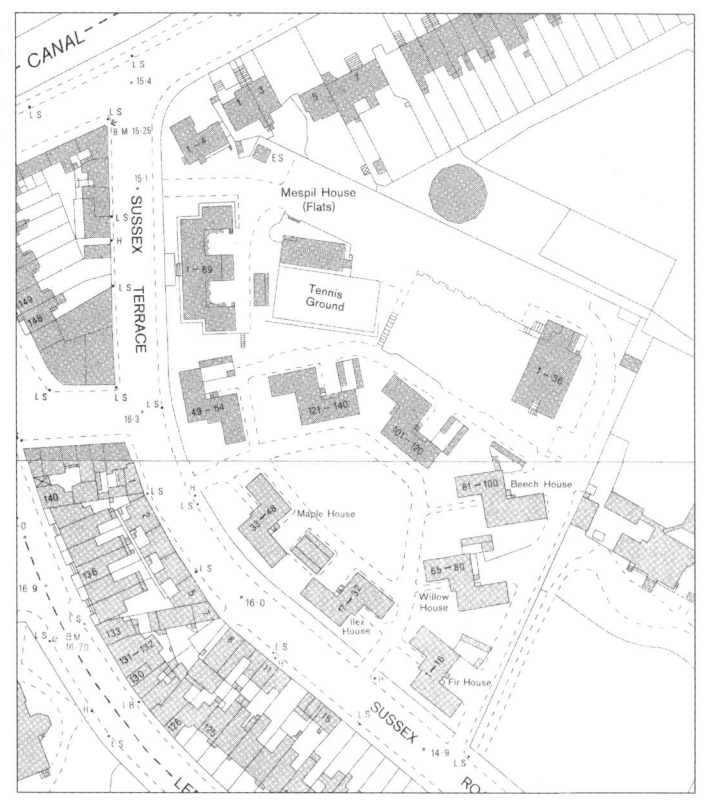

**104.** The Mespil apartments.

**105.** Ardoyne House on the edge of Herbert Park.
(Ordnance Survey plan, 1:1000, Sheet 3264–22, 1973.)

**106.** A view of Ardoyne House from Herbert Park.

value in living high off the ground. Rather more typical would be a complex such as that built at St Kevin's Court in Dartry in 1966. They might have been smaller than Ardoyne House, only three storeys, but the emphasis on luxury living was still important as this description from an *Irish Times* feature demonstrates:

> The young couple sit at a table on the balcony sipping their drinks. In the distance the blue mountains look inviting to the energetic. But in the foreground their attention is drawn to the two couples bashing a tennis ball on the green lawn courts below. A young man in sweater and slacks sprawls in a deck chair beside the courts; he waves to the couple on the balcony and then gets back to his book. It looks cool down there in the shade of the trees.
>
> It might be a holiday apartment block on the Costa del Sol. But if the sun shines hot enough in the next few months it might well be a new block of luxury flats in South Dublin, St Kevin's Court – a new luxury development which opened this week – has all the amenities described in the opening paragraph.
>
> (*Irish Times*, 6 April 1966, p. 6)

This was a small development of only six flats, two of which were three-bedroomed and the remainder had two bedrooms. They offered a high level of finish and design with built-in units and hardwood floors in an open-plan design. On a slightly larger scale but in a similar vein was a 1967 Donnybrook development. Brendan House was a three storey block facing onto Brendan Road with generous parking provision to the rear and individual garages. The complex comprised twelve two-bedroomed flats with gas fired warm air heating. The reason for keeping it to three storeys was that the developer did not want to install a lift and in this he was keeping to the belief, shared by Dublin Corporation, that people had no difficulty climbing three flights of stairs. It was not anticipated that these flats would appeal to people who had children but it is unclear what the elderly were supposed to do. St Kevin's Court did offer an intercom system so that residents could avoid 'one of the occupational hazards of flat dwellers' of having to run down three flights of stairs to answer the door.

It was not until the 1970s that flats or apartment building took off in the city and then only in the already successful residential areas and still at a modest scale. Greenmount Lawns, which was under construction in 1969, was one of the first to offer apartments for sale. Located in Rathgar, off

**107.** Brendan House on St Brendan's Road.

**108.** Apartments at St John's Court, Sandymount.

Greenmount Road, the developer offered what he described as maisonettes on two floors over a self-contained ground floor flat, rather similar to what the Corporation was building. There were three blocks with twenty-seven units. The potential buyer was invited to come and see this 'ultra-modern' and, of course, luxurious development which offered three bedrooms, a lounge with dining area and fitted kitchen while the ground floor flat consisted of one bedroom, lounge, kitchen and bathroom. The price at £9,250 (extra for corner sites) was for both a maisonette and apartment, though each was entirely separate, on the principle that the buyer could use one and rent the other. Not only was this a 'convenient, desirable and central location' but the developer offered two additional selling points. The first was that all services were underground but the second was that a phone was guaranteed. Thus was eliminated what the *Irish Times* referred to as 'obnoxious marks of the modern estate and which would have not have fitted in with the luxury of Greenmount' (*Irish Times*, 22 November 1969, p. 16). Another early example of owner occupancy was the Brennan and McGowan development on Eglinton Road in Donnybrook. 'Ballinguile' offered two- or three-bedroomed unfurnished but centrally heated flats for £6,850 in 1969 while twelve two-bedroomed units at St John's Court, on the junction with Park Avenue in Sandymount, were offered in 1970 at a price of £7,000. While the concept of owner occupancy had been accepted there were still major obstacles to the expansion of owner-occupied blocks. The first was that there was a marked reluctance on the part of institutional lenders to offer mortgages to those who wished to purchase an apartment (*Irish Times*, 31 January 1975, p. 25), which was not easily solved. The second, and related, problem was that it was difficult for flat owners to get property insurance. A later hiccup in the spread of the concept was a requirement that all new housing be provided with at least one fireplace or other solid fuel system if it was to be eligible for a grant (*Irish Times*, 17 May 1974, p. 23). While this was a sensible response to the first oil crisis of 1973, which exposed the difficulties of electrical heating, it posed significant problems for developers who had not factored in the cost of such provision into their plans.

The plan below shows that in the 1960s, the locations of these developments were mainly in the south-eastern inner suburbs with very few in Dún Laoghaire. Convenience was the selling point with the belief that these would appeal to people who valued the central location over the absence of a large garden. There were only 73 apartments started in 1970, rising to a high of 786 starts in 1979.

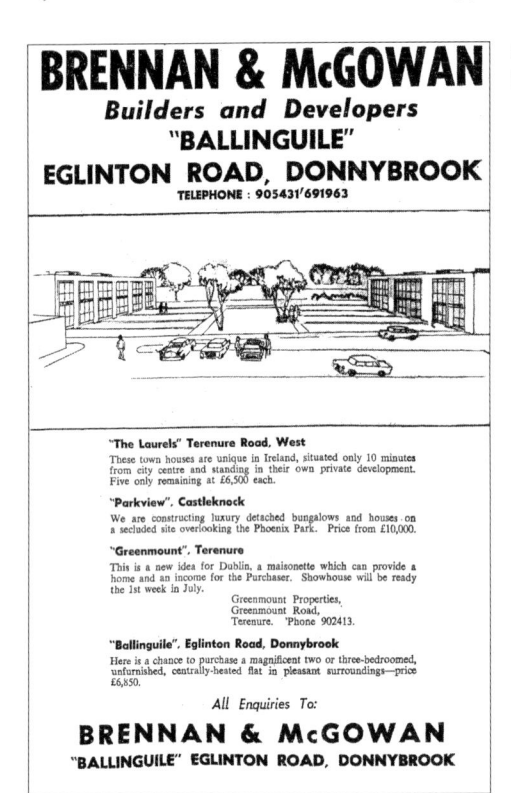

109. Advertisement for Ballinguile. (*Irish Times*, 29 May 1969.)

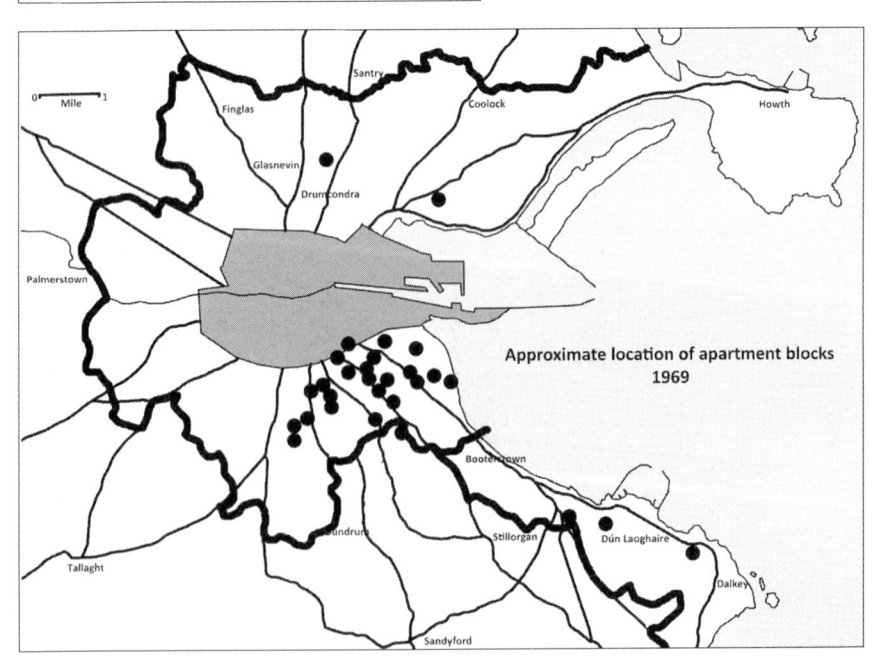

110. Approximate location of apartment schemes in 1969.

# A new concept in living for the '70s...

Greenmount Properties invite you to come and see this ultra modern development in Rathgar, only 20 minutes from the city centre. A gas-fired centrally-heated maisonette on two floors over a self-contained ground floor flat. The maisonette consists of three generous bedrooms, a large lounge with dining area, completely fitted kitchen and large bathroom. The ground floor flat consists of one bedroom, lounge, kitchen and bathroom. The construction is the most modern, with load-bearing cross walls, well insulated roof and cavity brick-faced external walls. Price £9,250 (extra for corner sites), substantial mortgages available. Showhouse on view today 11.30 a.m.-5.30 p.m. and Sunday, 11.30 a.m.-5.00 p.m.

Sole agents—Peter White, M.A., Estate Agents, 29 South Anne St., Dublin. Telephone 776544/3.

111. A new concept in apartment living. (*Irish Times*, 22 November 1969, p. 16.)

112. Apartments in Greenmount Lawns.

## Individual housing schemes

*Greenhills Estate*

One the first large scale private developments of 1950s bears out many of the points made above. Greenhills Estates was built around Cromwellsfort Road, close to Walkinstown but in the County Council area, in the early 1950s. The selling point for the development in 1954 was that they might be at the lower end of the market but they offered features that were usually only found in the more expensive houses. As they put it 'while costing no more than the average purchaser can afford [the houses] incorporates features which have hitherto been confined to the more exclusive type of dwelling. This is the first time that central heating, combined with insulation, has been attempted in this type of house in this country' (*Irish Times*, 15 February 1954, p. 3).

At an official opening of a further development in February 1955 (*Irish Times*, 9 February 1955, p. 4), it was reported that it was intended to provide 1,180 houses on a 110 acre (45ha) site with 11 acres (4.5ha) devoted to amenity use. This was a further manifestation of a growing trend towards larger estates in the private sector, catching up on what was well developed practice in the social housing sector. Now referred to as 'subsidy type' houses, these cost £1,770 and were built by Messrs M.D. and J.G. O'Callaghan.

Unusually for private houses, these were built in terraces of four and externally they were of fairly standard design. They were provided with outbuildings and gardens front and rear. The basic cost was £2,045 for a mid-terrace house and £2,095 for an end-terrace one. What reduced them to £1,770 was the availability of the State grant of £275 and purchasers could qualify for SDAA loans as well as supplementary grants. A deposit of between £160 was required with a ground rent of £10 per year. These houses ticked many of the boxes required to ensure sales at the time.

They did try to be different though inside and to offer something new on the housing market. It was not just the central heating and the insulation that made them different. The builders also focused on the provision of high quality parquet wood floors, removing the need for carpets, and the use of open-plan downstairs. This meant that kitchen and dining room area, though separate spaces, were integrated into a single room. The house was provided with built-in units in both kitchen and bedrooms and was supplied wallpapered. The central heating system was a solid fuel system with a back boiler and, combined with the insulation, was designed to heat the house efficiently to about 21°C in the dining room and about 16°C in the

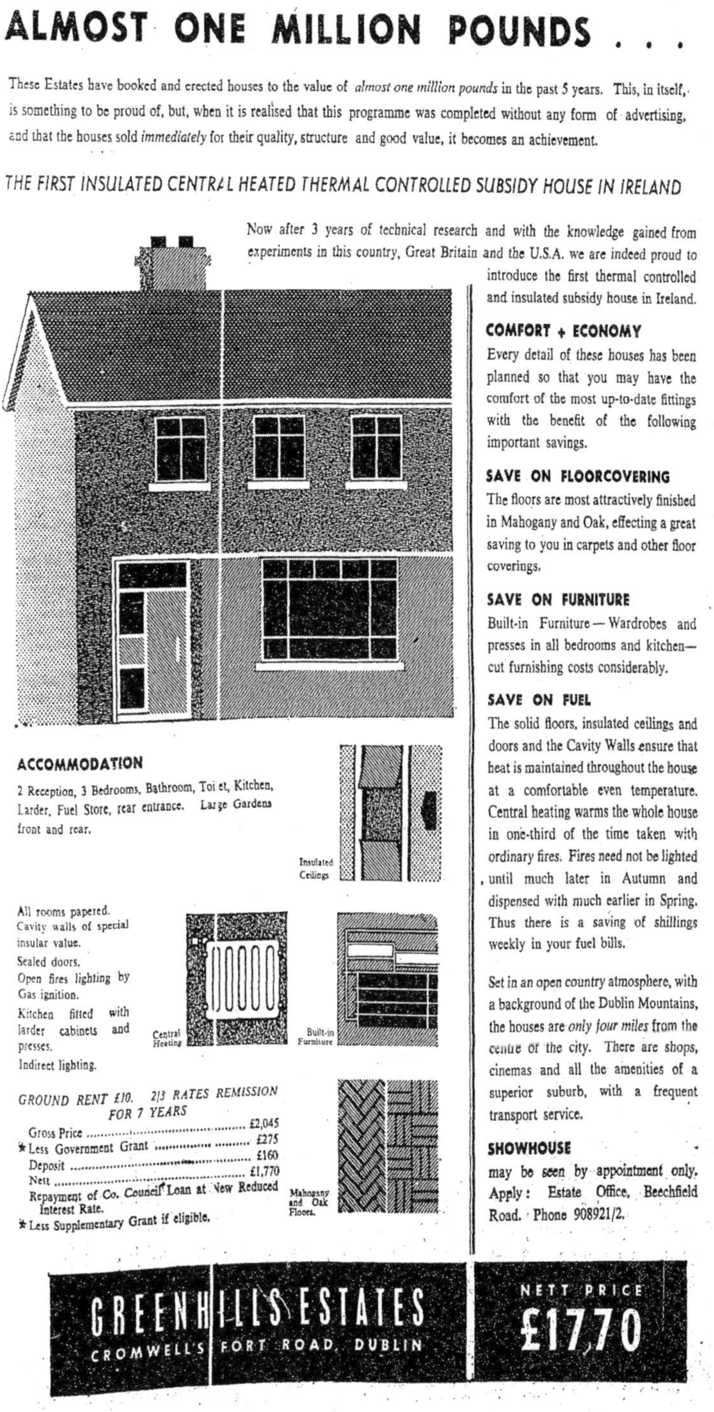

# ALMOST ONE MILLION POUNDS . . .

These Estates have booked and erected houses to the value of *almost one million pounds* in the past 5 years. This, in itself, is something to be proud of, but, when it is realised that this programme was completed without any form of advertising, and that the houses sold *immediately* for their quality, structure and good value, it becomes an achievement.

## THE FIRST INSULATED CENTRAL HEATED THERMAL CONTROLLED SUBSIDY HOUSE IN IRELAND

Now after 3 years of technical research and with the knowledge gained from experiments in this country, Great Britain and the U.S.A. we are indeed proud to introduce the first thermal controlled and insulated subsidy house in Ireland.

### COMFORT + ECONOMY

Every detail of these houses has been planned so that you may have the comfort of the most up-to-date fittings with the benefit of the following important savings.

### SAVE ON FLOORCOVERING

The floors are most attractively finished in Mahogany and Oak, effecting a great saving to you in carpets and other floor coverings.

### SAVE ON FURNITURE

Built-in Furniture — Wardrobes and presses in all bedrooms and kitchen — cut furnishing costs considerably.

### SAVE ON FUEL

The solid floors, insulated ceilings and doors and the Cavity Walls ensure that heat is maintained throughout the house at a comfortable even temperature. Central heating warms the whole house in one-third of the time taken with ordinary fires. Fires need not be lighted until much later in Autumn and dispensed with much earlier in Spring. Thus there is a saving of shillings weekly in your fuel bills.

Set in an open country atmosphere, with a background of the Dublin Mountains, the houses are *only four miles* from the centre of the city. There are shops, cinemas and all the amenities of a superior suburb, with a frequent transport service.

### SHOWHOUSE

may be seen by appointment only. Apply : Estate Office, Beechfield Road. Phone 908921/2.

**ACCOMMODATION**

2 Reception, 3 Bedrooms, Bathroom, Toilet, Kitchen, Larder, Fuel Store, rear entrance. Large Gardens front and rear.

All rooms papered.
Cavity walls of special insular value.
Sealed doors.
Open fires lighting by Gas ignition.
Kitchen fitted with larder cabinets and presses.
Indirect lighting.

GROUND RENT £10.   2/3 RATES REMISSION FOR 7 YEARS

| | |
|---|---|
| Gross Price | £2,045 |
| *Less Government Grant | £275 |
| Deposit | £160 |
| Nett | £1,770 |

Repayment of Co. Council Loan at New Reduced Interest Rate.
*Less Supplementary Grant if eligible.

**GREENHILLS ESTATES**
CROMWELL'S FORT ROAD, DUBLIN

**NETT PRICE £1,770**

113. Advertisement for Greenhills Estate. (*Irish Times*, 15 February 1954, p. 4.)

## LAUREL PARK ESTATE
## CLONDALKIN

Soundly built, centrally heated with convector heating unit, semi-detached houses. Situated just off the DUBLIN - NAAS ROAD. Nos. 51, 68, 83 Buses pass the door. 20 minutes from City centre. Convenient to churches, schools.

Accommodation—Two large reception cloakroom, lounge hall, large kitchen, fully fitted with built-in refrigerator, presses, three bedrooms with built-in wardrobes, fitted bathroom with hot towel rail; garage, fuel house and outside w.c.

SHOW HOUSE ON VIEW DAILY
AT BRIDES PARK ESTATE

### PRICE £1,800 NET. £100 DEPOSIT TO APPROVED CLIENTS
GROUND RENT £12-10-0

**P. LOUGHNANE, Builder,** Phone Clondalkin 342058

114. The home of your dreams. (*Irish Independent*, 6 February 1954, p. 15.)

115. An aerial view of the Laurel Park, Clondalkin, development. Note the standard building line. The rear gardens of *c.*12m were in line with what had been proposed as minimum by the draft development scheme of 1957.

bedrooms, though interestingly the inhabitant of the small bedroom had to put up with an electric fire for heating. These were three-bedroomed houses with two reception rooms, bathroom, kitchen, larder. The room sizes were in the middle range but as the *Irish Times* put it: 'from the point of view of the purchaser the builders claim that the house is a good proposition, compared with the normal type subsidy dwelling, as there is a substantial savings on items such as carpets, side board, wardrobes, and kitchen furniture and equipment as well as in fuel costs' (*Irish Times*, 15 February 1954, p. 3). All this and a house which was 'set in an open country atmosphere, with a background of the Dublin Mountains, the houses are only four miles (6km) from the centre of the city. There are shops, cinemas and all the amenities of a superior suburb, with a frequent transport service'.

Not far away in Clondalkin, the Laurel Park development was offering semi-detached houses for similar prices. These were described as the 'home of your dreams for £2 per week' (*Irish Independent*, 12 March 1954, p. 2). With three bus services, the builders claimed that the city centre could be reached in 20 minutes, something which was probably still possible at the time of development. It was said that no matter where you wanted to go the extra distance was negligible. It was close to shops, schools and churches. The price was £1,800 net (£2,075 without subsidy) but the suburban location allowed for a substantial house which offered in addition to three bedrooms, two reception rooms with cloakroom, large fully fitted kitchen with fridge, a fully fitted bathroom, with the height of luxury – a heated towel rail – a garage, outside wc and fuel house. It was centrally heated too by means of a convection system. At the time of this particular advertising campaign in 1954, it was claimed that 200 units had been already sold.

*Monastery Park*
Monastery Park, a neighbour to Laurel Park in Clondalkin, was a later 300 house development at a distance of about six miles (10km) from the city centre and one that capitalized on the improved building environment to come on the market in 1962. Like the earlier Greenhills development, there was an emphasis on being different and here the theme was American with small defensible front gardens replaced by open lawns. The houses were three-bedroomed in three different designs. The Colonial design was a quasi-bungalow, semi-detached, in that most of the space was on the ground floor with the master bedroom and bathroom on the upper floor. The other two bedrooms were part of the ground floor arrangement and it was emphasized

**116.** Advertisement for Monastery Park. (*Irish Times*, 1 March 1963, p. 6.)

that this gave greatest flexibility in terms of use as family needs changed. The laundry room was separate from the kitchen and the living room was an open-plan room with a dining area at one end. The house was not particular big but there was an emphasis on saving space by not having a large hall or entrance lobby. Central heating, although more common in private housing at this time, was only an optional feature in this design. For an extra £150, they offered underfloor electric heating in the communal rooms and convector heating in the bedrooms. This would prove to be an expensive choice later on.

> Externally the Colonial is an attractive house, its unusual roof, large windows, coloured panels and Tyrolean rendering combining well, produce an elevation which is normally found only in individually built homes. The front garden is turfed and Tarmacadam drive is laid. This is a feature which will apply to all the homes at Monastery Park. At the price of £2,300 nett the Colonial offers ample accommodation for medium sized families and certainly has far more in the way of fittings and equipment than many other houses in this price range.
> 
> (*Irish Times*, 17 August 1962, p. 4)

Thus the emphasis was on convincing the buyer than an estate house was not an estate house and that it offered more despite being rather small. At £2,300 it

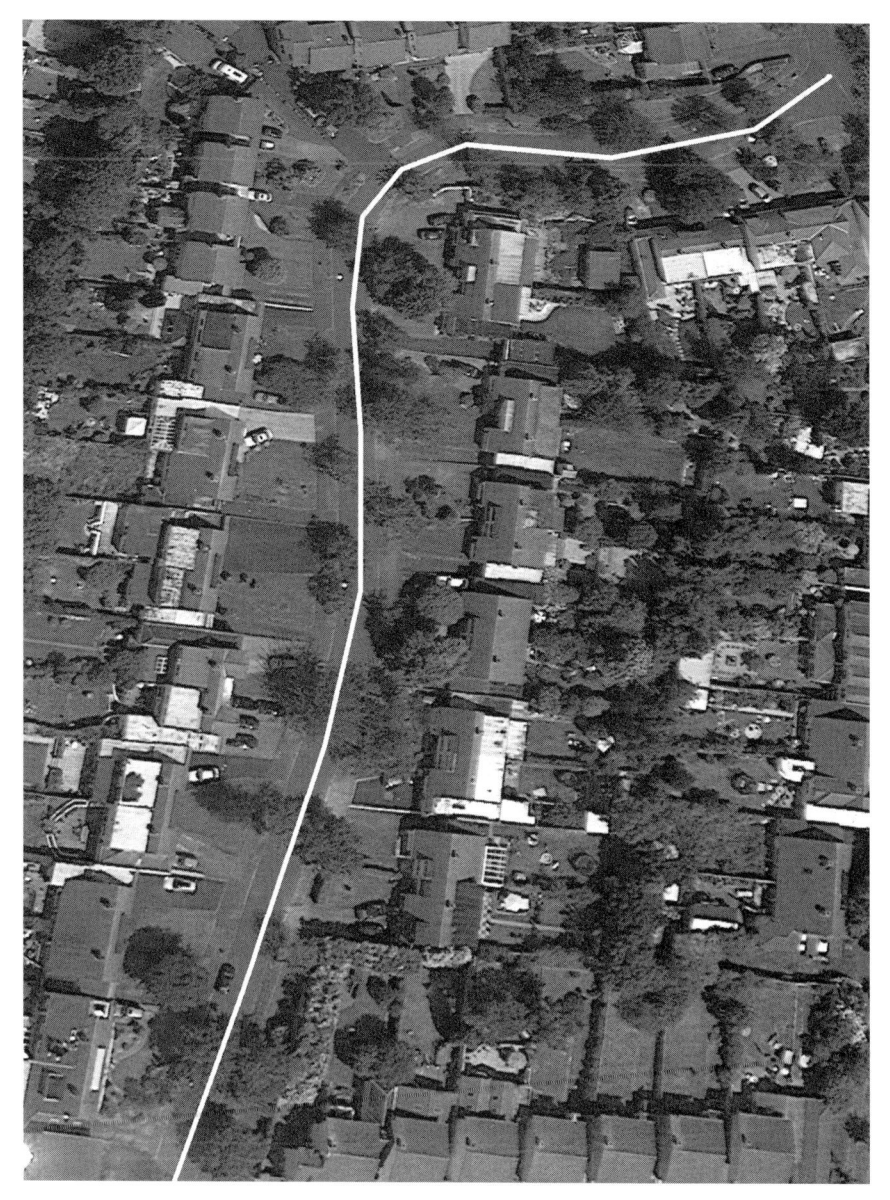

117. An aerial view of the mature landscape at Monastery Park. Note the relatively large amount of garden space, which is still maintained in open style at the front.

was competitively priced and purchasers could also be eligible for SDAA loans. Its companion house, the Beverley, was also semi-detached but dearer and larger and more conventional in design with a standard hallway and stairs leading to the bedrooms upstairs. This had central heating built in and the living space downstairs was divided into sitting and dining room cum kitchen by sliding doors. 'The large lounge, which faces the front of the house is separated from the dining room by glazed doors which can be thrown open to provide a room of enormous size when entertaining. The dining room and kitchen are of open-plan style and conveniently separated by units which form a useful breakfast bar. Additional storage units and a sink unit are standard equipment.' This cost £2,825 net and both houses needed a deposit of just £100.

The electric central heating system was promoted by the ESB on the basis that it was clean, quick and fully automatic and, at the time, cheap to run. Part of the modern look to these houses was the furnishing of the showhouses with A-Line furniture, very 1960s and appealing to the young or young at heart. This was wood veneer rather than wood and was designed never to chip, fade or crack as well as being resistant to cigarette burns.

The developers were testing the market and at the launch of the scheme, they had plans for a four-bedroomed house, the Montreal, but they did not build any initially, concentrating their efforts on the three-bedroomed house and covering as much of the market as they felt was reasonable – those within and without the subsidy range. The developers, Merit Homes (and note the UK connections of their selling agents), did well with the development and they were still selling them in 1963. By this time they had decided that central heating would now be standard in all the houses and the price was now advertised at £2,450. The Beverley was still on sale at £2,825 and they had introduced the Queen design, a detached three-bedroomed house at £2,625, and they had decided to go ahead with the Montreal, a four-bedroomed detached house at £3,300. All the houses made space for cars but in the form of a car port rather than a garage.

*Yellow Walls*
The American theme was continued in another suburban development, which was opened in May 1963. This was at the unusually named Yellow Walls development in Malahide where 100 houses were built in what was called 'ranch style' but could be just as easily referred to as a bungalow. These were large detached houses on a considerable footprint. These were centrally heated throughout initially by a warm air system but many houses had converted to oil fired central heating by the late 1960s. There was a wide hall, large lounge, four bedrooms, toilet, shower room and a kitchen with built-in units. As might be expected, there was a garage. The location was a selling point, only five minutes from the sea, and this was reflected in the asking price of £4,750,

though there were plans at the time to build three-bedroomed versions of the same house for £3,500. The area was the subject of a compulsory purchase order in 1965 when the County Council sought sites for 70 houses in the vicinity. This was contested by local farmers who claimed that as small holders they needed the land for their living. It was also contested by the local residents who did not wish to have council houses nearby. The Council argued that 70 houses were badly needed in the area and there was a problem getting suitable sites. It was back in 1961 when they had last built in Malahide and at that time they still left 40 families without suitable housing. The chair of the Housing Committee wondered if the opposition of some of the local residents might be overcome if the Council built an attractive scheme that was pleasantly laid out (*Irish Times*, 23 February 1965, p. 9). On this occasion the Minister for Local Government, Mr Blaney, refused permission to the Council but they returned to the matter and by 1969 they had received sanction and loan approval for 60 houses and 6 flats at an estimate cost of £190,000 (Dáil Debates, 238(10), col. 1459).

*Dundrum*

In 1967, one of the developments on offer on the southside was Dun Emer where over 120 semi-detached houses were under construction (see the advertisement earlier in this chapter). It was on the Sandyford Road, not far from Dundrum village where two major shopping developments were in prospect at the time. It was sold by Paramount Homesteads with no particular locational feature emphasized in their sales material. The estate was also 4 miles (6.5km) from the centre of Dublin and close to Dundrum but there were no references, as there would have been in a previous generation, to healthy air or good views. Instead it was described as a pleasant development. The houses were four-bedroomed with front and back (though small) gardens. There was a garage and the gardens were walled front and rear. Indoors, the developers followed the fashion for open-plan and there was no distinction between living and cooking spaces. Upstairs were the four bedrooms and bathroom. The bathroom featured tilings but only half way up the walls. A sign of the times was that they advertised that each bedroom had one electric socket. This house would have cost £4,400 net at the time. A smaller development, this time of twenty houses, was being built at Arnold Park, off Avondale Road in Killiney. Though further from the city, it had the advantage of being both close to Killiney and Dún Laoghaire. This development too comprised semi-detached housing but offered the additional advantage of a four acre (1.6ha) public open space behind which was unlikely to be built upon. Once again, while there was a hall provided and a cloakroom, the living space ran the length of the house. The kitchen was separate, with plastic covered 'easy clean floors' and wall units. It was suggested that it could be used as a dining space. The bedrooms and bathroom were upstairs, with a telephone box shower unit. What was interesting in a house of this price was that, while the house was delivered with wallpaper, the walls in the toilet, kitchen and bathroom were only distempered. It would have been usual to have at least some tiling as in Dun Emer. This had been a feature of middle-class housing since the 1930s and this would have been somewhat disappointing in a house costing £4,350.

*Offington Park*
Offington Park in Sutton was a high status development of detached dormer bungalows in Sutton. This was quite a suburban location on the Howth peninsula and in this case the developer emphasized the panoramic views of Howth Head and the sea. The four-bedroomed houses were on a large footprint giving a very large front garden. The design provided for a lounge cum dining area and a separate kitchen which was described as 'fully fitted'. The bathroom was tiled throughout and there were two toilets provided. These extra features and the location pushed the price up to £6,650 or 50 per cent more than the houses in Dun Emer.

*The Laurels, Terenure Road*
The concept of a 'town house' took on a new meaning in the late 1960s. Heretofore, the wealthy might have spoken about their town house as a base in the town away from their country pile. In 1968, Brennan and McGowan developed an 'in-town' development by which they meant a relatively high density, for the time, private housing development. The two storey houses, arranged in blocks of six, had three bedrooms, an L-shaped living room, described as 'spacious', and an 'airy' kitchen cum breakfast room, but they were also described as 'compact' though at a reasonable price in 1968 of £5,500 for housing in Terenure. The scheme on Terenure Road West, near the Presentation Convent, was in a desirable location and reasonably central. While the buildings themselves have a block look, the selling points focused on the quality of the interior – the French door leading to the garden, the gas fired warm air central heating, the kitchen units and the number of power points in the main bedroom. It was a development which had not quite grasped the potential of the town-house concept because not only was space

118. Dublin's most exclusive site at Offington Park. (*Irish Times*, 21 June 1967.)

**Offington Park, Sutton**

DORMER TYPE HOUSE

**DUBLIN'S MOST EXCLUSIVE SITE**

Situated with Panoramic Views of Howth Hill and Sea—Detached Luxury Bungalows on exceptionally large sites

SHOW HOUSE
Furnished by Lees
on view
Sat. 3 to 6 p.m.
Sun. 3 to 6 p.m.

- Fully centrally heated
- Loans arranged
- PRICE: £6,650 nett

**ACCOMMODATION**
This consists of:
SPACIOUS LOUNGE HALL
CLOAKROOM
LARGE LOUNGE WITH DINING ANNEXE
LARGE FULLY FITTED MODERN KITCHEN
TILED BATHROOM AND W.C.
4 BEDROOMS
SECOND W.C., ETC.

Builders: **GOUGH BROTHERS LTD.**
PHONE 322250

**PATRICK J. O'DWYER & CO.**
M.I.A.A., Auctioneers, Valuers and Estate Agents,
1 Clare Street, Dublin 2    Phone 66719, 63415

wasted in providing parking but gardens of 40ft x 20ft (12m x 6m) were provided in the front and 60ft x 20ft in the back (18m x 6m); details may be read in the *Irish Times*, 23 March 1968, p. 8. More houses could easily have been fitted onto the site without diminishing the concept. It was seen to be particularly attractive to young married couples as a starter home or to middle aged and elderly people who wanted a house with a minimum of demands.

*Shrewsbury Lawn, Cabinteely*
The final examples in this section are also taken from the southside but at the higher end of the market and closer to the then edge of the city. What is interesting about the Shrewsbury Lawn development was the attempt to avoid

**119.** Advertisement for Shrewsbury Lawn. (*Irish Times*, 24 December 1969.)

an 'estate look' by varying the design of the houses, rather as Mount Merrion had done in an earlier generation though on a much grander scale. Shrewsbury Lawn in Cabinteely was a fifteen acre site (6ha) on which it was intended to build fifty-six houses. Each was promised to be to a different design, thus escaping any suggestion of an estate and the environment of the development was enhanced by the retention of many of the trees on the site. The variations in design was done by modifying particular components within the framework of four basic designs and also by varying the amount of garden space. Garden space could be tailored to the demands of the purchaser so that those who saw a vast expanse of lawn as a chore could have a much smaller plot. Internally, the houses were in the American style with as few permanent partitions as possible and open-tread stairs to give even more sense of space. The houses were heated by a hot air system, with individual room controls, which could be fired either by a gas or oil fed boiler, but most houses were also given a functioning fireplace in the main space. These were big houses with four or five bedrooms and two bathrooms (a most unusual feature). The American theme was continued in the large amount of built-in furniture. While emphasizing the environmental quality of the suburban location, the developers claimed that the city centre could be reached in fifteen minutes. Hopefully, the remainder of their claims were not as dubious as this, as fifteen minutes would have, even then, been possible only if there was no other traffic on the road and all the traffic lights were set at green. This kind of exclusivity did not come cheap and the purchaser could have expected to pay between £9,250 and £11,000 – expensive, but similarly priced to other perhaps less distinctive developments.

### Shanganagh Vale

Shanganagh Vale, in Loughlinstown (later to become Cabinteely), was another development by Merit Homes and aimed at the upper end of the market also. In 1963, they offered two-storey four-bedroomed houses with a high level of specification. They were two types, the Vancouver and the Virginian.

The Vancouver was described as follows:

- a large and lavishly equipped four-bedoom home with a lounge that has a handsome log-burning fireplace, Parana pine panelling and a magnificent open stairway
- de-luxe kitchen and separate launderette
- separate dining area
- built in wardrobes in all bedrooms
- built in vanitory unit in guest bedroom
- built in dressing table in master bedroom
- part tiled fully equipped bathroom
- full comfort Caltex oil fired central heating
- entrance lobby with pram space.

This was a small development and a sense of exclusivity was emphasized by not building along the main roadway and ensuring that all houses were well set back from it. Much was also made of the association with Brown Thomas who had furnished the showhouse, with this being mentioned three times in the feature that appeared in the *Irish Times*. The Vancouver was priced at £5,150 net but loans of up to 95 per cent were available. For those on more modest budgets, the Virginian was available for £4,550 (*Irish Times*, 9 November 1963, p. 18). A bungalow development, described as long, low and lovely, was offered in 1964 and was more interesting in that they claimed it was designed on the Radburn system. This had long been seen as one of the gold standards in residential design in that it offered completely separate circulation systems for pedestrians and cars.

The system was developed in Radburn, New Jersey. It was originally intended to be a new town of 30,000 people but the economic depression post-1929 pushed its builder, City Housing Corporation, into bankruptcy and ended that possibility. It is currently a settlement with a population of about 3,000 people with a footprint of 149 acres (60ha) and which includes 430 single family homes, 90 terraced houses, 54 semi-detached houses and a 93-apartment unit, as well as a shopping centre, parks and amenities.

# THE Vancouver

## FURNISHED SHOWHOUSE AT SHANGANAGH VALE, LOUGHLINSTOWN CO. DUBLIN

A large and lavishly equipped 4-bedroom home with a lounge that has a handsome log-burning fireplace. Parana pine panelling and a magnificent open stairway.

Vancouver value—De-luxe kitchen and separate launderette
Vancouver value—Separate dining area
Vancouver value—Built in wardrobes in all bedrooms
Vancouver value—Built in vanitory unit in guest bedroom
Vancouver value—Built in dressing table in master bedroom
Vancouver value—Part tiled fully equipped bathroom
Vancouver value—Full comfort "Caltex" oil fired central heating
Vancouver value—Entrance lobby with pram space
Vancouver value—Sliding windows suitable for double glazing
Vancouver value—Two garages
Vancouver value—Landscaped front garden

Price £5,150 nett, leasehold 600 years. Ground rent £20 p.a.

THE VANCOUVER SHOWHOME furnished by Brown, Thomas and Co., Ltd., of Dublin, is open on Sundays between 11 a.m. and 9 p.m. and on every other day except Tuesday between 2 p.m. and 9 p.m. at Shanganagh Vale on the main Bray Road, 8 miles south-east of Dublin.

WHILE YOU ARE THERE ASK ABOUT THE VIRGINIAN

Another top value 4 bedroom luxury home at £4,550 nett. Ground Rent £18 per annum.

**95% MORTGAGES AVAILABLE**

120. Distinctive houses at Shanganagh Vale. (*Irish Times*, 9 November 1963, p. 18.)

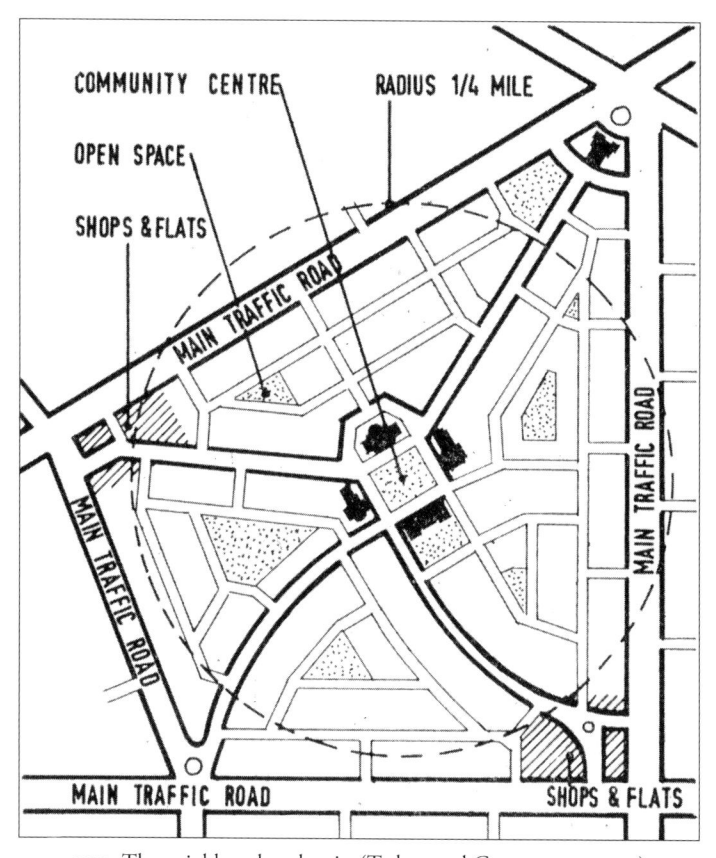

121. The neighbourhood unit. (Tetlow and Goss, 1970, p. 40.)

However, the concepts which were employed in the small community that was built resonated widely and influenced many planning schemes far away from New Jersey. Designed by its planners Clarence Stein and Henry Wright, and its landscape architect Marjorie Sewell Cautley, it drew on some of the Garden City ideas of Ebenezer Howard and especially those of his followers such as Patrick Geddes (no stranger to Dublin) as well as on the neighbourhood unit idea of Charles Perry. The latter had developed the idea of providing services within each neighbourhood in such a manner that they were easily accessible from all parts of the neighbourhood. Schools and churches were located centrally with internal streets designed only for local traffic. Radburn's creators claimed to have adapted Howard's ideas to the motor age (indeed it was called 'a town for the motor age') by building a settlement in which pedestrians and motor traffic never interacted at the same level. There was a nested hierarchy of roads whereby traffic was gradually funnelled towards its destination, keeping through traffic to an absolute minimum. In bringing this to its logical conclusion, houses were arranged in culs de sac. This aspect of Radburn, the idea of a hierarchy of road systems has been widely used. The associated but separate system of pedestrian access has not been as widely used, Cumbernauld new town in Scotland being perhaps one of the best examples. Designated in 1955, it had reached a population of about 34,000 in 1971 out of a target population of 70,000.

The principle was that there were pathways for pedestrians throughout the neighbourhood, which allowed them to interact and conduct their business without the need to engage with motor traffic. Where the pedestrian route interacted with the motor roads, this was dealt with by overpasses or underpasses. In keeping with the garden city concept, a high standard of landscape design was incorporated into the development. It is interesting that the Shanganagh Vale development should explicitly make reference to Radburn. The concept would not have been particularly well known outside the planning and architectural community. It had been part of the building manuals in the UK since the early 1950s (see following chapter) but this seems to be its first use in Dublin as a marketing tool, perhaps reflecting Merit Homes' UK connections. Shanganagh Vale was 'Radburn like' in that it provided separate circulation systems in a great deal of open and managed landscape space. However, in scale it came nowhere near the original concept of an entire community organized on this basis. While the concept had its many advocates, there were others who pointed out that the more secluded pedestrian routes, especially underpasses, were more vulnerable to anti-social behaviour than routes which passed along busy traffic roads.

Naturally, the Shanganagh Vale development mentioned 'luxury' as being an important design concern. In fact 'at every turn the brilliant design features show themselves, impressive dimensions give an air of grandeur, lavish fittings spell luxury and powerful oil fired central heating wraps every room in cosy warmth' (*Irish Times*, 23 July 1964, p. 19). The twenty-four houses (though this was added to later) in the initial 1964 launch were four-bedroomed bungalows and came in two designs, each with its own name – the Palma and the Caribbean. Each house came with oil fired central heating, built-in units, and a fully fitted kitchen; naturally, the living area was open-plan (24ft x 14ft) with a separate 'dinette'. In addition, there was a patio area for barbecues but privacy was assured by the provision of 6ft-high (1.8m) walls around each house and the fact that the footprint of each house was one third of an acre. At a distance of eight miles (13km) from the city and some distance from

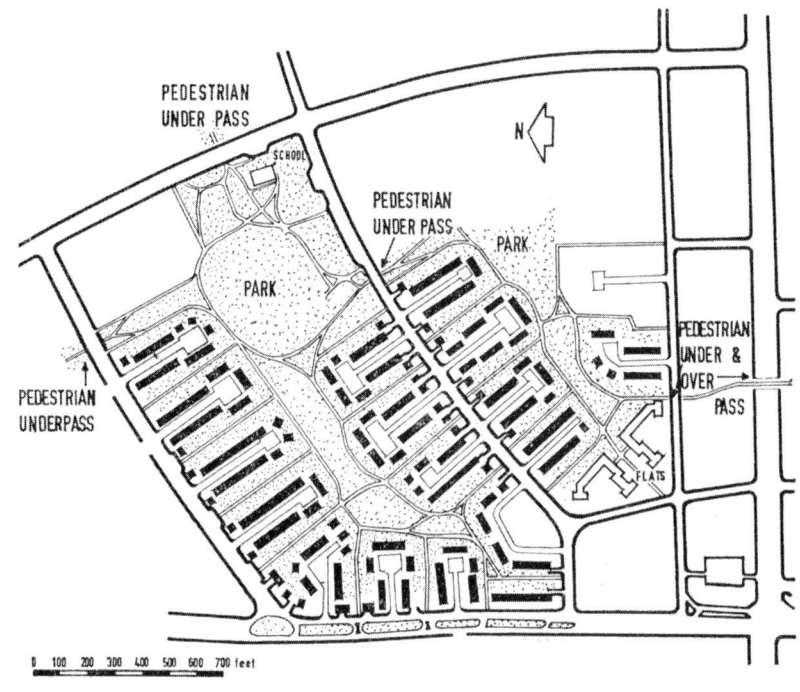

**122.** The layout of Radburn. (Tetlow and Goss, 1970, p. 42.)

**123.** The layout of Shanganagh Vale. (Google maps.)

schools and local shops, the assumption was that this was a car-owning community and the garage was built to accommodate two cars. A high standard of landscaping was provided and the development blended into the open countryside nearby. No prices were mentioned in the first advertisements, doubtless on the assumption that mere money would not stop discerning purchasers (described as 'top people') but by early 1965 it was revealed that luxury did not come cheap and they were available from £7,750 (*Irish Times*, 29 January 1965, p. 15).

*Bayside, Sutton*
Though most distinctive development was on the south side of the city, it was not exclusively so. One northside development which sought to capitalize on its coastal location was Bayside. Despite the great sweep of the bay, there were few locations close to the coast that were chosen for development until the city had moved out and absorbed the St Anne's Estate. Bayside, where 'there's room to live', was also interesting because it too claimed to be built on Radburn lines. It was intended to be much bigger than the Cabinteely project and with 800 houses planned it had the capacity to be a 'true' Radburn. The first 100 houses were not completed until 1968 but the project had been under development since 1963 as planning permission had proved difficult. The developers promised that cables would be underground with no outside service pipes on the houses either, giving a very clean look. Each façade was designed to be the same so there was no real concept of the 'front' or the 'back' of the house. There was to be a community centre and a church provided as well as shops of 1,000 sq. ft (93 sq. m), a supermarket of 4,500–5000 sq. ft (420 sq. m) and a petrol station and a public house. The latter proved to be a divisive feature and necessitated a hearing in the high court in 1973 before its provision was finally approved. The community centre was later interpreted as being the 'shopping community area'. Gardens were limited in size in most of the houses and instead communal green spaces were provided which would be landscaped. As a further novel concept, the estate was to be managed, initially by the Wates company but ultimately by a management committee of the residents, with each resident paying an annual service fee.

The Radburn concept was to be achieved by building the houses in pairs or terraces of three to six houses around a lawned court. Most houses were serviced by a cul-de-sac and through roads were kept to a minimum. The pedestrian ways were designed to provide easy access to the community centre with a minimum of interaction with the main roadways, though complete separation of pedestrians from cars was not envisaged. Under the slogan of 'no through road', the estate was thus described in 1972.

**124.** Bayside advertisement, citing 'Radburn' features. (*Irish Times*, 1 December 1972, p. 23.)

**125.** The layout of the Bayside estate. (Google maps.)

At Bayside your home enjoys the benefits of being on a cul-de-sac. And Wates have positioned the houses in small groups around miniature greens. Such care in planning has also produced spacious areas of parkland, a church, a shopping-centre and a primary school all within the development. In addition the new Bayside Railway Station will open next Spring. You will not find anything which compares, pound for pound, with a Wates house at Bayside. Because in buying your house you 'buy' the complete environment and nowhere else in Ireland is there such a carefully planned development.

(*Irish Times*, 1 December 1972, p. 23)

The prices were also lower than on the southside. In 1968 (*Irish Times*, 18 April 1968, p. 17), they offered four designs of house; three of them with three bedrooms with four bedrooms in the final offering; each also had two reception rooms. All houses had gas-fired hot air central heating systems and they offered built-in presses and a fitted kitchen.

- 4 Bedroomed Virginian        £5,055 net
- 3 Bedroomed Powerscourt      £4,500 net
- 3 Bedroomed Queenscourt      £3,875 net
- 3 Bedroomed Courtmead        £4,075 net

It was noted that the Virginian and Powerscourt had not been part of the original offering and had hitherto only been available in their development in Dundrum Heights. Later on the developers decided to introduce a two-bedroomed house. These, named the Killeek, went on offer in 1972 and the intention was to provide between 150 and 200 of these, which had a floor area of about 750 sq. ft (70 sq. m) and which were built in terraces of three to seven houses. Responding to criticism that these were flats, the developers made it clear that these were houses. They had their own garden and direct access to it from the ground floor. The perceived market for this house type was as a 'starter house' for couples without children and as an 'empty nest' home for retired people. By the time they came to build these houses, the price was £6,100, significantly more than the three-bedroomed houses they had been selling only four or so years previously. Bayside, therefore, offered quite a number of interesting innovations to the shrewd housebuyer, as long as s/he liked the open design concept in the American style with private space blending into public space and the absence of fences and walls.

## The ideal home

Developers liked the idea of American influences and the open-plan living space was a 'new idea' for the 1960s. But what of the purchasers? One sense

"We want to see how your Ideal Home stands up to actual conditions."

**126.** The ideal homes exhibition. (*Dublin Opinion*, 1959, p. 171.)

of what was seen as trendy can be obtained from looking at the offerings at the various ideal homes and similar exhibitions over the years. Having an exhibition at which professionals and producers could showcase their wares was not a new idea. The first such national event had taken place at the Olympia exhibition centre in London in 1908 and it was quick to get going again in 1947 after the war had ended. Attendances during the 1950s numbered into the millions and the influence of what was on display was significant, though not necessarily immediately. Both the London show and its Dublin version, which ran from 1950, attracted a great deal of interest.

In these early years, aside from the suggestion of Dr Ernest Walton, the Nobel Prize winner for his work on splitting the atom, that large scale central heating was a possible use for atomic energy and that an 'atomic pile located close to a town could quite conceivably heat many of the houses and supply them with hot water' (*Irish Times*, 24 November 1951, p. 9), most of the ideas for an ideal home were more modest. At the Dublin exhibition in 1953, it was open-plan that was the design winner. On display was a model two-storey house and the *Irish Times* writer, Caroline Mitchell, noted that 'whether or not you approve of the "open plan" on the ground floor, it is interesting to study it for, if nothing else, this "open plan" is a modern trend of importance' (*Irish Times*, 10 September 1953, p. 10). In this house, the kitchen was the focus because, as the *Irish Times* put it, 'in these modern days, this room is the one in which the housewife finds that she spends the majority of her time'. The kitchen was supplied with wide windows, fitted cupboards and sink units with stainless steel draining boards. The ceiling came with what would now be seen as those dreadful acoustic tiles.

From the kitchen the owner (or the housewife) would walk into a dining alcove and from there access was provided to the living room. There were no doors between the spaces but each was demarcated. The bedrooms did not seem particularly innovative, except that each was provided with built-in cupboards. Nor was there anything especially interesting about the bathroom except that it was taken that the bathroom should be separate from the toilet, as it had been in houses of an earlier generation. So it was really open-plan, fitted kitchens and wide windows that captured the imagination. Built-in units were found in all the 'ideal houses' at the time. The argument was that they took up less space and that a dressing table could be foregone by making use of the space between two built-in wardrobes for that purpose.

There were some interesting ideas too. In *Dublin, 1930–1950*, it was noted that tiling in a bathroom was seen as an indicator of house price and quality. Fully tiled bathrooms were rare and sometimes ceramic tiles were substituted by beauty board, a covered cardboard surface. Now, the man about the house was encouraged to do his own tiling since there was now available a special tile cement which would do the job, rather than having to grapple with traditional sand and cement (no wonder tiles were such a novel feature). Venetian blinds had long been on the market but in 1953, outdoor venetian blinds were being suggested. These were aluminium alloy blinds which slid down the front of the window, making them look something like the security screens that are used to close up modern shops. The venetian blind theme was also found in the furniture section where a chest of drawers was on offer with a venetian-blind type front and with the handles and knobs illuminated.

Hoover had introduced a floor polisher, which had two soft brushes and revolved at high speed. This was the forerunner of the industrial ones still seen today though they never really became commonplace domestically. Indeed there were lots of gadgets available to part the consumer from his or her money. In 1952 there was a combined tea pot and hot water jug in aluminium. The idea was to put the tea leaves in the base on top of which was put an inner container containing the hot water. This supplied water to the tea below and as each cup was poured a new supply of hot water was added to the tea. This was available from 6s. to 16s. A teabag would have made more sense but it was not until the middle 1960s that they began to be widely available in Dublin. These household items were destined to remain exotic and not part of the usual list of household appliances. Prices for the standard and perhaps more mundane items rose during the 1950s. The table below gives an idea of what the ESB felt were suitable Christmas gifts in 1952 and 1956. The iron, toaster and kettle had been available for a long time and, in so far as like is being compared with like, it seemed that prices for these were falling. Other items were surprisingly expensive and this probably reflected their relative novelty.

|  | 1952 | 1957 |
|---|---|---|
| Electric iron | £2 4s. 6d. | £1 9s. 0d. |
| Electric toaster | £1 15s. 0d. | £2 5s. 0d. |
| Electric fire |  | £4 3s. 0d. |
| Electric kettle | £3 18s. 6d. | £2 17s. 6d. |
| Pressure cooker | from £5 5s. 0d. |  |
| Electric convector heater | £7 12s. 6d. |  |
| Electric plate warmer | £6 6s. 0d. | £4 10s. 0d. |

Washing machines were expensive and automatic machines had not yet completely replaced the older manual ones. For those who could not afford one but who had a vacuum cleaner, help was at hand. A gadget was placed into the sink and using the vacuum cleaner air was pumped through three bars in the bottom of the sink to produce a soapy foam and agitate the clothes. One wonders if it also washed the floor. However, for those who could afford it, they were still advertising a device that could wash clothes or dishes, though not at the same time. These had been introduced in the late 1940s and it is fascinating to see that they were still around in 1952. As the advertising blurb

**An ELECTRIC GIFT is a Welcome Gift**

**UNDER £2**

| | |
|---|---|
| SMALL IMMERSION HEATER<br>An appliance with a hundred applications. | 15s. 0d. |
| CHRISTMAS TREE LIGHTS<br>Gay decoration for the festive season | from 16s. 11d. |
| STANDARD ELECTRIC IRON<br>An essential in every home. | £1.5.6 |
| MANTEL CLOCKS<br>A variety of models. | from £1.5.9 |
| ELECTRIC DOOR CHIMES<br>Complete with transformer. | from £1.6.6 |
| TABLE LAMP<br>The "Versatile" table or bedlamp. | £1.10.0 |
| ALARM CLOCKS<br>Latest alarm clock – an acceptable gift. | from £1.12.0 |
| ELECTRIC HEATING PADS<br>New comfort at bedtime. | £1.13.9 |
| ELECTRIC TOASTERS<br>Chrome finished, attractive and serviceable. | from £1.19.6 |

**UNDER £5**

| | |
|---|---|
| ELECTRIC HAIR DRIERS<br>A grand gift for a lady. | from £3.9.6 |
| 2 kW ELECTRIC FIRES<br>In a variety of colours. | |
| ELECTRIC MILKWARMER<br>With egg boiler and porringer | £3.12.6 |
| ELECTRIC KETTLES<br>Copper 3 pint model. | £3.15.0 |
| ELECTRIC PLATE WARMERS<br>For keeping meals 'just right' | £3.18.9 |
| PRESSURE COOKER<br>Hawkins 10½ pint cooker | £4.5.0 |
| 6 PINT ELECTRIC KETTLE<br>Boiling water day or night. | £4.7.6 |
| ELECTRIC BOILING RING<br>A welcome asset in any home | £4.12.6 |
| | £4.10.0 |

**UNDER £3**

| | |
|---|---|
| KITCHEN WALL CLOCK<br>A housewife's joy. | £2.0.6 |
| PERSPEX MANTEL CLOCKS<br>In attractive white and rose finishes. | from £2.5.0 |
| 1 kW ELECTRIC FIRES<br>Handy, attractive and economical. | from £2.9.0 |
| TABLE STUDY LAMP<br>Useful and decorative, complete with shade. | £2.10.0 |
| DOOR GONG<br>High quality two-tone door chime and transformer. | £2.10.6 |
| AUTOMATIC ELECTRIC IRON<br>Quick, safe and efficient | from £2.19.6 |

**E.S.B. SHOWROOMS**
DUBLIN AND BRANCHES

127. ESB Christmas advertisement for 1954.

put it: 'a single load of 8lbs of dry clothes can be washed, rinsed and fully dried for ironing in 30 minutes. The utensils used for a full four-course meal for five persons can be washed, rinsed and dried in five minutes; it also washes cutlery, glass and silverware, as well as pots and pans, without danger of breakages, cracking or chipping' (*Irish Times*, 13 September 1952, p. 6). This wonder could be had for a snip at £99. For some reason, it was felt useful to have a dual fuel washer also. The clothes were boiled (!!) by gas and then agitated by electricity.

In Dublin in 1953, the house owner would find it relatively difficult to get a plumbed-in washing machine. There was a Hoover available that took 3½ lbs (1.6kg) dry clothes for £30 but a 6lb (2.7kg) capacity was available for £40. Servis offered a 'round type' model with a power wringer and an emptying hose. It was said to move easily on castors and was available for £43. For an extra £4 16s. a model with a power-driven pump for emptying into the sink was available and thus washing the floor at the same time could be avoided.

The trend towards smaller rooms and lower ceilings continued in house design and there was a vogue for space-saving items such as small electric cookers that took only 11.4 inches x 11.5 inches (20cm). It would cook for three people and the oven could roast a 4lb (1.8kg) joint. It was advertised as being portable and its 25lbs (11kg) weight was seen as reasonable to move around a kitchenette. This cost £6 19s. 6d. The fridge was still not a standard item in kitchens in the early 1950s because it was expensive and even tiny ones could cost upwards of £40, while standard sizes were likely to cost more than £70. It became more of a necessity as shopping patterns changed and people moved from 'just in time shopping' to a daily or even a weekly shop. This practice though did not find favour with one Carmel Cregan in the *Irish Independent* in 1950 who in the course of a series of articles on food hygiene remarked:

> Even if the housewife has a refrigerator and good storage facilities, food should only be bought in small quantities, and certain foods should be purchased daily, particularly in hot weather. Meat, milk, fish, green vegetables and bread deteriorate quickly and in addition there is no absolute guarantee of their freshness when purchased. Cooked meats should be used the same day.
> 
> (*Irish Independent*, 30 December 1950, p. 5)

Freshness was the important selling point but so was the idea of value. As an ESB advertisement for 1954 put it, 'once installed, it will save money for you day by day throughout the year, as perishable food can be purchased when prices are keen, and stored until required for use. Food "left-overs" can be kept and transformed into further tasty meals, and new, exciting summer dishes can be prepared to delight your family. Gone forever also are the risks of food spoilage through hot weather or contamination by insects.' Clearly, this was before the days of 'use by dates'.

## THE ELECTRIC
# REFRIGERATOR

PROVIDES STORAGE

PROTECTS FOOD

SAFEGUARDS HEALTH

SAVES MONEY

REDUCES WASTE

Here is an attractive selection to suit all needs :—

**ELECTROLUX** Capacity 1½ cubic feet, for the small house or flat ; silent and serviceable, 5 years' guarantee. Cash Price—£39 15 0

**HOTPOINT** Capacity 3 cubic feet, low running cost, sealed unit, very reliable, 5 years' guarantee. Cash Price—£52 0 0

**PRESTCOLD** Capacity 3 cubic feet, for medium size family, fits easily into small kitchen, sealed unit, low running cost, 5 years' guarantee. Cash Price—£48 0 0

**BOSCH** Available in two sizes to suit larger families, good storage capacity.
3½ cubic feet capacity  Cash Price £55
5½ cubic feet capacity  Cash Price £73

128. Advertisement for fridges in 1953.

In the Olympia exhibition of 1952 there was a similar emphasis on designs for smaller places. There was a clothes drier which dried by bringing the clothes into direct contact with a warm plate and which was said to provide heat for four hours on one unit of electricity. This cost £5 15s. 6d. A cordless electric iron was available, which was heated on a special plate and then could be used. This was nothing more than an electric version of the old-fashioned smoothing iron but it was available for £11 5s. The pressure cooker had long been available in the United States but it was new to the UK and it was one of the featured products in 1952. Another innovation was an electric sandwich maker and from the Continent came a simple idea for keeping food hot. This was a plate under which were three night lights or tea lights. This was available for 21s. There was a dishcloth that simply held the dirt and did not absorb it

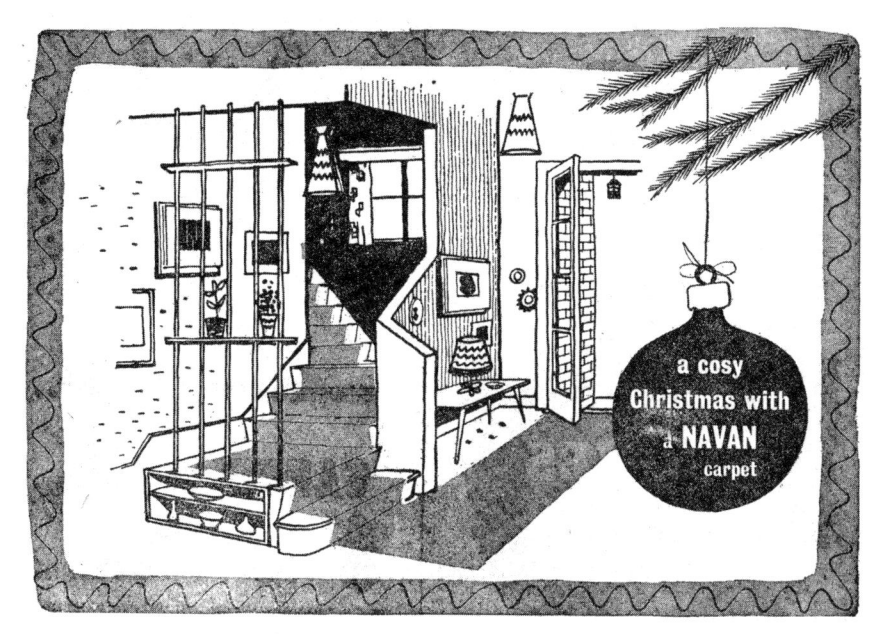

**129.** A cosy 1956 Christmas with a Navan carpet.

so that it could be easily washed. There was a barrier cream, 'the invisible glove', which could be rubbed into hands before undertaking dirty work, making them easier to clean. There was a paint stripper that was claimed to allow paint to be scraped off within 30 seconds of application but which would not harm the hands and which was not inflammable. What strikes the reader about many of these items was how long they took to be established. The warmer was a device that was still a novelty in Ireland in the 1990s and electric sandwich makers were more a creature of the 1980s than the 1950s. The paint stripper would be valued by any decorator struggling with today's environmentally friendly products, which merely tickle the paint.

Carpets were very much in vogue and were described in 1950 as the 'foundation of a well-furnished house' (*Irish Times*, 23 May 1950, p. 4), but the battle between carpet squares and fitted carpets was not yet over. The suggestion in 1950 was that it could cost £300 to carpet a small house of five rooms, stairs, hall and landings. However, this would include the extravagance of carpeting the bedrooms. The square was cheaper and it could always be turned if it got worn on one side. It took until the end of the 1950s for fitted carpets to become the norm, although people were warned not to try to do it themselves. Carpet squares were still seen to have a place, though, and it was felt that they were the best investment for tenants of rented houses and flats,

130. Polishing with Mansion floor polish in 1959.

presumably because they could take them with them when they changed abode.

There was still a place though for polished floors and Mansion Floor Polish was advertised in 1959 as the best product for both furniture and floors. It was suggested that it was just the thing for concrete floors and it came in three colours – clear, red and green. Of course, the advertisement reproduced here also suggested that polishing was effortless! Central heating became a standard feature of new private housing during the 1960s but until then, there was still competition between the various forms of standalone heaters that could be used to augment the fire. There were paraffin heaters, such as those provided by Valor, and electric fires and convector heaters provided by the ESB. It was suggested that a convector heater cost only 1½d. per hour while an electric fire cost less than 10d. per week to run. The convector heater had the added advantage of safety, it was said, in that if it turned over there was no problem.

Most houses still used wallpaper and the trend during the 1950s was towards brighter colours and bolder patterns leading ultimately to the horrors of 1960s wallpapers with its dazzling colours and 'in your face' patterns. 'A London firm shows a wide selection of papers, which includes a brilliant Scotch plaid, a chessboard with chessmen superimposed, and a black paper with a bright flower pattern. These brighter papers, they say, are not usually used for a whole room, they lend colour to the alcoves, while the rest is done in a quieter pattern. Another attractive development is companion papers – for instance, one in very pale pink, with white spots and pink moss roses, another identical, except that the roses are left out' (*Irish Times*, 13 March 1951, p. 4). The best that can be said is that it was 'different'.

## *All electric*

By the middle 1950s, all-electric houses were back in vogue. A small number of estates in Dublin had been built before the Second World War where the houses were designed to be all-electric but these were the exception. The ESB were keen to change that and offered an all-electric ideal home in 1955. Once again it was the kitchen that was the core of the house – the house was described as the answer to any housewife's prayer. Almost everything was in reach and equipment included a cooker, fridge, washing machine, iron, toaster, percolator, kettle and mixer. An extractor fan was included over the cooker. The washing machine was designed to take 9lbs (4kg) of dry washing.

As in other examples, the kitchen led into a breakfast room with the space demarcated by a serving counter and with a harking back to the Victorian great house, there was a signalling system for other parts of the house. The large dining room had a fireplace but this was only for show as electric fires were built into the surround. While the house was heated by electricity, an extra wall-mounted infra-red heater was provided in the kitchen for the winter months. The bedrooms were fully carpeted and all of the light fittings and the radio fitting could be controlled from the bed. The house was a four-bedroomed house with a separate bathroom and wc and at £7,000 for all of the features was at the upper end of the range for the time but not

131. Cookers on credit terms in 1954.

outrageously expensive. For the economy minded, it could have been had without the furniture and fittings for £3,535. Despite this attempt, all-electric houses never became popular and, indeed, many of the white goods did not become standard for some time. Judy Fallon reporting on the Ideal Home Exhibition in London in 1955 pointed out that:

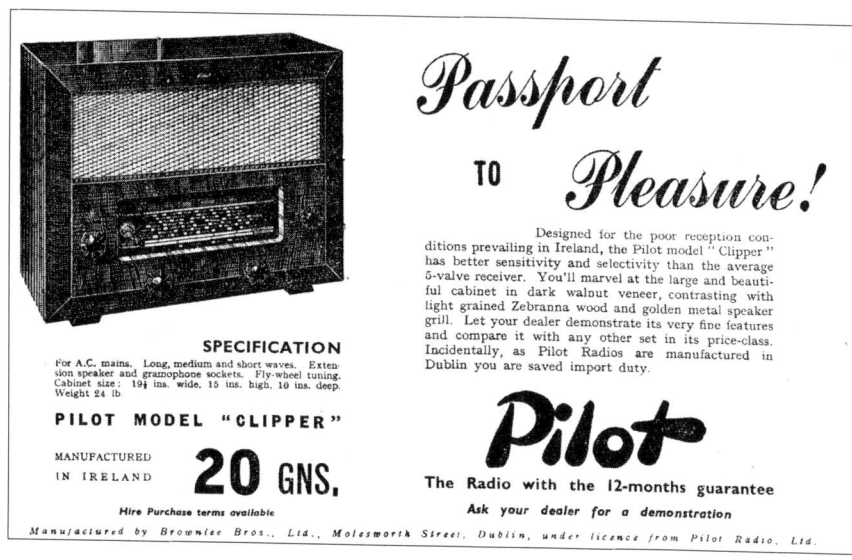

**132.** A 'Pilot' radio in 1950. Widely seen as the mark of quality.

In America, and in my own country, Australia, the housewife is far better served than her sister on this side of the world. Her kitchen is far more likely to be streamlined, and such things as refrigerators, washing machines, vacuum cleaners, food mixers, steel sinks and modern cookers are commonplace equipment in the average home. Over here in England, refrigerators are subject to a crippling purchase tax. Why? Because, according to officialdom, the climate does not make them a necessity, as it does in hot countries.

(*Irish Times*, 16 March 1955, p. 6)

She went on to note that the argument would apply only if one cooked and kept one's food in the middle of an open field in winter. In her view it was an old story (and one that continues to be heard) that:

**133.** The transition to television in 1960.

If men had to work in the house with the difficulties that women face and overcome every day, then all these fabulous inventions would become realities instead of dreams. Let the men do the cooking, washing, washing up, ironing, darning and sewing for a few months, and then we'd find miraculously that cookers, refrigerators, washing and washing-up machines, darning and other attachments for sewing machines, ironing machines and food mixers had somehow been adapted and altered so that they were available to every home.

The point about price was well made, for many of the items on display, although commonplace in the United States or even on the mainland of Europe, were very expensive and it would be hard to justify the expenditure. For example, she also discussed the 'Merry-Go' potato peeler, which allowed the user to power through 3lb (1.5kg) of potatoes in 60 seconds. It would also peel carrots, apples and onions and involved placing the device in the sink, attaching the hose to the tap and then turning the handle briskly. As she put it 'this very efficient little gadget retails for £6 12s. 6d. and although this is not astronomical, and although it does save waste by its economical peeling, I feel that there are many home budgets that perhaps may not be able to stretch to this for a vegetable peeler' (*Irish Times*, 16 March 1955, p. 6).

One item which had long been commonplace in the United States was the television. It had gradually crept into the living rooms of Dublin, replacing the Pilot radio as the standard means of entertainment. Its adoption had been slow because of the lack of a local television service and the patchy nature of fortuitous service from Northern Ireland or from Wales. Once RTÉ television came on air after 1962, there was a surge in television purchases and because it was very expensive, it was available both on credit terms and on rental terms. Indeed, television (and radio) rental shops became common features on many streets in the centre of Dublin.

Buying items on credit was normal in an era before credit cards. Large items such as washing machines and cookers were seen to be relatively expensive household items and in the 1950s, there was much emphasis on the fact that these could be had on easy credit terms. Thus a fridge which had a cash price of £56 7s. in 1954 was available for a down payment of £5 13s. 10d. and eighteen two-monthly payments £3 6s. 5d. At the time, the repayments on a tenant purchase house in Annadale would have been around £2 per week and it shows just how expensive were these items. Cookers were significantly cheaper but terms were also available for them and it was possible to get even small electrical items this way.

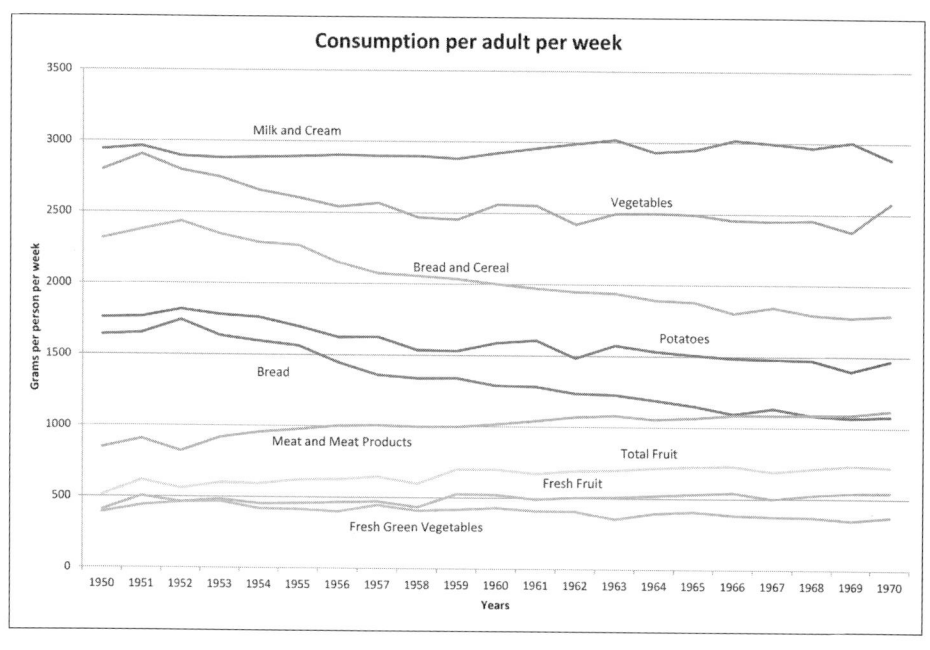

**134.** Trends in UK National Food Survey, 1950–70.

## Consumption and consumer products

There is little or no scientific information on what products and appliances were used in the preparation of meals. There was a nutrition survey undertaken in Dublin in 1944 but this was not repeated for 40 years. In the United Kingdom, a food survey was undertaken every year from 1940 until 2000 when it was replaced by the expenditure and food survey. It was a sample survey where householders were asked to record their purchases during a weekly period. It would be too much to suggest that what was going on in the United Kingdom could be applied to Dublin directly but the following trends might have wider applicability.

The data do not show any dramatic change in the eating habits of the UK population between 1950 and 1970. The consumption of both tea and coffee increased and while bread declined in use, the use of cereals increased. There was little change in the use of milk but consumption of both cheese and eggs declined while butter was increasingly used instead of margarine. The consumption of potatoes went down but this was not replaced by any major increase in fresh green vegetables though there was an increase in the use of both fresh and processed fruit. Perhaps the most significant increase was that of meat and meat products, though the same did not occur for fish.

**Table 35.** Consumption of food products in UK, 1950–70. Amounts are in grams per person per week.

| Year | Milk and cream | Bread | Bread and cereal | Potatoes | Vegetables |
|---|---|---|---|---|---|
| 1950 | 2,938 | 1,637 | 2,315 | 1,759 | 2,798 |
| 1954 | 2,887 | 1,596 | 2,288 | 1,761 | 2,655 |
| 1958 | 2,898 | 1,338 | 2,055 | 1,535 | 2,469 |
| 1960 | 2,921 | 1,289 | 2,000 | 1,588 | 2,560 |
| 1964 | 2,932 | 1,190 | 1,893 | 1,534 | 2,504 |
| 1968 | 2,966 | 1,086 | 1,793 | 1,472 | 2,454 |
| 1970 | 2,887 | 1,080 | 1,791 | 1,470 | 2,577 |
|  | Meat | Fresh green veg. | Fresh fruit | Total fruit | Eggs (no.) |
| 1950 | 846 | 392 | 409 | 513 | 3.50 |
| 1954 | 955 | 419 | 453 | 594 | 4.26 |
| 1958 | 997 | 408 | 433 | 596 | 4.42 |
| 1960 | 1,017 | 430 | 522 | 698 | 4.64 |
| 1964 | 1,054 | 393 | 520 | 713 | 4.73 |
| 1968 | 1,091 | 370 | 527 | 714 | 4.66 |
| 1970 | 1,121 | 372 | 543 | 723 | 4.66 |
|  | Tea | Coffee | Fish | Butter | Margarine |
| 1950 | 61 | 6 | 188 | 129 | 112 |
| 1954 | 80 | 10 | 161 | 116 | 136 |
| 1958 | 81 | 11 | 162 | 173 | 98 |
| 1960 | 79 | 11 | 166 | 161 | 104 |
| 1964 | 76 | 13 | 168 | 170 | 95 |
| 1968 | 73 | 15 | 161 | 174 | 80 |
| 1970 | 73 | 16 | 152 | 170 | 81 |

What is striking is that the range of goods that people consumed would be largely recognizable today. There was nothing particularly exotic or exciting in the goods on offer. Taking some newspapers from June 1955 revealed that people enjoyed Lamb Brothers' Spanish Gold marmalade with their breakfast, when they might also be tempted to try Ryvita crispbread with Marmite or perhaps Golden Syrup, a new product from Irish Sugar, on their toast. They would enjoy Bachelor's canned vegetables with their main meals or Crosse and Blackwell's Salad Cream for summertime. There was now a range of instant foods such as Bachelor's Chicken Noodle soup which took only seven minutes to prepare. It had the advantage of having all of the ingredients in the package

**135.** Advertisement for Lucozade from 1956.

but Royal Instant Pudding needed only the addition of milk and then the consumer could enjoy 'a great American favourite'.

They seemed to worry a lot about indigestion and constipation because there were many advertisements for Andrew's Liver Salts, Eno's Fruit Salts, Beecham's pills, Bile Beans, Rennies and Milk of Magnesia. Aspro or Disprin was available to take care of headache and Anadin was particularly good with Asian flu. Alternatively, people could take Yeast-Vite tablets and enjoy an instant pick-me-up. Lucozade was marketed more as a drink to help people recover from illness than a general energy drink. There was greater worry around colds, chills and infections than would be common today and it was described as tonic food beverage that rallied the sick and sent the convalescent on their way. There was competition from Ribena, which was also sold on the basis of its restorative powers. It was claimed that Ribena was used by many

**136.** (*left*) Chocolate as a food in the 1950s.

**137.** (*above*) The arrival of Palm Toffees. (*Irish Independent*, 6 June 1955, p. 1.)

famous hospitals and recommended by eminent doctors. These were all good reasons why it should be given to invalids.

This was a nation with a sweet tooth who enjoyed their Chivers Jelly, their chocolate, especially Rolo, and for whom the arrival of a sweet hitherto only available in England merited an ad on the front page of the *Irish Independent*. Walters' Palm toffees, which had been available in the UK for 150 years, were now available in Dublin. They were sold in seven varieties for 7*d*. per quarter pound or a chocolate variety could be had for 8*d*. per quarter. Cadbury's still advertised on the basis that their Dairy Milk was a food and the glass-and-a-half of dairy milk in each bar was as good as a glass of milk and two poached eggs. Biscuits were supplied by Jacob's and ginger nuts could be widely enjoyed. There were fruit whirls from Fuller's and, of course, Lemon's sweets.

The increasing trend towards DIY was encouraged by ads for Black and Decker tools. Rawlplugs make fixing to walls easier while their plastic wood

**138.** Advertisement for Afton Major from 1955.

was great for repairs. Washing was still a matter for Sunlight Soap or perhaps Lifebuoy, which made life healthier. Clothes could be made sparkling again by using Tide or Rinso. Rinso was sudsy and extra soapy and could be guaranteed to take the dirt out of clothes without wearing them out. It was also notable that it could be used in washing machines. Surf was great at cleaning clothes and keeping them white. Also 'sudsy' was Vim, which made short work of the home cleaning needs, especially seeking out dirt in those hidden crannies where a doctor would look for dangers. Jeyes Fluid could take care of all disinfectant needs and pots could be kept sparkling clean by the application of Brillo pads.

Smoking remained a normal activity and the variety of brands on offer included Player's (where it was the tobacco that counts), Gold Flake and Afton

Major (where it seemed important to mention that they were popular in Burma). But smoking was not without its difficulties and smelly breath could be improved by taking Amplex tablets or perhaps using Kolynos or Colgate toothpaste.

There was a concerted effort to promote tea drinking by the Tea Council of Ireland and Mi-Wadi was always available but for those who liked something stronger, there was Bulmer's Cider, Black and White Whisky or Sandeman's Port. The adventurous might try a new drink from Guinness, Cherry's Ale. It was brewed in New Ross but 'to Guinness standards'. It seemed important that women understood that gentlemen pay sincere compliments to anyone with a deep copper-brown tan and this could be obtained by Cooltan. The giant economy size tube at 4s. 6d. seemed to be the best bet.

Ten years later and it can hardly be said that things had changed much. The customer in 1965 was buying from much the same range of goods and brands. There was no sign yet of different types of products that might be suggestive of opening up to a wider world. Established companies introduced new products such as the Goldgrain Digestive Biscuit or Rich Tea from Bolands. Concern for biliousness and constipation seems to have diminished and products such as Andrew's Liver Salts were now being sold as refreshing drinks while Beecham's was now something for colds and flu. Freshness for all the family was now available from Max Factor Family Deodorant spray.

There was now vodka to add to the list of drinks that were popular with Smirnoff leading the pack with its 'leaves no trace on the breath' promise, though there was also Nordoff or Saratof. Gin was also seen to be a trendy drink and Asbach Uralt, the German brandy, arrived in 1966. Carling Black Label was another lager to try or Time beer from Smithwicks. Lots of varieties of tea continued to be available including Becker, Lyons, McGraths or Musgraves. There was no diminution in the advertising of cigarettes with the same brands being available – Player's Navy Cut, Woodbine, Gold Flake, Benson & Hedges (pure gold at 4s. 8d. for 20) and Rothmans to name but a few. There was also Kingsway at the same price which offered more length, more tobacco and more pleasure. Senior Service, an old favourite, was a bit cheaper at 4s. 1d. for 20.

There were more and more DIY products and Dulux gloss paint became available in Ireland. With the increase in car ownership came the need for Isopon, the fibre glass repair method for rust holes and damage and you could polish the finished job with M1, creamed solid wax. For smaller tasks, there was a new version of Bostik that was supposed to do the job better.

**139.** The Lyons tea range in 1965.

**140.** Irish Coffee chocolate from 1960.

Chocolate was no longer being sold as a food in itself but the perfect combination of coffee, milk and whiskey was now available. Processed cheese was the new convenience food and Golden Vale was advertised as Ireland's most complete food and a ½lb block contained as much nourishment as 10 eggs, ¾lb of beef and 4 pints of milk. Alternatives were Three Counties or Calvita from Mitchelstown Creamery and one was invited to be 'slim, trim and brimful of energy'.

## *Innovation*

In 1956, some house owners were given the opportunity to write about their perceptions of an ideal home and, specifically, whether an old house was better than a new one. There was nothing scientific about this; it was just a series of opinions (*Irish Times*, 26 May 1956, p. 4). Modern houses were faulted because space saving had gone too far and there was not enough storage. The idea of a stairs rising immediately from a small hallway was seen as both impractical and downright dangerous as the stairs were inevitably very steep. Despite the increasing use of architects to design homes, at least one occupant of a new house accused them of a lack of imagination. Kitchens for all their design were too small and far from being the centre of the home, they were an annoyance. However, older houses, while offering more space, were seen to be harder to heat and, by definition, they took longer to clean. Modern trends in furniture did not sit well in older houses but at least there was the opportunity to experiment with new layouts, something that the smallness of the modern house did not permit.

These people liked the open-plan arrangement that was now common in new houses unlike those who responded to the scientific survey undertaken some ten years later and discussed below. It may be that the love affair with open-plan, which was the new 'thing' in the 1950s, had cooled somewhat. Central heating was regarded as a must in all modern houses and respondents wanted houses to be adaptable to the changing needs of the family.

There was no impression of particular innovation in house design during the exhibitions of the remainder of the 1950s, though there were still plenty of gadgets on sale, both practical and impractical. A microwave oven was demonstrated in 1962 at the eye-watering price of £495. Rather, the focus was on making the house work better, with time devoted to the best heating systems or how to make the most of décor. Even by the early 1960s, there was still debate on how to heat a house now that the days of the coal fire in one room of the house, serviced by regular deliveries of Polish coal, were coming to an end (at least for some!). Advertisements extolled the virtue of every class and kind of heating appliance and door-to-door salesmen attempted to interest householders in one system or another.

Three types of heating systems were generally on offer in the Dublin of the early 1960s. There was the standard system with hot water radiators heated by a solid fuel, oil or gas boiler. Then there were air heating systems whereby air heated by a boiler was distributed through the house via ducts and, depending on the system used, there could be hot water or not. The final system was electric either by means of underfloor heating or simple storage heaters. The principle here was that the heat was built up in periods of low cost off-peak electricity and radiated into the house during the day. While there was concern that the electric systems could prove very expensive if not properly managed, it seems that there was not such a cost difference between them that one system stood out over any other in terms of value for money. That would change within a relatively short period of time.

There was a brief vogue for individual oil fired heaters as offering great value. However, as these had to be filled individually and as they made the house stink like a diesel engine, the idea was not universally popular. It would not be correct to give the impression that all Dubliners enjoyed central heating. It was a feature of new houses but there was still a long way to go before it would be retrofitted to older houses. The pollution of the 1980s, leading ultimately to the ban on smoky fuels in 1990, is testament to that. The 1981 census indicated that 56 per cent of households in the built-up area of Dublin still used solid fuel for heating and in only 35 per cent of households was central heating the dominant form of heating. It will not surprise that 60 per cent of these lived in the new suburbs with only 24 per cent of households in the county borough relying on central heating (Brady, 1986).

Fitted carpets continued to be seen as desirable but expensive and people were warned that unless attention was paid to the floor surface that the carpets might not give the expected wear. However, the discussion inevitably returned to the kitchen. This was where most was expected. Surprisingly, there were still people who could afford domestic help but this number was continuing to decline both because of the costs involved and the difficulty in getting people to take on the work. Therefore, the emphasis was on the kitchen being more comfortable and more efficient. The expectation was that a kitchen would have a cooker, toaster, washing equipment and a variety of gadgets but these had to be efficient both in use of space and in delivery of service because there was not much space in the average kitchen or as one writer put it: 'one cannot afford to load a small kitchen with useless stuff since there aren't even cupboards in which one may hide one's culinary calamities' (*Irish Times*, 17 September 1957, p. 6).

There was a sense in the exhibitions of the early 1960s that design had gone too far and that practicality had been sacrificed to achieve a particular effect. Judy Fallon in her piece on the Olympia show in 1961 bemoaned the latest style in bathrooms, which was for low rimmed bathtubs combined with carpets or floor matting. The combination would ensure sodden floor covering everytime they were used. She went on to say that the lower bathtubs demanded lower presses to fit in with the concept and she wondered who was going to sit on an 18-inch (46cm) high dresser in order to put on make-up. She found useful items but these were more in the equipment area rather than in design and she returned to a previous theme that these items were more expensive than they needed to be. However, she found useful the concept of a washing machine that though it needed to be hooked up to the cold tap (built-ins were still not yet the norm) did the entire cycle including drying of the clothes. For 86 guineas a similarly automatic dishwasher was available. One can suggest that Ms Fallon was not entirely convinced as to the utility of all that was on offer. She concluded her piece by saying that:

> If the tale of all these labour saving devices bothers you, I can only say that I came away from the exhibition with a frightening vision of the Ideal Home Owner of 1961. Who is: too lazy to read (hence television, tape recorders, long playing records); too lazy to cook; wash up; sweep rooms (vacuum-cleaner attachments in every room); step out of a bathtub (low-set tubs for lazy people); and even too lazy to teach the children (admonishments on the wall of the nursery, records of nursery rhymes and fairy tales etc.).
>
> This year's ideal home exhibition was bigger than ever before, they tell me but next year's will have to be 'bigger still'. That one will have to show us what to do with the time that all these 'Big Brother' machines are saving for us. But don't worry – the day of your Master of Arts degree in six easy longplaying records can't be far off.
>
> (*Irish Times*, 15 March 1961, p. 4)

A sense of a more realistic but still ideal home was offered when ICI decided to build an ideal house in Kilcroney, Co. Wicklow, in 1966. Granted this was a suburban house on its own land but many of the features could translate into more ordinary houses. Given the company that produced it, it is perhaps not surprising how plastic was used to displace more traditional materials. People liked the plastic guttering and downpipes. They liked the new approach to plastering, which reduced the work involved by a significant amount. They were keen on the notion of having metal work covered in a transparent lacquer. The bins were an early generation of wheelie bins and had what were described as cat-proof lids. It seemed that the emphasis was on the use of new, modern synthetic materials rather than on the use of traditional ones. In a talk given to the Institute of Patentees and Inventors in London in 1968, Mrs Mary Adams, deputy chairman of the Consumer's Association in Britain, set out her view of the ideal home. She clearly had a lot of fun developing her list but it was focused on new materials, time saving equipment and very much aimed at freeing women from the home, though she argued that: 'it might be simpler and quicker perhaps, to invent the new woman, ergonomically standardized, without biological disabilities and without built-in attachments to men and babies but, instead, armed with an unsentimental critical attitude to possessions and status. And possessed of a self-confidence which could remove mountains' (*Irish Times*, 27 January 1968, p. 1).

It is fun to revisit her ideas which she said 'begins with the perfect contraceptive pill and ends with the perfect jug'. She wanted new materials in the house, especially moulded plastics, fitted furniture, ample storage with American-style walk-in wardrobes. The house would be well ventilated but without windows to open and close and clean and everything would be controlled by remote control. The kitchen equipment would all be on hire and replaced when outmoded. She would have central heating with cool larders, no polish surfaces, no curtains, total revision of garbage and washing up. The beds had to be supremely comfortable with sheets plus single Continental type covers and they would be adjustable for sitting position, fully mechanized and with remote control.

The wishlist continued: cooking utensils, silicone-coated and designed for transfer to table; refrigerators with deep-freezes; telephones with inexpensive message recording; television with remote control. Mail order or out-of-town supermarket for basic orders; evening and weekend shopping; informative labelling (especially medicines and prescriptions); plastic bottles and containers for all fluids; small measures of basic groceries for the 3-million single person homes; easily opened packaging, and less of it; handbags with interior lighting.

She was remarkably prescient and much of what she outlined is commonplace today, even the interior lighting in handbags is available. People have not abandoned windows but otherwise there is little in her list that would surprise the homeowner of today. The wish to have smaller quantities in less packaging and more information on purchases is remarkably modern. It marked a shift from seeing the ideal home as the answer to a housewife's prayer and more to seeing a home as something that needed as little engagement from the dweller as possible.

It is somewhat disappointing, however, to find that over the course of the twenty years covered here that there was so little attention paid to redesigning houses to meet the needs of people. More attention was devoted to putting gadgets into standard houses and commentators seemed less enthused at the notion that the standard three-bedroomed semi-detached house would benefit from a radical rethink that would reflect changing society and its needs. For the 1969 Dublin exhibition, there was a subtle shift away from assuming that the exhibition was aimed at 'housewives'. After all, this was the same month that the *Irish Times* stirred the pot by inviting its readers to comment on the concept of women working outside the home though the responses showed that there was not a uniform view on this (*Irish Times*, 2 October 1969, p. 6). Otherwise though, there was little striking in the Ideal Homes exhibition as the 1960s came to an end. There were gadgets, though there seemed to be fewer of them. Mostly it was as described: 'This exhibition does provide an excellent opportunity to view, under the domed cupola of the Mansion House Round Room, a wide variety of cooking, beating, and freezing machines, as well as the entertainments and communications machinery – everything to serve that machine for living in we call home' (*Irish Times*, 11 September 1969, p. 6). The Building and Construction Exhibition (IBAC), which took place in the RDS in 1969, might have been the showcase for new designs. While a system built house at £4,000 and with a floor space of 1,042 sq. ft (97 sq. m) generated a lot of interest among the 63,000 visitors, most of the focus was on the interior and how it was laid out. Among many ideas was a fascinating concept to give interest to the television when it was turned off. This was achieved by what would now be called a screen saver which would produce multiple coloured patterns and designs in random formation (*Irish Times*, 20 October 1969, p. 6) and doubtless reduce the household to a catatonic state in no time at all.

## *Householders' perceptions*

A survey was undertaken by the Department of Social Science in UCD in association with An Foras Forbartha and the Irish Housebuilders' Association in 1968 (*Irish Times*, 14 December 1968, p. 8) and Galligan, Glynn and Ward (1968). The sample size was 249 housewives in Dublin Corporation houses and 219 in owner-occupied houses. The results for those in the council houses will be discussed later with some further comments on the survey methodology. This survey was a pilot study and could not be said to be representative of Dublin city housing but it is interesting. The focus was on new houses and thus the survey was carried out on three adjoining areas in the southern suburbs.

The answers were similar to those in the Corporation estate. Most people were satisfied with their house but there was a belief that the house could have been better designed. Eighty-seven per cent described structural alterations that they would like and while one third had already made changes, another 50 per cent intended to do so. Among the most sought after changes was a bigger kitchen with better placed built-in presses and more electrical sockets and more bedrooms. Almost 60 per cent did not like the trend toward open-plan and would have preferred separate reception rooms. The negative comments on the estate focused on inadequate bus services, shopping facilities and open space. They would have liked more variation in housing design and more space between houses. Nearly all wanted their own gardens with not much support therefore for American-style lawns which blended into the public space. In other words, despite the impact of twenty years of marketing, they still wanted a traditional house.

The social pattern of the city had been developing for many years and what went on during the 1960s was just a continuation of a process which was inevitable without the active intervention of the planning authorities. Indeed the *Irish Times* (24 December 1969, p. 14) captured what was going on very well in a feature in 1969 when they wrote:

> DUBLIN is growing fast – to the North, to the West but most of all towards the South. Although the tidy-minded town-planners do not approve, the greatest spread of residential development is inexorably moving through South-East County Dublin along a strip parallel with the coast. The reason for this surge of building activity, especially of new houses, is only too obvious: this is the most attractive, convenient, naturally well-endowed and serviced area in the entire region surrounding the capital city.
>
> (*Irish Times*, 24 December 1969, p. 14)

# The European context

## High-rise and suburban design

The professionals in Dublin Corporation were well aware of trends in continental Europe and the Americas, even if they had not the means to implement them in Dublin. After all, and it has been mentioned previously, Dublin was to the fore in showing enthusiasm for the developing garden city / garden suburb concept in the early years of the twentieth century. They were equally enthused by the discipline of town planning and accepted the need for town plans to manage an urban area long before this became the norm. It is a pity that their implementation did not live up to expectations. The long term association with Abercrombie provided a formal link with the developing thinking around suburban development and new town planning in the UK but informal contacts also ensured that people were well informed. This chapter will provide a brief survey of what they might have been considering during the 1950s and 1960s.

## Why not high-rise?

Apartment living had long been part of the urban experience of European cities, especially in central areas. Haussmann's Paris, for example, was redesigned on the principle of multi-household dwellings. It was a logical extension of the concept to build them higher as technology facilitated. Tall blocks were part of the design conversations of people such such as Le Corbusier by the 1920s and these new designs did not shy away from dramatic statements, such as those suggested by Ludwig Hilberseimer in *c.*1928 for the Friedrichstadt area of Berlin. Opportunities to do anything practical were limited except in the Soviet Union where, before the repression of the 1930s, there was an active and lively debate in the Soviet Union about how best to provide housing for people in the new socialist world with the desubanists, focused around Okhitovitch, suggesting that towns were unnecessary. There was a great interchange of ideas between those in the USSR and those in the rest of the world and people such as Le Corbusier both influenced Soviet thought and were influenced by it in turn.

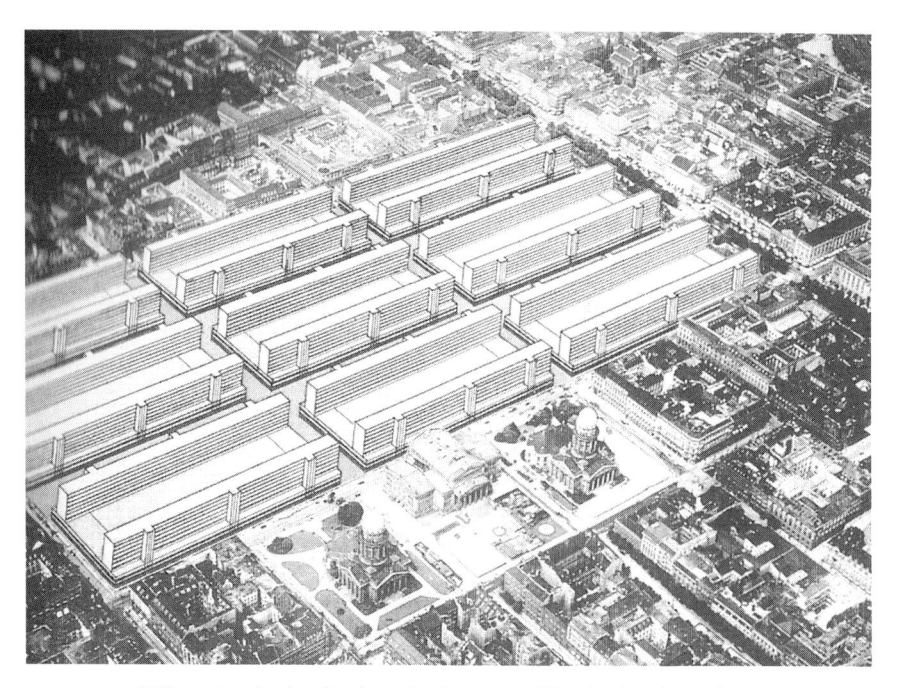

141. Hilberseimer's plan for the redevelopment of Friedrichstadt, Berlin, 1928.

142. Le Corbusier's design for a contemporary city of three million, 1929.

## *The USSR experience*

In the Soviet Union, the process was driven by ideology. An important principle of society was that life was to be lived communally and not as individuals. Obviously, how cities were designed was going to have a significant influence on this and one of the theoretical approaches that developed was that of the 'urbanists', developed by the economist and

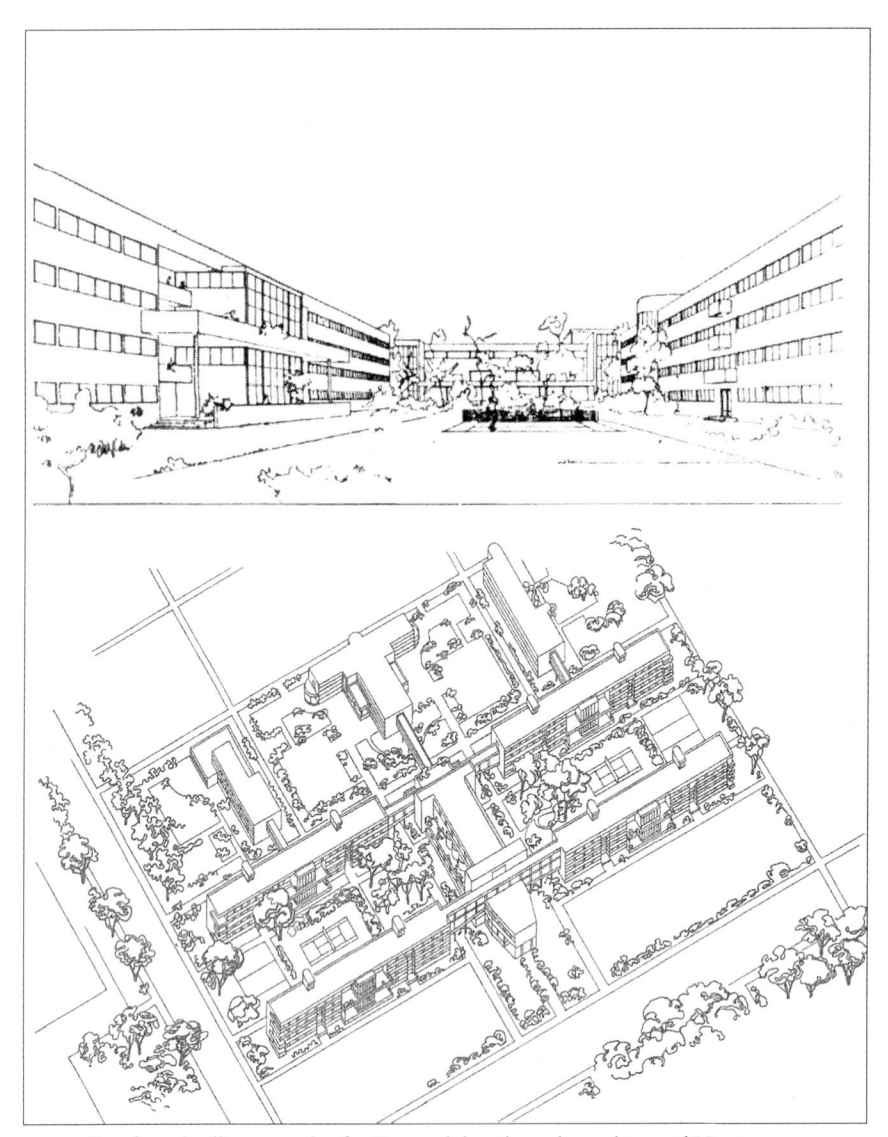

**143.** Plan for a dwelling complex for Kuznetsk by Alexander and Leonid Vesnin, 1929–30.

statistician Leonid Sabsovich. In his ideas on cities, towns should be small and all of the population could be housed in tall blocks that would provide only bedrooms for the adults. Essentially, a town of 30,000 people could easily be created without the need for streets and where everything was within walking distance. Centralized facilities would provide kitchens and canteens, education, recreation, libraries and so on. The principle was to liberate people

**144.** Early high-rise in central Moscow.

**145.** Standard housing style in suburban Moscow.

from the acquisition of objects that they needed only from time to time. These blocks were to rise to between fifteen and twenty-nine storeys, far beyond the technology of the times. The principles, in a more modest and practical expression, were incorporated into designs for particular cities such as those produced by the Vesnin brothers for Kuznetsk. This was a design for a city of 35,000 people with housing provided in two types – one housing complex for

2,100 people and another for 1,100 people. Each complex comprised a group of four-storey houses linked by passages to a communal area where a canteen, a conference hall, club rooms and a gymnasium were all provided.

The essence of these designs was that a communal lifestyle was possible when many people lived in the same place in close communication with each other. This also meant that it was possible to provide many services for people who are closely related spatially.

After 1932, there was a closedown of debate and there was little further discussion of the principles involved in the creation of new cities (see Miliutin, 1974). Instead, the focus turned towards existing cities and what was needed to provide for the huge housing needs of a rapidly growing urban population. It was decided that the rest of the country would draw from the practical experience of solutions that were implemented in Moscow. The high-rise, high-density solution met both the practical and ideological needs of the society and in the post-war period, much effort was devoted to developing the techniques of industrial building. It took some time before the post-war economy stabilized to the degree that building materials were available in sufficient quantities and for some years the absence of lifts limited the height of buildings to five storeys. Gradually, the techniques were developed to prefabricate more and more of the construction, and the scale of individual housing developments increased. By 1950, they were able to build suburbs such as those in the south-west district (along Leninsky Prospekt), which housed 100,000 people and where the housing was to a uniform design in 8 or 9 storey buildings. Though the design was uniform, there was some attempt at creating a visually pleasing environment and classical forms and references were often used. However, during that decade, there developed an intense debate as to whether such embellishment was at all necessary. This resulted in uniform housing developments right across the Soviet Union of pretty undistinguished blocks. The critic Yaralov wrote: 'there can be no artificial preservation of some features merely for the sake of these features. They are not an end in themselves. And if there is at work a process of their extinction in dwelling house architecture, then the process is inevitable and cannot be halted by any exhortations. And it is hardly worthwhile to feel sorry over this being so' (Ikkonikov, 1998, p. 271).

This led to a critical backlash and the desire to introduce at least some design into schemes. The response, though, was limited and muted because the demand for housing was such that by the early 1960s, the pressure was to build as much housing as quickly as possible and consequently as cheaply as

**146.** Prefabrication in building in Moscow.

**147.** Large scale use of high-rise in Moscow, late 1980s.

possible. To facilitate pre-fabrication, the number of designs was limited and some residential areas were built with one design only. As the 1950s moved into the 1960s, so the average height of buildings moved from five storeys to nine storeys. An important point is that these were almost all greenfield,

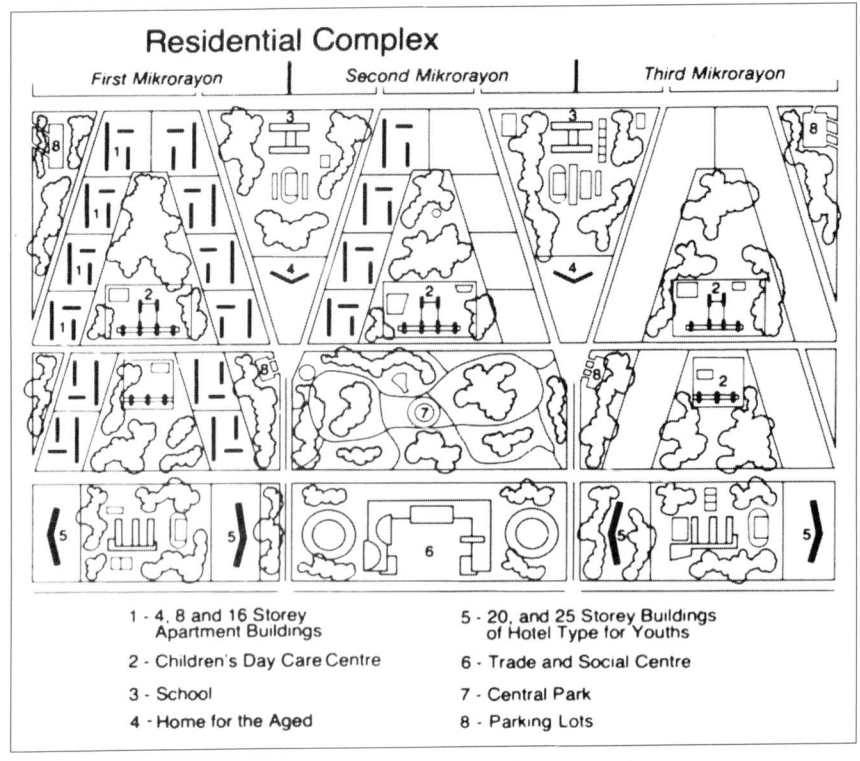

**148.** The microrayon concept. (Bater, 1980.)

**149.** A microrayon in Moscow. Note the provision of local services in the middle of the complex of apartments.

suburban sites in Moscow where there were no issues of clearance and this kept costs at a much lower level than they would have been had brown field sites been used. An important example was that of the Khimki-Khovrino area in the north-west of Moscow. This area grew to house over one-quarter of a million people. It is a mixture of lower spine blocks and towers; the patterns varied across the site in the attempt to avoid monotony. The towers were twelve storey in this case and the high-rise blocks were used to identify clusters of particular social importance. In the 1970s, the area was further developed by the addition of 18-storey blocks. They did not stop at that and by the late 1960s, they were experimenting with 25-storey panel blocks on Prospekt Mira. It was recognized that monotony was a problem in these developments and there was a general acceptance that the most useful resource in dealing with this was local geography.

The key to the success of these developments, if they were successful, was the provision of local services. The concept that evolved over time was that of the microrayon, the micro district. The principle was one of a hierarchy of provision. A microrayon occupied a footprint of between 10 and 60ha and contained a population of about 10,000. Day-to-day needs, such as grocery stores, personal services, cafés, clubs, playgrounds and building maintenance offices, were met within the cluster of housing. The standard required was that nobody should be more than 500m from these services. Less frequently needed services were provided to a group of microrayons and so on up the hierarchy of provision. It was theoretically possible to provide for the needs of a city-scale population with a footprint of only a few square kilometres.

Though the Soviet Union was a long way from Dublin culturally as well as in distance in the 1960s, their approach to housing set the parameters for high-rise. When built in the city centre, they were a solution to the problem of decentralization. This was less clearly an advantage in suburban areas and it was here that the additional feature of system building became important. By using industrial building techniques it was possible to build quickly and relatively cheaply, at the cost of monotony. There were other examples closer to home.

## *Other European examples*

Karl Marx-Hof, the name alone might have been enough to put off Dublin Corporation, was built by Karl Ehn in the suburbs of Vienna between 1927 and 1930. This was towards the end of the 'Red Vienna' period when the city

150. Karl Marx-Hof, Vienna, in the late 1990s.

151. Quarry Hill development showing the local bus station.

had its first period of democratic government, in this instance by the Social Democrats. The development was of 1,382 apartments, which ranged in size from 30 sq. m to 60 sq. m. It housed about 5,000 people with a great deal of

**152.** Unité d'Habitation, Berlin.

play area and garden space and with day-to-day facilities that included laundries, kindergartens, a library, medical services and commercial offices. Quarry Hill in Leeds was an early inner city regeneration project that attempted something on the lines of Karl Marx-Hof. It was designed in 1934 by R.A.H. Livett, the Director of Housing and later City Architect for Leeds. The development occupied 36 acres (14.6ha) and contained 938 flats built in seven- and eight-storey blocks, which were serviced by 88 lifts, quite an innovation for the time. At its peak, it housed about 3,000 people and, in keeping with the principle of providing day-to-day needs, it included a community hall, twenty shops, indoor and outdoor swimming pools, extensive courtyards, gardens and play areas, a nursery and a communal laundry. Despite this, it proved to be a disaster and was soon a byword for slum dwelling in Leeds and a decision was taken to demolish as early as 1973.

Le Corbusier's ideas would have been more politically acceptable in the Dublin of the 1950s but they too emphasized the idea of living in common. His ideas for the Voisin area of Paris (1925) or expressed in *The city of tomorrow* (1929) suggested a city with a small footprint which was achieved by the concentration of facilities and services into high-density zones. While the office and commercial sector would be housed in high-rise, the residential

**153.** Modern high-rise in Antwerp.

**154.** Modern high-rise in south-eastern suburban Prague.

155. Modern high-rise in central Berlin.

areas were lower rise blocks with central gardens. The assumption was that these garden spaces would both provide space for recreation as well as allotments for the growing of food. People would have their own apartments, though, and the communal nature of society was less emphasized than in the Soviet model. His Unité d'Habitation was the expression of these ideas on a smaller scale. At one view, these are just large apartment blocks but closer inspection reveals that they are designed to facilitate small communities by the provision of local services within the building and the laying out of the floors as individual streets, a concept later developed in the Roehampton scheme in London where the floors could be reached by trade vehicles.

Both concepts emphasized that high-rise and high density offered the opportunity to provide services in close proximity to residents, thus reducing the need for transport. The price to be paid was one of uniformity and discipline. Living in such close proximity could be achieved harmoniously only with a system of shared values and a buy-in from the residents. In the Soviet Union, this was ideologically imposed but in Corbusier's model, it is useful to recall that his plans were for the middle and upper class only. The workers he relegated to garden cities at some distance from his centre. In both

**156.** Roehampton in the mid-1960s.

systems, it was assumed that the residents were rational beings, motivated by logic and not by emotion. In other words, they could be expected to behave well and to make the system work.

High-rise became a feature of many European cities after the Second World War and remains so to this day, though not to the same dominating degree as in the Soviet Union or Eastern Europe. Much experience of building high blocks was obtained and the use of industrial or system building techniques increased. In the UK, the Roehampton development, which was completed in the late 1950s, was one of the largest in Europe at the time and came to be regarded as a model of its type. It, too, was suburban and brought city centre densities of about 100 persons per acre (247 per ha) to the London suburbs.

**157.** The Roehampton scheme today. (Google Earth).

**158.** The spine blocks in Roehampton.

It comprised 25 eleven-storey tower blocks, twelve-storey maisonette slab blocks, terraces of four-storey maisonette blocks and terraced houses. In all, it housed 9,500 people and these were provided with sixteen shops (see Tetlow and Goss, 1965). The Red Road complex was Glasgow's most ambitious foray into the world of high-rise (see Horsey, 1990). Begun in 1964, finished by 1969 and finally demolished in October 2015, it comprised eight multi-storey blocks, two of which were spine blocks, much wider in cross-section than they were deep, while the remainder were tower blocks. The spines were 28 storeys tall and the tower blocks rose to 31 storeys and were designed for a population of 4,700.

Even if Roehampton could be considered a success at the time, much of what was built in Europe after the Second World War lacked a number of the basic elements outlined above. The provision of services, a crucial justification for building high, was secondary to the provision of houses and the extent to which the population were prepared for the disciplines of high-rise is questionable at best.

## *Building suburbs in the UK*

Following the publication of the Tudor Walters report in 1918, detailed guidance was provided to local authorities in the form of housing manuals, the first of which was published in 1919. These set out standards for building and provided suggested templates for houses and estates. Despite this the assessment of the Dudley report in 1944 was that the housing that had been built between the wars lacked variety in the types of dwellings and the internal layout of houses was not suited to modern life.

As the Second World War came to an end, there was a need to undertake a great deal of rebuilding to replace the housing stock which had been lost. This resulted in the publication of a housing manual in 1944, designed for a transitional period, as they called it, when the rapid replacement of the housing stock was the priority. This was revised in 1949 as matters began to stabilize and this set the tone for local authority building into the 1950s and beyond. It, therefore, provides a useful comparison with the approach of Dublin Corporation.

The recommended size for a three-bedroomed house in the 1949 housing manual was between 900 and 950 sq. ft (84–8 sq. m) with houses for larger and smaller families on a pro-rata basis. The largest house anticipated was a four-bedroomed house at 1,175 sq. ft (109 sq. m). In the supplements to the manual produced in 1952 and 1953, there was emphasis on reducing the wasted space in the house by reducing the circulation space and concentrating on the aggregate living space – the combined area of the ground floor living room, sitting room and kitchen. The aim was to keep the previous standard for the living space but 'to plan a house in which the circulation space taken up by hall, passages and lobbies is reduced to a minimum' (Housing Manual, 1952, p. 2). This might mean, for example, the stairs rising from the sitting room and not from a separate hallway. By doing this there would be considerable savings in construction and a consequent reduction in rent. This became a feature of many private houses but with the explanation that it offered greater flexibility and made the house more airy.

The 1953 manual went further and concentrated on housing layout and planning. They were anxious that development costs be reduced – 'one penny saved on the cost per square foot of a house of about 900 sq. ft (84 sq. m) gross will save nearly a penny a week in the rent and reduce the cost of 3,000,000 houses by over one million pounds' (Housing Manual, 1953, p. 1). Suggestions were offered as to savings that could be made, for example, on frontage and better use made of corner sites. There was emphasis in this manual on linking the house design to the layout design. The point was made that development could not be independent of the landscape in which it was taking place. Providing accommodation was only one of the elements and a development could be seen to be successful only when access, daylight and space had been properly integrated. They promoted three basic designs for estates and examples of each are to be found in Dublin, though the first layout was the most favoured by Dublin Corporation in the early part of the period under discussion.

The first was the conventional street in which the majority of the houses fronted onto the road servicing the estate and the back gardens were enclosed. Access to gardens was either by a side entrance if the housing was semi-detached or perhaps a common tunnel running between terraced houses. The latter design had featured in some of the houses in Marino in the 1920s. The UK planners were concerned about this form of development because semi-detached houses wasted road frontage and access to the rear of terraced houses sometimes resulted in wasted space. Within the parameters of good design, they wanted the largest number of houses per area and they provided a number of examples of good and bad practice. The second basic design model was what they called a 'service cul-de-sac' layout. This was where all main traffic was confined to peripheral roads and road access to the house was limited to a cul-de-sac leading from the traffic route. Where this was coupled with an independent pedestrian system of circulation, then this approach came close to the Radburn approach and explicit reference was made to Radburn, though it was noted that it was not always possible to offer this kind of

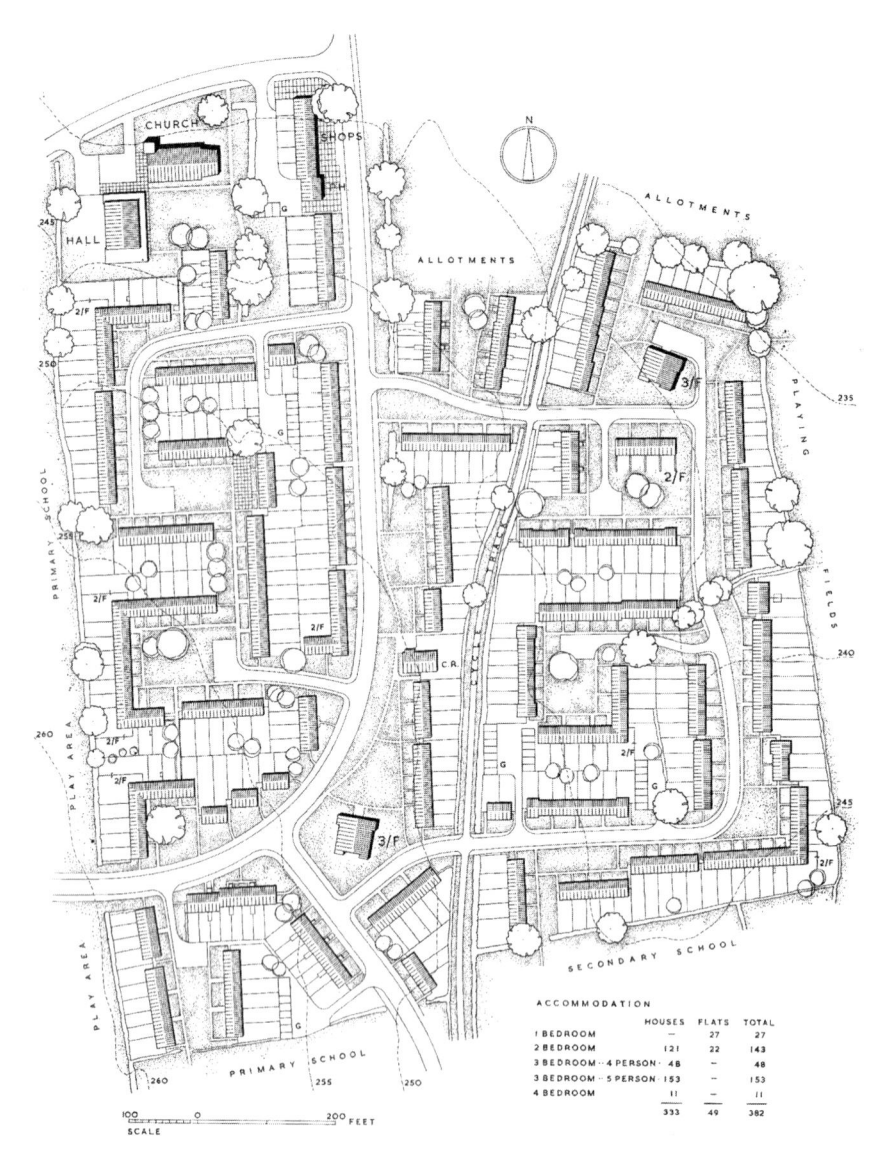

**159.** Conventional layout. (Housing Manual, 1953, p. 43.) In this layout most houses have access from the street. Each house has its own private enclosed back garden.

circulation system. It was mentioned in the previous chapter that the Radburn concept was used by some developers as a marketing tool in Dublin in the 1960s. The concept also had the advantage of requiring less road frontage since there was easy access to both front and back of the houses and therefore no need for front to back access. While they were not certain that there would be

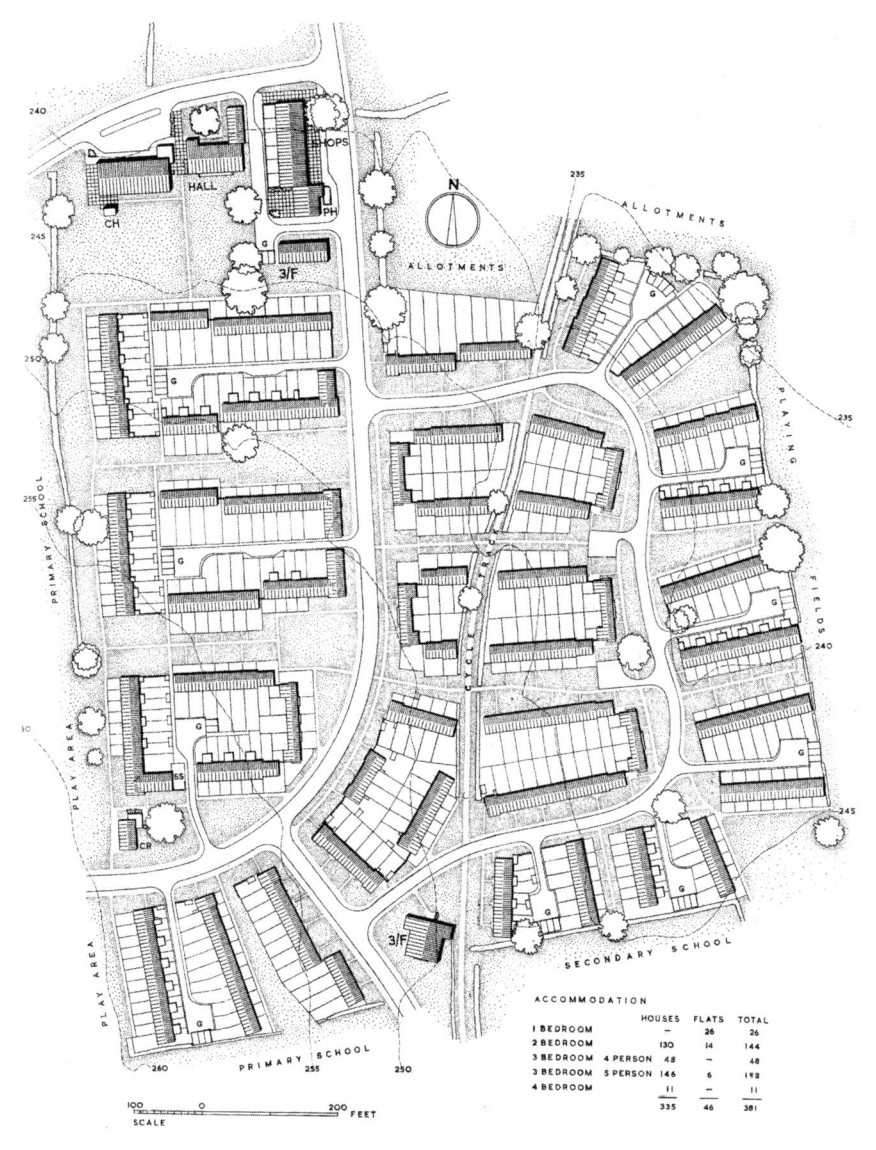

**160.** Cul-de-sac layout. (Housing Manual, 1953, p. 45.) In this layout, road traffic is confined to peripheral roads and short culs-de-sac.

any significant capital savings if a full independent pedestrian circulation system was provided, they acknowledged that the layout was safer for children, though privacy in private gardens would be reduced. The final design type was where the houses were sited at right angles to the road and approached by footpaths with a maximum distance of 150 ft (46m) from the nearest access

**161.** Double footpath layout. (Housing Manual, 1953, p. 49.) In this layout, all the houses are frontage-saving and at right angles to the road with footpath approach on both sides.

road. These had the advantage of being safer for children with lower development costs but they could result in inconvenience in the delivery of goods and the collection of refuse.

Dublin Corporation worked to much the same kind of specifications. Towards the end of the period, a size of 1,000 sq. ft (93 sq. m) was seen as being modest and most houses were built with at least 900 sq. ft (84 sq. m) (see the chapter on private housing for a comparison). Against that, family sizes were larger in Dublin, especially those which fell into the priority housing category and overcrowding would have been more of an issue here. While the conventional street was also used, there was increasing use of circulation systems that filtered traffic from the main routes and ensured that only local traffic needed to be on local roads. The cul-de-sac, which was nothing new in Dublin, became more and more common. There were some attempts at the footpath access layouts (see the discussion on Finglas earlier) but they were not popular with tenants and there was agitation to have roads installed.

Dublin suffered from the lack of variety spoken of above as the city came to rely on a small number of model houses that it varied only slightly from place to place. Unlike the UK, it did not depart greatly from the standard design until the late 1960s and it was only with the building of Darndale in the 1970s that more unconventional designs were attempted, though unsuccessfully in that case. In contrast, whether successful or not, British schemes were marked by variations in housing layout and design.

Barr (1958) noted that 'for so many years, the semi-detached house constituted the basic type of dwelling on a large majority of local authority housing estates' (p. 60). He complained that this housing type was wasteful of land and inadequate from the point of view of building up a town since the housing was too spread out. By 1953, the UK had come to the view that there was too much waste in land and money and that 'among the reasons which account for this dual waste in the schemes examined are the excessive use of semi-detached houses' (1953, p. 25). This was an important change from the 1949 manual which had recommended either semi-detached houses or terraces. There was a move towards terraces in the 1952 supplements which suggested that 'to achieve economy, the design of houses is of prime importance, but further savings may be possible in housing layouts, the construction of road and services, and the use of terraced forms of development instead of semi-detached houses'. This pleased Barr who noted that the substitution of terraced housing as a result of the economic gloom of the 1950s was a happy outcome. Dublin Corporation never adopted the semi-detached house as its standard and the terraced house was always the dominant housing type. The general form of provision was for small terraces of four to eight houses and semi-detached houses tended to occur only by accident in the sense that they were used at junctions and other locations where they made sense. The semi-detached house was a means of

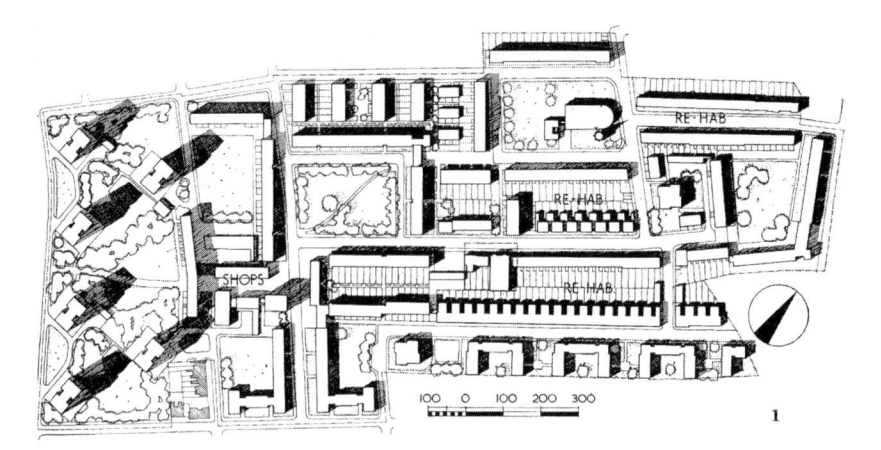

**162.** The Brandon Estate, Kennington. This had 1,005 dwellings, including 432 in 18-storey blocks but also four and six-storey maisonettes and refurbished standard houses. It was begun in 1956 and completed some four years later. (Barr, 1958, p. 165.)

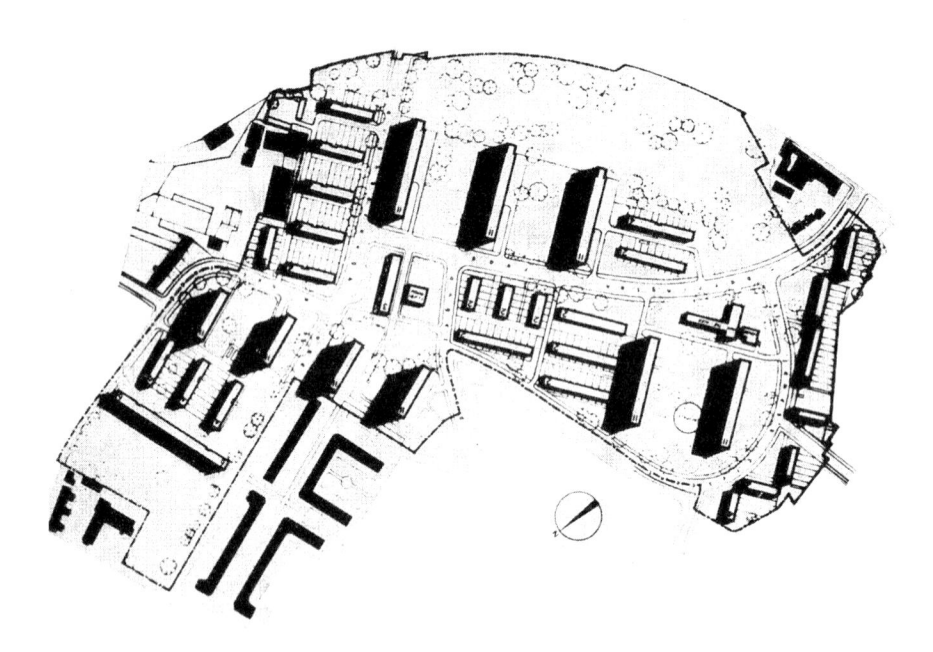

**163.** Loughborough Road Estate, London. This had 1,029 dwellings with 61 per cent in 11-storey blocks, 31 per cent in four-storey maisonettes and the remainder in houses. It was begun in 1954 and finished in 1957. (Barr, 1958, p. 167.)

**164.** Layout of Loughborough Road Estate, London, 1957. (Barr, 1958, p. 169.)

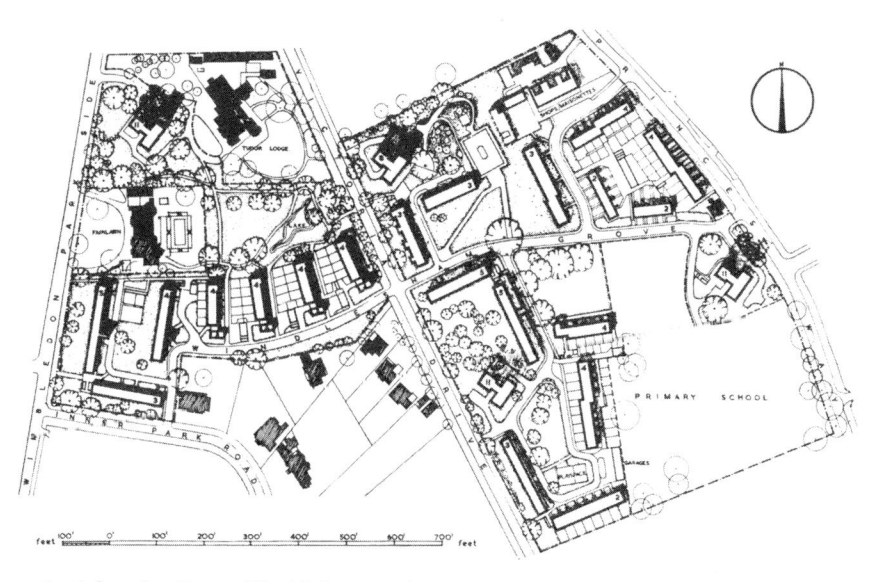

**165.** Ackroydon Estate, Wimbledon, London. This had 446 dwellings in a combination of high-rise blocks, four-storey maisonettes, 3- and 5-storey spine blocks and terraced houses. (Barr, 1958, p. 209.)

differentiating private from council housing areas and the Corporation often provided for semi-detached houses in its reserved areas or in plots which it provided for private building.

The UK moved more quickly to the concept of mixed development where houses and flats were provided in the same scheme. This permitted higher densities to be achieved while maintaining the concept of traditional housing for families and flats for smaller households. The 1949 Housing Manual suggested that 'unity and character are best achieved in low-density areas by the use of terraced and semi-detached houses in contrast with blocks of flats and public buildings and in other areas by a mixture of three-storey terraces and multi-storey flats and maisonettes' (p. 23). It went on to suggest that most families with children would prefer to live in two-storey house with gardens than in blocks of flats. They believed that people would also be happy with three-storey houses with gardens even if development had to be at relatively higher densities, such as in the 100–120 per acre range. They believed that 'the reintroduction into urban areas of this traditional type of house has much to commend it, not only on the ground that it provides more suitable family accommodation in high-density areas, but also because it enables an urban character to be given to the development' (1949, p. 47). The UK recognized early on that flat living was difficult for families and the Brooke Report (1952), *Living in Flats*, noted that 'for families with several children it is well-nigh impossible to provide in flats a wholly suitable environment'. There was a price though for the provision of houses in areas where a high density was needed. As the manual put it, 'to enable as large a number of two- or three-storey houses as possible to be built in such areas, the blocks of flats in them should be high. When families with children cannot be provided with houses, they should be offered accommodation on the lower floors of blocks of flats or maisonettes' (p. 82). This was for high-density developments. Developments in outer urban areas would still mainly comprise two-storey family houses but they allowed for bungalows and a few blocks of three- or four-storey flats to add interest and focus to the schemes.

One example which was offered was of a 48 acre (19ha) site in a high-density redevelopment area. The housing comprised three-storey terraced housing and eight-storey blocks so that approximately two-thirds of the rooms were in family houses and the balance in flats and maisonettes. This way they could achieve a density of approximately 100 rooms per acre (247/ha). However, this was only one combination and there was a wide choice of other combinations that would work.

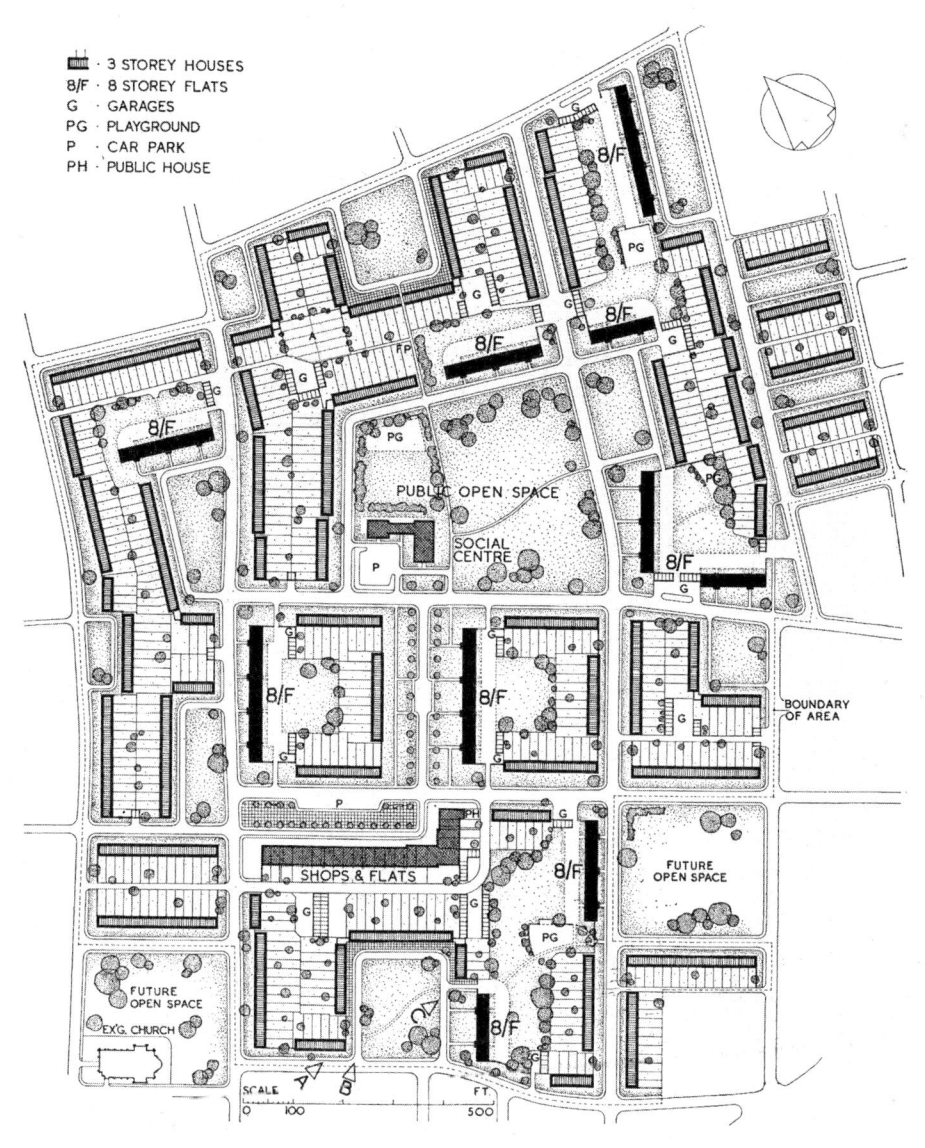

166. Redevelopment plan for a high-density area. (Housing Manual, 1949, p. 31.)

While there were many examples of such developments available to Dublin Corporation as templates, they chose not to follow this possibility to any great extent, the exception being some of the later sections in Kilmore and Edenmore. They preferred relatively low-rise flat developments in the central area and houses in the suburbs. This was despite the fact that in the

**Table 36.** Tenders approved in England and Wales, 1953–70.

|  | Percentage of dwellings approved |  |  |
| --- | --- | --- | --- |
|  | 5–14 storeys | 15+ storeys | No. of dwellings |
| 1953–9 | 6.4 | 0.5 | 971,678 |
| 1960–4 | 12.3 | 7.0 | 595,403 |
| 1965 | 10.9 | 10.6 | 162,540 |
| 1966 | 15.3 | 10.4 | 172,557 |
| 1967 | 13.3 | 9.7 | 170,545 |
| 1968 | 14.0 | 5.9 | 154,308 |
| 1969 | 9.7 | 3.8 | 112,201 |
| 1970 | 8.0 | 1.8 | 98,080 |

(Source: Cooney, 1974, p. 152)

development areas in the city centre, they were building for large families and not the mixed distribution more typical of the UK. Their reasoning was probably that they did not want to build above five storeys.

Dublin Corporation used flats in central areas to maximize the utility of the sites. In the UK up to 1950, multi-storey housing was generally rectangular blocks where access was along a balcony or via an enclosed staircase. They were generally from three to five storeys in height but they went higher too and some schemes contained eight- and ten-storey blocks. As time went on, the block designs became more ambitious with central access corridors and all manner of shapes. The heights also increased and by the early 1950s, there were eleven-storey blocks in London and from there they spread to the remainder of the country. The enthusiasm with which high-rise was adopted varied from place to place. In many cases, it seems to have been seen as a solution to the problem faced by cities running out of land and having to contemplate seeing their population located on land belonging to another authority with consequent loss of economic power and prestige. In Liverpool, the City Council was of the view that, so far as possible, the overspill of population into areas beyond the surrounding green belt should be minimized (Cooney, 1974, p. 160).

This led to a surge in high-rise as the figures from Cooney demonstrate. This was a relatively short-lived enthusiasm and the numbers were in decline in the second half of the 1960s for reasons explored above. This decline was given further impetus by the partial collapse of the twenty-two storey block at Ronan Point in the London borough of Newham in May 1968. This raised safety questions about other blocks which had been built by a variety of system building techniques. There was no such surge in Dublin. As has been seen above, Dublin Corporation was not greatly enthusiastic about flat blocks in excess of five storeys and did not see that they justified the cost. As in Dublin, flats were more expensive to build in the UK than traditional housing. The reasons attributed to this were:

- the need for public circulation areas and the provision of amenities which are not usual in houses such as laundry rooms, storage etc. A lift was regarded as a standard feature in any block over four storeys in height. This was believed to add something of the order of 10 to 25 per cent;
- the need for most complex services and a higher standard of specification for water and electrical systems;
- the structure tended to be more expensive to build and needed to meet higher standards in terms of walls, floors, roofs, insulation and fire safety;
- the building process was more complex.

It was this cost argument that won out in Dublin (see the discussion on Dominick Street above) but it can suspected that there was also still a desire to provide people with gardens.

In all, Dublin Corporation was building pretty closely to what was being undertaken in the UK with the exception that it tended to make less use of multi-storey flat blocks. They were always reluctant to go above five storeys and they felt that the increased costs were not justified by any increase in housing volume. The standards employed by the Corporation were at least as high as in the UK and they too recognized the need for developments to contain amenities as they were being completed. The fact that this did not always happen in Dublin was no different to the UK. As Barr (1958) noted: 'in many post-war estates, the shops are not being built for several years after the houses are occupied. This is a fatal mistake which should have been realized from experience after the First World War, but in such matters history continues to repeat itself. While a large shopping centre can subsequently establish itself in a community it is most difficult for local traders to do so, and local small groups of shops are of great social value if established at the same time as the estate is built' (p. 51).

# *The housing sector at the end of the 1960s*

## *Housing provision in the city*

The discussion on housing over the previous chapters showed that both public and private sectors had experienced a significant slowdown during the 1950s but whereas the private sector was quick to respond to the upturn of the 1960s, it took longer for social housing projects to come on stream. Private housing came to be concentrated in the southern suburbs of the city but there were favoured locations elsewhere such as on the western edge of the city, along the north coast or in northern suburban locations beyond the airport corridor. Social housing locations were largely determined by the administrative boundary of the city and the provision of waste drainage and this meant that it was largely northside, along the northern edge and in the north-western corner of the county borough. By the end of the 1960s, land for either public or private housing had run out and both sectors were actively in competition for what was available.

While many people now lived in four- and five-bedroomed houses, the size of individual rooms in houses in the private sector continued to get smaller, or space-saving as the estate agents would have put it, but there was an attempt to introduce some new design concepts such as open-plan and borderless gardens. It was also the period when central heating became no longer something only for the very well-to-do and most new houses incorporated it. The influences on house design were both American and British, and the aim was to make a large suburban estate not look like a large suburban estate. Social housing tended not to change that much in appearance and the old and trusted models were maintained for another couple of decades. However, it was the social housing sphere that produced the most exciting experiment of all – the foray into high-rise apartment living. Private housing largely avoided apartments but there were signs that people were prepared to adopt this kind of living, if only at particular stages of the life cycle.

By the end of the 1960s, Dublin Corporation had made a massive contribution to the housing stock of the city, having built 51,878 dwellings by February 1969 (Minutes, 3 February 1969). This is only a base number since it excludes the various assisted building schemes which the Corporation supported which allowed people to buy their own houses. Except for a few

**Table 37.** Approximate dates for Corporation houses and average cost per unit.

| Scheme | Date | Cost £ |
|---|---|---|
| Beggsboro | 1933–4 | 368 |
| Donnellys Orchard | 1933–4 | 364 |
| Malone Gardens | 1933–4 | 348 |
| Crumlin South | 1934–9 | 461 |
| Friends Fields | 1934–5 | 386 |
| Annamoe Road | 1935 | 359 |
| North Lotts | 1935–6 | 431 |
| South Lotts Road | 1936–7 | 485 |
| Ellenfield | 1937–9 | 650 |
| Crumlin North | 1938–50 | 570 |
| Harold's Cross | 1938–9 | 535 |
| Terenure | 1938 | 546 |
| Larkhill | 1939–40 | 617 |
| Cabra West | 1941–50 | 656 |
| Emmet Road | 1941 | 536 |
| Rutland Avenue | 1944–6 | 765 |
| Donnycarney | 1947–51 | 1,064 |
| Sarsfield Road | 1948–51 | 683 |
| Captain's Lane | 1949–51 | 889 |
| Ballyfermot Lower | 1950–3 | 833 |
| Sutton | 1950 | 736 |
| Howth | 1950–1 | 911 |
| Inchicore | 1950–1 | 736 |
| Brickfields | 1951–2 | 1,006 |
| Danespark | 1951–2 | 787 |
| Ennis Grove | 1951 & 1956 | 1,193 |
| Finglas West | 1951–65 | 1,649 |
| Bluebell | 1952–3 | 1,564 |
| Finglas East | 1952–65 | 1,461 |
| Milltown | 1952–3 | 1,559 |
| Ballyfermot Upper (Chapelizod) | 1953–9 | 1,535 |
| Donnybrook | 1953 | 1,694 |
| Wilkinstown | 1953–8 | 1,646 |
| Rathfarnham | 1954–6 | 1,668 |
| Coolock/ Raheny | 1956–8 | 1,783 |
| Finglas North | 1959–65 | 2,111 |
| Powerscourt | 1959 | 2,204 |
| Rathfarnham | 1962 | 2,472 |
| Edenmore | 1963–5 | 2,384 |
| Rathfarnham Village | 1964 | 2,746 |
| Coolock/Kilmore | 1965–not complete | 2,659 |

years at the end of the 1950s, the balance was always in favour of suburban housing in an approximate ratio of three to one. Some £16.94m had been provided in grants between 1932 and 1968, of which £4.27m was a direct payment while the remainder was a subsidy towards debt charges (Minutes, 5 February 1968).

The approximate sequence for the various developments and the average cost per unit is shown in the adjacent table derived from the Council minutes for 4 March 1969, pp 89–90. It shows the continuity of the building programme since the early 1930s and the steadily rising inflation in building costs.

## Owner occupancy

The 1971 census of population provided an opportunity to have an overview of housing in that year. The city had expanded beyond the boundaries of the county borough and the built-up area now extended into the county area to the south, and to a much lesser degree on the northside. There were few opportunities left to build within the city area and most of them were already earmarked for such development. This meant that in the city there were now 127,042 dwellings compared to 110,914 when the census was taken in 1946. Though the increase in the total number might have been relatively modest, the turnover in dwellings was considerable with much demolition in the city centre and replacement by suburban housing. Dublin Corporation rentals accounted for 41,819 dwellings in 1971. This was one-third of the housing stock and it is a clear statement of how important social housing had become in the city. The size of the remaining portion of the rental sector, however, was also important because many of them were likely to have been Corporation tenants in other circumstances. It accounted for 17.7 per cent which meant that about 51 per cent of accommodation in the city was some kind of rental. This was a big change from 1946 when 74.5 per cent of accommodation was rented, and, thus, the 1971 census marked the move into home ownership, which so characterizes the modern city. Some of this change resulted from the Corporation's late 1960s initiative to transfer much of its stock into the private sector by selling it to their tenants. The 1971 census indicated that 4,661 (3.7 per cent) were in the process of tenant purchase, another supported pathway towards ownership.

The balance between rental and ownership in Dún Laoghaire was roughly 45/55 in favour of ownership. Council housing accounted for around 23 per cent of the housing stock (3,108 units) and very little of this was in the process

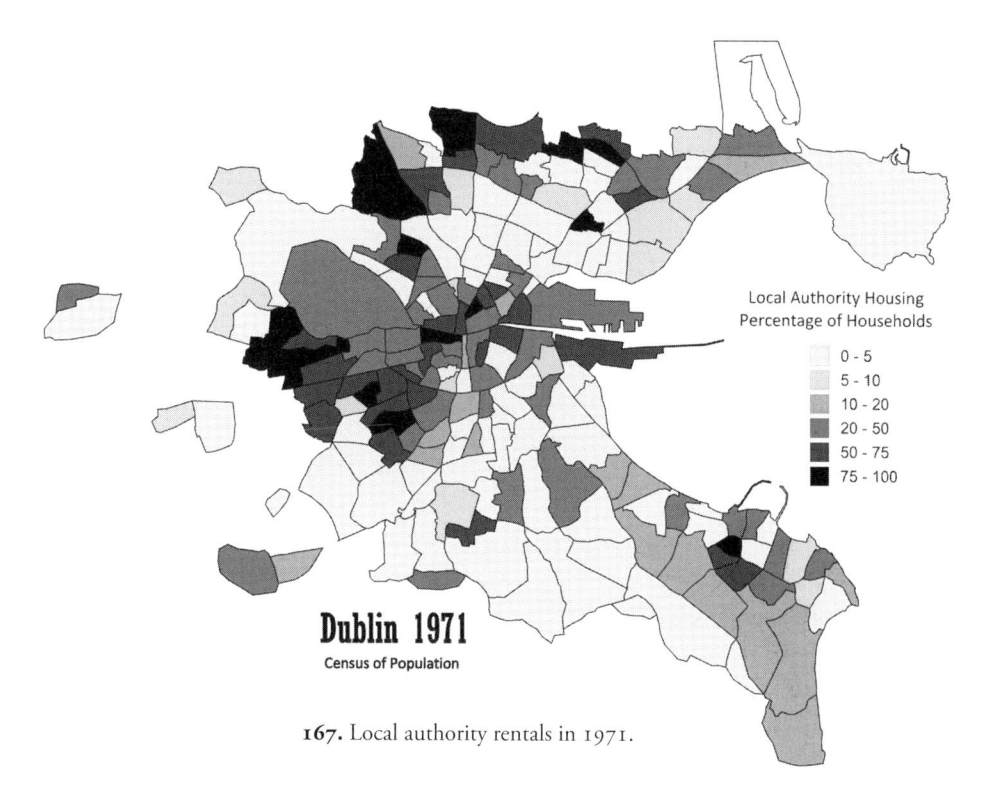

THE HOUSING SECTOR AT THE END OF THE 1960s 333

**167.** Local authority rentals in 1971.

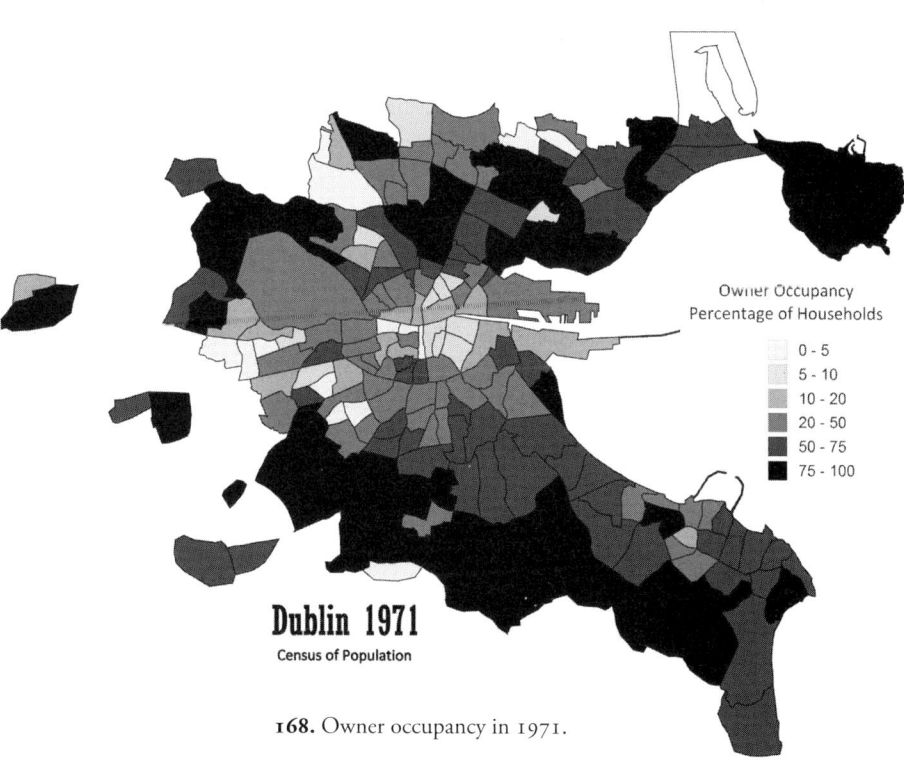

**168.** Owner occupancy in 1971.

**Dublin 1971**
Census of Population

Private Rental Market
Percentage of Households
- 0 - 5
- 5 - 10
- 10 - 20
- 20 - 50
- 50 - 80

169. Private rental sector in 1971.

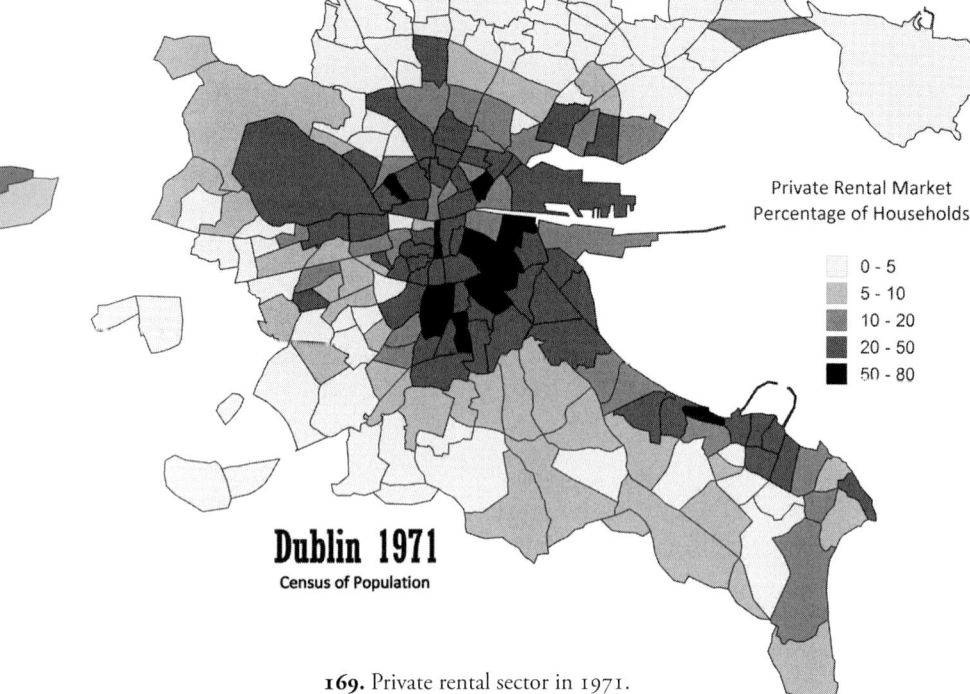

of being bought. Although the city had spread into the county area by 1971 and there were now 34,384 dwellings in the southern part of the built-up area, relatively little of this was social housing. Over eighty per cent was privately owned with only 6.4 per cent (2,189 units) rented from the local authority. This meant that Dublin Corporation accounted directly for 85 per cent of social housing rentals in the entire built-up area.

The 1971 census data were made available for some 200 small areal units, wards or district electoral divisions, and this provided an unprecedented level of granularity in looking at how the city was structured. There are some problems with the areas as research tools; one such is that the Phoenix Park is visible as a very large area on the maps but it has a very small population, mostly along its edge, and is not of major importance.

The dominance of local authority housing in the west of the county borough and along its northern edge was very marked, where it was in excess of 75 per cent. This was also the case in the inner city, defined as the area between the canals, where the incidence of local authority flats was very high. There were pockets of local authority housing in the Dún Laoghaire borough, as would be expected, and an interesting and isolated area of rentals in Donnycarney. The city was quite segregated in terms of housing tenure, though not necessarily housing history, and many parts of the city had little or no local authority housing nearby.

The map of owner occupancy is, for the most part, a mirror image of the local authority rental map. Over much of the southern suburbs, owner occupancy was at least 75 per cent of the housing stock and rose to almost all of it in many places. Despite having its own urban structure and a significant level of local authority housing, the distribution in Dún Laoghaire shows that the most characteristic form of tenure was owner occupancy. This was also the case in Glasnevin, Clontarf, part of Artane and Coolock as well as Castleknock. This was a function of the combined effects of the private housing sector and also the Corporation's policy of building houses for owner occupancy either in reserved areas or in tenant purchase schemes. The impact of these purchase schemes can be seen, for example, in the higher instances of owner occupancy in Finglas East but not in Finglas West. Owner occupancy was also strong in the south-eastern inner suburbs, the areas of the old Pembroke and Rathmines townships, but there the relative importance was decreased by the importance of the private rental sector.

## *Private rental sector*

The private rental sector was always an important feature of the housing market. At its best, it was an important safety valve for the social housing programme in that it provided housing to people who might otherwise have ended up on the housing list, without any prospect of being housed. For many years, Dublin Corporation encouraged the provision of rental properties which could be afforded by those with modest incomes but smaller families. At its worst, it was the problem that Dublin Corporation had to solve. By 1971 the tenement problem was being brought under control but in previous generations it was the failure of private landlords to maintain decent rental accommodation that caused so much of the problem that Dublin Corporation had to solve. The map shows that rental properties were most concentrated in the inner city and older inner suburbs and they were not a major feature of the newer developments. In the former areas, the rental properties were not occupied by potential Corporation tenants alone. Many older, middle-class people would have rented their properties in earlier generations, owner occupancy being very much a recent phenomenon in Dublin. There was a large zone that encompassed Merrion Square, Mount Street and reached into the Baggot Street and Ranelagh areas while it was also a significant feature (40–50 per cent of housing units) in Ballsbridge, Rathmines and parts of Rathgar. In the latter cases, it represented the growing 'flatland' of Dublin. Rental accommodation was also very important in the south inner city, especially east of the Liberties. The Iveagh Trust was the most notable provider in this area but there was the full range of rental properties available, though in most cases it served the lower end of the market. Dún Laoghaire also had its areas of private lettings, in the harbour area especially and in the coastal part of Monkstown consisting mainly of large subdivided Victorian villas.

On the northside, the map captured the private rental areas off Mountjoy Square with its decaying Georgian houses and the much better accommodation in Oxmanstown, a development of the Dublin Artisans' Dwelling Company. The lone island in the north-western part of the city was the privately-built housing estate for rental developed by Associated Properties Ltd in Wadelai. In 1971 much of the original estate was still rented but this was soon to change considerably as the property company actively encouraged renters to buy their properties.

## *Multiple occupancy*

The census recorded the total number of dwellings in purpose-built blocks of flats or other buildings which had been structurally sub-divided into separate housing units. For all of the importance of the Ballymun development in the 1960s, Dublin remained a city of conventional single family houses. In very few areas did multiple occupancy rise above 10 per cent and it was close to zero across huge swathes of the city. Only in the inner city, where Dublin Corporation had always built flat blocks, and in the southside inner suburbs were these an important aspect of the urban landscape. Dún Laoghaire had its own concentration of this housing type, again mostly local authority developments. The uniqueness of the Ballymun experiment and its peripheral location really stand out from the map. There was nothing like the concentration of flat developments anywhere else outside the inner city.

## *A new city?*

As has already been noted in Chapter 1, the 1960s changed the housing profile of the city. Some 41,000 new housing units had been added in the ten years

**Dublin 1971**
Census of Population

Multiple Occupancy
Percentage of Households
- 0 - 20
- 20 - 40
- 40 - 60
- 60 - 80
- 80 - 100

170. Multiple occupancy in 1971.

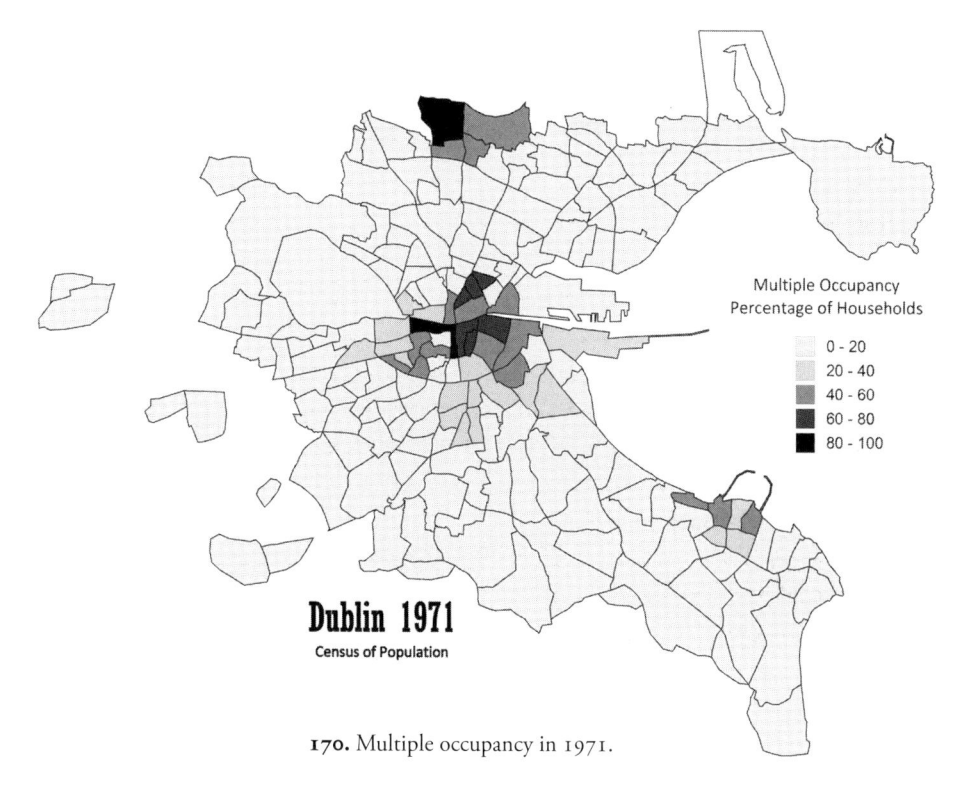

since 1961 or fifteen per cent of the total. Widening the time frame to 1946 showed that forty-four per cent of housing was less than 25 years old. There had also been demolition of old housing as part of slum clearance and this now formed a relatively small part of the stock. Only twenty per cent pre-dated 1900, of which only four per cent was older than 1860. The effect of demolitions had a larger statistical impact because so many of the 'dwellings' that disappeared were in multi-dwelling houses.

Table 38. Age of housing stock in Dublin as of 1971.

|         | Built-up area | County borough | Dún Laoghaire | North suburbs | South suburbs |
|---------|---------------|----------------|---------------|---------------|---------------|
| pre 1860 | 7,101        | 5,312          | 1,253         | 101           | 435           |
| 1860–99 | 23,590        | 19,769         | 2,834         | 133           | 854           |
| 1900–18 | 16,524        | 14,209         | 1,418         | 103           | 794           |
| 1919–40 | 37,310        | 31,553         | 2,785         | 237           | 2,735         |
| 1941–60 | 54,242        | 37,106         | 3,267         | 568           | 1,301         |
| 1961+   | 40,589        | 19,056         | 1,725         | 3,553         | 16,255        |

Note: The unit of measurement is the housing unit and this is not directly comparable with the concept of dwelling used in the 1961 census. There could be many dwellings in a housing unit, especially in the inner city.

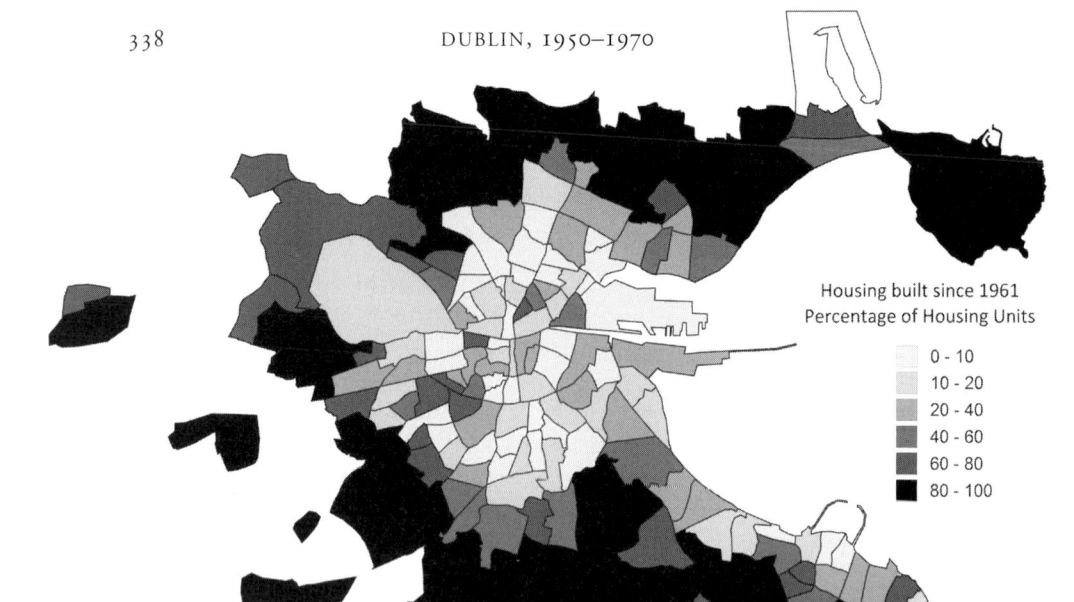

**Dublin 1971**
Census of Population

171. New housing in the city.

Figure 171 confirms the peripheral nature of new housing since 1961 with new housing dominating the outer suburbs and with only a few inner city renewal projects having a major impact on the housing stock. A new development zone or belt had been added to the city during the decade as the city expanded into greenfield areas. Most of the northern part of the city comprised new housing and there was a similarly imposing addition to the southern part of the city, but outside the county boundary in this case. All of this building, combined with inner city clearance, helped to continue the improvement in the condition of the housing stock. The census provided some information on the quality of housing provision such as the nature of the water supply, the provision of sanitary facilities and the extent to which a housing unit was provided with a bath or with electricity. It shows that there was very little very poor housing left, though that fact would have been of cold comfort to the people living in that housing.

Almost every housing unit had electricity and the number of housing units without a flush toilet (not necessarily indoors) was very small indeed as was the number of units without access to an indoor water supply. While the bath

**Table 39.** Some indications of housing quality in the entire city, 1971.

| Facility | Housing units | Per cent |
| --- | --- | --- |
| Inside water supply – public main | 176,726 | 98.5 |
| Outside water supply – public main | 1,711 | 1.0 |
| Inside water supply – private well | 722 | 0.4 |
| Outside water supply – private well | 76 | 0.1 |
| No piped water | 171 | 0.1 |
| Flush toilet | 178,913 | 99.8 |
| Chemical closet | 146 | 0.1 |
| Dry closet | 274 | 0.2 |
| No toilet or closet | 73 | 0.0 |
| Housing units with bath | 157,083 | 87.6 |
| Housing units with electricity | 179,125 | 99.9 |

was not yet a universal feature, it was approaching this. It will come as no surprise that its absence remained a problem of old, subdivided houses, concentrated in the inner city. In these areas it was possible to find locations where fewer than one third of housing units had a fixed bath.

## *Adequacy?*

More than any question, this depends on the perspective of the reader. The building programme of the Corporation was impressive but it was not universally seen as being sufficient. The issue lay in the housing list and the categories of people for whom the Corporation took direct responsibility. Not everyone on low income could expect to be housed; the reality was that people had to have large families in overcrowded conditions before the assessment of the medical officer would be that housing was required. Young married couples had little hope of being housed by the city except for the annual lottery and they would have to do as best they could until they had at least three children. This was not a capricious policy on the part of the authorities. The only income that the city had was from rates and this was a significant burden on both business and all non-council tenants and homeowners. Whatever portion of this income could be devoted to housing had to be supplemented by State grants and the extent to which this could be done was always extremely limited.

The waiting list was reviewed in 1966 and this resulted in the number of active applications dropping from 5,192 to 4,700 (Report 71/1966). Some 3,881 persons who were on the previous list did not reapply. However, in that year there were 502 new applications. In September of 1967, an analysis of the approved waiting list showed the following distribution (Minutes, 4 December 1967).

| Approved waiting list | |
|---|---|
| Persons per application | No. applications |
| 1 | 445 |
| 2 | 224 |
| 3 | 1,240 |
| 4 | 1,497 |
| 5 | 720 |
| 6+ | 626 |

By August 1968, there were 5,410 applicants on the approved list. These were people who met the approved requirements and who had been certified by the Chief Medical Officer as being in need of rehousing. The others remained on the non-approved list where they would remain until either their circumstances changed or the priorities altered to encompass their circumstances (Minutes, 21 August 1967). By the same date there were 4,662 cases on this list and by February 1969, there were 5,301 cases on this list, of whom 456 were single people (mostly older persons) and 231 were couples. Not everyone who needed housing would apply to be put on the waiting list since for some it was a pointless exercise but not everyone on the approved waiting list would receive housing in a timely manner. The view of the City Manager when reporting in December 1967 was that it was not expected that everyone on the list would be housed by December 1968.

So, how the Corporation's programme was viewed depended on the perspective of the viewer. In 1968, two Labour Councillors (Dermot O'Rourke and Gerard English) took the view that public agitation was needed and they called for city-wide protests by Labour supporters as a way of forcing the government into action (*Irish Press*, 13 November, p. 7). They suggested that only by such increased agitation would the officials of the Corporation be given the necessary help and encouragement by the Department of Local Government to expand the housing programme. This led to a rebuke by the Housing Committee for the two councillors (Report 164/1968) but their action was symptomatic of a feeling that there was a crisis for those outside the remit of the Corporation. Into this space came the Dublin Housing Action Committee and a very useful treatment of this group is offered by Hanna (2013). They saw the political advantage of public protest and direct action by squatting. They did not advocate squatting in Corporation dwellings, but they did not condemn it, but rather they encouraged it in what they saw as habitable accommodation, mostly in the city centre, which was lying vacant as it waited for redevelopment. As they 'outed' landlords who were evicting tenants or behaving badly, they wanted the government to curb property speculation, declare a housing emergency and requisition all vacant accommodation for housing. In highlighting a need to curb property speculation, they found themselves on the same side as the City Manager. From their headquarters in 30 Gardiner Place the group sought to organize all homeless people in a mass movement of militant action. They claimed to be a non-political, non-sectarian association of homeless people but their activities were curtailed by the Forcible Entry and Occupation Act which was passed in 1971.

A study was undertaken by the Department of Social Science in UCD and published in 1969 (Ward, 1969) and was introduced in the chapter on private housing. It was based on a random sample of 249 residents of a newly developed Corporation suburb in north Dublin. The suburb was not identified except to say that it had an old village and a limited amount of pre-war and immediately post-war private housing. It adjoined a large owner occupied development which was built at about the same time. The sample size was small, even though the authors went to some trouble to make sure that the reader was aware of the size of the resulting sampling error. Nonetheless, it provided an interesting snapshot of peoples' perceptions of their new area. And these perceptions were generally positive. The respondents had been in the area for less than four years and they felt that they had settled well into their new environment. Most had come to the area because they needed more space in their accommodation or because their housing had been condemned. Close to 60 per cent now lived in four-roomed houses while the remainder were in five-roomed houses. They recognized that their homes were a great improvement on what they had come from but there were niggles with regard to design which could have been solved with some dialogue between the developers and the potential residents. More than anything, the residents wanted a bigger kitchen.

There were complaints about the distances that husbands now had to travel to work but the biggest irritant was that shops did not come at the same time as the development and the distances from church and school was greater than people felt was reasonable. There was a loss of support systems in that a little more than half of the housewives had less contact with their families than they had prior to the move. This was not a problem for most but there was a small percentage of people (<10 per cent) for whom this sundering of their social networks was a problem and they were unhappy and experienced a variety of difficulties.

As the decade came to a close, the Corporation was running out of land on which to build. In October 1967, the Corporation had 4,040 sites for normal housing on which building had yet to commence and a further 1,100 sites were being acquired. In addition, they had about 2,000 sites which they could either devote to social housing or to private housing. In the private sector, it was estimated that there were about 7,000 sites available, divided evenly between city and county. The work which was being done on the development of the sewerage system on the periphery of the city would yield about 23,000 sites. In a detailed report to the Council, the Manager took the unusual step of denouncing speculation. He noted that speculative builders had difficulty in getting suitable land for private building and owners had pushed up the prices for land dramatically in the belief that they would have no difficulty in passing on the cost to the purchasers. This meant that small builders and voluntary associations were finding themselves priced out of the market and it was increasingly difficult for some sections of society to afford housing. This was particularly so for those on modest income who were kept off the housing list by virtue of their being able to afford their own accommodation.

Not surprisingly, this was also causing problems for the local authority in that the price of land was rising and they often found themselves gazumped even when a deal had been done with a landowner. This phenomenon was occurring not only to land which was ready for development but also land which had any prospect of development. Speculators were buying land in anticipation that it could be turned into development land at some time in the future. As a result the Council was being forced to pay exorbitant prices.

The Manager took the view that the price of land should reflect its agricultural value plus a reasonable amount to reflect its good location. The fact that it had been turned into development land by virtue of the action of the local authority in providing roads or sewerage should not provide a profit to the landowner since they had contributed nothing to the development. In the view of the Manager: 'The purchase of land for building should not be regarded as the El Dorado for monied interests, many of whom do not make any contribution towards its development. They hope to make a profit on it which will ultimately fall as a burden either on the tax payer or on the house purchaser' (Minutes, 8 May 1967).

In terms of what needed to be done, the Manager suggested a direct intervention into the land and housing market to take the heat out of it.

Working in concert, the councils would build up a land bank sufficient for their own needs and for the provision of private housing of modest size (1,000 sq. ft / 90 sq. m). This would be costly to begin with but as more and more land was made available, the price would fall so that it returned eventually to its real value.

Since both the city and Dún Laoghaire were running out of land it was suggested that the authorities co-operate in the provision of sites so that sufficient land would be made available for immediate requirements for both social and private housing. In order to ensure that the maximum benefit was obtained, there was also a need to relax some of the restrictions on the assistance programmes available to private buyers. In particular, there was a residency requirement in relation to the supplementary grant and it was now suggested that this be abandoned (discussed above, p. 121) and that the grant to be paid regardless of where the applicant lived. While this would be a cost to the County Council to begin with, the rate income that would accrue from these houses would be sufficient to offset any losses after about two years. In all, the strategy suggested was that:

> this will facilitate a combined effort by all three authorities in the making available of sites and in the provision of houses for all those of modest means who are anxious to provide their own house. I would hope that we would reach the position ultimately where people who are sorely in need of houses would know with reasonable certainty that a house would be available to them within a particular period.
>
> It is intended that priority should be given to existing tenants who vacate houses and make them available for those in the lower income groups and secondly for those who are on the approved waiting list for houses.
>
> In order to supplement the available capital for house building, some means might be devised whereby people who are anxious to provide themselves with houses would be given the maximum incentive to save and local authorities might arrange to accept deposits on houses in advance of the date on which the houses are provided.

The Manager was prescient in his concern about land speculation and the hoarding of land in anticipation of development. He did not quite appreciate that it might be possible to direct development towards where land had been hoarded and thus alter the spatial development of the city. It was also the case that the councils were never going to be able to control or even dampen down the speculation in land prices; there was simply too much money to be made and too many wishing to make it. Nor were there large scale transfers of sites but Dublin came to experience the phenomenon of development sponsored by Dublin Corporation or Dún Laoghaire borough taking place in the County Council area.

The Housing Committee Breviate for May 1968 showed the process underway as they approved a layout plan prepared by Consultant Architects, Morris & McCullough, for a proposed housing development at Tallaght (Report 73/1968). It also showed the continuing efforts to encourage house purchase as they recommended that applications be invited for proposed sales schemes for houses at Coolock/Kilmore, St Columbanus Road and Ballygall Road East from Corporation tenants and persons on the approved waiting list. In the case of the Tallaght area, the Corporation was prepared to be more flexible than usual and recommended that applications be not limited to Corporation tenants and those on the approved waiting list but that all applicants could apply. They also continued to support reserved area building by recommending that 32 sites for private dwellings at Martin's Lands, Kimmage, and 38 at Finglas be allocated to small builders for the erection of houses to be sold to persons who would be nominated by the Corporation. The breviate for November 1968 (Report 164/1968) showed the continuation of these actions. They approved a sketch layout for the proposed new Housing Area at Darndale, where it was proposed to provide approximately 3,000 houses. This was going to be a very interesting development with the Corporation departing from conventional design to one that promised better social integration. Unfortunately, it delivered nothing of the sort. The layout also provided for shopping centres, churches, schools, playing facilities and an industrial area of approximately 16 hectares. They also noted that the Department of Local Government was agreeable to the Corporation's proposal to utilize the services of the National Building Agency Ltd in connection with the development of the Corporation's lands at the Bawn/Tallaght area.

All this demonstrated the Corporation's new and continuing strategy. While they continued to build on the remainder of their sites within the city area, they were now building in Tallaght and, with the experience of Ballymun behind them, they were prepared to use the services of the National Building Agency. They were continuing to provide private housing for tenants who could surrender their leases and free them up for people lower down the income spectrum. They were relaxing their residency rules for the developments outside their functional area and they were trying to keep the building industry going by providing special allocations to small builders.

On a previous occasion, they had agreed to a mix in Kilbarrack that would include 1,210 rental houses, 288 flats, 212 sites for tenant purchase and 140 in the reserved areas (Report 8/1967). This continued with its development in Howth (Balglass) where it agreed to 112 sites on the basis of a 50/50 split between tenant and private housing (Report 57/1968). A similar split was agreed for Holylands while a proposal was accepted by the McInerney Company to build 358 houses at Old Bawn. There would be 150 semi-detached houses at £3,525, 96 end-terrace houses at £3,475 and 112 terraced houses at £3,435 each. One hundred of the houses would go to Dublin County Council while the remainder were to be made available to Dublin Corporation. The spatial geometry and geography of the city had quickly become more complex but there was continuity in the range of housing initiatives that were available as the city moved into 1970.

# The social areas of Dublin, 1971

## Social structure

Jimmy O'Dea, the legendary comedian and actor, used perform a piece entitled 'thank heavens we are living in Rathgar' which was a quick tour through the social areas of the city.

> There are some quite decent suburbs, I am sure.
> Rathmines is not so bad or Terenure.
> we've heard of spots like Inchicore,
> But really don't know where they are;
> For, thank heavens, we are living in Rathgar.
> Someone must live in Kilmainham,
> So it's hardly fair to blame 'em,
> And in Dartry they are almost civilized.
> But in Fairview, goodness gracious,
> Fellows tennis in their braces;
> In Drumcondra all their shirts are trubenized.

As the above extract indicates, there were quite definite impressions of the social composition of the various parts of the city and of the differences between them. There is nothing unusual in this. It is a characteristic of western cities, even those with a large social housing component, to be structured into different residential areas with distinctive characteristics where social status or social class is an important differentiating factor.

Dublin's social structure had been developing over the previous 150 years and its future shape had become clear from the 1930s. It was fixed from that point that the most desirable residential areas were in a south-eastern wedge that radiated from the old Pembroke and Rathmines townships. These areas ultimately joined up with the residential areas of the coastal (Dún Laoghaire) borough. This was in contrast to the western part of the south city where the decision by Dublin Corporation to build social housing on a very large scale, a decision that they came to regret almost immediately, gave that part of the city its distinctive character. The northside was more complex because the impact of the Drumcondra and Clontarf townships was not as decisive on the social geography of the city. Their spatial extent was quite small and they were not spatially contiguous by the time they were absorbed into the city. When that is combined with a building programme by Dublin Corporation which was spread more widely than on the southside, it is possible to understand why the social geography of the northside came to be more complex with greater mixing of different social areas.

As a means of drawing this book to a close, this chapter will attempt to summarize the city as it was in the beginning of the 1970s, providing an opportunity to compare it with the city described in Chapter 1 and also in *Dublin, 1930–1950*. The county borough, the area controlled by Dublin Corporation, was subdivided into 141 wards for the 1971 census in comparison to the 42 there previously while the county area was divided into 80 district electoral divisions (deds) replacing the 49 deds previously used to describe the county.

From a technical point of view, it was necessary to decide on what comprised the city. It had long extended beyond the county borough and there were urban suburbs in the county area. At the same time, not all of the county area could be considered urban in 1971 and it would have distorted what follows to include it and so for this analysis it was decided to add those parts of Blanchardstown, Lucan/Clondalkin, and Tallaght, which were described as urban by the CSO, to the data for the county borough and Dún Laoghaire. The city thus defined comprised 199 areas with a population in 1971 of 798,230. At this point it is useful to explain two concepts which will turn up in the discussion. A household is a number of people who are economically linked. Most households comprise families but household members need not be related. Two students sharing a flat would comprise a household if they shared their living expenses. In Dublin in 1971, there were 194,258 households who were housed in 179,406 housing units. A housing unit is a structurally separate dwelling and for the most part they were conventional houses – 152,241 or just under 85 per cent of the total.

The data were initially made available as computer printout and were referred to as small area population statistics (saps). Welcome as these were, there were some methodological issues relating to their use. These are not discussed here but an appendix is provided for those who wish to explore them. Also, while the saps were a huge step forward in making data available, they were not without their limitations. They did not provide any information on income, family structure, journey to work or education though some of these omissions were rectified in later censuses. The first section of this chapter will be devoted to looking at a series of maps that show different aspects of the structure of the city. These will examine age profiles, economic structure, social composition and some data on housing. Housing has already been discussed in an earlier chapter. It will be seen that the same patterns emerge from time to time and the argument will be developed that these patterns are manifestations of a couple of larger concepts or processes. It will be argued that it is possible to summarize these different patterns and so summarize the city by a small number of maps.

## *The people in 1971*

The saps presented a substantial amount of demographic information for 1971. Total numbers were given for the number of males and females in five-year age bands and these totals were further sub-divided into single, married and widowed categories.

The overall pattern of population change can be seen in the maps below; later maps will deconstruct the various elements that combine to produce this distribution. In 1971, Dublin was a city with a very variable experience of population change. Most of the county borough areas were, at best, static but many had lost population. The most significant population losses were in the inner city, a combination of the natural aging of the population and Dublin Corporation's redevelopment programme. On the southside the areas in decline included much of the High Street and Coombe areas as well as around Harcourt Street and Harcourt Road. The gains were mainly towards the northern edge of the borough in the housing estates of Ballymun, Beaumont, Kilmore, Donaghmede, The Donahies and on into areas of extensive building in Baldoyle, Sutton and Howth. There were pockets of growth elsewhere such as in Finglas West, Glasnevin/Ballygall, and in parts of Raheny but with the exception of the Nutley Lane area of Donnybrook there was little growth within the southern part of the county borough. Dún Laoghaire was a mixture of growth and decline. There was substantial growth in parts of Monkstown as well as in Dalkey/Killiney.

With the exception of the areas described above, growth was a suburban phenomenon, particularly on the edge of the city. It was at its most substantial on the northern fringe of the city at Coolock and in the new southern suburbs of Dundrum/Ballinteer, Dean's Grange and to the far south in Ballybrack. Growth was also substantial in adjacent locations and there was a band of areas which grew by more than five per cent which reached from Terenure in the

# THE SOCIAL AREAS OF DUBLIN, 1971

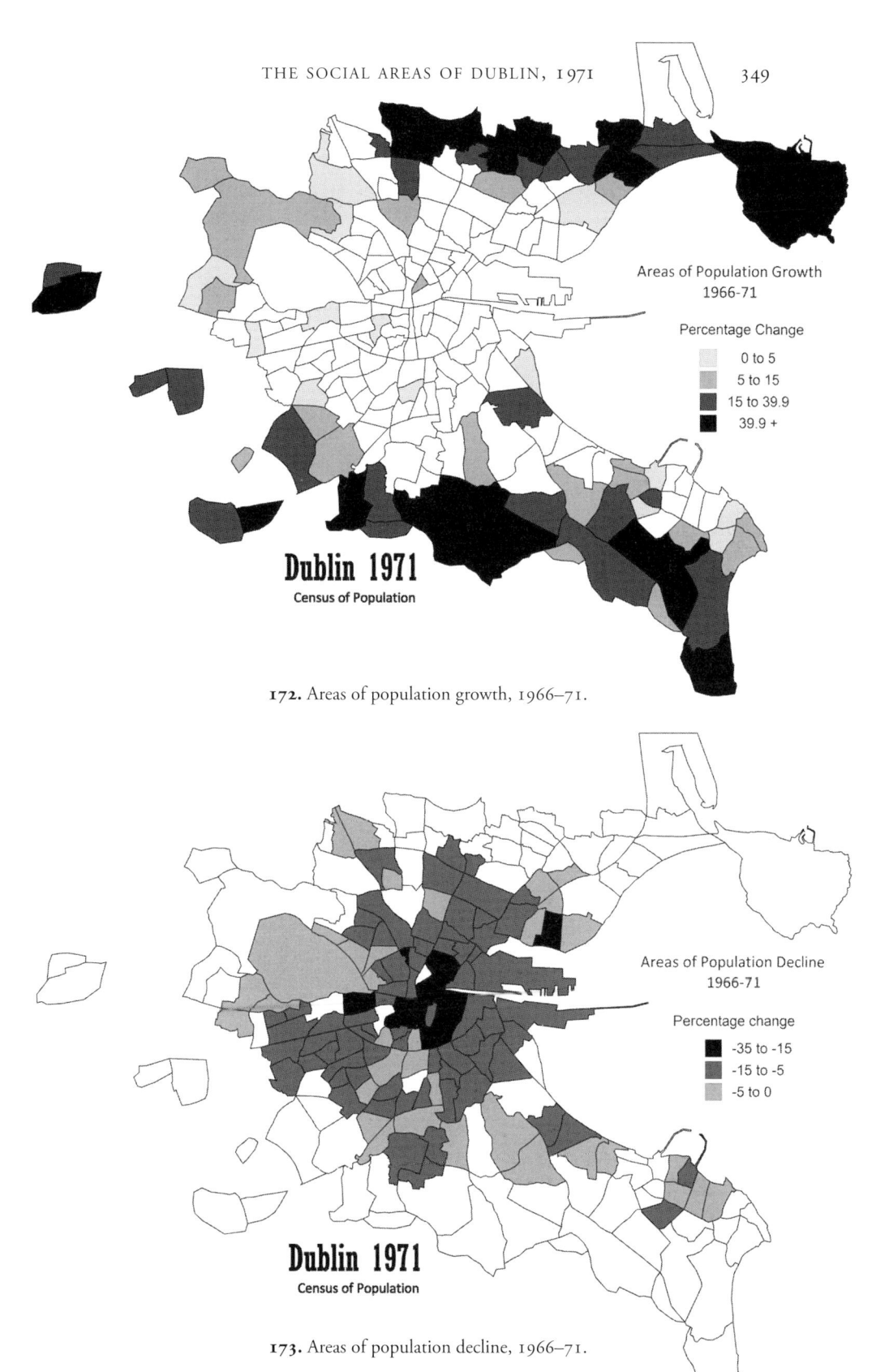

**172.** Areas of population growth, 1966–71.

**173.** Areas of population decline, 1966–71.

west, along the southern edge of the city to the coast at Killiney. It included Churchtown, Mount Merrion and Foxrock. However, it is worth noting that some areas of the southern suburbs, relatively recent suburbs such as those around Rathfarnham and Clonskeagh, had stopped growing and had moved into decline, probably as a result of their movement out of the family formation stage of the life cycle. The map also shows the beginnings of development in the new suburbs to the west of the city with strong growth in Blanchardstown, Clondalkin and Tallaght. The footprint of development was still small and the final shape of the communities had yet to emerge.

The growth in population was due largely to family formation and the development of new family oriented residential areas. Some 87,527 children were added to the city between 1966 and 1971, though their location varied considerably from a minimum of 55 in one area to a maximum of 2,501 in another. Figure 174 shows the extent to which the *under 4 years group* was important in the age structure of an area. An area with a high percentage was still growing and, conversely, areas with few children under the age of four years were moving to a different stage of the life cycle. Generally, children of this age accounted for seven per cent of the population but while most areas had some children, the map shows that strong growth was highly concentrated on the northern edge of the city. There were also large numbers in the Old Bawn area of Tallaght as development of this new town proceeded ahead of the other chosen locations. In most areas in the south of the county borough and in parts of Drumcondra, Glasnevin, Fairview and Clontarf, the proportion was well below the average and in one instance fell as low as 2.4 per cent. This was true of most areas in the south county borough, especially the south inner city and its western edge. On the northside these areas were also largely outside the canal ring and found in Drumcondra, Glasnevin, Fairview and Clontarf.

Another way of looking at population growth is to calculate a *fertility index*. In terms of the data available, the best that could be done was to calculate a ratio which would indicate how many children were born during 1966–71 per woman in the usual child bearing ages of 15–44. So, this is a measure of active family formation in each area; it is crude but it serves the purpose. As would be expected there is a degree of similarity between the pattern shown in the map of young children but the patterns are not identical and the insights given are somewhat different. The number of children born per woman varied from a low of almost zero (0.08) to a high of 1.63 with an average for the city of 0.50. The areas with the lowest fertility rate were generally also those with the

THE SOCIAL AREAS OF DUBLIN, 1971　　　351

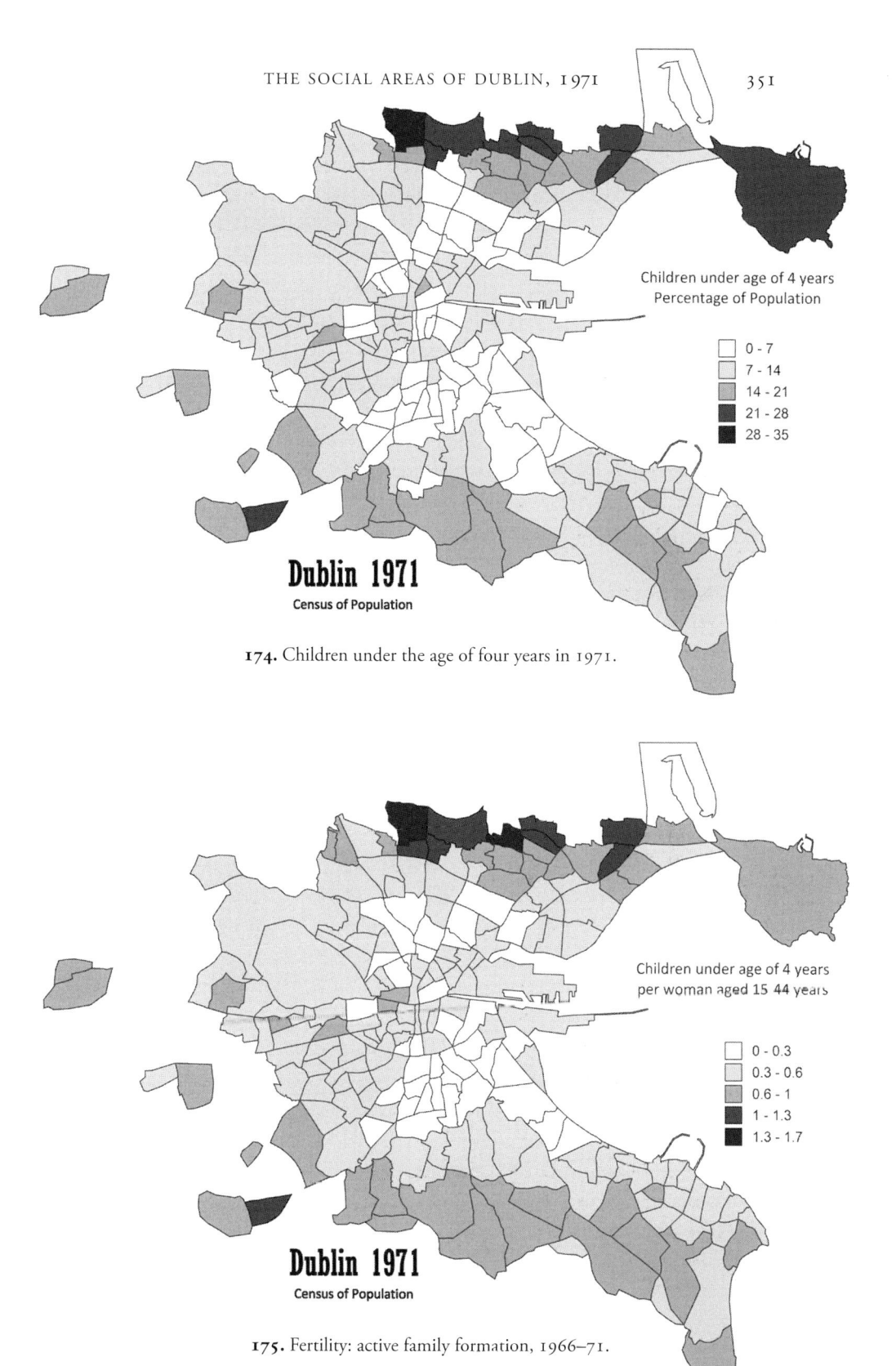

174. Children under the age of four years in 1971.

175. Fertility: active family formation, 1966–71.

smallest proportion of children under 4 years and women in these areas have either completed their families or were in other roles. Fertility below the city average was found in much of south Dublin, especially in the Dún Laoghaire and Dalkey/Killiney areas as well as in Rathfarnham and Terenure and was also a feature of much of the western edge of the city. Above average ratios were found along the northern fringe, especially in Ballymun, Santry and Kilmore where mothers had between 1.3 and 1.6 children each over the five-year period. These were recently developed areas and the high proportion of children under 4 years combined with a high fertility rate was the natural consequence of a population made up predominantly of young couples. Similar fertility levels were found in Old Bawn (Tallaght) and Templeogue. Howth, though it had a high proportion of children under 4 years in its population, did not exhibit a particularly high fertility rate and the high number of young children is probably due to the addition of numbers of new families to the area. In overall terms, the northern and southern fringes of the city had above average fertility with the highest levels along the northern edge and in Tallaght and Templeogue.

At the other end of the age spectrum are those areas with a significant number of people *over the age of 65 years*. There were 67,704 such persons in 1971 and their numbers varied from none in one area to one in five or six of the population in others. The newness of the areas around the edge of the city and the fact that they were largely greenfield developments was emphasized by the fact that they had very few older people. With the exception of Blanchardstown, part of Lucan, and parts of Sutton there were few older people on the periphery of the city; instead the proportion was higher along the coastal corridor from Killiney northwards to Sandymount and they had a strong representation in Rathgar, Rathmines and Donnybrook. There were more old people than average for the city in Glasnevin, Drumcondra, Whitehall, parts of Clontarf and in areas towards the city centre via Fairview. Only in seven areas in the city was the proportion over 18 per cent, but in only three cases, two of which are in the Dún Laoghaire area, can it be truly said that these were 'older' areas. The other areas were dominated by hospitals, which tend to inflate the concentration of old people, such as Our Lady's Hospice in Harold's Cross, the Royal Hospital in Donnybrook, St James's Hospital in Kilmainham, St Brendan's in Grangegorman and St Mary's in the Phoenix Park.

One way of summarizing the various age distributions is to calculate an index of dependency. It is usual to look at the population aged between 15

People aged over 65 years
Percentage of Population

0 - 5
5 - 10
10 - 15
15 - 20
20 - 33

Dublin 1971
Census of Population

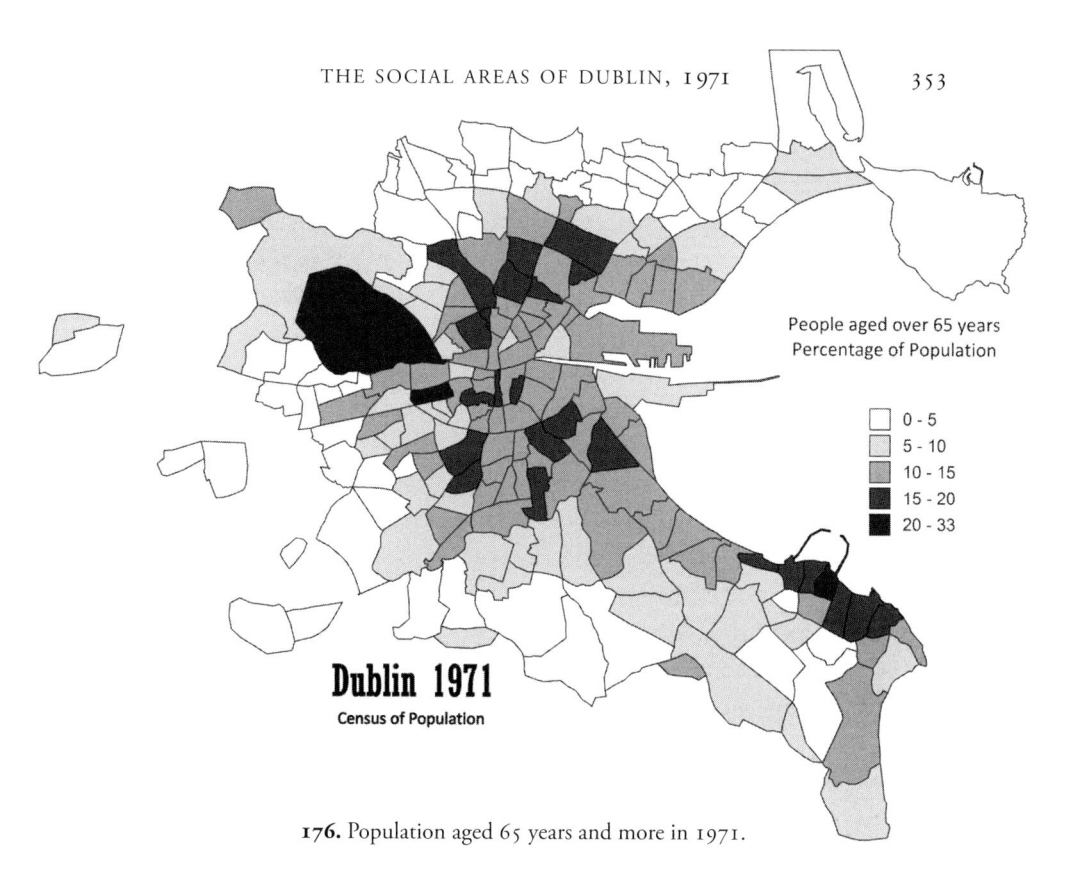

176. Population aged 65 years and more in 1971.

and 64 years as the economically active population. These are the people who are potentially earning money in the labour force and who have the resources on which others depend. The next map shows the number of *children under the age of 14 per 100 persons in the 15–64 age group*, a measure of youthful dependency in each area. The city average was 89 children per 100 potentially economically active people but this varied considerably from one area in which there were only 10 children per 100 to those where there were in excess of 200. The highest ratios were found in a small number of areas on the northern edge of the city, mainly in Kilmore/Coolock, Ballymun and parts of Finglas and in Walkinstown/Templeogue on the southside. These areas had over twice the number of children as adults. The pattern had something of a concentric nature with most of the inner suburbs and city falling into the lowest category where there were less than 60 children per 100 adults. The only parts of the inner city which showed a higher index than this were parts of Dolphin's Barn, the north quays and Summerhill, Ballybough and the North Strand. Somewhat higher ratios were observed beyond the inner city in the western edge of the city in Ballyfermot, Crumlin, Drimnagh and Walkinstown. These areas shared a youthful dependency ratio of between 60 and 130 children per

100 with the greater part of the south county. On the north side of the city the incidence of below average youthful dependency extended in an arc around the inner city and included Cabra, Drumcondra, parts of Whitehall and Clontarf. Higher ratios were found along the coast through Dollymount, Sutton and Howth and in a band across the north city between the low and high ratios mentioned above.

The second dependency index is a calculation of the *number of people of 65 years and over per 100 person aged 15–64 years* in the population, giving a measure of older age dependency. Not surprisingly there were fewer old folk than there were children and the city average was 24 older persons per 100. The lowest ratios, where there were fewer than 15 old people per 100, were found at the edge of the city, especially on the northside in a wide band of areas from Finglas through Ballymun, Santry, Kilmore, Coolock and parts of Raheny and Howth. On the southside a more or less continuous band of areas around the western and southern edges of the city displayed the same values from Ballyfermot in the west southwards including Walkinstown, Terenure, Templeogue and Dundrum.

The 'older' areas of the city were found on both sides of the Liffey in a dispersed pattern but one of the largest concentrations comprised Marino, Drumcondra and Glasnevin where there were at least 35 older people per 100 active people. The very highest values were associated with hospitals.

The census provided information on the marital status of the population: the numbers single, married or widowed in each age group. One of the more interesting statistics is to look at the *proportion of single people* under 35 years in an area. At noted before, Dubliners did not rush into marriage, though 87 per cent of those aged 35+ were married. Just over one-third of those aged 20–35 years were single but with quite a degree of variation across the city. The most interesting deviation from this was found in the south city in places such as Ranelagh, Rathmines and Donnybrook where over 70 per cent of the under 35s were single. This was the largest single concentration of its kind in the city but there were smaller clusters on the northside around Phibsborough and Drumcondra and parts of Cabra. These were the flatlands of the city where housing was available for those in small households, generally from the private rental sector. However, these were also non-family areas as property values generally ensured that housing in these places was beyond the reach of young married couples. The expected pattern was for many of these people to move eventually to suburbs such as those on the edge of the city where fewer than 25 per cent of their age group remained single.

THE SOCIAL AREAS OF DUBLIN, 1971    355

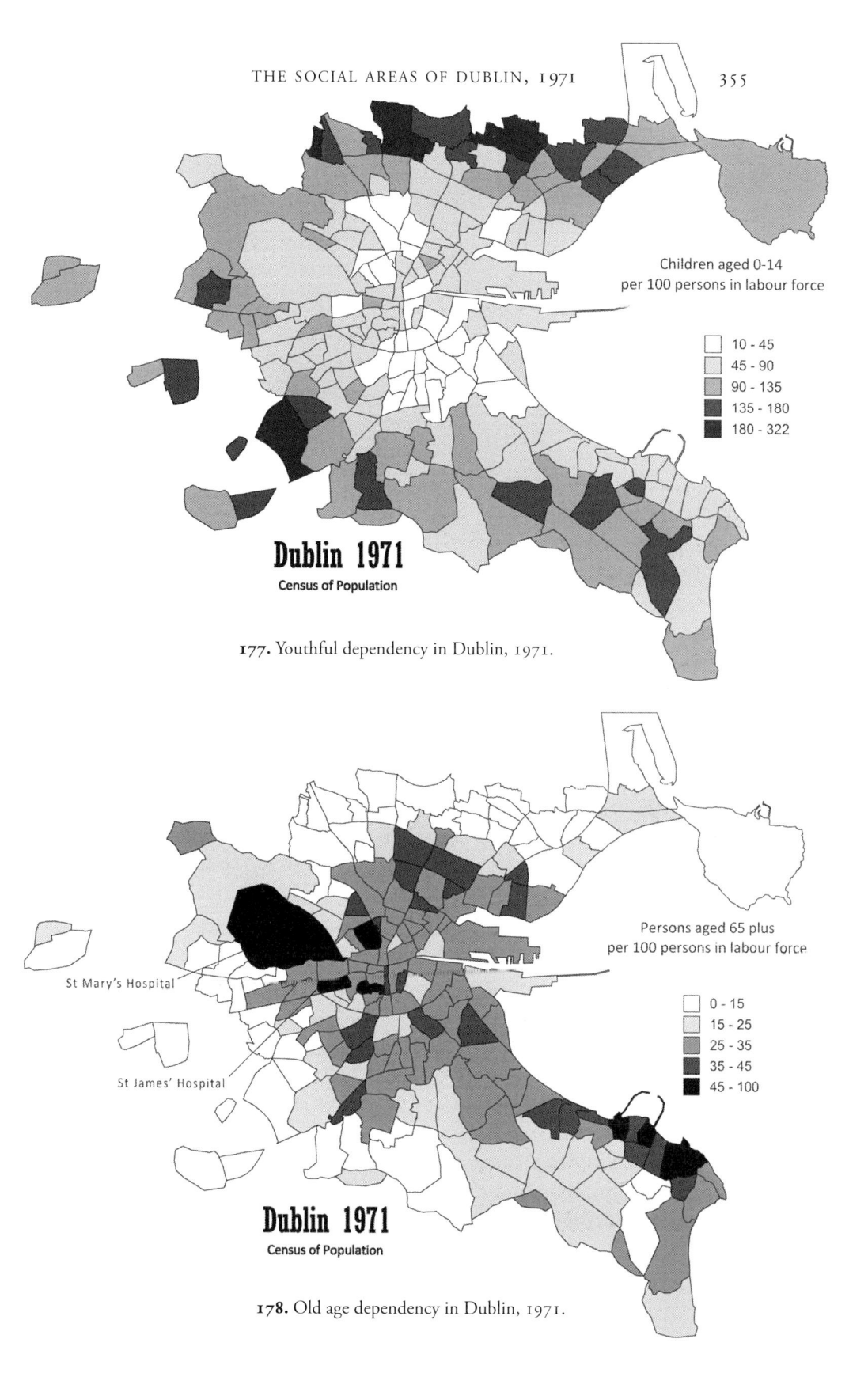

177. Youthful dependency in Dublin, 1971.

178. Old age dependency in Dublin, 1971.

**179.** Young and single in Dublin, 1971.

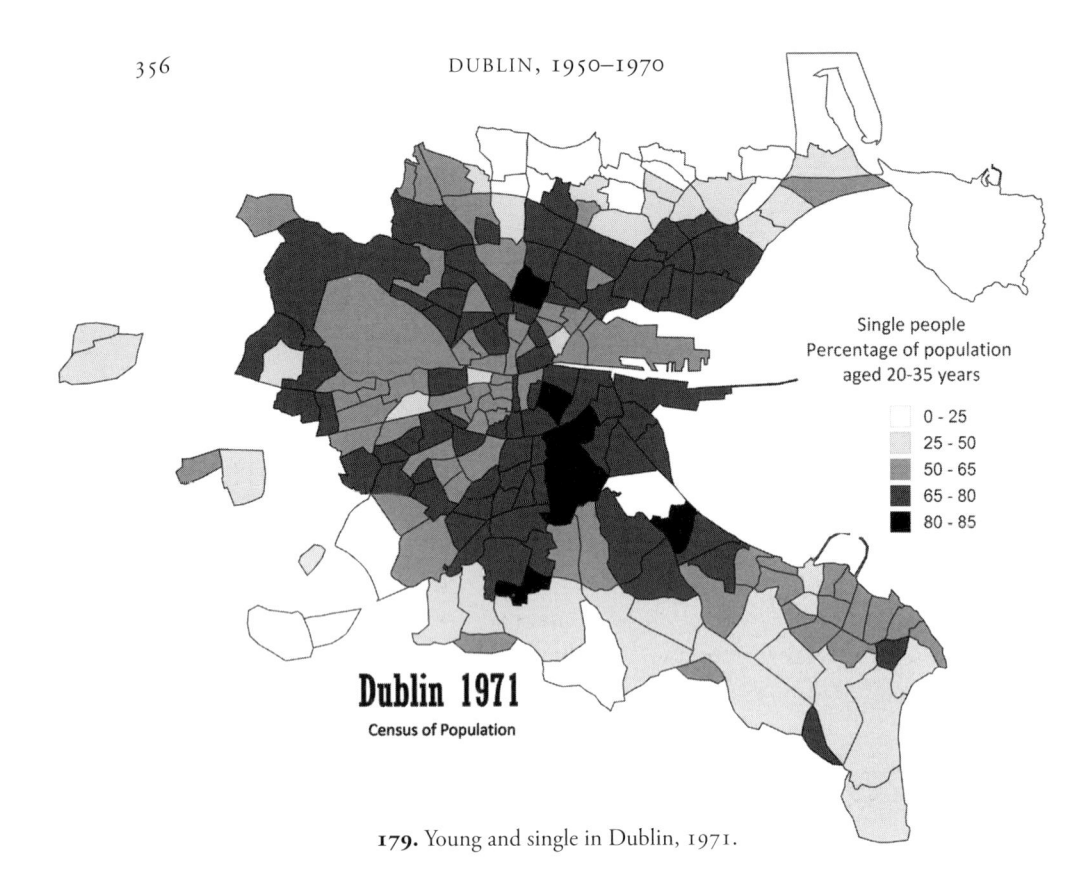

## *Social status in the city*

People disagree on so many things, yet there seems to be a general consensus as to what is high status in occupational terms and what is low status. In practice, when researchers have measured the concept of social status, they have tended to use a concept which is more definite than labels such as 'working class' or 'upper class'. The concept of 'socio-economic status' has been widely used whereby people are ranked in terms of their occupation. It is a useful concept since income, occupation, and the status of the occupation are generally related, though there are exceptions, and the ranking by socio-economic level would probably be agreed by most social scientists (Duncan & Duncan, 1955, p. 159). The saps provided a classification of each area in terms of socio-economic group, the basis of which was to group people who have similar occupations with regard to the level of skill and/or educational attainment required to do the job. No claims were made by the CSO that it was an ordinal scale though an examination of the composition of the categories suggests that it was a good approximation of such a scale. It makes sense, however, to place the employers & managers category (see below) above the lower professional category since the former contain such occupations as senior officials in the civil service and local authorities and senior ranks of the Garda. The CSO defined the lower professional group to contain the following: teachers, nurses, pharmacists and dispensers, other medical workers, authors, journalists and editors, actors, entertainers and musicians, painters, sculptors and commercial artists, social workers, technical and related workers.

There is an issue in the distinction between the lower grade non-manual occupations and the skilled manual occupations. The former may earn less than the latter but have the higher status 'white-collar' rather than 'blue-collar' label. Everyone in a family was given the socio-economic status of the head of the household, which in 1971 was deemed to be the father or man-of-the-house, regardless of the wishes of the household. This was changed in later censuses to be that of the person first named. The information was presented for eleven specific groups and a residual category with information for both males and females. For each sex group the numbers of gainfully occupied, not gainfully occupied and children under 14 (the school leaving age) was given. Since each person was allocated to the category of the household head, the value of these breakdowns in revealing more of the city's structure is somewhat limited.

The socio-economic structure of the city is given in the table below, though the first two categories were omitted since they refer to farming employments. It can be seen that the most common grouping was that of the skilled manual employees which contained most of the craft employments such as plumber or fitter. This group was followed closely by that of the intermediate non-manual category which comprised 22.1 per cent of the population of the city. This group contains a wide variety of occupations including shop assistants, typists, bookkeepers and clerical workers. The other non-manual category was a catch-all grouping and included a wide range of disparare employments such as bus drivers and conductors, chefs and waiters as well as sportsmen, barbers, postmen and street vendors. This lack of a clear identity makes this category less useful than others.

The proportions of employers and managers, lower and higher professionals were very similar but with a tendency for numbers to decrease as one goes up the scale. There can be little argument that these represent the higher social groups in the city. At the other end of the scale the semi-skilled and unskilled manual occupations are also uncontroversial in their composition and they accounted for almost one in five of the population.

**Table 40.** Socio-economic groupings in the city in 1971.

| Social group | Number | Per cent |
|---|---|---|
| Higher professionals | 38,526 | 5.3 |
| Self-employed/managers | 45,397 | 6.2 |
| Lower professionals | 35,327 | 4.8 |
| Salaried employees | 27,103 | 3.7 |
| Intermediate non-manual employees | 160,966 | 22.1 |
| Other non-manual employees | 115,949 | 15.9 |
| Skilled manual employees | 168,844 | 23.1 |
| Semi-skilled manual employees | 66,924 | 9.2 |
| Unskilled manual employees | 70,362 | 9.6 |

An overall view of the extent of residential segregation can be obtained by the calculation of an *index of dissimilarity*. The calculation of this index and its associated index, the *index of segregation*, is described in Duncan and Duncan (1949). The *index of dissimilarity* (Id) is a measure of displacement in that it compares the extent to which two groups are different in their residential pattern by calculating the proportion of one group that would have to move if they were to attain the same pattern of distribution across all the areas of the city as the other group. It is an interesting concept and the formal definition given above can be simplified to read as the extent to which any two socio-economic groups tend to live in the same area.

**Table 41.** Index of dissimilarity for socio-economic groups in Dublin, 1971.

| | Social group | 1 | 2 | 3 | 4 | 5 | 6 | 7 | 8 | 9 |
|---|---|---|---|---|---|---|---|---|---|---|
| 1 | Higher professionals | | 20 | 29 | 28 | 41 | 59 | 59 | 70 | 71 |
| 2 | Employers/managers | | | 24 | 14 | 34 | 52 | 51 | 65 | 68 |
| 3 | Lower professionals | | | | 21 | 19 | 41 | 41 | 57 | 60 |
| 4 | Salaried employees | | | | | 27 | 44 | 43 | 59 | 62 |
| 5 | Inter. non-manual | | | | | | 27 | 26 | 43 | 47 |
| 6 | Other non-manual | | | | | | | 11 | 21 | 24 |
| 7 | Skilled manual | | | | | | | | 25 | 29 |
| 8 | Semi-skilled manual | | | | | | | | | 12 |
| 9 | Unskilled manual | | | | | | | | | |

The Id for the various occupation groups show that Dublin is segregated in terms of socio-economic status and that the degree of residential dissimilarity generally increases with social distance. The index goes from 0 to 100. The smaller the number, the greater the degree to which the two groups live in the same areas. Taking the higher professional group, the Id between them and the employers and managers is 20 but it rises to 59 for the skilled manual group and continues to rise until 71 per cent of unskilled manual workers would have to move across the city if their distribution were to match that of the higher professionals. Clearly, these groups hardly co-exist spatially at all. Though the progression to higher residential dissimilarity with increasing social distance is generally observable the rate of change is not constant. Thus, still comparing the higher professionals, there is little difference between them and the lower professionals and between them and the salaried employees, or between them and the other non-manual groups and the skilled manual groups. Other anomalies exist; the employers are more residentially similar to the salaried employees than they are to the lower professionals who are the next closest to them in status.

Also of interest is the Id between the other non-manual group and the skilled manual group which is only 11. This may be because though these groups may mark the distinction between 'white collar' and 'blue collar' occupations, the level of earnings of these groups expressed in terms of residential choice was not such as to make them residentially dissimilar. The provision of social housing would also tend to blur the distinction here.

This tells nothing about where people live, just that they live in different areas but it indicates that Dublin was just as residentially segregated as any other city in the western capitalist orbit, even with large programmes of social housing.

A neat way of making a further summary is to calculate an *index of segregation* (Is). This shows how dissimilar one group is compared to all other groups and, in effect, shows the extent to which one group keeps to itself. The Is for each of the social groups is presented below. Duncan and Duncan (1955) suggest that the distribution of these values should be in the form of a U-shape with lower indices for the social groups in the middle of the spectrum. This, they suggest, is because residential segregation is greater for those occupation groups with clearly defined status than for those whose status is more ambiguous, that is, groups which might have a higher standing but a lower income and vice versa. The results for Dublin did not produce a perfect U but the essence of what Duncan and Duncan suggest was confirmed. The higher professionals keep themselves to themselves but the degree of spatial exclusivity declines for the other social groups until it reaches the other non-manual group, after which it begins to rise again. However, though the unskilled group are at the other peak of the U, they have nothing like the residential exclusivity of the higher professionals and employers and managers. The reason for this may lie in the role of the local authority in providing housing which results in the unskilled being better housed than their incomes would support and therefore are less segregated than would otherwise be the case.

**Table 42.** Indices of segregation, 1971. The higher the index, the more spatially segregated is the social group.

| Social group | Index |
| --- | --- |
| Higher professionals | 50 |
| Employers and managers | 42 |
| Lower professionals | 31 |
| Salaried employees | 33 |
| Intermediate non-manual employees | 20 |
| Other non-manual employees | 16 |
| Skilled manual employees | 19 |
| Semi-skilled employees | 32 |
| Unskilled employees | 37 |

There are some methodological issues with these indices but they are useful in indicating the degree and extent of residential similarity at a city-wide scale though they say nothing about its distribution. It is important not to fall into the trap of equating social distance with spatial distance and to assume that the more socially distant two group are, the greater the spatial distance between them. This may be the case, but the index cannot compute this, since it merely indicates the extent to which two social groups live in the same area but says nothing about where these areas might be. In short, there is no substitute for the map as a means of ascertaining the distribution of socio-economic status. It is not proposed to map all of the social groups but rather to present four maps which show the more dissimilar groups.

*Higher professionals*
On average, 5.2 per cent of the population were higher professionals but the distribution ranged from none at all to just under 25 per cent of the population. South Dublin is clearly where this group liked to live and nowhere on the northside did their presence exceed 15 per cent. Their preferred areas,

where there was more than three times the city average, were Mount Merrion and Foxrock but also Ballsbridge, Donnybrook, Sandymount, Clonskeagh, Killiney, Blackrock, parts of Rathfarnham and Sandyford. Few ventured closer to the city centre than the canal ring, though there were some who chose to live in the Merrion Square area. Though south Dublin was generally preferred there were a number of areas in Dún Laoghaire which were not favoured such as Sallynoggin and the area close to the harbour. Neither was the north side of the city favoured territory with only Howth, Sutton and Clontarf having appreciable numbers but never to the same extent as in south Dublin. In addition, some chose to live in Drumcondra, largely along Griffith Avenue or the Drumcondra Road, in Glasnevin and in Castleknock.

*Lower professionals*
The lower professionals were more widespread on the northside and generally seem to have a more dispersed pattern but while they accounted for over 13 per cent of the population in some places, there were places from which they were completely absent. On the north side of the city, they favoured Howth, Clontarf and Glasnevin but above city averages (4.6 per cent) were found all along the coast to Sutton and in Drumcondra, Glasnevin, and along the Navan Road which skirts the Phoenix Park. They were more likely to be found in the inner city than are the higher professionals but not in any particular clusters; the heavier concentrations in the Grangegorman area and the Kilmainham area can best be explained in terms of hospital staff living-in or being there on enumeration night. On the southside, the greatest concentrations of lower professionals were not in the same places as the higher professionals, even though they were mainly concentrated in south Dublin. Most favoured areas such as parts of Ballsbridge but also including Sandymount, Terenure and Rathfarnham, Templeogue, and Dundrum. It is noticeable that the new town of Tallaght had very few professionals of either group.

There is a stark contrast between the distribution of semi-skilled people and the two maps which have gone before. Despite the fact that the semi-skilled socio-economic group account for 8.1 per cent, on average, of the city's population, they were noticeably absent from the areas favoured by the professional groups in south Dublin. In many of these areas barely 1 per cent were semi-skilled people. Instead, the main concentrations of semi-skilled people were in the inner city and in a wedge which reached towards the western edge. This group made up over 20 per cent of the population in areas around Pearse Street, Sean McDermott Street, the northern docks area and

**180.** Higher professionals in Dublin, 1971.

**181.** Lower professionals in Dublin, 1971.

Ringsend. Levels of between 15 per cent and 20 per cent were characteristic of a wedge of areas which ran from the Liberties, through Dolphin's Barn and into Crumlin and also of another wedge which ran from Cabra into much of the Finglas area on the northern edge of the city. Most of the northern fringe of the city had above average concentrations of semi-skilled workers as did much of Coolock and Raheny. In general terms, semi-skilled workers were not a feature of south Dublin, except in the Sallynoggin and harbour areas of Dún Laoghaire. They would appear to be rather more ubiquitous on the north side of the city though there are quite a number of areas where they are hardly present.

The unskilled manual group is at the bottom end of the social spectrum and though it had a city average of 8.6 per cent, in over 41 per cent of the city's areas they accounted for less than 5 per cent of the population. In parts of the inner city, notably the Sean McDermott and Sheriff Street areas, they accounted for at least 20 per cent and perhaps as much as one-in-three of the population. They were similarly well represented in the area from James's Street to Dolphin's Barn with a further concentration in Ballyfermot. In addition to these areas of major concentration they accounted for at least 7 per cent in almost all of the inner city and in most of the suburbs to the west and north of the county borough, especially in Ballymun and Coolock but also with a considerable presence in most of Finglas and Cabra. In the south city, with the exception of the areas mentioned above, there were few areas with more than 7 per cent unskilled people. These were in Dún Laoghaire, where there was also a concentration of semi-skilled, Ballyboden and Tallaght. Most of the new town areas, with the exception of Blanchardstown, had noticeable numbers of semi- and unskilled manual workers.

Although, strictly speaking, car ownership should not come under the heading of social groups, the perceived relationship between the ownership of a car and social groups make it logical to discuss them together. The only piece of information given on car ownership was on the total number of cars in an area. This figure could be expressed in many ways but since it was usually a household item at the time it seemed best to express it in terms of the number of cars per household. In the city as a whole there were 103,955 cars or 0.54 cars per household but there was a considerable range around that average. In some areas there were hardly any cars at all with one area having six cars per 100 households, while at the other extreme quite a number of areas had in excess of one car per household though households with two or more cars were relatively uncommon. The pattern of car ownership shows very clearly that in

**182.** Semi-skilled workers in Dublin, 1971.

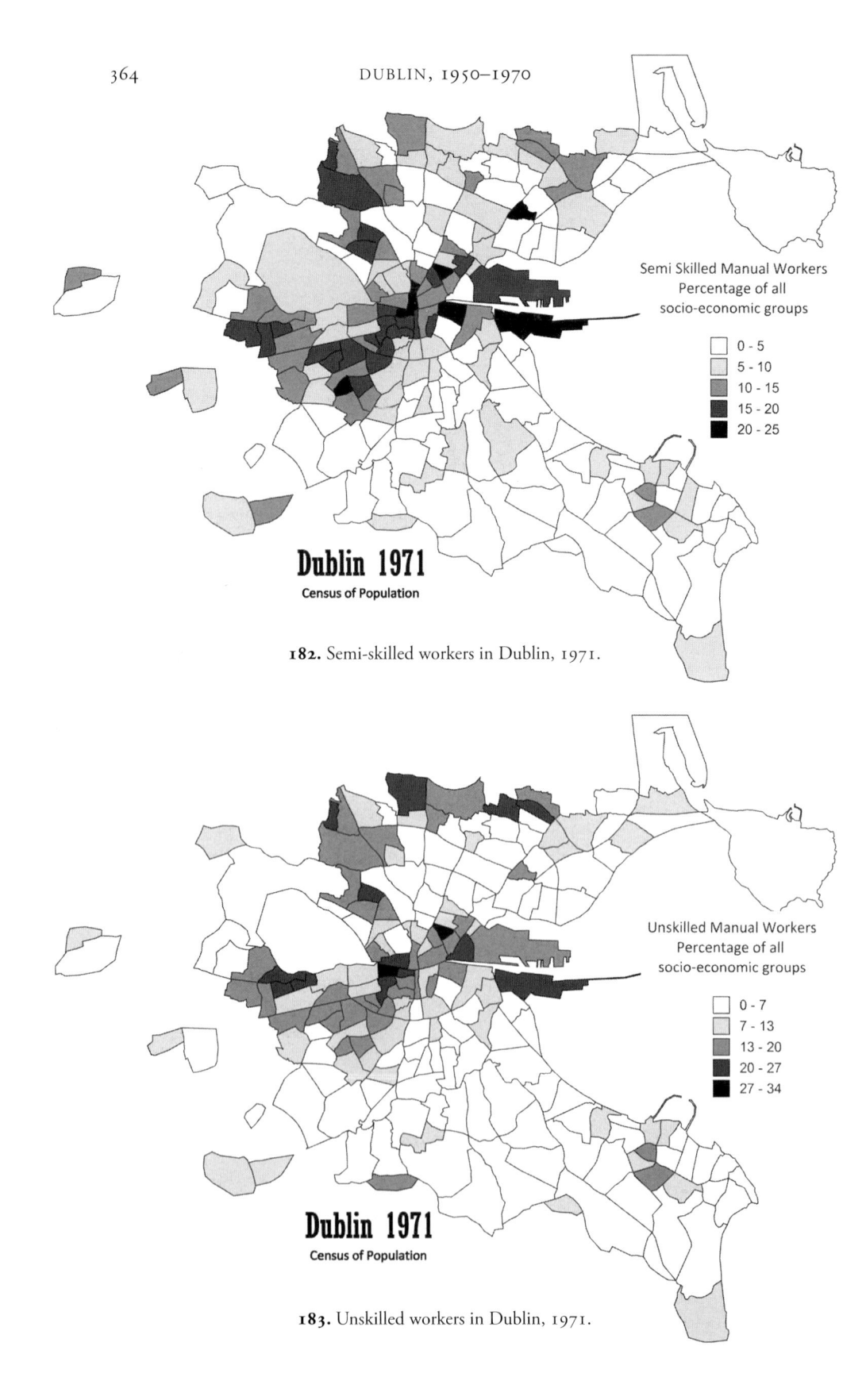

**183.** Unskilled workers in Dublin, 1971.

**184.** Car ownership in Dublin, 1971.

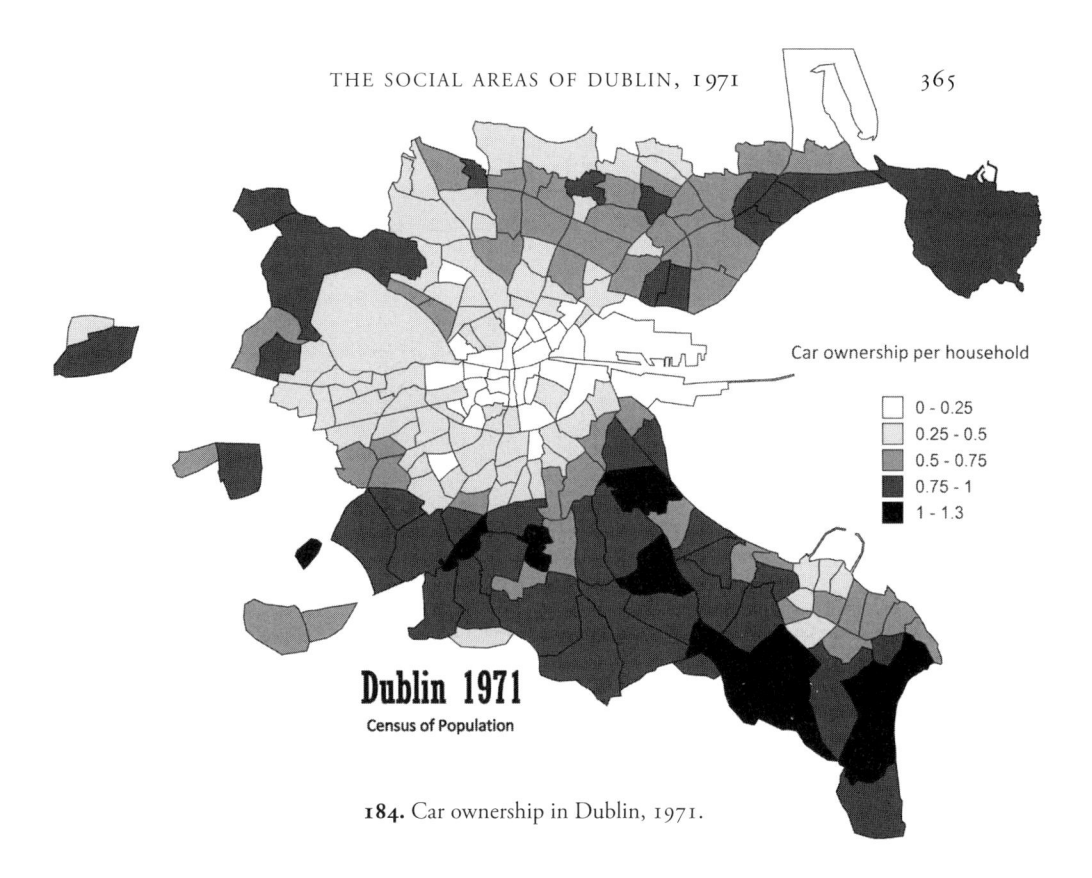

the inner city car ownership was very low with less than one household in four having a car. At the other extreme, households with in excess of one car were concentrated in the south city in places such as Terenure, Templeogue, Rathfarnham, Donnybrook, Ballsbridge, Mount Merrion, Foxrock and Killiney. It is only in parts of Dún Laoghaire that ownership slipped to or below the city average. The north side of the city was much more 'average' with relatively few areas rising above the level of 0.75 cars per household. These were Howth, Sutton, where ownership exceeded 1 per household, Clontarf and Castleknock as well parts of Beaumont. In the new towns, car ownership was generally above average but given the poor levels of public transport in these areas in 1971, life must have been difficult for the one in three households, at least, without a car.

## Household characteristics

The saps offered a variety of data on the size of households and the number of rooms occupied by households. It is possible to determine the number of persons in households that occupied between one and ten plus rooms, the number of such private households, and the number of permanent housing units which had between one and ten plus rooms. Rooms in this context includes a kitchen but excludes a kitchenette, scullery, bathroom, toilet, or any office or shop space. Data were also provided on the size of households and it is possible to determine how many households had between 1 and 12 plus persons as well as the number of housing units which were occupied by between 1 and 12 plus persons. An index of persons per room and persons per household was also provided. It is possible to generate a very large number of indices from these data and produce every conceivable ratio but common sense dictates that the analysis focus on a small number of what are considered the more significant.

An overall picture of household size can be obtained from an examination of the average number of *persons per household*. The average for the city was 3.94 but with a considerable variation from a low of 2.10 persons to a high of 6.32 persons. The map shows that household numbers were smallest in the south inner city and in the adjacent areas of Rathgar, Rathmines and parts of Ballsbridge. In these areas there tended to be between two and three persons per household on average. This could identify an empty-nest population where the parents are left alone in the house after the children are gone but it is also possible that this identifies the 'flatland' of the city where the young people of the city, often migrants, live either while attending higher education or going to work until such time as they enter the property market and move to the suburbs. There is no direct evidence from the map for this view but it is based on a general knowledge of this area and also from the fact that there are few other areas in the city where household sizes are so small.

Household sizes comprised less than four persons in most of the south county borough and it is only in the social housing areas on the western edge where sizes were greater. Similar household sizes were also the norm for a coastal strip which stretched from Sandymount to Killiney but, for the most part, household sizes were bigger than this in the remainder of the south county. South of Glasnevin, Drumcondra and Clontarf, household sizes were less than four persons but the figure rose north of these areas until it reached its highest levels on the edge of the city. Indeed, with only one exception, the largest households were on the edge of the city in what would be predominantly social housing areas. These included the newly developed areas of Coolock and Kilmore as well as much of Finglas while on the south of the city much of Ballyfermot and Walkinstown had over 5 persons per household.

*Persons per room* is a measure of the amount of space available per person and might be crude indicator of overcrowding in the city although that would depend on being able to establish what ratio was desirable or the level at which it could be argued that a problem existed. However, a family of two adults and two children in a standard three-bedroomed house would have an index of 0.66. The lowest value for the city was 0.55, rising to a high of 1.51 against a city average of 0.89. If it is remembered that Dublin Corporation's priority housing group in the 1940s was families living with six or more per room then some sense of progress may be obtained; it does not matter that the definition of a 'room' was a bit different. Values of between 0.50 and 0.75 persons per room, below the city average, were widespread throughout the southern city and south of a line from the inner city to Terenure and Templeogue there were few areas where the value rose above this. The places where there was in excess of one person per room included Sallynoggin, Nutgrove Avenue and Ballyboden. Ratios under 0.75 were less common on the north side of the city but were found in Howth, Sutton, Clontarf, Drumcondra and Glasnevin. In contrast, over much of the inner city more than one person per room was the norm and it rose to over 1.25 persons per room in the Sean McDermott Street and Sheriff Street districts as well as in the area around Parnell Square, and in the area around Arran Quay and Watling Street on both sides of the Liffey. These areas were part of a cluster of higher than average areas which ran westwards from the north docks and Ringsend area, took in the Liberties and Dolphin's Barn and reached to the Local Authority areas of Crumlin and Kimmage and Ballyfermot, all areas of major social housing schemes. On the northside, it was new suburbs such as Finglas and Kilmore that had the highest figures, followed by Ballymun and Coolock.

It will be useful later in this analysis to include measures of the distribution of large and small households since it might be expected that these will help to understand something of the stage-in-the-life-cycle process as it operated in Dublin. Housing units with two people or fewer might be taken to indicate that they contain households at one end or other of the life cycle. They could consist of young couples in the pre-family stage who have moved into their own house but they could equally well describe those households who are in the final stages of the life cycle. These 'empty-nest' households would comprise one or both parents continuing to live in the family home after the children have moved away. There are other forms of one or two person households which must be considered and which largely explain the difference in the totals

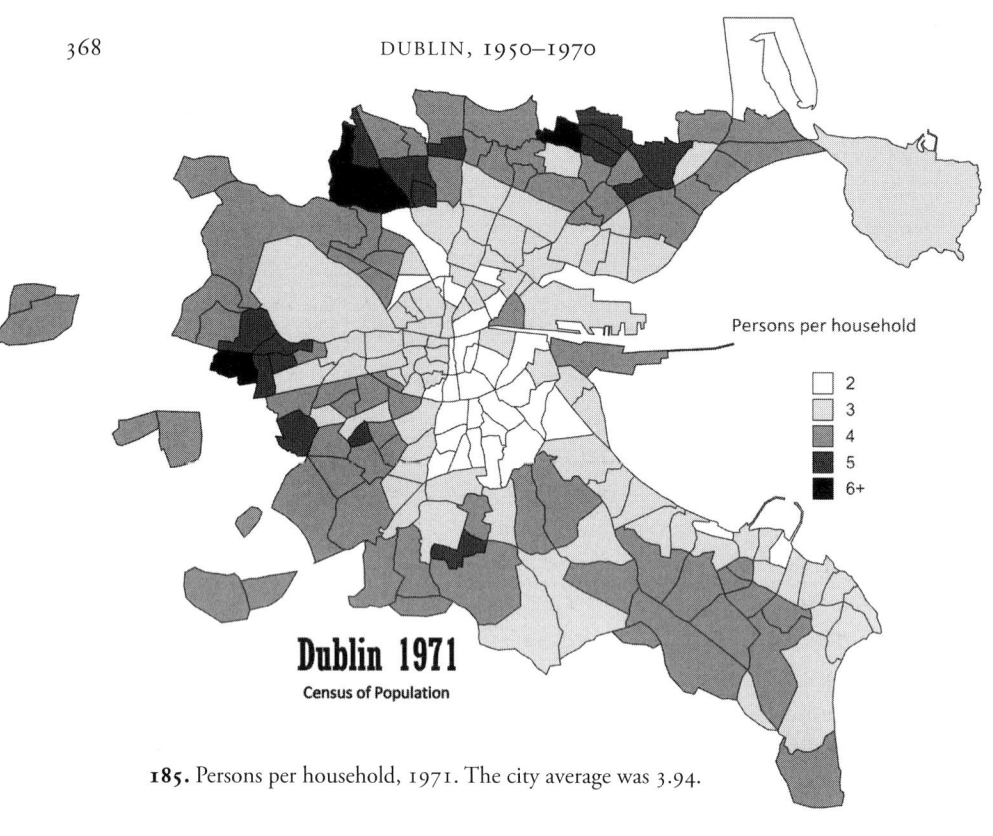

**185.** Persons per household, 1971. The city average was 3.94.

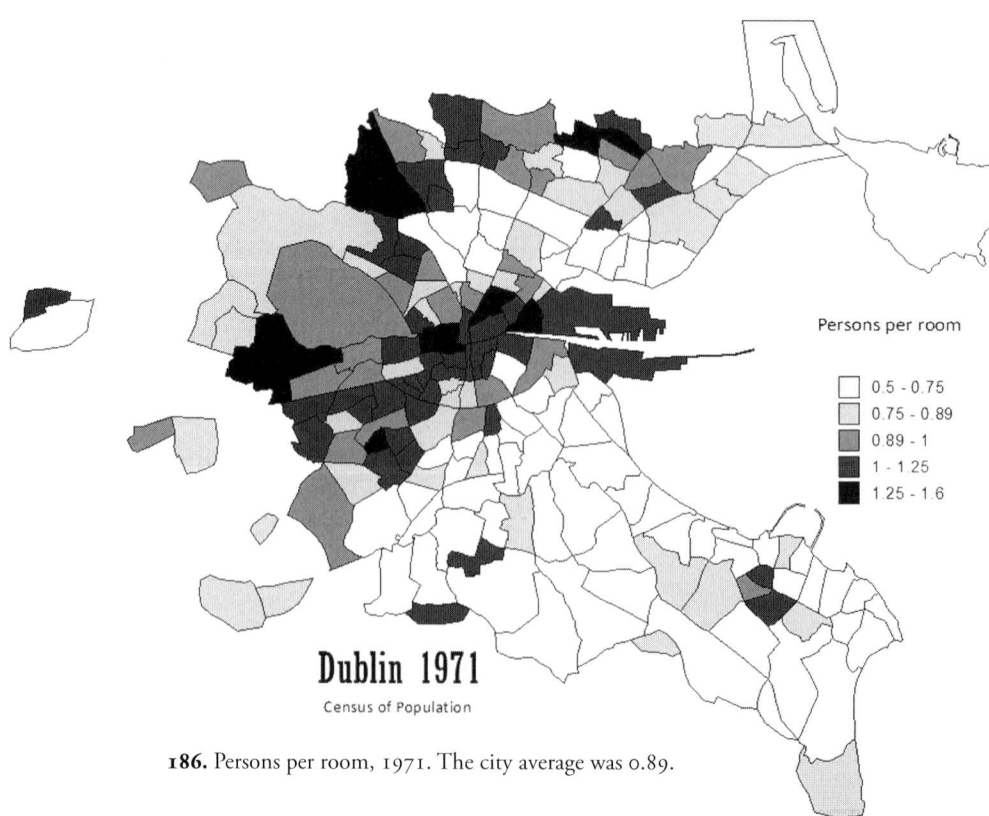

**186.** Persons per room, 1971. The city average was 0.89.

between housing units and households. These comprise people who live in conventional houses with multiple households. These are not classified by the CSO as separate housing units if the rooms assigned to each household are not structurally separate. Essentially the difference lies in whether bathroom facilities are shared. These housing units are typically what would be known to Dubliners as 'flats'. They consist of dwelling houses which have been 'converted' into a number of units, of which a large proportion would be bedsits for 1 or 2 persons. In an earlier generation many of these houses would have been the typical Dublin tenements but few of them would be occupied by one or two persons. The typical tenant in 1971 in one of these houses was young and single and might still be in education or at the early stages of a career. Living in a flat would be a short-term aspect of their lives until such time as they became more settled.

The proportion of *housing units with two persons or less* varied considerably around a city average of just over 28 per cent. The lowest incidence was just over 1 per cent but the highest rose to almost 75 per cent and the maps shows that there was a concentric pattern of sorts to the distribution. The greatest concentrations, in excess of 60 per cent, were in the south inner city and south inner suburbs. On the northside, the greatest concentration extended northwards in an uneven fashion beyond the inner city into Glasnevin but it decreased towards the edge of the city until it fell below 12 per cent, reaching almost zero in some cases. The areas which had the lowest concentration included Walkinstown/Templeogue, much of Ballyfermot, much of Finglas, and a belt of areas across the northern edge of the city which includes Ballymun, Santry, Kilmore and Coolock.

The census also permitted the analysis of *households with two or less members*. Just over one in three Dublin households were of this type but the distribution varied from just over 1 per cent to almost 88 per cent but there was little difference in the spatial pattern of this indicator and the one discussed above. There was also information on old people living alone such as the number of those over 65 years of age living alone or in two person or three person households. There were 16,923 people in these kinds of households in 1971 and their number varied from a solitary person in one area to 279 in another. There are a number of ways in which this information could be expressed such as a percentage of the total population or as a percentage of all those over 65 years of age.

**187.** Housing units with one or two persons, 1971.

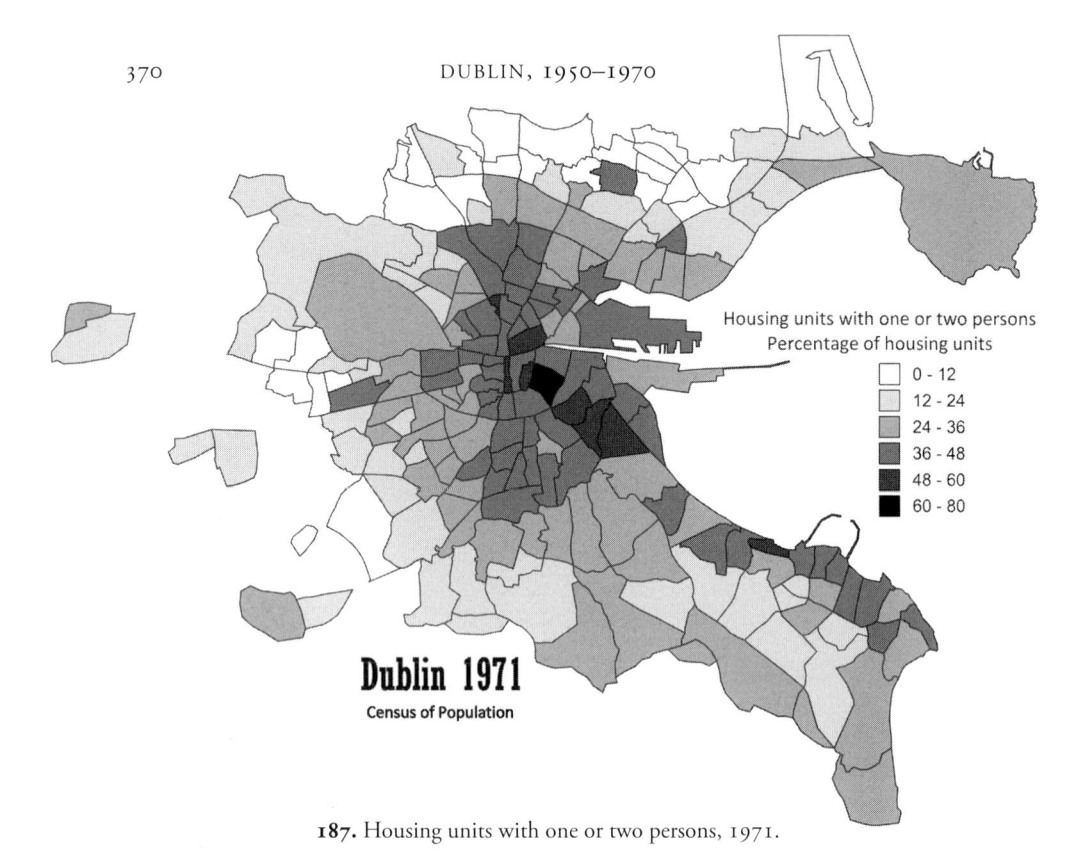

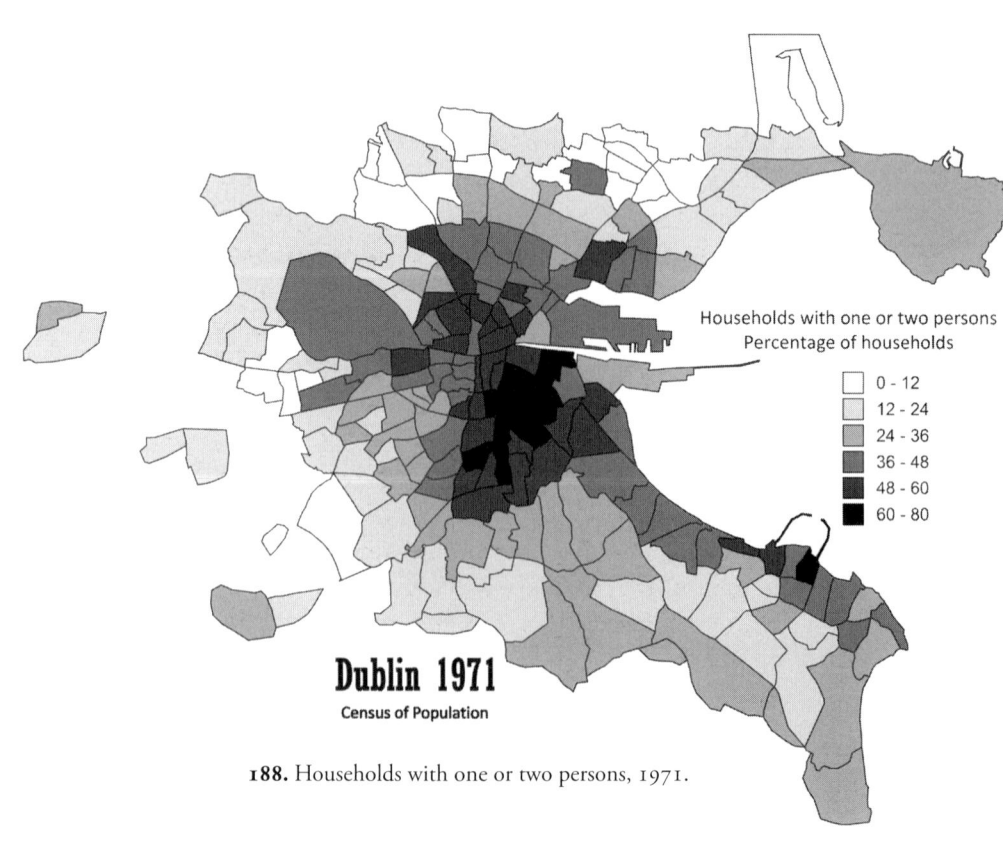

**188.** Households with one or two persons, 1971.

## *Labour force*

A considerable amount of information was provided on the composition of the labour force for each area but the usefulness of much of this information was quite limited. Information was provided on the numbers of males and females working in each of 10 industrial groups. These categories were far too broad to reveal much about the jobs which people did; manufacturing industry alone covers a wide variety of activities. Their usefulness was further reduced by the fact that a person was assigned to the sector in which the product or service was finally used rather than the sector in which it was produced. Moreover, since a wide variety of skills and levels existed in each employment, the usefulness of any such categorization to an analysis of the social and economic structure of a city is questionable. Information was also provided on a variety of occupational groups for males and females. This was a bit more useful in that it gave an indication of the person's actual job but it did not differentiate between those actually in employment at the time of the census and those unemployed. This leaves the data on gainful employment and it is this which is explored below.

In 1971, the figures showed that out of a total of 255,607 males, some 204,700 or just over 80 per cent were in employment. As would have been expected, there were fewer women employed; the percentage for the city was 56 per cent. Being 'not gainfully employed' did not mean that the person was unemployed. The largest group in non-gainful employment were those, largely women, engaged in home duties. There were only 476 men so described in the entire city. Then there were those who were still at school. A total of 28,457 males and 22,522 females were described as still being at school. This was 11.1 per cent of males and 7.5 per cent of females, giving an average for the city of just over 9 per cent. This map (figure 189) shows an interesting distribution. The low values show where there were fewer young adults in school but it must be remembered that not all areas would have many people in that age category. The lowest instances were in the inner city, as might be expected, and in some of the newer suburbs such as Ballymun where there would not have been many in the relevant age groups. In contrast, most of south-eastern Dublin was at or considerably above the average, a characteristic also observed in Clontarf and Drumcondra. Interestingly, there were some higher outliers in parts of Finglas. The pattern is suggestive of an association with better off areas, with the Finglas values reflecting the extent of the social mix there.

The data for the *gainful employment of women* in the labour force suggested that 35 per cent of all women over the age of 14 years were in employment, high compared to the national figure of 27.3 per cent but a decline on the figures shown in Chapter 1, due in large measure to increasing numbers staying on in school beyond the legal leaving age of 14 and improving longevity. The range across Dublin was from a low of just over 8 per cent to a high of over 64 per cent. Areas above the city average were concentrated within the inner city on both sides of the Liffey as part of a zone which reached into the suburbs on either side. On the northside this zone was hammer shaped with a wedge from Cabra to Fairview forming the head and a narrow sector between Phibsboro and Drumcondra forming the shaft while on the southside the zone reached into Ballsbridge, Rathmines, Rathgar, and Harold's Cross. The areas of highest participation rates were found in the city centre, the area around Baggot Street and a part of Rathmines. There were few other occurrences of rates in excess of 40 per cent beyond this central nucleus. In contrast, the areas with lowest rates, less than one in four, were found on the periphery of the city with the lowest rate of all in Ballymun. It seems reasonable to suggest that in the areas with the lowest rates that most women were involved in home duties and, given what has been said above about the numbers of young children, engaged in child rearing. The pattern of areas where there were more employed women suggests a strong association with 'flatland', as described above, though not entirely confined to that. It will be interesting to see in the later analysis if it is associated with the social status of an area or its family structure.

Another of the non-gainfully occupied categories which the census reported was that of *engaged in home duties*. Some of the old certainties may have been under threat in parts of Dublin but male/female roles were stereotypical in 1971. Home duties was a predominantly female activity and the map here shows those engaged in this activity as a percentage of the entire female cohort. It shows that in the new suburban areas where there were large numbers of children and where the fertility rate was high that most women had taken on the role of homemakers. Rates in excess of 70 per cent were seen in areas on the northern and western edges of the city. The contrast was with the south inner city and the areas which had high percentages of employed women. This would suggest that homemaking was a minority activity for women in these areas and that they were either still in education or working for gain.

The other categories, as noted above, were not particularly informative but it might be interesting to note that 2,668 males were engaged in agriculture,

THE SOCIAL AREAS OF DUBLIN, 1971 373

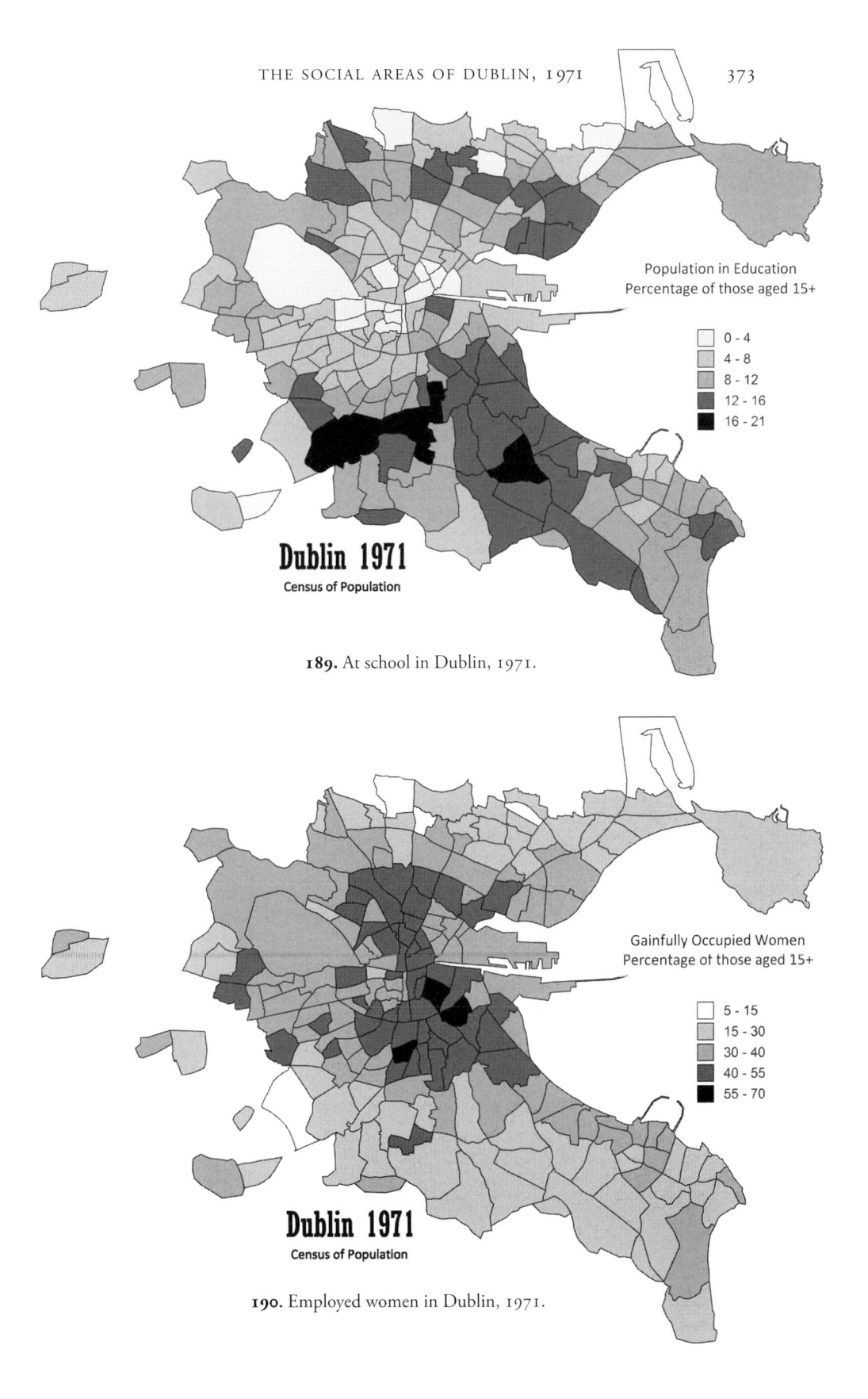

189. At school in Dublin, 1971.

190. Employed women in Dublin, 1971.

**Women in Home Duties**
Percentage of Women aged 15+

- 25 - 40
- 40 - 55
- 55 - 70
- 70 - 85
- 85 - 90

**Dublin 1971**
Census of Population

191. Women engaged in home duties, 1971.

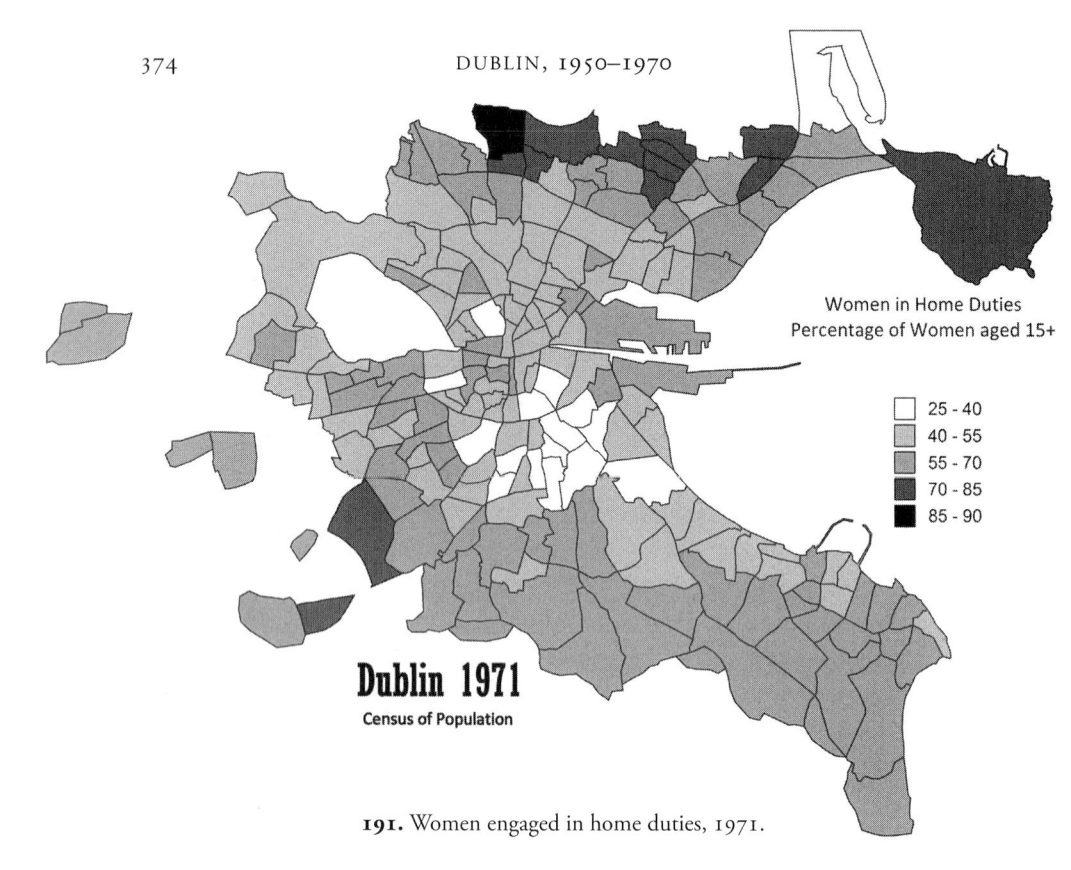

forestry and fishing as were 116 females. While Howth had a small concentration of fisherfolk, this group was spread right across the city and there was an almost equally large concentration around Blanchardstown.

The saps provided a further set of labour force data which gave information on the nature of a person's employment in broad terms. It classified people as to whether they were employers, employees, relatives assisting, unemployed, or retired.

**Table 43.** Employment status in 1971.

| Category | Number | Per cent |
| --- | --- | --- |
| Employer | 19,676 | 6.3 |
| Relatives assisting without payment | 994 | 0.3 |
| Employee | 274,025 | 88.5 |
| Out of work | 15,074 | 4.9 |
| Retired | 21,118 | |
| Others not gainfully occupied | 225,547 | |

Note that the percentages are based on the total of those at work or unemployed.

Employers of one kind or another made up, on average, 6.3 per cent of the labour force of the city but their distribution varied from a low of 1.6 per cent in one area to a high of 19.4 per cent. The areas that housed most employers were on the south side of the city and they included most of the desirable addresses in the city such as Ballsbridge, Mount Merrion, Foxrock, Dalkey and Killiney, Terenure, Rathfarnham and Churchtown. In only one area of the northside did the presence of employers rise above 12 per cent and this was in Sutton. At the other extreme there were relatively few employers (< 4 per cent) in the west of the city in places such as Ballyfermot or Crumlin or indeed in Tallaght. On the northside, Finglas, part of Cabra, and much of Coolock fell into the same category as did the docklands north and south of the Liffey. On the whole the south side of the city, especially south of the county borough, but including Ballsbridge and Sandymount, was the more favoured location for employers and there were relatively few areas of the northside over 8 per cent.

The average unemployment rate for the city was 4.9 per cent; full employment effectively given that zero unemployment will never be achieved because of structural and seasonal imbalances in the economy. This is hard to believe from today's perspective and it was even then a somewhat better situation than for the State as a whole, which had an average unemployment rate of 5.1 per cent (Eurostat, 1980). In Dublin this varied from an almost zero rate (0.8 per cent) to areas where it affected almost one in five of the working population. The worst unemployment rates were found in the inner city in the areas around Arran Quay and Oxmanstown, Patrick Street, and the Sheriff Street and Sean McDermott Street areas as well as further along the quays where rates were over twice and in instances over four times the city average. On the whole, higher rates were an inner city phenomenon with only isolated pockets of values in excess of 8 per cent outside this area. Most notably these occurred in Coolock, Ballymun, parts of Finglas and Ballyfermot and in Sallynoggin (Dún Laoghaire). In overall terms, unemployment of over 4 per cent was a characteristic of the inner city and the western edge of the county but with pockets of higher rates more widespread on the north of the city than south of the Liffey.

## Miscellaneous characteristics

Finally, the saps provided a small amount of information on a number of the characteristics which do not fit easily into any category. The first of these provided very broad information on the extent to which the population was

**192.** The distribution of employers in Dublin, 1971.

**193.** The unemployed in Dublin, 1971.

**194.** Non-Roman Catholics in the population, 1971.

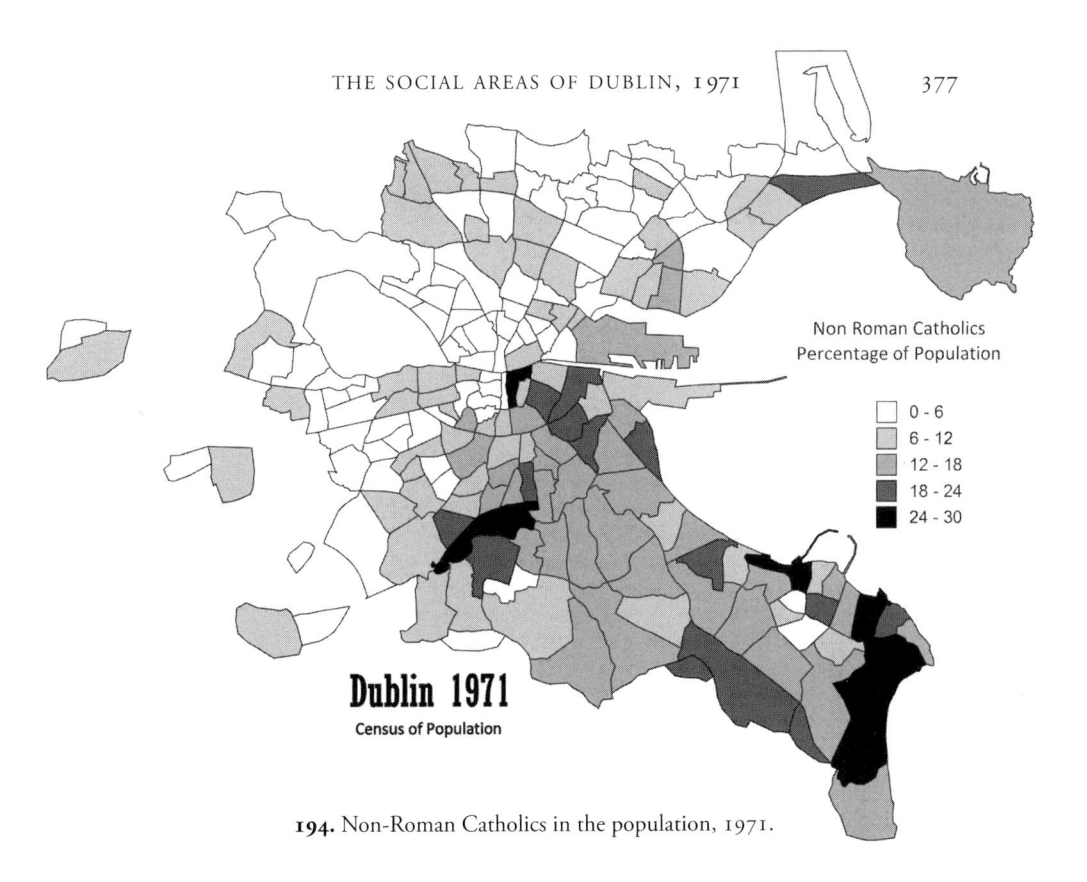

Catholic or not. Only 70,132 people were described as non-Roman Catholic which was 8.8 per cent of the population of the city. However, while this percentage was as low as 1.4 per cent in one area where there were only 38 non Catholics, there were areas where upwards of 30 per cent of the population were not of the Roman Catholic church. Most notable was the Dún Laoghaire area, which included Dalkey and Killiney, Cabinteely and Foxrock, where over 18 per cent of the population were non-RCs. Another cluster of importance existed in Rathfarnham while there was another large concentration in the city centre and parts of Sandymount. The northside had only one area where the non-Catholics reached more than 18 per cent of the population and that was in Sutton. In all cases these are old Church of Ireland enclaves that had retained their population while other parishes had lost theirs.

The last characteristic of note relates to the ability to speak the Irish language. People responding to the census questionnaire were asked to say whether or not they could speak Irish. The quality of the data is doubtful since it was nothing more than a purely subjective assessment by the respondent with no attempt at even an ordinal scale of fluency. Just under 23 per cent of the population claimed fluency in Irish but this varied from 4.5 per cent to

43 per cent. No pattern emerged from the map though there seemed to be two major clusters where Irish speaking was higher than average. The first of these was on the north side of the city and included such areas as Glasnevin, Drumcondra and most of Clontarf/Dollymount. On the south side of the city, while there were a number of disjointed occurrences of values in excess of 30 per cent, the major cluster was in the Ballsbridge, Donnybrook and Mount Merrion areas, popular areas for civil and public servants.

The reader will have noticed from the discussion above that individual indicators often exhibited similar spatial patterns. The suggestion has been made that some are associated with particular overall concepts such as social class or family type. The discussion here now moves to consider whether it is possible to summarize the various indicators discussed above under a small number of individual headings.

## *Factorial ecology*

There is a well-developed methodology for doing this which goes variously under the heading of 'factor analysis' or 'factorial ecology'. It was particularly popular for a while in geography during the time when the subject was more quantitatively focused than it is today. The methodology will not be discussed here but it is explored in Appendix 2 for those who wish to take it further. The underlying principle is that a city is not a haphazard collection of people but that there are forces that sort particular kinds of people into distinctive areas. Originally, it was suggested that it might be possible to summarize the city in terms of a single concept. Thus Burgess' (1926) approach in the 1920s saw the city as being structured in terms of the social status of its population, with the suggestion that social status encompasses different family types. He suggested, in some circumstances, that this might result in the city's social areas being organized into a series of concentric circles with the higher status areas in the outer or suburban ring. Later work by Hoyt (1939) suggested that it was more likely that social areas would be arranged in wedges or sectors and that the city would be like a pie with the different social groups arranged in particular slices. However, it was the work by Shevky, Williams and Bell (1949 and 1955) in the 1950s that showed that most cities were more complex and that they were structured by more than one process. They suggested that the city was structured into different social areas that were determined by (a) social status; (b) family status and (c) ethnic status. They also suggested that the forces that sorted the people in the city into these different areas were independent of each other. Thus one set of forces or processes sorted people into different areas based on their social class while another set of forces sorted them into different family types.

Shevky and Bell wrapped a theory of increasing social scale around their analysis but the theory was unconvincing and it left open the question as to the universality of their findings. This generated many studies of cities around the world and, perhaps surprisingly, the outcome was that it was felt that they had generally got it correct. Cities did have a structure that was capable of being summarized into a small number of factors or indicators and social status and family type were generally the most important. It was also found that cities were not all exactly the same. Each city was a combination of those elements which were generic to all cities in the western world, the effect of capitalism, and those elements which reflected the particular circumstances of the history and planning of the city. In particular, the extent of the role of the city authorities in developing the city was important.

The first study of Dublin was undertaken by Brady and Parker (1975) but the outcome discussed below is a development of that analysis based on a reworking of the data. Both studies confirmed that Dublin could be explained in terms of a small number of composite indicators or factors. One of these was social status and each area could be placed on a scale from high to low. Dublin was also structured into different family areas, largely as a result of the manner in which the development of housing was undertaken. There were other aspects which were peculiar to Dublin but these will not be discussed here.

## Socio-economic status in 1971

The map shows the city divided into six different types of social area. These are identified by combinations of the indicators described above. These have emerged from the analysis as having the same basic spatial pattern so that areas which are high on one indicator tend to be high on other similar ones. The six areas are on a scale from what can be called high status areas to lower status areas. The population of the areas in the highest group can be best described as belonging to the business or higher professional social groups. Exactly 34 per cent of the population in the highest status areas belong to these social groups compared to a city average of under 12 per cent. These areas were particularly favoured by those who have their own businesses as distinct from being in employment and employers accounted for 14 per cent of those in the

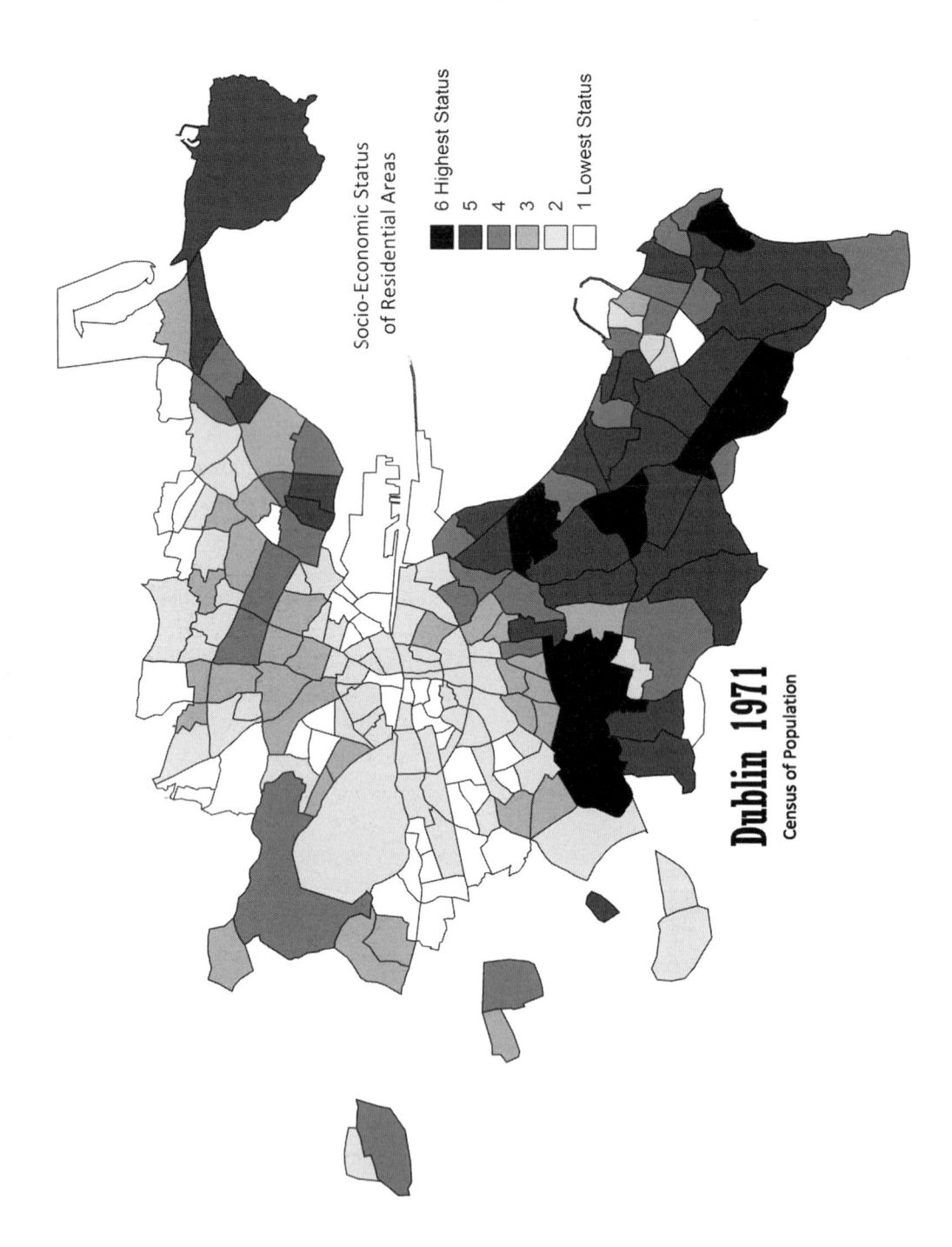

195. The socio-economic status of Dublin's areas, 1971.

labour force, over double the city average. Salaried employees and lower professionals may also be present in these high status areas but the association with the latter group is a little less strong indicating that the lower professionals may also locate outside these 'good' areas. The quality of life is good with households enjoying housing with more than 7 rooms, generally having a car and with their children staying on at school after the minimum school leaving age of 14 years. Since religious differences in Ireland can often be seen in an ethnic context, it is interesting to note that the non-Catholic population of the city tends to be associated with these high status areas, precluding the emergence of any distinctive ethnicity characteristic such as has been found in Amsterdam. In fact an average of 21 per cent of the population belong to churches other than the Roman Catholic, which is also over twice the city average of 8.8 per cent.

At the other end of the spectrum were found the 'blue' collar workers and the lower end of the non-manual employee groups. Low status areas are associated with skilled employees and semi-skilled employees but not the unskilled group to the same extent. In contrast, less than 1 per cent were in the higher professional category or the employers and managers socio-economic group. These areas are strongly associated with local authority housing and there is a suggestion of less personal space with more persons per room on average. The converse of having children at school after the age of 14 years is to have them in the labour force and this is borne out by the high proportion of people in gainful employment.

The map shows the distribution of socio-economic status in Dublin for 1971 and it shows that the 'best' areas of the city were on the south side of the city, though these exist in a number of distinctive clusters rather than a single area. The best areas were identified as the Dublin 4 areas of Ballsbridge and Mount Merrion, parts of Dalkey and Killiney and, of course, Foxrock. To the west there was another cluster in the Rathfarnham and Terenure areas which also leads into Templeogue. However, these are islands in a sea of generally higher status on the south side of the city. Very few areas south of the county borough boundary fell into the lower three categories and these are mostly found in Dún Laoghaire in the area behind the harbour and in the local authority area of Sallynoggin. The areas tending to middle rather than higher status include most of Dundrum but also parts of Ballybrack and Shankill as well as some parts of Blackrock and Dún Laoghaire. However, the general picture is one of prosperity south of the border.

**Table 44.** Characteristics of high- and low-status areas.

| |
|---|
| High status area – high instance of: |
|     Employers and managers |
|     Households with more than 7 rooms |
|     Higher professionals |
|     Cars per household |
|     Salaried employees |
|     Lower professionals |
|     Persons over 14 years at school |
|     Housing units with owner occupiers |
|     Non-Roman Catholics |
| |
| Low-status areas – high instance of: |
|     Other non-manual employees |
|     Semi-skilled employees |
|     More persons per room |
|     Unskilled employees |
|     Housing rented from local authority |
|     Skilled employees |
|     Unemployed people |
|     Population in employment |
|     High economic dependency |

    The north side of the city was much more poorly endowed with high-status areas with no areas at all of the first rank and only six of the second rank. These areas were found along the coast in Clontarf, Dollymount, Sutton and Howth. It was that part of Clontarf around Vernon Avenue that scored highest and this is an area of large houses with a relatively high Church of Ireland population and has its origins in the former township of Clontarf. With the exception of Castleknock on the western edge of the city, the northside's middle-status areas were close to its areas of high status with a salient leading west into the remainder of Clontarf and into Drumcondra and Glasnevin while much of the remainder of the coastal belt fell into the top three categories. If the north side of the city had much fewer areas of high status than the southside it had a more distinctive grouping of middle-status areas. These areas (3 & 4) include Phibsborough, Glasnevin, Drumcondra, Whitehall and the remainder of the coastal strip.

    On the south side of the city, Harold's Cross, Rathmines, Ranelagh and the northern parts of Ballsbridge emerged as being of middle rank and scored either a 3 or 4 on the scale. Social areas are difficult to alter; the forces promoting or ensuring inertia are very strong. Change, though, is more likely in areas such as where there is quite a mixture of occupational groups and consequently less clarity around identity. With these exceptions the remainder of the south county borough fell mainly into the two lowest classes and this included the inner city and the suburbs of Kimmage, Crumlin and Inchicore with Ballyfermot, Drimnagh and Dolphin's Barn emerging as the lowest-status areas. On the northside the lowest-status areas were more widespread and stretched from Cabra into Finglas and then along the northern edge of the city including places such as Ballymun, Kilmore and Coolock and in the city centre in the Sean McDermott Street, Sheriff Street, and north docks area, which is mirrored on the southside by Ringsend.

The impression given by the map is that the northside of the city is indeed of lower socio-economic status than the south side of the city, giving some justification to the folklore. Certainly there are fewer areas in the top two categories and their spatial extent is nothing like that of the southside. In more positive terms this means that the northside is less polarized with areas of very different socio-economic status side by side. This is not to say that there is more mixing of the social groups; proximity does not necessarily result in interaction as Boal (1971) clearly demonstrated for Belfast, but people of the various social groups are more likely to see each other and each other's houses on the north side of the city than on the south side. It is worth a mention that many southsiders place Ballyfermot on the north side of the city in a mental tidying up of the city.

As a final point it is worth noting that Tallaght fell into the lower social categories and was different to Clondalkin which was middle status in character at this time as was much of Lucan.

Viewing the distribution as a whole it is hard to see any distinctive pattern. The southside comes closest to having a sectoral pattern with a narrow band of the middle status areas dividing the lower status north and north-west from the prosperous south-east. This would lend some justification to the Berry (1965) view that socio-economic status varies in sectoral patterns while family status follows a concentric pattern, thus integrating the Burgess and Hoyt models. However, even this improbable sectoral system breaks down on the northside where no pattern is distinguishable. The lack of pattern may be due to the eclectic way in which Dublin developed and the combined influences of independent townships, a cash-poor Dublin Corporation area and a lack of local government structures to plan for the city as a whole.

## Youthfulness and growth

The second set of indicators described areas at particular stages of the life cycle. At one extreme were the areas of the city which were undergoing rapid growth. These were areas with a high fertility index and where children under the age of four represented a significant element of the population. These tended to be greenfield areas that had been developed recently and which were therefore dominated by new housing. The adults tended to consist of married couples in a traditional arrangement where most women worked in the home. All of these things combined to produce a high youthful dependency ratio. There was no particular association with socio-economic group though.

This rapid growth and large numbers of children was a very spatially concentrated phenomenon with few areas in the highest category and all bar one on the northern fringe of the city in Ballymun, Kilmore and Coolock. Almost one in four of the population of these areas was born in the previous five years. Fewer than 16 per cent of the women were in the labour force, which was less than half the city average of 34 per cent, while 4 out of 10 people aged over 14 years worked in the home which is 50 per cent greater than in the city as a whole. This suggests that these were solidly traditional young family areas.

An equally small number of areas fell into the next category and most of these were also on the edge of the city. Baldoyle, Beaumont, and the remainder of Coolock fell into category four and these served to create an almost continuous band of growth areas along the northern fringe. The southern city exhibited this phenomenon to a lesser degree with only four areas in the top two categories, namely Old Bawn (Tallaght), Templeogue, Dundrum and Glenageary. In addition there were a number of dispersed occurrences of category 4 which are found in the remainder of Tallaght, Clondalkin, Firhouse, Dundrum, Stillorgan, Dean's Grange and parts of Killiney and Ballybrack.

It might be expected that at the other end of the spectrum would be areas which have moved into the final stages of the life cycle, characterized by large numbers of old people and almost no new growth. However, this extreme was not found. This is not surprising because decline and renewal take place at varying rates unlike growth which can be achieved in a very short time period. People die at different ages, they move house to different extents and so the turnover of a population will never be as smooth or sudden at this end of the spectrum. The areas at this end of the spectrum were those where a high

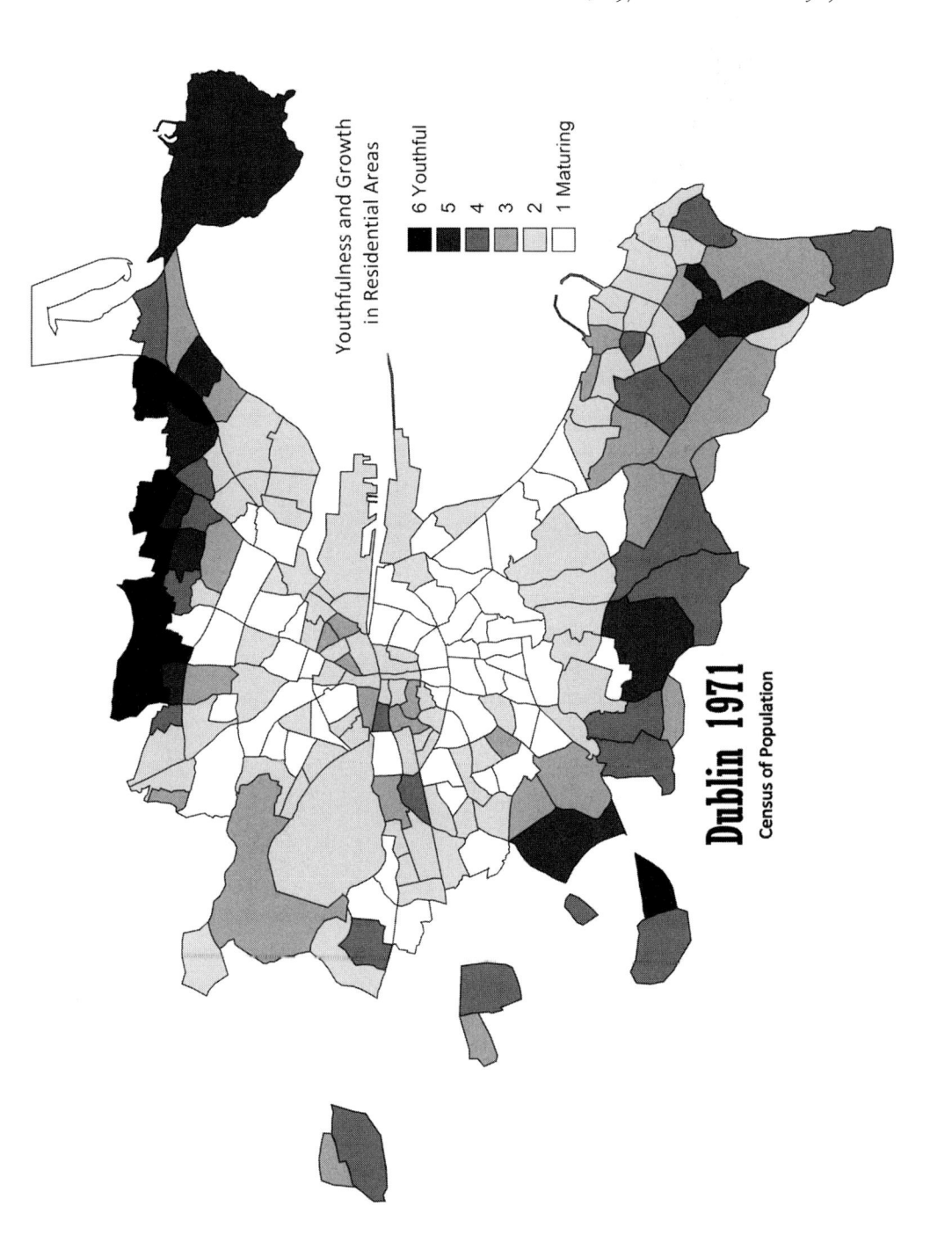

196. Areas of youthfulness and growth in Dublin, 1971.

proportion of the 20–35 age group were unmarried and where there were considerable numbers of women in the labour force. In the areas of category 1 just over 28 per cent of the population was in this age group with an average of 75 per cent of them still single. Over 4 in 10 women of working age were in the labour force. These are not young family areas, with less than one third of the proportion of children under the age of 4 years found in the areas at the other end of the spectrum. Moreover, the fertility ratio was only 0.28. Households were generally small with a tendency to be of two people or less.

Part of the zone described by these characteristics was undoubtedly the flatland of the city where young single people lived in small households in houses which had been converted into flats. The opportunity to create this flatland landscape would have come about by the maturing of the area, the death of older residents and the purchase of their properties for renting. The association with renting would tend to support this. Not all the areas need to have taken on this character and many areas might simply have become mature without becoming part of flatland; the specific flatland indicators are just not strong enough to separate them out. Thus the presence of young single people could also be explained as children in grown up families who

**Table 45.** Characteristics of youthful and maturing areas.

| |
|---|
| Youthful areas – high instance of: |
| Fertility |
| Population under 4 years |
| Married population |
| Housing units built since 1961 |
| Engaged in home duties |
| Youthful dependency ratio |
| Relative importance of post-1961 housing |
| Children of school-going age |
| |
| Maturing areas – high instance of: |
| Single population |
| Women in labour force |
| Population between 15 and 64 years |
| Households with less than 2 persons |
| People over 65 years |
| Housing units with less than 2 people |
| Housing privately rented |

have not yet left home. The women could, therefore, be expected to be in the labour force. The problem lies with the lack of indicators which would differentiate between the two types of area.

Most of the south county borough fell into the two lowest categories, suggesting that population decline would soon be characteristic of most of the south inner suburbs. The exceptions were Ringsend and the western half of the south inner city as well as parts of Kilmainham, Crumlin and Kimmage. The remainder of the southside had some growth potential remaining, though much of Dún Laoghaire fell into category 2.

The greater part of north inner city was in category 2 or 3 which meant that it had not quite yet moved into the final maturing phase. This latter phase was characteristic of most of the area north of this – east of Castleknock, Cabra, south Finglas, Phibsborough, Drumcondra, Glasnevin and parts of Clontarf.

By concentrating development in recent years the city authorities had ensured that growth was concentrated into a small number of bulging areas. Elsewhere, removed of this growth, the city was getting older. Few areas in 1971 had moved into the terminal stages of the life cycle but the seeds of this change were evident from this map. It would have taken a policy of in-fill development to produce any change but this was not a feature of the period from 1971–81, though it would happen later.

## *Other aspects of the socio-economic structure of the city*

The two elements described above would be common to the structure of most cities in the western world but there were also elements which are particular to Dublin. One described areas which contained a residual community of old people who had a distinctive household and housing character. The households tended to be small both in terms of the number of people and also in the physical size of the housing unit. People were found in 1 or 2 person households living in housing units that contained only themselves. They might have been living alone or with other old people and the size of their housing units tended to be on the smaller scale.

The other structural element showed areas with the highest concentration of multi-family dwellings, better described as flat blocks. Households tended to have three or less rooms with some of the units having two rooms or less. It housed the lowest social groups, the unskilled manual employees and the unemployed, and there was only a weak association with semi-skilled employees. An association with persons per room would suggest that accommodation might be tight. This was generally local authority housing and it tended to be found in areas where there are relatively few conventional houses. Within the inner city it was in the Sheriff Street, Summerhill, Aungier Street, Patrick Street and Usher's Quay areas that the greatest concentrations were found though most of the inner city fell into the top categories. In these areas 81 per cent of housing was in the form of multi-family dwellings and 72 per cent of it was rented from the Local Authority with a further 20 per cent from private rental sources. While the highest incidence of this form of housing is generally confined to the inner city, the Ballymun area emerged as an area of very high concentration. This area, as has been shown, has an unusually high concentration of flats for a peripheral area and is out of line with the rest of the city.

## *Dublin's distinctiveness*

Dublin is not greatly different to other Western cities. The forces that sort and sift its people into different kinds of social areas are a reflection of the operation of the housing market, both public and private. Different socio-economic groups tend to occupy different areas and this is mediated through the housing market. In a city where there is a large and pretty anonymous population people need clues as to where they should live. They tend to gravitate towards others who are similar in terms of background and position in life. This leads to certain areas being seen as 'good' or 'suitable' and the reflection of this in house prices tends to reinforce that image. While it is not necessarily true that everyone will purchase up to the maximum price that they can afford, it is sufficiently the case to ensure that the sort of differentiation observed above will happen. Equally, where the local authority builds large estates for its client population, these too will take on a distinctive character. Only particular types of people can get onto the housing list and these are the people who will come to give a distinctive character to these areas. The better-off could not live in these areas even if they wanted to.

Similarly, in a city which has grown relatively rapidly and in which there has been a tendency to build houses on greenfield sites, it is almost inevitable that areas will have different family characteristics. It might be desirable from the point of view of a balanced community to have people at various stages of the life cycle to ensure the efficient use of resources in any area but this did not happen in Dublin. In fact, it was soon to become even more polarized in the new towns to the west where such was the demand for primary schools that shift systems were common into the 1980s. The problem with unbalanced communities is that resource provision will always reflect that imbalance. Thus the demand will be first for primary schools but that will soon translate into a demand for secondary schools. In both cases the demand will falter after twenty years and it will not be immediately clear what to do with these schools. Later on, as the population ages, the demands will change and it will be some time before houses are freed up once again for a young population.

Dublin did not have any ethnic areas in 1971 for the simple reason that there was no population of non-Irish sufficiently spatially concentrated in the city. It would be a different picture today where analysis of the most recent censuses suggests that there are now areas in the city with a very distinctive ethnic characteristic but this is volatile and changing from year to year.

So, two maps, social status and family type, summed up the city in 1971. The social status picture was not going to change. The housing market sees to that and peoples' investment in housing and their interest in seeing that grow ensures that no policy instruments of State or local Government are allowed to threaten that. Therefore, a map of social status in 2015 would not be greatly different to the one here, except in detail. Naturally, the city's growth has expanded its footprint but high-status areas remain where they always were and have simply expanded radially as Homer Hoyt argued that they would. A few new high-status areas have been added as a consequence of a shift to inner city apartment living but Foxrock is still Foxrock. The other map has changed, however. There have been population shifts and areas have aged and developed. There was much in-fill during the 1980s and 1990s, particularly as great tranches of institutional land came onto the market. This changed the distribution of family types and probably evened out some of the contrasts. The biggest change though would be the emergence of a multi-cultural city with different ethnic groups in particular locations and not always where they might have been expected to be found.

# The wider urban context

## The car, the office and the suburbs

This text has largely been about housing but what else was happening in the city? These matters will be dealt with in a forthcoming volume but it is reasonable to suggest that the increased availability of the motor car was one of the more important forces driving change. As Dubliners found themselves with a little more money in the better economic climate of the 1960s, their thoughts turned to houses and to cars. Car ownership increased and, not surprisingly, people wanted to use their cars for everyday activities. The city had long wrestled with problems of congestion. Despite the excellent work of the Wide Streets Commissioners in the eighteenth century, the city was clogged on a regular basis because of the need for much city traffic to cross the Liffey. Any increase in car ownership brought renewed concern about the issue and there was a great deal of consideration (though, perhaps fortunately, not much building) of solutions. This was still an era when it was felt that it was both possible and desirable to modify the city's streetscape to accommodate the car. This required that new roads be created, either by the significant widening of existing routes but also by cutting brand new highways through the city centre. This seemed to be the modern thing to do and there was only limited concern for the impact that this would have on the historic landscape. This concern was diminished greatly by the suggestion that most of the new routes would go through areas which were in decline and in need of regeneration. There were no qualms though about bringing a highway into the environs of St Patrick's or Christ Church cathedrals or in doing likewise at the top of O'Connell Street along Parnell Street. For a while, there was quiet satisfaction that a new use could be found for the canals by filling them in and using the space for wide and spacious roads. It was probably fortunate that not enough money was available for these projects in the early 1960s, otherwise the city would have got what was built in cities such as Glasgow. Glasgow got the M8 in the late 1960s, linking it with Edinburgh. This runs through the city centre on an elevated platform and bisects the city along a north-south axis. Dublin did not escape unscathed but by the time that projects were being seriously considered for implementation, opinion was beginning to swing away from accommodation and more towards management of the motor car as it was realized that no amount of road building would ever be sufficient to meet demand.

It was not just in the matter of road provision where the motor car had an impact. Cars improve accessibility and make it possible to access and use a far greater swathe of the urban environment than would be possible using public transport. Public transport suffered from under investment and it was in any event focused on a congested city centre. There needed to be a reorientation of the city. This coincided with the adoption by retailers of the self-service concept from the United States and the supermarket arrived. This idea allowed larger and larger stores to be managed by small staff numbers. Suburban locations suited these operations better and the shopping centre concept allowed the development of the idea of one-stop shopping. Now that people had cars, could they not do all of their shopping in suburban locations? Car parking was easier to provide, land was cheaper, shops could be laid out all on one floor. This suited both retailer and shopper and it was not surprising to find both the supermarket and the shopping centre ideas take hold quickly once car ownership reached critical mass. The city centre's dominance was also challenged by the move of industry to suburban locations, following the same logic as retailing. Unless a company could derive particular benefit either from the prestige of a city centre location or from the capacity for its employees to have face-to-face contact with others, they were better off in the suburbs. Here operations could take place on one floor, there was plenty of room for storage and warehousing and their staff could come to work by car. Very soon Dublin began to see a change toward being polycentric.

This greatly increased the problems that the city centre had to contend with. It was already congested and difficult to access and much of Dublin had seen better days. There had to be a fight back and the only solution was to try and replicate the suburban model in central areas. This meant building central shopping centres with easy access and ample parking. Not much of this was built during the 1960s but the focus was on the area around Moore Street. The north city needed regeneration to a far greater degree than south of the Liffey and the poor state of the urban fabric offered possibilities. This would ultimately become the ILAC centre but not as quickly as Dublin Corporation might have hoped.

The increased ownership of cars was one indication of a changing society and economy. Another was a boom in commercial employment during the 1960s. Dublin needed more office space and new purpose-built office blocks began to appear in the city centre. The issue though was that this precipitated a clash between the modernizers and the conservationists. The best-preserved Georgian landscapes were in the south-eastern sector of the city which had avoided the decline and decay that was so evident elsewhere. Part of the reason was that this area had become a favoured area for shopping and commerce but the nature of these activities had not been such as to demand significant redevelopment, at least until now. There was plenty of space elsewhere in the inner city where office blocks could be built. Indeed the north inner city needed such redevelopment to breathe life into its commercial heart. No developer, however, was going to risk his investment by building in an area associated with decay and decline without significant State support and this was not forthcoming. The safe and sensible thing to do was to build in the proven and desirable area of south-eastern Dublin and that is what they did. The scale of what they wanted to build could not be accommodated by remodelling Georgian houses and the approach was to demolish and build anew; renewal rather than renovation. It took a while for a conservation movement to gather momentum and even longer to get significant public support. Dublin was a city that had been quite prepared to build urban motorways; it seemed odd that it would baulk at building office blocks, which would be both modern and provide employment. There was less appreciation of the value of the historic streetscape than there would be now for reasons that were complex and interwoven. It cannot be said that the conservation movement had great success during the late 1960s; most of the projects that were proposed were built but with modifications in some cases. There was an awakening, though, of public interest in urban heritage and the slogan of 'away with the old and in with the new' did not get such a ready audience in the 1970s.

It was the office blocks that became the new signature buildings of the city. In previous generations, citizens had looked towards the civic authorities for buildings that would express the pride and power of the city. This now passed to the commercial sector and there was little civic building of a monumental type. There were important infrastructural developments but a main drainage system tends not to capture the imagination as much as a skyscraper. There was fun with the 'bowl of light' on O'Connell Bridge, which occupied Dubliners on and off between 1953 and 1963, and Nelson, after over a century of agitation, was finally removed from his position in 1966. Otherwise, it fell to the State to add to the landscape of commemoration by the completion of the Garden of Remembrance and the siting of the long-awaited statue of Thomas Davis. These were small-scale changes and nothing came of the larger plans such as that for the concert hall, another long promised project. This was given new impetus following the assassination of President John F. Kennedy in 1963 but the initial energy was not enough to bring the project to completion.

From now on, most of the growth of the city was going to be in the suburbs, beyond the confines of Dublin Corporation. The baton now passed to Dublin County Council on whose land most new development would be concentrated. As a latest manifestation of the fractured governance of the city, much of that building would be by Dublin Corporation as developer as it continued its programme of inner city slum clearance and general housing provision. By 1981 there were 956,125 people within the city of Dublin, of whom 458,575 were male and 497,550 were female. This city was no longer a continuous spatial entity as the development plans for the new towns to the west of the city envisaged green belts between the city and the new towns and between the new towns themselves. These towns had grown substantially during the 1970s with the result that there were now considerable satellite populations to the west of the city. However, the degree of separation should not be exaggerated as the green belt was breached in many locations. In the case of Tallaght the green belt was no more than a couple of hundred metres wide and Clondalkin had an umbilical cord which linked it to the city. Lucan remained distinct from the city but Blanchardstown was linked to the city as early as 1971 and, while it grew in size, development also continued along the roads from the city removing any impression of isolation. The increase in the spatial extent of these areas could readily be seen by a comparison of the maps for 1971 and 1981 and while the city did not yet reach the county border to the west, it was not far from it. Development was not confined to the new towns and the villages of Swords, Malahide and Portmarnock were extensively developed during this period. Though they remained spatially distinct from the city because of the airport corridor, they were nevertheless suburban areas of the city, very much part of the commuting belt and developed because of their high amenity value. Some housing developments took place further north in places such as Skerries and Rush, and also in Bray in the south.

There was going to be a great deal of house building and by 1981 over one in four houses in the city would be less than 10 years old. Those built prior to 1918 now accounted for just over 17 per cent.

During the 1970s the idea of home ownership became firmly rooted with the result that the greater part of housing was now owner occupied, whether owned outright or mortgaged. The policy of tenant purchase, introduced at

**Table 46.** Age of housing stock, 1981.

| Period built | Number | Per cent |
|---|---|---|
| Before 1918 | 41,698 | 17.2 |
| 1919 to 1940 | 38,009 | 15.7 |
| 1941 to 1960 | 54,722 | 22.5 |
| 1961 to 1970 | 42,594 | 17.5 |
| 1971 to 1975 | 35,707 | 14.7 |
| 1976 to 1981 | 29,996 | 12.4 |

the end of the 1960s, had a dramatic impact and local authority housing had slipped to just 18 per cent of the stock by end of the decade. Things had changed dramatically since the 1950s and those who first introduced the idea of tenant purchase in the 1920s would have been pleased that the city now comprised property-owners who would be less likely to turn to communism. In fact, the early 1980s was to see a further push towards ownership with greater incentives given to Corporation tenants to surrender their tenancies and move into the private market. As a result, new building by Dublin Corporation fell to almost nothing.

The 1970s had the potential to be interesting for other reasons too. The development plan for the city included an underground system as well as the more usual zonation for business, industry and housing. The controversy over Wood Quay and its Viking remains was going to blow up, just as Dublin Corporation felt that it might get its civic offices at last. There was talk of hypermarkets and of regional-scale shopping centres that would hoover up all of the business of the city into one suburban location. The city might change beyond all recognition!

# Appendix 1

## Detail of selected aspects from the censuses of population

**Table A1.** Population in Dublin wards, 1951–61. (Census of population, various years, volume 1.)

| Wards | 1951 | 1956 | 1961 | 1966 |
|---|---|---|---|---|
| Arran Quay | 24880 | 22874 | 20242 | 19091 |
| Artane | 2317 | 6088 | 9318 | 16542 |
| Baldoyle | 1158 | 1549 | 1642 | 2097 |
| Ballybough | 12847 | 10576 | 9533 | 9965 |
| Beann Eadair | 5756 | 5823 | 6077 | 7377 |
| Cabragh East | 19215 | 16245 | 14749 | 14647 |
| Cabragh West | 20617 | 21061 | 19530 | 19733 |
| Clontarf East | 14098 | 18170 | 19917 | 21017 |
| Clontarf West | 21777 | 20544 | 19588 | 20210 |
| Coolock | 473 | 2055 | 8131 | 15596 |
| Drumcondra North | 16550 | 15529 | 14556 | 14944 |
| Drumcondra South | 15440 | 14752 | 13870 | 13914 |
| Finglas East | 6794 | 15149 | 20053 | 24557 |
| Finglas West | 602 | 4879 | 11745 | 18718 |
| Glasnevin | 9152 | 8176 | 7835 | 7732 |
| Inns Quay | 20390 | 16133 | 13649 | 13078 |
| Mountjoy | 17521 | 14247 | 13123 | 11402 |
| North City | 7454 | 5391 | 4195 | 2966 |
| North Dock | 17192 | 14809 | 13977 | 13548 |
| Phoenix Park | 2893 | 2600 | 2231 | 1907 |
| Raheny | 1063 | 1947 | 3288 | 6256 |
| Rotunda | 13617 | 8882 | 8241 | 6757 |
| Santry | 134 | 1970 | 3404 | 5792 |
| Ballyfermot | 13209 | 29364 | 31892 | 33910 |
| Crumlin | 37122 | 35406 | 32729 | 32024 |
| Crumlin West | 968 | 1483 | 1460 | 1699 |
| Kilmainham | 18179 | 18189 | 17086 | 17585 |
| Kimmage | 25379 | 24036 | 22243 | 22197 |
| Mansion House | 14453 | 11218 | 9859 | 8827 |
| Merchant's Quay | 25412 | 22593 | 19394 | 19225 |
| Pembroke East | 18987 | 18452 | 18330 | 18670 |
| Pembroke West | 15801 | 13731 | 12855 | 12582 |
| Rathfarnham | 8214 | 10705 | 12742 | 14466 |

**Table A1.** Population in Dublin wards, 1951–61. (Census of population, various years, volume 1.) *(contd)*

| Wards | 1951 | 1956 | 1961 | 1966 |
|---|---|---|---|---|
| Rathfarnham South | 599 | 2556 | 3176 | 3358 |
| Rathmines East | 18461 | 16331 | 16255 | 16732 |
| Rathmines West | 24539 | 21275 | 21016 | 22065 |
| Royal Exchange | 10475 | 7357 | 6165 | 5293 |
| St Kevin's | 9614 | 7462 | 6512 | 5900 |
| South Dock | 10341 | 7584 | 6914 | 5818 |
| Terenure | 12679 | 12107 | 12253 | 12536 |
| Usher's | 23938 | 20568 | 18765 | 19316 |
| Wood Quay | 11245 | 9610 | 8908 | 8723 |
| | | | | |
| Blackrock 1 | 4386 | 4175 | 4185 | 4244 |
| Blackrock 2 | 6530 | 5728 | 5500 | 5578 |
| Blackrock 3 | 2863 | 2816 | 2711 | 2774 |
| Blackrock 4 | 5679 | 5526 | 5754 | 6786 |
| Dalkey | 2331 | 2748 | 2774 | 3167 |
| Dún Laoghaire 1 | 6592 | 6228 | 6306 | 6705 |
| Dún Laoghaire 2 | 8307 | 8772 | 9022 | 9826 |
| Dún Laoghaire 3 | 8408 | 9083 | 8962 | 10147 |
| Dún Laoghaire 4 | 2466 | 2477 | 2578 | 2545 |
| Dún Laoghaire Total | 47562 | 47553 | 47792 | 51772 |
| | | | | |
| Dublin City | 551555 | 539476 | 537448 | 568772 |
| Dún Laoghaire | 47562 | 47553 | 47792 | 51772 |
| | | | | |
| North Inner City | 117857 | 97459 | 88479 | 84970 |
| South Inner City | 105478 | 86392 | 76517 | 73102 |
| Inner City | 223335 | 183851 | 164996 | 158072 |

**Table A2.** Age of dwellings in Dublin wards, 1961. (Census of population, 1961, volume VI.)

| Wards | Pre-1860 | 1860–99 | 1900–18 | 1919–39 | 1940–5 | Post-1946 | Total dwellings |
|---|---|---|---|---|---|---|---|
| Arran Quay | 1157 | 2389 | 744 | 179 | 4 | 288 | 4839 |
| Artane | 18 | 14 | 12 | 70 | 32 | 1820 | 1969 |
| Baldoyle | 19 | 62 | 40 | 63 | 9 | 134 | 330 |
| Ballybough | 794 | 1173 | 448 | 302 | 19 | 89 | 2863 |
| Beann Eadair | 99 | 329 | 300 | 410 | 40 | 311 | 1506 |
| Cabragh East | 61 | 767 | 673 | 2253 | 52 | 102 | 3954 |
| Cabragh West | 15 | 67 | 27 | 498 | 2048 | 1060 | 3733 |
| Clontarf East | 124 | 366 | 266 | 1439 | 216 | 2267 | 4690 |
| Clontarf West | 141 | 381 | 392 | 1936 | 39 | 1720 | 4627 |
| Coolock | 14 | 17 | 12 | 17 | 9 | 1408 | 1480 |

**Table A2.** Age of dwellings in Dublin wards, 1961. (Census of population, 1961, volume VI.) *(contd)*

| Wards | Pre-1860 | 1860–99 | 1900–18 | 1919–39 | 1940–5 | Post-1946 | Total dwellings |
|---|---|---|---|---|---|---|---|
| Drumcondra North | 19 | 19 | 30 | 2272 | 218 | 506 | 3072 |
| Drumcondra South | 146 | 698 | 787 | 1580 | 20 | 325 | 3571 |
| Finglas East | 16 | 38 | 44 | 307 | 125 | 3680 | 4237 |
| Finglas West | 23 | 27 | 18 | 18 | 27 | 1949 | 2074 |
| Glasnevin | 52 | 622 | 878 | 423 | 14 | 101 | 2111 |
| Inns Quay | 1521 | 1531 | 517 | 288 | 15 | 5 | 3904 |
| Mountjoy | 2208 | 490 | 371 | 313 | 99 | 199 | 3691 |
| North City | 916 | 138 | 55 | 24 | 2 | 0 | 1140 |
| North Dock | 657 | 940 | 334 | 815 | 164 | 328 | 3275 |
| Phoenix Park | 115 | 200 | 15 | 15 | 2 | 4 | 353 |
| Raheny | 11 | 19 | 14 | 125 | 26 | 613 | 808 |
| Rotunda | 1820 | 38 | 5 | 83 | 1 | 356 | 2303 |
| Santry | 2 | 1 | 3 | 4 | 6 | 823 | 842 |
| North City Total | 9948 | 10326 | 5985 | 13434 | 3187 | 18088 | 61372 |
| | | | | | | | |
| Ballyfermot | 16 | 25 | 68 | 313 | 95 | 5094 | 5619 |
| Crumlin | 12 | 12 | 67 | 3961 | 1768 | 810 | 6649 |
| Crumlin West | 4 | 5 | 12 | 82 | 29 | 194 | 326 |
| Kilmainham | 312 | 541 | 625 | 1049 | 76 | 1102 | 3729 |
| Kimmage | 95 | 106 | 72 | 2765 | 241 | 1153 | 4455 |
| Mansion House | 1500 | 394 | 116 | 592 | 19 | 6 | 2633 |
| Merchant's Quay | 1250 | 1859 | 604 | 1026 | 32 | 400 | 5189 |
| Pembroke East | 468 | 1162 | 1055 | 973 | 162 | 899 | 4737 |
| Pembroke West | 1402 | 1397 | 832 | 401 | 19 | 190 | 4251 |
| Rathfarnham | 106 | 352 | 361 | 814 | 58 | 1336 | 3053 |
| Rathfarnham South | 1 | 1 | 0 | 25 | 27 | 557 | 611 |
| Rathmines East | 590 | 2279 | 792 | 660 | 58 | 202 | 4622 |
| Rathmines West | 1697 | 3351 | 857 | 623 | 13 | 109 | 6707 |
| Royal Exchange | 1114 | 294 | 69 | 137 | 36 | 163 | 1821 |
| St Kevin's | 1284 | 430 | 194 | 52 | 14 | 4 | 1980 |
| South Dock | 1423 | 513 | 17 | 3 | 2 | 98 | 2057 |
| Terenure | 81 | 168 | 660 | 1378 | 57 | 737 | 3086 |
| Usher's | 483 | 1014 | 613 | 1085 | 198 | 866 | 4269 |
| Wood Quay | 418 | 1444 | 485 | 159 | 36 | 55 | 2619 |
| South City Total | 12256 | 15347 | 7499 | 16098 | 2940 | 13975 | 68413 |
| | | | | | | | |
| Dublin City | 22204 | 25673 | 13484 | 29532 | 6127 | 32063 | 129785 |
| Dún Laoghaire | | | | | | | |
| | | | | | | | |
| North Inner City | 9199 | 6918 | 2503 | 2144 | 332 | 1882 | 23176 |
| South Inner City | 7472 | 5948 | 2098 | 3054 | 337 | 1592 | 20568 |
| Inner City | 16671 | 12866 | 4601 | 5198 | 669 | 3474 | 43744 |

**Table A3.** Housing facilities in Dublin wards, 1961. Number of dwellings with specified facilities. (Census of population, 1961, volume VI.)

| Wards | Total dwellings | Shared tap | Fixed bath | Shared sanitary | In flats |
|---|---|---|---|---|---|
| Arran Quay | 4839 | 768 | 1139 | 1203 | 1954 |
| Artane | 1969 | 18 | 1872 | 26 | 39 |
| Baldoyle | 330 | 4 | 189 | 7 | 11 |
| Ballybough | 2863 | 583 | 1087 | 907 | 1131 |
| Beann Eadair | 1506 | 47 | 1093 | 92 | 150 |
| Cabragh East | 3954 | 333 | 3522 | 554 | 802 |
| Cabragh West | 3733 | 31 | 3527 | 44 | 90 |
| Clontarf East | 4690 | 148 | 4339 | 278 | 398 |
| Clontarf West | 4627 | 253 | 4235 | 414 | 521 |
| Coolock | 1480 | 7 | 1396 | 17 | 13 |
| Drumcondra North | 3072 | 63 | 2885 | 86 | 111 |
| Drumcondra South | 3571 | 314 | 2958 | 470 | 628 |
| Finglas East | 4237 | 22 | 3835 | 44 | 34 |
| Finglas West | 2074 | 11 | 1919 | 14 | 11 |
| Glasnevin | 2111 | 233 | 1658 | 376 | 519 |
| Inns Quay | 3904 | 1216 | 989 | 1782 | 2235 |
| Mountjoy | 3691 | 1231 | 1058 | 1697 | 3218 |
| North City | 1140 | 431 | 276 | 624 | 996 |
| North Dock | 3275 | 161 | 1527 | 405 | 929 |
| Phoenix Park | 353 | 20 | 145 | 41 | 69 |
| Raheny | 808 | 8 | 759 | 14 | 17 |
| Rotunda | 2303 | 1134 | 890 | 1391 | 2175 |
| Santry | 842 | 4 | 808 | 10 | 7 |
| North City Total | 61372 | 7040 | 42106 | 10496 | 16058 |
| | | | | | |
| Ballyfermot | 5619 | 38 | 5390 | 69 | 176 |
| Crumlin | 6649 | 49 | 6361 | 80 | 185 |
| Crumlin West | 326 | 1 | 292 | 11 | 3 |
| Kilmainham | 3729 | 70 | 2298 | 153 | 377 |
| Kimmage | 4455 | 39 | 4145 | 83 | 156 |
| Mansion House | 2633 | 515 | 1434 | 956 | 2378 |
| Merchant's Quay | 5189 | 578 | 1841 | 1270 | 1984 |
| Pembroke East | 4737 | 226 | 3459 | 505 | 1327 |
| Pembroke West | 4251 | 429 | 2837 | 997 | 2259 |
| Rathfarnham | 3053 | 37 | 2675 | 88 | 334 |
| Rathfarnham South | 611 | 2 | 576 | 5 | 9 |
| Rathmines East | 4622 | 544 | 3891 | 1091 | 2016 |
| Rathmines West | 6707 | 870 | 4720 | 1929 | 3812 |
| Royal Exchange | 1821 | 602 | 459 | 989 | 1556 |
| St Kevin's | 1980 | 449 | 896 | 1018 | 1411 |
| South Dock | 2057 | 397 | 866 | 950 | 1627 |
| Terenure | 3086 | 153 | 2715 | 280 | 420 |
| Usher's | 4269 | 316 | 2181 | 631 | 1733 |
| Wood Quay | 2619 | 689 | 955 | 967 | 1399 |
| South City Total | 68413 | 6004 | 47991 | 12072 | 23162 |
| | | | | | |
| Dublin City | 129785 | 13044 | 90097 | 22568 | 39220 |

**Table A4.** Housing tenure in Dublin wards, 1961. Number of dwellings. (Census of population, 1961, volume VI.)

| Ward | Total dwellings | Rented from LA | Tenant purchase | Privately rented | Owner |
|---|---|---|---|---|---|
| Arran Quay | 4839 | 694 | 8 | 3179 | 724 |
| Artane | 1969 | 79 | 68 | 95 | 1708 |
| Baldoyle | 330 | 91 | 83 | 41 | 109 |
| Ballybough | 2863 | 551 | 2 | 1472 | 787 |
| Beann Eadair | 1506 | 283 | 2 | 322 | 824 |
| Cabragh East | 3954 | 1082 | 403 | 825 | 1576 |
| Cabragh West | 3733 | 2264 | 21 | 174 | 1141 |
| Clontarf East | 4690 | 161 | 25 | 683 | 3721 |
| Clontarf West | 4627 | 1010 | 717 | 610 | 2114 |
| Coolock | 1480 | 918 | 29 | 30 | 499 |
| Drumcondra North | 3072 | 1041 | 198 | 199 | 1600 |
| Drumcondra South | 3571 | 196 | 528 | 868 | 1934 |
| Finglas East | 4237 | 1104 | 316 | 630 | 2157 |
| Finglas West | 2074 | 1895 | 13 | 36 | 110 |
| Glasnevin | 2111 | 4 |  | 734 | 1337 |
| Inns Quay | 3904 | 599 |  | 2346 | 829 |
| Mountjoy | 3691 | 1322 |  | 2082 | 241 |
| North City | 1140 | 208 |  | 765 | 84 |
| North Dock | 3275 | 1189 | 5 | 1197 | 836 |
| Phoenix Park | 353 | 15 | 3 | 218 | 58 |
| Raheny | 808 | 30 | 1 | 52 | 711 |
| Rotunda | 2303 | 622 | 41 | 1511 | 110 |
| Santry | 842 | 8 |  | 28 | 755 |
| North City Total | 61372 | 15366 | 2463 | 18097 | 23965 |
| Ballyfermot | 5619 | 4903 | 54 | 214 | 405 |
| Crumlin | 6649 | 4285 | 22 | 1162 | 1151 |
| Crumlin West | 326 | 79 | 17 | 27 | 195 |
| Kilmainham | 3729 | 1888 | 255 | 603 | 831 |
| Kimmage | 4455 | 3548 | 2 | 249 | 575 |
| Mansion House | 2633 | 692 | 1 | 1580 | 149 |
| Merchant's Quay | 5189 | 1155 | 182 | 2862 | 920 |
| Pembroke East | 4737 | 893 | 15 | 1446 | 2267 |
| Pembroke West | 4251 | 333 | 59 | 2591 | 1189 |
| Rathfarnham | 3053 | 207 | 36 | 538 | 2193 |
| Rathfarnham South | 611 | 365 | 18 | 25 | 198 |
| Rathmines East | 4622 | 54 | 2 | 2236 | 2255 |
| Rathmines West | 6707 | 640 | 3 | 3851 | 2032 |
| Royal Exchange | 1821 | 370 | 0 | 1233 | 100 |

**Table A4.** Housing tenure in Dublin wards, 1961. Number of dwellings. (Census of population, 1961, volume VI.) *(contd)*

| Ward | Total dwellings | Rented from LA | Tenant purchase | Privately rented | Owner |
|---|---|---|---|---|---|
| St Kevin's | 1980 | 101 | 0 | 1542 | 269 |
| South Dock | 2057 | 67 | 1 | 1760 | 139 |
| Terenure | 3086 | 460 | 101 | 831 | 1664 |
| Usher's | 4269 | 1771 | 70 | 1437 | 933 |
| Wood Quay | 2619 | 204 | 1 | 1805 | 575 |
| South City Total | 68413 | 22015 | 839 | 25992 | 18040 |
|  |  |  |  |  |  |
| Dublin City | 129785 | 37381 | 3302 | 44089 | 42005 |
| North Inner City | 23176 | 5230 | 60 | 12822 | 4380 |
| South Inner City | 20568 | 4360 | 255 | 12219 | 3085 |
| Inner City | 43744 | 9590 | 315 | 25041 | 7465 |

# *Appendix 2*

## *The socio-demographic spatial structure of Dublin, 1971*

The description of the city presented in the chapter on social areas was a factor analysis of the form that was used to study cities from the 1960s onwards. The approach has fallen out of favour in geographical research in recent years as the subject has moved from its brief flirtation with quantitative methods to the post-modern approach of uncritical qualitative reporting. Therefore, most of the texts are from an earlier era but they are none the worst for that because the essential issues with the technique remain.

The age of factor analytic studies of urban social structure began with the work of Shevky and Williams (1949). Their study of the social areas of Los Angeles was clearly meant to be a case study for in their preface they noted that the work which they were undertaking was an attempt to establish the basis for developing a comprehensive knowledge of Los Angeles. However, in the course of this research they discovered that they had found a means of describing the residential structure of the city in terms of three axes of differentiation. They also came to the conclusion that these ideas could be applied more widely and in the introduction to the 1955 theoretical presentation of their ideas, Shevky and Bell stated that 'the second major purpose of this monograph is to demonstrate the use of the typology as an analytic framework for the comparative study of certain aspects of the social structure of American cities' (p. 2). Their approach generated lively criticism and their theoretical framework was the focus of particular attention. This was so because of the time gap between the publication of the research report on Los Angeles and the more general study of 1955 and it was generally believed that Shevky, Bell and Williams had developed their early ideas out of their empirical work and, when they found that the notions of three axes gained some currency, built a theoretical framework to fit them. Abu-Lughod (1969) puts the point very well when she says 'the theory, inadequately explicated as it was and appended uneasily to serve chiefly as an elaborate rationalization for Shevky's perspicacious and, as it later developed, happy hunches' (p. 199).

## *Social area analysis*

The Los Angeles study was important because it suggested that there were three forces or processes which sorted out population. These were social class, family type and ethnicity. It was not clear from their writing why this should be the case though they provided a very long and detailed description of changes in American (*sic*) economy and society.

The city was seen to be structured in terms of three processes and they produced a scale on which any of the areas of the city could be placed. These three axes of differentiation could be measured by seven variables or indicators. The first three, which measured social rank, were occupational status, educational status and income. Occupation status measured the relative importance of manual employments in the labour force while educational status was a measure of those over 25 years of age who had completed grade school. The final indicator was chosen as rent per capita, the total monthly contract or estimated rent for the total population.

Information was obtained from census tract returns enabling a composite index to be developed for each area. They argued that the variables chosen were important factors in social stratification because they were indicators of position in society. Thus the higher the number of people in an area with grade school education only, the lower the social rank of that area while the smaller the number of craftsmen, operatives and labourers the higher the social rank of that part of the city.

In their discussion of the second axis, urbanization, they noted that the distribution of the social class groupings appeared to have internal structural differences. They found that the working population in one area was largely male, young and associated with large numbers of children while another was 'heavily weighted with younger women in paid employment, a larger proportion of persons in working ages and fewer children' (p. 41). These differences were explained as being an expression of the fact that the areas of the city differed in terms of their 'urbanization' which was measured in terms of fertility, women in the labour force, and the relative importance of single-family dwellings.

The impression given is that there is a climax lifestyle called 'urbanization' which an area reaches when fertility is low, when the number of women in the labour force is high and when people do not live in single-family dwellings. It is a strange concept since it implies that family life has little place in the city and it seems to suggest a bleak future for most urban communities. Moreover, there was a suggestion that this axis of differentiation had some relationship with social status in that fertility is highest among populations at the lowest occupation and income levels. However, later formulation of these constructs implied that social rank and urbanization are independent axes of differentiation.

The final axis of differentiation was that of segregation. They believed that groups could become spatially isolated in the city especially if the social position of such groups was such that they felt the need for cohesion and solidarity. When the degree of isolation reached a level at which it became an expression of discrimination by the host population then it could be termed segregation. Segregation was measured in terms of the relative proportion of highly isolated populations per census area. Such populations included the categories 'Negroes', 'Mexicans', 'Orientals' as well as those of Russian origin. This axis of differentiation was also related to social rank and the areas with greatest segregation were largely concentrated in the lowest social levels.

The purpose of the 1949 study was to develop a social typology of the city and not to map its social areas. They wanted to identify particular types of social areas that would be particular combinations of the three axes. They developed a typology of social areas in Los Angeles whereby the social rank and urbanization axes were divided into three intervals describing 'high', 'medium' and 'low' status with each of these further subdivided in terms of whether they experienced 'high' or 'low' segregation. This yielded 18 social area 'types' of which they discovered 16 in the Los Angeles area and the remainder of the study is taken up with a consideration of the importance of these social areas. Maps are presented of the typology but the spatial patterning of such social areas is not considered and there is, therefore, no assessment of the extent to which their results add to or detract from the work of Burgess and Hoyt.

## *The statement of theory, 1955*

When they published their statement of theory, they also made some changes to how the axes should be understood though their number remained the same. The theory was based on an idea of societal change and the various areas of the city could be seen in terms of how far they had progressed along this path to change. Since the theory was very quickly challenged as having no relationship with what was being observed on the ground, there is no need to go into it here.

In practical terms the typology was modified to provide four divisions of social rank and urbanization while retaining two categories of segregation. Furthermore, the authors recognized that the variables used in the analysis might not adequately describe the concept of social rank or urbanization and, in fact, might only indirectly measure these concepts or fail to do so fully. It was, therefore, possible to exercise a degree of choice in the measures used providing that the key indicators were represented. In particular, it was noted that urbanization as it was measured by the choice of indicators did not directly capture the process of change in the ranges of relations in cities although they noted that occupation was the key determinant of social rank. Finally, a note at the end of the report shows that there was disagreement between Shevky and Bell as to the naming of the axes. Bell preferred the term economic status to social rank, status referring to the fact that each social area's position is determined with reference to each dimension while economic was preferred to social because it was closer to what was measured by the construct. He also preferred family status to urbanization because he believed that this was what the indicators measured rather than the more general concept of urbanization. It measured the extent to which family life was central to each area and it made more sense to refer to an area as having low family status rather than low urbanization. Ethnic status was his chosen label for the third element because 'in addition to emphasizing the concept of position, the use of the term "ethnic status" rather than "segregation" reduces possible confusion with the index of isolation and the group segregation ratio which are also a part of this method of analysis' (p. 68).

But, interestingly, despite the quick discounting of the theory, researchers who analysed their own cities using mathematical techniques were surprised to find that most cities, especially those in the US, could be described in terms of concepts such as Shevky and Bell suggested. It appeared that they had hit on something useful. For a detailed discussion of this, the reader is referred to Timms (1971).

There was now a problem though in that there was no theoretical basis for using only the indicators that Shevky and Bell suggested. Why not use more indicators and see if there were other forces at work in the city? And thus, factorial ecology or simply factor analysis was born. Factor analysis is a heavyweight mathematical tool that allows a large number of indicators to be summarized into a small number of composite indicators made up of different combinations of the original ones. In terms of the city, it allows the researcher to compare the patterns that are exhibited by different indicators and to group similar ones together. The belief is that by doing this it will be possible to identify the underlying process or forces which caused these indicators to have the same patterns. It is not an easy technique to use because there are many decisions to be made which can influence the

## Wards and District Electoral Divisions 1971

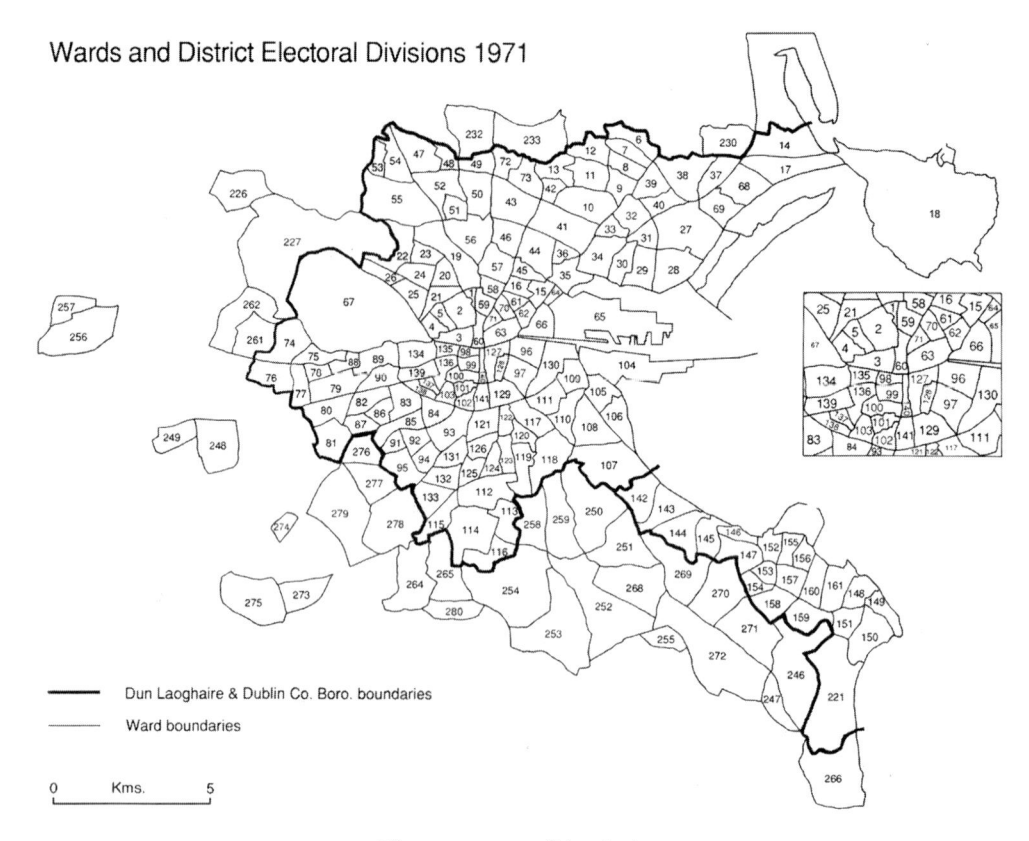

**197.** The census areas of the city in 1971.

result but at least the advent of high speed computers has made the computational element painless.

The first study of Dublin was undertaken by Brady and Parker (1975). This was the first to make use of the small area population statistics and other analyses followed, both of the 1971 data, and the data for subsequent censuses.

## *Definition of city*

Brady and Parker's (1975) paper was described as a preliminary analysis and was based on a definition of the contiguous built-up area. This had the advantage of spatial coherence but it left out what was developing in the new suburbs beyond the green belt. On balance and on later reflection, it was decided for this analysis to add those parts of Blanchardstown, Lucan/Clondalkin and Tallaght that were described as urban by the CSO in the 1971 saps. The city so defined loses the neatness of the contiguous built-up area and advances the claims of emerging suburbs such as Swords, Malahide and Portmarnock to be included also. The decision to exclude these was arbitrary but was based on the principle that the western communities were included because their development was part of a major planning strategy compared to the more organic suburban development elsewhere. The northern suburbs were also smaller individually in 1971 and with poor communications to the city could be argued to be more spatially distant from the contiguous built-up area than were those to the west. The city thus defined comprised 199 district electoral divisions (deds).

## *District electoral divisions*

There is a sufficient body of research to show that the geographical scale employed in an analysis can influence the result, though the extent of that influence is a matter of debate (see Davies, 1984). In this discussion it is noted that while Berry and Spodek (1971) found a remarkable degree of stability in their study of Bombay carried out using wards, circles and sectors, Perle's study of Detroit (1979) was less comforting. That study compared results from an analysis of 62 sub-community areas with the results obtained from 444 census tracts. Perle found that there were major differences in factor interpretations and concluded that the different scales provided different perspectives on the structure of the city. However, it is worth noting that Davies considered that Perle may have been too critical and his re-interpretation of the results suggested the major axes of differentiation were relatively invariant. He cited his own study of Cardiff (1983) for further evidence that the larger or more dominant axes of variation are often similar at different scales. This is just as well as the problem of aggregating areas into meaningful blocks has been considered at length by Openshaw (1973, 1978), among others. His work shows that while results may vary with different scales and/or combinations of areas, there is no satisfactory way of determining which is best and that all that can be done is to report the results for different scales. The pragmatic approach to this problem is to recognize that the scale of the deds will have an effect on the results and to keep this in mind when comparing results with those of other cities.

There was a considerable degree of variation in the size of the Dublin areas, from a minimum of 571 to a maximum of 10,906. These are extremes, however, and there are only four areas with populations less than 1,000 and only two greater than 8,500. In fact the distribution of population values is not significantly different to that of a normal distribution with a mean of 4,011.

Davies also raised the question of the shape of areas since this will influence the appearance of the distribution to the eye and perhaps affect its interpretation. From time to time researchers have asked that census data be made available on the basis of regular grid squares but this was not possible in 1971. The shapes of the Dublin areas are so variable that nothing could be done to make the shapes more regular. Instead, the boundaries of the individual deds were shown on all of the distribution maps.

A final consideration relates to the homogeneity of the deds themselves. If this concept is to be interpreted strictly it would require that each area should show little or no internal variation in terms of any significant characteristic. This will never be met in any form of geographical research where the criteria for choosing areal boundaries has more to do with not crossing main roads than with ensuring internal homogeneity. A more accommodating interpretation is offered by Tyron (1955), which suggests that homogeneity should be an indication that the probability of any individual having a particular characteristic will be the same in any part of a census area. Timms (1971) puts it as follows: the criterion of homogeneity is not that all the people inhabiting a given area should be the same but that their probability of being of a particular characteristic should be alike in all parts of the area (p. 42). Most of the deds in Dublin would probably meet the less rigid definition and there are few, if any, that contain glaring social differences. There is no research to support this assertion, however, and it is based more on experience than analysis. That said, there are some deds (269–271) on the county side of the Dún Laoghaire borough boundary where there is a gradation from social housing to private housing, with the social housing closer to the boundary. The maps of social housing tend to overemphasize the extent of social housing in this area.

## *The factor analysis*

### *The choice of variables*
The absence of any generally accepted theory of residential differentiation which would predict the axes of social differentiation has required that researchers choose a wide range of indicators for any factor analysis so as to ensure the identification of all of the main structural elements. This choice is fraught with difficulties since the nature of any factor analysis is such that the type of input will influence the output so that only those axes that form part of the data set will finally emerge. The temptation is therefore to put every possible indicator into the analysis in the hope that every angle will be covered. However, some guidance was available for this analysis. The preliminary analysis by Brady and Parker (1975) indicated that Dublin was structured in terms of socio-economic status, a fact further emphasized by the analyses of the indices of differentiation given above. Family type also emerged from that analysis as a separate and independent structural aspect of the city, confirming that the urban structure of Dublin was similar to that observed in other Western cities. Particular housing characteristics sometimes emerged in British cities as additional structural elements where these had a distinctive spatial character and this was also the experience with the Dublin analysis. The distribution of these areas was not closely associated with either of the socio-economic or family status measures and so formed independent, though minor, axes in the city.

There were also a number of methodological issues that it was necessary to address and which had implications for the final choice of variables. It has already been shown that there is considerable variation in the size of the deds and it seemed wise to remove this variability by expressing each indicator as some proportion or ratio. The logic for this is that the focus of the study lies in the relative importance of each indicator within each area, contributing as it does to the character of that area, rather than in the absolute occurrence of the phenomenon in city terms or indeed the proportion of city totals found in each area. The distinction between the use of weighted indicators or raw data is important since Brady and Parker (1987) have shown the impact on the analysis is fundamental.

The most obvious way of weighting the data is to express them as percentages of some total but this creates its own difficulties. The use of the same denominator in the creation of a series of indicators will tend to increase the correlation between those variables (Dent and Sakoda, 1973). The question that then arises is whether this correlation is spurious since it is different from that which would have been obtained from the original data. The answer to this must be that it depends on the reasoning for the use of weighted indicators. Kuh and Meyer (1955) argue that if the percentages or ratios are the major focus of attention then the correlations obtained are correct and meaningful. A problem would only arise if the real object of attention was the raw data and if their expression as percentages or ratios was a necessary requirement for some analysis. This seems very sensible since it is indeed the percentages that make the data meaningful. It is not the fact that there are 405 cars in an area that builds up the picture of an area but rather that there are 1.25 cars per household. Nevertheless, while it can be argued that the use of percentages is justifiable and that the correlations so obtained are meaningful it seems sensible to reduce the denominator effect by varying the denominators used. This has been done with the data set wherever possible, making use of the fact that the reported totals for sets of indicators do not add to the total population because of non-response. Ratios were also used in a number of circumstances where it was felt that they would be helpful though they tend to make the explanation of factor loadings more difficult.

Davies has argued (1975, 1978) that closed number sets should also be avoided. A closed number set results when a researcher includes all of a set of attributes such as every social group or every form of housing tenure. The result of this is that if the indicators in such a set are expressed as percentages their total must sum to 100 per cent. Since the total is known, the degrees of freedom associated with the final member of the set is zero and its position on an axis will be predicted from the position of the others. Quite simply, over counting results and the correlations are biased. The effect is greatest in small data sets but Davies (1984) indicated that where a large data set is being investigated, and the factors are identified by many variables, the bias in the position of the axes may be quite small – especially if there are many categories in the closed number variables (Davies, 1984, p. 104). He also suggested that sometimes it is necessary to include all the categories to make the process of explanation easier. Brady and Parker, in unpublished work (1987), investigated the effect of closed number systems on factor loadings using the 1981 census data for the city and the results would suggest that the impact of closed number systems is as Davies suggested. Examination of the Dublin dataset showed that it was not a problem as long as the number of categories was sufficiently large. Nevertheless, it seemed sensible to avoid the problem of closed numbers sets even if a case can be argued for their presence. This was done by excluding the variable from such a set which had the weakest pattern of correlations with the other members of the full data set. Such an indicator was therefore less likely to explain much about residential differentiation and its removal would have little overall impact. However, in cases where it was felt necessary to include all of the categories another approach was adopted. All indicators can be calculated on the basis of the overall total of households or family units or whatever. This will include a number of non-responses though, and it is more desirable to base calculations on the number of people who gave answers since this has the advantage of varying the denominator as much as possible as well as making the analysis more meaningful. Where adopting this procedure would involve the creation of a closed number set it was decided to base the calculation of the indicators on the total, which would include the 'not stated' and use the 'not stated' category as the one that was eliminated from the analysis.

Building on the experience of the 1975 study it was also decided not to differentiate between males and females except in exceptional circumstances. The 1975 study separated males and females on such indicators as gainful employment, socio-economic status and age. In no case did a sex differentiated variable load on a different factor to its counterpart and the strength of the loadings, although not the same, was not sufficiently different to warrant the use of separate indicators by sex. Taking all of the above considerations into account the final data set for the analysis was as shown below.

### Housing conditions

1. Percentage of housing units built prior to 1860.
2. Percentage of housing units built 1860–99.
3. Percentage of housing units built 1900–18.
4. Percentage of housing units built 1941–60.
5. Percentage of housing units built since 1961.
6. Housing units built 1941–60 as a percentage of the city total.
7. Housing units built since 1961 as a percentage of the city total.
8. Percentage of all housing units with poor water supply.
9. Percentage of housing units without a bath.

### Housing tenure

10. Percentage of housing units being rented from the local authority.
11. Percentage of housing units rented privately either furnished or unfurnished.
12. Percentage of housing units which are owner occupied.
13. Multi-family dwellings as a percentage of all housing units.
14. Conventional housing as a percentage of all housing units.

### Demographic characteristics

15. Children under 4 years of age as a proportion of the total population.
16. Children of school-going age as a proportion of the total population.
17. People of working age as a proportion of the total population.
18. People aged over 65 years as a proportion of the total population.
19. Fertility Index calculated as the number of children born in the previous five years to women in the age group 15–44 years.
20. Married people as a proportion of those aged 15 years or over.
21. Single people between 20–35 years as a proportion of the population in that age group.
22. Ratio of those aged 0–4 years to those aged 15–64 years.
23. Ratio of those aged over 65 years to those aged 15–64 years.

### Social class

24. Proportion of higher professionals in each area.
25. Proportion of lower professionals in each area.

26  Proportion of employers and managers in each area.
27  Proportion of salaried employees in each area.
28  Proportion of other non-manual employees in each area.
29  Proportion of skilled manual employees in each area.
30  Proportion of semi-skilled employees in each area.
31  Proportion of unskilled employees in each area.
32  Number of cars per household.

### Household characteristics

33  Persons per household.
34  Persons per room.
35  One- or two-person households as a percentage of all households.
36  One- or two-person housing units as a percentage of all housing units.
37  Percentage of households in housing units with 3 or less rooms.
38  Housing units with 2 or less rooms as a percentage of all housing units.
39  Households with more than 7 rooms as a percentage of all households.
40  Households of more than 6 persons as a percentage of all households.
41  Households of 1 to 3 persons, all over 65 years of age as a percentage of those aged 65 years plus.

### Labour force composition

42  Percentage of those aged over 14 years who are gainfully occupied.
43  Female participation in the labour force as indicated by the percentage of females over the age of 14 years who are gainfully occupied.
44  Percentage of those aged 14 years and over who are at school.
45  Percentage of those age 14 years and over at home duties.
46  Percentage of the gainfully occupied who are described as being out of work.
47  Ratio of those gainfully occupied to those not gainfully occupied.

### Miscellaneous characteristics

48  Proportion of population who are non-Roman Catholics.

The set of 48 variables was felt to be a fair representation of the data provided in the saps while not being so large as to be unwieldy. It was also considered an improvement on the data set previously used. Cattell (1978) suggested that there should be four times as many cases as variables. On this criterion, this analysis has about the correct number but, in any event, Davies (1984) suggested that such a high ratio might not be really necessary. Happily, Perle (1979) indicated that ecological structures are little affected by the number of variables used. Moreover, as long as the variables chosen are always a good selection of what is available, the major axes will be constant, though of course the characteristics will reflect the variables. This was confirmed by Sweetser (1965) who noted that 'ecological factors are invariant under substitution, addition and subtraction of variables' (p. 379). Larger data sets permit better understanding of the major axes but also tend to produce more minor axes. The cost, therefore, of a large data set is having to decide the extent to which these minor axes are relevant in the study of the city.

Unfortunately, there are deficiencies in the scope of the information provided by the saps. The biggest omission is that of 'quality of life' data which would describe such attributes as access to services, levels of crime, environmental problems, etc. Knox (1978), for example, has shown the way in which access to primary medical care is differentially available while Herbert (1982) suggested that different crimes have different geographical patterns. Useful as this data might be, it is not clear whether or not its inclusion would result in additional axes of differentiation or whether it would amplify existing ones. Certainly Knox's analysis would suggest that access to services such as GPs would be related to the socio-economic complexion of an area. Others suggest that attitudinal data would also be important. Thus Herbert (1982) suggests that the ethos of an area is an important attribute in explaining such things as delinquency. The quality of the environment could be measured by using attitudinal data such as that employed by Palmer, Robinson and Thomas (1977) in their analysis of countryside images. However, while the point that the data set is limited must be conceded, the possibility of any of this kind of data ever being provided in the form of saps must be nil. Indeed, the battle will be to keep what is there at present.

## *The factoring model*

The use of factor analysis became the primary method of determining the major axes of differentiation despite the fact that the use of the technique is full of pitfalls for the unwary. In fact some statisticians have said that it is not worth the time taken to carry it out and understand it since it tells one nothing more than could be derived from an examination of the correlation pattern of the original variables. This may be so for statisticians but for those outside that discipline the technique is still useful as a fast way of identifying clusters of inter-related variables. The discussion of the individual maps and their distributions which took place above could lead a researcher into correctly identifying the major axes of differentiation but only with some considerable difficulty. The use of factor analysis provides a speedier way of determining which variables are inter-correlated and to what extent, as well as providing a more objective way of producing a map of the major axes than overlaying many different maps and removing the 'noise' to produce one final map. It has been described by Harman (1960) in one of the classic works on this area as follows:

> The principal concern of factor analysis is the resolution of a set of variables linearly in terms of (usually) a small number of categories or 'factors'. This resolution can be accomplished by the analysis of the correlations among the variables. A satisfactory solution will yield factors which convey all the essential information of the original set of variables. Thus the chief aim is to obtain scientific parsimony or economy of description (p. 4).

It is incorrect to speak of factor analysis as if it was a single technique when there are quite a number of common factoring methods including Principal Axes Factoring (PAF), Alpha Analysis and Image Analysis to name three. In addition, there is the conceptually and mathematically different technique of Principal Components Analysis (PCA), which is generally bundled together with the common factoring techniques under the heading of 'factor analysis'.

Of the methods available, PAF and PCA analyses are by far the most widely used in the study of areal differentiation. It is beyond the scope of this appendix to explain in detail what each of these methods does and anyway to do so would be to re-invent the wheel since there is an excellent discussion in Rummel (1967) that provides a non-theoretical discussion while the mathematics of factor analysis are simply explained by Goddard and Kirby (1976) and those of principal components analysis by Daultrey (1976).

The choice lies essentially in the assumptions that the researcher wishes to make about the data set being analysed. A PCA analysis is an orthogonal transformation of a data set whereby a set of inter-related variables is transformed into a set of independent constructs or components. These components are linear combinations of the original variables and are derived in decreasing order of importance so that the first derived account for the maximum amount of variation in the original data set. In essence, nothing is lost in this analysis since the number of components derived is the same as the original number of variables and all of the variance is accounted for. The implications of this for someone seeking to use the technique in a study of spatial structure is that it assumes that all of the variation in the data set entered into the analysis is capable of being explained by the other variables in the set. It assumes that there are no other axes of differentiation that are not measured or only incompletely measured by the data set in use and which might account for some of variation of some of the variables.

Principal Axes Factoring does a very different job. It assumes that the variation of a variable can be decomposed into what is explained by the other variables in the data set (communality) and a remainder which can be described as 'noise' or unique variance. It is, therefore, an inferential approach since there are assumptions made about the nature of the relationship between the variables. The analysis then proceeds to extract linear transformations of these variables to produce independent constructs which are comprised of linear combinations of the original variables. However, unlike PCA, it is not an exact solution since only a portion of the original variance will be present in the solution derived. Therefore, the number of factors which will be produced is also indeterminate. In using a PAF it is necessary, *a priori*, to estimate the degree of common explained variance to replace the 1.0 that would otherwise be found in the diagonal of the correlation matrix. A variety of methods can be used but the most commonly used is the squared multiple correlation coefficient. The implications of this method for the student of residential structure is that it permits an acceptance of the fact that the data set is only part of the universe of indicators and that some of the variance of individual variables might be explained by other indicators than those available. This can result in some variables which are poorly explained by the other variables being lost from the analysis.

The choice is essentially an arbitrary one with both methods used extensively and without any guidance available as to which one to choose. Even Davies' (1984) text on Factorial Ecology, the most comprehensive study of the use of these techniques in urban analysis, hedges on this question and suggests that the investigator should be aware of what s/he is doing. For the reasons suggested above, the study of Dublin for 1971 made use of the Principal Axes Factoring method.

Central to the analysis is the calculation of the correlation matrix between the variables. The correlation co-efficient generally used is Pearson's Product Moment Correlation Coefficient. Its use assumes a linear relationship between the variables and requires, *inter alia*, that the data be normally distributed while the factor model requires that the data have a multi-normal distribution. If this requirement were to be rigidly enforced it would present a major problem to researchers since the procedures for testing this are cumbersome and much of the available data would not in any case meet the requirement. Nevertheless, there a sufficient body of opinion to permit this requirement to be relaxed. Harman (1976) suggests that flexibility is possible providing that no distinctly non-normal variable is included in the analysis while Cattell (1978) suggests that the factor model is sufficiently robust to account for the general elements of structure even when the linearity requirement is not met. A standard method of coping with non-normality in data is to employ some transformation to the data set. Thus the squaring of all the data values or the taking of their square root might be of use in shaping the distribution of values to the normal shape. This is not as easy as it seems, as Pringle (1976) noted, and commonly used transformations may not always produce normality in a data set. However, while transformations may meet the requirements of normality, it is much more difficult to say what it does to one's understanding of the data. For example, if it is found that the square of a person's income is highly correlated with their propensity to take foreign holidays, does this mean that income and the propensity to take foreign holidays are also related? The question is whether in transforming the data something of its character and nature is lost so that the correlations obtained from the data are worse than if the data were untransformed to begin with. Therefore, while statistical transformation is important, it must be weighed against the difficulties that the use of these transformed variables will cause in interpreting the factors. This is a point accepted by Harman and suggests that transformed variables should be transformed back to original values after the critical part of the analysis, a feature not available in any package. On the other hand, Bennett (1977) argued that there was little statistical justification for the effort involved in transforming data and presented empirical results to justify his viewpoint. Opinions differ on this but it is hard to ignore the advice of Davies (1984), who suggests that the evidence to date is not convincing either for or against transformation and that the most sensible thing to do is to try and avoid really badly skewed variables by either dropping them from the analysis or rescaling them in some way.

As insurance against this, researchers have sometimes turned to the use of ordinal measures of correlation such as Spearman's Rho. However, Moser and Scott (1962), in an early analysis of city structure, point out that the results obtained differ little from those obtained with Pearson's Coefficient. The 1975 preliminary analysis made use of Spearman's Rho but a subsequent re-analysis using Pearson's coefficient yielded no significant differences in the major axes of differentiation. No transformations were applied to the data for the reasons described above but the advice given by Davies above was followed with regard to very badly skewed variables.

## The analysis

The analysis therefore consisted of a Principal Axes Analysis on 48 variables measured over 199 areas using Pearson's product moment correlation co-efficient. Four factors were extracted which together explained 74.2 per cent of the common variance of the data set, the largest of which explained just over one-third of the variation. The number of factors to be extracted is a further problem to be discussed. While a PCA will produce the same number of components as there were original variables, the researcher will rarely be interested in all of them. Similarly, while a PAF will produce less factors than variables, it will inevitably produce more factors than are needed. This is because parsimony is almost always the reason for undertaking a factor analysis, at least in urban studies, so that a large data set can be reduced to manageable proportions. This begs the question as to how many are enough. No difficulties would arise if there were hypotheses about the number of axes to expect but in their absence recourse has to be had to rules of thumb for although there are statistical and quasi-statistical methods available, none have received widespread acceptance.

One of the most common of these is to choose only those factors which have an eigenvalue of greater than 1. Each variable in an analysis adds one unit of variance to the total so that the total number of eigenvalues equals the number of variables in the analysis. Therefore, this rule would extract only those factors which explain at least as much of the variance as would have been explained by one (1) of the original variables. This seems quite sensible since factors with smaller degrees of explanation could hardly be argued to be of much significance but there is a problem with its use. This is that the cut-off level in explained variance terms of such a criterion will depend on the number of variables in the analysis. Thus in a 100 variable analysis, a cut of 1.0 eigenvalues will retain any factor that explains more than 1 per cent of the variance while the same cut-off in a 10 variable analysis would exclude any factor which did not explain at least 10 per cent of the variance. For this reason a minimum in terms of 'per cent explained' is often preferred with 5 per cent being a common cut-off level. It is no less arbitrary than the 1.0 eigenvalue but its meaning in size terms will be the same from study to study so that all factors extracted have at least the same relative importance.

**Table A5.** Explantory power of the chosen factors.

| Factor | Percentage | Cumulative |
|---|---|---|
| 1 | 34.5 | 34.5 |
| 2 | 25.9 | 60.4 |
| 3 | 10.7 | 71.1 |
| 4 | 5.1 | 76.2 |
| Total | 76.2 | 76.2 |

A graphical alternative is to make use of Cattell's (1966) Scree Test in which the eigenvalues of the factors are plotted against the factor numbers. The cut-off point is taken where the most significant break of slope occurs on the plot. However, if this approach is not to fall foul of tricks of the eye it would require that the changes in slope be measured, reducing the simplicity of the approach. In the final analysis, the researcher must make a choice and in this case the scree test is rejected because of a lack of faith in graphical solutions. An eigenvalue cut off of 1.0 was also rejected as it would have included factors that just about explained 2 per cent of the variance. Instead, it was decided to extract those factors which explained at least 5 per cent of the variance.

## *Rotation*

The solution obtained from the initial factor analysis may not prove to be satisfactory. This is because a researcher is looking for a result that sees each variable load strongly on the fewest possible number of axes, preferably on one only, while the model will try to extract factors which successively account for the greatest proportion of variation. Thus most, if not all, variables will load on the main factors as the axes are positioned so as to align themselves to the greatest possible extent with the clusters of variables. In simple terms, this might result in an axis between two clusters of variables rather than through one of them. The resulting matrix of loadings is therefore less clear than desirable and interpretation is made difficult. In these circumstances it is usual to apply a rotation to the axes in order to simplify the structure so that each axis, in so far as is possible, uniquely identifies a cluster of variables. However, while rotation is appropriate for PAF solutions, there is debate about the degree to which rotations should be applied to Principal Component Analyses. It is generally argued that as there is only one solution to a Principal Components analysis any rotation will result in a suboptimal result.

A variety of rotations are available, each of which simplifies the data structure in its own particular way but the basic division is between orthogonal and oblique rotations. The factor solutions produced by a PAF analysis are orthogonal which means that each factor is statistically independent of the others. In graphic terms, this means that each axis is at right angles to every other axis. In an orthogonal rotation the set of axes is rotated around a common origin until some criterion is met but the orthogonal relationship between each axis is maintained. Of the orthogonal rotations, quartimax, equimax, and varimax are the best known. The quartimax rotation aims to align the axes in such a way as the variables loads highly on one factor but is almost at zero on the others. However, the mathematics of this method is such that it tends not to discriminate well between axes unless the structure is very strong and tends to produce a solution where the first rotated factor is a general factor with many variables loading highly on it while the subsequent factors tend to be subclusters of variables. The Equimax rotation is a compromise between the quartimax and varimax rotations. Since, in most cases, the purpose of the research is to identify specific and distinct clusters of variables the varimax rotation is preferred (Kaiser, 1958). This operates by maximizing the variance in individual factors so that each variable has as high loadings on as few factors as possible. This yields a solution where factors are as distinct as possible and as such is commonly used in studies of urban structure.

There may be times when it is inappropriate to maintain the orthogonality of the axes. For example, it may be that social class and family status are not independent axes of differentiation but are instead correlated to some degree. The evidence from American cities was that the ethnic status dimension was not independent of the other two. An oblique rotation permits this structure to emerge since each axis is aligned maximally with a single cluster of variables irrespective of the relative angle between the axes. The size of this angle is transformed into a measure of the correlation between the axes or factors. As the factor axes are optimally aligned with clusters of variables, it should produce higher loadings on factors but there is a cost in terms of ease of explanation. Oblique rotation takes place in two sets of coordinate spaces and produces what are called *primary axes* and *reference axes*. The reference axes give a slightly better interpretation of the clusters of interrelated variables than do the primary axes but the difference is not great. Where the problems of interpretation arise is that each set of axes produces two matrices of 'loadings'. The *primary factor pattern* produces a matrix of loadings that indicate to which factor the variable best belongs. They vary between 0 and 1.0 and the closer to 1.0 the more a variable is associated with that particular factor. However, these are not strictly loadings in the sense that they represent the correlation of the variable with the factor and their use is more in identifying factor membership than in interpreting the exact relationships between variable and factor. That is the job of the *primary factor structure* matrix, which is a series of correlations between the variables and the factors. The composition of the factors will not be as clear-cut as on the pattern matrix but these loadings may be squared to produce estimates of the communality of the variables.

Of the family of oblique rotations, the direct oblimin method, which attempts to minimize the factor pattern, is the one which has received most favour and this method was applied to the four factors extracted from the Dublin data to determine whether there was any correlation between the axes. The results show that although there was a correlation between Factor 1 and Factor 3 and between Factor 2 and Factor 4, these were very low, with less than 10 per cent of the variance of one explained by the other. Thus an orthogonal solution would satisfactorily describe the structure and given the relative ease with which a varimax rotation can be interpreted it was decided to rotate the factors using varimax in preference to an oblique rotation. Factor scores were produced for the rotated matrix and these form the basis of the maps discussed below.

**Table A6.** Explanatory power of rotated factors.

| Factor | Percentage | Cumulative |
|---|---|---|
| 1 | 24.2 | 24.2 |
| 2 | 21.5 | 45.7 |
| 3 | 21.4 | 67.1 |
| 4 | 9.1 | 76.2 |
| Total | 76.2 | 76.2 |

## *Socio-demographic structure, 1971*

The interpretation of factor scores is a subjective matter and relies on the ability of the researcher to make sense of the pattern of loadings that the analysis has produced. Loadings vary from -1.0 to +1.0 and can be interpreted as correlation coefficients so that the square of the loading indicates the proportion of a variable's variance which is explained by that factor. As an aid to interpretation it is usual to ignore variables that fail to meet a threshold loading. This threshold is arbitrarily defined but is often set at between 0.4 and 0.5. Using the larger threshold would omit a variable that has less than 25 per cent of its variance explained by the factor in question, the logic being that it plays only a minor role in the factor's composition and may only be noise confounding explanation rather than enhancing it while the smaller threshold would exclude variables with an explanation of 16 per cent or less. The procedure adopted in this book was to use the lower threshold and to ignore loadings which are less than 0.4. The scores were grouped into six equal intervals which means that groups 3 and 4 represent average conditions in the city. This produced the maps that have been discussed in earlier chapters.

# Sources and bibliography

## Sources

This volume builds on the topics developed in the five previous volumes of the series and especially with the two previous thematic volumes that deal with Dublin in the twentieth century. The reader is encouraged to explore these volumes in building up a comprehensive view of the city.

- *Dublin through space and time*
- *Dublin, 1910–1940: shaping the suburbs*
- *Dublin, 1745–1922: hospitals, spectacle and vice*
- *Dublin Docklands reinvented: the post-industrial regeneration of a European city quarter*
- *Dublin, 1930–1950: the emergence of the modern city*

As usual, the bibliography below aims to provide the reader both with details of the sources used in this volume but also to act as a guide to wider reading in the area.

This volume was as reliant as ever on maps to illustrate the ideas being discussed. Unfortunately, the 1950s and 1960s have rather sparse offerings. The revision of the 25 inch (1:2,500) series of Ordnance Survey plans was complete by the mid-1940s and they were not revised again. Local revisions were produced by organizations such as Dublin Corporation but they were not for public release and the quality of the output, though sufficient for their purpose, was variable. These OS maps remain the most useful scale for the purposes of this book but they become somewhat dated by the time discussion moves to the 1960s. They were replaced by the 1:1000 series towards the end of the 1960s and this meant that there was now a highly detailed map resource available. The issue was that they were too detailed and too many sheets were needed to look at even a small urban area. This is perhaps to look a gift horse in the mouth but it remains the case that the 1:2500 was a more useful scale for urban analysis. In the 1930s the Ordnance Survey began to produce its Popular Edition maps of the city of Dublin at a convenient scale. There is a provisional edition (265b) dated 1933 and then an edition at 1:25,000 which has an imprint of 1948. Publication of these maps became a more regular feature during the 1950s and 1960s and provide a very useful overview of suburban development. The degree of revision varied from edition to edition and it is important not to assume that the printing date means that the map is current as of that date. The scale of maps also varied from 1:25,000 to 1:20,000 and 1:18,000. This is not a major issue but it means that temporal comparisons sometimes require some digital manipulation. As the city began to grow so the 1:63,360 sheet of the Dublin District became more useful. A number of editions of this map were produced from the 1950s into the 1970s and they provide a really useful overview of the growth and expansion of the city.

To these must be added the extremely useful Geographia plans which provide a view of the city for approximately 1935, 1948, 1958 and 1968 at a scale of 4 inches to the mile (about 1:15,800).

Unfortunately the golden age of the postcard was long over by the 1950s. These had proved particularly useful in the earlier volumes of this series but their geographical scope became steadily more and more limited. The views now concentrated on the main streets with relatively few images of lesser locations. A surprising number of guides to Dublin were produced during the 1950s and 1960s. Many were produced by the Irish Tourist Association for Dublin Corporation and were detailed accounts of the city. Some of them are explored in the volume. Though the kernel of them did not change all that much, they changed at the margins and they add to our understanding of a developing city. To these can be added the commercial guides of which there were a number, though Ward Lock, which had produced excellent guides since the latter years of the nineteenth century, disappeared from the Irish market in the early 1960s.

This volume, like the others in the series, relies on ephemeral material quite a lot because it is trying to build a picture of what it was like to live and use the city during the 1950s and 1960s. The advertisements that are contained in the various guides and often on the margins of maps are central to understanding how people spent their time and on what they spent their money. To these may be added the information on the margins of theatre programmes and other events. The availability of this material is very much hit and miss and a matter of luck. While the tradition of the better hotels producing guides for visitors resumed after the war, they were but a poor reflection on what had been provided previously.

A census was undertaken in 1951, 1956, 1961, 1966 and 1971 and though only the printed volumes are available, they remain a valuable source. The amount of detail in the 1951 census is limited and even more so in the 1956 version. Much of the information was presented at the level of the city but there was some detail available at a smaller spatial scale. The big change came in 1971 when it was decided to publish census results for small spatial units – almost 200 in the case of Dublin. These permitted a much finer look at the city and the author was one of the first to get the opportunity to work with these data. The first set was not sold in digital format and the author had the pleasure of spending an entire summer translating the information onto punched cards for computer analysis.

As noted in the previous volume, the debates in the Oireachtas should never be overlooked. There was much discussion there about matters relating to the development of the city and information was provided in debates and answers to parliamentary questions which is not easily available elsewhere. However, the great joy of recent times and a huge improvement for the researcher is the availability of newspapers online. The archives of the *Irish Times*, *Irish Press* and *Irish Independent* and a host of local newspapers are now available electronically. For a time, only the search engine for the *Irish Times* was of any value but there was been a huge improvement in the ease with which all the publications can accessed.

This archive allows for a huge increase in productivity and enables us to follow up stories in a way which would have been hit and miss otherwise. Another repository of great use is that of Dublin Corporation, referred to as Report x/19xx, and held in the City Archive. While surprisingly little of the record of the work of committees of the Corporation has survived, it is fortunate that these committees reported regularly to the entire Corporation and that these reports were printed and bound for the members.

## *Bibliography*

Aalen, F.H.A. and Whelan, K. (eds) (1992) *Dublin city and county: from prehistory to present.* Dublin: Geography Publications.

Abercrombie, P. (1944) *Greater London plan.* London: Stationery Office.

Abercrombie, P. and Forshaw, J.H. (1943) *The county of London plan.* UK: Macmillan and Company Ltd.

Abercrombie, P., Duffy, G. and Giron, L.F. (1942) The Dublin Town Plan [with comments], *Studies: An Irish Quarterly Review,* 31(122), pp 155–70.

Abercrombie, P., Kelly, S. and Kelly, A. (1922) *Dublin of the future: the new town plan.* Liverpool: University Press of Liverpool.

Abercrombie, P., Kelly, S. and Robertson, M. (1941) *Dublin sketch development plan.* Dublin: Dublin Corporation.

Abrams, C. (1961) Urban renewal project in Ireland (Dublin), prepared for the Government of Ireland by Charles Abrams, appointed under the United Nations Programme of Technical Assistance. NY: United Nations.

Abu-Lughod, J. (1969) Testing the theory of social area analysis, *American Sociological Review,* 34, pp 198–212.

Aldridge, H.R. (1915) *The case of town planning – a practical manual for the use of councillors, officers and others engaged in the preparation of town planning schemes.* London: National Housing and Town Planning Council.

Allan, C.M. (1965) The genesis of British urban redevelopment with special reference to Glasgow, *Economic History Review,* 18, 2nd series, pp 598–613.

Alonso, W. (1964) *Location and land use.* Cambridge: Harvard University Press.

Artifex (1930) Greater Dublin: complexities and possibilities, *Dublin Magazine,* 5(1), pp 37–43.

Baillie Scott, M.H. *et al.* (1910) *Garden suburbs, town planning and modern architecture.* London: Fisher Unwin.

Ballymun Amenity Group (1974) *Ballymun: the experiment that failed.* Dublin: Ballymun Amenity Group.

Bannon, M.J. (1973) *Office location in Ireland and the role of central Dublin.* Dublin: An Foras Forbartha.

Bannon, M.J. (1978) Patrick Geddes and the emergence of modern town planning in Ireland, *Irish Geography,* 11(2), pp 141–8.

Bannon, M.J. (ed.) (1985a) *The emergence of Irish planning, 1880–1920.* Dublin: Turoe Press.

Bannon, M.J. (1985b) The genesis of modern Irish planning. *In*: Bannon, M.J. (ed.) *The emergence of Irish planning, 1880–1920.* Dublin: Turoe Press, pp 189–260.

Bannon, M.J. (1988) The capital of the new State. *In*: Cosgrave, A. (ed.) *Dublin through the ages.* Dublin: College Press.

Bannon, M.J. (ed.) (1989a) *Planning: the Irish experience, 1920–1988.* Dublin: Wolfhound Press.

Bannon, M.J. (1989b) Irish planning from 1921 to 1945. *In*: Bannon, M.J. (ed.) *Planning: the Irish experience.* Dublin: Wolfhound Press, pp 13–70.

Bannon, M.J., Eustace, J. and O'Neill, M. (1981) *Urbanization: problems of growth and decay in Dublin*. Report 55. Dublin: National Economic and Social Council.

Barlow (1940) *Royal Commission on the distribution of the industrial population. Chairman: Sir Montague Barlow*. UK: HMSO.

Barnett, J. (1986) *The elusive city: five centuries of design, ambition and miscalculation*. New York: Harper and Row.

Barr, A.W. (1958) *Public authority housing*. UK: Batsford.

Barrett, H. and Phillips, J. (1987) *Suburban style: the British home, 1840–1960*. London: Macdonald & Co. Ltd.

Bater, J. (1980) *The soviet city*. UK: Edward Arnold.

Behan, B. (1963) *Hold your hour and have another*. London: Hutchinson.

Behan, D. (1961) *Teems of times and happy returns*. London: Heinemann.

Behan, D. (1965) *My brother Brendan*. London: Leslie Frewin.

Bell, C. and Bell, R. (1969) *City fathers: the early history of town planning in Britain*. London: Barrie & Rockliff.

Berry B.J.L. and Spodek, H. (1971) Comparative ecologies of large Indian cities, *Economic Geography*, 47, pp 266–85.

Blackwell, J. (1982) Government, economy and society. *In:* Litton F. (ed.) *Unequal achievement: the Irish experience, 1957–82*. Dublin: Institute of Public Administration, pp 43–62.

Boal, F.W. (1971) Territoriality and class – a study of two residential areas in Belfast, *Irish Geography*, 6(3), pp 229–48.

Bolger, D. (ed.) (1988) *Invisible cities, the new Dubliners: a journey through unofficial Dublin*. Dublin: Raven Arts Press.

Bowley, M. (1945) *Housing and the State, 1919–1944*. London: Allen & Unwin.

Brady, J. (1986) The impact of clean air legislation on Dublin households, *Irish Geography*, 19, pp 41–4.

Brady, J. (2001a) Dublin in the nineteenth century – an introduction. *In:* Brady, J. and Simms, A. (eds), *Dublin through space and time*. Dublin: Four Courts Press, pp 159–65.

Brady, J. (2001b) Dublin at the turn of the century. *In:* Brady, J. and Simms, A. (eds), *Dublin through space and time*. Dublin: Four Courts Press, pp 221–81.

Brady, J. (2001c) The heart of the city – commercial Dublin, c.1890–1915. *In:* Brady, J. and Simms, A. (eds), *Dublin through space and time*. Dublin: Four Courts Press, pp 282–340.

Brady, J. (2004) Reconstructing Dublin city centre in the 1920s. *In:* Clarke, H., Prunty, J. and Hennessy, M. (eds) *Surveying Ireland's past, multidisciplinary essays in honour of Anngret Simms*. Dublin: Geography Publications, pp 639–64.

Brady, J. (2005) 'Geography as she used to be', *Geographical Viewpoint*, 31, pp 29–39.

Brady, J. (2006) Dublin – growth and economic prosperity, 1995–2005. Archived paper for XIV International Economic History Congress. Helsinki. http://www.helsinki.fi/iehc2006/papers3/Brady.pdf

Brady, J. (2014) *Dublin, 1930–1950: the emergence of the modern city*. Dublin: Four Courts Press.

Brady, J. (2015) Dublin – a city of contrasts. *In:* Fogarty, A. and O'Rourke, F. (eds) *Voices on Joyce*. Dublin: UCD Press, pp 77–95.

Brady, J. and Simms, A. (eds) (2001) *Dublin through space and time.* Dublin: Four Courts Press.

Brady, J. and Simms, A. (eds) (2006) G.A. Boyd *Dublin 1745–1922: hospitals, spectacle and vice.* Dublin: Four Courts Press.

Brady, J. and Simms, A. (eds) (2008) N. Moore *Dublin Docklands reinvented: the post industrial regeneration of an industrial quarter.* Dublin: Four Courts Press.

Brady, J. and Parker, A.J. (1975) The factorial ecology of Dublin – A preliminary investigation, *Economic and Social Review,* 7(4), pp 35–54.

Brady, J. and Parker, A.J. (1986) The socio-demographic structure of Dublin 1981, *Economic and Social Review,* 17(4), pp 229–52.

Brady J. and Lynch, P. (2009) The Irish Sailors' and Soldiers' Land Trust and its Killester nemesis, *Irish Geography,* 42(3), 261–92.

Brady, J.V. (1917) *The future of Dublin – practical slum reform.* Dublin: Dollard.

Brooke, H. (1952) *Living in flats: report of the flats subcommittee of the central housing advisory committee.* London: HMSO.

Buchanan, C. (1963) *Traffic in towns – a study of the long term problems of traffic in urban areas –* Reports of the steering group and working group appointed by the Minister of Transport. London: HMSO.

Buchanan, C. (1963) *Traffic in towns.* The specially shortened edition of the Buchanan report. UK: Penguin.

Burnett, J. (1978) *A social history of housing, 1815–1970.* London: David & Charles.

Butler, R.M. (1916) The reconstruction of O'Connell Street, *Studies: An Irish Quarterly Review,* 5, pp 570–6.

Butler, R.M. (1927) Dublin past and present. In: *Dublin Civic Week Handbook.* Dublin: Civic Week Council, pp 26–33.

Cahill and Co. (1939) *Dublin by day and by night. A new guide to the city.* Dublin: Cahill.

Callanan, M. and Keogan, J.F. (2004) *Local government in Ireland: inside out.* Dublin: Institute of Public Administration.

Cameron, C.A. (1913) *Reminiscences.* Dublin: Hodges, Figgis & Co.

Cameron, C.A. (1914) *A brief history of municipal public health administration.* Dublin: Hodges, Figgis & Co.

Cattell, R.B. (1966) The scree test for the number of factors, *Multivariate Behavioural Research,* 1, pp 140–61.

Cattell, R.B. (1978) *The scientific use of factor analysis.* New York: Plenum Press.

Central Housing Council (1925) *Housing week,* official programme and guide. Dublin: Central Housing Council.

Chang Yee (1953) *The silent traveller in Dublin.* London: Methuen.

Cherry, G.E. (1974) *The evolution of British town planning.* Leighton Buzzard: Hill.

Cherry, G.E. (1988) *Cities and plans.* London: Edward Arnold.

Citizens' Housing Council (1937) *Interim report on slum clearance in Dublin, 1937.* Dublin: Citizens' Housing Council.

Citizens' Housing Council (1938) *Report on slum clearance in Dublin, 1938.* Dublin: Citizens' Housing Council.

City of Dublin Vocational Education Committee (1993) *The old township of Pembroke, 1863–1930.* Dublin: City of Dublin VEC.

Colman, H. (ed.) (1947) *Eire to-day.* Dublin and London: Metropolitan Publishing Company.

Congress Committee (1932) *Advance programme.* The thirty-first international Eucharistic Congress. Dublin.

Cooke, P. (ed.) (1989) *Localities: the changing face of urban Britain.* London: Unwin Hyman.

Cooney, E.W. (1974) High flats in local authority housing. *In:* Sutcliffe, A. (ed.) *Multi-storey living – the British working-class experience.* UK: Croom Helm, pp 151–80.

Corden, C. (1977) *Planned cities: new towns in Britain and America.* London: Sage Publications.

Corpus Christi Parish (1991) *Golden Jubilee, 1941–1991* [private publication, no details].

Cosgrave, E. and Strangways, L.E. (1907) *Visitor's guide to Dublin and neighbourhood.* Dublin: Sealy, Bryers & Walker.

Costello, P. and Farmar, T. (1992) *The very heart of the city: the story of Denis Guiney and Clerys.* Dublin: A&A Farmar.

Cowan, P.C. (1918) *Report on Dublin housing.* Dublin: Cahill & Co. Ltd.

Craft, M. (1970) The development of Dublin: background to the housing problem, *Studies: An Irish Quarterly Review,* 59, pp 301–13.

Craft, M. (1971) The development of Dublin: the southern suburbs, *Studies: An Irish Quarterly Review,* 60, pp 68–81.

Crawford, J. and Gillespie, R. (eds) (2009) *St Patrick's cathedral Dublin: a history.* Dublin: Four Courts Press.

Creese, W.L. (1967) *The legacy of Raymond Unwin: a human pattern for planning.* London: MIT Press.

CSO (1958) *Censuses of population 1946 and 1951.* General Report. Dublin: Stationery Office.

CSO (2000) *That was then, this is now. Change in Ireland, 1949–99.* Dublin Stationery Office.

CSO (2012) *Older and younger.* Profile 2. Dublin: Stationery Office.

Dalton, G. (1994) *My own backyard – Dublin in the fifties.* Dublin: Wolfhound Press.

Daly, M.E. (1984) *Dublin: the deposed capital, a social and economic history, 1860–1914.* Cork: Cork University Press.

Daly, M.E. (1985) Housing conditions and the genesis of housing reform in Dublin 1880–1920. *In:* Bannon, M.J. (ed.) *The emergence of Irish planning 1880–1920.* Dublin: Turoe Press, pp 77–130.

Daultrey, S. (1966) *Principal components analysis: concepts and techniques in modern geography 8.* Norwich: Geo Abstracts.

Davies, W.K.D. (1971a) Varimax and the destruction of generality: a methodological note, *Area,* 3(2), pp 112–18.

Davies, W.K.D. (1971b) Varimax and generality: a reply, *Area,* 3(4), pp 254–9.

Davies, W.K.D. (1972) Varimax and generality: a second reply, *Area,* 4(3), pp 207–9.

Dawson, C. (1901) The housing of the people with special reference to Dublin, *Journal of the Statistical and Social Inquiry Society of Ireland,* 11, pp 45–56.

Dawson, C. (1913) The Dublin housing question – sanitary and insanitary, *Journal of the Statistical and Social Inquiry Society of Ireland,* 13, pp 91–5.

Dawson, J.A. (1983) *Shopping centre development: topics in applied geography.* UK: Longman.

Dawson, J.A. (ed.) (1980) *Retail geography.* UK: Croom Helm.

DeCourcy, J. (2000) Bluffs, Bays and Pools in the medieval Liffey at Dublin, *Irish Geography*, 33(2), pp 117–33.

Dennis, J. (1989) From 'rookeries' to 'communities': race, poverty and policing in London, 1850–1985, *History Workshop*, 27, pp 66–85.

Department of Local Government (1948) *Housing – a review of past operations and immediate requirements.* Dublin: Stationery Office.

Department of Local Government and Public Health [various] Annual Reports, Dublin, Stationery Office.

Dickinson, P.L. (1929) *The Dublin of yesterday.* London: Methuen & Co.

Dillon, T.W.T. (1945) Slum clearance: past and future, *Studies: An Irish Quarterly Review*, 34, pp 13–20.

Dix, G. (1978) Little plans and noble diagrams, *Town Planning Review*, 49(3), pp 329–52.

Dix, G. (1979) Patrick Abercrombie: pioneer of planning, *Architectural Review*, 990, pp 130–2.

Dixon, D. (2014) *Dublin – the making of a capital city.* UK: Profile Books.

Douglas, R.M. (2009) *Architects of the resurrection: ailtirí na haiséirghe and the fascist 'new order' in Ireland.* UK: Manchester University Press.

Doyle, L. (1935) *The spirit of Ireland.* London: B.T. Batsford Ltd.

Dublin and District House Builders' Association (1939) *The contribution of private enterprise to Greater Dublin's needs* [pamphlet]. Dublin: Sackville Press.

Dudley, Earl of (1944) Design of dwellings. The Dudley Report. *Report of the design of dwellings sub-committee of the central housing advisory committee and study group of the ministry of town and country planning.* UK: HMSO.

Duncan, B. and Duncan, O. (1955) Residential distribution and occupational stratification, *American Journal of Sociology*, 60, pp 493–503.

Duncan, O. and Duncan, B. (1949) A methodological analysis of segregation indices, *American Sociological Review*, 20, pp 210–27.

Dyos, H.J. and Wolff, M. (eds) (1973) *The Victorian city.* London: Routledge.

Eason, C. (1899) The tenement houses of Dublin, their condition and regulation, *Journal of the Statistical and Social Inquiry Society of Ireland*, 10, pp 383–98.

Edwards, A.M. (1981) *The design of suburbia.* London: Pembridge Press.

Egan, M.J. (1961) *The parish of St Columba, Iona Road, Glasnevin* [private publication].

Evans, H. (ed.) (1972) *New towns: the British experience.* UK: Charles Knight.

Farrer, R. and Turnbull, A. (1951). *Ulster and Dublin.* London: W&R Chambers.

Ferriter, D. (2006) *What if? Alternative views of twentieth-century Ireland.* Ireland: Gill & Macmillan.

Ferriter, D. (2007) *Judging Dev: a reassessment of the life and legacy of Eamon de Valera.* Dublin: Royal Irish Academy.

Ferriter, D. (2010) *The transformation of Ireland: 1900–2000.* UK: Profile Books.

Festinger, L., Schachter, S. and Back, K. (1950) The spatial ecology of group formation. *In:* Festinger, L., Schachter, S. and Back, K. (eds), *Social pressure in informal groups*, pp 33–59.

Fishman, R.L. (1984) The origins of the suburban idea in England, *Chicago History*, 13(2), pp 26–35.

Fleming, M.C. (1965) Economic aspects of new methods of building with particular reference to the British Isles, the Continent and America, *JSSSI*, 21(3), pp 120–42.

Foster, R.F. (1989) *Modern Ireland, 1600–1972*. Penguin: London.

Galligan, M., Glynn, M. and Ward, C. (1968) *New homes: a pilot social survey*. Dublin: An Foras Forbartha.

Garrett, A. (1970) *From age to age: history of the parish of Drumcondra, North Strand, St Barnabas*. Dublin: Blackrock Printers.

Garvin, T. (1996) *The birth of Irish democracy*. Dublin: Gill and Macmillan.

Gaskell, S.M. (1987) *Model housing*. London: Mansell.

Gaskell, S.M. (ed.) (1990) *Slums*. Leicester: Leicester University Press.

Gaughan, J.A. (ed.) (1981) *Mount Merrion, the old and the new*. [no publisher], Naas.

Gauldie, E. (1974) *Cruel habitations: a history of working class housing, 1780–1918*. London: Allen & Unwin.

Genders, R. (1947) *Holiday in Dublin*. Worcester: Littlebury and Company.

Gibberd, F. (1972) The master design: landscape; housing; the town centres. *In:* Evans H. (ed.) *New towns: the British experience*, pp 88–101.

Gill and Co. (1932) *Gill's guide to Catholic Dublin*.

Greater Dublin Commission (1926) *Report of the greater Dublin commission of inquiry*. Dublin: Stationery Office.

Guild, R. (1989) *The Victorian house book*. New York: Rizzoli.

Guinness, D. (1967) *A portrait of Dublin*. New York: Viking Press.

Gumley, F.W. (1982) Remembering … *Dublin Historical Record*, 35(3), pp 95–8.

Hall, P. (1985) The rise and fall of the planning movement: a view from Great Britain, *Royal Geographical Society of Australia, South Australian Branch, Proceedings*, 85, pp 45–53.

Hall, P. (2002) *Cities of tomorrow*. Oxford: Blackwell Publishing.

Hanna, E. (2013) *Modern Dublin: urban change and the Irish past, 1957–1973*. UK: Oxford University Press.

Harkness, D. and O'Dowd, M. (1981) *The town in Ireland*. Belfast: Appletree Press.

Harris, R. and Larkham, P.J. (eds) (1999) *Changing suburbs: foundation, form and function*. London: E. & F.N. Spon.

Harrison, B. (1966) Philanthropy and the Victorians, *Victorian Studies: An Irish Quarterly Review*, 9, pp 353–74.

Harvey, J. (1949) *Dublin – a study in environment*. London: Batsford.

Haverty, A. (1995) *Elegant times – a Dublin story*. Dublin: Sonas.

Hayward, R. (1949) *This is Ireland – Leinster and the city of Dublin*. London: Arthur Barker.

Herbert, D. (1970) Principal components analysis and urban social structure: a study of Cardiff and Swansea. *In:* Carter, H. and Davies, W.K.D. (eds), *Urban essays: studies in the geography of Wales*. UK: Longmans, pp 79–100.

Herbert, D. (1982) *The geography of urban crime*. UK: Longmans.

Hobson, B. (ed.) (1929) *A book of Dublin*. Dublin: Corporation of Dublin (1st edition).

Hobson, B. (ed.) (1930) *A book of Dublin*. Dublin: Kevin J. Kenny (2nd edition).
Hoppé, E.O. (1926) *Picturesque Great Britain: the architecture and the landscape*. London: E. Benn.
Horner, A.A. (1985) The Dublin region, 1880–1980. *In:* Bannon, M.J. (ed.) *The emergence of Irish planning, 1880–1920*. Dublin: Turoe Press, pp 21–76.
Horner, A.A. (1992) From city to city-region – Dublin from the 1930s to the 1990s. *In:* Aalen, F.H.A. and Whelan, K. (eds), *Dublin city and county*. Dublin: Geography Publications, pp 327–58.
Horsey, M. (1990) *Tenements and towers – Glasgow working-class housing, 1890–1990*. UK: HMSO.
Houghton, J.P. (1949) The social geography of Dublin, *Geographical Review*, 39, pp 237–77.
Housing and Public Health Committee (1937) *London housing*. London: King and Staples Ltd.
Housing Inquiry (1885) *Report of the Royal commission appointed to inquire into the housing of the working classes*. Minutes of evidence etc., Ireland, British Parliamentary Papers, cd. 4547, London.
Housing Inquiry (1914) *Report of the departmental committee appointed by the Local Government Board for Ireland to inquire into the housing conditions of the working classes in the city of Dublin*. British Parliamentary Papers, 19, 1914, cd.7272/7317–xix, London.
Housing Inquiry (1944) *Report of inquiry into the housing of the working classes of the city of Dublin, 1939–43*. Dublin: Stationery Office.
Housing Manual (1944) *Housing Manual 1944*. Ministry of Health, Ministry of Works. UK: HMSO.
Housing Manual (1949) *Housing Manual 1949*. Ministry of Health. UK: HMSO.
Housing Manual (1952) *Houses 1952. Second supplement to the Housing Manual 1949*. Ministry of Housing and Local Government. UK: HMSO.
Housing Manual (1953) *Houses 1953. Third supplement to the Housing Manual 1949*. Ministry of Housing and Local Government. UK: HMSO.
Howard, E. (1898) *Tomorrow: a peaceful path to real reform*. London: Swan Sonnenschein.
Hoyt, H. (1939) *The structure and growth of residential areas in American cities*. Washington DC: Federal Housing Administration.
Hubbard, E. and Shippobottom, M. (1988) *A guide to Port Sunlight village*. Liverpool: Liverpool University Press.
Hughes, J.B. (1914) Poverty in Dublin, *Irish Messenger Social Action Series*, 13. Dublin: Irish Messenger Office.
Hunter, M. (1981) *The Victorian villas of hackney*. London: Hackney Society.
Hyland, J.S. (Ltd) (1898) *Ireland in pictures*. Chicago: J.S. Hyland and Co.
Igoe, V. (1990) *James Joyce's Dublin houses*. London: Mandarin Paperbacks.
Ikonnikov, A. (1988) *Russian architecture of the soviet period*. USSR: Raduga Press.
Johnston, J.H. and Pooley, C.G. (eds) (1982) *The structure of nineteenth-century cities*. London: Croom Helm.
Johnston, M. (1985) *Around the banks of Pimlico*. Dublin: Attic Press.
Jordan, D.P. (1995) *Transforming Paris – the life and labors of Baron Haussmann*. USA: Free Press.

Jordan, T. (1857) The present state of the dwellings of the poor, chiefly in Dublin, *Dublin Statistical Society*, 2(1), pp 12–19.

Kelleher, D.L. (1918) *The glamour of Dublin*. Dublin: Talbot Press.

Kelleher, D.L. (1919) *The glamour of Cork*. Dublin: Talbot Press.

Kelly, J. and MacGearailt, U. (eds) (1990) *Dublin and Dubliners*. Dublin: Educational Company of Ireland.

Kelly, P. (1990) Drumcondra, Clonliffe and Glasnevin township, 1878–1900. *In:* Kelly, J. and MacGearailt, U. (eds), *Dublin and Dubliners*. Dublin: Educational Company of Ireland, pp 36–51.

Kennedy, T. (ed.) (1980) *Victorian Dublin*. Dublin: Albertine Kennedy Publishing.

Khan-Magomedov, S.O. (1987) *Pioneers of soviet architecture*. London: Thames and Hudson.

Killen, J. (1992) Transport in Dublin: past, present and future. *In:* Aalen, F.H.A. and Whelan, K. (eds) *Dublin city and county*. Dublin: Geography Publications, pp 305–25.

Knox, P.L. (1982) *Urban social geography: an introduction*. London: Longman.

Kopp, A. (1970) *Town and revolution: Soviet architecture and city planning, 1917–35*. NY: Braziller.

Kostof, S. (1991) *The city assembled: elements of urban form through history*. London: Thames and Hudson.

Kostof, S. (1992) *The city shaped: urban patterns and meanings through history*. London: Thames & Hudson.

Lawless, P. and Brown, F. (1986) *Urban growth and change in Britain: an introduction*. London: Harper & Row.

Le Corbusier (1929: 1987) *The city of tomorrow*. Translated by Frederick Etchells. US: Dover Books.

Lichfield and Associates (1966) *Preliminary appraisal of shopping centre redevelopment in Dublin Centre*. Report No. 1. London: Nathaniel Lichfield and Associates.

Lincoln, C. (1992) *Dublin as a work of art*. Dublin: O'Brien Press.

Local Government (1938) *Report of the Local Government (Dublin) Tribunal*. Dublin: Stationery Office.

Long, H.C. (1993) *The Edwardian house*. Manchester: Manchester University Press.

Luddy, M. (1995) *Women in Ireland, 1800–1918: a documentary history*. Cork: Cork University Press.

Lynch, K. (1990) *City sense and city design*. Cambridge, MA: MIT Press.

MacLaren, A. (1993) *Dublin, the shaping of a capital*. London: Belhaven Press.

Magowan, R.S. (1961) *Dublin and Cork*. London: Spring Books.

Malone, P. (1990) *Office development in Dublin, 1960–1990*. UK: University of Manchester.

Marley Committee (1935) *Departmental committee on garden cities and satellite towns*. Ministry of Health. UK: HMSO.

May, S. (1944) Two Dublin slums, *The Bell*, 7(4), pp 351–6.

McCartney, D. (1999) *UCD: a national idea: the history of University College, Dublin*. Dublin: Gill and Macmillan.

McCullough, N. (1989) *Dublin: an urban history*. Dublin: Anne Street Press.

McDonald, F. (1985) *The destruction of Dublin*. Dublin: Gill and Macmillan.

McDowell, R.B. (1957) The growth of Dublin. *In:* Meenan, J. and Webb, D. (eds), *A view of Ireland*. Dublin: British Association for the Advancement of Science.

McGrath, F. (1931) The Sweep and the slums, *Studies: An Irish Quarterly Review*, 20, pp 529–54.
McGrath, R. (1941) Dublin panorama: an architectural review, *The Bell*, 2(5), pp 35–48.
McManus, R. (1996) Public Utility Societies, Dublin Corporation and the development of Dublin, 1920–1940, *Irish Geography*, 29(1), pp 27–37.
McManus, R. (1998) The Dundalk Premier Public Utility Society, *Irish Geography*, 31(2), pp 75–87.
McManus, R. (1999) The 'building parson' – the role of Reverend David Hall in the solution of Ireland's early twentieth-century housing problems, *Irish Geography*, 32 (2), pp 87–98.
McManus, R. (2002) *Dublin, 1910–1940: shaping the city and suburbs*. Dublin: Four Courts Press.
McManus, R. (2004) The role of public utility societies in Ireland, 1919–40. *In*: Clarke, H., Prunty, J. and Hennessy, M. (eds) *Surveying Ireland's past, multidisciplinary essays in honour of Anngret Simms*. Dublin: Geography Publications, pp 613–38.
McManus, R. (2005) *'Such Happy Harmony': early twentieth century co-operation to solve Dublin's housing problems*. Dublin: Dublin City Public Libraries.
McManus, R. (2006) The growth of Drumcondra 1875–1940. *In:* Kelly, J. (ed.) *St Patrick's College, Drumcondra, 1875–2000: a history*. Dublin: Four Courts Press, pp 41–66.
McManus, R. (2008) *Crampton built*. Dublin: G.&T. Crampton.
McManus, R. (2011) Suburban and urban housing in the twentieth century, *Proceedings of the Royal Irish Academy*, 111C, pp 253–86.
McManus, R. (2012) 'Decent and artistic homes' – housing Dublin's middle classes in the 20th century, *Dublin Historical Record*, 65 (No. 1 & 2), pp 96–109.
McManus, R. (2012) Upper Buckingham Street: a microcosm of Dublin, 1788–2012 (with Sinead O'Shea), *Studia Hibernica*, pp 141–79.
McManus, R. (2013) An introduction to Dublin's first citizens (with Lisa-Marie Griffith). *In:* McManus, R. and Griffith, L. (eds) *Leaders of the city. Dublin's first citizens, 1500–1950*. Dublin: Four Courts Press, pp 15–34.
McManus, R. (2013) Lord Mayor Laurence O'Neill, Alderman Tom Kelly and Dublin's housing crisis. *In:* McManus, R. and Griffith, L. (eds) *Leaders of the city: Dublin's first citizens, 1500–1950*. Dublin: Four Courts Press, pp 141–51.
McNiffe, L. (1997) *A history of the Garda Síochána*. Dublin: Wolfhound Press.
Meenan, J. (1957) Dublin in the Irish economy. *In:* Meenan, J. and Webb, D. (eds), *A view of Ireland*. Dublin: British Association for the Advancement of Science.
Meghen, P.J. (1963) *Housing in Ireland*. Dublin: Institute of Public Administration.
Meller, H. (1990) *Patrick Geddes, social evolutionist and city planner*. London: Routledge.
Mikhail, E.H. (ed.) (1982) *Brendan Behan*. London: Macmillan.
Miliutin, N.A. (1974) *Sotsgorod – the problem of building socialist cities*. MIT Press. This is a translation by Arthur Sprague of the original text in Russian.
Miller, M. (1989) Raymond Unwin and the planning of Dublin. *In:* Bannon, M.J. (ed.) *The emergence of Irish planning, 1880–1920*. Dublin: Turoe Press, pp 189–260.
Miller, M. (1992) *Raymond Unwin, Garden Cities and town planning*. Leicester: Leicester University Press.

Milne, K. (ed.) (2010) *Christ Church cathedral Dublin – a history*. Dublin: Four Courts Press.
Mingay, G.E. (1986) *The transformation of Britain, 1830–1939*. London: Routledge.
Ministry of Local Government (1925) *House designs. Prescribed by the Minister of Local Government under the Housing Act, 1924*. Dublin: Stationery Office (5 volumes).
Moody, T.W. and Martin, F.X. (eds) (1967) *The course of Irish history*. Cork: Mercier Press.
Mumford, L. (1961) *The city in history*. London: Penguin.
Municipal Boundaries (1881) *Report of the Municipal Boundaries Commission (Ireland)*. British Parliamentary Papers, vol. 50, c.2827, Dublin.
Murphy, F. (1984) Dublin slums in the 1930s, *Dublin Historical Record*, 37 (3/4), pp 104–11.
Murphy, R.E. (1972) *The central business district*. London: Longman.
Murphy, R.E. and Vance, J.E. (1954a) Delimiting the CBD, *Economic Geography*, 30, 189–222.
Murphy, R.E. and Vance, J.E. (1954b) A comparative study of nine central business districts, *Economic Geography*, 30, 301–36.
Murphy, R.E., Vance, J.E. and Epstein, B.J. (1955) Internal structure of the CBD, *Economic Geography*, 31, 21–46.
Muthesius, S. (1982) *The English terraced house*. New Haven: Yale University Press.
National Planning Conference (1944) *The handbook of national planning and reconstruction*. Dublin: Parkside Press.
Nesbitt, R. (1993) *At Arnotts of Dublin, 1843–1993*. Dublin: A&A Farmar.
Nevin, E. (1963) *Wages in Ireland, 1946–1962*. Paper 12. Economic and Social Research Institute. Dublin: Economic and Social Research Institute.
Nowlan, K.I. (1989) The evolution of Irish planning, 1934–1964. In: Bannon, M.J. (ed.) *Planning: the Irish experience*. Dublin: Wolfhound Press, pp 71–85.
Ó Fearghail, C. (1992) The evolution of Catholic parishes in Dublin city from the sixteenth to the nineteenth centuries. In: Aalen, F.H.A. and Whelan, K. (eds) *Dublin city and county*. Dublin: Geography Publications, pp 229–50.
Ó Maitiú, S. (1997) *Rathmines township, 1847–1930*. Dublin: City of Dublin Vocational Education Committee.
O'Brien, F. (1940) The trade in Dublin, *The Bell*, 1(2), pp 6–15.
O'Brien, J.V. (1982) *Dear dirty Dublin, a city in distress, 1899–1916*. Berkeley: University of California Press.
O'Brien, M. (1950) The planning of Dublin, *Journal of Town Planning Institute*, 36(6), pp 199–212.
O'Donoghue, D. (1998) *Hitler's Irish voices: the story of German radio's wartime Irish service*. Belfast: Beyond Pale Publications.
O'Rourke, H.T. (1925) *The Dublin civic survey*. Liverpool: Liverpool University Press.
Oliver, P., Davis, I. and Bentley, I. (1994) *Dunroamin: the suburban semi and its enemies*. London: Pimlico (Random House).
Olsen, D.J. (1976) *The growth of Victorian London*. London: Penguin.
Openshaw, S. (1973) *An empirical study of scale or principal component and factorial studies of spatial amount*. Proceedings of Quantitative Methods Study Group, Institute of British Geographers, Birmingham.

Openshaw, S. (1978) A geographical solution to scale and aggregation problems in region building, *Transactions of Institute of British Geographers*, 2, pp 459–72.

Orbach, L.F. (1977) *Homes for heroes, a study of the evolution of British public housing, 1915–1921*. London: Seely, Service.

Osborough, N. (1996) *Law and the emergence of modern Dublin*. Dublin: Irish Academic Press.

Owen, D. (1965) *English philanthropy, 1660–1960*. Cambridge, MA: Harvard University Press.

Palmer, C., Robinson M. and Thomas, R. (1977) The countryside image, *Environment and Planning*, A7, pp 739–49.

Park, R.E. and Burgess, E.W. (1925) *The city*. Chicago: University of Chicago Press.

Parker, A.J. (1973) Intra-urban variations in retail grocery prices, *Economic and Social Review*, 5(3), pp. 393–403.

Parker, A.J. (1973) The structure and distribution of grocery stores in Dublin, *Irish Geography*, 6(5), pp 625–30.

Parker, A.J. (1974) An Analysis of retail grocery price variations, *Area*, 6(2), pp 117–20.

Parker, A.J. (1974) Changing retail grocery prices in Dublin, *Irish Geography*, 7(1), pp 107–11.

Parker, A.J. (1975) Hypermarkets: the changing pattern of retailing, *Geography*, 60(2), pp 120–4.

Perle, E.D. (1979) Scale changes and impacts on factorial ecology structures, *Environment and Planning*, A9, pp 549–58.

Pevsner, N. (1968) Model dwellings for the labouring classes, *Architectural Review*, 93, pp 119–28.

Pooley, C.G. (1984) Residential differentiation in Victorian cities: a reassessment, *Transactions of the Institute of British Geographers*, 9(2), pp 131–44.

Pooley, C.G. (1985) Housing for the poorest poor: slum-clearance and rehousing in Liverpool, 1890–1918, *Journal of Historical Geography*, 11(1), pp 70–88.

Pooley, C.G. (ed.) (1992) *Housing strategies in Europe, 1880–1930*. Leicester: Leicester University Press.

Pooley, C.G. and Lawton, R. (1992) *Britain, 1740–1950: an historical geography*. London: Edward Arnold.

Powell, C. (1974) Fifty years of progress, *Built Environment*, 3(10), pp 532–5.

Powell, C.G. (1980) *An economic history of the British building industry, 1815–1979*. London: The Architectural Press.

Power, A. (1993) *Hovels to high-rise: State housing in Europe since 1850*. London: Routledge.

Power, S. (2000) The development of the Ballymun housing scheme, Dublin, 1965–9, *Irish Geography*, 33(2), 199–212.

Pringle, D. (1976) Normality, transformations and grid square data, *Area*, 8, pp 42–5.

Pritchett, V.S. (1967) *Dublin – a portrait*. London: Bodley Head.

Prunty, J. (1998) *Dublin slums, 1800–1925: a study in urban geography*. Dublin: Irish Academic Press.

Prunty, J. (2001) Improving the urban environment. *In*: Brady, J. and Simms, A. (eds), *Dublin through space and time*. Dublin: Four Courts Press, pp 166–220.

Rahilly, A.J. (1917) The social problem in Cork, *Studies: An Irish Quarterly Review*, 6, pp 177–88.

Ratcliffe, J. (1974) *An introduction to town and country planning.* London: Hutchinson.
Ravetz, A. (1974) From working class tenement to modern flat. *In:* Sutcliffe, A. (ed.) *Multi-storey living: the British working-class experience.* London: Croom Helm, pp 122–50.
Reith (1946) *Reports of the new towns committee. Ministry of town and country planning and Department of health for Scotland.* Chairman: Rt Hon. Lord Reith of Stonehaven. Interim Report cmd 6759, second report cmd 6794, final report cmd 6786. UK: HMSO.
RIBA (1931) *Dublin.* Handbook for delegates. Conference of the Royal Institute of British Architects.
Robertson, M. (1933, 1934) *A cautionary guide to Dublin.* Dublin: Royal Institute of the Architects of Ireland (RIAI).
Rockey, J. (1983) From vision to reality: Victorian ideal cities and model towns in the genesis of E. Howard's Garden City, *Town Planning Review,* 54(1), pp 83–105.
Rocque, J. (1756) An exact survey of the city and suburbs of Dublin. Dublin.
Rogers, H.B. (1962) The suburban growth of Victorian Manchester, *Journal of the Manchester Geographical Society,* 58, 1–12.
Rosenau, H. (1983) *The ideal city, its architectural evolution in Europe.* London: Methuen, 3rd edition.
Rothery, S. (1991) *Ireland and the new architecture, 1900–1940.* Dublin: Lilliput Press.
Royal Commission (1881) *Royal Commission to inquire into boundaries and municipal areas of cities and towns in Ireland,* Report, Part II (Dublin, Rathmines, Pembroke, Kilmainham, Drumcondra, Clontarf, Kingstown, Blackrock and Dalkey). C.2827.
Rummel, R.J. (1967) Understanding factor analysis, *Journal of Conflict Resolution,* 11, pp 447–80.
Ryan, J. (1975) *Remembering how we stood – Bohemian Dublin at the mid century.* New York: Taplinger Publishing.
Schaffer, F. (1970) *The new town story.* UK: MacGibbon & Key.
Scott, W.A. (1916) The reconstruction of O'Connell Street, Dublin: a note (including sketch), *Studies: An Irish Quarterly Review,* 5, p. 165.
Scuffil, C. (ed.) (1993) *By the sign of the dolphin: the story of Dolphin's Barn.* Dublin: Dolphin's Barn Historical Society.
Shaffrey, M. (1988) Sackville Street/O'Connell Street, *GPA Irish Arts Yearbook,* Dublin, pp 144–56.
Sheehan, R. and Walsh, B. (1988) *The heart of the city.* Dingle: Brandon.
Shevky, E. and Williams, M. (1949) *The social areas of Los Angeles.* Chicago: University of California Press.
Shevky, E. and Bell, W. (1955) *Social area analysis.* Chicago: University of Chicago Press.
Sies, M.C. (1987) The city transformed: nature, technology and the suburban ideal, 1877–1917, *Journal of Urban History,* 14(1), pp 81–111.
Simms, A. and Fagan, P. (1992) Villages in County Dublin: their origins and inheritance. *In:* Aalen, F.H.A. and Whelan, K. (eds) *Dublin city and county.* Dublin: Geography Publications, pp 79–119.
Simpson, M. and Lloyd, T. (eds) (1977) *Studies in the history of middle-class housing in Britain.* Newton Abbot: David & Charles.

Skilleter, K.J. (1993) The role of PUSs in early British planning and housing reform, 1901–1936, *Planning Perspectives*, pp 125–65.
Slater, T.R. (ed.) (1990) *The built form of western cities.* Leicester: Leicester University Press.
Smith Morris, E. (1997) *British town planning and urban design.* UK: Longman.
Spence, N. (1982) *British cities: an analysis of urban change.* Oxford: Pergamon Press.
Stationery Office (1939) *Official Industrial Directory.* Compiled by the Department of Industry and Commerce. Dublin: Stationery Office.
Stationery Office (1941) *A guide to the social services – a summary designed for the information of individuals and groups.* Dublin: Stationery Office.
Stationery Office (1948) *National nutrition survey. Part 1. Methods of dietary survey and results from Dublin investigation.* Dublin: Stationery Office.
Stationery Office (1955) *National commission on emigration and other population problems, 1948–54.* Dublin: Stationery Office.
Stedman-Jones, G. (1971) *Outcast London: a study in the relationship between classes in Victorian society.* Oxford: Clarendon Press.
Stenhouse, D. (1977) *Understanding towns.* Hove: Wayland Publishers.
Stevenson, G. (2006) *The 1930s home.* London: Shire Books
Stevenson, J. (1984) *British society, 1914–45.* London: Penguin.
Stuart, M. (1972) *The city: problems of planning.* London: Penguin.
Sutcliffe, A. (1972) Working-class housing in nineteenth-century Britain: a review of recent research, *Society for the Study of Labour History*, Bulletin 24.
Sutcliffe, A. (1981) *Towards the planned city: Germany, Britain, the US and France, 1780–1914.* Oxford: Basil Blackwell.
Sutcliffe, A. (ed.) (1974) *Multi-storey living: the British working-class experience.* London: Croom Helm.
Sutcliffe, A. (ed.) (1980) *The rise of modern urban planning, 1800–1914.* London: Mansell.
Sutcliffe, A. (ed.) (1981) *British town planning: the formative years.* New York: St Martin's Press.
Sweetser, F.L. (1965) Factorial ecology: Helsinki 1960, *Demography*, 2, pp 372–86.
Swenarton, M. (1981) *Homes fit for heroes.* London: Heinemann.
Talja, S. (2014) *Sport, recreation and space in urban policy. Helsinki and Dublin from the 1940s to the 1980s.* Historical studies from the University of Helsinki XXXIII. Finland: Helsinki.
Tarn, J.N. (1968) Some pioneer suburban housing estates, *Architectural Review*, 143, pp 367–70.
Tarn, J.N. (1973) *Five per cent philanthropy.* Cambridge: Cambridge University Press.
Tarn, J.N. (1980) Housing reform and the emergence of town planning in Britain before 1914. In: Sutcliffe, A. (ed.), *The rise of modern urban planning, 1800–1914.* London: Mansell, pp 71–98.
Taylor, N. (1973) *The village in the city.* London: Temple Smith in association with New Society, 1973.
Telesis Consultancy (1982) *A review of industrial policy.* Report 56. Dublin: National Economic and Social Council.
Tetlow, J. and Goss, A. (1965) *Homes, towns and traffic.* London: Faber and Faber.

Thomas, R. and Cresswell P. (1973) *The new town idea.* Unit 26 of urban development course. The Open University. UK: Oxford University Press.

Thompson, F.M.L. (1988) *The rise of respectable society: a social history of Victorian Britain 1830–1900.* London: Fontana Press.

Thompson, F.M.L. (ed.) (1982) *The rise of suburbia.* Leicester: Leicester University Press.

Thrift, N. and Williams, P. (eds) (1987) *Class and space: the making of urban society.* London: Routledge.

Timms, D. (1971) *The urban mosaic – towards a theory of residential differentiation.* Cambridge: Cambridge University Press.

Townroe, B.S. (1924) *A handbook of housing.* London: Methuen.

Tudor Walters Report (1918) *Report of the committee appointed by the President of the Local Government Board and the Secretary for Scotland to consider questions of building construction in connection with the provision of dwellings for the working classes in England, Wales and Scotland.* London: HMSO.

Tyron, R.C. (1955) *Identification of social areas by cluster analysis.* Berkeley, CA: University of California Press.

Unwin, R. (1912) *Nothing gained by overcrowding.* London: Garden Cities and Town Planning Association.

Unwin, R. and Parker, B. (1909) *Town planning in practice* (1994, reprint). Princeton: Princeton Architectural Press.

Ward, C. (1969) *New homes for old. Human sciences in industry, study number 3.* Dublin: Irish National Productivity Committee.

Ward, S. (2002) *Planning the twentieth-century city.* UK: Wiley.

Watchorn, F. (1985) *Crumlin and the way it was.* Dublin: O'Donoghue Press International.

Waterman, S. (1981) Changing residential patterns of the Dublin Jewish community, *Irish Geography*, 14, pp 41–50.

Watson, I. (1989) *Gentlemen in the building line: the development of South Hackney.* London: Padfield Publications.

Whelan, W. (2003) *Reinventing modern Dublin.* Dublin: University College Dublin Press.

Whelan, Y. (2001) Scripting national memory: the Garden of Remembrance, Parnell Square, *Irish Geography*, 34(1), pp 11–33.

Whelan, Y. (2001) Symbolizing the State: the iconography of O'Connell Street, Dublin after Independence (1922), *Irish Geography*, 34(2), pp 145–50.

Whelpton, E. (1948) *The book of Dublin.* UK: Rockcliff.

Whitehand, J.W.R. (1987) The changing face of cities: a study of development cycles and urban form, *IBG Special Publications*, 21. Oxford: Basil Blackwell.

Wilson, W.H. (1994) *The city beautiful movement.* Baltimore, MD: Johns Hopkins University Press.

Wright, L. and Browne, K. (1974) A future for Dublin. Special Issue, *Architectural Review*, November, pp 268–330.

Wright, M. (1963) *The Dublin region. Advisory regional plan and final report.* Dublin: Stationery Office.

# List of illustrations

| | | |
|---|---|---|
| 1. | The cost of living. | 16 |
| 2. | The limits to taxation! | 19 |
| 3. | A happy new year! | 20 |
| 4. | Commission on emigration. | 24 |
| 5. | Northern inner city wards for the 1966 and 1971 censuses. | 28 |
| 6. | Southern inner city wards for the 1966 and 1971 censuses. | 29 |
| 7. | Age distributions for males and females in Finglas West, 1961 and 1966. | 31 |
| 8. | Age distributions for males and females in Cabra East, 1961 and 1966. | 32 |
| 9. | Age distributions for males and females in North Dock, 1961 and 1966. | 33 |
| 10. | Hillside housing estate, Dalkey. | 38 |
| 11. | Late nineteenth-century DADC housing on John Dillon Street. | 40 |
| 12. | Vacant lots being used as car parks. | 40 |
| 13. | Functional areas in Dublin city centre. | 50 |
| 14. | New offices for Esso in Stillorgan, completed in 1960. | 51 |
| 15. | Dublin in the 1940s. | 57 |
| 16. | Dublin in the early 1950s. | 58 |
| 17. | Dublin in the mid-1960s. | 59 |
| 18. | The demand for housing. | 64 |
| 19. | Tender request for flat blocks on Botanic Avenue, 1961. | 71 |
| 20. | The Botanic Avenue scheme as completed. | 71 |
| 21. | The first phase of Ballyfermot. | 76 |
| 22. | Ballyfermot completed. | 76 |
| 23. | An example of housing style in Ballyfermot. | 77 |
| 24. | Tender for residential shops in 1957 in Ballyfermot. | 79 |
| 25. | Finglas before development. | 83 |
| 26. | Finglas development in the late 1950s. | 83 |
| 27. | Standard houses at Ballygall Crescent. | 85 |
| 28. | Houses at right angles to road at Ballygall Crescent. | 86 |
| 29. | Housing on Ferndale Road, Finglas. | 88 |
| 30. | Aerial view of Finglas West and Kildonan Park. | 90 |
| 31. | Mellowes Park in Finglas West built by W. & T. Crampton in 1960–1. | 91 |
| 32. | General tender for shops in Finglas West in 1961. | 91 |
| 33. | Site of the Milltown clearance. | 93 |
| 34. | Compulsory purchase order for Milltown clearance, 28 July 1953. | 93 |
| 35. | Wilkinstown/Walkinstown before development. | 95 |
| 36. | Walkinstown as completed. | 95 |
| 37. | The vista at Walkinstown Green. | 96 |
| 38. | Outline of the Bonnybrook, Kilmore and Edemore scheme as of the mid-1960s. | 97 |

| | | |
|---|---|---|
| 39. | Housing on St Brendan's Park, Raheny. | 100 |
| 40. | Housing on Adare Park, Bonnybrook. | 100 |
| 41. | Housing on Cromcastle Park, Kilmore. | 101 |
| 42. | Housing on Edenmore Avenue. | 101 |
| 43. | Invitations for tenders in the 1950s. | 111 |
| 44. | Invitations for tenders in the 1960s. | 111 |
| 45. | Housing on Bóthar Ainninn. | 113 |
| 46. | Advertisement inviting applications for Coolock houses. | 115 |
| 47. | Layout plan for the Kilmore development. | 115 |
| 48. | Houses on Kilmore Avenue. | 116 |
| 49. | The developments of the Red Park Utility Society, Tolka Estate and Ballygall Public Utility Society. | 118 |
| 50. | Advertisement by Ballygall Public Utility Society. | 119 |
| 51. | The need for austerity. | 129 |
| 52. | Advertisement for leasehold interest in SDAA houses. | 135 |
| 53. | The layout of the completed scheme in Sallynoggin. | 137 |
| 54. | Housing in Sallynoggin. | 137 |
| 55. | Alpine Gardens Public Utility Society. | 139 |
| 56. | Advertisement for Annadale scheme. | 156 |
| 57. | The Annadale development to the north-west of the Croydon part of the Marino scheme. | 156 |
| 58. | Housing on Annadale Drive. | 157 |
| 59. | Housing in the Annadale scheme in 2014. | 157 |
| 60. | Advertisement for St Anne's housing scheme. | 162 |
| 61. | The St Anne's area before development. | 163 |
| 62. | Layout for St Anne's housing scheme. | 163 |
| 63. | Example of housing in St Anne's. | 165 |
| 64. | Kilmore purchase houses advertisement. | 165 |
| 65. | Housing maintenance. | 167 |
| 66. | Kimmage Road East. | 173 |
| 67. | Terenure Road West. | 173 |
| 68. | Ballymun Avenue. | 174 |
| 69. | Glasnevin Avenue. | 175 |
| 70. | The connection between Glasaree and Ferndale roads. | 177 |
| 71. | Layout plan of O'Devaney Gardens. | 179 |
| 72. | Aerial view of O'Devaney Gardens in 2014 as it awaits demolition. | 180 |
| 73. | Dominick Street before redevelopment. | 181 |
| 74. | Dominick Street with its flat complexes. | 181 |
| 75. | New design for flats as used in Donnybrook. | 184 |
| 76. | Tower access design on Macken Street – city centre location. | 184 |
| 77. | Front view of tower access design on Chamber Street. | 185 |
| 78. | Rutland Street flats, 1969. An alternative flat design. | 186 |
| 79. | The same design used in four blocks in Charlemont Street. | 186 |
| 80. | The tower access design in Gardiner Street before the redevelopment of the west side of the street. | 187 |

## LIST OF ILLUSTRATIONS  435

| | | |
|---|---|---|
| 81. | Upper Rutland Street, Summerhill, waiting for redevelopment in the late 1970s. | 189 |
| 82. | Hardwicke Street before redevelopment. | 190 |
| 83. | Hardwicke Street flats. | 190 |
| 84. | Expressions of interest for the Ballymun development. | 192 |
| 85. | Fenian Street housing collapse. | 194 |
| 86. | The flat complex on Kilmore Road. | 201 |
| 87. | The UCD land available for development, shaded grey. | 203 |
| 88. | Expression of interest in alternative housing approaches. | 206 |
| 89. | Ballymun from the air. | 221 |
| 90. | Aerial photograph of the Ballymun development. | 222 |
| 91. | A tower block in Ballymun. | 224 |
| 92. | A view of a spine block. | 225 |
| 93. | The view from the main roundabout, shopping centre on the left. | 225 |
| 94. | The completed scheme at Ballymun. | 227 |
| 95. | The town centre in Ballymun. | 230 |
| 96. | Enjoying the amenity in Lee Bank, Birmingham. | 235 |
| 97. | Landscaping in Ballymun in 1980 around the blocks, a decade following completion. | 237 |
| 98. | Mature landscaping along Ballymun Road in 2005. | 237 |
| 99. | Dun Emer in Dundrum. | 245 |
| 100. | Range of developments available. | 247 |
| 101. | Belgrove Lawn. | 248 |
| 102. | Portmarnock by the sea. | 249 |
| 103. | The Mespil complex in the early 1970s. | 253 |
| 104. | The Mespil apartments. | 253 |
| 105. | Ardoyne House on the edge of Herbert Park. | 254 |
| 106. | A view of Ardoyne House from Herbert Park. | 254 |
| 107. | Brendan House on St Brendan's Road. | 256 |
| 108. | Apartments at St John's Court, Sandymount. | 256 |
| 109. | Advertisement for Ballinguile. | 258 |
| 110. | Approximate location of apartment schemes in 1969. | 258 |
| 111. | A new concept in apartment living. | 259 |
| 112. | Apartments in Greenmount Lawns. | 259 |
| 113. | Advertisement for Greenhills Estate. | 261 |
| 114. | The home of your dreams. | 262 |
| 115. | An aerial view of the Laurel Park, Clondalkin, development. | 262 |
| 116. | Advertisement for Monastery Park. | 264 |
| 117. | An aerial view of the mature landscape at Monastery Park. | 265 |
| 118. | Dublin's most exclusive site at Offington Park. | 269 |
| 119. | Advertisement for Shrewsbury Lawn. | 270 |
| 120. | Distinctive houses at Shanganagh Vale. | 272 |
| 121. | The neighbourhood unit. | 273 |
| 122. | The layout of Radburn. | 275 |

| | | |
|---|---|---|
| 123. | The layout of Shanganagh Vale. | 275 |
| 124. | Bayside advertisement, citing 'Radburn' features. | 277 |
| 125. | The layout of the Bayside estate. | 277 |
| 126. | The ideal homes exhibition. | 279 |
| 127. | ESB Christmas advertisement for 1954. | 282 |
| 128. | Advertisement for fridges in 1953. | 284 |
| 129. | A cosy 1956 Christmas with a Navan carpet. | 285 |
| 130. | Polishing with Mansion floor polish in 1959. | 286 |
| 131. | Cookers on credit terms in 1954. | 288 |
| 132. | A 'Pilot' radio in 1950. Widely seen as the mark of quality. | 289 |
| 133. | The transition to television in 1960. | 289 |
| 134. | Trends in UK National Food Survey, 1950–70. | 291 |
| 135. | Advertisement for Lucozade from 1956. | 293 |
| 136. | Chocolate as a food in the 1950s. | 294 |
| 137. | The arrival of Palm Toffees. | 294 |
| 138. | Advertisement for Afton Major from 1955. | 295 |
| 139. | The Lyons tea range in 1965. | 297 |
| 140. | Irish Coffee chocolate from 1960. | 297 |
| 141. | Hilberseimer's plan for the redevelopment of Friedrichstadt, Berlin, 1928. | 305 |
| 142. | Le Courbusier's design for a contemporary city of three million, 1929. | 305 |
| 143. | Plan for a dwelling complex for Kuznetsk by Alexander and Leonid Vesnin, 1929–30. | 306 |
| 144. | Early high-rise in central Moscow. | 307 |
| 145. | Standard housing style in suburban Moscow. | 307 |
| 146. | Prefabrication in building in Moscow. | 309 |
| 147. | Large scale use of high-rise in Moscow, late 1980s. | 309 |
| 148. | The microrayon concept. | 310 |
| 149. | A microrayon in Moscow. | 310 |
| 150. | Karl Max-Hof, Vienna, in the late 1990s. | 312 |
| 151. | Quarry Hill development showing the local bus station. | 312 |
| 152. | Unité d'Habitation, Berlin. | 313 |
| 153. | Modern high-rise in Antwerp. | 314 |
| 154. | Modern high-rise in south-eastern suburban Prague. | 314 |
| 155. | Modern high-rise in central Berlin. | 315 |
| 156. | Roehampton in the mid-1960s. | 316 |
| 157. | The Roehampton scheme today. | 317 |
| 158. | The spine blocks in Roehampton. | 317 |
| 159. | Conventional layout. | 320 |
| 160. | Cul-de-sac layout. | 321 |
| 161. | Double footpath layout. | 322 |
| 162. | The Brandon Estate, Kennington. | 324 |
| 163. | Loughborough Road Estate, London. | 324 |
| 164. | Layout of Loughborough Road Estate, London, 1957. | 325 |
| 165. | Ackroydon Estate, Wimbledon, London. | 325 |

|     |     |     |
| --- | --- | --- |
| 166. | Redevelopment plan for a high-density area. | 327 |
| 167. | Local authority rentals in 1971. | 333 |
| 168. | Owner occupancy in 1971. | 333 |
| 169. | Private rental sector in 1971. | 334 |
| 170. | Multiple occupancy in 1971. | 337 |
| 171. | New housing in the city. | 338 |
| 172. | Areas of population growth, 1966–71. | 349 |
| 173. | Areas of population decline, 1966–71. | 349 |
| 174. | Children under the age of four years in 1971. | 351 |
| 175. | Fertility: active family formation, 1966–71. | 351 |
| 176. | Population aged 65 years and more in 1971. | 353 |
| 177. | Youthful dependency in Dublin, 1971. | 355 |
| 178. | Old age dependency in Dublin, 1971. | 355 |
| 179. | Young and single in Dublin, 1971. | 356 |
| 180. | Higher professionals in Dublin, 1971. | 362 |
| 181. | Lower professionals in Dublin, 1971. | 362 |
| 182. | Semi-skilled workers in Dublin, 1971. | 364 |
| 183. | Unskilled workers in Dublin, 1971. | 364 |
| 184. | Car ownership in Dublin, 1971. | 365 |
| 185. | Persons per household, 1971. | 368 |
| 186. | Persons per room, 1971. | 368 |
| 187. | Housing units with one or two persons, 1971. | 370 |
| 188. | Households with one or two persons, 1971. | 370 |
| 189. | At school in Dublin, 1971. | 373 |
| 190. | Employed women in Dublin, 1971. | 373 |
| 191. | Women engaged in home duties, 1971. | 374 |
| 192. | The distribution of employers in Dublin, 1971. | 376 |
| 193. | The unemployed in Dublin, 1971. | 376 |
| 194. | Non-Roman Catholics in the population, 1971. | 377 |
| 195. | The socio-economic status of Dublin's areas, 1971. | 380 |
| 196. | Areas of youthfulness and growth in Dublin, 1971. | 385 |
| 197. | The census areas of the city in 1971. | 404 |

## List of Tables

|     |     |     |
| --- | --- | --- |
| 1. | Value of major domestic exports, 1950–5. | 17 |
| 2. | External trade, 1940–58. | 18 |
| 3. | Population change in the State, 1946–71. | 24 |
| 4. | Urban structure, 1971. | 25 |
| 5. | Urban structure – towns less than 30,000 population. | 25 |
| 6. | Population change in Dublin county borough and Dún Laoghaire, 1951–66. | 26 |
| 7. | Urban (aggregate town areas) population change in entire county, 1961–71. | 26 |
| 8. | Areas of growth and decline, 1951–66. | 30 |

| | | |
|---|---|---|
| 9. | Dublin in 1951, sex ratio and marriage rate. | 35 |
| 10. | Wards with highest proportions of old housing in 1961. | 39 |
| 11. | Wards with highest proportions of new housing in 1961. | 39 |
| 12. | Quality of housing facilities in Dublin city, 1961. | 43 |
| 13. | Percentage of 1961 households with higher occupation densities, along with 1946 figures. | 45 |
| 14. | Examples of different patterns of tenure, 1961. | 46 |
| 15. | Occupational structure in Dublin | 52 |
| 16. | Involvement in the labour force, 1951–66. | 55 |
| 17. | Housing provision by Dublin Corporation, 1945–63. | 65 |
| 18. | Dwellings occupied and net vacancies, 1950–60. | 67 |
| 19. | Relationship between family size and rooms occupied, 1959. | 69 |
| 20. | Location of construction projects, 1961. | 70 |
| 21. | Housing programme for four years as envisaged in January 1951. | 74 |
| 22. | House building in Finglas East and West, 1953–65. | 87 |
| 23. | Later additions to Finglas East. | 87 |
| 24. | Tender costs in a range of cottage developments, 1948–1956. | 107 |
| 25. | Tender costs in a range of flat developments, 1948–1956. | 107 |
| 26. | Supplementary grants paid, 1953–62. | 124 |
| 27. | Loans and supplementary grants. | 134 |
| 28. | Rent per month in 1961. | 145 |
| 29. | Rents payable under the March interim scheme. | 150 |
| 30. | Tenant purchase schemes in progress or predicted, 1952. | 158 |
| 31. | Projects for which funding was sought in 1955. | 191 |
| 32. | Housing provision in January 1964. | 197 |
| 33. | Displaced families, June 1964. | 198 |
| 34. | Executive salaries in 1967. | 250 |
| 35. | Consumption of food products in UK, 1950–70. | 292 |
| 36. | Tenders approved in England and Wales, 1953–1970. | 328 |
| 37. | Approximate dates for Corporation houses and average cost per unit. | 331 |
| 38. | Age of housing stock in Dublin as of 1971. | 337 |
| 39. | Some indications of housing quality in the entire city, 1971. | 339 |
| 40. | Socio-economic groupings in the city in 1971. | 358 |
| 41. | Index for dissimilarity for socio-economic groups in Dublin, 1971. | 358 |
| 42. | Indices of segregation, 1971. | 360 |
| 43. | Employment status in 1971. | 374 |
| 44. | Characterisics of high- and low-status areas. | 382 |
| 45. | Characterisics of youthful and maturing areas. | 386 |
| 46. | Age of Housing stock, 1981. | 394 |

# Index

Page numbers in *italic* refer to illustrations.

Abbotstown Avenue, 89
Abbotstown Drive, 89
Abbotstown Road, 89
Abercrombie, P., 13–14, 61, 98, 159, 304
Abu-Lughod, J., 401
Ackroydon Estate, Wimbledon, *325*
Adams, M., 301
Adare Avenue, 99
Adare Drive, 99
Adare Green, 99
Adare Park, 99, *100*
Afton Major cigarettes, *295*, 296
agriculture, 16–17, 47–9, 51, 56, 202
Albert Building Group, 109
Albert Place West, 105
Albion Securities, 252
A-Line furniture, 266
Alpha Analysis, 410
Alpine Gardens Public Utility Society, *139*
Amsterdam, 381
Andrew's liver salts, 293, 296
Anglesea Group, 109
Anglesea Public Utility Society, 108
Annadale, 107, 154–6
    housing scheme, 155–7, 162, 167
    tenant purchase schemes, 158, 290
Annadale Drive, *157*
Annamoe Road, 331
Antwerp, *314*
apartments, 177, 251–9, 271, 304, 315
    blocks, height of, 252, 255
    location, *258*
    price of, 252, 257
    rents, 252
    three-bedroomed, 251–2, 255, 257
    two-bedroomed, 252, 255, 257
Ardán Naomh Áine, 162

Ardglas (Ballymun), 220
Ardilaun, Lord, 158
Ardoyne House, 252, *254–5*
Armagh Road, 109
Arnold Park, 267
Arran Quay, 39, 367, 375, 395–6, 398–9
    housing, 39, 43, 45
Artane, 335, 395–6, 398–9
    housing, 39, 45–6, 60
    housing facilities, 43
    population, 30
Asbach Uralt, 296
Ascal an Mhuillinn, 162
Ascal Bhaile Bheite, 162
Ascal Bhaile Thuaidh, 162
Ascal Cnoc Síbile, 162
Ascal Mac Uáid, 162
Ascal Nainicín, 162
Ascal Naomh Áine, 162
Ashgrove Park, 138
Associated Industrial Consultants, 250
Associated Properties Ltd, 85, 336
Association of Municipal Authorities in
    Ireland, 166
Athlone, 164
auctioneers, 241–2
Aungier Street, 388
Australia, 289
Austria, 36
Avondale House, 68
Avondale Road, 267

B.&R. Builders, 247
Back, K., 170
Baggot Street, 336, 372
Balbutcher, 216
Balcurris, 216

Balcurris Road, 220, 227
Baldoyle, 348, 384, 395–6, 398–9
  housing facilities, 43
  population, 30
Balency and Schuhl, 208, 214
Balency method, 207, 220
Balglass (Howth), 345
Ballinguile, 257–8
Ballinteer Road, 248
Ballsbridge, 336, 365–6, 372, 378, 381–2
  housing facilities, 42
  occupations, 361, 375
Ballyboden, 363, 367
Ballybough, 106, 353, 395–6, 399
  housing, 45
  housing facilities, 43
Ballybough House, 68
Ballybrack, 136, 348, 381, 384
Ballyfermot, 366–7, 369, 375, 382
  age profile, 353–4
  boundary extension, 64
  housing, 39, 66, 75–82, 107
    overcrowding of, 44–5, 75
    tenure of, 46–7, 399
    vacancies, 67–8, 81
  housing facilities, 43, 398
  housing scheme, 66, 73, 75, 111
  housing stock, 39, 41, 397
  isolation, 81–2, 179
  maps, *76*
  occupations, 363
  population, 30, 78, 395
  rents, 143, 146
  shops, 78–80
Ballyfermot Avenue, 78
Ballyfermot Crescent, 78
Ballyfermot Drive, 78
Ballyfermot Hill, 172
Ballyfermot Lower, 331
Ballyfermot Newly-weds Association, 143
Ballyfermot Parade, 78
Ballyfermot Road, 75, 78
Ballyfermot Upper, 74, 77, 158, 331
Ballygall, 120
Ballygall Crescent, 84, *85–6*
Ballygall House (Hillcrest), 118

Ballygall Parade, 84
Ballygall Place, 84
Ballygall Public Utility Society, 87, *118–19*, 176
Ballygall Road, 118, 120
Ballygall Road, East, 84, 176, 344
Ballygall Road, West, 84
Ballymun, 193, 214–35, 344, 348, 352–4, 363, 367, 369, 371–2, 375, 382–4, 388
  'the Ballymun neurosis', 238
  central heating, 225, 238
  development, 192, *221–2*, 224, 225, 336
  housing schemes, 105, 192–205, 213–14, 223
  landscaping, 235–7
  lifts, 232, 234, 238
  problems, 177, 239
  recreational areas, 234, 238
  rents, 149
  reputation, 175–7, 205
  shops, 229–30
  system building, 15, 147, 191, 207, 211
  tenants, selection of, 238
  town centre, *230*
  young families, 232–3
Ballymun Avenue, see Glasnevin Avenue
Ballymun Drive, see Glasnevin Park
Ballymun Estate Tenants Association, 230, 231, 233
*Ballymun: the experiment that failed*, 238
Ballymun Park, see Clonmel Avenue
Ballymun Residents' Association, 204
Ballymun Road, *237*
Ballyneety Road, 75
Ballyshannon Avenue, 99
Ballyshannon Road, 99
Bank of Ireland, 128
banks, 126, 128
Bannon, M.J., 51–2
Barets, 208
Barets system, 207
Barr, A.W., 323, 329
Barry Avenue, 89
Barry Drive, 89

Barry Green, 89
Barry Park, 89
Barry Road, 89
Barryscourt Road, 99
Basin Street, 189
Basin Street, Upper, 71
bathrooms, 117, 138, 161, 210, 215, 248, 257, 263, 267–8, 270–1, 280, 287, 300, 366
Bayside, Sutton, 276, *277*, 278
Bayside Railway Station, 278
Beann Eadair, 395–6, 398–9
Beaumont, 348, 365, 384
Beaumont Road, 114
bedrooms, 226, 247, 260, 263–4, 268, 271, 280, 285, 287, 303
Beecham's, 293, 296
Beechlawn Avenue, 116
Beechlawn Close, 116
Beechlawn Green, 116
Beggsboro, 331
Belfast, 49, 382
Belfield, 202–3
Belgium, 36, 237
Belgrove Lawn (Chapelizod), *248*
Bell, W., 378–9, 401, 403
Belton Estate, 136
Belton Park, 176
Beneavin Road, 87
Beneavin Drive, 135
Beneavin Park, 135
Beneavin Road, 135
Benmadigan Road, 75
Berlin, 304, *305*, 313, 315
Berry, B.J.L., 383, 405
Birmingham, 234–5
Blackditch Road, 78
Blackrock, 61, 125, 241, 361, 381, 396
Blackwell, J., 22
Blanchardstown, 240, 347, 352, 363, 393, 404
    development, 105, 136, 350
    housing scheme, 105
Blaney, N., 65, 147, 169, 201, 207, 267
Bluebell, 106–7, 331
Boal, F.W, 382

Boland, Gerard, 103
Boland, Kevin, 151–2
Bolton Street, 193
Bombay, *see* Mumbai
Bonnybrook, 96–7, *100*
Bosch, *284*
Botanic Avenue, 70, *71*
Bóthar Ainninn, *see* St Brendan's Park
Bóthar an Easa, 162
Bóthar Bhaile Mhuire, 162
Bóthar na Naomh, 162
Brady, J., 379, 404, 405–6
Braemor Grove, 135
Braithwaite Street, 70
Brandon Estate, Kennington, *324*
Bray, 393
Brendan House, 255–6
Brendan Road, 255
Brennan and McGowan, 248, 257, 268
Briarfield (Kilbarrack), 104
Brickfield Drive, 108
Brickfields, 108, 112, 331
Bride Street, 105
Bridgefoot Street, 191
Briscoe, R., 130, 132
Britain, 22, 48, 53, 64, 211, 301
British Association for the Advancement of Science, 49
Brooke Report, 326
Brookwood Avenue, 114, 174
Brookwood Lawn, 175
Brookwood Rise, 174
Brown Street, South, 106
Buckingham Street, 170, 187–8, 191
budget (1956), 17
builders, 15, 84, 103, 114, 121–2, 240–3, 260, 263, 271
    private, 27, 38, 103–4, 110, 170, 242
building
    costs, 106, 182, 216, 241, 332
    trade, 215, 229, 243
        carpenters, 243
        labourers, 243
        masons, 243
        painters, 243
        plasterers, 243

Building and Construction Exhibition, 302
buildings
    condemned, 124, 193, 196
    dangerous, 195–200, 205
building societies, 125–6
bungalows, 114, 244, 248, 266, 271, 274, 326
Bunratty Avenue, 99
Bunratty Drive, 99
Bunratty Road, 99
Burgess, E.W., 378, 383, 402
Burke, P.J., 216
Burma, *see* Myanmar
bus fares, 82, 89, 187
    high, 80, 178–9
Byrne, A., 170, 179, 187–9
Byrne, L., 193

C. Mooney Gardens, 107
Cabinteely, 247, 270–1, 276, 377
Cabra, 29, 354, 363, 372, 375, 382, 387
    housing schemes, 62, 77, 94
    vacant houses, 68
Cabragh [Cabra] East, 29, 395–6, 398–9
Cabragh [Cabra] West
    housing, 38, 45, 396
        tenure of, 46, 399
    housing facilities, 43, 398
    population, 395
California Hills Park, 79
Cameron, Sir Charles, 194–5
Cameron Estate, 172
Camus, 208
Cappagh Avenue, 89
Cappagh Road, 89, 110
Captain's Lane, 73, 107–9, 111, 331
Cardiff, 405
Cardiffsbridge Avenue, 89
Cardiffsbridge Road, 89
Carna Road, 78
Carnlough Road, 169
carpets, 299–300
    Navan, *285*
cars, 75, 217, 229, 248, 266, 271, 277, 382, 392–4, 407

ownership of, 13, 276, 296, 363, 365, 390–1
parking, 217, 229–30, *237*, 269, 391
per household, 409
Casement Green, 89
Casement Grove, 89
Casement Park, 89, 138
Casement Road, 89
Castlekevin Road, 99
Castleknock, 245, 248, 335, 361, 365, 382, 387
Castletimon Avenue, 99
Castletimon Drive, 99
Castletimon Green, 99
Castletimon Park, 99
Castletimon Road, 99
Cathal Brugha Street, 177
Cattell, R.B., 409, 411–12
Ceannt Tower, 231
census
    1936, 44
    1946, 42, 44–5, 52, 332
    1951, 23, 25–6, 30, 35, 55, 395–6
    1956, 23, 26, 395–6
    1961, 23, 44, 337–8
        age distributions, *31–3*
        housing, tenure of, 46, 399–400
        housing facilities, 43, 398
        housing stock, 37, 39, 396–7
        labour force, 55
        occupations, 52
        population, 26, 395–6
        rents, 144–5
    1962, 400
    1966, 23–4, 26, 28–34, 37, 55, 395–6
    1971, 336, 347, 354–8, 360–75, 376–7, 379, *380*, 381–2, *385*, 386–90, *404*, 405
        age profile, *351–3*, *355–6*
        car ownership, *365*
        education, *373*
        home ownership, 240, 332
        housing, *333–4*, *337*, *339*, *368*, *370*
        Irish speakers, 377
        labour force, *373–4*

multiple occupancy, 336
occupations, *362, 364*, 52
population, 24, 26, *349*
rentals, 333–4
wards, 28–9, 347
1981, 299, 407
central heating, 246, 286
Ballymun, 224–6, 252
Donnybrook, 257
Dundrum, 247–8
flats, 215
gas-fired, 278
Greenhills Estate, 260, 263
housing, 215, 217–18, 244
Monastery Park, 264–6
oil-fired, 271, 274
system building, 211, 220
Terenure, 268
Central Statistics Office, 23, 36–7, 44, 356–7, 369, 404
Chalet Building Company, 109, 113
Chamber Street, *185*
Chamber Street/Cork Street, 66
Chapelizod, 247–8, 331
Chapelizod Hill, 172
Charlemont Street, 105, *186*
Chief Medical Officer, 199
children, 233, 322
young, 232, 236, 350, 352, 372
Children's Allowances Acts, 149
children's allowance scheme, 23, 141, 149–50
Christ Church cathedral, 14
Christian Brothers, 60, 120
churches, 94, 96, 187, 210, 215, 219, 230–1, 263, 273, 276–7, 341, 344
Church of Ireland, 377, 382
Church Street, 196
Churchtown, 350, 375
CIÉ, *see* Coras Iompair Éireann
Cill Eanna, *see* Eannafort Road
City and County Management (Amendment Act) 1955, 142
city averages, 372, 375, 379–80, 383
city centre, 14, 28, 183, 242, 244, 352, 372, 377, 382, 390–1

demolition, 332
flats, 70, 178–9
City Hall, 169, 204, 233
City Housing Corporation, 271
City Manager, 66, 72, 81, 121, 125–8, 142–3, 168–9, 340
assistant, 70, 141, 146–8, 166, 169, 207
Ballymun scheme, 193, 216, 218
Coolock scheme, 172
differential rents system, 143, 149–52
Finglas schemes, 176, 183
Gardiner Street scheme, 182
property speculation, 341–3
reports of, 67–8, 140, 182–3
City Manager, St Anne's, 159
Claddagh Green, 78
Claddagh Road, 78
Clanbrassil Street, 14, 105
Clanbrassil Street, Upper, 106
Clancy Building Group, 108
Clarke, T., 170
Clarkin, A., 112
Clifden Road, 78
Cloiginn Avenue, 78
Cloiginn Park, 78
Cloiginn Road, 78
Clondalkin, 60, 136, *262*, 263, 350, 384–5, 393
Clonmel Avenue, 172, 175
Clonsilla, 105
Clonskea [Clonskeagh], 241, 350, 361
Clontarf, 13, 45, 161, 365–7, 371
age profile, 350, 352, 354
home ownership, 241, 335
housing, overcrowding of, 45
housing scheme, 154
occupations, 361
social housing, 160, 346
socio-economic groups, 382, 387
tenant purchase scheme, 154
Clontarf/Dollymount, 378
Clontarf East, 29, 395–6, 398–9
housing, 39, 46
housing facilities, 43
population, 30

Clontarf West, 395–6, 398–9
CMO, see Chief Medical Officer
Coggin, S., 172
Coiste Teaghlachais, 218
Colepark Avenue, 78
Colepark Drive, 78
Colepark Green, 78
Colepark Road, 78
College Green, 14
Collins Avenue, 14, 60, 112, 176, 218
Collins Drive, 84
Collins Green, 84
Collins Park, 112, 135
Collins Place, 87
Collins Row, 84
Committee of the Whole House, 148, 215, 224
community development, 79–80, 208, 231
  McInerney, 106–7, 138
compulsory purchase orders, 66, 69, 71, 73, 84, 93–4, 102, 104–5, 109, 138, 196, 267
Connacht, 23–4
consumer products, 291–8
  advertisements, *284, 286, 293, 295,* 299
  cigarettes, *295*–6
  detergents, 284–5, 295
  DIY, 294, 296
  electrical appliances, 281–4, 287–8, 290, 300
  food and drink, 291, 296–8, *315*
  gadgets, 281, 284–5, 290, 301–2
  hire purchase, *288*
  medicines, 296
  personal hygiene, 296
  tobacco, 47
Consumer's Association in Britain, 301
Coolatree Road, 135
Coolock, 27, 94, 96, 164, 172, 335, 348, 354, 363, 366–7, 369, 375, 382–4, 395–6, 398–9
  development, 60, 73
  housing, *100*, 107, *115*
  housing facilities, 43
  housing scheme, 73, 94, 114–16, 120, 170

housing stock, 39, 41, 68, 114
population, 27, 30
Coolock Avenue, see Beechlawn Avenue
Coolock Close, see Beechlawn Close
Coolock Drive, 99
Coolock Green, see Beechlawn Green
Coolock/Kilmore, 114, 200, 331, 344
Coolock/Raheny, 106–7, 191, 331
Coolock village, 96
Coombe, 105, 348
Cooney, E.W., 328
Co-operative Home Building Society Limited, 110
Copenhagen, 208
Coras Iompair Éireann, 82, 98, 179
Corish, B., 72
Cork City, 25, 140, 205
Cork City, Bishopstown, 125
Cork City, Blackrock, 125
Cork City, Douglas, 125
Cork City, St Mary's, 125
Cork City Council, 129
Cork Street, 196
Corporation Place, 68
Corporation Tenants' Association, 144
Cosgrave Group, 110
Costello, J.A., 128–9
Coultry Road, 220, 227, 232
County Dublin, 25, 146
Cregan, C., 283
Cremona Road, 78
Cromcastle Drive, 99
Cromcastle Avenue, 99
Cromcastle Green, 99
Cromcastle Park, *101*
Cromcastle Road, 99
Cromwellsfort Road, 260
Crosspan, 248
Crumlin, 29, 179, 353, 363, 367
  housing, 44–5, 397
    tenure of, 46, 399
  housing facilities, 43, 398
  housing scheme, 38, 62, 68, 73, 78, 112
  occupations, 375, 382
  population, 387, 395
Crumlin North, 331

Crumlin Road, 108, 111
Crumlin Road, Lower, 112
Crumlin South, 331
Crumlin West, *see* Walkinstown
CSO, *see* Central Statistics Office
Cubit, 229
Cubitt system, 220
Cuffe Street, 71, 188
culs-de-sac, 136, 274, 276–7, 319, 321, 323
Cumbernauld (Scotland), 274
Curtis and Farrelly, 113–14

DADC, *see* Dublin Artisans' Dwelling Company
Dáil, 65, 72, 103, 131–2, 145, 147, 159, 212, 234
Daleview (Ballybrack), 136
Dalkey, 247, 375, 377, 381, 396
Dalkey/Killiney, 348, 352
Dame Street, 14
Danespark, 331
Daniel Morrissey and Sons, 242
Darndale, 323, 344
Dartry, 346
Daultrey, S., 411
Davies, 405, 407, 409, 411–12
Davis, T., 392
Dean's Grange, 348, 384
Deanstown Avenue, 89
Deanstown Drive, 89
Deanstown Green, 89
Deanstown Park, 89
Deanstown Road, 89
Decies Road, 75
deds, *see* district electoral divisions
De La Salle Brothers, 79
Dempsey, 107
Denmark, 207
Denzille Street, 171
Department of Agriculture, 202
Department of Finance, 202
Department of Local Government, 66, 110, 127–8, 130, 148, 183, 196, 202, 207, 222, 236, 340, 344
Department of Social Welfare, 23

department stores, 229–30
Dermot O'Dwyer House, 170
Detroit (MN), 405
de Valera, E., 17, 19
differential rents, 81, 117, 139–54, 183
differential rent system, 80, 143–4, 146–7, 150, 164
Diggis Street, Upper, 188
dining rooms, 120, 260, 266
district electoral divisions, 347, 405–6
Dodder, River, 92
Doherty, P., 109
'Doherty Group', 109
Dollymount, 354, 382
Dolphin House, 195
Dolphin's Barn, 107, 178, 353, 363, 367, 382
Dominicans, 79
Dominick Street, *40*, 180–2, 329
Dominick Street, Lower, 70, 179, 189
Dominick Street and District Development Association, 179
Dominick Street Upper/Dorset Street, 71
Donaghmede, 348
The Donahies, 348
Donnellys Orchard, 331
Donnybrook, 257, 331, 348, 352, 354, 361, 365, 378
  apartments, 255
  cottages, 74
  flats, 70, *184*
  tenant purchase scheme, 158
Donnycarney, 68, 331, 335
Dorset Street, 106
Dorset Street, Lower, 106
Doyle, P.S., 131–2
Drimnagh, 353, 382
Dromawling Road, 135
Drumcondra, 346, 366–7, 372, 378
  age profile, 350, 352, 354, 371
  housing, 108, 110, 251
  socio-economic areas, 361
  socio-economic groups, 346, 382, 387
  tenant purchase schemes, 62, 154, 164
Drumcondra North, 395, 397–9
Drumcondra Road, 361

Drumcondra South, 395, 397–9
Drumfinn Avenue, 78
Drumfinn Park, *see* Pairc Droim Finn
Drumfinn Road, 78
Dublin, modern city, 13, 15
*Dublin 1930–1950*, 16, 27, 34, 39, 280
Dublin Airport, 13, 61
Dublin Airport corridor, 330, 393
Dublin and District House Builder's Association, 241
Dublin Artisans' Dwelling Company, 41, 336
Dublin–Belfast Road, 98
Dublin Brick Company, 112
Dublin Building Operatives Public Utility Society, 121
Dublin City
  1800s, 14, 38, 41
  1940s, 13–16, 57
  1950s, 15–34, 36, 58
  1950s–1960s, 16–37, 39–60
  1960s, 15, 17, 33, 59
  1970s, 347–9
  boundary, 25, 92, 117
    extension of, 25–6, 64, 82, 92
  distinctiveness of, 388–9
  economy, 52
  northside
    age profile, 354
    boundary extension, 64
    car ownership, 365
    development, 13, 60, 350
    home ownership, 47, 332, 365
    household characteristics, 369
    housing, 47, 104, 120, 367, 369
    housing schemes, 73, 82, 92, 104, 135, 330
    Irish speakers, 378
    labour force, 372
    occupations, 360–1, 363, 375
    religion, 377
    rentals, 336
    socio-economic groups, 13, 346–7, 361, 375, 382–3
    suburbs, 26, 240, 405
  planning, 13, 55–61

  population, 29, 34, 60
  southside, 361, 372, 382, 387
    age profile, 353–4
    boundary extension, 64
    car ownership, 365
    development, 267, 269, 276
    fertility, 352
    household characteristics, 369
    housing, 47, 255, 278, 336
      development, 15, 64, 92, 267, 269, 347
    Irish speakers, 378
    occupations, 360, 363
    socio-economic groups, 13, 360–1, 363, 375, 381–3
Dublin City Council, 66, 68, 124, 129, 180, 193, 209
  housing, 65–6, 70
  meetings of, 141–3, 147–8, 204, 212
  rental rates, 142
  reports of, 74
Dublin City Council, Ballymun, 218, 227
Dublin City Council, Finglas, 176
Dublin City Council, St Anne's, 159–60
Dublin City Council, tenant purchase schemes, 155
Dublin Civil Servants' Building Society, 109
Dublin Corporation
  building programmes, 27, 38, 62, 154, 339, 347
  cottages, 107
  flats, 65, 92, 107, 188
    schemes, 67, 73, 180
  housing, 65, 72, 109, 154, 218, 331, 340–1
    costs, 106
    list, 112
    maintenance, 167
    policies, 13
    programmes, 62–76, 78–113, *115–56*, 158–77, 201, 208–9, 213, 227, 242, 328–9, 335, 344
    reconditioning, 74, 158, 188–9, 191
    schemes, 15, 88, 92, 106–13, *115–16*, 136, 174, 176, 197–8, 303

landscaping, 215, 219, 229, 235–7, 276
naming of, 162, 170–6, 239
social interaction, 172, 174
vacancies, 67
social, 102, 106, 191, 202, 206, 260, 330, 332, 334, 346, 359, 367
Ballymun, 204
Dún Laoghaire, 136
inner city, 178
size, 123
social mix, 62, 77, 87, 342, 405
southside, 13
stock, 41, 69, 112, 114, 133, 139–40, 164, 166, 182, 228, 330–2, 337, 394
subsidised, 125, 242
vacancies, 67, 69, 148, 150, 197–8
meetings, 205, 226–7
planning rules, 246
ratepayers, 143, 150–1, 153–4, 166, 171
rates, 88, 117, 125, 134, 140–2, 145–6, 150–5, 166, 182, 218, 252, 339, 375
rental properties, 148, 252, 332, 335, 399–400
rents, 80, 138, 140–54, 161, 166, 169, 187, 232, 252
economic, 63, 69, 143–4, 148, 153, 164, 183
fixed, 81, 141–4, 150–1, 153
minimum, 146–7
sub-tenants, 69
tenants
continuous, 168–9
new, 80, 152, 195
priority, 63
rehousing, 47, 64, 138, 191, 196–200, 340
tender requests, 109, *111*, *115*, *135*, *139*, 161, *192*, 212
waiting list, 66, 68, 105, 114, 116, 210, 339–40
approved, 114, 116, 134, 340, 343–4
wards, 28–9, 347, 395–7, 399–400

Dublin County
housing, 44
population, 23, 25
rent, 145
Dublin county borough, 25, 347–8, 363
home ownership, 240
labour force, 55
marriage, 35
population, 25–7
Dublin County Council, 105, 117, 121, 260, 267, 343, 345, 393
housing, 117, 267, 332
housing areas, 107, 136–9, 141, 326
Dublin Housing Action Committee, 198, 340–1
*Dublin in the Irish economy*, 49
Dublin Laundry, 112
Dublin Mountains, 61, 263
Dublin Opinion, *16*, *19–20*, *24*, *64*, *129*, *167*, *279*
Dublin Typographical Housing Group, 108
Dudley report, 318
Duncan, B., 358–9
Duncan, O., 358–9
Dundaniel Road, 99
Dundrum, 139, 241, 247, 267, 354, 361, 381, 384
housing, 139, 241, 247, 268
Dundrum/Ballinteer, 348
Dundrum Heights, 278
Dundrum Road, 112
Dundrum village, 267
Dunedin Estate, 136
Dun Emer (Dundrum), *245–6*, 267–8
Dún Laoghaire, 336, 343, 347–8, 352, 361, 363, 365, 377, 381, 387, 396–7
age profile, 36
domestic servants, 53–4
home ownership, 47, 125–6, 240, 332, 335
housing, 44, 136, 138, 241, 257, 267, 337
labour force, 54–5
marital status, 35–6
monthly rent, 145

Dún Laoghaire *(contd.)*
  occupations, 52
  population, 26–7, 34
  social housing, 136
Dún Laoghaire borough, 13, 25, 344, 346, 405
  home ownership, 240
  housing, 120, 138, 207, 334
  population, 25
Dún Laoghaire Home Builders' Public Utility Society, 138
Dunmanus Road, 169
Dunne, S., 145–6
Dunsink Avenue, 89
Dunsink Drive, 89
Dunsink Gardens, 89
Dunsink Green, 89
Dunsink Park, 89
Dunsink Road, 89
duplexes, 92

Eannafort Road, 171
East Wall, 117
*Economic development*, 21
Edenmore, 41, 72–3, 96, 98, 104, 327, 331
  housing scheme, 72–3, 96, 98–9, 104, 164
  housing stock, 41
  rehousing, 197
Edenmore Avenue, 99, *101*
Edenmore Crescent, 99
Edenmore Drive, 99
Edenmore Gardens, 99
Edenmore Green, 99
Edenmore Grove, 99
Edenmore Park, 99
Edenmore Road, 111, 113–14, 164
Eden Quay, 99, 117
Edinburgh, 236, 390
education, 23, 55, 306
Educational Building Society, 243
EEC, *see* European Economic Community
Eglinton Road, 257
Ehn, K., 311
electrical appliances
  cookers, 287–8, 290, 299

dishwashers, 290, 300
refrigerators, 263, 283–4, 287, 289–90, 301
washing machines, 281–4, 287, 289–90, 295, 300
electricity, 187, 226, 247, 283–4, 287, 338–9
Electricity Supply Board, 251, 266, 287
  advertisements, *282–3*
Electricity Supply Board, Christmas gifts, 281
Electricity Supply Board, hire purchase, *288*
Electrolux, *284*
Ellenfield, 331
emigration, 21, 23–4, 27, 34, 48, 56, 66–7, 164
Emmet Buildings, 68
Emmet Road, 331
employees, 112, 374, 388, 391
  semi-skilled, 363
  skilled, 382–3
  unskilled manual, 358
employers, 53, 112, 144, 154, 359, 374–5
employers and managers, 357–60, 382–3, 409
employment, 22, 48–54, 56, 371, 382, 392
  non-gainful, 54, 371
  occupations, 47, 52, 152, 356–7, 403
  women, 373
England, 328
English, G., 340
Ennafort Road, 171
Ennis Grove, 331
ESB, *see* Electricity Supply Board
ESSO, *51*
Europe, 14, 191, 211, 290, 318
European Economic Community, 21–2, 52
exports, 17–18, 47–8, 52, 56

factor analysis, 378, 401, 405–15
  rotation, 414
factorial ecology, 378–9
Fairview, 346, 350, 352, 372
Fallon, J., 288–9, 300
*Families in flats*, 236
Fatima Mansions, 68

Fearon, 107
Fenian Street, 171, 193–4, *194*
Ferndale Avenue, 87, 176–7
  residents of, 176
Ferndale Road, *88*, 135, 177
Ferrycarrig Avenue, 99
Ferrycarrig Road, 99
fertility, 352, 372, 386, 402
fertility index, 350–1, 384, 386
Festinger, L., 170
Fianna Fáil, 14, 132
Finance Committee, 73–4
Fine Gael, 103, 132
Finglas, 82–3, 155, 179, 366–7, 369, 371, 382, 387
  age profile, 353–4
  cottages, 70
  development, 29, 41, 60, 62, 70, 85, 118, 245, 344
  housing schemes, 82–91, 96, 103, 110, 183, 191
  housing stock, 41
  occupations, 363, 375
  rehousing, 197
  vacant houses, 68
Finglas East, 107, 331, 335, 395, 397–9
  cottages, 74
  housing, tenure of, 46–7
  housing facilities, 43
  housing scheme, 65, 73, 82, 86–7, 117, 144
  housing stock, 39
  isolation, 88
  population, 30
  shops, 89, 91
  tenant purchase, 158
Finglas East Development Association, 88
Finglas Housing Society, 117
Finglas North, 331
Finglas Park, 117, 119
Finglas Place, 87
Finglas Road, 84, 87–8
Finglas West, *31*, 157, 191, 331, 335, 348, 395, 397–9
  cottages, 74
  housing, tenure of, 46–7

housing facilities, 43
housing scheme, 65, 73, 82, 84, 87–8
housing stock, 39
population, 27, 30
shops, 84, 91
Finland, 22, 236–7
Firhouse, 384
*First programme*, 21
First World War, 329
Fitzgerald, D., 183
Flanagan Group, 109
'flatland', 336, 354, 366, 372, 386
flats
  bedsits, 252
  blocks of, 63, 178, 185, 200, 217, 233, 236, 251, 329, 336
    families, 238, 326, 387
    height, 182–3, 191, 200, 210, 238
  complexes, *181*, 191
  design of, *184–7*
  size of, 180, 210–11
  three-bedroomed, 210–11, 215, 257
  towers, 183, 227–8, 232–3, *237*
  two-bedroomed, 185, 252, 255
Foley Street, 68
An Foras Forbartha, 302
Forcible Entry and Occupation Act 1971, 341
Fort Leith Estate (Edinburgh), 236
Foxfield Avenue, 171
Foxfield Drive, 171
Foxrock, 241, 350, 361, 365, 375, 377, 381, 389
France, 36, 207
Francis Street, 41
Frank Kenny and Co., 73
Freeman, T.W., 47–8, *50*, 51
free-trade agreement, 22
Friedrichstadt (Berlin), 304, *305*
Friends Fields, 331

Gaeltacht Park Resident's Association, 204
Gallagher, M., 102–3
Gallagher and Company, 102
Galligan, Glynn and Ward, 302

Gardaí, 357
  houses, 214
Garda station, 229
garden cities, 273–4, 315
Garden of Remembrance, 392
Gardiner Street, 68, 71, 170, 182, 185, *187*, 187–8
  flats, 68, 71, 187
Gardiner Street, Lower, 178
Garryowen Road, 78
Garvin, J., 110, 127, 132, 193, 205, 241
GDP, *see* gross domestic product
Geddes, P., 273
general election (1965), 244
General Housing Society, 110
General Valuation (Griffith), 154
Glasanaon Place, 87
Glasanaon Road, 84, 87
Glasaree Road, 84, 176–7
Glasgow, 233, 318, 390
Glasilawn Avenue, 117
Glasilawn Road, 117
Glasmeen Road, 117
Glasnamana Road, 117
Glasnevin, 367, 369, 382
  age profile, 350, 352, 354
  housing, 45, 118, 366, 397
    tenure of, 46, 335, 399
  housing facilities, 43, 398
  Irish speakers, 378
  occupations, 361
  population, 29, 395
  socio-economic groups, 382, 387
Glasnevin Avenue, 105, 174–6, 203, 205
Glasnevin/Ballygall, 348
Glasnevin North, 205
Glasnevin Park, 176
Glass Industry Housing Society, 112
Glenageary, 247, 384
Glenayle Road, 172, 174
Glendassan Road, 172
Glenfarne Road, 172
Glenroan Road, 172
Glenwood Road, 172
Glin Avenue, 99
Glin Drive, 99

Glin Road, 99
Gloucester Place, 107, 170, 191
Golden Lane, 105
Gold Flake cigarettes, 295–6
Gracefield Avenue, 135
Grafton Street, 14
Grand Canal, 251
Grange, 245
Grangegorman, 352, 361
grants, 63, 112, 119, 122–5, 139, 257
Great Clarence Street, 171
Greater London Council, 236
Greencastle Avenue, 99
Greencastle Crescent, 99
Greencastle Drive, 99
Greencastle Park, 99
Greencastle Road, 99
Greenhills Estate (Walkinstown), 260–3
Greenmount Lawns (Rathgar), 255, *259*
Greenmount Road, 257
Green Property Company, 230
Grenville Street, 170, 188
Griffith Avenue, 60, 361
Griffith Drive, 87
Griffith Parade, 87
Griffith Road, 87
gross domestic product, 22
G.&T. Crampton, *38*, 73, 87, 107
Guild Street, 71
Guinness, 51, 251, 296
Gurteen Avenue, 78
Gurteen Park, 78
Gurteen Road, 78
Gygax group, 110

Hadens and Cubitt (London), 214
Hall, Canon D., 117
Hanna, E., 198, 340
Hard Street, 188
Harcourt Road, 348
Harcourt Street, 348
Hardwicke Place, 81, 188
Hardwicke Street, 107, 170, 188, *190*
Harmonstown, 104
Harmonstown Avenue, 135
Harmonstown Grove, *see* Brookwood Lawn

Harmonstown Halt, *163*
Harmonstown Rise, 172
Harmonstown Road, 98, 135, 172, 174
Harold's Cross, 331, 352, 372, 382
Harvery, J., 109
Haussmann, Baron Georges-Eugène, 304
Haymarket, 105
Henry, W., 109
Herbert, D., 410
Herbert Park, 252, *254*
Hernon, P.J., 159
higher professional group, 358–62, 379–81, 408
high-rises, 15, 178, 180, 182, 191–239, 304, 308, 330
    Antwerp, *314*
    Berlin, 315
    centralized facilities, 306, *310*, 310–11, 313
        canteens, 306, 308
        club rooms, 308
        conference halls, 308
        gymnasiums, 308
        laundries, 313
        USSR, *310*
    communal areas, 233, 308
    end of, 229–39
    height of, 328
    lifts, 233, 236, 255
    Moscow, *307*, 308, *309*, 311
    Prague, *314*
    spine blocks, 225, 227, 317–18
    tower blocks, 224, 317–18
    town centres, 216
high status areas, 382–3
High Street, 348
Hilberseimer, L., 304, *305*
Hillside Housing Estates (Dalkey), *38*
Hill Street, 70
Hogan['s] Place, 170, 171, 191
Hollyfield Buildings, 68
home duties, 54, 374, 386, 409
home ownership, 15, 46–7, 149, 164, 166, 169, 171, 174, 193, 240–75, 277–303, 332, 393–4, 399–400
    State grants, 119–20, 124, 260, 339

Hoover, 281, 283
Hotpoint, *284*
householders, perceptions of, 302–3
households, 347
    1–2 persons, 369–70, 386
    2 persons, 409
    characteristics, 365–71, 409
    income of, 149, 151–4
    multi-, 304
    multi-family, 387–8, 408
    persons per, 217, 366–9, 387, 409
    private, 37, 366
    size of, 366, 387
    small, 354, 386
houses
    all-electric, 287–8
    building of, 15, 82, 207, 211, 335, 343, 393
    detached, 245, 247–8, 266
    five-bedroomed, 246, 270, 330
    four-bedroomed, 15, 139, 241, 246, 248, 266–8, 270–1, 274, 278, 287, 318, 330
    garages, 84, 116–17, 119, 205, 248, 255, 263, 266–7, 276
    Georgian, 14, 179, 181, 185, 187–8, 336, 392
    multi-dwelling, 337
    new, 39, 338, 383
        building of, 140–1, 193, 303
        demand for, 241, 244
        design of, 257, 298–9
        Edenmore, 72
        loans, 126, 134
        northside, 41, 338
    older, 39, 41–2, 127, 134, 168, 251, 298–9
    owner-occupied, 303
    prices of, 13, 122–3, 125, 133, 240, 244, *247*, 250, 260, 263–8, 270–1, 276, 278, 287–8, 388
    selling, 344
    selling to tenants, 164–9
    semi-detached, 114, 116, 123, 205, 245, 271, 302, 323, 326, 345
        Ballyfermot, 77

houses *(contd.)*
  semi-detached *(contd.)*
    Ballygall, 120
    Dundrum, 267
    Finglas, 110, 119–20
    Laurel Park, 263
    Monastery Park, *263, 265*
  terraced, 77, 120, 245, 260, 271, 323
    Ballyfermot, 75
    Ballygall Crescent, 84
    Dundrum, 278
    end of, 117, 119
    Marino, 319
    Milltown, 92
    Old Bawn, 345
    rents, 161, 205
    three-bedroomed, 15, 112, 117, 120, 138–9, 161, 215, 241, 244–5, 247, 263, 266–8, 278, 302, 318
  town, 248, 268
  two-bedroomed, 77, 263, 278
housewife's prayer, 302
housewives, 280, 283, 287, 289, 302–3
housing
  1950s–1960s, 37–8
  1960s, 330–45
  advertisements, 109, 114–15, 119, 135, 139, *156*, 161–2, 192, 205, 212, 251, *258*
  'all-electric', 289–90
  amenities
    ballrooms, 229
    bowling alleys, 229, 231
    butchers, 78
    chemists, 78
    cinemas, 229, 231, 263
    community centres, 204, 226, 231, 276
    community halls, 229, 313
    concert halls, 393
    crèches, 231
    dairies, 28
    drapers, 79
    fish and chip shop, 79
    grocers, 28, 78–9
    hardware shops, 79
    kindergarten, 313
    libraries, 216, 231, 306, 313
    medical clinics, 216, 229
    medical services, 313
    newsagents, 28, 78
    nurseries, 231, 313
    open spaces, 96, 98, 223, 234, 236, 303
    parkland, 204, 277
    parks, 135, 161, 223, 271
    petrol stations, 229, 276
    play areas, 217, 219, 230, 232, 313, 344
    playgrounds, 75, 223, 228
    playing fields, 96, 223
    post-offices, 231
    public halls, 216
    recreational areas, 159, 306, 315
    residential shops, 79, 89, 92, 161
    schools, 79, 96, 187, 210, 215, 219, 226, 230, 263, 273, 276–7, 341, 344, 408
    supermarkets, 229–30, 276, 391
    swimming pools, 216, 229, 231, 313
    tobacconists, 28, 78–9
  condemned, 69, 72, 193, 196–8, 200, 341
  costs, 106, 138, 182, 240
  dangerous, 197, 200
  designs, 330
    American, 263, 266, 270, 278, 301, 303, 330
    Beverley, 265–6
    Caribbean, 274
    Colonial, 263–4
    Courtmead, 278
    Killeek, 278
    Montreal, 266
    open-plan, 278, 280, 298, 330
    Palma, 274
    Queen, 266
    Queenscourt, 278
    standard, 85, 244, 302
    Virginian, 271, 278
  European, 304–29

gardens, 15, 62, 223, 251, 303, 313, 315
　Ballyfermot, 79
　Bayside (Sutton), 276, 278
　Dundrum, 267
　Finglas, 84–5, 117
　Monastery Park, 263
　Monkstown, 138
　Mount Merrion, 139
　St Anne's, 159
　Terenure, 268–9
garden space, 77, 265, 270, 313
innovation, 298–302
lack of sites, 343–4
local authority, 334–5, 382, 388, 394
multi-family, 388
multiple occupancy, 336–7
new, 104, 122, 148, 150, 197
overcrowding of, 44, 199
owner occupancy, 46, 122, 240, 245, 251, 257, 332, 334–5, 382, 393, 408
persons per room, 367–8, 382, 409
private, 121–35, 154–5, 264, 323, 330, 335, 342, 345, 405
private builders, 13, 15, 27, 104, 109–10, 113, 125, 154, 176, 205, 218, 240, 326, 342–3
　prices, 106
　schemes, 13
　Walkinstown, 113
social, 366
temporary, 134, 196–7, 205
tenders, 72, 78, 84, 86, 91, 98, 107, 111, 114, 182, 196, 217, 328
tenure of, 46–7, 335, 399–400, 407–8
USSR, 305–11
Victorian, 244, 287, 336
Housing (Amendment) Act 1952, 119, 123
Housing (Amendment) Act 1954, 123
Housing (Loans and Grants) Act 1962, 124
Housing Act 1948, 122
Housing Act 1950, 155
Housing Act 1966, 123, 152

Housing Amendment Act, 1948, 108
Housing Committee, 66, 73, 77, 110, 114, 130, 180, 182–3, 195–6, 199–200, 202, 340
Housing Committee, Ballymun, 204–5, 209, 211–12, 219, 224, 226, 229, 235
Housing Committee
　differential rent system, 140, 150, 164
　loans, 132–3
　rental rates, 142–3, 150
　tenant purchase schemes, 166, 168
Housing Committee, Yellow Walls, 267
Housing Committee Breviate, 344
housing facilities, 41–3
　baths, 62, 300, 338–9, 408
　　fixed, 41–3, 62, 339
　　public, 42
　indoor plumbing, 62
　shared tap, 43
　shopping, 96, 230
　toilets, 62
　water supply, 41, 338–9, 408
Housing Inquiry 1913, 194
Housing Inquiry 1914, 195
Housing Inquiry 1939–43, 140
housing market, 133, 210–46, 260, 335, 342, 388–9
　buyers, 241–2, 244, 257, 264
　speculators, 14, 167, 240, 242, 341–4
housing problem, 136, 207, 238, 332
housing profile, 336–41, 343
housing stock, 37, 63, 116, 335, 338
　age of, 38, 337, 384–6, 394, 396–7
　new, 39, 41
　old, 39, 41, 148, 298, 337
Housing Tribunal 1938, 64
housing units, 37–8, 41, 62, 65, 232, 336–9, 347, 366, 408
　1–2 persons, 367, 369–70, 386–7, 409
　1–12 persons, 366
　2 or less rooms, 409
　3 or less rooms, 409
　owner occupiers, 382, 408
　rentals, 408
　since 1961, 386, 408
Howard, E., 273

Howth, 73, 105, 245–6, 331, 345, 348, 365, 367, 382
  age profile, 352, 354
  occupations, 361
Howth Head, 268
Howth Road, 114
Hoyt, H., 378, 383, 389, 402
Hungary, 237
Hyde Road, 138

IBAC, *see* Building and Construction Exhibition
Id, *see index of dissimilarity*
Ideal Homes Exhibition, Dublin, 278–87, 298, 301–2
Ideal Homes Exhibition, London, 279–80, 288
ILAC centre, 391
*Illustrated London News*, 194, 244
Image Analysis, 410
IMI [Irish Management Institute] survey, 250
imports, 18–19
Inagh Road, 78
Inchicore, 78, 106, 331, 346, 382
*index of dependency*, 352–5
*index of dissimilarity*, 358–9
*index of segregation*, 358–60
industry, 17, 48–54, 56, 344
  baking, 47
  brewing, 47
  chemical, 48, 52
  clothing, 47–9, 52
  development of, 20, 214
  distilling, 47
  electrical, 52
  electronic, 52
  engineering, 47–8
  footwear, 48, 52
  mechanical engineering, 52
  pharmaceutical, 52
  services, 48–9, 53, 56
inner city, 371, 397, 400
  age profile, 350, 353–4
  apartments, 389
  development, 178, 392

employment, 372
flats, 15, 63, 67, 70–1, 178, 180
households, 366–7, 388
housing, 44–5, 47, 334
housing facilities, 41–2
housing stock, 39, 41, 339, 397
occupations, 361, 363
population, 27–8, 56, 63, 348, 353, 396
redevelopment, 28, 104, 189, 313, 338, 392
rentals, 335–6
socio-economic groups, 382, 387
unemployment, 375
wards, 28–9, 44
Inns Quay, 395, 397–9
  housing, 39, 45–6
  housing facilities, 41–3
Institute of Patentees and Inventors, 301
intermediate non-manual employees, 357–8, 360
*Into the West*, 233
Irish economy, 16–23, 49, 55
*Irish economy since 1922*, 21
Irish Estates Management Ltd, 107, 251
Irish Ex-servicemen's Utility Society, 108
Irish Ex-servicemen's Public Utility Society, 109
Irish Glass Bottle Company, 112
Irish Housebuilders' Association, 302
*Irish Independent*, 79, 115, 119, 156–7, 169, 212, 234, *262*, 262–3, 283, *294*
Irish Medical Association, 238
*Irish Press*, 110, 120–1, 134–5, *135*, 165, 192, 207, 212, 231–2, 234, 238, 340
*Irish Times*, 53, 144, 160, 185, 245–6, 250–1, 255, 257, 263, 269, 280, 302–3
  Ballyfermot, 80–1
  Ballymun, 219, 228
  building trade, 241, 243
  housing advertisements, 139, *206*, 212, 245, 247–9, *258–9*, *261*, *264*, 269–70, *272*, 277
  slum clearance, 188
  social housing, 103
  St Anne's, 159
*Irish Times Pictorial*, 188

Irishtown, 107
Is, *see index of segregation*
Italy, 22
Iveagh Trust, 336

J.A. Kenny and Partners, 224
J.A. Lawler, 114
James' Street, 68, 363
Jamestown Road, 82, 84
Jennings, 73, 77–8, 107
Jesperson, 208
John Dillon Street, *40*

Karl Marx-Hof (Vienna), 311, 313, *312*
Kelly's Field, 138
Kennedy, J.F., 393
Kennedy, T., 22
Keogh, 176
Kevin Street, Lower/Bishop Street, 71
Khimki-Khovrino (Moscow), 311
Kildonan Park, *90*
Kilbarrack, 60, 96, 102, 345
  housing scheme, 104–5, 121
Kilbarron Avenue, 99
Kilbarron Drive, 99
Kilbarron Park, 99
Kilbarron Road, 99
Kilcroney, Co. Wicklow, 300
Kildonan Road, 84–5, 89
Kill Avenue, 138
Killester Park, 135
Killiney, 366
  age profile, 352, 385
  home ownership, 244–5
  housing, 247, 267, 350
  occupations, 361, 375
Kilmainham, 346, 352, 361, 387, 395, 397–9
  housing, 45–6
  housing facilities, 43
Kilmore, 99, 164–5, 327, 348, 352, 354, 366–7, 369, 382–5
  housing scheme, 94, 96–7, *97*, 105
  housing stock, 41
Kilmore Avenue, *116*
Kilmore/Coolock, 353

Kilmore Crescent, 116
Kilmore Road, *201*
Kilshane Road, 89
Kimmage, 172, 179, 344, 367, 382, 387, 395

Liverpool, 328
Livett, R.A.H., 313
*Living in flats*, 326
loans, 66, 120, 124, 127, 130–1, 134, 139
local authorities, 146, 206, 214–15, 342–3
  grants, 119, 123
  housing, 62, 107, 110, 131, 152, 155, 201, 205–7, 231, 360, 388
  loans, 126
  rentals, 334, 382, 388, 408
  supplementary grants, 119
  tenants, 46, 240, 333, 382
Local Government (Planning and Development) Act 1963, 244
Local Loans Fund, 129
London, 214, 244, 279–80, 287–8, 315, 324–5, 328
lord mayor of Dublin, 110, 112, 130, 159, 179, 207, 215
Los Angeles, 401
  social areas, 402
  study, 401–2
  urbanization, 402
Loughborough Road Estate (London), *324–5*
Lough Conn Avenue, 78
Lough Conn Drive, 78
Lough Conn Road, 78
Lough Conn Terrace, 78
Lough Derg Road, 98
Lough Ennel Avenue, 98
Lough Ennel Drive, 98
Lough Ennel Park, 98
Lough Lein Gardens, 98
Lough Lein Park, 98
Loughlinstown, 271
Lough Mask Avenue, 98
Lough Mask Crescent, 98
Lough Mask Drive, 98
Lough Mask Green, 98
Lough Mask Road, 98

Lough Ree Avenue, 98
Lough Ree Road, 98
Lourdes House, 170
Love Lane, 187, 191
lower professionals, 357–62, 382, 408
Lucan, 240, 245, 247, 352, 393
Lucan/Clondalkin, 347, 404
Lynch's Place, 71
Lyons estate, 202

Macken Street, 171
Macroom Avenue, 99
Macroom Road, 99
Magnificat Family Guild, 112
maisonettes, 185, 187, 196, 257, 317, 326
Malahide, 245, 247, 266, 393, 404
Malahide Road, 98, 111, 113
Malone Gardens, 331
Mansion House, 30, 302
    housing, 39, 45–6
    housing facilities, 41, 43
Maples, Mr and Mrs, 193
Marian Home Building Society, 110
Marino, 62, 154, 158, 164, 319, 354
    housing scheme, 62, 110, *156*, 167
Markievicz Park, 79
Marrowbone Lane, 68, 196
Martin's Lands (Kimmage), 344
Maywood Crescent, *see* Maywood Lawn
Maywood Lawn, 171
McAuley, C., 98
McAuley Avenue, 98
McAuley Drive, 98
McAuley Park, 98
McAuley Road, 98
McDonnell and Dixon, 92
McInerney, F., 102–3
McInerney and Sons, 77, 107, 345
McInerney Company, 345
McKee Road, 117
McKelvey Avenue, 89
McKelvey Road, 89
McMahon Building Group, 109
McManus, R., 121
McNamara. B., 180
McVeigh, E., 246

Meath Street/South Earl Street, 191
Meenan, J., 21, 49
Mercer Street, 188
Merchant's Quay, 395, 397–9
Mercy Sisters, 98
Merit Homes, 266, 271
Merrion Square, 14, 336, 361
Mespil apartments, 252–3, *253*
Mespil development, 251
microrayon, *310*, 310–11
Milltown, 74, *93*, 107, 157, 331
    housing scheme, 73, 92, 116
Milltown Drive, 135
Mitchell, C., 280
Mitchelstown Creamery, 298
Moeran Road, 120
Molloy, B., 231, 234
Monastery Park, 263–6
Monkstown, 336, 348
Moore Street, 391
Morris & McCullough, 344
mortgages, 125–6, 167, 169, 257, 393
Moscow, 308–11
Mountjoy, 28, 395, 397–9
    housing, 39, 41, 46
        overcrowding, 44–5
    housing facilities, 41–3
Mount Merrion, 60, 381
    development, 60, 350
    housing, 139, 241, 270
    occupations, 361, 375
Mount Pleasant Buildings, vacant flats, 68
Mount Street, 336
Mounttown, 138
Moycullen Road, 78
Mullen, F.J., 202
Mullen, M.J., 183, 226
Mumbai (Bombay), 405
Murphy, T.J., 159–60
Muskerry Road, 78
Myanmar, 296

National Association of Tenants' Organizations, 153
National Building Agency Ltd, 214, 220, 222, 224, 344

National Convention of the National Association of Tenants' Organizations, 169
NATO, *see* National Association of Tenants' Organizations
Navan Road, 361
NBA, *see* National Building Agency Ltd
Nelson's Pillar, 392
Netherlands, 36, 237
Nevin, E., 249
Newfoundland Street, 81, 170, 178
Newly-wed Scheme, 199
Newmarket, 105
New Street, 105
new towns, 365, 389, 393
    Ballymun, 228
    Cumbernauld (Scotland), 274
    Old Bawn, 350
    Tallaght, 361
1916 Rising, 159
Non-Manual Groups, 359–60
non-Roman Catholics, 377, 381–2, 409
North Avenue, 139
North Brunswick Street, 105
North Circular Road, 74–5, 178
North City, 28, 395, 397–9
    housing, 39, 41–5
    population, 30
North Clarence Street, 178
North Dock, 395, 397–9
    housing, 39, 43, 45
    population, *33*, 33–4
North Dublin Drainage Scheme, 82
North Dublin Sewerage System, 202
Northern Ireland, 290
North Gloucester Place, 170, 178
North Great George's Street, 188
North Inner City, 396–7, 400
North Lotts, 331
Northside Shopping Centre, 102
North Strand Road, 70, 74, 107, 353
Norton, W., 65
Norwood Tennis Club (Ranelagh), 241
Nutgrove Avenue, 367
Nutley Lane, 348

O'Brolchain, R., 146
occupational insurance scheme, 23
O'Callaghan, M.D. and J.G., builders, 260
O'Connell Bridge, 392
O'Connell Street, 171, 390
O'Dea, J., 346
Odeon Building Society, 112
O'Devaney Gardens, 68, 107, 178–80, *180*, 196
O'Donnell, P., 126
O'Donnell Group, 110
Office of Public Works, 77, 159–60
offices, 229, 313, 391–2
Offington Park, 246, 268–9, *269*
O'Hanlon, A.G., 204
O'Hogan Road, 75
oil crises, 22, 52, 257
Old Bawn, 344, 345, 350, 352
Old Finglas Road, 114
Oliver Bond House, 68
Olympia Exhibitions, 279, 284, 300
O'Mahony, J., 53
O'Mahony, T.C.G., 110
O'Moore Road, 75
Openshaw, S., 405
OPW, *see* Office of Public Works
Oranmore Road, 78
Ordnance Survey, 60
    maps, 57–9, *83*, *115*
        Ardoyne House (1973), *254*
        Ballymun (1971), 227
        Ballymun Avenue (1969), *174*
        Dominick Street (1939), *181*
        Dublin (1954), 60
        Finglas (1939), 83
        Finglas (1959), *83*
        Glasaree and Ferndale roads (1974), *177*
        Glasnevin Avenue (1979), *175*
        Hardwicke Street (1939), *190*
        Kilmore (1959), *115*
        Kimmage Road East (1948), *173*
        Mespil Complex (1973), *253*
        Milltown (1936–7), *93*
        O'Devaney Gardens (1972), *179*

Ordnance Survey *(contd.)*
  maps *(contd.)*
    Sallynoggin (1959), *137*
    Terenure Road West (1959), *173*
    University College Dublin (1962), *203*
    Walkinstown (1943), *95*
    Walkinstown (1969), *95*
O'Rourke, D., 340
Oscar Traynor Road, 98–9, 102, 116
O'Sullivan, E., 84
Other non-manual employees, 357–60, 382, 409
Our Lady's Hospice (Harold's Cross), 352
Oxmanstown, 41, 336, 375

PAF, *see* Principal Axes Factoring
Pairc an Mhuillinn, 162
Pairc Droim Finn, 79
Pairc na Naomh, 162
Palmer, C., 410
Paramount Homesteads, 267
Paris, 208, 304, 313
Park Avenue (Sandymount), 257
Parker, A.J., 379, 404, 406–7
Parkview (Castleknock), 248
Palmerstown, 60
Parnell Square, 367
Parnell Street, *40*, 390
Patrick Doyle Road, 92
Patrick Street, 41, 375, 388
PCA, *see* Principal Components Analysis
Pearse Square, 171
Pearse Street, 361
Pearson's Product Moment Correlation Coefficient, 411–12
pedestrians, 271, 273–4, 277
Pembroke, 13, 42, 335, 346
Pembroke East, 395, 399
Pembroke West, 39, 395, 397–9
Pender, M., 81
pensions
  invalidity, 23
  old age, 23, 36–7
Perle, E.D., 405, 409
Perry, C., 273

Phibsboro, 372
Phibsborough [Phibsboro], 354, 382, 387
Phibsborough Road, 106
Philipsburgh Avenue, *see* Annadale
Phil Shanahan House, 68, 170
Phoenix Park, 159, 178, 248, 334, 361, 395, 397–9
  housing facilities, 43
  housing stock, 39
Pimlico, 71
Planning Appeals Bill 1967, 103
Player's Navy Cut cigarettes, 295–6
Plunket, B.J., 158
Plunkett Avenue, 89
Plunkett Crescent, 89
Plunkett Drive, 89
Plunkett Green, 89
Plunkett Grove, 89
Plunkett Road, 89
Poppintree, 105
population
  age profile, 29–37, 350, 352–4, 384–7, 408
  change, 23–4, 28–34, 348–50, 387
  demographics, 30, 351–3, 408
  Dublin wards, 395–6
  education, 22
  families, 401
    income, 123, 140, 142, 147, 150
    new, 27, 34, 145, 231–2, 236, 350, 352
  housing, tenure of, 399–400
  Irish speakers, 377–8
  marital status, 34–5, 354, 356, 386, 408
  middle class, 42, 54, 56, 133, 158, 251–2, 268, 315, 335
  occupations, 47–9, 52, 357, 360–1, 363, 379
  religion, 377, 382, 409
  social areas, 346–88, 402–3
  social networks, 341–2
  social ranking, 356, 401, 403, 409
  socio-demographics, 346, 403, 415–16
  socio-economic groups, 356–65, 378–84, 388, 405, 408

urban/rural, 24–5
women, 34–6
working class, 56, 118, 127, 136, 139, 146–7, 155, 188, 356
Portland Row, 106
Portmarnock, 247, *249*, 393, 404
Portugal, 22
Post Office Staff Society, 108
Power Group, 110
Power's Court, 66, 178, 189, 196
Powerscourt, 278, 331
Prague, *314*
Presentation Convent, 268
Principal Axes Analysis, 413
Principal Axes Factoring, 410–11, 413–14
 analysis, 414
Principal Components Analysis, 410–11, 413–14
Pringle, D., 411
Prospekt Mira (Moscow), 311
Public Health Act 1878, 195
public utility societies, 85, 108–9, 113, 117–23, 138–9, 155, 170

Quarry Hill (Leeds), *312*, 313
Queen's Square, *see* Pearse Square

Radburn (NJ), 271, 273–4, 319–20
Radburn system, 271, *275*, 276–7, *277*
radio
 Pilot, *289*, 289–90
 rental shops, 290
Radio Teilifís Éireann, 22
Raheny, 102
 development, 60, 72–3, 245
 housing, 39, *100*, 161
  tenure of, 46, 397, 399
 housing facilities, 43, 398
 housing scheme, 60, 72–3, 103
 population, 29–30, 348, 395
Railway Street, 170, 187
Ramillies Road, 78
Ranelagh, 105, 241, 336, 354, 382
Raon an Mhuilinn, 162
Raon na Naomh, 162
Raon Naomh Áine, 162

Rathfarnham, 29, 350, 377, 397–9
 age profile, 352
 car ownership, 365
 cottages, 70
 housing, 38, 45–6, 70, 109
  tenure of, 46, 397
 housing facilities, 43
 housing scheme, 60, 66, 105, 109, 331
 housing stock, 38
 occupations, 361, 375
 population, 30, 395
 socio-economic groups, 361, 382
 tenant purchase schemes, 158
Rathfarnham Lower, 74
Rathfarnham South, 396–9
Rathfarnham village, 331
Rathgar, 251, 255, 336, 346, 352, 366, 372
Rathmines, 335–6, 346, 352, 354, 372
 'flatland', 244, 251, 336
 housing, 13, 42, 366
 socio-economic groups, 42, 346, 382
Rathmines Avenue, 191
Rathmines East, 396–9
Rathmines West, 396–9
Ratoath Avenue, 89
Ratoath Drive, 89
Ratoath Road, 89
RDS, *see* Royal Dublin Society
Red Cross, 159
Redmond, 107
Red Park Utility Society, 117–18, *118*
Red Road (Glasgow), 233, 318
rehousing, 103
rentals, 27, 46, 334–5, 354, 399–400
renting, 46, 149, 154, 205, 386
rents, maximum, 144, 146, 148–51
Revenue Commissioners, 19
Rialto, 178
Ringsend, 363, 367, 382, 387
Ringsend Park, 196
roads, 14, 215, 217, 223, 273–4, 390–1
 motorways, 98, 392
 networks, 13–14
 ring roads, 14, 98
Robertson, M., 27
Robinson, M., 410

Rockford (Stradbrook), 138
Roebuck, 241
Roehampton Alton Estate (London), 239, 315, *316–17*, 318
Roman Catholic Church, 14, 377, 382
Ronan Point, Newham (London), 328
Rooney, 107
Rory O'Connor House, 170
Rosemount (Kilbarrack), 104
Rossmore Avenue, 78
Rossmore Road, 78
Rotunda, 28, 395, 397–9
    housing, overcrowding of, 44–5
    housing facilities, 41–3
    housing stock, 39, 41
    population, 30
Royal Dublin Society, 302
Royal Exchange, 396–9
    housing
        overcrowding of, 44–5
        tenure of, 46
    housing facilities, 41, 43
    housing stock, 39
    population, 30
Royal Hibernian Hotel, 110
Royal Hospital (Donnybrook), 352
RTÉ, *see* Radio Teilifís Éireann
Rummel, R.J., 411
Rush, 393
Rutland Street, *186*
Rutland Avenue, 70, 331
Rutland Street, Upper, *189*

Sabsovich, L., 306
Sackville Street, 171
salaried employees, 358–60, 382, 409
salaries, 249–51
Sallynoggin, 136–7, *137*, 361, 363, 367, 381
Sandyford, 361
Sandyford Road, 246, 267
Sandyhill Road, 220, 227, 232
Sandymount, 61, *256*, 256–7, 352, 361, 366, 375
Santry
    age profile, 352, 354
    development, 60, 105, 369
    home ownership, 46
    housing, 39, 105, 397
        tenure of, 46, 399
    housing facilities, 43, 398
    population, 29–30, 395
Santry River Park, 98
Saorstát Civil Service Public Utility Society, 121
An Saorstát Public Utility Society, 121
saps, *see* small area population statistics
Sarsfield Road, 73, 75, 106–7, 331
Schachter, S., 170
schools
    primary, 389
    secondary, 22, 389
Scotland, 274
scree test, 413
SDAA, *see* Small Dwellings Acquisition Act
Sean McDermott Street, 68, 177, 361, 363, 367, 375, 382
Second World War, 16, 65, 136, 154, 249, 287, 316, 318
Section 23, 199
Section 25, 199
self-employed/managers, 358
semi-skilled manual employees, 358, 360, 382–3, 409
semi-skilled workers, 364
servants, domestic, 34, 53–4
Service Housing Society, 109
Sewell Cautley, M., 273
sewerage system, 82, 342
Shanganagh Vale, 271–5, *275*, 276
Shangan Road, 220, 227
Shankill, 381
Shanowen Park, 135
Shantalla Drive, 135
Shantalla Road, 135
Sheriff Street, 363, 367, 375, 382, 388
Sherry, P., 109
Shevky, E., 378–9, 401, 403
shopping, 14, 16, 28, 89, 267
shopping centres, 28, 52, 96, 187, 210, 391, 394

Ballymun, 215–16, 218, 225, 229–30
Bayside (Sutton), 277
Darndale, 344
Edenmore, 102
shops, 313, 317, 329, 341, 391
Ballymun, 216–17, 219, 226, 230
Bayside (Sutton), 276
Bonnybrook, 96
Clondalkin, 263
Coolock, 96
Edenmore, 96, 101
Finglas, 84, 89, 91
Greenhills, 263
housing schemes, 73, 78, 96
Kilmore, 96
retail space, 229
Shanganagh Vale, 276
St Anne's, 162
Shrewsbury Lawn (Cabinteely), 269–70
Sisk, 214, 229
Sisters of Charity of St Vincent de Paul, 80
Skarne, 208
Skerries, 393
skilled manual employees, 357–60, 409
slums, 75, 82, 161, 191
clearance of, 27, 29, 34, 38, 41, 56, 92–3, 188–9, 195–6, 207, 337
Leeds, 313
small area population statistics, 347–8, 356, 365, 374–5, 410
Small Dwellings Acquisition Act, 66, 122, 125–7, 129–34, 160, 166, 176, 242
houses, 135
loans, 66, 125, 127, 131–4, 241–2, 260, *265*
schemes, 138
support, 243
Smithfield, 105
social area analysis, 401
Social Democrats, 312
South City, 43, 397–8, 400
South Dock, 28, 396–9, 400
housing, 39, 43, 45–6
population, 30
South Dublin Co-operative Housing Society, 120

South Inner City, 397, 400
South Lotts Road, 331
Soviet Union, *see* Union of Soviet Socialist Republics
Spearman's Rho, 412
Spiddal Park, 78
Spiddal Road, 78
Spodek, H., 405
Springdale Road, 99
Stafford, T., 216
St Agnes' Park, 109
St Anne's, 66, 73–4, 94, 157–9, *162–3*, *165*, 276
cottages, 74, 158
tenant purchase, 157–8
St Audoen's House, 68
St Barnabas Public Utility Society, 117
St Brendan's Hospital (Grangegorman), 352
St Brendan's Park, 98, *100*, *113*, 113–14, 171
St Brendan's Road, *256*
St Bridget's Gardens, 68, 81, 170, 178
St Canice's National Housing Society, 120
St Columba and Glasnevin Residents' Association, 70
St Columbanus Avenue, 92
St Columbanus Place, 92
St Columbanus Road, 92, 116, 344
Stephen's Lane, 189
St Gall Gardens, North, 92
St Gall Gardens, South, 92
St George's Church, 190
St George's Public Utility Society, 82
Stillorgan, *51*, 241, 384
St James's Hospital, 352
St John's Court (Sandymount), 257
St Joseph's Mansions, 68
St Jude's Gardens, 170
St Kevin's Court (Dartry), 255
St Kevin's, 396–8, 400
housing, 39, 45–6
housing facilities, 43
population, 30
St Laurence's Mansions, 68, 170
St Margarets Road, 89

St Mary's Hospital (Phoenix Park), 352
St Mary's Mansions, 68
St Mary's Terrace, 106
St Mobhi Public Utility Society, 121
St Patrick's Cathedral, 390
St Stephen's Green, 14
St Teresa's Gardens, 68, 107, 170
St Vincent Street West, 70
Stein, C., 273
Stockholm, 208
Stormanstown House, 98
Streets Committee, 202
suburbs, 347, 350, 354, 363, 366, 371–2, 382, 392–3
    Ballyfermot, 67, 75
    cars, 390–1
    development in, 67, 77, 178, 191, 245, 263, 266, 268, 270, 391, 394
    Finglas, 60
    growth of, 393
    high-rises, 304, 308, 311
    home ownership, 47, 335
    housing, 67, 70, 330, 338, 394
    housing conditions, 41–2, 178
    housing stock, 337
    industry, 52, 391
    population, 25–6, 63
    rehousing in, 63–4, 104, 191
    shopping centres, 391, 394
    southside, 60
Summerhill, 68, 188–9, 353, 388
Sundrive Building Group, 110
Sundt, 208
Superintendent Medical Officer for Health, 194–5
supplementary grants, 122–4, 134, 343
    categories, 124–5
    Coolock, 116
    Finglas, 119–20
    qualifying for, 130, 133, 164, 260
Sutton, 268, 367, 377, 382
    age profile, 352, 354
    car ownership, 365
    housing scheme, 60, 331, 348
    occupations, 361, 375
Sweden, 207

Sweetman, G., 18, 131
Sweetser, F.L, 409
Swords, 245, 393, 404
Sycamore Road, 135
system building, 72, 200, 205–28, 311
    Ballymun, 15
    field trips, 207–9
    Moscow, 308–*9*

Tallaght, 347, 383–4, 393, 404
    housing scheme, 105, 136, 344, 350
    occupations, 361, 363, 375
Taney (Dundrum), 247
Tara Street, 42
taxation, 17, 19, 166
Taylor, N., 232
TB, *see* tuberculosis
Tea Council of Ireland, 296
television, 290, 300–2
    Pilot, *289*
    rental shops, 290
    RTÉ, 290
Templeogue, 352, 354, 361, 365, 367, 381, 384
Temple Place, 188
Temple Street, 188
tenant purchase schemes, 106, 151–2, 155, 158, 161, 164, 166, 168, 335
    Drumcondra, 62
    Finglas, 82
    Marino, 62
tenements, 194, 244, 335, 369
    clearance of, 75, 80
    collapses, 193, 195, 198
    compulsory purchase of, 73
    reconditioning of, 63, 187, 189
Terenure, 172, 241, 346, 348, 352, 354, 361, 365, 367, 375, 381, 396–8, 400
    housing, 45, 268, 331
    tenure of, 46
    housing facilities, 43
Terenure Road West, 172, 248, 268
Thomas, R., 410
Thomond Road, 75
Thornville (Kilbarrack), 104
Thurles Vocational School, 53

Timms, D., 403, 405
Tolka [Valley] Estate, 111, 114, 117–18
Tolka Valley, 60, 88, 105
Tonlegee Avenue, 172
Tonlegee Close, *see* Glenayle Road
Tonlegee Gardens, *see* Glenwood Road
Tonlegee Grove, *see* Glenfarne Road
Tonlegee Road, 98, 172
town planning, 304
Town Planning and Streets Committee, 82
traffic, 13–14, 79, 85, 136, 219, 270, 273, 319, 390
Transitional Development Fund, 73
Treacy, S., 170
Trim Road, 99
tuberculosis, 199
Tudor Walters Report, 318
Tyron, R.C., 405
Tyrone Place, 189
Tyrone Square, 189

UCD, *see* University College Dublin
UK, *see* United Kingdom
Ulster, 23–4
Ulster Museum, 251
unemployment, 80–2, 130, 243, 375–6
Union of Soviet Socialist Republics, 304–11, 315–16
Union Place/Grove Road, 70
Unité d'Habitation (Berlin), 313, *315*
United Kingdom, 326, 328–9
    building manuals, 274
    credit restrictions, 243
    flat complexes, 234
    food consumption, 292
    high-rises, 209, 233, 238–9, 316
    housing costs, 228, 323, 329
    Housing Manual, 85
        1944, 318
        1949, 318, 323, 326–7, *327*
        1952, 318–19, 323
        1953, 318, *320–2*
    housing stock, 164
    local authorities, 236, 247, 318
    National Food Survey, *291*
    new towns, 82, 274, 304

    rebuilding, 318
    salaries, 53
    suburbs, 318
    trade, 22
United States of America, 15–16, 48, 284, 290, 391, 403
University College Dublin, 15, 193, 202–3
    Albert Agricultural College, 202–4
        site, 207, 212
    Department of Social Science, 302, 341
    Faculty of Agriculture, 202
unskilled employees, 360, 382, 409
unskilled group, 360
unskilled manual workers, 359, 364
urban areas, 402–3
US, *see* United States of America, 403
Usher's Quay, 388
Usher's Ward, 43, 45, 396–8, 400
USSR, *see* Union of Soviet Socialist Republics

Vancouver, 271
Vardy, M., 193
venetian blinds, 280–1
Vernon Avenue, 382
Vesnin, A., 306–7
Vesnin, L., 306–7
Vicar Street, 183
Vienna, 311–13
Voisin (Paris), 313
Vote 28 – Local Government, 212

Wadelai, 85, 336
Wales, 290, 328
Walkinstown
    boundary extension, 64
    cottages, 74
    housing facilities, 43
    housing scheme, 75, 94, 113
    housing stock, 39
    population, 30
    tenant purchase, 158
Walkinstown Avenue, 75, 94
Walkinstown Crescent, 94
Walkinstown Drive, 94

Walkinstown Green, 94–6, *96*
Walkinstown Parade, 94
Walkinstown Park, 94
Walkinstown/Templeogue, 353, 369
Walkinstown Utility Society, 120
Walton, E., 280
Waterford City, 206
Waterford county borough, 25
Watermill Road, 111, 113
Wates Company, 276
Watling Street, 367
Wellmount Avenue, 89
Wellmount Crescent, 89
Wellmount Drive, 89
Wellmount Green, 89
Wellmount Park, 89
Wellmount Road, 89
Wentworth Place, 171
west Dublin, 13, 60–1, 330, 350, 393

Westgate West, 170
West Germany, 48
Westmoreland Park, 105
Whitaker, T.K., 21
Whitefriar Street, 107, 178
Whitehall, 68, 352, 354, 382
White Paper on Housing, 218
Wide Streets Commissioners, 14, 390
Wilkinstown, *see* Walkinstown
Wilkinstown Avenue, see Walkinstown Avenue
Williams, M., 378, 401
Wood Quay, 394, 396–8, 400
Woodvale Public Utility Society, 109–10
Wright, H., 273

Yellow Walls (Malahide), 266–7
York Street, 188
youthful dependency ratio, 355, 384, 386